WOMAN ON TRIAL

WOMAN ON TRIAL

LAWRENCIA BEMBENEK

HarperCollins*PublishersLtd*

Tons of appreciation to editor Marq de Villiers for facilitating communication so effectively. His hard work, expert advice, experience and humor made it all not only possible, but a pleasure as well.

— L. B.

Cover photo: This courtroom picture was taken during my post-conviction motion for a new trial. (Milwaukee Journal Photo.)

First Edition

Canadian Cataloguing in Publication Data

Bembenek, Lawrencia
  Woman on trial

ISBN 0-00-215746-2

1. Bembenek, Lawrencia. 2. Escapes — United States. 3. Trials (Murder) — United States. 4. Woman murderers — United States — Biography. 5. Prisoners — United States — Biography. 6. Fugitive from justice — United States — Biography. 7. Refugees, Political — Canada — Biography. I. Title.

HV6248.B4A3 1992   364.1'523'092   C92-093398-X

---

92 93 94 95 96 ❖ AG 5 4 3 2 1

To my parents who are the sun and moon in my life. To all my true friends, who have supported me and helped me beyond words.

Now here you see, it takes all the
running you can do to keep in the
same place. If you want to get
somewhere else, you must run
twice as fast as that.

— Lewis Carroll

WOMAN ON TRIAL

THE VERDICT

"All rise."

The jury walked in.

I sat down with my hands folded in front of my face, biting my knuckle as I watched them enter, one by one.

My counsel had said to me, "*Watch their faces!* If they look at you, you're home free. If they don't ... you're in trouble."

It was silent, like a death watch. I heard no sound but the shuffle of a single pair of shoes and the sinister, insistent hum of the TV cameras at the back of the courtroom.

The heavy woman with the long, brown hair wouldn't look at me.

The elderly black man watched his feet as he entered the jury box.

"Oh no," I heard my counsel whisper.

More jury members followed in a solemn line. Not one of them returned my gaze. I broke the skin on my knuckle with my tooth.

"God, no," my counsel said again.

The jury forewoman was short, dark-haired, rigid. She had squinted at me through schoolteacher eyeglasses while I testified. She wasn't looking at me now.

"Ladies and gentlemen of the jury," Judge Skwierawski was saying, "have you reached a verdict?"

"We have, Your Honor," her nasal voice replied.

1

The judge opened the envelope. His ruddy, bearded face did not change expression. He read calmly:

"We find the defendant, Lawrencia Bembenek, guilty of first-degree murder."

I felt my life begin and end in that single instant.

Guilty! The word sliced into my consciousness with the heat of a lightning bolt, slashing like a razor.

Guilty! It made a sound inside my head like bones breaking.

I could taste blood in my throat, and I clenched my jaw shut. Suddenly, I was standing at the bench, in front of Skwierawski, unaware that I had just walked there.

The judge was saying something. I saw his mouth form the words, his jaw move, I saw the hairs of his beard, but it was all movement and bleakness and silence, and I heard nothing.

"No," I said. "Oh, no."

I felt my pulse hammering. How could there be blood in my heart when there was room only for this pain? Tears welled up.

"I must sentence you to life imprisonment."

I heard sobs behind me. I told myself not to turn around, to try to hang on. *Don't turn around and look at them, or you will die.*

My counsel was speaking, saying something about some kind of appeal bond, which Skwierawski was denying, and my eyes traveled in slow motion to the jurors. I half-expected to see that they had turned into headless demons. Even then, none of them would look at me.

"Laurie?" the bailiff said, and even his eyes were red. My counsel had his arm around my shoulder for a second, and then I was gone, led to my captors, moving slowly, not knowing what I was doing. My purse and coat were two feet behind me, but I couldn't stop for them.

A crowd of deputies surrounded me and cuffed my hands to a chain around my waist. The chain felt big enough to shackle the world.

I felt so very small.

Then I was in a room, on a chair, all alone, and the tears came.

■　　■　　■

When I was a little girl, nine years old, I almost drowned. I was in a swimming pool, on vacation in Canada with my parents. I clung to an inflatable ring, and I accidentally floated into the deep end. The ring slipped away from me. Suddenly I couldn't reach the bottom, and I was under the water. Panicking, I tried to get my face above the surface, desperate for air, but I went down again and again and again, and I started to scream inside my mind. Then my mother's hand came out of the sky and grabbed my flailing arm, hauling me out of the pool, to safety. To safety.

Mom, mom, help me! Please help me! I'm drowning again!

But my mother was behind the wooden courtroom railing, seated next to my dad, her hands rigid and her heart breaking.

And then they came, and they took me away.

1

WHO I AM

I'm the person you don't know. You may think you know me, but you don't. You know only some creature from the media, from the hype and hysteria that surrounded my arrest and trial in 1981 for the murder of my husband's ex-wife.

Bambi, the ex-bunny! The killer! The fugitive!

I'm no Joan of Arc, nor am I what you think. I was a person who trusted too many people too much, who was naive, who made many bad decisions, who has grown up in a way I wouldn't wish on your worst enemy. But I'm not a bad person, and I'm not a killer, either.

I have learned some things I wish I'd never learned. I've learned that the media is sentimental and cruel, feeding on self-serving thoughts of its own lofty role in our system, but in reality filled with lies and lazy ignorance. I have no wish to make enemies of the press; I have more than my share of enemies already. But the press convicted me before my trial, turned me into some kind of crazed killer bimbette in drop-dead clothes, out of a wish for a story that they only imagined was there.

That's not me. None of that is me.

You may have read that I was a cop, once, but did you know I was an artist? You almost certainly have heard that I was a "bunny" for Playboy (as if four weeks as a waitress should define a life!), but did you know that my favorite color is periwinkle blue, and that I love animals, foreign films and jazz? There are articles about my jobs, about my dismissals, about my appeals being denied, about my filing for bankruptcy, but no articles to say I enjoyed books by Marilyn French and John Steinbeck, that I played the flute for twelve years, that I've been painting since I was old enough to pick up a brush, that I used to plant a garden, and that I love the smell of wood and burning leaves. If I was free, I would want to work for Greenpeace. I'm a person, not a headline. I'm a prison-reform activist, a feminist, a lifer. I'm a daughter, a friend, a lover, a sister—maybe like yours.

Jail isn't what you think, either, not in a million years. This is not the late show. This is where women are imprisoned for prostitution while rapists go free; women caged for cocaine use while cops are on drugs; women incarcerated for fraud while witnesses commit perjury. Some women are here for stealing, but they've had everything taken from them: their freedom, their children, their humanity.

No one is safe here. Not your children, your mothers, your sisters.

I was once asked what I miss about the streets. I rambled on and on about the small things that people take for granted—frying an egg, raiding the refrigerator, driving a car. But that's not it. It's privacy. To have my love letters read, my every thought authorized, my property and my very body open to inspection—God! Is there a world without strip-searches, walkie-talkies blaring and the footsteps of the guards?

Privacy, privacy is what I miss.

When I had my freedom, I didn't even know that was all I needed.

I have cruel dreams of being free again. I dream I'm at my mother's bedroom window. My mom! Always calm and fresh, like the rain on the tiger lilies by the backyard swing, her skin cool and clean. I dreamed I saw her at the park, in her sleeveless blouse, with the wind swaying the branches above her. Safe arms to come home to. Only to wake at the sound of the blaring bell, and realize I am still here.

I've been inside for ten years now. My life is passing, my body breaking down. I don't know if there's hope left in me. I try not to cherish the anger, but the anger keeps me going.

Because I did nothing wrong.

I don't know if you can believe that. But it's true all the same.

■　　■　　■

Okay, lighten up, Bembenek!

■　　■　　■

The hoopla that surrounds this case, even now! The circus! So many partisans! So many enemies! When I was on the run, after I escaped from prison and took refuge in Canada, a Milwaukee radio station printed up thousands of Laurie Bembenek masks. All you had to do was call and they'd send you an LB Mask, made from a hideous old picture of me taken at the *Milwaukee Journal* in connection with my lawsuit years before. They blew it up and punched the eyes out so you could wear it. I got a copy later. And a naive friend asked, "But don't they have to have your permission to do that?" Yeah, sure! Permission from me! I've had every ounce of power wrestled away from me.

I was called "Bambi." It was a nickname I acquired at the Police Academy in Milwaukee. Nobody could pronounce Bembenek, though it seemed easy enough to a Polish girl from South Side Milwaukee, seeing as it's pronounced exactly the way it's spelled. Most recruits at the Academy acquired some sort of goofy nickname. It was a paramilitary environment, and to break the tension, there was a lot of horseplay and kidding around. There was a Jones, and we called him Jonestown, after the poisoned Kool-Aid place. Bradford was called Brackley, for some reason. Me they called Bambi.

That was only at the Academy. No one else called me that. I was always Laurie to my friends, or LB. It was the media that picked it up.

There were T-shirts after I escaped. *Run, Bambi, Run!* they said. My friends were baffled. My friend Kathy Braun, my best friend from prison, wrote and asked, "What? What is this Bambi thing?" She thought it was so funny.

My friends tell me that when they're making calls on my behalf, perhaps asking someone to write or do something for me, they'll ask, "Are you familiar with the Laurie Bembenek case?"

Often, the answer is no. Then they'll ask, "You know, the woman they call Bambi?"

"Oh! Bambi! Of course!" They remember that. So, in a way, the nickname is helpful. It's a double-edged sword. Some people say I shouldn't criticize it too much, because it's now used sympathetically and even affectionately as often as not. But it perpetuates a trivial image. A "Bambi" is a frightened little deer in the woods. Not exactly a feminist nickname, is it? It's awfully close to "bimbo."

The media image I was tagged with at the beginning of my case follows me still. Recently, a sympathetic reporter from the *Toronto Star* saw some of my paintings and asked me whether I'd been painting long. He was surprised when I told him I'd worked as a display artist for two or three years and had painted all my life. Yet for four or five weeks out of my life I worked at the

Playboy Club, and he certainly knew that, but he didn't know that I'd taken the job because I had been black-listed by the MPD and ordered to pay back the unemployment compensation I'd received.

When I first got to Toronto, after my recapture, the *Sun* ran an editorial saying, "She posed for a Playboy centerfold. Do we want that kind of person here in Canada?" In truth, it was just a waitressing job, but people somehow assume that a centerfold goes along with it. And so the myth is perpetuated, and becomes "fact."

After that, a few of the male guards came running up to my cellblock asking for my autograph.

"Why?" I'd ask.

"You were in the magazine ... *Playboy.* You were a centerfold ...!"

They didn't believe me when I told them I'd never posed for any such thing.

Now, if you rode a horse once, fifteen years ago, would they call you a former equestrian? Of course not.

But a bimbo seems to live forever.

■　　■　　■

Many characters have paraded through my life, for good or ill. Some of them I think of fondly, others I try not to think of at all. Some became friends; others did me harm and caused only pain. You'll meet them in what follows; some will touch you, some will very likely make your skin crawl.

You'll meet the boy I loved, who couldn't abide to see me change. You'll meet the man I married ... I thought I loved him too, but knew nothing of the shadowy world in which he lived. You'll meet the pitbull private eye who became obsessed with my case; the conman and manipulator who tried to destroy me; the convict who "confessed" to the murder for which I was convicted; the armed robber who might actually have committed that murder but who shot himself to death in the middle of a hostage-taking incident years later. You'll meet the members of the Milwaukee Police Department: some good officers and decent people, but too many of them crude and brutal men who were interested only in survival and self-profit. You'll meet the friends I made in jail, the man who helped me escape, the woman who betrayed me, the counselors who helped me, the friends who supported me, the family who loves me, the lawyers who have worked for me, some of whom I have recently learned to trust.

So many people! Some passing through my life and disappearing in a cloud of malice and acrimony; others chipping out a small niche for themselves in the place I keep the good memories, where I keep my family and my friends.

But in the end, I'm the one in jail. It's my life that is slowly seeping away, precious water sucked into the arid deserts of uncaring bureaucracy.

Here they put me, and here I still am.

■　　■　　■

I had a happy childhood, I think, though I was alone a lot. I grew up in a South Side Milwaukee neighborhood that was largely Polish and German. My mom and dad are Catholics, good people. I have two sisters, Colette and Melanie, but they are ten and thirteen years older than me, so we were never kids together.

I used to read a lot when I was a kid, because I was alone so much. I had a best friend in the neighborhood named Lori Schultz who lived just down the alley. She had four brothers, and we used to roughhouse with those kids all the time. But if she wasn't around or was busy, I was alone. I spent a lot of time reading and drawing, and my parents encouraged that.

Like most adults, I keep in my mind only a few powerful memories of those years.

Here's one: I had a bad attack of appendicitis when I was four and a half, and I remember it as if it were yesterday. It was my first disillusioning lesson in breach of contract, too.

That night, I remember, my sister Colette was babysitting—again. She was not too happy about that. We sat at home watching Red Skelton and, being typical kids, had fun chowing down on Malomars, salami and popcorn.

I started to complain about a stomachache. My sister, naturally enough, thought it was the food. I remember squeezing my little bunny slippers together, it hurt so much. I have a high tolerance for pain, and don't show it much. This can be a curse, because if you're not hysterical, people don't believe anything's wrong. My sister told me to stop crying or she'd put spiders in my bed—she was mad! By the time my parents came home I was really wailing. "My side, my side ..." My temperature was raging and they took me to the hospital, flat on my back down a corridor strapped to a table, right into the operating room. I felt really small. My dad said if I was brave he would get me a wooden rocking horse ...

I woke up with a huge scar; it looks like a caterpillar, and I don't like to wear a two-piece bathing suit to this day. Still, I was brave, very brave about the whole thing. But when I got out, my dad decided arbitrarily that I was too old for rocking horses, and he never bought me one.

My mom remembered, though. Years later, when I was married, she bought me a Christmas tree ornament that was a little wooden rocking horse. She looked at me, and I at her, and we both wanted to cry. It was a wonderful moment.

Later, I became interested in playing the flute. I started about the third or fourth grade, and I continued until I was out of high school. I'd practice two or three hours a day. Partly because of so much practice, I guess, I was better than average. When I was thirteen or fourteen, I studied with Professor Israel Borouchoffe at the university; I was the youngest person to study at the University of Wisconsin–Milwaukee. I was a bit of a prodigy, I guess.

Becoming a musician had been my mom's dream when she was young, but in those days parents didn't want to waste that kind of money on a girl, so her brother got to be a musician instead. She wanted to give this gift to me. It was her dream that I join the Milwaukee Symphony some day.

The thing about music is that it consumes your life. You must devote so much time to it. I was with one concert band for four years, and then another for four more years. My whole life as a kid seemed to be music lessons, band practice, playing for one concert or another, field drill. I never saw a parade when I was a kid—I was always in them! I went as far as I could without becoming bored, without losing all other aspects of my life.

I started my schooling at St. Augustine, a grade school. I made some good friends there. When you grow up with kids, you remember so much about them. You remember when John threw up in church in third grade, and all the trivial and wonderful stories that children retain.

Next I spent a year at St. Mary's Academy, a Catholic high school.

Ah, Catholic schools ...! Every morning we had to go to church before school. In those days, the girls had to wear chapel veils. If you forgot your chapel veil, one of the nuns would pull her hankie out of her pocket and you had to sit there with her hankie over your head. It was really humiliating.

Even as a kid, I noticed that something was screwy, really wrong, about organized religion. It seemed to be all about money and was male-dominated. The priests drove brand-new Cadillacs. I was in the rectory only once, and it was like being ushered through the gates of heaven—an awesome place, expensively furnished, with walnut paneling, thick carpeting and velvet drapes. The nuns, of course, had taken a vow of poverty and were not permitted any possessions; their house was spartan in comparison. I was just a kid, but I knew something was terribly skewed. We weren't even allowed to give the nuns small presents for Christmas.

In our neighborhood ... well, Catholics didn't allow contraception, so there were commonly huge families of thirteen or fourteen kids. Another kid? It's

God's will.... I felt wealthy compared to some of my friends. I was the last of three children, and my dad was in the construction industry, which was booming at the time. We were comfortable. My friends all wore hand-me-downs.

On the other hand, I was drawn to large families, because their homes were so alive with noise and kids, laughing and playing and roughhousing. Because my sisters were so much older, I was the only child in my little house, and it was always so quiet. My mom would have classical music on, and everything was just so, perfect, and then I'd go over to the house of one of my playmates and there'd be fourteen kids screaming and fighting. It seemed like a lot of fun.

I loved big families for another reason. When you're the only one at home, you're the only object of attention. So if you're five or ten minutes late, they know, they're waiting for you. My parents were strict with me. But heck, at my friend's house we could be an hour late and her mom never even noticed! What a difference! Her mom had ten other kids to take care of. They just didn't get the attention I got, and of course I saw that as an advantage.

The problem with some brands of Catholicism is that everything is a sin. Even thinking about sin is a sin. You grow up guilt-ridden, shame-based. I broke with that as much as I could, but some of it still comes back to haunt me ... it's ingrained.

At St. Augustine, I had an outrageous experience with a priest that has colored my thinking about the church and religion ever since.

This priest taught a catechism class to sixth- and seventh-graders. He told us that among advanced theologians there is apparently a theory that Mary Magdalene was Jesus's mistress. But you don't tell that to sixth-graders! At that time, I was a true believer. I loved Jesus with all my heart. It was blind faith. The way that man talked about Jesus seemed so wrong and dirty and shocking, it made me want to cry.

I started to challenge him—I always had a big mouth. I would look around to see if my classmates were similarly shocked. Oh, over there would be someone picking her nose, and someone else would be sleeping and yawning. Most were not even listening.

I tried to tell my mom all this, but I couldn't understand it well enough to know what was going on, so I didn't explain it well. I just knew something was really wrong.

The priest was also in charge of the gym classes, which were held in the church basement, and he would make more strange comments there. He would say stuff like, "If you girls do enough of this exercise, you'll all look like Marilyn Monroe."

I was thinking, What is this guy saying? Developing girls are so self-conscious as it is. All these references to our body parts? I knew it wasn't appropriate. It gave me the creeps. Everything he did was to embarrass us, to put us down as girls. Some of the girls had their periods already, and when they felt too sick to take the gym class he'd ridicule them for that.

One afternoon, when I was twelve, I was sitting on the basement floor, wearing pants, with my feet up on a bench along the wall. He looked over and yelled, "Bembenek, get your feet off the wall!"

Well, I was a smartass and never did like authority. I lifted my feet in the air but didn't move them. Technically, they weren't on the wall anymore.

He turned around and glanced at me again and lost his temper altogether, and in front of all these little kids, he hollered, "Goddamn it, Bembenek! I told you to get your fucking feet off the wall, you look like a slut!"

I looked at him ... I didn't even know what a "slut" was! All the little girls dropped their jump ropes and stood there with their mouths hanging open at this sight of a priest swearing and taking the Lord's name in vain in a major way.

I knew, however, that whatever a "slut" was it was really bad, and I wasn't that. So I stood up and I said, "I am not a slut!"

And he said, "If you look like one I'll treat you like one!"

Nice man.

"Go back up to the classroom," he shouted. "Get out of my sight. You disobeyed me."

I looked at him, and I just couldn't keep my mouth shut. I said, "Oh yeah, and you know what you are!"

I didn't know what I was saying. I didn't know what "gay" was, never mind "pedophile" or "misogynist." I just knew he was bad. I had to say something, so I said it and started to walk away.

Then I heard my girlfriends yelling, "Run, Laurie!"

I turned around, and this guy was coming after me. There was a tunnel between the church and the school building, and I took off on my spindly little legs and ran through the tunnel. He was a big, oafish guy and couldn't run very well, and I was a little sprinter. To this day I wonder what he would have done if he'd caught me.

I went to the playground, panting against the church wall like a little criminal, then later I hid in the girls' washroom.

I was miserable. I told my mom I'd gotten into trouble at school again, and explained what had happened. My mother was shocked. When my dad came home, I told the story again. I don't want to say anything against my parents, because I love them, but they were brought up not to make any waves, to leave things alone, to clean it up, not make things worse. If that had been my kid, I'd have run right to the *Milwaukee Journal*, and to the first lawyer I could find, and I would have taken that creep into court so fast ... but people weren't sue-happy in those days.

They decided to go and see the pastor. On the way to my flute lesson after supper, we stopped at the rectory, but the pastor was so drunk he wasn't even coherent. He had changed too much water into wine, I guess.

My mom and dad decided I should leave the school, but I refused to go. I said no, I want to graduate, I don't want to leave my friends. If I left, it would be admitting I had done something wrong, and I hadn't.

It was my first really powerful lesson in independence.

■　　■　　■

I went through something of a rocky adolescence, as many teenagers do. My parents, who were very strict, were not ecstatic about my behavior. In the ninth grade I suddenly wanted to stay out as late as my other friends. They could stay out until eleven, but I had to be home by nine. We could not agree on anything. I was a bit of a wild child, I guess. Some of my rebellion was a fascination with the tail end of the sixties, when disobedience was fashionable; we all still wanted to be hippies. My sister had a boyfriend with long hair, and I wanted one too. I thought my two sisters were just the coolest things on earth, and I wanted to do everything they did. I wanted to wear the shirts from India with the little mirrors all over them and burn incense and wear sandals and smoke hash and be like them. And of course I was too young to do any of those things, really.

My mom went through menopause when I was going through adolescence—talk about raging hormones on Taylor Avenue!

We battled it out all the time. I wanted to wear make-up and she wouldn't let me. I couldn't even get a phone call from a boy. And of course the more they prohibited me, the more I wanted to rebel.

They decided it would be a good idea for me to go to an all-girl school and wear a little plaid skirt. Scholastically, St. Mary's Academy was the best school around; I was reading Keats and Shakespeare and studying Latin. But it wasn't a well-rounded atmosphere—there was no band, the school offered only a few sports and a small Art Department.

When you're an adolescent, you really have no way to meet boys aside from school. In an all-girl school, you're stuck. I guess St. Mary's was a good preparation for prison in that way. But like the prisoner who most wants what she can't have, we were obsessed with boys, because there weren't any. I don't think you can develop normally in an all-girl setting. I remember these dreadful dances, the boys bused over—it was so embarrassing. We were all so shy. Everyone stood on one side or the other of the gym, too scared to talk to anyone, not knowing how ...

Finally my rebelliousness persuaded them they were wasting their money, and they transferred me to the public system, to Bay View High. Then I was bored; we were reading books I'd read two or three years earlier. I lost interest in my studies. But I did other things. I joined the band. And I joined the girls' track team. We were the first girls' track team in the state, which shows you how backward things were. Before that, the only thing for girls to do was cheerleading. I was always long and spindly, but I could run like the wind, and I ran the 110-yard hurdles.

The boys all got to take shop; the girls had to take sewing and cooking. I have a domestic deficiency to this day—I can't cook. (Of course, ten years in prison doesn't help!) I hated being dictated to on that level. I wanted to take woodworking and shop; I loved the smell of wood, making things from wood. I never did understand why I couldn't do these things ... I couldn't understand why women were denied choices just because they were women, and why housework was gender-specific. I was a feminist before I'd ever heard the word.

■   ■   ■

I got my first job when I was sixteen and still in school. There was a program in my senior year that allowed students to work if they didn't need a full load of courses. I had enough credits to graduate early, but who wants to hire a sixteen-year-old? Instead, I decided to take one or two easy credits in my senior year— ceramics was one—and work after school. I went to school for half a day, worked half a day. First I worked for a jewelry store, then as a waitress down-town. What an education! That part of town was full of pimps and prostitutes, drunk sailors, mentally ill people wandering around. Later I was a waitress in a mall department store on the south side and worked for K–mart in the shoe department. I regret now that I didn't go all the way through to university, but I guess I was a typical teenager of the time.

I looked into the job of police aide—this is not exactly a police officer but more like a clerk. But my birthday didn't fall on the right date—I was either too young or too old by a couple of months, so I missed it.

The summer I graduated from high school was the best of my life. I was soon going to be eighteen and able to drink legally. Everything seemed possible.

My best friend, Joanne, decided to go to the University of Denver, so it was our last summer together. As a graduation present, I got permission for the first time to go to Daytona Beach for the college madness. Joanne and I went together. It was the first time I'd been to Florida.

I met a guy there who was from Milwaukee, Danny, and I ended up going out with him for four years. I loved him so much! It's too bad we were so young when we met. If we'd been older, it might have worked out, and everything would have been different. But it was too early. I felt I was in transition from one life to another. I wasn't ready. He wanted to get married, but marriage was the last thing on my mind.

On a whim that summer I took a test and won a scholarship to a local business college, Bryant & Stratton, where I took an associate degree program in Fashion Merchandising Management. The hours were peculiar and so I managed to hold down three part-time jobs at the same time. At night I tended bar. In the afternoons, I worked at a pharmacy, as a cashier, and whenever I had a few spare hours, I did inventory for a baby clothing company, Carter's.

It was during this period that I started modeling.

■　　　■　　　■

Talking about this period of my life is tough for me, even now. So much garbage has been written about me and how I look, as if that's all there is. After my arrest, even local women's groups couldn't seem to see past the descriptions of my clothes and my face and my body. And it still happens. A Vanity Fair reporter, speaking to me in jail this year, denied that I could have been unhappy during this period. "You were drop-dead gorgeous, you had everything going for you, how can you sit there and tell me you were depressed?" he demanded.

All they ever want to do is ask me about sex. All they ever do is think back to that one cheesecake calendar photo I did for Schlitz (in which I was Miss March 1978, but fully clothed, after all), which they have turned in their minds into some kind of symbol for my life. Why must they try to imprison me in my body as well as in these grim, gray places they have put me for the past decade?

■　　　■　　　■

When I was growing up, people would often say to me, "You're so tall, you should be a model!" You hear that often enough and you're just a kid and you get curious. So I looked into it.

14

There are so many false, preconceived notions about the life of a model. I thought it would be really glamorous, and to a certain extent it was. But you know what? It's not exactly cerebral.

I couldn't understand why I was not happier doing it, this job that I thought I wanted, but it was completely unsatisfying. I was treated like a mannequin. Everyone condescends to you. The photographers are prima donnas of the worst kind.

I was pretty naive around then. I was a teenager, and my politics weren't really together yet. I was dabbling, not yet knowing what I wanted, who I was. I wouldn't do lingerie shows and I never did nude modeling. I knew I had to be able to come home and show my dad the photos without being embarrassed. The calendar was the most risqué thing I ever did. I was eighteen when I posed for that thing; it's fifteen years old. Why do they keep bringing it up? I never did anything like it again.

For a while, I worked for The Limited, a store that sold better ready-to-wear fashions. I was selling their designer dresses, at three and four hundred dollars each. Employees were required to wear their clothing, but even with forty percent off it was expensive. It was easy to become addicted to the very latest things—I had all kinds of clothes. My closet's probably still stuffed with all that junk.

In 1978 I started working for Boston Store, as a display artist. I really liked that. I was up and down on ladders all day doing displays and fixtures, that sort of thing, helping to move all the wretched excess of the capitalist system! I was happy. It was creative, and without the pressure of sales. I liked the store and all the employees. To this day some of them write to me. I also taught a health-and-beauty course to eighth-graders, and worked part-time at Vic Tanny's Health Club.

But I was impatient. I was always impatient. I wanted a little authority, a little responsibility, but I discovered that the store didn't accept anyone under twenty-four into their management program. I was only nineteen, and twenty-four seemed decades away. Then the store was bought out, and there were major changes. I started thinking about police work again.

I had always had police work in the back of my mind. My dad had been a cop for a while, an MP in the U.S. Army and later with the Milwaukee Police Department.

My dad never, ever, told me I couldn't do something just because I was a woman. Never. He was extraordinary that way. My mom doesn't think he's the most progressive guy in the world, and in some ways he's not. But he never treated his daughters in any way but with encouragement.

■　　■　　■

At the same time, my relationship with Danny was beginning to sour. That relationship ... oh, it almost became habit. We couldn't live with one another, we couldn't live without one another. It was difficult. I was living at home. I could barely afford things like car payments. Wages were so low I was working at two jobs, from eight to five at Boston Store and then from six to ten at Vic Tanny's. This wasn't uncommon—lots of people, especially women, worked at a couple of jobs to survive. I couldn't afford to move away from my parents.

Danny and I were not officially living together. Practically, you understand, but not really. I look back on those years with him as perhaps the happiest years of my life. We had no adult responsibilities. We had trivial priorities like learning the latest disco dance step and trying to outdo each other in getting a darker tan. I wish I had such problems now! He had a married brother in Chicago and we'd visit him all the time. We'd go out and have fun there. We'd have fun all the time. When I think of it, ah ... really ...

No, I mustn't think of it, not now.

I became very unhappy. I began to dislike modeling. My other jobs were going nowhere. I didn't know what I wanted. I didn't know why I was unhappy. And it was ridiculous. I had the world by the tail, but I never realized it. I didn't know how really miserable it was possible to be.

I turned twenty-one. It was then that I applied to the Police Department. We know what happened after that.

Very wise decision on my part, right?

2

OFFICER BEMBENEK

Around my twenty-first birthday, I came across a notice in the newspaper that indicated special applications were being solicited for the Milwaukee Police Department. In order to meet federal requirements, women and minorities were being urged to apply. Eagerly I made the trip downtown once again.

■　　■　　■

Oh God, why was I there? Why didn't the ghosts of the future frighten me off? Why didn't I flee? I would have, should have, if I'd only known ... I'd listened to my dad talking about the cops, telling stories—none of the bad stuff, of course, only the romantic stories. Why didn't I shut my ears?

My dad wasn't a cop for very long, really. Now he says he hated it, hated the corruption and the special pleading and the double-dealing. Maybe he thought it would be different for me ...

By trade he's a carpenter, and an excellent one; he's a big man with big carpenter's hands. I worked alongside him sometimes, and he told me I could have been a carpenter, too. I was good with wood. I'm no cabinet maker, but I'm not shabby either.

I could have been a carpenter, and not a cop. I could have been a carpenter, and not a convict.

But I've been inside ten years now, ten years of watching the branches, the green wood, through small windows, past bars, the green wood against the open sky.

And I know that might-have-beens are a trap for the unwary.

■　　■　　■

I was scheduled for a short interview with a sergeant at the station in my district. Dressed casually in jeans and a T-shirt, I parked my car and entered the building. I hadn't been there for years.

I sat down on a hard bench and overheard the boisterous cops behind the desk, arguing over who should pick up the fish-fries for supper that night. One of them noticed me and smiled.

"Don't tell me you're waiting for an interview? You mean a pretty little thing like you wants to be a big, bad policeman?"

"Police *officer*," I corrected him. Off to a good start.

Another cop sneered. "Hey! Assign her to my squad! I'll teach her a few things!" An outburst of guffaws followed. These are the kinds of remarks all women grow accustomed to.

To my relief, the sergeant then called me into his small, stuffy office. He was a polite, middle-aged man, the buttons bulging on his blue uniform shirt. He explained that character references would be required and then a background investigation would follow.

A few months went by and I was notified by mail that I was eligible to take a written exam. At the exam, I tried to analyze every question to establish what exactly it was they were looking for. My answers must've been acceptable because I was notified after several months that I'd passed.

A physical agility test was next. It included tests of speed and strength. I read the list of events and it didn't appear to be too difficult, with the exception of a test to scale a six-foot wall.

I searched the city for a similar wall to practice on. I thought a schoolyard or an institution of some sort might suffice, but cyclone fences weren't the same.

The night before the test I couldn't sleep. I kept thinking about that crazy wall as I tossed and turned. As the gray light of dawn began to filter in through my windows, I abandoned the effort to sleep and wearily rose from my bed. My parents were already awake, rinsing out the coffeepot at the kitchen sink and plugging in the toaster. I dressed quickly, saying a silent prayer before leaving the house for the Police Academy where the test was to be held.

"I promise to go to church every Sunday from now on if only I pass ..."

I ran dashes and long distances. I hung in a chin-up position until my eye-balls bulged, and then I had to drag a 150-pound dummy a certain number of feet in under ten seconds. The grip-strength of my hands was tested on a meter. The wall was the last event.

As I stood in line with the other contestants, a young woman behind me began chatting about her progress that day. She was worried about passing. I confessed my fear of the wall. It was a relief to know that I wasn't the only one harboring an insecurity or two. The young woman said her name was Judy.

I drove home happily. I'd passed every test, even going over the wall like a squirrel. I was certain the hardest part was over.

Another month passed. I received notice of a medical exam. All female applicants had to have a pelvic exam. I grimaced at the thought of it.

The next thing I knew, I was standing in a line with a cup of freshly-peed urine, clad in a drafty, white paper sheet, feeling like I had just joined the army. The examining doctor asked me if I was on birth-control pills. Was it any of his business? I answered the question anyway. Later, I realized that the question would indicate whether or not a woman was sexually active—yet there was no similar indicating question for men. I knew the Police Depart-ment had in the past dismissed its officers for "sexual conduct outside the sanctity of marriage," and also for "cohabitation." Such things were techni-cally illegal in Wisconsin in 1979 even though no one was ever arrested for "living together."

A few months elapsed, and then I was granted an oral examination before the Fire and Police Commissioners. They presented hypothetical examples, rating each answer I gave.

They asked me why I wanted to become a police officer. Tough question to answer without sounding naive or insincere. I tried to answer honestly. Ner-vously, I looked at each Commission member for some sign of reaction, but they simply continued silently to write their evaluations.

The last situation described to me was this:

"You are in a squad and you're the senior officer. You get dispatched to a 'man with a gun' call. When you arrive, the scene is a three-story apartment building, and a crowd of people block the entranceway. A woman runs up to your squad and identifies herself as the sister of the man inside with the gun. She informs you that he has himself locked in, has turned on all the gas inside the apartment, has a shotgun and refuses to come out. She adds that he is also presently under psychiatric care. What do you do?"

I thought I managed to answer this complicated question logically, while the Commission members returned my stare, expressionless. I suggested calling for other squads, clearing the crowd away from the entrance, contacting the man's doctor if possible and turning off the gas in the apartment.

"What if every step you took failed?" they countered. "What would you do if the man still refused to come out?"

"Then we'd just have to go in," I replied, and then thought, "Oh no!"

The Commission thanked me for my time. Later, I found out that I had scored very high, despite my doubts, placing sixth. I was excited. It was now only a matter of time before I got my appointment date to the Police Academy. My last small exam was straightforward, vision testing and a test for color-blindness.

Almost a year had passed since I'd filled out the application.

I had to sit back and wait. Patience was never one of my virtues, and as time went by I grew restless. I was losing interest in my work at Boston Store. I didn't resign, though, because I was entitled to vacation time, and I'd decided to try to synchronize this time off with Danny's spring break from school.

We were having problems. He seemed to be distancing himself from me. We couldn't seem to make it through an evening without a heated argument. He'd been unenthusiastic about my career plans, to say the least. He merely shrugged when I talked about the Academy. Were we just a habit now? But we were in love, we believed. We'd been dating for four years. I loved him, and I thought that if we could just be alone for a while we could save what had meant so much to both of us for so long. We talked about going away together for a week or two.

It wasn't to be. Just after confirming our vacation plans, I was notified of my appointment date at the Milwaukee Police Academy: March 10, 1980.

Danny and I had just returned from a ski trip. I went in the back door of my house, wet skis under my arm, and my dad met me. He had the envelope from the city. He'd been so eager for the news that he'd already opened it. I read the letter and showed it to Danny, smiling and happy.

"March 10?" he exclaimed suddenly. "Laurie! That's right on top of our vacation!"

We argued for a while, fruitlessly, but then he left, slamming the door behind him.

It had taken me so long to get this appointment! I'd worked hard for it. I wanted this career. Why couldn't he understand? Maybe, I thought optimistically, we could squeeze in a vacation before my starting date. I could quit my job earlier than I had planned.

I'd just finished putting away my boots, goggles and ski poles in the hallway closet when the phone in the kitchen rang. It was Danny.

We argued some more, but he refused to compromise. It was impossible for him to get away from school and his part-time job any other time, he said. "Now we face a cancellation penalty from the travel agency."

Half an hour later he called me back to announce that he had a replacement to go with him on our special vacation—a buddy from his neighborhood.

That seemed to be that. He had chosen to precipitate a break.

■   ■   ■

Still, I had three weeks before starting at the Academy and had paid vacation time from Boston Store. I really wanted to go somewhere. I knew it would be another year before I could get away again.

I was at the Police Administration building downtown for some last-minute errand when I ran into Judy Zess, the woman who'd worried so about passing her physical agility tests. We were both quitting our jobs early. I told her I was planning to take a vacation before starting at the Academy.

"I'd like to go on a vacation too. Someplace warm! After this it's going to be a lot of hard work. Did you say you had reservations somewhere?"

"Yeah. I managed to book a hotel in Miami at the last minute—a few days ago. Getting the flight was harder."

"Are you going alone?"

"I guess I am."

"If I could get a flight I could join you in Miami! That is, if you'd like some company. We'd have fun."

"Sounds like a good idea," I said.

A week later I flew down to Florida, and Judy met me there. The weather was a little cool but we still had a pleasant time. Judy's intelligence and frankness impressed me. She spoke French fluently and told me that she'd studied in Switzerland as a foreign exchange student.

Aren't first impressions wonderful? Two years later this woman would testify against me.

There was one odd incident during our vacation, though I didn't pay it much attention at the time. A man staying at our hotel had been meeting Judy for drinks and sitting with her at the pool. He told me Judy had said she was obsessed with the desire to sleep with me. I was shocked. I laughed it off. She must have been joking. I felt it was too absurd to repeat to Judy, so I didn't confront her.

■   ■   ■

21

Fun ended at the Milwaukee Police Academy doors. I hadn't expected such a military atmosphere. Marine Corps Basic Training couldn't hold a candle to the twenty-one weeks of grueling misery that the Academy put us through. I felt as though the intention was to drain the recruit of identity, of anything that contributed to individualism or personality. We were blue machines, carbon copies of one another. We were programmed into a blind obedience—a selfless dedication.

The Department rules and regulations were originally written for men, since at that time there were no women police officers. At the Academy, unwritten rules for female recruits were arbitrarily introduced and arbitrarily enforced. No make-up, fingernail polish or long hair allowed. It's difficult to ignore years of socialization, so I felt almost naked without all of those things at first. For both men and women, hair could not touch the shirt collar and sideburns had to be cut to reach mid-ear. Hair on the sides could not cover the ears. Inspection every morning allowed our commanding officers to make sure we all appeared perfect. The black shoes we wore had to be shined, our navy-blue uniforms lint-free and our brass buckles polished.

In addition to having our appearance scrutinized at inspection, our memories were tested. We had to memorize the Daily Bulletin, which listed all the crimes that had occurred in the city the previous day, all the felonies, misdemeanors, missing persons and stolen cars. We learned descriptions, the names of victims, the license numbers of cars. It was demanding and at times ridiculous. There were no excuses or exceptions. Our jobs were on the line.

We had strenuous physical training daily, including running, weight lifting, calisthenics, volleyball and self-defense. I threw myself into this because I enjoyed it immensely. I did well. I found myself alongside some of the best guys in the class when it came to running and weight lifting. It was competitive and challenging, and I think some of the male recruits enjoyed competing with me. We were a class of fifty-five, nine of us women.

We studied subjects like Accident Scene Procedure and Report Writing. Our classes included Traffic Law, Criminal Investigation, Search and Seizure Law, Defensive Driving and a course in the Rules and Regulations of the Department. We used shotguns and handguns. We were certified in first aid and Cardio-Pulmonary Resuscitation.

Camaraderie developed. Nicknames emerged. "Bambi" made her appearance.

At noon every day there was a movie—a different lesson each day, different crime scenes and situations. I suffered through an emergency childbirth film—a huge close-up on an eight-by-nine-foot screen, of an explosion birth. The vulva tore.

"Jesus! You could drive a truck through that thing!" laughed one of the male recruits. Typical subtle humor.

I almost made it through the movie, my disinclination to bear children completely reinforced by this time. I cringed at every labor pain. Then the placenta emerged, and I was out the classroom door. When I returned, white-faced, the men teased me about leaving.

"You missed the best part of the film! They showed us how you can use your shoelace to disconnect the umbilical cord by tying a knot around it," a recruit informed me, grinning.

"What?"

"Suppose a lady decides to give birth on a street corner or in an elevator and you don't have your first-aid kit?"

"I'll tell you what I'm going to do," another recruit assured him. "I'm going to take off my shoelace, tie that lady's knees together and go Red Lights 'n Siren to the hospital where she belongs!"

"Thank God cops don't have ambulance duty anymore," I said. Milwaukee had abolished that practice several years before.

The female officers got back at the men a few days later. The noon movie was called *The Mansfield, Ohio Exposé*. A public washroom in Mansfield was the target. To the dismay and embarrassment of the male recruits, we viewed acts of oral and anal sex between men who frequented this restroom. There was a great deal of hand stimulation and hilarious defiances of gravity. The men arrested included married teachers, lawyers, family men and one well-known athlete. The female recruits had a good snicker at the roomful of red-faced men at the end of the movie.

I had another problem with the film, though. It was intended to reinforce the Police Academy's disapproval of a recent bill challenging state law on sex between consenting adults. Like the archaic "illegal cohabitation" standards, there was still a "fornication" law on the state books. The Mansfield film served as a statement from our superiors that legalizing any sex between consenting adults would encourage homosexuals, lesbians and child-molesters—all that they considered "deviant."

During one class, an instructor known for his lurid vocabulary lectured us on street language. His name was Blackburn.

"Now," he began, "assuming that probably all of you officers come from good, God-fearing homes, and that you are all intelligent, educated people, you'll find out when you get out on the street that there are a lot of seedy individuals. You'll have to get used to the language they use, because they'll use it to shock you—to get you to lose your temper. Don't give anyone the satisfaction of knowing that they pissed you off."

He walked around the room. "Especially you female officers! You'll have

23

to resign yourself to being an unusual sight for most people. The public is used to seeing the neighborhood policeman. You might face a bit more harassment on the street."

I watched him pace back and forth. "I'm not saying you have to take whatever anyone dishes out. If abusive swearing disturbs other people, then you can make an arrest for disorderly conduct. But if their comments are not made in front of other people, you have no right to arrest them. They can say anything they want to you. If you lose your temper and a fight starts over something they said to you, you won't have a leg to stand on in court. It will be an open-and-shut case of police brutality."

He stopped in front of a female recruit. "For instance—say two fellas come up to you while you're walking your beat and say: Well! What do we have here? A pussy cop!"

She blushed, but he continued.

"Hey! Why are you carrying around that night-stick? Can't you find a man?"

Her name was Linda Palese. She turned three shades of red and everyone in the class laughed. Then he turned and looked at me. I stopped laughing.

"Bembenek! Is your mother still hooking?"

"Just on weekends, sir," I replied, playing his game.

It was an exercise in self-control, of course, to illustrate what can happen on the street. I understood what he was trying to get across. Blackburn was an excellent instructor, a twenty-two-year veteran of the department. His experience was valuable, his war stories humorous and his intentions basically good.

Palese never came back after that. Maybe she just realized that she didn't like the job.

Blackburn was always looking over my shoulder, always scrutinizing my work, appearance and attitude. He especially liked to catch me in a transgression and make me file what we called a "Matter of" report—a standard disciplinary device. I recognized this immediately, so purposely kept on my toes when he was around.

In April we received our four-week evaluations. I got good marks from all the sergeants and instructors but was told that they were particularly impressed with my physical performance on the track and in the gym. There were only three men who ran faster than me.

After our evaluation, a heavyset guy by the name of Duthie was gone. No one in the class knew if he was dismissed or if he resigned. It put a scare into a few of us.

Meanwhile, Blackburn continued to catch me doing chin-ups on doorjambs in the hallways and threw reports back at me that were written in blue ink instead of the required black ink. He saw even the smallest mistakes, and never failed to come down hard on me for them.

After some weeks, when he'd summoned me to his office for more correction, he sat back in his chair looking at me. I returned the gaze.

"Off the record, Bembenek—you know I've been picking on you to a certain extent."

"Have you sir?" I asked innocently.

"Yes. I think we're on the same wavelength. I was testing you to see what kind of stuff you're made of. I thought I might be able to get your goat, make you lose your temper, your self-control ... perhaps even make you cry. But you're doing all right, Bembenek. You'll be okay."

About a week later, another female recruit officer resigned. Her name was Janet Shadewald. I liked her and thought she was going to make a good cop. Again, no one knew what happened. I passed her in the hallway one morning and could see she had been crying. She was in civilian clothes and was carrying the contents of her locker. I wondered if she was dismissed or if she had resigned.

At home, I was preoccupied with studying and memorizing Miranda, the Carroll Rule, the Plain View Doctrine, the basic circumstances of a legal search, the Fourth Amendment and many other lessons. I had exams coming out of my ears, along with memorizing the Daily Bulletin, the hot car sheet and cancellations of items when suspects were apprehended. I had to ask my mom to help me wash and iron my uniforms because I was beyond help in that department. "What I need is a wife!" I thought cynically.

In the midst of this whirlwind, Danny returned from vacation. He seemed like a different person. I asked him if he'd met another woman while he was away, but he denied it. We argued constantly.

"I hate that dyke haircut," he snapped. "Why do you want that macho job?"

"My hair will grow back. But why do you assume I'm changed? It's only my appearance."

"It's not just that," he insisted. "That job is interfering with us. First it interfered with our vacation and now it's interfering with our social life, because you're always busy studying or too tired to go out. And you've changed. You're swearing too much. It's not ladylike."

Maybe, I thought, I had changed. I wasn't seventeen anymore. Perhaps I'd outgrown him.

"Since when has that mattered? You swear a lot," I said.

"That's different, Laurie. I'm a man."

"You drive me crazy!" I shouted.

Great dialogue, right?

Our fights became more frequent, each one increasing the futility of our efforts to restore harmony. Every time we argued, he would bring up the subject of my job.

So I was forced to choose between the man in my life and a career I wanted.

Mostly what I felt was anger, I had trained on my own for the job for a long time and passed a series of difficult tests. But instead of being proud of me, he was filled with resentment. I wondered if he wasn't jealous because of the high salary I was earning.

I began to examine him through the prism of some of my new attitudes, as well as my older, more feminist attitudes. He seemed so ... outdated. He was hopelessly traditional, conventional, with all the sexist double standards of our time.

He tried to persuade me that a wedding in his church, followed by a marriage with children, was the only life for us. I told him I didn't want to marry, didn't plan to have children, ever, and even if I did eventually marry I'd want to be secure in a career first. I didn't feel it was my obligation to get married in his church, I said, and in any case, I didn't intend to change my name.

Did I love him? If I did, it must have been for physical reasons. We had so many differences, religious and political, and our goals seemed always to conflict. In the end, I just couldn't give up everything that was "me." And so, on a quiet Saturday afternoon, I picked up the phone and we said goodbye.

3

FIRST INTIMATIONS OF TROUBLE

Blackburn continued to single me out. One day he had a lesson in observation to teach the recruits. After his usual class, he walked to the back of the room and ordered everyone to remain seated, facing the front.

"Okay officers!" he shouted. "You've all been staring at a suspect for over an hour now—namely *me*. Officer Bembenek, describe that suspect."

"Shit!" I thought. Facing the front of the room, I stood up quickly and tried to recall what he was wearing. I hadn't paid much attention. But I still had an advantage—my training from the fashion world. I knew that the cheap old goat only owned about three suits. To give myself more time to think, I started with the obvious physical description, starting at the head and going down.

"White male, six feet, two inches and about 170 pounds ... short gray hair, mint-green polyester plaid sports coat ... white shirt and tie, green pants, brown shoes ... and I would say the suspect had to be between fifty-five and fifty-nine years of age," I recited.

"I'll get you for that last one, Bembenek!" he said, and the class laughed. He was only in his forties.

Another time we had an exercise with a film series called *Shoot—Don't Shoot*. It illustrated the minute amounts of time available for decision-making in emergencies. An officer has only a split second to decide whether or not to use his (or her) gun. The film's choice: shoot at a suspect, or not shoot and risk death.

I was told to pick up the imitation handgun and stand before the screen. The film began. The first scene showed a squad answering a family-trouble complaint.

I "entered" a yard full of small children. It was very hard to discern movement. There was a sudden, loud **BANG**. A five-year-old kid had a gun that I didn't see, and shot me. The sergeants rewound the film and let the class review it.

"Well, Bembenek—you're dead!" Blackburn declared. "Now, my question is: would you have pulled out your gun and shot a five-year-old child had you seen the gun in time?"

I was uncertain. "Um. Yes, sir."

"Do you mean to tell me that you would have pulled out a gun and shot a small child?"

"Yes, sir," I answered apprehensively.

"Damn right, officer! Don't sound so unsure of yourself! I don't care if an eighty-five-year-old woman points a gun at you! You don't have time to ask them if they plan on shooting it or not!" He looked at me. "Let's give you the next film to try, Bembenek."

The next situation had me approaching a car stopped for speeding. It was a convertible with the top down, an old woman behind the wheel. As I approached, before I even reached the door, she turned around and—**BANG**! I was shot again. I began to think the situations were downright impossible.

"Watch the hands! Watch the hands!" Blackburn was bellowing. "Officer Bembenek, you don't seem to be doing so well. Shot to death twice today! Why don't we give you one more chance. Let's run the next film and see how you manage this one."

"Damn it!" I thought, rattled. The class was chuckling. I was determined to do well on the next situation.

The film showed a squad car in the area of a bank that had just been robbed. Several people had described the suspect: she was armed and dangerous, a black female, five feet, seven inches. She was wearing a white blouse, yellow skirt and white boots. She was on foot.

The film had me leave my squad. I began walking through a crowded square not far from the bank. A black woman fitting the description was walking straight toward me. When she saw me, she reached into her purse and began to pull something out. Quickly I drew my imitation handgun and—**CLICK**—pulled the trigger to shoot her.

A second later she started to powder her nose with the compact she withdrew from her purse. Everyone laughed.

A replay of the film allowed the class to see that she was wearing a yellow blouse, white skirt and yellow boots—close but not correct. Blackburn explained that the sequence of situations had been intentionally arranged to show how a chain of events can affect observation adversely.

"Every recruit ever tested overreacted the very same way," Blackburn said.

The didactic methods were effective, but I thought they bordered on brainwashing. It took me years to understand the politics behind the ideology being inculcated. We were only presented with one explanation of crime, and we were expected to buy it completely, without question.

Department attitudes towards women were appalling. I tried not to be aggressively feminist when discussing cases of rape, but it was hard—I'd never thought rape was anything to joke about. For several years I'd been a member of various feminist groups: NOW, Women Against Rape, the Women's Political Caucus. I'd contributed money, written letters and marched in protests. I'd even attended a rally against Police Chief Harold Breier for refusing to establish a special sexual-assault unit to replace the hopelessly insensitive, male-dominated Vice Squad. (This was before I joined the force, of course!)

One day in class the subject of a highly publicized sexual assault was brought up. The case involved a young woman who was pressing charges against several members of a local motorcycle gang, the Outlaws. She was the girlfriend of one of the members and had been sleeping with him at the gang's clubhouse one night when the rest of the bikers arrived. Three of the Outlaws repeatedly and viciously raped her.

"It's really a shame the way the law works," was the Sergeant's viewpoint. "Here you've got this broad who's a dancer at some bar—she's got a lousy reputation already but now she's screaming rape. She was sleeping with one of these bums but the way our law works? Even if her choice was Guys One, Two and Three: Yes, but Guys Four, Five and Six: No—she could actually press charges! She could have numbers Four, Five and Six prosecuted!"

Most of the other men in class thought this was funny, but Kocher's attitude outraged me. I couldn't shut up.

I raised my hand. "Sir, there's another way to look at this. Say that there's a man around town who is very rich. Say this man carries a lot of cash on him, which is unwise, and has even been known to flash his money around and give some away to strangers. Knowing all this, would that give you the right to steal from him? No! The same holds true for sexual assault. No one has the right to forcibly take a woman's body."

Kocher raised his eyes and changed the subject. Afterwards he would occasionally comment to me on the progress of certain women's issues. One morning he walked in and smiled. "Did you read the paper this morning, Bembenek? Another one of the states refused to ratify!" He was referring to the Equal Rights Amendment.

"Male-dominated legislature," I simply replied.

A black male officer by the name of Hicks was gone that day. The class was shrinking. There were hushed comments and worried glances.

■ ■ ■

Then I was invited to a party. From where I look now, I can feel that invitation as if it were yesterday, and I want to scream down the years, No! Don't go! Only dire things will happen! But, of course, time is my enemy, and I cannot hear ...

■ ■ ■

It was late April, and the party was given by a recruit called Boville as a house-warming. It had been such a long time since I had been out that I decided to go. I asked Judy if she planned on going, but she hadn't been invited. Later that day, on break, I was talking with a black recruit named Thomas about a new record album. Thomas asked if he could borrow it. I said yes and asked him if he was going to Boville's party. He said he was planning to but didn't know where it was. I offered to drop off the album on my way to the party and give him Boville's address.

"Where are you going to be after work?" I asked him.

Just then the intercom came on and we were called back to class. Over the drone of the speaker, Thomas told me an address. I scribbled numbers onto a notebook cover.

I returned home later that day and my phone rang. A girlfriend was in town for the weekend.

"Can we get together?" she asked. "What are you doing tonight?"

"I've been invited to a party—a guy from work. You can go with me but you won't know anybody."

"That's okay. I'd like to go. Can you pick me up?"

"I have one place to stop first, to drop off an album, but then I can pick you up. Sure."

I changed out of uniform, showered and put on a denim skirt with a striped T-shirt. I found the album and rushed out of the house. The address Thomas gave me was on the North Side of town.

When I arrived, I gave Thomas the record and Boville's address with the nearest intersection listed on the same slip of paper. Another recruit, White, was there. I only stayed a few minutes because I had to pick up my friend.

The party was crowded, hot, blasting with music from the fifties. It wasn't my kind of get-together. I stood in the basement with my Dixie cup of beer, watching someone do "the twist." My friend looked bored. Some of my class-mates were there, but we couldn't talk over the loud music. My friend and I decided to leave.

As we stood in line to use the bathroom upstairs, a drunk lurched up to me and announced that she was Officer Tim Klug's wife. With no provocation she began insulting me.

"You work with my husband, don't you? Well! You can't let much more hang out of that T-shirt, can you?" She was swaying badly.

What was this? "Look," I said. "I don't know what your problem is, but why don't you go sit down before you fall down?"

"I saw the way Tim looked at you when you walked in!" she continued. "Why don't you stick that badge of yours up your ass?"

My friend nudged me and whispered, "Let's just go, Laurie."

"I didn't say one goddamn word to your husband tonight, so you got no beef with me," I snapped. I wanted to smack her but I knew better. She was a fellow officer's wife, and I couldn't lose control without hell being raised at work. My friend and I worked our way through the crowd and left by the back door. I needed to cool off.

■　　■　　■

About a week later, I was summoned to Sergeant Orval Zellmer's office in the Internal Affairs Department. He informed me that I was about to become the subject of a confidential internal investigation. I was confused. For what?

Two sergeants—Zellmer and Figer—read me Rule 29 from the Department regulations. This is the section that deals with untruthfulness. They asked me if I understood it and told me I was being given an order not to discuss what was about to be said with anyone.

I sat with my hat in my lap, nervous and worried. What was going on? This sounded serious. I couldn't begin to imagine what it was all about.

They asked me about my off-duty activities the week before, and Friday evening in particular. I couldn't even remember at first and had to look at a cal-endar to see that it was the night of Boville's party. I wondered what right they had to ask about my off hours, but they ordered me to answer.

It was either capitulate or lose my job.

I told them about the friend I'd gone with, and supplied her name and address. They asked which recruits had been at the party, and whether they'd been with their wives. What was served to drink? Was marijuana smoked? Did I ever smoke pot?

In the middle of the questioning I suddenly remembered I'd forgotten to tell them about stopping off at Thomas's on the way to the party. But if I brought that up, it would only complicate matters further. It didn't seem important anyway.

They asked a few questions a second and third time, pushing for discrepancies. I was then informed that they were going to search my locker. They escorted me to the women's locker room and poked through my belongings—my purse, my lunch bag and my jacket.

When we got back to the sergeants' office they told me to "Matter of" everything I'd told them. Several hours had passed.

Finally, Zellmer told me that someone had made an anonymous complaint, saying that I was at Boville's party with my badge pinned to my shirt, smoking a joint. The caller said I'd declared that I couldn't be busted because I was a cop. Zellmer said that the description given by the caller was correct—they'd described my red-and-white striped T-shirt and blue jean skirt. That was it—the whole evidence. On that, Zellmer had acted. I couldn't believe it. It was ridiculous. Why would anyone say such a thing, and how could the Department give so much weight to an anonymous complaint?

I repeated what I'd already said: the only disagreeable incident during my short stay at the party had been the one with Klug's wife.

After I was released to return to class, the sergeants called down a few more officers, announcing their names over the intercom. I regretted having told them who was at the party, but no one had done anything wrong. I was sure Zellmer wouldn't find any inconsistencies in our reports, since the truth was the truth. I was sorry I'd bothered to go to that party—it wasn't worth the trouble.

The others were curious to know what I'd been doing in the office all that time, and they began to worry and talk about me among themselves. I got the impression that some thought I was snitching on them—about Lord knows what. A recruit approached me during break and told me that Judy had been saying I was no longer her friend because I couldn't be trusted. I wanted to confront her, but I was prevented from telling anyone what had taken place in Zellmer's office because of the gag order I was given.

A few weeks went by. Judy and a group of her friends had tickets to see Rufus and Chaka Khan at the Milwaukee Auditorium. "The tickets are only seven dollars," Judy told me. "Do you want to go with us?"

"Okay. Are we meeting at your house?"

"We're going out for some Mexican food first. I'm going to change at my boyfriend's house, so I'll call you before I leave."

I met Judy and her friends Norm and Jan at a restaurant for drinks and gua-camole. After about the third margarita we left.

Our seats at the concert were terrible; we could barely see the stage. Judy and Jan left to look for better seats. When they returned, they suggested we move to a different section. It was a wild concert, with crowds of people in the aisles dancing and drinking and smoking.

We had just sat down in our new seats when I left to use the bathroom. Norm wanted to get more beer so we left together. He got in line for refreshments as I departed to find the women's room. The drinks had made me a little fuzzy.

The line in the washroom was unbearably long. When I walked past the beer stand later Norm had already gone. I hoped I'd be able to find our new seats.

I strained to see over the people. The smoke was thick and the music very loud. To my surprise, I saw a man standing behind Judy, gripping her in a head-lock. At first I thought it was a friend of hers, joking. Then another man appeared and they dragged Judy and Jan out of their seats and down the row. I struggled to get through the crowd, trying to see in the dimly lit auditorium. Near the doorway I saw one of the men take Jan's purse away from her. He pulled out what looked like a small bag and I thought I heard him shout, "You two are under arrest!" but the music was so loud I couldn't be sure.

I sobered up and turned to look back at the seats to see if Norm was there. He was. He appeared to have fallen asleep. I squirmed between bodies to get back to our seats, calling frantically, "Norm! Some guys just took Judy and Jan away—I think they were cops."

Norm started. "What do you mean ...?"

"Well, they were dressed in plain clothes, but I heard them say that Judy and Jan were under arrest—I think. We've got to find them to see what happened."

Norm agreed, but by the time we got back out into the main hallway, Jan and Judy were gone. Searching seemed futile in a crowd that size. Not knowing what else to do, Norm drove me back to my car, which was parked at the restaurant. We both drove home.

I let myself into my house, crept upstairs and got into bed. The phone rang. It was Norm.

"I tried calling downtown to find out where that dingbat and her girlfriend are but I guess they've already been booked."

"For what?"

"Possession, I think," Norm said. "That stupid Jan had a nickel bag in her purse."

"Oh God," I groaned, hanging up the phone. I was sorry I'd gone. My mother had tried to talk me out of it earlier. Shouldn't I reconsider? I was a police officer now and I should be more careful. I just laughed and told her she was being overprotective. What could happen at a concert? I was so naive.

The following day I drove to the Academy with the reluctance of a grade school student approaching the principal's office. Even before roll call I was summoned to Zellmer's interrogation room. The same procedure followed—I was read Rule 29 and the questioning began. It lasted hours this time. They wanted to know every move I'd made before, during and after that concert.

I felt like a criminal—or worse—kept in that tiny office and ordered to repeat my story over and over. The lunch hour came; I was escorted into another room and locked in.

When the sergeants returned, I had to write a "Matter of" report. Zellmer brought up all kinds of irrelevant issues, like my trip to Florida with Judy. Afterwards, I was again ordered not to discuss the interrogation with anyone.

Finally, toward the end of the day, the sergeants allowed me to return to the classroom. To my surprise, everyone knew of Judy's arrest. A couple of veteran officers had in-service classes at the Academy that day and had gossiped to the recruits at lunch. I worried that my superiors would blame me for blabbing. As it was, everyone played "twenty questions" with me, and I had to avoid them as much as I could.

After work that night I headed to the airport. I'd been invited to a friend's wedding in New York. I sat back on the plane and ordered a double Scotch. As we left the ground and Milwaukee disappeared out of view, all I could think of was losing my job. It looked so bad—first that stupid anonymous complaint, and now this!

"God! Any normal person would think I'm crazy to want this insane job," I thought. "I can't even have a private life. Wait till I get back—they'll probably have my dismissal papers all ready for me. And where the hell is Judy? Still in jail? What did she say to them to make them come down on me so hard?"

The weekend in New York was miserable. My friends were concerned. They felt I had changed. They couldn't understand how a job could mean that much to anybody.

On Monday, when I returned, matters proceeded exactly as I had expected. I was summoned to Zellmer's office and the interrogation resumed.

The sergeant asked if I had had contact with anyone over the weekend—namely Judy. They seemed almost disappointed when I explained that I had been in New York. I was ordered to write a report on my trip. I sat there wishing it would all end.

Then an odd issue was raised. Officer Thomas—did I ever smoke pot with him or stay at his house? No, and no, I said. I couldn't understand what they were accusing us of. They ordered me to add more statements to the report I'd just written, standing over my shoulder to make sure I worded everything to their liking.

Everything was being blown out of proportion. They acted as if this was a grand jury investigation.

The next day I was sent to the Captain's office. I was ordered to give a verbatim statement, which was recorded by a stenographer. Everything, the whole story, over and over ... Boville's party ... the concert with Judy Zess.

The Captain asked me if I was aware that, at that very moment, Paul Will, Jr. from the Vice Squad downtown was at the DA's office trying to obtain a warrant for my arrest. I answered no—how would I know that? And for what? I couldn't tell if they were trying to bluff—it sounded so crazy—or if they were really going to charge me with something.

I was too young and inexperienced to know that as soon as criminal charges were threatened I had the right to demand representation. I could have refused to cooperate, under the protection of the Fifth Amendment. But how would I know? I was totally baffled by the whole thing. Criminal charges? What criminal charges? My job was on the line and I was scared, so I cooperated. I thought that if I didn't, it would have looked like I had something to hide.

It was a busy week for Zellmer. Recruit officers were continually being called down to his office—the majority of them female and/or black. I found out that, while I was in New York, Thomas had had a party at his house that was now under investigation. I was glad I'd been out of town or Zellmer probably would have tried to connect me with that in some way, too. I kept my airline ticket stub as proof of my trip.

That night I was surprised to see Judy Zess's photo in the newspaper, along with an article about her efforts to get her marijuana case reopened. She wanted to withdraw her plea. She said she'd been denied an attorney and had been forced to plead guilty.

4

FIRED!

I went downtown to the Milwaukee Police Association office, hoping the union attorneys could answer some of my questions. I didn't know where else to turn. They were glad to talk to me but told me that they really couldn't do anything until my superiors took some sort of action—like dismissal or suspension. Newly graduated officers were officially on probation and had no appeal rights for a whole year.

The other problem was timing. For eight years they'd been working on a Bill of Rights for police officers. It would include the right to representation before interrogation by commanding officers, the right to remain silent until represented and the right to know the nature of the investigation before interrogation—all things I could have used right then. The governor was about to endorse the bill, then it had to be signed into the state journal. It would be in effect in about a week. A week too late for me.

I got the impression that the union was rather ineffectual. They seemed more interested in Department gossip than anything else. Someone at the union office passed on a rumor they'd heard about Boville's party. Naturally, by the time the story got to them it was even wilder than the original hearsay. They were told that a female recruit had been caught walking around the party with nothing on but her bikini underpants—with her badge pinned to them!

The union officials asked me to keep them informed and wait for the Department to make its move. The president added that as soon as he could give me the actual date on which the bill would be signed, he'd tell the union attorney, Ken Murray, to give me a call. He advised me to call in sick until the bill was passed to avoid further interrogations.

"I can't wait for that bill to be passed," Tom Barth, the union president, said.

"Did you ever imagine that cops would have fewer rights than criminals? Keep your chin up—maybe Breier's witch-hunts will cease."

When I returned home, I received a call from Judy. "Judy!" I exclaimed. "I've been trying to get hold of you for days! Where the hell have you been?"

"I've been staying at Bill's until things around my house cool down. Was my dad pissed!"

"I saw the article in the paper. Jesus, have they been giving it to me at work! I've been going nuts. What on earth happened with you?"

"Those assholes," Judy said. "They're trying to get away with charging me on a possession case. Can you believe it?"

"But I don't understand," I said. "You didn't have any pot with you that night?"

"Well ... Jan and I were smoking a joint, but I threw the roach down and they recovered it. They picked up a soda cup from under my chair and used that. There was a roach in the cup. Do you want to hear the ridiculous amount they recovered?"

I said nothing.

"Point zero six of a gram of marijuana! It was just a little tiny butt! My lawyer thinks the whole thing is ludicrous. Especially since the pot wasn't in my possession! They're only supposed to charge people who are in possession. Jan, the dummy, was the one with the dope in her purse."

"Why have they been hassling me at work? Zellmer has been working me over like a homicide suspect!"

"Laurie, I didn't even tell them you were with us that night. Jan might have said something, but she doesn't know your full name. I just told them we were with Norm."

"Then I don't understand their hot pursuit."

"They probably think we were all in on it. You know how they are! Their rules say that even if you're *aware* of a violation, you're just as guilty as the violator."

She was right. Had I simply been aware of the marijuana in Jan's purse, that would have been sufficient grounds for dismissal.

Since I hadn't heard from the union, I went to work the following day as usual, only to be called to the offices again. I was almost getting used to it. This time I was informed we were going to the Deputy Inspector's desk. He was higher in rank than the Captain. I half expected to see the Chief of Police himself sitting there.

The Deputy Inspector hit me with both barrels. "Officer Bembenek," he said, "I've reviewed the reports from your sergeants concerning several different instances, and I'll tell you right now, I'm making my recommendations to the Chief to have you dismissed. You have no integrity or moral responsibility! You don't even have the decency to admit when you've done something horrendously wrong! You obviously think we are playing games here. Well, Officer, we are not playing games."

He stared at me. I sat in front of him, not allowed to say anything. I felt two inches tall. I wanted so badly to say, "No! No! You're wrong!"

He continued. "What we're basically doing here is giving you the option to resign. It would look a great deal better on your employment record to resign rather than to be dismissed by this Department. So you think it over. You really have no choice. You don't deserve to wear the honored badge of this Department! You are nothing but a liar! You were at that party walking about with a marijuana cigarette, wearing your badge on your dress! You've smoked marijuana with members of this class and lied about it when we have affidavits to prove it! You don't have much more time on this Department, Officer Bembenek. I suggest that you simply resign."

I looked at his fat, round, expressionless face. I felt defeated and helpless. The room was silent.

"Respectfully request permission to speak, sir," I asked meekly, trying to establish a courageous facade.

The Inspector nodded.

"I can't imagine what instances you are referring to. I attended a party at a fellow recruit officer's home—but, sir, you've got to believe me! You can ask anyone who was there! I did no such thing! It's got to be a m-m-mistake," I stammered. "All I can tell you is that all my life I've only wanted one thing, and that is to be a police officer. My father was a police officer. I would never do anything as foolish as what you've accused me of. You've got to believe me!"

The Inspector said nothing, just hoisted his plump body up from the chair and announced, "Dismissed."

I stood, returned the salute and left, with the sergeants on my heels like two Dobermans. It was useless.

On my way back to the classroom, Sergeant Zellmer cornered me. I was as tall as he. He scowled and said, "Bembenek, you really had us fooled. You say your father was a police officer? I suggest you tell him what you did and ask him how we adjudicate matters on this Department! I'm satisfied that it will be taken care of in a matter of days. Think seriously about resigning."

Two days passed without another interrogation, but I still jumped whenever the intercom came on. Other recruits were being questioned, and there was still trouble brewing. We were all too scared to talk to each other in the relaxed, friendly way we used to. No one trusted anyone.

I wondered why Boville wasn't in any trouble—it was his party and his house! But then Boville was a white male, just what the Chief of Police wanted for his Department.

I made up my mind not to resign. I wasn't going to give in to those bastards when I hadn't done a damn thing wrong. They would have to take my job away from me.

My marksman scores on the firing range, previously very good, went to hell. Even my performance in the gym reflected my depression.

I called the union and was told that the police officers' Bill of Rights would be in force in three days. I told Murray about the rest of the confrontations that had occurred. He again suggested I call in sick, so I did, for the next three days.

Some time went by with no mention of the investigation. I thought optimistically that since the information on which the accusations against me were based was erroneous, I'd not be dismissed. Some of the tension lifted and the recruits became friendly and talkative again.

My evaluations went from bad to worse, though. It angered me, because some of them bore no relation to my performance. I knew I was being victimized. For example, I'd made a point of trying to raise my hand in class and participate more than before. But the comment in the "Willingness to participate in classroom discussions" section was "Poor."

After some time, I regained some of my fight. One afternoon, we were shown a slide presentation with pictures of the Police Department administration in living color.

I raised my hand.

Sergeant Kocher nodded in my direction. "Officer Bembenek?"

"Sir, why aren't there any women within the administration? I don't see a female above the rank of patrol officer. Not even a sergeant."

"No female officers have been members of the Department long enough," he answered.

That's an understatement! I thought bitterly, but I kept the thought to myself. I wondered why the female cops didn't organize a separate support group, since the black officers could rely on the NAACP or The League of Martin.

Graduation was drawing near and field training assignments were listed. Field training allowed a recruit to work on the street with a seasoned officer prior to graduation. Each recruit was assigned a Field Training Officer, or FTO, who would submit an evaluation afterwards. Field training lasted three weeks—one week on third shift, referred to as "late," and two weeks on second shift, referred to as "early." It was now July.

I was assigned to District Number Five, which included an all-black neighborhood and some of Milwaukee's East Side, extending to the lakefront. My FTO was Rosario Collura. His squad partner was Michael Jourdan.

Crossing my fingers, I reported for my first day of field training. There was so much to learn. Collura told me to drive the squad car and be on the lookout for any traffic violations. I was apprehensive, because at the Academy they hadn't taught us how to use the squad radios or the walkie-talkie. I bit my lip and hoped I'd get through it correctly. To add to my problems, I was unfamiliar with the district, let alone our assigned squad area in the ghetto.

After driving around for about half an hour, Collura began to tell me where to turn and which streets to take. We ended up in an alley. He turned to me.

"Stop the car. Okay, Bembenek—what's your 10-20?"

He was asking me what my location was in police code. I knew how important location was; they always stressed it at the Academy. If you didn't know where you were, you couldn't call for help. After making all those turns in such an unfamiliar area, I could do nothing but guess. Fortunately, I was correct.

I soon learned that I was training in a very busy district. On my first day we were sent to numerous shootings, armed robberies and other serious crimes that never made the news.

"Take the shotgun and cover me!" Collura told me as we pulled up in front of a house where an armed man had been arguing heatedly with his wife. The shotgun was in a zippered pouch attached to the back of the front seat.

I took a position behind a tree at the front yard opposite Jourdan. Collura went in and arrested the man. No shots were fired.

Half an hour later we responded to an armed robbery of a store. The owner had shot one of the robbers and we chased the wounded man down an alley, following a trail of blood. A car picked up the wounded suspect and tried to make a run for it, but they were apprehended by another squad that blocked the end of the alley.

When we weren't busy, Collura and Jourdan had their fun. I was instructed to write all the reports after each incident. The forms had to be filled out in duplicate with carbon paper, so if a mistake was made, the whole thing had to be redone. I'd be writing an Offense Report or an Accident Supplementary

Report in the booking room and Collura would come flying past, saying, "You're not done yet? Finish it at home—we got another hitch. Let's **GO!**" I'd jump up and fly out after him, papers scattering.

Usually I got home from "early" shift well past midnight. I'd sit up until two or three at the kitchen table, writing reports, updating the hot car sheets and Daily Bulletin cancellations, knowing that I had to appear in court the next morning because Collura was sending me to every case he could think of. Although I was earning a lot of overtime pay, I wasn't getting much sleep.

I didn't know how much more I could take.

Collura's vocabulary was worse than Blackburn's. The vulgar verbal abuse was uncalled for. We were standing roll call when the sergeant ordered us to draw our guns and unload for inspection. As we reloaded, I took a second longer than the veteran officers. In the silence, my gun was the last to click as I snapped the cylinder back into place.

The sergeant was aware of that last, late click. "Was that you Jourdan?" he asked.

"Nope—it was the dumb cunt," Collura said. Snickering followed.

Department rules supposedly made it mandatory to treat fellow officers with respect, especially when in uniform. Apparently this didn't apply to Collura or Jourdan. Once, Collura and I were in a squad, driving through an alley behind the station house, when Collura pulled up next to a civilian.

"Hi, Rosie!" the man said, using Collura's nickname. "I see you have a new partner."

"Yeah," Collura smiled. "I was going to let her drive, but I didn't want the seat to be all wet and sticky!" They laughed.

I was furious, but he was the senior officer, so I said nothing. I told myself he was just trying to get my goat and that I'd only have to work with the creep for another week. When I switched to "late" shift, I'd be assigned another FTO.

My stubbornness only provoked Collura. He sent me into situations I was untrained for just to watch me fall on my face in ignorance.

I understood that field training was a period of rigorous instruction that was supposed to prepare recruits for the worst—it was supposed to be tough. But there's only so much a rookie can be expected to know. Instruction was supposed to be a part of the training. Collura apparently preferred the school of hard knocks.

I was lucky I knew how to change a flat tire because that was Collura's next little trick.

We were sent to a family disturbance. We found a woman throwing her boyfriend out of her house, along with everything she owned that was breakable.

The street was littered with broken glass. I was glad I wasn't driving, because as we pulled up a sliver of glass punctured a tire.

We stopped the fight and arrested the woman on a Disorderly Conduct charge. After the wagon pulled away from the scene, my FTO told me to open the trunk of the squad.

"You'll find a broom in there."

"A broom?" I blinked.

"Yeah!" Collura snorted. "I figure you'd look more natural with a broom in your hand! Now sweep up all this glass."

The crowd of people that had gathered outside to watch the fight still stood in the street. Sheepishly, I swept the glass into the gutter.

"That's good, Bembenek!" Collura hollered to me. "Now, you want equal rights? You can change that tire next!"

Gritting my teeth, I took the jack out of the trunk. I wondered if Collura had been talking to Sergeant Kocher.

"That's cold-blooded!" a black woman said to Collura, laughing. "Making a lady change a flat tire."

"Hey! She wants a man's job, let her do a man's job," he said.

Later, I called a few recruits to see if they were as exhausted as I was from field training. To my surprise, they weren't. No other recruits had even been allowed to drive a squad. I had more overtime than anyone I knew. One of my friends said that they'd had a flat tire too, but their FTO had called a Department tow truck team to change it. This made me wonder what was going on.

Finally, toward the end of my hellish two weeks, Collura took me aside.

"Bembenek, I'm putting my ass on the line for telling you this, but you've been a good shit, so I figure I owe ya."

"What?" I asked suspiciously.

"Well ... okay, don't let this get around, but I was ordered to give you a hard time—which I did. The stripes were hoping that you'd just give up and resign. Did some shit come down at the Academy or something?"

"Way back in April, or May," I replied. "I thought it had all blown over."

"Oh." Collura glanced around nervously. "Hey—all I have to say is, you took an awful lot these past two weeks. Good luck, kid."

That was the last time I would ever see Collura. Five years later he would be shot and killed on duty.

The next day, I thought about what he'd said. Why was discipline so different for the women and blacks on the one hand and for the white males on the other? Collura and Jourdan always had wine or beer with their lunch, on duty, despite the fact that it was against Department regulations. They overlooked a

42

lot of marijuana, but Judy was arrested with less than a gram that wasn't even in her possession. They made sexist, vulgar remarks to me in front of sergeants, and nothing was done.

Sergeants Eccher and Dagenhardt (nicknamed Dragonheart by Fifth District officers) handed me a good evaluation report at the end of my field training.

Graduation day arrived, and I participated in the ceremony, with my parents attending. I received a basic certificate from the Department of Justice's Law Enforcement Standards Board, and a certificate of completion from the Milwaukee Police Department's Police Academy.

My permanent assignment was Second District, on the South Side of town. At least I would be familiar with the terrain, and I considered this new assignment a chance to start fresh. Still, I'd heard rumors that the lieutenant on late shift had no use for female officers and didn't even try to hide his prejudice. I was warned to stay out of his way.

It was August, and I felt that I had finally made it through my troubles. Who cared about a single hateful lieutenant when I had survived the worst? Or so I thought at that time.

If the Deputy Inspector really felt I didn't deserve the "honor" of a Milwaukee Police Department badge, he could never have laid eyes on the "Finest" of Second District. What a place! What a force! Many of the cops were brutal, lazy, apathetic and corrupt. Second was a slower district with less crime, except in one poverty-stricken Hispanic area, but the less the cops had to do, the less they cared to do. I saw *hundreds* of rule violations. Squads would park in the cemetery at night after the bars closed and sleep away three or four hours on late shift, or drink in "squad parties." Cops walking a beat were getting free drinks at bars. Some were selling pornographic films from the trunks of their cars, or seeing girlfriends on duty while their wives thought they were at work. They used brutal, unnecessary force on suspects already in handcuffs—in the booking rooms, away from the public eye. They used and sold drugs. They demanded and got blowjobs from prostitutes. They paid their informants with drugs. They released drunk drivers from accident scenes to avoid the overtime it took to process, test and book them. What I didn't observe personally, I heard about, because corruption was common knowledge. Rank made no difference. But obviously sex and race did.

In this environment, the rookie is in a precarious position. If I witnessed a rule violation, as I did, I was just as guilty as the violator if I didn't turn him in. So if I didn't make my Commanding Officer aware of it, in the eyes of the Department I was violating a rule myself. And if I did ... I still had to take orders from these veteran officers. Try calling for backup in a life-threatening situation and have nobody show up!

I wasn't going to be their Serpico.

Then, of course, there's the comradeship between patrol officers, the "us against them" feeling. Collura was the first one to tell me: "Never trust stripes!"

"After all," he had said, "if we don't take care of our own, who will?"

At least Jourdan and Collura worked hard, for all their faults.

Despite everything, I began to enjoy the work, and the advantage of having a permanent assignment. I especially liked to walk my beat alone, a duty that appeared more frequently on my schedule. Then I could be my own boss and didn't have to worry about seeing rule violations or being at the command of some shiftless senior officer. I felt I was adjusting very well to police work.

My friends during this period were mostly from the Academy, working the same late shift I was. My old civilian friends worked "normal" hours, and it was getting harder to relate to them. My new friends were all cops.

An officer I will call Suzy, with whom I'd had drinks once before, called me one afternoon. We had a lot to discuss, since she had field-trained at Second District and was now working at Five, where I had field-trained. We swapped talk about how our work was going, the problems of adjusting to the late shift and of losing contact with old friends.

We started meeting for lunch, and once in a while we'd visit Judy to sit poolside with a bottle of wine. Suzy usually got very drunk, and I began to worry about her. Once she took me aside.

"Listen, I don't mind seeing Judy now and then, Laurie. But believe me, Zess is trouble with a capital T."

I wondered what she meant. Judy was working then as a waitress. She hadn't gotten into any trouble since the concert. If there were any signs I should have recognized at that time, I failed.

Suzy was irritable at times; there seemed to be a great deal of anger inside of her, though at what I couldn't say. She was struggling to raise a daughter, who frequently woke her up during the day as she tried to sleep. I felt sorry for her.

She was dating a man named Steve but told me that she was just using him for his money. Her real love was an old flame, Seymour, who lived in Chicago. She told me she'd lived with him years before her ill-fated marriage. She occasionally drove to Chicago to see him, but it was a strain.

Around this time she mentioned that she'd met and was dating a Department detective, but then she quickly changed the subject, as if mentioning him had been a mistake.

Meanwhile, men had virtually vanished from my life. I didn't want to jeopardize my job again, so I didn't go out with any cops, and I couldn't seem to find the time to date men who weren't cops. This hardly helped my reputation at the Department—I got wind of a rumor that I was a lesbian. After all, I lifted weights!

The rumor was reinforced one night when my squad partner decided to drive past the gay bars in the district to harass the patrons. He enjoyed himself, whistling through the squad loudspeaker microphone, making comments. He spotted two women on the sidewalk, embracing. They were just hugging, but my partner turned the squad spotlight on them.

"Youse could be arrested for that, ya queers!" he yelled.

Blinded by the light and embarrassed, they parted and walked to their own cars.

"Why are you doing this?" I asked finally. "Don't we have more important work to do? They aren't hurting anyone, but plenty of people in this city are, right now."

"They're queer," he sneered. "You wouldn't happen to be a dyke, would you?"

I could tell by the look in his eye and the tone in his voice that I was not going to win this argument, so I dropped the subject after assuring him that, no, I wasn't a "queer," to use his jargon.

■　　■　　■

Summer began to pass by quickly. My parents had a foreign exchange student staying at our house from Japan, but I wasn't home much. On my days off I looked at several condominiums in town that were for rent with an option to buy. My birthday was uneventful. I turned twenty-two.

At the end of August, I called my district station to confirm my work schedule. The Captain picked up the phone to inform me, nonchalantly, casually, that the Chief had sent out an order for my dismissal.

The bomb had finally fallen.

They didn't even have the guts—or the courtesy—to do it to me in person.

They'd got me for—what? For being a woman? For not shutting up and taking their sexist garbage? Because I asked too many questions? How could I know?

I knew it wasn't because I had lied or broken rules—clearly cops weren't being dismissed for that. I knew it wasn't because I'd done anything wrong. I knew it wasn't because I wasn't a good cop. I think I was, or was becoming one. I would have been, if they'd let me stay.

The following morning, a day-shift sergeant came to my house to take away my badge and my gun and other Department property.

I fumbled with a screwdriver, trying to take off my newly bought mahogany grips from my Department thirty-eight caliber Smith and Wesson.

When my dad returned home from work that afternoon, I told him the news and cried in his arms.

5

FRIENDS

So much time had gone by since the party in April and the concert in May that the dismissal came as a terrible shock. The charges that had been filed against me were typed on the dismissal order I was handed: untruthfulness and filing a false official report. The order did not list the details of the charges and I could only guess what they involved. When had I lied? In what official report?

I called Suzy and tearfully told her the news. She, too, was shocked.

"Where are you?" she asked.

"I'm at Judy's. I can't bear to hang out at my house. My parents are too upset. They were counting on me ... "

"Stay where you are. I'll be right over," Suzy said, and in half an hour she was knocking on the door with wine, cheese, soup and beef sandwiches in her arms.

"Have you talked to the union yet?" Suzy asked.

"I've got an appointment with them tomorrow," I said. "What's that called? A 'grievance for reinstatement'?"

Suzy nodded. "What are you going to do for money?"

"That's the worst part—this ruins everything. I can forget my plans to buy a condo. I was supposed to close the deal next week, but now that's shot. I have my pension fund and I could apply for unemployment."

"You're lucky you didn't move out already. Think of what a mess that would have been! If you're interested, I need a babysitter for Aimee. Right now, a cop's wife is watching her at night, but it's a real pain because I have to drop Aimee off and pick her up everyday on the opposite side of town. It's hard to find someone to babysit late shift. She's four years old—she wouldn't be a real problem. At least it would get you out of the house and hold you over financially for a while."

I thought it over. I knew I had little experience with or tolerance for small children, but I guessed it would be better than nothing, so I agreed.

The following day, the union attorneys seemed optimistic when I saw them. First, they wanted to review my files, in order to establish the reasons for my dismissal. It took several letters from the union before the seventy-year-old Chief finally agreed to allow me to review my records.

When I appeared for my appointment at the Police Administration building, it was already September. I walked in to see Thomas, Bonnie Avanti and Pat Lipsey there. They had all been dismissed the same week I had, for various reasons. All three were black.

We sat outside the Chief's office for about three hours while the lawyers, Tom Barth and Ken Murray, were in conference with Breier. After waiting all that time, we were told to go home. The Chief wasn't going to allow us to see our files after all.

Several Second District officers phoned me. They wanted to know the details of my dismissal, and some were concerned about a rumor accusing me of turning in my co-workers for rule violations.

"Why would they say that?" I asked a caller.

"Oh, they always say that about anyone who gets fired. They're all paranoid, that's all—afraid the cop that gets dismissed wants to get even."

By now I was babysitting every night and on weekends for Suzy. She was in bad shape. She drank more than anyone I knew: three or four bottles a week of Jack Daniels. She'd drink late in the day—too late to get up for work—so she'd snort a few lines of cocaine to sober herself up.

I knew myself that late shift was hard to get used to. When I was working, I couldn't have a drink any later than lunchtime if I didn't want to feel groggy and listless on the job that night. I could see how hard it was for a single mother, trying to hold down a job.

Suzy was buying her coke from several different people, but the majority from a guy named Jimmy, who drove a white Corvette and occasionally spent the night with her. She was hooked. Despite her constant complaints about money—she was behind in the rent and ate off paper plates—she still spent a great deal on drugs.

I know I should have disassociated myself from people like Suzy and Judy when it became obvious what they were like, but there were many dumb reasons why I didn't. My firing had disoriented me. I was disillusioned and confused, which made me lonely and desperate for friends—even the wrong kind.

I'd also started drinking too much to be in any real control of my life. I don't know why I turned to alcohol, other than the fact that it was so socially acceptable. It was there, I guess, and everyone else did it. I certainly didn't learn to drink at home, because neither of my parents did. All I knew was that when I drank, life didn't seem so cruel. I could feel better about everything and I could believe everything was okay.

■　　■　　■

Toward the end of September, I was informed that Chief Breier had agreed to let those of us who were dismissed view our files after all. About the same time, my unemployment compensation started to arrive. I also received a subpoena to testify at Judy Zess's jury trial on the possession charge.

Again I returned to the Police Administration building with my union attorney, Ken Murray. He told me to take a notebook and write down anything important, because Breier stipulated that I review my papers alone, without Murray's help.

So I sat in front of a detective, Bob Rivers, who handed me my file, page by page. Page by page, he read it! It took me weeks of union negotiation to persuade the Chief to release my own files to me, and this nosy detective had the nerve to blatantly read through it all right in front of me.

I regretted that Murray wasn't allowed to help me, because the pile of reports seemed meaningless and confusing—until the shocking discovery of a signed statement against me by Judy Zess! She'd specifically included me in her marijuana smoking at the concert that night, though of course she knew it wasn't true. It was like getting a knife in the back. Why did she do it? Was she angry that night because she was getting fired and wanted to drag me down with her? Was it as simple as that? I was shocked and furious.

I stopped off at her apartment to confront her. She was her usual cheerful self, asked me to sit down, and began to tell me about the progress of her appeal.

"Judy," I interrupted. "I was allowed to see my records today. Downtown."

"So?"

"How could you make those statements against me? You told me you didn't even say that I was with you! How could you do that to me?"

Judy never skipped a beat.

"Laurie, you don't understand. I was drunk. They told me that if I didn't write all those things down, and sign it, that they were going to wake up the

Chief and take me to see him! Jan mentioned your name, and then I was confused. They kept me there all night! I just ... I just wanted to go home."

"Bullshit," I said angrily. "You tell them that I was smoking with you two assholes, when I wasn't even there?"

"You've got to believe me!" she protested. "Why do you think I appealed the damn thing? They had me under the hot lights practically. I didn't know what I was doing! They dragged me in there—I fell down and ran my nylons. Then they stood over my shoulder and told me what to write. My rights were violated! I told them that I wanted an attorney but they said, 'No! This is an internal matter!' " Judy was pleading with me. "You've got to believe me."

I didn't know what to think.

"Judy, what the hell am I supposed to do at my appeal when they fling your report at the Commission? What am I supposed to say then?"

"I'll go with you. If you need my testimony, I'll tell it just like it was. They were interrogating me all night! I didn't leave until 6:00 AM! I just spent four thousand dollars on a lawyer to take this thing back into court, because it wasn't fair! It wasn't right!"

"I got your subpoena," I said. "Now I'm supposed to testify for you? How did I even get dragged into this whole thing? I didn't see anything anyway!"

"Look, I'll even give you a signed affidavit if you want one," Judy promised. "You've got to believe me."

I sighed.

"What else was in your files?" she asked.

"Oh, they had so much crap in there! All unsubstantiated hearsay. None of it is concrete! Then White gave them some statement about the night I dropped off a record album at Thomas's house. White says he thinks Thomas and I were having an affair, and that's the reason I stopped there! How could he say something like that? Why would he? And how could the Department take it seriously? Since when is it a crime to go to a black person's house?"

"What was in it for White? Why would he give Zellmer a statement?" Judy asked.

"Maybe White's job is hanging by a thread, too, and he thought it would help. He's supposed to be Thomas's friend."

"What did the union say?"

"I'm going to file a grievance, but I don't know what good it will do," I said, "seeing as I was still on probation when they dismissed me." I shrugged. "Seems to me the only people getting pounced on by Internal Affairs are the women and the blacks. Just look at how many are gone so far, from our class alone. The year isn't even over with yet. I bet there'll be more."

"What did Pat Lipsey get fired for?" Judy asked.

"She doesn't know the specifics. Her charges read 'For the good of the service.' Can you believe that? I saw her downtown today. Thomas was there, too."

"I've got a good idea!" Judy interjected in her usual, erratic manner. "Why don't we drive out to the Playboy Club in Lake Geneva and apply for a job out there? A friend of mine knows one of the managers."

"Nah."

"Why not?" she insisted.

"What's wrong with your job at Sally's?"

"They're cutting my hours. I gotta get a different job. I won't be able to pay the rent pretty soon. Hey—why don't you move in here with me? I'd really like to live with you."

"I can't. The way things are going, I'm lucky I live at home. I got a notice yesterday from the unemployment office—the bastards are appealing my compensation eligibility now! The hearing is next month. If I can't even get unemployment, I won't be able to make my car payments, or anything."

"I thought anyone who gets fired is eligible for unemployment," Judy said.

"No. They said they have to determine that the employee didn't intentionally get fired in order to receive benefits."

"That's nuts!"

"I know. I think the city always appeals these things."

That night, Judy and I sat around at Suzy's house with a few of her friends. I was bored with the card game, so I called another cop friend of mine to see if he wanted to stop over. He agreed to come, but explained that he couldn't stay too late because he had to work that night. I fell asleep on Suzy's couch, watching TV, before he left.

The next day he called me. He sounded different.

"Is something wrong?" I asked him.

"Yeah. Well ... something is bothering me."

"Shoot."

"Laurie, I don't want to really get too involved. You know. With you and Suzy."

"What? What about Suzy?" I persisted.

"You seem to think she's your friend, but I'd be careful with her if I were you. Last night, after you fell asleep on the couch, I stayed for a few hands of cards. Suzy and Judy were laughing and getting super drunk, you know, and then when Suzy walked me out to my car, she was saying some really bad things about you."

"Like what?"

"She started out by asking me if I liked you very much, so I told her we were just friends, and then she was telling me some very vicious gossip about you—the real reason you got fired. It was stupid, sexual talk."

I was appalled.

"I know she was really looped, but that's no excuse. She said she heard it from some detective downtown."

"Why would she repeat that crap? If she only knew what they all say about her!"

"I know. Well, I didn't want to tell you, but I wanted you to know. I'd rather not go there anymore."

"Okay. Sure," I said. I hung up the phone.

I dialed Suzy's number but there was no answer. Then I remembered that she'd told me she planned on going to Chicago for the weekend to see Seymour. She had accumulated a lot more time off than the others from my class because she had been on the city payroll previously, as a metermaid.

A few weeks passed before I saw Suzy so I never did get a chance to talk to her about her indiscretion. I decided it was useless to ask her about something she'd said while intoxicated anyway.

One evening I was playing pool at a tavern and called her to see if she'd meet me there so we could talk. Unsure if she was scheduled to work that night or not, I let the phone ring. I was about to hang up when Suzy answered, sounding drunk and upset. I tried to hear what she was saying over the noise of the crowd in the bar.

"Hello? Suzy? This is Laurie. Are you there?"

She was crying hysterically.

"What's wrong? Are you okay?"

"Fuck it!" she screamed. "Fucking men! They're all the same! Assholes!"

"Suzy—get hold of yourself! What happened?"

"No! No! I was supposed to meet Fritz tonight and I had too much to drink because I lost track of time, so big deal! Big deal! So the fucker left! He didn't even wait for me—and now he just hung up on me!"

Then I heard the phone being thrown across the room.

I had no idea who Suzy was talking about. She'd never mentioned Fritz. I didn't know what she'd do next, so I ran out of the bar, jumped into my Camaro and drove to the other side of town. I kept thinking about the time Suzy came over with soup and cheese and wine, the day I told her I was fired. Now she needed me.

I hoped she wouldn't try anything stupid. She once told me that years ago, after a fight with Seymour, she'd taken an overdose of sleeping pills and had to have her stomach pumped.

When I got to her house, the front door was open. She had passed out on her bed, an empty bottle of Jack Daniels on the floor. Her breathing was regular, her pulse normal.

I looked around the room for any prescription bottles, but there were none. I checked her wall calendar to see if she had to work that night, but saw that "Overtime Off" was scribbled in.

I picked up what was left of the telephone, turned off the house lights and covered Suzy with a blanket. I looked in on Aimee and left, locking up the house.

The following day, Suzy remembered nothing. She wondered aloud what had happened to the telephone. I told her about our conversation, but she simply laughed it off.

"Jesus! Sometimes I get crazy when I'm tanked," was all she said.

That month, Judy again asked me about moving in with her, and I again told her it was impossible. She repeated her idea of applying for a job at the Playboy Club.

I wasn't keen, but I was in rough shape financially, especially since my unemployment compensation was being appealed. My life was a mess. It wasn't always pleasant babysitting for Suzy, and I didn't know how much longer I could stand it. Suzy's erratic drinking, moods and rages were more and more disturbing. She began to expect me to show up, with little notice, when she wanted to take off for a few days with a boyfriend. She went to homecoming weekend at La Crosse, Wisconsin with some man, but refused to tell me who it was. She complained about what a mess the house was, as if I was her housekeeper, too. I grew tired of her irritability.

I just didn't feel like my old self. I was directionless. I was drinking too much, applying for jobs all over town without luck. If I lost the unemployment compensation appeal, I'd be ordered to repay almost two thousand dollars to the city. I had no health insurance, and I had car payments. I didn't know what else to do.

I didn't even know what I looked like anymore. My hair had started to grow back, but my nails remained short and unpolished, and I almost never wore make-up. I usually dressed in jeans and shirts. I had unconsciously adopted a somewhat androgynous appearance, so different from the sophisticated, "feminine" polish of my modeling days. The whole sex and identity issue disturbed and confused me. Nothing seemed to be working for me.

So, on more or less a whim, I decided to return to traditional work and took a waitressing job at the Playboy Club at Lake Geneva for a month.

■　　■　　■

Biiiig mistake!

I waited on tables and learned to do the bunny dip. I wore that stupid little costume for only four weeks, and I collected money to pay back what they said I owed. And I apparently turned myself forever from Lawrencia Ann Bembenek into Former Playboy Bunny Bembenek. It was a waitressing job. Can we let it go now?

■　　■　　■

I had another blow in mid-October. I got a letter from the police union stating that they intended to drop my case. Although I'd paid my dues, it was just too expensive for them to pursue reinstatement. I had not completed my probationary period. Too bad all the interrogations took place before the police officers' Bill of Rights was passed. Most unfortunate. Too expensive. Too bad.

I felt everyone had given up on me.

My unemployment hearing was next. Ken Murray agreed to represent me there, even though the union had dropped my grievance.

I arrived at City Hall to find about twenty-five cops there—four sergeants, some Vice Squad officers, stenographers and others. I felt very small and alone. Finally, Judy and my attorney arrived.

The hearing took four long hours. All kinds of people testified—including the stenographer who took my verbatim statement—whether their testimony was relevant or not. Vice Officer Paul Will took the oath. He said I was arrested the night of the concert, along with the others, but was released after they'd determined that I was not in possession of marijuana.

"There must be some way to prove that I wasn't arrested!" I whispered to Murray. "Can't Judy testify? I wasn't even apprehended! Wouldn't there be a clearance or an arrest record on me if I was arrested?!"

"Calm down, Lawrencia," Murray said. "Let me handle it."

When it was over, I was informed that the decision on whether or not to grant me unemployment compensation would be mailed to me at a later date.

Judy's jury trial on the possession charges followed. The trial went on for over three days, and my testimony was delayed over and over again. The witnesses were sequestered, so initially I sat outside the courtroom. Finally, I was called to testify and entered the room. I was amused to see that the young court reporter was my ex-boyfriend's buddy, the guy who'd taken my place on the vacation we had planned.

I answered questions from Judy's lawyer, was briefly cross-examined, and was asked to step down. Watching the Vice officers testify, I noticed that their stories varied a lot from the reports they handed in—varying even further from how they had testified at my unemployment hearing. I wasn't surprised. I knew that police officers are encouraged to testify about what would have been correct procedure, not what really happened. It was a technique that was subtly reinforced at the Academy, where officers were not formally taught to lie, but it was suggested that if they couldn't remember exactly what had occurred, then they should describe what they should have done.

I was to watch this technique again and again. Judy ended up with a hung jury.

6

FRED SCHULTZ

*M*onths passed in a blur. I felt as though I was inside a bottle, looking out: fingers pressed against the glass walls, closed off, closed in, suffocating. I felt oppressed by failure. I clung to the few relationships that I had, because they were all I had. By now I knew who Suzy and Judy were. It's true they were amoral—boozing and screwing around and doing dope. It's easy to say now I should have fled, but I was at a loss. And I was lonely. I was mixed-up, confused, miserable about everything.

My life seemed to be falling apart. I tried to pick up the pieces, to stabilize, but I couldn't. Every time I tried to do something, I took one step forward and three steps back. I tried to get work, another job, any job. It was really demoralizing. I applied everywhere. Nobody would hire me.

I sometimes wonder how different my life would have been had I found a full-time job, made new friends and become engrossed in that ...

I discovered that I'd been blacklisted by the police. I almost got a job working as a security guard in a factory. The guy was impressed with my Police Department experience and hired me. But the day I was to start, the job suddenly didn't exist ... the position was mysteriously filled. It happened so many times. There are jobs, but the jobs suddenly don't exist. No one tells you anything. You get jacked around. It was so frustrating.

The police union abandoned me. The unemployment hearing went against me after the police presented their side to the Commissioners, and I was

56

ordered to pay back the compensation I'd earned. Nothing I did helped or worked. The air was thin, and I was panicking ...

So I thought, Okay, that's it, I'm going to give up trying in Milwaukee. I enlisted in the Air Force. But that effort failed, too ...

■　　■　　■

Judy was working as a sales consultant for a local waterbed store by then. Her bills were accumulating because of her court case, so she told me about a devious scam she had thought of.

"I called all the guys I've been sleeping with," she said. "I told them all I was pregnant and needed an abortion! At two hundred dollars apiece, I raked in about eight hundred dollars!"

"That's really low," I said.

"Oh, don't worry!" she said. "I have to make a living. Besides, one of them was that detective's son—Huey. He's a busboy at Sally's. He was scared that his daddy would find out."

"So what else is new?" I asked, wanting to change the subject.

"Oh—I know what I was going to tell you. The DA decided to drop the charges of possession. With a hung jury, they would have had to re-try the case. That's good news, isn't it? Now it's like you were fired for a non-existent crime!"

"True."

"So what are you going to do now? Look for another job? Or try to get back on the Department? You'd have to reapply and go through all those tests again, and the Academy."

"No. I couldn't do that. I've been working part-time at the gym. I'm considering the Air Force," I said.

"The Air Force? You're crazy!" Judy laughed. "What do you have? A uniform fetish?"

■　　■　　■

It was at this time that I met Elfred Schultz, Fred, Suzy's "Fritz." He was at Suzy's house one night, one of those many nights we'd had too much to drink, and I stayed over in Suzy's spare room, sleeping in my clothes.

The next morning I awoke and walked into the kitchen. Fred was sitting at the kitchen table. I was dying of thirst and poked about in the fridge. My head ached. Suzy was still sleeping.

"God," I groaned, "I wonder how many brain cells I killed last night."

"Probably both of them!" Fred said, laughing in a great bray, an outrageous laugh. I disliked him at once.

"You're going to have to trade that laugh in for a smaller model," I told him. "It's enough to wake the dead." Every word was an effort. I decided I had to get away from this guy and go home, so I gathered up my keys and purse, ready to leave.

He was still sitting on the kitchen table. "Will you go out with me?" he asked.

"Save your breath, Schultz. You'll need it to blow up your inflatable date tonight," I said.

"See?" he persisted, following me out to my car. "We have something in common already! I like Rodney Dangerfield, too!"

I drove home, irritated.

More weeks went by. No jobs appeared. I went to parties. I drank too much. I tried to have a good time, but I was miserable. I should have returned to school full-time, but didn't have any money and didn't know how I'd pay for it.

The Air Force seemed more and more like the answer to my problems. I was programmed into a Delayed Entry Plan.

Downtown one night, I ran into an officer from my Academy class. He told me that he had heard about the dismissal and he expressed his condolences.

"Man, we thought you were going to make it. We all had our fingers crossed for you. Then when we graduated, we thought you had made it. It's a damn shame. You were good."

"Thanks," I sighed.

"What are you doing now?"

"I enlisted in the Air Force. I'm scheduled to go in February. I train in Texas but then I get stationed in Illinois at Chanute. It sounds like a good deal. You get trained for a job that you can work at as a civilian when you get out."

"You're crazy! What are you doing that for? You could be doing so many other things."

"Like what? Everywhere I apply, they find out I was fired."

"I can't believe the number of people that have been fired." He shook his head.

It felt good talking to him. He seemed to be on my side.

"I can remember when you first went down for all that shit about Boville's party," he said. "I heard that it was a Police Aide that was smoking pot at that party, outside the house. She had blond hair, too. That's where it all started."

After all this time!

"What? Why didn't somebody say something to Internal Affairs? I got blamed for something I didn't do and all you punks were sitting back when you knew what really happened?"

"We were scared to say anything! Besides, we didn't know you'd take a rap for it! What are we talking about here? Rumor! It was all rumor! Nobody could talk!"

I walked away from him in anger and went inside an East Side club. Suzy's friends Russ and Jim were gathered at one end of the bar, looking at some snapshots with another guy named Eddy. They were photos of naked women standing on picnic tables. The background appeared to be some sort of a public park, with a huge crowd of people, including kids.

"Where was this?" I asked, looking over Jim's shoulder.

"Lake Park."

"Here? In Milwaukee?" I asked.

"Yeah! Don't tell me you never heard of the Tracks picnic?"

"No."

"They have this every year," Eddy said. "A whole bunch of cops were there."

"You mean all these people were taking their clothes off in a public park and no arrests were made?" I was incredulous.

"For what?" Russ asked.

"For what? For indecent exposure! Disorderly conduct! That's lewd and lascivious behavior! It's against the law!" It wasn't hard to think of possible charges; this was Milwaukee, after all.

"Oh. Well, most of the cops there were off duty." Jim shrugged. "Besides, they were all having a great time! Maybe they were paid off. Who knows? They'd have to be crazy to start anything—there were too many drunk fools."

Russ nodded. "See, they always get off to a wild start by having a free beer tent, and then something like a pie-eating contest, and then this Wet T-shirt contest. The crowd always begs the girls to take everything off."

"I can't believe this," I said. "In a public place where everyone can see? Outside? No one was arrested?"

"You think these pictures are good, you should see the ones from last year," Eddy told Jim.

"The Tracks ..." I began.

"It's a bar on Locust. A lot of detectives hang out there," Eddy said. "They had a Wet Jock contest, too. Look at all the crazy guys that took their clothes off."

He showed me pictures of a row of naked men on a table.

"Well, you see one, you've seen them all," I said sardonically. "Anybody could use these pictures to blackmail them. How could they do this?"

"You must know some of these cops," Jim said to me. "Here, look."

■   ■   ■

My tests for the Air Force turned out favorably. I was looking into a program that trained cadets to be fire fighters at airports. They told me that municipal airports only hired people trained by the Air Force. All my friends thought I was nuts to consider the Armed Forces.

"What do you want to be?" one friend asked. "Another Private Benjamin? Sometimes I think you've got a screw loose. You're going to be miserable."

■   ■   ■

Maybe I did have a screw loose. But my dismissal from the Police Department still rankled, and in December, I decided to talk to a representative from the Equal Employment Opportunity Commission, known as the EEOC. Maybe they could do something. I knew it wasn't just me. There were too many things wrong, too many good people getting fired for too many trivial excuses.

After reviewing the records of my dismissal, the EEOC rep said he felt I had a good case for sex discrimination. He explained that I'd have to show how male officers were disciplined differently than females. I told him about all the rule violations I'd witnessed. The key, he said, was to show that the Department administration knew about these violations. I told him about the Tracks picnic photographs, and his eyes lit up. He referred me to an Assistant U.S. Attorney.

The attorney said he was documenting the way that minority and female police officers were handled by the MPD. A pattern was becoming obvious, he said. Federal guidelines made the hiring of minorities mandatory, and these numbers the Department reported. Of course—there was federal funding at stake. The numbers dismissed or forced to resign, however, went unreported and unnoticed. He had come to believe those numbers were substantial.

I couldn't see how the Police Department could possibly maintain they weren't aware of what was going on. But just in case, I was going to make sure they did; I'd push their noses in it. For starters, I borrowed the photos of the Tracks picnic and turned them in to Internal Affairs. Some of the people in the snapshots were wearing T-shirts that said "The Tracks Picnic 1980," which was explicit enough. When Zellmer saw the photographs, his eyes almost popped out.

"Why are you here?" he asked me.

"Because," I said virtuously, "I was fired for little more than rumor, when cops out there are getting away with things ten times worse! I don't think it's fair. You tell me how this picnic could have gotten so out of hand, right out in the open in a public park. Where were the squads?"

■　　■　　■

Suzy called to tell me that she was leaving for a vacation in California with Aimee.

"Have a good time," I said. "How was your Thanksgiving?"

"Oh, all right I guess. I spent it with Fred at his parents' house. But he's my problem. I just want to get away and be alone for a while."

"Why? I thought you two were getting along so well."

"I've been hearing a lot about him from certain people, and I don't like what I'm hearing," Suzy said. "For one thing, he's been screwing almost every female officer on this Department! But he gives me the 'You're the only one I love' snowjob."

"Like who?" I asked.

"Like Pam and Lori, for starters. Then there are a few nurses, a cheerleader, a Karen, an Elaine ..." she said, disgusted. "What I can't figure out is, when does the guy sleep?"

"Who's been telling you all this?" I asked.

"Remember that guy with the deep, gravelly voice that I used to talk to on the phone? Now don't ever say anything, but that's Fred's roommate, Stu. He's a cop, too. Fred's been living at Stu's house ever since his divorce, and let me tell you, our Mr. Buns has been a very busy little boy. I might just tell him where to go."

"What's the difference, Suzy? You're just as bad. You go out with other guys."

"Oh, I know. But guess what Stu said? He said that Fred's divorce was his fault. Fred was fooling around with someone named Karen while he was still married. Stu said Fred's ex-wife is a really nice lady!"

It got really complicated, according to Suzy. After Fred and his wife, Chris, were separated, Stu began dating her. Stu gave Chris Karen's full name, birth date and address and told her that if she really wanted Fred to meet her financial demands, she should threaten to notify the Department about his girlfriend.

■　　■　　■

I know now the whole thing was sordid and I should have stayed out of it. It wasn't as if I hadn't been warned about Fred. But I was drawn in by his over-whelming personality. He was manipulative and consuming, but he was also full of jokes and laughter, the life of any party he went to. In my depression, he seemed fresh and alive and new, a way out.

I've pondered this so much! I've read what people say of me, that I was part of the fast lifestyle, that I dressed like a slut (that word again!), that my protestations of naiveté are a hazy sham and a cover. They all spin these webs of words, but I look into the net and I don't see me there. I see only a creature that others have invented.

Fred was another of my failures. But I didn't know that, then. He allowed me to forget my depression, for a while.

I was so lonely!

■　　■　　■

One night I was sitting after midnight in my favorite Mexican restaurant with a friend. The door opened and a frigid blast of air hit us. I turned to see two detectives walk in.

"Cops!" I said to my friend.

"How can you tell?"

"By their white socks!"

It was a dimly lit room, but I recognized Fred by his obnoxious laugh. He saw me and walked to the bar.

"Isn't it against Department regs for you to be here on duty?" I asked with a grin.

"Shhhh!"

"I've heard 'Milwaukee's Finest' love to frequent this place," I said. The usual pleasantries were exchanged.

"I'd really like to get together with you sometime," he said. "I hear you're athletic. I need a jogging partner. Maybe you'd like to go running with me? We can talk. Please. I want to talk to you about Suzy."

"I guess so. Give me your number. I'll call you," I said.

I never had to. Fred called me, and we went jogging. It was bitterly cold as we ran in the sand along a frozen Lake Michigan shoreline. We talked as we ran, mostly about Suzy. I wasn't really listening to him.

"How far have we gone?" I asked between breaths.

"Why? Want to quit?"

"No." The air bit my face, it was so cold, but I didn't want to stop running until he did. Running was the only thing I did for myself anymore.

Fred was so convincing—on his best behavior. I began to think that my first impression of him was wrong. He wasn't that bad, and he was right about Suzy. Everything Stu had told Suzy about Fred was no doubt said from jealousy. After all, Stu was dating Fred's ex-wife. We ended our run and hopped back into his van.

"Where to?" he asked.

"I'd really like to shower. We can go to my parents' house and have some coffee. You can wait while I change into some jeans."

Later, we went to a tavern owned by a friend of his. I had a marvelous time, feeling great after the brisk run. Fred was persuasive and charming. I was mesmerized.

"Would you like to go with me to a party tomorrow night?" he asked me on the way home. "I'd be honored to have you accompany me."

"Whose party?"

"It's the annual Christmas party that the Municipal Court throws," Fred explained. "I don't have a date and I'd really enjoy your company."

"I'd love to," I said.

The evening of the party, Fred arrived with an armful of red roses.

"Thank you—they're lovely. Did you read the headline tonight? Here. Take a look." I showed him an article in that day's paper about my sex discrimination complaint against the Police Department. "That's an awful photograph."

"This is great!" Fred said. "But I hope you know what you're up against."

I just smiled. I thought I did know.

After the Christmas party, we went dancing at a local club. Fred made me think we were so alike, so compatible, that I felt I had known him all my life. We enjoyed the same things. He never disagreed with anything I said.

I was growing fond of him. But I'd be leaving soon to join the Air Force, and I was to be a star witness in a sex discrimination suit, so I didn't pay much attention. I was just enjoying myself for a change.

7

ROSE-COLORED GLASSES

How pleasant it is between two people when everything is new! The need for acceptance brings gentle consideration, caution and polite words. No suspicion or accusations; no angry remarks. Fred flattered me, agreed with me, was interested in all my activities. He seemed to want the same things out of life as I did. He didn't want any more children. He wanted an independent partner, a career woman. On top of that, he was a cop. Although he was ten years older than me, I felt that I had found my perfect match. My glasses couldn't have been any more rose-colored.

Still, I was so sure I was leaving for the Air Force that I tried to close my heart—just my luck to meet someone wonderful right before I was scheduled to begin a four-year hitch.

One cold afternoon we sat by the fireplace at his parents' house, drinking wine and talking.

"I think you love me as much as I love you," he suddenly said.

I thought I was in love with him, but this was the first time he'd ever mentioned love, and it startled me.

I looked down.

"Yes, I do. But I'm going away, for four years ..."

"You're not going anywhere," he said softly.

"I am," I said.

"But you can't!" he protested. "We get along so well, we like all the same things, we feel the same way about everything! This past month has been so wonderful since we started going out. Laurie, I feel like—"

"Maybe we'd better go," I interrupted. I felt bad enough.

We walked outside, and as he locked up the house, I climbed into his van.

Approaching the van from the passenger side, Fred put his hand up on my window before passing by. I put my hand up on the other side, lining it up with his on the window, with just the glass in between. I smiled at first, but then saw that there were tears in his eyes. After a moment, he turned and walked around the van to his door. I wanted to cry, too. How sad, I thought, that just when I finally found a man who was everything I had always wanted, I was leaving.

■　■　■

Many years later I cried again, wishing it had ended that way. I don't know who it was who said, "Be careful what you wish for in life—it just might come true."

■　■　■

Christmas was happy. It was that year I received the little rocking horse from my mother. It was a tiny, wooden thing, painted bright red and white, with a mane and tail of fine yarn.

Fred and I dated frequently. We went to midnight mass together and he once accompanied me to a NOW dinner. One evening he invited me to Stu's house for dinner; he was a good cook and loved to prepare meals. As we lingered over the food, Fred complained bitterly about Stu, who was not home. He was upset over Stu's affair with Chris, Fred's ex-wife.

"Is he still friendly with her?" I asked.

"Are you kidding? He's sleeping with her! I always see his car there all night. The bastard even answers her phone! In my old house! Right around the corner from here!"

"You'd think Christine would have better taste," I commented. "But really, Fred, what's it to you?"

"Chris is probably just keeping him around to do all her heavy work around the house," Fred said angrily. "I just hate the fact that my kids are around that guy all the time!"

■　■　■

In January, a cop friend called me late at night with a warning.

"Laurie, keep your car off the street at night."

65

"Why? What are you talking about?" I asked, startled. I sat up in bed and rubbed the sleep out of my eyes.

"It's the guys. Boy, are they pissed. We were standing roll call last night, and one of the officers told us that, all because of you, we have to make our marks now."

Beat cops and squads were required to "make their mark" every hour while on duty, which means using a callbox to contact the station. The purpose was to keep track of all officers. If an officer failed to make her or his mark, she or he could be injured or incapacitated, and the station would investigate. At Second District, none of the late-shift officers ever made their marks.

"He also told us to be super careful, because of that discrimination thing you filed. The guys are being investigated."

"You know how unfair it is!" I said. "I had to show that white, male officers get away with violations that females are disciplined for!"

"Laurie, I don't want to know what you said. You're my friend, all right? All I'm telling you is, be careful. They were all grumbling and saying that they were going to shoot you, or blow up your car and all kinds of shit. Square business!"

"It's not my fault that those assholes made corruption commonplace! Then someone tells the whole shift! Christ!"

"Don't tell anyone I called you. In fact, they were getting on me a little bit because we're friends, but I denied seeing you for a long time. I don't know what you're doing, Laurie ..."

"So? The guys have to make their marks now! Just like every other station. Big deal!"

"Don't you get it? You can't make your mark if you're sleeping. You can't make your mark if you're drinking."

I hung up the phone and called Fred, but Stu said he wasn't home from work yet. A few minutes later, my phone rang again.

"Hello?" I thought it might be Fred.

"Bembenek, your mother's dead," a male voice growled. Then there was a click, followed by a dial tone.

I got out of bed and started to dress. Looking out the window through the snow, I noticed something strange about my car. Something was on the hood.

I threw on a jacket and ran outside. There was a big, black, dead rat on the windshield of my car, tucked under the wiper like a parking ticket. Wincing, I pushed it off with a stick and tossed it down a sewer.

"What's wrong?" my mom asked when I got back into the house. Before I had a chance to answer, my phone rang again. My heart pounded as I ran upstairs to answer it. It was Fred.

"Where are you calling from?"

"I just got home," he said. "Stu left me a note that you called."

"Fred! I'm in trouble." I told him about the phone call.

"Keep your car in the garage at night until we straighten this out," Fred said. "It will probably just blow over. Those guys are a bunch of windbags. I've got more bad news. Stu came home from work last night, and we got into a fistfight."

"Are you okay?"

"I kicked his ass! The chump! The only thing is, now I have to be out by the end of this month. I don't know where to go."

"I'll help you move, if you find a place." I paused. "Wait a minute. Judy has been bugging me for months to move in with her. She can't afford that two-bedroom place. You might be able to move in with her."

"I don't think so."

"Well, suit yourself. I just thought I'd make you aware of the possibility."

"Forget all that," Fred said, brightening. "Would you like to take my kids to a movie today?"

"I guess so," I said, still feeling uneasy about the rat.

"Good! We'll have lunch and then go to a matinee."

Later that day we pulled in to the driveway of the large house that Fred built several years before. His two boys came flying out the front door and a huge Great Dane bounded after them. I thought we were leaving so I remained in the van, but Fred went into the house. The boys plopped themselves down in the back of the van by the windows. They were playing with a small electronic game. Sean was eleven years old, with very dark hair and brown eyes. He looked like he had a tan even in the middle of winter. His seven-year-old brother, Shannon, looked just like Fred, with fair skin, blue eyes and blond hair.

Moments later, Fred's ex-wife Christine looked out the front door of the house as Fred left. She smiled, waving at me. Surprised that she was so friendly, I waved back.

The children impressed me with adult manners and polite behavior. I had underestimated them. We lunched at Taco Bell and then sat through a modern version of *Flash Gordon* in a movie house filled with active, screaming children. It was exhausting.

The threatening phone calls continued.

■　　■　　■

A few weeks later, my Air Force recruiter called. He sounded indignant.

"You didn't tell us you had a lawsuit pending," he said.

"Technically, it's not a lawsuit yet. It's still in the complaint stage with the Equal Employment Opportunity Commission," I explained. "Why?"

"Because the Air Force can't accept anyone with any litigation pending. Nothing. Not criminal litigation, not a civil action, a divorce proceeding, a custody petition. Nothing. Not even a complaint or claim with a government agency that involves hearings."

"So what are you telling me?" I asked. "I can't leave for basic training next month?"

"Not unless your complaint is dismissed or decided by then."

I met Fred downtown for lunch and told him the news.

"That's great!" he exclaimed. Then, seeing my frown, he added, "I mean, I'm sorry if you're disappointed, but this means that you're not leaving! That's all that matters to me!"

I didn't know what to do. I couldn't drop the claim, I just couldn't. There was too much riding on it. Also, others depended on me ... I had time, money, emotion and energy invested in the suit.

Some of it, of course, was a thirst for vengeance; I wanted to get back at the department. I'd had more threats: my car tires had been slashed; I had to change my phone number after a number of harassing calls. But there was more to it than that. If I dropped the case, I knew nobody would pick up the ball. They were all scared.

There were other considerations, too. I was organizing a group of ex-recruits to put together a Class Action suit against the Police Department. I was also cooperating by now with a U.S. District Attorney, James Morrison, to be a federal witness against the Chief of Police. All this was going on. How could I just drop it all and go? For four years in the Air Force?

I made up my mind.

I told Fred over a long lunch.

"So I guess I won't be leaving next month. I just have to get my career back on the ground. I have to have a direction. I have to work. I'd be so unhappy if I didn't." It was well after three in the afternoon. The wine made me feel warm.

"You know, Laurie," Fred said softly, "we're so much alike. When are you going to ask me to marry you?"

I just laughed. I was stunned.

"Then I'll ask you. Do you want to get married?"

I was caught in the mood of the moment, and my heart swelled.

"Of course," I finally replied. "I'd love to get married."

So we eloped the following day—a sunny January 31—and were married by a judge in Waukegan, Illinois. On the way back, we stopped at a park and took some pictures.

The rest of that day we spent, prosaically, moving Fred's belongings into Judy's condo. We'd move my things after the honeymoon. I didn't feel any different. I didn't feel "married." I was a little disappointed by my lack of excitement. I wore a gold wedding band that matched Fred's.

■   ■   ■

So there it is. I'd given up a loving relationship with a man I really loved for a job in the police force, then after a year I had neither the man nor the job. I'd applied to the Air Force but they wouldn't take me because I was involved in litigation. I'd given up the Air Force. Again, everything went wrong. I lost everything in the long run. What a series of dreadful decisions!

Several times I'd come to a fork in the road, and I took the wrong turn every time.

I felt that things couldn't possibly get worse. What did I know? It always does.

On my bulletin board in prison I had a cartoon of Garfield the cat. In the first panel, Garfield was up a tree. He was saying, "So I'm stuck up a tree, it can't get any worse." In the next panel it starts to rain, and he's saying, "So it's raining, it can't get any worse." Then, in the last panel, Kaboom! He gets hit by lightning. There it is. That sums it up. That's the way my life was. If I could go back I'd do it differently, but then, I didn't know what to do.

■   ■   ■

When I told my mom and dad that we'd just gotten married, they thought we were joking. Then they were a bit angry that we hadn't told them of our plans, but eventually they relented.

"We're legally married and everything," I said. "We just didn't have a reception, so we might have a little thing in spring."

"You're having a little thing in spring?" my mother asked me facetiously. "Is that why you eloped?"

"Impossible!" I said, laughing. "I married him for his vasectomy!"

"I suppose you insisted on keeping your name," my mom whispered. "You've been pontificating about that for years."

"You know better than to argue with me about that," I said. "Yes, I kept my name. For feminist reasons."

"I hope you know, Fred, you got yourself an independent little cuss here," my mom said, as I groaned at her choice of words. "But I don't understand. Laurie always said that she didn't like the domestic scene!"

"Fred loves to cook, and he can even sew! He just replaced the zipper that I broke in my Calvin Klein jeans! It's a nice role-reversal."

Before we left for our honeymoon, Fred called Christine to tell her the news. Unexpectedly, he handed me the phone.

"I heard you collect butterflies?" I asked, not knowing what else to say.

"I put them on velvet and make wall-hangings," she said.

"Maybe I can buy some tropical butterflies and bring them back for you." It was awkward.

"That would be nice," Chris replied. "Could I talk to Fred again?"

He finished talking on the phone and then hung up.

"I guess Chris felt a little uncomfortable, talking to you," he explained.

"Why did you hand me the phone like that? I didn't know what to say, either!"

"You'll be seeing a lot of each other because of the kids," Fred told me.

"I just don't have any experience with this kind of situation. Give me time."

We spent our honeymoon in Jamaica. On the way back, Judy picked us up at the airport. She told us we were in store for a disappointment. She'd been evicted, so we were out with her.

"Oh, Zess! We just moved in!"

"At least everything of yours is still in boxes," she said. "I'm sorry!"

■   ■   ■

One night, while Fred was sleeping, Sgt. Zellmer paid me a visit, with another cop in plain clothes. They wanted to know if I was willing to testify against the officers suspected of wrongdoing. I explained that I had suffered threats and I didn't want to testify against anyone. I told them they didn't need me anymore in their investigation. I'd given them some leads and made them aware of what was going on. That was the extent of my part in the whole mess. They had photographs! What more did they need? They left.

■   ■   ■

While we were still in the apartment, I had an odd conversation with Judy.

"You'll never guess who keeps bothering me," she told me. "That big hulk who lives on the thirteenth floor. I can't remember his name. I think it's Tom. Anyway, the guy is huge! I call him The Hulk."

"Does he want to go out with you?"

"I think so. I don't want to be seen with him!"

"Is he a bodybuilder?" I asked. I'd seen him on occasion, usually on the elevator.

"Yeah. I was talking to him down at the pool in the summer. He was trying to get a tan for some kind of contest. He told me he was Mr. Wisconsin a few years back."

"Really?"

"He doesn't work out at your club, though. He goes to the Wedgewood gym. That I remember."

"Did you know I bought Fred a membership to my club as a wedding present? We're going to start working out together."

"What *don't* you do together?" she said, with a peculiar whine to her voice. "I still can't believe you two just ran off and got married."

"Why?"

"I don't know if I like this arrangement. When I asked you to move in, I meant just you—not you and a guy."

"Okay. Why don't we give it a try until we have to move. Then, if you really feel that it's not cool, we'll get a place of our own. Don't you like Fred?"

"He's okay," she answered. "He's just ... the way he always brings you flowers and is cooking all the time."

She continued to speak almost as if she was irritated or jealous. I couldn't see why. She had no reason to be.

■　　■　　■

At the end of February, Fred came home one night with an upset look on his face that was becoming uneasily familiar.

"Is something wrong?" I asked.

"I had the property settlement today," he said. "On top of that, Chris sold my dog without even telling me!"

"One thing at a time. What are you talking about?"

"Never mind. I don't even want to talk about it," Fred snarled. He paced back and forth, slamming our kitchen cabinet doors like a child and mumbling, half to himself, "I paid three hundred dollars for that dog! My Great Dane! Too hard to take care of a dog! She's just too goddamned lazy!"

"Whatever you say," I commented, bewildered.

My in-laws were to become my next big problem. I wasn't accepted into the family with the open arms I'd expected. I didn't know it, but Fred's divorce

71

had caused a nasty family feud, and by marrying him I had joined the ranks of the enemy. Fred neglected to explain any of this to me, so the first display of rejection shocked me.

Kathy was his brother John's wife. They lived across the street from Fred's parents. If we dropped in on them to talk to John, Kathy would take one look at me, excuse herself and leave the room to go upstairs. Kathy despised Fred with a passion, and decided I should be treated with hate by association. I didn't catch on immediately, until it got back to Fred that Kathy had been expressing her disapproval to John and to Fred's mother.

"Why does Kathy dislike me?" I asked Fred.

"Well, perhaps part of it is that she's real thick with Chris."

"But so what? Chris doesn't hate me, and I didn't do anything to Kathy! I only tried to be polite!"

My parents, on the other hand, warmed to Fred in the beginning. They gave us many things that we needed and invited us over frequently.

I took on more hours at the health club, and filled out an application to join the Fire Department. Within a few weeks, however, I was turned down. The Fire Department had a rule that prohibited any member of either the Police Department or the Sheriff's Department from applying for a job after being dismissed. Applicants had to wait at least a year after dismissal to apply.

Around that time, I was surprised to learn that a black friend of mine, Officer Darlene Anderson, had resigned. She was in my Academy class—a sharp, streetwise woman. She told me she could no longer endure the harassment that superior officers subjected her to. I wondered how many black or female officers were left from our class.

In March, our landlords at the highrise finally gave us a notice to vacate, and we resumed our search for an apartment. Most of those we saw were either too big, too expensive, too small or outside of the city limits. (Cops must reside in the City of Milwaukee.)

Judy said she wanted to continue living with us. She said that she couldn't afford an apartment on her own.

She had started dating "The Hulk," whose name was Tom Gaertner. He would come up to our floor occasionally and knock on our door, always very late at night, after Fred had already left for work. I found him arrogant, an opinionated boor. He was very aggressive and rude.

He hated cops. They were, in his opinion, "the lowest scum of the earth."

I argued with him. "I know there are some jerks in blue. I myself got the shaft from the Police Department. But you can't generalize like that. What am I supposed to say? My dad was a cop, I was a cop, and I'm married to a cop. You can't say they're all bad. That's just as bad as when people call weight lifters 'dumb jocks' or 'steroid-heads.'"

One night over dinner, Fred talked in detail for the first time about his previous marriage. His version was that he "barely knew" Chris at college in La Crosse. Fred insisted that after a drunken, one-night stand, Chris announced she was pregnant.

"I never could believe it was me," he said. "We just passed out that night! But no! She tells her parents, who rushed to tell mine, and we were both rushed to a church in Appleton! White wedding gown and all!

"We were strapped for money because of the baby, and because of the baby, Chris said she couldn't work!"

He claimed he told Chris he didn't want any more children, but two years later she surprised him with another pregnancy, saying it would save their marriage.

"Why didn't you take the responsibility for contraception?" I finally asked Fred.

"I did! Only too late!" he insisted. "I went for my vasectomy. I couldn't trust her maternal impulses. Then she refused to work because of the kids."

"When did you build the house?" I asked, referring to the tri-level that Chris was living in.

"I was only seven credits away from my Bachelor's degree when I stopped school temporarily to build a house. See, I had a car accident that I got money from. That, together with an inheritance, enabled me to start building.

"I spent Christmas Eve of that year nailing the last of the roof shingles. One day Chris just announced that she didn't love me anymore. She said she never loved me, and didn't want to sleep with me anymore! Said I should go out and get sex somewhere else! She didn't care! I never beat her, I never gambled, I never cheated on her or drank. All I did was work! So she says I was never home!

"I hadn't even finished installing the skylights yet when she kicked me out. I paid cash for her new bedroom set and it wasn't even delivered yet. I never slept in the damn bed!"

"Fred, you say Chris uses the kids as an excuse for financial dependence now, so it's hard to believe she didn't consider the effect the divorce would have on them."

"Are you kidding? She said that she didn't care. And that the first kid was never really mine to begin with! Look at Sean—he looks nothing like Shannon."

■　　■　　■

The World According To Fred. It was all lies, of course, created from some detached, internal frame of reference. He left himself blame-free, as he would do years later, with me. He conveniently failed to mention that he abused Christine horribly, both physically and verbally, and had many affairs with other women. It was unbelievable that Chris tolerated him for ten years. Still, had someone told me then what he was really like, I wouldn't have believed it. If love is blind, then I needed a seeing-eye dog.

■　　■　　■

For the next few months, Fred was so intense and possessive that he nearly smothered me. He said he was determined to make sure that he spent enough time with me, and as a result he didn't give me enough space. He almost consumed me. I wished I had more time to myself. I wondered why Fred didn't have any friends of his own. Other men I knew needed their "night out with the boys." Not Fred. My friends became his friends. Later, I found out this wasn't exactly true. Fred was "out with the boys" while he was working; it was more like whole aspects of his life were kept secret, hidden from me—he never talked about that part of his life.

After a long search for another apartment, we finally found a place. It wasn't as luxurious as the one we were forced to leave, but it was less expensive and was bigger, with two bathrooms and a large living room, a loft and three bedrooms. I appreciated the spacious closets and the spare room. Judy, who had been bad with money in the past, seemed to have settled down. She was doing well at her job in sales at Wonderful Waterbeds. She promised that in April she'd sign a year's lease with us and pay her share of expenses faithfully.

I was wallpapering our bathroom one afternoon when Fred came home, looking heavy-hearted. He'd finally gotten the decision on the marital property settlement. He began to cry. We were alone; Zess was out somewhere.

"How can one person financially rape another person legally?" he complained, weeping. "What I built with my own two hands and what I paid for isn't even mine anymore! It's all hers! She's using the kids! She's just using them!"

"Calm down," I said. "What are you talking about?"

"The judge said I had to keep paying the mortgage on that goddamned house—$383 a month! While she's allowed to live there, rent free! I also got socked with child support payments of $365 a month! That's almost $800 a month! Out of my pocket!" He was weeping.

His annual income as a detective was about thirty-two thousand dollars a year, which averaged to around twenty-six hundred dollars a month. My job and the carpentry work Fred and I did on the side added to this income, so the alimony and child-support payments were tough, but not that much of a hardship.

"I'm even required to pay her attorney's fees!" Fred complained. "Besides that, she's entitled to my pension when I resign from the Police Department—whether or not she remarries!"

I didn't know what to say to him. The whole matter was so foreign to me. I simply allowed him to continue.

"The hideous fact of the matter is, Chris misrepresented her earnings in court, but there's no way to prove it. She just stood up and said that she can't work full-time because of the children! Again—the children! When I know for a fact that she's been earning almost six dollars an hour and has been working forty hours a week for the past nine months!"

"How do you know this?" I asked.

"I saw her check stub! The last time I picked up Sean to take him to a game after school, I waited for him in the kitchen—"

"And you were snooping?"

"No! I wasn't snooping! The stub was lying right there on the kitchen counter along with a mess of other papers. She's such a slob."

"Can't you prove it? There must be a way to subpoena her wage statements."

Fred shook his head. A tear rolled off his face and fell to the floor.

"I suppose I could. But that would mean I'd have to reopen the case, and that would cost me more in attorney's fees, and all that takes time. Meanwhile, the bitch is robbing me blind!"

He calmed down a bit. "She's just using the kids, Laurie. Two weeks ago, she was trying to make me feel real guilty, asking me if I could give her more money. She said the kids didn't have enough to eat! Can you imagine? Then I find out from Sean that all she did was fill the liquor cabinet for a party she was having! I always fall for it!" He began weeping again.

I was bewildered. How could such a financial slaughter happen? It didn't seem possible. I felt he must be exaggerating. Did my inexperience make me wrong? Both my sisters were divorced, and they ended up with nothing. I thought of Suzy, with her child support payment of eighty-five dollars a month. I couldn't believe there hadn't been some provocation, and I knew already how Fred tended to distort the facts.

In the back of my mind I was annoyed with his sniveling. If he was so poverty-stricken, why did he push me into getting married so fast? Sometimes the things he did made no sense.

The phone rang. It was the manager from the health club where I worked part-time with more bad news. Talk about bad timing!

An odd chain of events had led up to an incident that almost cost me my job. He told me the story.

He was in a laundromat doing his wash when a woman approached him and "came on to him like a bulldozer." He told her he managed the health club. She said she was a cop.

"Oh yeah? I've got a girl working for me that used to be a Milwaukee cop," he said. "Maybe you know her. Her name is Laurie Bembenek."

"I know her," she snapped, suddenly cold. "She's married to my ex-boyfriend!"

"No shit? What's your name?" he asked.

"Pam Fischer," she answered, and left abruptly.

Later, Pam gossiped to an executive of the health club chain that she had worked with me—although I'd never even met her—and that I was dismissed from the MPD for sitting on a married guy's lap at a party, smoking pot. Yet another version of the Department rumor! The wife of this executive phoned and demanded that I be fired. She didn't want someone "of that moral character" working for the club.

I had some difficulty keeping my job because of her.

Later that month, I met with a different representative of the Equal Employment Opportunity Commission, who was even more optimistic about my complaint than the first. I turned in signed statements, supporting my case, that I'd been collecting. The most important was signed by Judy Zess, and described the coercion she was under when she wrote the reports about the concert incident.

The reports dated May 2, 1980 that I filed in regards to the incident on May 1, 1980 were written under coercion and after long hours of interrogation and under mental duress. I was intoxicated and confused at the time.

The written reports dated May 3, 1980 that Lawrencia Bembenek filed in regards to that same incident of May 1, 1980 were factual and truthful.

On Dec. 15 the criminal charges of POCS (Possession of a Controlled Substance) issued against me were dropped after a jury trial within the Circuit Court of Appeals before Judge Patricia Curley during October, 1980. I was represented by Attorney Jack Gimbel.

I feel that both Lawrencia Bembenek and I were discriminated against because we were dismissed on false charges and allegations that were asserted and substantiated by nothing more than hearsay evidence. Harold Breier and his administration opposes women and minorities on the job. White male police officers are afforded preferential treatment in regards to disciplinary action.

Judy L. Zess

The representative wanted a list of police officers from my Academy class who had either resigned or were dismissed.

Meanwhile, a *Milwaukee Journal* analysis of city data produced even bleaker statistics, according to findings that were dated March 31, 1980. Female and minority officers just didn't last on Chief Breier's Department.

From my Academy class alone, the list was grim. With only one year having passed since our appointment dates, five black men, four white women, three black women and one white man were already gone. The white male was considerably overweight and resigned because he couldn't match the physical standards the Academy demanded. Out of eleven female recruits who joined the department when I did, eight were already without a job. Others would follow.

8

SASSON

We were still living out of boxes; Fred had never gotten around to unpacking. One afternoon, when I was irritable and short-tempered from a frustrating afternoon downtown filling out job applications, I began unpacking cartons and labeling the ones that were seasonal. Judy walked in.

"My! Aren't we organized!" she said.

"Look at this mess! Fred told me he'd unpack these things, but he never got around to it—all this stuff has been just sitting here. You've got to get Fred a key to the storage area so we can put some of these boxes away."

"When he comes home, I'll take some of my shit down there, too," Judy said. "I've got Christmas ornaments and a fake tree in a box that's taking up too much room in my closet."

"I wish you'd get a copy of that key made soon, anyway. You keep saying you'll do it."

"Calm down," she said. "I'll go to Sears this weekend. Hey! Tom's talking crazy lately! I think he's in love."

Fred came in the door, bristling with anger. He was upset because Stu Honeck had done some inept repairs to his precious house. Why couldn't he leave them alone? He seemed obsessed with Christine and with that wretched house. I tuned him out.

■   ■   ■

My parents came over to our apartment for dinner on their thirty-sixth wedding anniversary. They'd seen the place several times when they came over to drop things off, but had never stayed long. I wanted to make the evening special, so I bought some slim blue candles, and folded cloth napkins into pretty designs I had learned when I was a display artist. I finished decorating the table with a huge bunch of fresh flowers.

Fred made a salad, soup, beef, fresh vegetables and rolls. I bought a fattening German layer cake for dessert. Judy had made herself scarce and went out with Tom for the evening.

The evening was pleasant and relaxed. The only inconvenience was the toilet in Judy's bathroom. It was plugged and would overflow if flushed. I caught my mother as she was about to use it, and directed her to the apartment's other bathroom. "That's what's wrong with this complex," I told her. "Ever since we moved in here, there's been trouble with the plumbing. And problems always seem to take weeks to fix."

"That's a shame," my mother said. "Especially with the rent you pay here."

"One time I was all set to do a stack of dishes and the landlord called to warn everyone not to run their water! Soap was all over everything. I was so mad. All five apartments had the water shut off. The place downstairs was flooded."

My parents left late, after hugs and warm wishes, taking their cake with them.

■　　■　　■

The day of my Fact-Finding Conference with the EEOC finally arrived. The City Attorney, Ritter, was there, along with Lieutenant Tromp and the Commanding Officer of the Second District Station, Captain Pape. My complaint and the separate charges were presented orally, step by step. The City Attorney was given the opportunity for rebuttal.

I maintained that I was dismissed for reasons of sex discrimination. The report I'd filed the previous May regarding the concert was truthful, I said, and I submitted the signed statement from Zess. I pointed out that the charges issued against her had been dropped. I showed that there were numerous contradictions among the reports filed by the arresting officers—differences in descriptions and some outright falsehoods. One I recalled was in an Offense Report that said, "... cleared by the arrest of Lawrencia Bembenek," when I was neither arrested nor apprehended at that concert.

Ritter denied that, saying he had witnesses to verify my arrest.

Witnesses! Sure! But this one I knew I could prove. I told him to refer to his copy of my Verbatim Statement transcript, given before Captain Beste of the Police Academy. There he'd find the question:

"Are you aware of the fact that at this time, Paul Will from the Vice Squad is downtown right now trying to obtain a warrant for your arrest?"

To which I had replied: "No."

Ritter apologized. Then he shifted tactics. I was correct about not being arrested, he said. But still, my complaint of being subjected to sexist harassment was not "specific" enough.

He wanted specific? What about the names I was called?

"The word 'cunt' refers only to a woman, doesn't it?" I asked. "That was uncalled for and was done to me deliberately."

"You can't prove intent," Ritter said.

"I know it was deliberate because my FTO later informed me that he was told to give me a hard time—per his superiors."

"I ask, then, that you identify your Field Training Officers," Mr. Bronson from the EEOC said.

I told him their names.

Ritter chipped in. "Might I explain to the Commission that Field Training is a vigorous period of training that occurs before the recruit is allowed to graduate. It is only natural that the FTO gives his recruit a hard time. There's nothing sexist about it. It prepares the recruit."

"The name-calling ...?" Bronson asked Ritter.

"Street jargon and bad language come with the job," Ritter said. "Male recruits might be called 'pricks.' Besides, if Miss Bembenek was so concerned about it, she should have made supervisory personnel aware of it."

"I did!" I argued. "I talked to two sergeants about it, but they brushed it off like it was nothing."

"Did you file a 'Matter of' about it?"

"No. But there were times when the verbal abuse occurred in front of a sergeant! One time it happened at roll call. My point is that disrespect for a fellow officer is a rule violation."

"Are you aware of any other females that received similar treatment during Field Training?" Bronson asked me.

"Yes."

"You don't have to name them at this hearing, but would you be willing to identify them at a later date?"

"Yes."

The hearing continued for several hours. The city's final point was to the effect that my basis for a charge of discrimination was unfounded. They said I claimed that male officers were not disciplined for rule violations that got females fired, yet I hadn't presented a single incident involving a male officer that was identical to the action against me.

"Do you mean to say I'd have to tell you about a case exactly like mine, but involving a male cop?" I asked Bronson after the hearing. "Where a male filed a false report but didn't get fired for it? We're getting off the point here—the report I filed was not false!"

"But that would illustrate a clear case of discrimination."

"That's ridiculous!" I said. "I don't have access to personnel files!"

"That's why the City Attorney has such an advantage over you. I know what kind of game they're playing. Even though I'm an impartial fact-finder, it's obvious. Ritter could come up with fifty cases where disciplinary action had been taken against male officers."

"What about all the rule violations by men that I reported to Internal Affairs? They did nothing about all that."

"Laurie, they'd still argue that those are immaterial because it's not a relevant comparison."

"It's relevant by sheer fairness! What if I knew of several cases where male officers filed false reports?" I asked. "Like regarding sleeping on duty? I know they slept on duty. The reports they filed had to be false."

"They could still counter your assertion by saying that the brass didn't know those reports were false."

"This is impossible! They judge whether a report is false or not—even when it's the truth! It's so unfair! That female Puerto Rican from Second District took a rap for falling asleep on duty! They all sleep!" I sighed. "So. It's not enough to prove that a male officer filed a false official report. I also have to show that the commanders knew it was false and did nothing about it. That's impossible."

"I know how frustrated you must feel."

"I have a newspaper article about a Fifth District police sergeant, Clarence Martin, who was dismissed. It was his third offense for filing a false official report."

"They'll defend that by saying that his status accounted for the difference. You weren't a sergeant." Bronson managed a tired smile. "Cheer up. All is not lost."

"What now?" I asked wearily.

"We'll be contacting you soon. A 'Cause' or 'No Cause' determination will be made. If we find cause, the Commission will pursue this matter through the Department of Justice. If no cause is found, then you'll have the right to sue—at your own expense—in the federal court system. So it's far from over."

"Okay. Thank you," I said, picking up my file. I left and walked through the chilly air to my car.

■　　■　　■

The following week, the weather grew warmer. Fred suggested we have a barbecue. He'd go over to the house on Ramsey and retrieve one of his grills. Christine had three, he said.

We drove over to Ramsey Street, and I sat in the van as Fred ran up to the house. Stu's car was parked in the driveway. Sean and Shannon ran up to the van to say hi. They chattered on and on about a game they were playing. Fred returned within a few minutes with no grill.

As we drove away I looked at Fred. I was afraid to ask what had happened this time.

"She's got three goddamn grills and she won't even give me one! And I bought them all to begin with!" Fred complained.

"Did you tell her—"

"I couldn't tell her anything! Stu was right there, sticking his lousy two cents in. I didn't want to start anything with that turkey."

"Oh."

"And she had the nerve to ask me for money for her crummy electric bill, just because I used one of my power saws in the garage the last time I was there."

He squealed the van around a corner. "She kept all those bills in my name, so if she doesn't pay it, my credit rating goes to hell. Let me tell you something. Sean has been telling me that she's been missing work more and more lately. It's always the day after Stu's been over. I think she's starting to get too hungover for work. That's why she wants more money. Well, I'm not paying for her parties with Stu. She can go to hell!"

"So what about the grill?" I asked.

"I'll wait until she's not home and go in and take one," Fred snarled.

So much for the calm, fun-loving man I thought I'd married. He was always complaining about Christine, though he'd rarely even mentioned her before we got married.

Judy was not home much anymore. She spent most of her time with Tom, who was training for a bodybuilding contest in California. She told me he was on a special diet and was working out all day. I asked her what Tom did for a living, but she simply replied that he was a bodybuilder. I wondered about her answer, briefly, since he drove a Corvette and owned a boat. Later, she changed her story and said that he was living off an inheritance.

Soon she began to drop hints and talk idly about Tom asking her to move in with him. I reminded her about the lease.

■　　■　　■

A few days later, after I'd been doing laundry at my mother's house, she found something at the bottom of the tub. It was Fred's wedding ring from his earlier marriage, inscribed from Chris to Fred. I went back to the apartment. Fred and Judy were eating lunch when I let myself in.

"I have something of yours," I told Fred crossly, pulling the ring out of my pocket. His mouth opened slightly.

"Where did you find that?"

"My mom found it—at the bottom of her washing machine. Why were you carrying that around?"

"You're overreacting to this," Fred replied. "I don't know how it got there."

"Get real," I groaned.

"I don't! You don't believe me? Your mother must have got you all riled up."

"She was angry when she found it. As a matter of fact, so am I. Wouldn't you be?"

"Who cares what your mother thinks? You're married to me now!"

"Am I?" I asked. "It sure doesn't feel like it! It's always Christine this and Christine that. She has more to say about the things you do than you're willing to admit!"

"Bullshit!" Fred yelled.

"It's true! You always say you're going to do something but you never end up doing anything."

"You don't understand!" Fred claimed.

"All I understand is that she must have something on you and it must be something good, because when she puts her pretty little foot down, Fred jumps! You couldn't even get a grill from her."

"What do you want me to do?" Fred argued. "I've done all I can do. That's just the way the divorce laws are set up in this state!"

"I've been talking to some friends of yours and they told me that you just gave everything away without a struggle. A goddamn surrender! Goddamn it, why? What has that woman got on you?"

Fred sat down in a chair, looking tired and defeated.

"You just don't know, Laurie. She had me by the balls. She could've had my job." He wouldn't explain further.

He looked up at me, slowly. "Do you know what I'm going to do with this?" he asked, holding up his old wedding band. "I'm going to get rid of this right now." He tossed the ring into a bag of garbage.

"I'm sorry," I said.

"I'm sorry, too."

To make up, Fred suggested we visit friends of his in Florida, Dennis and Karen. He figured he could even make some money while we were there, working with Dennis, putting up aluminum siding.

"When do you want to go?"

"How fast can you pack?" Fred asked, grinning.

■　　■　　■

On the way to Florida, I learned a curious piece of information. I'd brought up the subject of Judy's mysterious boyfriend, Tom.

"You know," I said, "he says he hates cops so much, yet the other day Judy was telling me he used to have a best friend who was a Glendale officer."

"Really? What was his name?"

"His name sounded like those designer jeans—Sassoon? Sasone?"

"Not Sasson!" Fred exclaimed.

"I guess so. Why?"

"I shot and killed a Glendale cop in 1975 named Robert G. Sasson," Fred told me. "Don't you remember reading about it in the newspaper?"

"No. I was in high school then."

"It turned out that he was a bad cop who was dealing drugs. I was in a squad on that side of town when a call came over the radio: officer needs assistance, 10-17. The location was vague. They said somewhere on Silver Spring Road. We kept listening. The dispatcher came back and confirmed the location as a tavern called The Northway Tap. So anyway, we arrive, and a woman in the parking lot waves to us. She tells us to go in through the back door because the front was locked. It was Sasson's wife, Camille."

"Who locked the front door?"

"Wait. Let me tell it. This woman is pretty sloshed. I had a rookie with me, so he followed me in through the back entrance of the bar. There was a frosted, glass partition right by the door. Rounding the partition, all I see is a guy in a yellow baseball uniform kneeling over a black dude on the floor. This is about six feet away from me. As soon as we approach him, he stands up and puts his semi-automatic to the rookie's chest!"

"Holy shit!"

"That's what I said! I pulled my piece and loaded four slugs into the baseball uniform. It all happened so damn fast. Then the broad is screaming: 'That's my husband! He's a cop!'"

"What ...?"

"We found out later he was trigger-happy. That wasn't the first time an incident of that nature involved him. He drank too much and usually got in trouble with his gun."

"Wow."

"He had connections in after-hours places. It all came out during the investigation that followed his death."

"Why did you handle a call outside Milwaukee?" I asked.

"Oh. The Northway is in Glendale but the guy who called the cops was from out of town—so, by mistake, he called the Milwaukee Police instead of Glendale."

"What happened at the inquest?"

"I went before the DA who reviewed the case and ruled it justifiable homicide."

"Was that the end of it?"

"Camille Sasson filed a lawsuit against the county and was granted seventeen thousand dollars."

"Sasson is Tom's friend?"

"Could be," Fred said. "Pretty big coincidence if it isn't the same guy. This is going to be ticklish, living with Judy, if Tom is around. Don't say anything about it."

■　　■　　■

Here's a pretty kettle of seafood! Many rumors have swirled about over Sasson's death. Why were the Milwaukee cops called? Why are there rumors of cover-up? Why were the stories floated about Sasson's bad habits? Where is the proof that drugs were involved? What about the witnesses who said Sasson did not have a gun to anyone's head? That Fred must have known he was a cop? That he was trying to wave to Fred? What did Chris know about this? Was she holding some secret knowledge over Fred's head?

No one knows the truth to any of this, except that there is nothing straightforward about what the Milwaukee Police Department (or some of its officers) were up to. The whole thing smelled very bad. But I didn't know that then.

■　　■　　■

Of course, Fred messed up our vacation, too. He insisted on surprising Dennis and Karen instead of calling to let them know we were on our way. When we arrived, we found Karen's parents staying with them; they had no room for us. Nor did Fred do any work. He was gone every day with Dennis, leaving me alone with Dennis's mother.

We had to hurry back to Wisconsin so that Fred could return to work. We arrived home weary from all the driving, and noticed that some of Judy's appliances were missing from the kitchen. When I asked her about it, she said she was letting Tom borrow some things he needed, because he'd left the girlfriend he was living with.

■   ■   ■

The following week, Fred and I were invited by Christine to a party for Shannon's first communion. Fred was opposed to going. He said Christine's parents, Alice and Earl Pennings, would no doubt be there, and there were still too many hard feelings from the divorce. On the other hand, Fred's mother insisted that we both attend, because of the children.

I suggested that Fred simply go alone.

But Fred called Christine to say he wouldn't be going. He blamed me. He said I'd told him I'd be "too uncomfortable" around her.

I was furious.

"Damn it, Fred! Why did you have to put it all on me? I wasn't eager to go, but you didn't have to say I'm the reason we were refusing the invitation! It's just not true!"

"What was I supposed to say?"

"Why use me as an excuse? Why don't you just be honest—"

"Don't talk to me like I'm a child!" he interrupted.

"But he's your kid! Why won't you go?"

Fred pouted in silence.

But then I knew. Of course. Stu would be there!

"You're jealous! Why do you care so much?" I asked.

As I suspected, Fred never did call Chris back to straighten things out.

■   ■   ■

One morning, on my way out the main entrance of the apartment building, I checked the mailbox. To my pleasant surprise, my income-tax refund had arrived. Happily, I stuffed the envelope into my purse. I knew what I would spend it on.

I called Judy from work to ask her about a jeweler she was acquainted with. "Can you still get me a deal on a diamond ring?"

She said she could, and told me to meet her at Tom's. I called Fred to tell him that I'd be late.

"I'm going jogging with Judy at the lake."

"Good!" said Fred. "I'm going, too!"

Not wanting to ruin the surprise, I put him off.

"Look, Freddy. Remember that talk we had? You can't be with me twenty-four hours a day. You're smothering me. I need time away from you. Okay?"

"Well ..."

"I'll see you later," I said firmly.

"Call me as soon as you're through jogging," he demanded.

"Yeah," I placated him.

"How long will you be?" he insisted.

"You sound like my mother!" I groaned. "Lighten up!"

"Sorry," he mumbled.

Judy and I were gone longer than I'd expected, because when I arrived to pick her up at the high-rise, she wasn't ready to leave. She was alone, and she told me to wait in Tom's kitchen while she changed clothes. She had already started keeping some jeans and shirts there.

The kitchen looked just like the kitchen in our old place. I was thirsty and I poked about for something to drink. I opened the refrigerator door and quickly slammed it shut. It was either full of large bags of marijuana, or Tom was storing a year's supply of oregano for the U.S. Army.

So that's what he did for a living.

I said nothing to Judy, and we set off for the jeweler on the other side of town. I bought Fred a diamond solitaire ring for less than half of what was marked on the price ticket. I thanked Judy for arranging the deal. Fred's birthday was in June, and I wanted to surprise him—I'd never given him more than a simple wedding band. We were a little better off now. My hours at the club had been doubled and Fred had gotten a raise, so I didn't feel it was an extravagant purchase.

During our drive home, Judy began to talk about Tom.

"I really don't think I should move in with him. He's really so much older than me. What I want to do is go to California next summer. Besides, Tom's landlords aren't too thrilled about seeing me because I got evicted from two different condos at the high-rise. Ha!"

87

"What are you talking about? You signed a year's lease with us. By the way, the rent is due in a few days."

"Oh. I'll be a day or two late with my half," Judy said airily. "I don't get paid until after this weekend."

"We'll send our half with a note saying that you'll be late."

When I dropped Judy off at the high-rise, I ran inside to use Tom's phone and called Freddy. I felt like a stupid seventeen-year-old. As it rang, I thought with disgust, "I hope I don't get grounded for being late."

"Where are you?" Fred was furious.

"I'm on my way home now," I explained. A little more than two hours had gone by. He had the nerve to hang up on me! I drove home thinking that it was a mistake to have bought him the ring.

As I walked in, Fred bombarded me with accusations. While I was gone he had broken some things in anger and thrown them about. In the middle of his rampage, I calmly produced the ring box, tossing it down on the table in front of him. Instantly, he stopped. A pained expression replaced the rage.

"I feel about two inches tall," he whispered. His eyes lit up as he pried the top open. Blushing, he slipped the ring on, next to his wedding band.

■　　■　　■

A few days later, Judy called me at the gym. She was frantic.

"Laurie! Tom found out!"

"What?"

"Did Freddy kill a Glendale cop back in 1975?"

"Yes."

"That was Tom's best friend! We were at a dinner party the other night. The guy's widow was there. What was his name?"

"Sasson."

"Yeah! Camille started talking about it for some reason, and then she mentioned how the cop who killed her husband had been promoted to detective, and then she said Fred's name! I almost shit! Why didn't you ever tell me?"

"Judy, I just found out about it myself. Fred told me on the way to Florida. What did Tom say?"

"Oh! First, he just looked at me. Then he asked me what Freddy's full name was. He knew anyway. He is pissed!"

"I don't know what to do! It all happened before my time!"

"I don't know what to do either," Judy said. "You know how Tom hates cops to begin with."

As a result, Judy began to move out, presumably at Tom's request. But she did it in a sneaky way; she'd come by when neither Fred nor I were in the apartment and take a few things. She knew our work schedules. She knew I was always gone all day Saturdays. I knew she was avoiding us. Every time we returned, something else was missing. We had no real way to reach her, because she kept Tom's phone number a secret, and she was never available at work when we called. She still owed us her half of the rent for May, and we started to wonder how we'd find another roommate. The two of us didn't need three big bedrooms. I was worried.

I was also worried about Tom.

"That guy scares me," I told Fred. "He's so huge! He looks like he could squash your head like a melon."

Fred agreed. "Leave it to Judy to get involved with a creep like that. You didn't have to tell me he's a drug dealer. I had a funny feeling about him right from the start. I think I'll have to start calling you at night after I leave for work to make sure you're okay. Don't ever forget to lock the door."

"Judy still has a key," I told him. "Can't we change the lock or something?"

"She still has her damn furniture in the apartment and she'd go complain to the landlady. I don't think we can change the lock."

"What else can we do?" Fred asked. "Judy also still has the key to our basement storage-cage. She was supposed to make copies of that key and never did. If we do move, we have to get our boxes out of there."

We didn't hear from Judy again until she came home one night with Tom. Fred had already left for work. It was after eleven when I heard the door. I had to release the chain on the door for them. I was civil, thinking that it would do no good to start an argument. But Judy started in on me anyway, which led to an argument about the lease. I followed her to the door.

Tom stepped between us. I stopped talking in the middle of my sentence.

"Listen," he demanded. "We don't give a good goddamn about your finances. All I know is that your husband is nothing more than a scared, motherfucking punk that killed my best friend! The trigger-happy pig!"

I blinked. Tom was six feet, two inches, 250 pounds. But I just glared back at him, irrationally fearless.

"That all happened a long time ago," I said. "Before I met Freddy. Before I met you. Before you met Judy. So I'm not going to stand here and discuss Sasson. There's no point to it. I wasn't there when it happened, and neither were you. So who are you to judge?" I turned to look at Judy. "Get the rest of your shit. And get out."

After Fred got home from work the next day, I told him what had happened the night before, and we once again began looking for another apartment. Luckily, the landlady didn't care; she knew three young people who needed a place. I was sad that none of my friends had seen the apartment—somehow they never seemed able to find the time to visit. Years later, they said they'd kept refusing to visit because they disliked Fred so much.

We found a one-bedroom efficiency across from a park, not far from where my mom and dad lived, and we quickly signed for it. It was just the right size for the two of us.

About a week after Judy moved out, I read in the newspaper that Tom had been arrested by federal agents and charged with Possession With Intent to Deliver Cocaine. I woke Fred.

"I hope Tom doesn't think that you or I set him up. We didn't exactly part friends."

"How would we have done that?" Fred said. "We only had a hunch as to what he was up to. Oh well, it serves Judy right. I'm surprised she wasn't with him!"

A few days later, Judy arrived. She'd been crying. She came to drain her waterbed and retrieve the rest of her property. As I helped her hook up a garden hose, Fred went into our bedroom to use the phone. He'd been calling Chris. He was irritated because he'd heard that she'd taken the kids out of town without telling him, in violation of the divorce stipulation. I heard him shouting at her.

"What pisses me off is that I've asked you three times now to let me know when you take the kids up to your folks' house. If one of my boys needed emergency surgery, they'd have to have their father's permission to operate. What if you got in an accident?

"And another thing! My goddamn family won't accept Laurie because I remarried, but they sure are accepting that lowlife bastard you've attached yourself to." Fred paused. "Yes, I mean Honeck. Don't you see he's only dragging you down? That rotten guy spends time with my kids? Then you come bitching to me that you need more money! Listen, I know how often you take off work when you're too hungover to go in ..."

There was a silence, and I heard Fred laugh angrily.

"Yes! I know how often you call in sick. How I found out is my own business. We haven't settled this matter about my visiting rights." He paused again. "Ten miserable years and I'm paying through my teeth! Don't give me that crap, Chris. I know how much you make. I intend to expose your income to a judge just as soon as I can! I'll see you in court!"

I closed Fred's door and looked in on Judy while she drained her bed. I wanted to make sure she wasn't getting water all over the rug. Also, I was curious to know what had happened to Tom and if she intended to stay at his apartment. She still looked upset.

"Boy, is Fred having a good fight," she said. "Christine?"

"Yes. I'm bored to tears with all these arguments of his," I told her. "I'm just glad it isn't my problem."

"What's she like?"

"I've only met her a few times. She seems all right." I changed the subject. "Are you moving back home?"

"No. I'm staying at Tom's."

I left to sit outside on the porch. Fred came out after a while, smiling.

"Guess what?" he asked.

"I hate to ask." I squinted in the sun. Auto chrome in the parking lot gleamed.

"Chris is mad because someone turned in Honeck for sleeping with her."

"Really?"

"Yeah! And you know what's even funnier?"

I waited for an answer.

"They're both sure it was you!"

"Me?" I gasped.

"Ha ha! Isn't it hilarious?" He sat down with a smirk on his face. "I'm sure it wasn't you."

"What do you mean?"

"Because it was *me*!" he said, and started to laugh.

I could think of nothing to say. It was like the time when Fred told Chris he wouldn't go to the party for Shannon because of me. I refused to talk to him for the rest of the day.

9

MURDER

The following day, I went to several job interviews. When I got back, I checked our answering machine to find out if anyone had called. A peculiar voice started to growl after I pushed the Play button.

"Fuck you, motherfucker," the voice said.

I stopped the tape and rewound it for Fred to hear. He walked over to the phone and a look of disgust came over his face.

"Who is that?" I asked.

"Don't you know? It's Honeck."

"How did he get our number? What's going on?"

"The asshole is probably drunk. I'm sure Chris cried on his shoulder about the little fight we had," Fred said nonchalantly.

"How did he get our new phone number?" I demanded angrily. "This is a brand new, unpublished, unlisted number!"

"I don't know." Fred shrugged.

"You gave our new number to Chris, didn't you, and Stu got it from her!"

"So?"

"So? I thought you said you wouldn't give our number to her again! Didn't we have enough weirdos calling us and threatening us at our old place? Damn it! Honeck's got our new number."

Fred continued dressing for work, strapping on his shoulder holster.

"Stop it, Laurie. I refuse to argue about this. We've been through this all before. I had to give our number to the boys the last time I saw them. They're my kids! They have to know how to reach me!"

"You told me that they could call you at work in the morning—but you gave them our number!"

"I had to give it to Chris, and that's final."

"First you said you gave it to the boys. Now you say you gave it to Chris! I hate it when you lie to me! The phone is in my name, and I get the bills. You'd think I'd have a right to know who the hell gets my number!"

"So we got an obscene phone call! Honeck's not going to do anything. Why weren't you as indignant when your 'friend' Judy came by yesterday? How could you even talk to her after what she did to us?"

"That's irrelevant. But if you must know, I was fishing for information about Tom's arrest. I was being nosy."

■　　■　　■

The next day was taken up with more fruitless job interviews. After the first one, for a security firm, the interviewer told me I'd seemed unenthusiastic or disinterested. I guess I was becoming disillusioned; I no longer really expected anyone to hire me. Then I went to a different place and spent two and a half useless hours in a room, scratching in answers with a lead pencil to a computerized psychological exam.

I returned home around five. After dinner, my parents came over as planned, with some empty cartons, and my mother stayed to help me pack. Fred sat around for a while, watching us wrap things in newspaper. He grew tired and excused himself to get some sleep before work.

I packed in a rather half-hearted way. My mother, always able to sense my moods, tried to reassure me.

"We'll get this all done tonight. It certainly is a job, isn't it? But it will be so much better, living without Judy. You'll see, hon."

"Oh, yes, I'm sure it will be," I replied. "But we just unpacked, and now we have to pack again! I feel like a tumbleweed."

"What's your new place like?"

"It's small. It faces a nice park. Good neighborhood."

We packed for a while, and it grew warm and dusty in the room. I opened a can of beer. My mother looked around the apartment. "What's left?" she asked.

"The spare room. Most of that stuff is Freddy's junk—four hundred socks, ninety-eight T-shirts, all that sort of stuff. I told Fred that even Ripley wouldn't believe it! Would you like the honor of packing that room? I'll finish up here."

"Sure."

"It's a good thing I didn't bring my bench and all my weights over here. I was going to set them up in that spare room and start bench-pressing again on a regular basis. That would have been heavy stuff to move."

"You can leave it in our basement. There's plenty of room for it. That way, whenever you feel like working out, you can come over," my mom told me.

After we finished packing, I woke Fred for work. My dad arrived to drive my mom home, and I hugged them both, thanking them again for all their help.

Fred sleepily wandered out of the bedroom, half-dressed.

"I'm surprised you managed to pack everything tonight!" he said.

"You slept for about four hours," I told him.

He glanced at his watch. "Are you still planning on going out with Marylisa tonight?"

"No, I don't think so. I'm too tired and dirty. Besides, I have to work tomorrow morning."

"Did you call Marylisa?" Fred asked.

"Yeah. I tried her apartment earlier, but her roommate told me she went straight to Jeff's after work, and I don't have his number. So she must have forgot about our plans anyway. It doesn't matter."

Fred finished dressing, straightened his tie, and I walked with him to the door. "Are you on a South Side squad tonight?"

"Probably," he replied. "We'll stop by again for some coffee if we're not busy. Otherwise, I'll call you. I still worry that Judy and Tom might pay you a visit after I'm gone."

Some nights, Fred would drive past our apartment if he was in the area, to see if a light was still on. I'd usually keep the coffee warm until I went to sleep.

I put some jazz on the stereo and got ready for a shower. I was a bit disappointed that I couldn't reach Marylisa, because we had planned to see a special show at a club called The Tropicana.

■　　　■　　　■

Oh Marylisa, why didn't you call? That night, of all nights, I should have gone out. I should have stayed up to party, enjoyed the fast life, stayed out late in the company of friends, been seen drinking in a bar, in many bars, made a noise, danced, done anything. But how could I have known I would need an alibi? Instead, I listened quietly to jazz and went to bed.

Someone, somewhere, was thinking of murder that night.

■　　　■　　　■

94

I'd just stepped out of the tub and was brushing my teeth when the phone rang. It was Fred. Turning off the stereo, I asked him to call me back. I was dripping wet and my mouth was full of toothpaste.

He called me back after roll call. We talked for a few minutes, but his lieutenant approached his desk so he was forced to hang up abruptly.

I was reading a novel in the dim light of a small bedside lamp when my eyelids grew heavy. Again the phone rang and it was Fred. The fleeting thought went through my mind: Does he call so frequently out of concern, or to check up on me? We said good night. I turned off the light, and fell asleep.

Much later, I heard the phone ringing again. I had no idea what time it was. Still in bed, I reached over to pick up the receiver, dazed from sleep.

"Hello?" My voice wouldn't work.

The voice on the other end sounded like something out of a dream. Clutching the phone, I began to drift off to sleep.

"Laurie! Are you awake?" I recognized Fred's voice.

I nodded, forgetting that he couldn't see me. The tone of his voice sounded so different that it alarmed me slightly.

"Are you awake? Wake up!"

"What's wrong?" I asked, sitting bolt upright.

"Laurie, Chris has been shot. She's dead. I'm going over to the house now to see if the boys are okay. Are you all right?"

"Of course." But it really didn't register. I hung up, rolled over and fell back to sleep. I didn't fully understand what was going on; I thought it had been some kind of dream. Then the ringing woke me again. At once I remembered the previous phone call and jumped out of bed.

"Laurie?"

"I'm awake now. Freddy, was I dreaming, or ...?"

"No. Chris is dead. Somebody broke into the house—two guys, we're not sure. Maybe burglary. There was one guy—Sean saw one guy."

"My God."

"The kids are fine. They're next door here at the neighbors. Billy is coming to pick them up after the police talk to them."

"God, I—I don't know what to say."

"The stereo and the strongbox were moved, so we think they were in the process of stealing them. We don't know. Maybe Chris tried to struggle with them." Fred was talking rapidly, but with no emotion in his voice.

"Are you coming home? What should I do? Should I call your mom and dad?"

"Just get up and make some coffee. My partner and I will be coming over."

"Okay." I hung up the phone and quickly pulled my furry robe over my shoulders. For a second, I felt as though the whole thing was a joke, but I dismissed the thought. Fred wouldn't joke about such a matter. But it was so hard to believe ...

I stumbled down to the lower level of our apartment, squinting as I turned on the overhead light. I groped for the coffeepot, but suddenly realized that everything was packed in boxes, and I couldn't begin to guess where it was.

I plopped down on a box next to the table in the kitchen and tried to clear my head. None of it seemed real. It didn't make any sense. What was I going to do about work in the morning? Should I call in sick? How could I make coffee with everything packed? I wished Fred would come home and tell me that he was mistaken, that perhaps Chris had been injured, but not dead.

Not dead.

Not ... murdered.

What was I going to do with the two kids? What about moving? My head spun. It was all so complicated. I felt like crying. What a nightmare. I picked up a bottle of brandy from an open box near the table and took a swig, grimacing at the taste.

For what seemed like an eternity, I stared out the dark window and jumped at every headlight that drove up, thinking it was Fred and his partner. I called my mom and dad. I was hoping Fred might have called them and told them when he'd be coming home. Fred had just talked to them but hadn't said where he was calling from. My dad asked me if I'd like to wait for Fred at their house, but I decided I should stay at the apartment.

The sun began to rise. It was about four o'clock when I heard the buzzer downstairs. I ran outside, onto our second-floor balcony, hoping that it was Fred, but when I looked down I saw two detectives.

"Could we come in? We have some questions."

I left the apartment and hurried down the stairs to the main entrance to open the door. They followed me back upstairs, introducing themselves as Detectives Abram and Templin.

We sat down by the table in the lower-level kitchen. They explained that they hated to disturb me, that it was routine. One lit up a cigar.

"I'll do anything to help," I said.

They asked about Stu Honeck, and whether Fred was jealous of Stu's relationship with Christine. I told them about the obscene phone call, saying that it sounded just like Stu's voice. The phone interrupted us several times, and I had to leave the room to answer it. My mother called back, and Fred's mother called to see if her son was there.

Finally I asked if they knew what was keeping Freddy. "He called me a long time ago and said that he'd be coming right home. It's been over an hour, I think."

"He's probably talking to the cops at the scene."

A message came over their radios.

"Negative," he answered into it. "We're 10-6 at the same 10-20." This meant they were still busy at my address. I got the feeling that they were being evasive, and I wondered if Fred was in some kind of trouble.

The phone rang again. It was Freddy. "Something's weird," he said. "They're trying to keep me at the scene. Is anybody there?"

"Yeah."

"Are they asking you questions about me?"

"Yeah."

"Well, don't worry. I'll be home soon."

I walked back down into the kitchen. A hazy, gray light washed in through the windows. The detectives stood up.

"One more thing. Did you buy an off-duty weapon when you were on the Department?"

"No. All I had was a Department issue."

"Did you buy a gun once you got off the Department?"

I shook my head, no.

Why were they asking me about guns?

"Okay," one of the detectives said. "That about wraps it up." Then a smirk crossed his face and he asked an even stranger question. "By the way, you don't own any green jogging suits, do you?"

"I own a sweat suit. I work for a health club," I answered, puzzled. "Two sweat suits. A gray one and a red one."

"Mind showing us?"

"Well, they might be packed. Let me just check the hall closet," I said, as I led them upstairs. "I was supposed to work today. Should be one here. Here it is." I held the red suit up for them to see.

"Fine. We were told to ask. Routine, you know? Thanks again."

They were told to ask me about jogging suits? Why?

After they left, I went back down to the kitchen to wait for Fred. Another half hour passed. I was restless and upset. I needed someone to talk to, so I made a few phone calls to pass the time. I called my friend Joanne and told her what had happened. Remembering that the call was long distance, and afraid that I was tying up the line, I ended our conversation.

I heard a noise and rushed to the window. No one was there. I sat back down again. It was dreadful. If someone could break into Christine's and kill her, they could just as easily break into our apartment. Irrational fear filled me. I wondered about all the threatening phone calls I had received.

Where was Fred?

I went back to the phone. Who else could I call? Judy. I knew she was accustomed to phone calls at all hours of the night. I got Tom's number from Judy's mother. Judy was alone in his apartment.

"First Tom gets busted, and now this! What's happening to us?" she said. "Now you have two kids to take care of?"

Finally, I heard a car pull up, and within a few minutes the buzzer downstairs rang. I hurried down the stairs to let them in.

"Laurie, this is my partner, Durfee," Fred said, smiling. He didn't appear in the least upset. It was as if he was treating the murder of his ex-wife like any other homicide.

I almost tripped on the hem of my robe as I led the way up the two flights of stairs to our apartment. I went into the kitchen, assuming they were right behind me. I turned, however, and saw that when they came in the door they had immediately begun walking down the hall toward the bedrooms. I thought Fred was showing Durfee to the bathroom, but when I retraced my steps and reached the top of the stairs, I saw that they were in the doorway of our bedroom. Their backs were to me.

Durfee had Fred's off-duty revolver in his hand, chamber open, checking the rounds and dumping them into his hand. He smelled the barrel. "Nope," he said, nonchalantly. "This gun hasn't been fired. Fred, why don't you clean this thing once in a while?"

"Yeah," I heard Fred say. He turned to look at me. "I just wanted to check out this gun right away, and make our report on it. That way there'll be no questions asked. Get dressed, we have to go downtown to ID the body."

"Right now?" I asked.

"Yeah."

"Besides, Fritz," Durfee was saying to Fred, "we think the guy used a forty-five tonight."

I gathered up some clothes and went into our bathroom to change. I was still taken aback at Fred's composure. It was pretty odd of him to march in and have Durfee check his off-duty gun. Wasn't it?

We got into the squad and proceeded downtown because Fred's car was still parked across from the Police Administration building. It was cool outside, and I shivered in my cotton shirt. Durfee chatted with me about the Department; he seemed like a nice guy.

When we arrived at the morgue, Fred and I were alone with the body. He approached the cold, stainless-steel table. It was dreadful. Chris was dressed in a pair of panties and a T-shirt with an Adidas logo. Her lifeless hands had been tied at one time, but someone had untied them and long strands of rope hung loosely at her wrists. A blue scarf was around her neck, and Fred explained that it had been used as a gag. She was about five feet, eight inches and 145 pounds. Fred rolled her body over to look at the bullet wound in her back. It was huge. I wondered if she had been sexually assaulted, since her legs weren't bound together, but I said nothing.

Fred motioned for me to come closer.

"Look at this. This is called radial expansion. See how the muzzle of the gun left its imprint in the skin? That gun was right up to her skin."

I bent over the body to see what Fred was referring to. Various scientific terms I'd learned at the Academy came to mind. I remembered being taught that all body fluids settle into the lowest parts of the body after death, giving the skin a bruised appearance in those places.

My mind was numb. I was exhausted. That was Christine in there! That had been Christine!

We walked up the stairs. Fred talked with the coroner while I waited in a small office with Durfee. He was writing notes in his memo book. I paged through a newspaper that was left on a desk, listening to Fred answer questions about Christine.

"How would you describe her, physically?" a man asked.

"Very athletic!" Fred quickly replied. "Oh yes—very athletic. She was on the swim team at college. Very athletic."

Fred's answer echoed in my mind, because it contradicted what he had often told me. Very athletic? He once told me he couldn't even get her to go jogging with him. He'd told me Chris was lazy, fat, unmotivated. Now he told the coroner just the opposite. Then I heard him say, "It was common for her to run around the house in nothing but a T-shirt and panties."

We walked to the cafeteria. Fred asked me to wait for him there while he punched out his time card and reported to the top floor. Durfee had informed him that some inspector needed to see him. Before he and Durfee left, Fred popped open his briefcase to toss in his memo book. I noticed that his off-duty gun was in his briefcase, even though he was still wearing his service revolver.

Sipping weak coffee from one of the machines, I sat at a table looking through the windows. I knew that the Police Chief's office was on the same floor that Fred had been summoned to, and I recalled the day I'd waited there with my lawyer from the union.

It was still too early to call the gym. I glanced through a magazine that I'd picked off the rack near the cashier. To pass the time, I read my horoscope: "June for Leos is going to be a great month! A newness; finances good."

■   ■   ■

A newness! Is that what it was? June 1981 was the beginning of something new, all right. The beginning of a series of events that made my previous problems look like blessings. The beginning of the end, for me.

Or so I thought, for so many years.

10

THE HOUSE ON RAMSEY STREET

After spending a day with Fred's parents, we took Sean and Shannon home to the apartment, which was still filled with cartons. The boys seemed fine, to my surprise, chattering about the murder as if it were nothing more than a television cops-and-robbers show.

A description of the suspect sought by the police was announced on the evening news. Channel four reported that Sean had described his attacker to the police as a white male with a six- to eight-inch ponytail, five feet, ten inches to six feet tall, wearing a green jogging suit.

"But it *wasn't* a green jogging suit," Sean protested to me and Fred. "It was a green army jacket, without camouflage."

"Sometimes the news gets things wrong," Fred explained to his son.

Numerous calls poured into the police stations. People claimed to have seen a white, male jogger frequently in the area. Others called to say that there had been a substitute mailman in the neighborhood fitting that description.

"Dad?" Sean began with difficulty. "We were all standing there, after it happened—the policemen, and Stu ... well, Stu said 'I bet Freddy did this!' But I know you didn't, daddy!" Sean burst into tears.

I looked at Fred, now hugging Sean, and he returned my angry gaze.

"That wasn't right," I whispered. "To say something like that, in front of a kid."

Later that day, Fred began frantically rooting through the boxes in the spare room. I was irritated that he was making the room a shambles, and asked, "What are you doing?"

"Trying to find my leather jewelry box. Where is it?"

"I have no idea," I told him. "My mother packed this room, so she packed all of your things. Why? You're making a mess."

"It's got to be here," he persisted.

"Why do you need your jewelry box?"

"Because! I have a ring of keys in there, one of which is the key to the house on Ramsey. I wasn't supposed to have a key to the house at all—Christine didn't want me to have one. So, one day when I picked up the boys I made copies of Sean's house key. I hid one in my jewelry box."

"One?"

"I had one on my key chain with my car keys, but I had to give it to the police, so they could get back into the house to dust for prints."

I was disturbed at Fred's easy admission of the sneaky way he'd obtained keys to the house, against Christine's wishes. He tore open another box.

"Here it is! Now we have to get more of the kids' clothing. Some pajamas and toothbrushes. Let's go."

While Fred and I went over to the house on Ramsey Street, the boys had supper at my mom's house. I told Fred that it might be unwise to bring them along, thinking that it would traumatize them. When we opened the door, I was almost bowled over by the odor of dog piss in Chris's house.

"Christ!" Fred exclaimed. "Does it stink! That dog has been gone for almost four months now. She should have used rug shampoo. I was so embarrassed when the cops were in here—a brand-new home and it's a regular pigpen!"

I stared at Fred, confused by his animosity and shocked that he wasn't more tolerant, considering the fact that Chris was no longer there to defend herself or her house. We left the first level and walked up the stairs. Pointing to the boys' bedroom, Fred complained further.

"This room is such a mess that the cops assumed a big struggle took place here. But Sean said no, that's the way it always looks!"

We stepped over piles of game and puzzle pieces, paint brushes, dirty underwear and toy trucks. I started to pack some of their clothes into a paper bag. Fred paced like a mad tiger, and I assumed he was either stirred by memories or still disgruntled by the condition of the house. Crayons were ground into the carpeting, and one Mickey Mouse sheet on the bunk bed was stained from bed-wetting. I opened a window for some fresh air.

"Don't let this scare you," Freddy said. "The boys were never allowed to live like pigs when I was living here! You have to discipline kids!" He walked out of the room like an incensed landlord, running his hand over the door and looking around for possible damage to the walls and furniture.

I followed him into a den.

"This strongbox is right in the middle of the room for some reason," he commented. "But there are only papers and documents inside. The stereo was moved, too, but I really don't know if that necessarily means anything."

"Burglars?"

"The cops didn't find a point of entry. The patio door is a possibility, but who knows? One lieutenant told me that a detective case-knifed the door in back, just to see if it could be done. Knowing Chris, she probably didn't even lock the damn door. That was one of her bad habits." Fred sighed. "Honeck claims that when she drove him home, he asked whether or not she locked the back door, and she told him no, because she was going to be right back. So maybe it was open long enough for someone to get in."

"But what time was that?" I asked.

"He claims that it was around 9:30 PM."

"Then that doesn't make any sense, because the shooting was so many hours later."

"True, 2:00 AM. Unless Honeck's lying about the time that Chris dropped him off."

"Why would he lie?" I asked, noticing Fred's preoccupation with Honeck.

"Well," Fred said, "if they were fooling around that night. Let's say they went to his house when Chris drove him home. If it was later, around midnight? She spends an hour or so over at his house, comes home, and someone is already in the house."

"But you told me that Stu had spent the night here before, so why would they bother to sneak off to Stu's house?"

"That was before I turned Stu's ass in," Fred said. "If Internal Affairs was watching her house, they'd want to leave."

"I thought Stu worked early," I said, referring to second shift.

"He does, but he had that night off or something." Fred went into the bathroom to retrieve the boys' toothbrushes and bathtub toys. I followed him cautiously, disliking the feeling of going through someone else's drawers and closets.

"Why would Stu lie about what time she drove him home?" I asked again.

"To look better in front of the Department, so he wouldn't take a rap for sleeping with her. How much more innocent can you get than a wholesome curfew of 9:30? Unless he couldn't remember what the hell time it was. What really pisses me off is that she left my kids alone in the house. Even if it was early."

"Why would Chris drive Stu home at all? He lives right around the corner.

It would be more trouble to pull your car out of the driveway and then park it—I'd just walk home, wouldn't you?"

"Who knows."

I stared at a wad of unraveled gauze draped down the side of an open cabinet. This was the remains of Sean's attempt to administer first aid as his mother lay bleeding on her bed. He'd tried to pack the wound with gauze, before calling for help. Chris had died so swiftly that his efforts were futile. Why hadn't the cops taken it away?

Fred pushed back the shower curtain and stared at the tub.

"Do you see why I couldn't live with that woman? I built a perfectly good clothes hamper, right into that cabinet. It leads to the laundry room. But no! She had this filthy habit of filling the bathtub with dirty clothes! To hide it, she'd pull the shower curtain closed." He stopped, and felt the clothes in the bathtub.

"What?"

"They're not wet."

"So?"

"So ... something doesn't make sense. Do you remember what Stu and Chris were doing during the day?"

"No."

"They were working in the garden." Fred pointed out a window. "See that? Stu brought over his Rototiller, to rework the ground, and they were putting in railroad ties as patio steps."

"Which means?" I asked, tired of Fred's riddles.

"You were with me at the morgue—Chris was perfectly clean. Her hair was freshly shampooed. It shone under the lights. She didn't look like someone who had been working in the garden all afternoon. When I saw Stu, he was cleaned up, too. They both showered somewhere, and it wasn't here. Don't you see? If Chris had showered here, these clothes in the tub would be on the floor. She wouldn't put them back into a wet tub. I bet she spent some time at Honeck's house for a shower and a roll in the hay, and he's not saying."

"What if they don't find traces of semen at the autopsy?" I asked. "I don't think you should jump to conclusions. There might be a few holes in Honeck's story, but it doesn't spell homicide. Besides, Orval Zellmer lives right across the street from Honeck. He's the king of Internal Affairs. If Honeck was under suspicion for sleeping with Chris, I doubt if she'd frequent his house."

"When I lived with Stu, you were there quite a few times. Zellmer can't tell who's coming or going. Too many people live there. I'm tellin' ya—Internal Affairs had a car on Christine's house. I just don't know when," Fred insisted.

"Then they must have been asleep if they didn't see anyone break in that night!"

I followed him down into the kitchen. He opened a cabinet that squeaked loudly.

"I can see where all the money was going," he snapped, continuing his macabre post-mortem critique. "Just think! The bitch was telling me that she didn't have enough food for the boys. She's got more booze in here than the corner bar. Damn!" He slammed the door shut. I watched in disbelief as he whirled around to open the freezer. "Not enough goddamn food?" he repeated, his face red.

Chris's small, suede purse lay open on the kitchen counter. Fred picked it up and noted aloud that her bank book showed a total of three thousand dollars. There were several checks, still uncashed, in a brown envelope. Her leather wallet held sixty dollars.

"Do you realize she's got more in this purse than I have in the bank?" Fred demanded. He continued to rummage through the purse and pulled out a pack of birth-control pills. "Look at this!" he bellowed, waving them in the air.

"Stop snooping!" I said finally. "Let's just go. You're getting yourself all worked up over nothing. If I didn't know any better, I'd say you're actually acting jealous. My God, Fred, she's dead!"

He ignored me, studying Christine's kitchen calendar. I got up from the chair and walked out of the house. Fred caught up with me and pointed to some wires that ran parallel with the roof.

"At one time, this was an excellent alarm system. But right after Chris kicked me out, the garage door interfered with one of the circuits, which knocked out the whole system."

"Why didn't she have it fixed? It might have saved her life. Why? Why? Why did she sell my Great Dane? That dog could have saved her life, too! All for a lousy buck. I think I'll hand her purse over to the police. Maybe they can go through her address book to list people to interview."

■　　■　　■

We spent the following days talking to landlords. The efficiency across from the park was too small for us now that we had two children. A two-week extension at the three-bedroom apartment was a relief, but we couldn't stay there, because that building didn't allow children.

Christine's parents, Alice and Earl Pennings, insisted that her body be buried in Appleton, where she'd been raised.

The weekend of the funeral I was miserable. I felt entirely out of place. Fred neglected me. He never introduced me to anyone. He'd rise from his metal folding chair next to mine to shake the hand of another relative and stand in front of me, leaving me to stare at his rear end. I was the only person wearing black, and wondered if this old tradition was no longer followed. Kathy arrived with John, dressed in a short, orange, sleeveless dress and a white, crocheted poncho. She sobbed hysterically while she leaned on her husband. Christine's mother, Alice, graciously attempted to comfort Kathy, saying, "Come on now. We must be strong."

Fred's children were the only ones who sat with me during the buffet. Fred had disappeared into the bar and his family filled a different table. The two kids laughed and played with their food until I asked them to behave. I guessed that, unlike their father, they were too young to understand what had happened. Finally, Fred returned to our table with a drink in his hand.

"Did you get me a drink?" I asked.

"I forgot. I mean, I didn't know you wanted one."

"Daddy," Sean interrupted, "I wanna go swimming."

"Later."

"Can I get a soda?" Shannon asked, his blue eyes round and large.

After the boys scampered away, I turned to Fred. "I thought you'd never come back! Not to sound self-absorbed, but thanks for leaving me all by myself."

In the main room of the funeral parlor sat a huge bunch of pink roses, as big as a bush. It was so large that it dwarfed the other sympathy bouquets, and we wondered who had sent it. When we got close enough to see the card, we read: "To My Chris, Love, Stu."

"There have to be over two hundred roses on this thing!" I exclaimed. "It must have cost a fortune."

"Honeck sure is playing this to the hilt," Fred said in a whisper. " 'To My Chris!' Yuck! Methinks he doth protest too much!"

You, too, Fred, I thought.

The coffin was as pink as the bouquet of roses, which struck me as particularly poignant. Fred and I knelt before the body, respectfully silent. Simultaneously, we noticed an engagement ring sparkling on Christine's hand. After we returned to our seats, Fred turned to me. "You saw it, too? That ring wasn't on her hand when we saw her at the morgue! She only had a small pinkie ring on. And it wasn't in her jewelry box, because I went through that to see if anything had been stolen. I don't know how that ring got there, but I bet it happened today.

"Chris never said a word to me about getting married again! That would have been the first thing she would have thrown in my face—if it were true! Especially since I remarried! But this is the first I've heard of it! The kids weren't even aware of it. Of all people, the kids would have known." Fred paused, looking around the dimly lit room. "Let's find Stu and see what he has to say."

Honeck, when we found him, began telling us about two detectives who'd arrived at his house to warn him that he was going to be questioned about his relationship with Chris. He said he was told that the Department was going to want to know whether or not he was having sex with her. I decided I had heard enough. I went outside.

■　　■　　■

During the drive home from Appleton, Sean and Shannon asleep in the back seat, Fred announced that he had agreed to allow Attorney Kershek to handle the problem of the estate paperwork.

"Isn't that ... wasn't that Christine's divorce lawyer?"

"Yeah, but I talked to him today. He's cool."

"Cool?" I thought, bewildered at Fred's capriciousness. He had previously complained that, because Kershek was related to Christine, his representation of her throughout the divorce had been much more vigorous than that of an ordinary lawyer. Now Fred said, "He's cool."

Fred suggested that we move into the house on Ramsey. I disliked the idea. Not only was it the murder scene, but it held all the memories of his past marriage—wedding gifts, baby pictures, all the work he'd done during their days, months and years together. He continued to argue about it, even as I tried explaining my point of view. His solution was to delay the matter until we could reach an agreement. We still had another week to stay at the apartment. After that, we would stay at my parents' house while they were on the west coast. Meanwhile we could discuss it further, even though I was set against the idea.

■　　■　　■

I was at work at the gym one afternoon the next week when two detectives arrived to talk to me. They were trying to persuade everyone involved with the case to take lie-detector tests—Fred, Judy Zess, Stu Honeck, me—in order to "clear" everyone.

My first impulse was to agree, since I had nothing to hide. Then, something about their smiling faces made me think twice. I didn't put it past them to dig for information they could use against me at my discrimination hearings.

I talked to the cops about the test. I told them about a recent experience I'd had with a similar test—I'd taken one for a security job I'd applied for. The results had been confusing and inconclusive, which made me reluctant to try again with a far more serious matter at hand. Finally I said I'd call them back after seeking the advice of a lawyer.

I phoned Fred's lawyer, Reilly. "Absolutely not! I wouldn't advise it. They can misconstrue the results," he said. "Don't trust them. They can't force you to submit to a polygraph either."

Fred disagreed with this advice. "I'm going to take the damn test," he said.

"That's foolish," I said. "Reilly said—"

"I've got to do it," he said, interrupting. "For the children. The Department promised that anyone who agrees to the poly will be cleared if they pass. They won't bother me any more."

"Judy's not taking one either," I said. "Who knows what they'll ask you once they have you strapped in that chair? You could get fired."

Fred went ahead. He returned that evening, exhausted, unnerved and looking pale. They'd watched him via a video camera while he took the test. The questions they'd asked him referred to experiences he'd had as far back as age sixteen. He told me he'd admitted smoking pot in college at La Crosse, and lying on a traffic accident report once, by saying that he was wearing a seatbelt when in fact he was not. He claimed they asked him numerous questions about his temper—if he had ever physically abused Christine, or if he had ever used excessive force while on duty.

"I told them I punched Christine ... once," Fred told me.

■   ■   ■

The next day, I dropped Sean and Shannon off at my mom's house on the way to the gym. When I returned to pick them up that afternoon, I was happy to see my mother in a good mood. She liked children so much.

"How did the kids behave?"

"Fine! They're at the playground."

We talked about our apartment. "We canceled the efficiency place, for obvious reasons," I said. "Four of us couldn't live there. But I don't want to live on Ramsey. Fred just can't understand why not."

"I know how you must feel. That was his house from a previous marriage, for heaven's sake!"

"Maybe only women feel this way," I said.

"How was the funeral? I thought about you all weekend."

I shrugged. "Fred's mother came up to me, hugged me, and cried, 'You're all he has now'!"

"Now?" My mother blinked. "What an odd thing to say. Like as if when Chris was alive, Fred had her, too?"

"That's how it struck me."

"Oh well, don't dwell on it. It was probably said in grief."

I brooded for a while. There was something I felt awkward about, even with my mom.

"It's this situation," I finally said. "Suddenly having two kids dropped in my lap."

"So?"

"I didn't want children."

"I know that ... but these are two small boys that went through an awful, a terrible ordeal! They need a home with their father."

"But—"

"Laurie, stop being so selfish."

"But I married Fred! I didn't marry his kids!" I protested. "I like Sean and Shannon, they're nice kids. But I know what kids mean. It means babysitters and money for school and chauffeuring them all over and chocolate fingerprints on everything!"

"You're scared. Give it a chance! You don't know it will be all that bad!"

"They're not my kids! I'm still trying to adjust to being married—now I'm an instant mommy. Sean is only about ten years younger than me. It was different for you, mom. You had a marriage that was like a World War II novel. You got engaged, dad was drafted, and you waited faithfully for him for four years. He came back, you got married, you had kids. Simple and acceptable."

"It wasn't that simple," she said quietly.

I said nothing.

"I'll help you as much as I can with the boys. They can stay here when you're at work." I saw Sean and Shannon opening the gate of the white picket fence that enclosed the back yard.

"Thanks," I said.

To be honest, I resented the kids. Two children tagging along after me made me feel suddenly older—too old. I wasn't ready for this. It got ridiculous. I peered into the mirror, expecting to see wrinkles around my eyes.

One morning, Fred was playing in a baseball game at a local park. I fed the boys breakfast, got them dressed and piled them into my car to go watch the game. The children and I walked past some men from the other team when we entered the park. I was wearing a plaid T-shirt and cotton shorts, and I was mortified to hear wolfish comments directed at me.

"Mommy! Mommy!" one of the men panted, and the others whistled. I bit my lip and kept walking, telling myself not to let it bother me. But it did.

At the same time, I felt guilty about not being more compassionate, so I decided to try harder to put my needs aside. The boys insisted they loved me, and it was such a pure, unconditional response that it touched me deeply.

I was strict, seeing to it that they ate a balanced diet and picked up their toys. They, in turn, interpreted my discipline as a sign that I cared, according to the child psychologist they were seeing. His name was Ken Ploch.

The two boys had been suffering from recurring nightmares, so of course my first instinct was to wake them. Ploch disagreed. He said they should be left alone to dream undisturbed; it was the only way they could release what was bottled up inside them, to dream it out. With Fred working nights, the kids would often crawl into bed with me because they were so frightened. I would wake up in the morning to discover Sean and Shannon under the covers. I'd done the same thing when I was a child, and it touched me.

To my dismay, however, Ploch also recommended that we move into the Ramsey house—just the opposite of what I had expected (and hoped) that he'd say. He said it would get the kids back into familiar surroundings and routines, with their pals; that it would make the transference of a maternal figure easier for them. This was a suggestion I didn't want to hear. I still didn't want to live there.

Meanwhile, the constant arguments with Fred, the continual bickering, went on. He couldn't seem to let that house—or Christine—alone.

One Saturday, I pulled a pair of jeans over my black leotard and threw on a light jacket, getting ready to leave for work at the gym. Fred told me that he had to go over to the house on Ramsey. He said Christine's mother, Alice, had called and asked if she could come into town to pick up a few of her daughter's personal belongings. Fred had told her that he would meet her there at ten.

According to Fred, when he pulled up in front of the house, a crowd was already in the driveway. He said that Alice and Earl Pennings stood there, with the lawyer Kershek, Christine's brother Michael, Christine's sister Barb and Barb's husband Bruce Christ, and Stu Honeck. Fred claimed that Stu had already used his house key to let everyone into the house. Fred said that, despite his frantic efforts to get the situation under control, he was outnumbered. The family quickly loaded up their cars. Stu even unhooked the HBO unit and removed the antenna. They even loaded up Chris's car and were planning to drive that away, too.

Fred made the incident sound more like grave-robbing than retrieving personal effects. He claimed he told Kershek that no one had given Honeck permission to unlock "his" house, and that as far as he was concerned, everyone was trespassing, to which Kershek allegedly snorted, "So call a cop." Fred said Kershek informed him that Alice planned to petition the court to be appointed co-representative of the estate. He said he tried explaining that he was planning to sell Chris's Mercury Bobcat to start a college fund for the boys, but someone drove away in it.

The following day, Fred said he'd stop at the Ramsey house to clean and disconnect the kitchen appliances.

"Probably half the food in that fridge is spoiled already. We have to move this weekend, remember?"

He paused, waiting for a response from me. When there was none, he said, "What I'm trying to get at is, we have no other recourse than to move into that house."

"Why?"

"We've been through this."

"Why can't we rent a place until you sell the house?"

"Rent? Again? How many security deposits have we lost so far? Besides, we're paying a mortgage on a house we're not living in. We have my sons to consider. We're worse off financially, now, than we ever were. And the house is close to their school—St. Roman's."

"Wouldn't a public school be cheaper? Do you know what tuition is at a private school?"

"We'll talk about that some other time. Right now, all I'm telling you is that we have no other choice but to move into my house," Fred said.

I felt cornered. Fred seemed to have a strange, almost frantic obsession with the house. I wondered if he'd ever part with it.

Still, I did look forward to leaving that troublesome apartment. We'd often tried to contact the landlady about maintenance problems, but the complex of buildings was so large that we were easily avoided. A repair person was always "coming," but this phantom never appeared. The heat vents in the apartment were blasting ninety-degree air into an already warm living room, so we ran the air-conditioner for relief. The hallway closet door had come off its hinges, and the toilet in the bathroom formerly occupied by Judy, had been out of order since the time my parents came over for dinner on their anniversary. Water was running inside the tank. I taped a small sign on the door so the children wouldn't forget to avoid it.

Just before we moved out, into my parents' house, a young woman from across the hall knocked on the door, asking if she could borrow a plunger.

"You're lucky you're moving out," she said. "These places look so nice, but they're falling apart!"

■ ■ ■

During this period, I finally had some good news. I'd taken a physical agility exam as part of the application process for a job as campus guard, or Public Safety Officer, at Marquette University. During the test, I'd run into a former Milwaukee cop who'd been in my Academy class. We'd had a beer together after the test at a bar nearby.

A few days later, I learned I had the job—Marquette University wanted to hire me! I was to start working second shift, which meant I could still keep my other job at the gym. The pay was very close to what I had made as a city cop.

I told Fred the good news about my job when he returned home. Shortly afterwards, he disappeared in his van. I thought nothing of it—I guessed he'd just gone to park it elsewhere, but when he returned, he proudly displayed a shiny, new bicycle.

"Purple!" he said. "Your favorite color!"

"What?"

"It's for you—to celebrate your new job."

Fred always went out and bought things on impulse. It wasn't great for budgeting, but I could hardly complain. It was a nice gesture.

■ ■ ■

The following week, Fred went to the Ramsey house to retrieve something, only to discover that Christine's mom, Alice Pennings, had had all the locks changed.

"That's Criminal Damage to Property! Trespassing! Breaking and Entering!" he yelled, speaking in Police Department capitals. "So Alice doesn't want us to live there? Fuck her. I know how to get into my own damn house," Fred told me. "Hell, I'm a carpenter."

He went back, broke in and changed the doorknob on the back door. He said that he noticed Honeck drive by. Although I'm not sure how Fred knew this, he said that Stu promptly drove away and called Alice in Appleton, to report that despite having hired a locksmith, Fred was back in the house.

Fred told me that the Pennings called Kershek, who was vacationing in

California. Kershek called Fred's lieutenant, attempting to persuade him to press charges against Fred for breaking and entering. It was a civil matter, the lieutenant said.

Why were the Pennings so vehemently against Fred? What did they have against him? What did they know that I didn't?

Then Alice insisted that Fred make an offer to purchase the estate's half of the house.

"In other words," Fred complained, "they expect me to buy half of my own house from my children!"

Still, he couldn't leave the house alone. One day he was taking apart the bed in Christine's bedroom. It was a massive, cannonball-style headboard made from walnut. As he began to lift the mattress from the box spring, a penis-shaped vibrator fell to the floor.

"I can't believe the police didn't discover it!" he said. "But it's no wonder, the crime scene that night was a regular circus, with almost every squad on the South Side climbing over one another in the house."

At Fred's request, two detectives arrived to write up a report about the vibrator, but didn't seem interested enough to confiscate the thing.

"They could have taken it to the Crime Lab, and tested it for traces of pubic hair or semen," Fred explained. "But they acted like, 'Who cares'?"

Sean complained that an envelope containing almost one hundred dollars was missing from his room. The money was part of a fund-raising effort for baseball uniforms for St. Roman's. Fred reported this to the police as well.

Although there was no mention of it in the newspapers, Fred told me the police were pestering a man they considered a suspect in Christine's murder. He lived across the street from the Ramsey house.

"He's been described as sort of a nut," Fred explained. "A strange guy, living alone ... history of emotional problems."

"Seriously?" I asked.

"It looks pretty suspicious. I heard that right after the shooting he reported that a thirty-eight caliber revolver had been stolen from his garage."

"But the gun used on Chris was a forty-five, right?"

"No—ballistics determined that it was a thirty-eight."

"Then why was the bullet hole so huge?" I asked. "We saw it at the morgue—remember?"

"They said the wound was that large because of the close proximity from which the gun was fired. Right up to the skin."

"So this guy reported a gun of the same caliber stolen, even before the police knew it was a thirty-eight?"

"Yeah. He also made a statement to a neighbor that he's missing his green jogging suit."

"He must be crazy."

Fred agreed. "He works second shift at a factory, has long brown hair. He paints cars as a hobby, so he'd also have a painter's mask."

"The murderer was wearing a mask?" I asked.

"Well, according to Shannon he was. But then Shannon also says he saw a silver six-shooter with pearl handles."

I shook my head. "He's the one who saw a green jogging suit, too. I think Sean is more credible. He's older, and he's a smart boy. Sean said he saw an army jacket. That's more plausible."

Fred nodded. "The guy consented to a polygraph. The first two were inconclusive, but he passed the third time. He claims to have an alibi." Fred grew silent and appeared moody.

"What's on your mind?"

"Honeck. The whole thing is so goddamn goofy. That surprise engagement! I just re-read Sean's police report at work. He told the cops that on that night, when Chris tucked him into bed, she looked upset about something. Maybe Stu asked Chris that very night if she would marry him, and she refused. Maybe that's why she was upset. You know, Stu was so positive that Chris wasn't seeing other men. He even told the police that she wasn't dating anyone else. But that's not true! Sean told me that she had lots of other male visitors. And I found some cards and letters hidden away in her knitting basket—letters and greeting cards from different guys, signed Bob, Frank, George ... and a Mother's Day card from Stu. A real corny one.

"Know what I think? I wouldn't be surprised if Stu was turned down that night, went home, got one of his guns, let himself back in with his key. Who knows? He only lives a minute away."

"Except Stu claims Chris drove him home," I said.

"Sean says that Stu went home by himself! He knows how loud his mother's car was, because the muffler on Christine's Bobcat was so bad. He told me that Stu and Chris left the house earlier, to return the Rototiller, but that was around dinner. It was still light outside. Sean is positive that Stu left later by himself."

I could only take Fred's word for all this. "I don't get it," I said, puzzled.

"There are too many things that aren't right. Honeck claims he had one vodka gimlet with Chris, while he was there for dinner. Yet there was an empty gallon of wine in the kitchen on the counter, with two wine glasses right next to it."

"Did they dust the glasses for prints? Maybe Chris had drinks with someone else after Stu left."

Fred snorted. "The assholes didn't dust those glasses until I asked them to—the same day they came over to look at the dildo I found. What kind of police work is that?"

"That bottle of wine could have been left there from some other day," I said. "What if it was an old bottle?"

"There was a sales receipt from the liquor store in a bag on the floor. It was dated May 27 and listed a price that matched the price-sticker on the bottle."

"Did the autopsy discover alcohol in the blood?" I asked.

"I don't know yet. Besides all that, Stu says in his police report that just after he got home Chris called him and they spent another hour or so on the phone. Why would you call someone just after spending almost the whole day with them?"

"Unless you were ironing out a disagreement."

"Another thing—they never determined the time of death. They were supposed to use a rectal thermometer at the scene. Everyone's going on the assumption that her death was close to the time that Honeck called the paramedics. It could have been earlier."

■   ■   ■

At least on the job things were going well. I loved the work. Our uniform was a white shirt and blue pants, with Public Safety Office patches and badges. The security force used a couple of squad cars—the campus was large—and we followed usual police procedures, with which I was well acquainted.

All the men on the job were experienced. I was the only female officer on my shift. My lieutenant was a former state trooper, and there were ex-police officers from other cities as well. The person I liked most was the director of the department, the person who had hired me. Her name was Carol Kurdziel. Her opinions were feminist, and she didn't mince words. She showed some sympathy for my dismissal from MPD; she said she was "aware of the chief's ways."

I adjusted well to the new job and was happy to be busy working again. Kurdziel showed me what I'd scored on the psychological exam I took when I applied. The results described me as being confident, assertive and independent, but also indicated that my feelings were easily hurt. As I read the exam results, I told Kurdziel about my situation with two new children. She sympathized, urging me to call her anytime if I wanted to talk. The business card she handed me listed her home phone number.

But off the job ... there was Fred. One day he came home from work, to my parents' house, where we were staying, looking frazzled.

"They're questioning me at work," he blurted out.

"About what?"

"They asked me if I had a key to the Ramsey house. I told them that I gave it to a cop that same night. Then they wanted to know how many keys I had. So I told them: two. One on my key ring, and the other one back here."

"They must know Honeck had a key, too?"

"I don't know. It was like they were trying to establish whether or not you or I had access to the house, because there was no sign of forced entry." Fred looked worried.

"You or *me*?" I replied, in disbelief. "Why? I didn't even know you had a key! The first I heard of a key was when you started tearing open all those boxes, looking for it."

"I know. I kept it a secret, because I wasn't supposed to have a key to that house."

"Did you explain that to them?" I asked.

"No. That would make me look bad."

"You? Jesus Christ! What about me? You make it sound like I had a key to the place! Why did you even tell them that you had the extra key?"

"I couldn't lie," Fred replied, piously. "If the police saw us in the house later on, I would have had to explain how we got back in, anyway."

I wanted to believe him, but this thing of his volunteering information and letting the blame fall on me for so many things kept repeating itself, and I grew angry.

"No wonder they were hassling me to take a polygraph!" I said. "It's all your fault. First you tell Chris that we wouldn't go to Shannon's communion because of me! Then you drop a dime on Honeck for sleeping with her and let them both think it was me! You were just too chicken to take the blame yourself!"

"Bullshit!" Fred shouted at me.

"Bullshit, nothing! It's been nothing but trouble ever since we got married!" The months of stress caught up with me, and I started to yell. "My mother told me divorced men were nothing but trouble. I should have listened to her! I thought you were different!"

"What are you telling me?" Fred snarled.

"I'm telling you I'm tired of being your fall guy and I want out of this whole nasty situation. I'm not moving into that house on Ramsey! I'm not playing Susie Homemaker to kids who aren't mine! I'm tired of being treated like dirt by your family and I'm tired of this whole thing."

"Either you come with me to live on Ramsey in my house, or I'm leaving you," Fred threatened.

"Fine!" I replied. "I'll live right here with my parents. Go to your damned house."

Fred stood up, as silent as a stone. I was sitting on a lawn chair in the yard, my arms wrapped around my knees. As I watched him walk back into my mom and dad's house, I began to regret my words.

Fred came back out with Shannon. He knew I had a soft spot in my heart for the child, because he looked just like his dad with his large, blue eyes and shaggy, blond hair.

"Kiss Laurie goodbye," Fred announced. "We have to go."

Shannon looked puzzled, because my face was red from crying. Then he smiled and leaned over to hug me, which really affected me, as Fred had intended.

"You really disappoint me, Laurie," Fred whispered, taking his son's hand and walking away.

■　　■　　■

I remember going inside and sitting down with my sketchbooks. For a few hours I worked on a drawing of my mom and dad. As I drew the familiar faces, I remembered wishing so often that I was the oldest child instead of the youngest. I drew lines of weariness around the eyes of my beloved parents, then quickly erased them—only to draw them in again. The lines were real, the worry was real, the age was real. If only I could take away the worry as easily as I brushed away the lines!

■　　■　　■

I heard feet on the stairs. My mother entered the room with a cup in her hand. She'd been in the basement, canning quart jars of dill pickles. A kitchen towel was thrown over her shoulder and she wore a crisp gingham apron.

"I heard the fight, Laurie," she said. She smelled of dill and brine—good smells. "I had the windows open because of the steam. Is there anything I can do?"

We talked for a while, until it grew dark. Then we walked downstairs and sat at the table in the kitchen. A little while later Fred came home, Sean and Shannon following him in the door.

My parents took Sean and Shannon for ice cream so Fred and I could be alone. He begged and pleaded that I change my mind about living on Ramsey.

He promised a regular babysitter, a housekeeper, a guard dog, a burglar alarm. He was bursting with his usual optimism. Soon my determination weakened; in another half hour I found myself apologizing.

I agreed to live in the house on Ramsey for the time being. We wouldn't move in until after it was cleaned and redecorated, and while we lived there, the house would be put on the market to be sold. It was a last resort. It was all I agreed to.

11

THE BOMBSHELL FALLS

I was on campus with Thomas Conway, my sergeant at Marquette, when I got a radio message to report back to headquarters for a phone call. It was Fred's lawyer, Reilly.

"Hi, Laurie," he began. "Fred wanted me to call you. He's at the Crime Lab. He wanted me to let you know—they found blood on his service revolver."

"Thank you," I said slowly, hanging up the receiver.

How could that be? Fred had at least two guns. His off-duty gun was a small Smith and Wesson, thirty-eight caliber with wood grips and a two-inch barrel—a very common style. His service revolver, also a thirty-eight, had a four-inch barrel and big, black rubber grips. He always wore the larger gun to work. Now the Crime Lab had found blood on his service revolver. Why? Why had they even looked? Throughout the remaining hours on my shift I wondered about it, thinking that there had to be a logical explanation.

Fred met me at the door when I returned home. He looked frantic.

"What's this all about?" I asked him.

"It was type A blood. I'm type A. But so was Chris," Fred said. I had no idea whether or not this was true. "The only difference is, mine is negative and Christine's was positive."

"Which ...?"

"They can't tell a subgroup like that from dried blood."

"Fred, this ... has to be a frame." I didn't know what to say.

"Maybe it's my blood on that gun, from a fight I got into at work. We got dispatched to a disturbance at Montreal's ..."

"You didn't tell me you were hurt at work."

"I wasn't hurt that bad. But I picked a scab on my arm. That must be it. They've been crawling all over me since we were at the lab. They might as well be accusing me—but I was on duty that night! Then they were ridiculous enough to suggest that you might have been able to switch guns with me that night. Isn't that stupid?"

"*Me*? What are you talking about?" The conversation began to take on an unreal quality.

"You didn't have an alibi that night ..."

"Are you crazy? This is a homicide! An alibi?"

"I know, but ... the way they were questioning me."

"It's your gun! They found blood on the gun you were wearing that night. Why would they be asking questions about me?"

"I passed the polygraph. You refused to take one."

"But—"

"Maybe I'm overreacting, Laurie. All I know is that Reilly told me not to cooperate with them anymore. They'll see that it's my blood on that gun."

I looked at him, trying to make some sense out of what he'd said. The only logical explanation in my mind was that it was his blood on the gun. I didn't like the fact that I was under suspicion, but I thought that it was because Fred was on duty that night, so when they found the blood, it was only routine for them to question my whereabouts. The detectives had talked to me that night. They would find out it was Fred's blood. They must!

That weekend we had the task of cleaning the house on Ramsey before moving in. Several friends of ours came along to help, and so did my mom and dad. The children did all they could. It took six of us over ten hours to finish.

While I was wiping the dust from some kitchen cabinets, I found a coffee mug containing a handful of Fred's old bullets. He said he hadn't even known they were there.

We packed away all of Christine's personal possessions. There were about fifteen different macramé wall hangings, pictures, lampshades and plant hangers that must have taken hours to make by hand. Fred wondered out loud why Alice and Earl didn't come and get her artwork and take it home with them.

■　　■　　■

It was only a few days later, just after Fred's birthday (I remember the boys and I got him a pet hamster as a present) that the next and most devastating bombshell landed. I'd been on duty for several hours when I realized I'd left my radio at the station. I'd been using the squad car radio. Back at headquarters, I noticed the sergeant's door was closed, which was unusual. I stared at the lettering that read "Public Safety Department" and knocked. When Conway opened the door, he had an odd look on his face.

"What's wrong?" I said. "I just came back for my radio."

Beyond Conway was Fred's lieutenant and another huge man. They pulled me inside and flashed their badges.

"Of course, you know Lieutenant Ruscitti. I'm Detective Frank Cole. You're under arrest for first-degree murder."

What? I couldn't believe I'd heard him. What was going on? I stood in shocked silence as they handcuffed me and stripped me of my badge, cap and ring of university keys. I was in handcuffs! It was totally unreal. I couldn't react. Murder! Me?

"Is there any other property you'll be needing from her?" Cole asked Conway. Conway looked like he wanted to cry. He shook visibly. I was still in shock. "Just, just her uniforms," he stuttered. He looked at me like he wanted to die.

"They're in my locker," I said to him. "Want to write down the combination?"

As I told him the number, he wrote it down wrong and I had to repeat it. "I'm sorry, Laurie," he said.

When I was a kid, I'd always managed to appear calm and composed, even when I felt hysterical inside. It was some kind of defense mechanism, I suppose; my feelings were so easily bruised! I guess it had become second nature. I must have seemed unnaturally composed to the two cops. Apparently they were taken aback by my calm, because Ruscitti said, "You aren't even surprised, are you?"

"Actually, I'm shocked!" I said. I knew they'd try needling me, and I knew enough not to make any statements at all.

"Well, you knew it had to be—right?" Ruscitti nodded, and he spoke with the comforting tone of voice a priest might use.

"I don't know what you're talking about," I said.

"Suit yourself. Let's go." They walked me outside to an unmarked squad car. Cole had to be at least six feet, seven inches tall and three hundred pounds. I never saw anyone so big. I didn't understand why this was happening, but I was sure it was all a mistake. When we got to the Police Administration building, instead of taking me to the booking room, they marched me into the Deputy Inspector's office and removed the handcuffs. They were unusually nice.

"We really hate to do this," Cole explained, "but it's our job. You're such a beautiful young lady. We're going to have a department photographer come up here in a minute to take your mug shots. That way, we'll have proof that we didn't beat you up or anything. Is that okay with you?"

I nodded, my stomach in knots.

"Would you like a cigarette?"

"I don't smoke."

"All right. Now then, Lawrencia ... we think your husband set you up for this. You know he did it. We can make it easier for you. We know you were both in on it."

"I don't understand," I replied, thinking, Fred? He wouldn't. He didn't. They're crazy!

"If you won't go for that, let us just tell you a few things," Cole said matter-of-factly. "We have evidence, Lawrencia."

I said nothing.

"Enough evidence to lock you up for the rest of your life."

I couldn't believe what they were saying.

"First of all, we know how much alimony your husband Elfred had to dish out to Christine every month. We know what his salary is—after all, he worked for us. That didn't leave you very much to live on, did it? We don't blame you."

"We also know you threatened Christine," Ruscitti said.

I never threatened anybody, I thought.

"We also have the ballistics on Freddy's gun. It all points to you," Cole added.

That blood on the gun? I thought.

"Our theory is, you two cooked up a plan to scare Chris but you fucked up, and killed her instead."

"That's ridiculous!" I blurted.

"You wanted to scare Chris out of that house so that you and Elfred could live there."

I stared at them. How could a grown woman be scared out of her own house? If they only knew about the fights Fred and I had about that damned house.

"We have your shooting scores from the Academy," Cole said. "You're an excellent marksman. Why don't you just admit it?"

"Don't you think we can prove it?" Ruscitti asked. "Hey, you better start talkin', 'cause we're the only friends you have in the world right now! If you tell us what happened, we can talk to McCann and recommend that the charges be knocked down to manslaughter." They opened their memo books, ready to write.

"It's my right to remain silent until I get an attorney," I said.

My lack of response angered them. Cole slammed his pen down on the table.

"Okay, Bembenek. No more games. You want it? You got it. But know this: since you refuse to talk to us, I'm planning to see to it that you also get charged with attempted murder for what you tried to do to that little boy."

That was like a slap across the face. The murderer had struggled with Sean the night of the shooting, trying to strangle the child in his bed. What kind of monster did they think I was?

Frank Cole stood up; he towered over me like a human sequoia. Three years later he would collapse and die of a heart attack, just before Thanksgiving, at the young age of fifty-one.

They left the room as a matron walked in to search me. After that, a photographer took pictures. I was about to take my hair down when Cole said, "Just a minute," approaching me with a ruler. I had about a two-inch blond ponytail in my hair because I needed a neat appearance in uniform for work at Marquette. Cole made a big production out of measuring my ponytail, though the ponytail on the suspect was described as being about six inches longer than mine.

A Hispanic man walked into the room. "I'm a friend of Elfred's," he told me, smiling. "I'm here to give you some advice. Mr. Cole and Mr. Ruscitti aren't bullshitting you when they tell you they can knock this thing down to manslaughter. The DA listens to us. All you have to do is cooperate."

I just looked at him.

"You're only twenty-two years old," he said. "Do you want to spend the rest of your life in prison with all them queers?"

I said nothing.

"We talked to your mother. She's very nice."

My mom had told me that two detectives stopped by the house to question her, about a month ago. She said that she told them she didn't have time to talk to them.

"What do you think she's going to say when she reads the headlines about you?"

"My mom and dad are on vacation," I said. "Can I call a lawyer?"

He frowned. "So. You're a tough cookie, huh?"

"No."

"Look, why don't you just tell us what happened? You don't have the kind of money it takes for a criminal attorney. You'll get some crummy Public Defender and end up in the slammer for the next eleven-three."

"I know I'm allowed a phone call, so may I make one?"

Cole walked back into the room, and the Hispanic cop shook his head at him.

"We've dispatched a squad over to your house on Taylor Avenue, to inform your husband of your arrest."

■   ■   ■

On day two or three they were taking me to booking, and I heard somebody say "Laurie!" I looked and I couldn't see because they had taken my glasses, but there was a tall figure and he said he was Richard Reilly. That was Fred's divorce lawyer. Fred had obviously hired him in a panic when I got arrested.

"Hi!" he said. "Hi! I'm Richard Reilly, and Fred retained me to represent you ..." Reilly took me aside. "Did you make any statements in there?"

"No. This is all a mistake, isn't it? They're going to let me go home now, aren't they?" I pleaded with him. I couldn't think straight.

"They didn't have a warrant for your arrest," he told me. "It certainly appears to be a mistake, but they mean business. Look, just hang in there right now, and don't say anything to them. Do you understand? Not anything! I'll get back to you as soon as I can."

The next thing I knew, I was in a small, dimly lit cell in the City Jail of District One, which was designed to be used as a twenty-four-hour "holding cell." The matrons kept my glasses, and I didn't have my contact lenses, so everything was blurry. I had been to the jail many times when I was a police officer, but never like this. I hoped I wouldn't see any cops I knew from the Academy.

I lay down on the metal cot, still in my Marquette uniform. There were no bars on the cell, just a heavy metal door with a tiny slot. It felt claustrophobic. I stared at four cement walls, a steel toilet and a tiny ceiling light, its bulb enclosed in a wire cage.

There was nothing to do but think, sleep and look out the door slot by pressing the side of my face against the door. I could see nothing but the wall opposite my cell door, as the hallway out there was not very wide.

Late at night there was a great deal of noise. Hundreds of arrests had been made at the beginning of Milwaukee's Summerfest lakefront festival. From what I could hear, the talk in the cellblock described arrests for smoking pot. Most of the other prisoners were from Chicago.

I knew something was wrong, and I worried that Reilly hadn't contacted me as he'd promised. I was stiff and tired. I tried doing some floor exercises just to stay limber, but there was little room to do anything.

Having been in the same clothes all those days without a shower, I felt dirty and smelled of perspiration. There was constant crying and screaming from the other women prisoners. I wondered what day it was, and heard the matron walking down the hallway.

"What day is it, please?"

"Friday," came the answer. I'd been there since Wednesday.

■   ■   ■

I was arrested without a warrant. I was sitting there in jail in this bullpen in my uniform for three days before a complaint was sworn out. I was sitting there thinking, Naaaah, this is crazy, they're gonna see that this isn't right. For three whole days I sat there, in a panic, not knowing what to do. They took away my glasses; I couldn't see anything. All the time I was thinking, This is wrong, they're gonna come now and let me go and say, You know, we made a big mistake, you know what I mean? I didn't even know what day it was, whether it was day or night. It was horrible. The only way I knew another day had passed was when the matron came to the door with a cup of coffee and a bologna sandwich at five in the morning; that's all there was all day. I didn't know what to do. I knew I could make a phone call, but who should I call? I'd never even thought about being arrested before! I didn't want to waste it. I was confused, thinking of calling James Shellow, a prominent lawyer who had overturned the conviction of a man charged with shooting two cops. The case had caused a big stink, and after that the cops changed the rules about carrying guns. Shellow got this guy off ... should I call him? Or Fred? I didn't even know whether they had notified Fred. Should I call him, or Shellow? I didn't know what to do.

■   ■   ■

Finally, my cell door opened with a grinding, mechanical noise. The matron announced that my lawyer was in the visiting room.

"Can I go home now?" I asked Reilly as I sat down anxiously behind the clear partition.

"You've been charged with first-degree murder," he said in a droning voice. "Our next step will be to go before a judge, who is going to set your bail at ten thousand dollars. That amount is a gift. Bail for most murder cases is set around one hundred thousand dollars. Or more."

"Why is mine so low?"

"Well, they have an extremely circumstantial case. Perhaps the judge considered that, and this low bail is his comment on the case. Also, I've proposed that the conditions of the bail stipulate that you live at home with Elfred or your parents, and the children will stay out of town with their grandparents. Fred is at some bank right now. He wanted me to tell you he loves you. He's been trying to get in to see you. He said he's behind you 100 percent. Your parents are on vacation?"

"Yes."

At least they won't see the newspapers. You've been all over the front pages for the past few days."

"Oh, no."

■　　■　　■

The media circus had already begun. The bunny bimbette killer—this walking metaphor, this person who wasn't me—made her first appearance. I was sitting in shock, waiting for them to admit they'd made a horrible mistake, and on the streets they were selling newspapers crucifying me.

■　　■　　■

"Okay, like I said, I appeared before the judge for you, but we're going to have to go again. You'll have to be brave and face the cameras. The judge will ask you if you wish to waive your right to a preliminary hearing within ten days. It is my advice that you waive that right, because it will give us more time to prepare."

My mind spun with legal terms unfamiliar to me then.

"Incidentally, Fred was sent home from work for a few days. He went to Marquette to pick up your car. Oh, and Carol Kurdziel gave me a call. You've been suspended with pay."

"Oh." Only half of what he was saying was registering.

"Now, I have several questions for you. Are you all right?"

I nodded.

"Okay. Do you now, or did you ever, own a wig?"

"Yeah. I had two short, blond wigs that I wore when I worked at Second District, instead of getting my hair cut. I sold one of them to my friend Suzy."

"Where is the other one?"

"Somewhere. Either at the house on Ramsey, or at my mom's house—I don't know. We've moved so many times."

"Did you make the statement 'I hate those fucking kids' in regards to Fred's children?"

"Of course not!"

"How do you feel about Sean and Shannon?"

"At first, I wasn't thrilled about the whole idea. But it's working out. I like them. Why are you asking me these things?"

"We'll talk about it in detail, later. Did you ever tell anyone that you'd like to hire someone to kill Christine?"

"No!"

"Okay. That's it for now. I'll be back to accompany you to the hearing. For now, just sit and watch TV and try not to think about too much. You look very upset. I'll see you later."

As I left the room, I thought of his last recommendation: "Sit and watch TV?" What TV? Of course I'm upset!

Before my appearance in front of the judge, I was placed in a bullpen outside of the courtroom. Every few seconds, someone opened the peephole on the bullpen door to peer in at me, out of curiosity. I refused to look up, feeling like a caged animal on display, but listened to the door on the peephole slam over and over again. I was still in my Marquette uniform.

Just as Reilly had predicted, there were a lot of cameras in the courtroom. I felt just terrible after being locked up for three days without a shower or comb. My hair was a head of tangles and my mascara was smudged under my eyes. Everyone in the room was a fuzzy blur, because I still didn't have my glasses.

My preliminary hearing was scheduled for a day a few weeks away. The next day, I was transferred from the City Jail to the County Jail. An emotional paralysis overwhelmed me as I was instructed to change into a light cotton dress issued by the jail. I longed to go home.

I had wondered whether County Jail was like prison, but it was much worse. The cellblock was filthy, with garbage strewn haphazardly in the corners—cigarette butts, moldy bread crusts and dried vomit. An obviously insane woman sat in a corner and sang continually.

There was a small television set against one wall. I watched the six o'clock news. Pictures of me flashed across the screen. All I could hear was "ex-Playboy Bunny." I cracked my knuckles nervously, wondering if my mom and dad were home yet. I felt I was drowning.

One of the deputies walked into the cellblock and asked me whether I was going to be able to post bail. I asked if I could call my husband, since I'd never received permission to make the one phone call I was allowed. When I finally reached Fred, I cried. He said no bank would lend him much, even though he had collateral. He said my parents weren't home yet. The deputy instructed me to hang up the phone.

I sat down on the floor, trying to reconcile myself to the fact that I wasn't going anywhere. The whole thing still felt like a bad dream.

Suddenly, the sheriff motioned to me, and I walked to the door again. "Do you want your relatives to post bail?" she asked.

"Of course!" I cried, wondering who had come to rescue me. I changed back into my Marquette uniform, my face wet with tears.

My Aunt Mary and Cousin Julie came to get me, and we rushed down a back flight of stairs and left the building. I was never so glad to see anybody in my entire life. I'll never forget the family's kindness.

Finally, home. Fred sobbed as I walked in the door. We embraced in the middle of the kitchen and stood that way for a long time; I was afraid to let go. I said the first thing I wanted to do was take a long, hot shower.

Fred told me that the night of my arrest he'd gone to work as usual, but they'd already assigned a replacement for him. They told him he was too emotional to work and that he should go home. They considered his status "on medical leave without pay." Fred didn't know when he'd be allowed to return.

That night, we sat up and watched the late news. None of the stations realized I was out on bail. I watched in disbelief as Channel six did a story on my life, showing my yearbook photo from high school and some pictures from my days as a fashion model. It was unreal. But it was just the beginning.

"You think the TV was bad? Wait until you see the newspapers, Laurie. Are you strong enough to look at them? I saved all of them."

I looked at the huge front-page photographs and headlines and winced. I threw the papers in a corner.

"My God! Did you see this? They're giving me a press trial! How can they do this?"

Fred handed me a drink. "Half of it's just not true. They say that police recovered a red wig from the plumbing of our three-bedroom apartment. That's not true. It came from the apartment across the hall. They say that we moved into my house on Ramsey—we aren't living there yet! Then they say that you were also charged with attempted murder, which isn't true."

"They keep quoting 'a source' but don't say who the source is. 'A source says she owned a green jogging suit!' A source says this, a source says that," I said. "Who is this source? It's so unfair! People read this and believe it!"

"There's nothing we can do about it. Reilly doesn't want you to say a word to the newspapers."

"Why not?" I exclaimed, outraged. "Why can't I tell my side of the story?"

Looking through another paper, I gathered that the police were basing their whole case on the ballistics report that said the murder weapon was Fred's off-duty revolver. It was impossible! Fred and Durfee checked that gun that same night! What about the blood on the service revolver? Did they mix up the guns?

"The papers even mentioned the fact that you refused to take a lie-detector test," said Fred. "So did Judy. So did Stu."

"It says here that a wig hair was found on the body," I said.

"There were at least two female police officers at the crime scene that night," Fred claimed. "They were probably wearing wigs."

"I can't deal with this anymore," I said. "I'm going to bed. This isn't real."

"The department had so many other suspects," Fred said. "Every one a man! Then they arrest you out of the clear blue. It's like they had blinders on—the investigation scope grew more and more narrow. They didn't want to listen to a thing I had to say. I could see it coming, but I thought maybe I was mistaken."

He came over to me and held my hand. "You must promise me."

"What?"

"I've never seen you so distraught. You must promise me that no matter how depressed you get, you'll never do anything stupid. You'll never do anything to yourself."

I nodded.

"We're going to beat this thing," Fred was saying. "It's wrong. But we have to do it together. Your parents will be back tomorrow."

"Oh God! Freddy! I'd rather die than tell them!"

"We must. Do you want me to?"

Feeling helpless, I nodded again.

My parents took it very badly, but I was barely aware of the events around me. I walked around like a zombie, a ghost. All I could do was sleep. Even small tasks seemed insurmountable. It was nightmarish.

Letters began to pour in from all over. Old friends, classmates, neighbors and former boyfriends sent letters of support, prayers and money. A friend in Madison said she was trying to organize some women's groups to help me.

The biased newspaper articles still continued, and in my anger, I granted an interview with a female *Milwaukee Journal* reporter. She had treated me fairly when she wrote the story about my discrimination claim the previous December, so I felt I could trust her. The article described me as a feminist. I raised the possibility that I was being framed and I detailed the harassment I'd undergone after filing my discrimination suit.

Reilly was furious, but admitted the article was not bad. I explained to him that I couldn't stand it anymore—standing by and watching all the lies being printed about me. He scolded me as if I were a child, and made me promise I wouldn't talk to any more reporters.

Soon we discovered that the police had searched my locker at Marquette, without a warrant, confiscating everything. They labeled everything "evidence," including my purse. I needed my purse, because it held all of my money, credit cards, bank books and identification. The police refused to release any of this.

Reilly was making me nervous. Something about him made me uneasy. My preliminary hearing was fast approaching, and he was talking about waiving it entirely. When we finally met, Fred had insisted on sitting in on my meetings with Reilly. After all, he was Fred's lawyer, too.

I didn't have a good rapport with Reilly. In a way, I guess it was a personality conflict; maybe it was me. But his partner was on the Police Commission, and that made me uncomfortable. And then my parents got the feeling that Reilly might be in conflict of interest in representing me after representing Fred during Fred's divorce—after all, the police considered Fred a suspect, too. Still, I was in shock after my arrest, plummeted into this ... depression ... and I couldn't act on my feelings. I knew I wasn't comfortable with him, but somehow I couldn't do anything about it. My parents went to see him and were also uncomfortable with him. They thought he already had me convicted. I don't know whether he thought I was guilty or what. It was hard to communicate with him.

Eventually, Reilly informed me that my preliminary hearing had been postponed—a request that came from District Attorney McCann, who said he was going to Florida on vacation. He gave the case to an assistant named Kraemer. Of course, the newspapers promptly reported that I had requested the postponement.

At that point I gave up on Reilly and started looking for a new lawyer. My parents and Fred helped me with the search. They decided it would be easier to get someone from out of town who couldn't have a conflict, so they went to Don Eisenberg, in Madison. Initially, I was impressed with his personality and style. He was confident, friendly and informative—the complete opposite of Reilly. My heart fell somewhat, though, when he informed me that Reilly's fee was only a fraction of what his own representation would cost—a twenty-five thousand dollar retainer fee, for starters.

I told my family that the fee was out of the question, but they insisted they'd raise the money, even if they had to mortgage their house. Fred agreed. I phoned Reilly to tell him I'd hired a different attorney. He sounded irritated, and with a tinge of sour grapes, he ended our conversation by saying, "Good luck. You'll need it."

Reilly turned over a set of files to Eisenberg's office, all of which were labeled and alphabetized, and all of which were empty.

Eisenberg was pleased that McCann had requested a postponement, since it would give him more time to review the facts. He said it was the most absurd thing he ever heard when I told him Reilly had planned on waiving my preliminary hearing.

"We are going to get this case dismissed at the prelim," Eisenberg said. "You won't even be bound over."

Sean and Shannon were staying with Fred's mom and dad, having a good time because their cousins lived right across the street. Fred said that the boys complained to him that they missed me. They tried calling me on the telephone and mailed me cards.

Fred's dad was very understanding. He stopped at my parents' house to give me a hug and expressed his support and belief in me. It meant very much to me, and I thanked him sincerely. I wondered how Fred's mother felt.

Then Carol Kurdziel called. She'd called a couple of times before, more or less as a friend, I thought, to see if I needed someone to talk to. This time she called to tell me that she was having budget problems. One of her officers had resigned to begin classes at the Milwaukee Police Academy. Several others were studying, and state law wouldn't allow them to work overtime, so they were unavailable. My salary was being tied up, because I'd been suspended with pay. She wanted to apply my salary to a body that could be there. That left me with two options: either I could resign, or request a leave of absence without pay. The latter choice, she explained, would allow me to return to work when it was possible. Eventually I decided on the leave of absence, composed a brief letter to Marquette and mailed it quickly before I changed my mind.

I made a brief appearance before a judge, with my new lawyer, to arrange for another hearing date. There was a small crowd, and, to my surprise, the judge refused to allow television cameras in the courtroom. A preliminary hearing was scheduled for September.

Sean and Shannon were unhappy that they couldn't live with us, but since those were the conditions of my bail we didn't dare question it. Sean remembered that my birthday was coming up in August and asked Fred if they could buy something for me. They chose a red-and-blue blouse and a stuffed dog. I was touched, but also frustrated, because I couldn't thank the boys in person. Instead, I wrote them a short note on a Thank You card, enclosing a snapshot of me wearing the new blouse and holding the dog. I mailed the card to Sean and Shannon, at John Schultz's address in Pewaukee.

Kathy and John turned my letter over to the District Attorney. But Sean sent a card saying, "Laurie we love you no matter what happens."

Eisenberg finally managed to persuade the DA to release my purse from the evidence bureau. When I got it back, all the items were separated into small plastic bags.

■　　■　　■

With nothing to do and too much time on our hands, Fred and I made plans to go camping with friends from my Boston Store days, Wally and Donna.

Just before we left, Donna appeared with that day's newspaper and pointed out a front-page article. A familiar face peered at me—it was Judy Zess. I read the small print under the headline. She had been attacked by two men, who had robbed her at gunpoint. The robbery took place in the parking lot of the high-rise where we'd shared an apartment. The article speculated that the men might have been after money and drugs left behind in Gaertner's apartment after his arrest. I didn't know she was still at Tom's. I wondered how she could afford it.

Judy's description of one of her assailants struck me at once—it was incredibly similar to the suspect described by Sean and Shannon. The man had been wearing a wig, used a thirty-eight, and had handcuffed her. His name was Fred Horenberger. All weekend I wondered about it, weighing the possibility of these two men being tied in with the murder of Christine. Fred suggested that the whole thing might have been fabricated by Judy. I couldn't decide what to make of it.

The weekend was a disaster. It was intensely hot and humid, the woods thick with huge mosquitoes and biting flies. Several times Fred blew up at me for trivial reasons, and once at Donna and Wally.

Once we were back on the road, with Fred driving in silence, Donna whispered to me.

"Look. We planned this weekend for you, Laurie, because we figured you needed it. But this guy!" She pointed a thumb at Fred. "Where on earth did you meet such a jerk?"

When we returned from camping, we moved all of our stuff out of the house on Ramsey and stored it in the basement of my mom and dad's house. Fred and I set up reasonable living quarters upstairs. With half of our belongings still in boxes, I felt disorganized and scattered, but I was glad all of our property was finally under one roof.

Fred's friends Dennis and Karen called us from Florida. They'd been interviewed by police, who asked them if Fred and I had been plotting anything openly. They were appalled. Then my best friend, Joanne, gave me a call. Two detectives had driven to Stevens Point, Wisconsin, over four hundred miles, to question her. They asked the same questions.

"I was so mad!" she told me. "They kept acting like I was lying or something! I told them I never saw you in a green jogging suit—I don't think you own anything green. They knew we were on the track team together in high school."

An acquaintance of Fred's called to tell us the cops had asked him if I'd bragged recently about buying another handgun. This baffled me. Why would the police still be asking about another revolver if their report indicated that the murder weapon was Fred's off-duty gun? Could the ballistics report on the gun be incorrect?

After persistent urging from me, Fred filed for unemployment benefits. It was obvious that it would be a long time before he would be allowed to return to work. The city, naturally, wasted no time denying him benefits, and Fred demanded a hearing to appeal the denial. I told him not to worry.

"I've been this route before. You have to file a written rebuttal, disproving their reasons for denying the benefits."

Living with my parents was difficult. They went to bed very early and woke up early to get my dad off to work. Fred and I liked to stay up late and sleep in the morning. Everyone was frustrated, full of stress. No one was acting normally.

■   ■   ■

Normal? How could anything be normal? I was to stand trial for killing the ex-wife of my husband, a husband I was coming to bitterly regret marrying, supposedly over a house I had no wish to live in, with kids I had never asked for. They were poisoning my friendships with ugly questions. I had been forbidden contact with the children—not my children, but children I cared about all the same. Wigs and jogging suits and guns ... it was all crazy. It meant nothing. I didn't do this dreadful thing!

And I was angry, too. People were telling lies about me. What gave them the right?

I watched Fred fall asleep in front of the television set. Outside, the branches scraped against the window. I fingered my wedding ring.

The nightmare cannot last forever.

I told myself that.

It cannot, it cannot.

12

THE PRELIMINARY HEARING

The night before Fred's unemployment hearing, Fred's tax attorney called Darryl Laatsch phoned. He'd just received a notice announcing a custody hearing, scheduled for the following day.

"Alice Pennings has petitioned the court for custody of Sean and Shannon. But the law requires at least five days' written notice. They can't just plop this in our laps the night before. You have to be served. You weren't, were you?"

"This is the first I've heard of it!" Fred replied.

"From what I gather, Alice is petitioning the court as an extension of the divorce stipulation that gave Christine custody. But Alice wasn't a party to the divorce, so I don't know what she's doing," Laatsch said. "I wouldn't worry about it. It's next to impossible to take children away from a natural parent. It doesn't happen overnight."

We got other legal opinions as well. They all said it could never happen, and we were relieved—until Fred decided to call Sean and Shannon at John and Kathy's house.

I was on the extension phone as Fred talked to Sean. The child told his father that a strange man had been at John Schultz's house that week to talk to him and his brother, Shannon. He didn't know the man's name or where he was from. Fred immediately thought: reporter.

"I told you not to talk to anyone without my permission, son! Was the man from a newspaper?"

"I don't know, dad," was Sean's tearful reply. "I mean, no."

"Did the man give you his name?"

"No, but Uncle John told me to talk to him," Sean cried.

"Calm down, Sean. I'm sorry I hollered at you. I'm not mad. I'm angry at Uncle John for not telling me about this. It's just that I don't want any reporters interviewing you or Shannon."

"Okay."

"What did he ask you?"

"He asked us about the night mommy was killed, and he asked us if you or Laurie ever spanked us or hit us."

"Where is Uncle John?" Fred asked, his concern growing.

"At grampa's," Sean replied. "Oh! The man gave Aunt Kathy a little card and I think she put it on the refrigerator door. Do you want me to get it?"

"Yes!" Fred said. "That's good, Sean. Now listen—this is important. Hang up the phone, get the card, and call me right back. Don't run off and play or forget to call daddy back."

About twenty minutes passed. Fred paced back and forth in the kitchen, waiting for the phone to ring. I sat at the kitchen table and finally suggested that he try to call back. Sean answered.

"Why didn't you call daddy back?" Fred asked.

"Because Aunt Kathy wouldn't let me!" the child wailed.

"Is she there right now? Let me talk to her."

There was a long wait. Kathy wasn't coming to the phone. Fred looked at me, and I felt sick. Something was wrong.

"Hang up, Fred!" I whispered. "Go down there! You'll never get this straightened out over the phone. Go!"

Fred hung up the phone. He ran out of the house and jumped into his van. I wished I could go along.

He came back about three hours later. He plopped down on a chair and told me what had happened.

"I think John has had a nervous breakdown!" he said. "When I got to Pewaukee, I pulled the van into my mom's driveway because Sean told me that John was across the street. The boys' bikes were in the yard, so I thought they might all be having supper. Here we were, sitting around the table—"

"Who?" I asked.

"My dad, my mom, me and the kids. Anyway, my brother comes flying in through the door of my dad's house with the Pewaukee cops! He was like a madman!"

"What?"

"I'm not kidding! Remember when Kathy wouldn't come to the phone?

135

She went running to John and told him that I'd threatened to kill her and her whole family! She said I was on my way!"

"You did not! I was right here!"

"So, when the cops arrived, they could see nothing was wrong. John was hysterical. He was screaming that I'm not his brother anymore, and that he didn't want my kids in his house ever again—you should have heard him."

"God."

"You know what they've been doing? John and Kathy have been conspiring with Alice to take Sean and Shannon away from me. They were cooperating with this custody action all along. Kathy panicked when she knew she was about to be discovered."

"Not your own brother!" I couldn't believe it.

"Yeah! Oh, was my dad pissed! He demanded that the police leave his house and told them they had no right to come storming in without a warrant. But fucking John just led the way! My dad told John that he was taking him out of his will and everything!"

I was staring at Fred with my mouth open. What a melodrama! "Did you ever find out who that guy was who talked to the kids?"

Fred nodded. "Lee Calvey."

"Calvey? He's the 'Guardian ad litem'! He's supposed to be the impartial party—"

"I know," Fred said, rubbing his temples with his fingers. "I'm going to take a couple of aspirins and go to bed. I've got to get up early tomorrow and go downtown to see about this custody hearing."

I walked into the den, where my parents were watching television. My dad was cleaning some coins for his collection. He looked up and put his magnifying-glass down.

"What's going on with Fred?"

"Don't ask," I said with exhaustion, sitting cross-legged. How could I explain what was going on when I barely understood it myself? There was a lawyer for the estate, a lawyer for the kids, a lawyer for me, a lawyer for Fred, when just a few years back I didn't even know what a lawyer looked like! Life had begun to seem like one big courtroom.

■   ■   ■

The next day, it rained like it was the end of the world. It was dark and humid all morning. After Fred left for the courthouse, I went to the basement recreation room and stayed there all day, painting and listening to the radio over the loud crashes of thunder.

I was just making a fresh pot of coffee in the kitchen when Fred walked in, soaking wet. He was weeping.

"They took my kids away from me," he said. "I have to turn them over by three."

So much for the lawyers and their advice.

"I can't stay. I have to pack some of their clothes and go back out to Pewaukee."

When he got back, he explained what had happened. When he'd got to the courtroom, Alice and Earl Pennings were there with Barb and Bruce, John and Kathy and Stu Honeck. Fred met Darryl Laatsch inside the court. They were about to approach the bench when the Pennings and Stu Honeck's father went into Judge Curley's chambers. Fred and Laatsch were not allowed to follow them. When they came out, the judge announced his decision. Laatsch's objections were overruled. His motion to dismiss was denied.

The newspaper article about the hearing later quoted Laatsch as saying, "It was utter lawlessness."

"They said they wanted to take the boys up north, for their own safety," Fred explained. "They thought you were trying to influence them."

"I haven't seen Sean or Shannon since before my arrest. Those are the conditions of my bail!" I said resentfully. "How could this happen? Was your brother there?"

Fred sneered. "Yeah. Well, at least now my mother believes me. She was so busy being palsy-walsy with Kathy that she wouldn't even believe me when I told her I thought something was going on behind my back. Now that the kids are gone ... now reality has slapped her in the face.

"I was a bit late dropping off Sean and Shannon. I wanted to buy them ID bracelets before they had to go. Stu actually called the Pewaukee police, saying that he represented the MPD and that there was a 'hostage situation' going on! They sent a squad."

"How were the boys taking it?" I asked.

"Crying. Said they would run away."

"What are you going to do now?"

"I already called Eisenberg. He referred me to Joe Balistreri. I know Joey. He's a good attorney. Darryl has enough on his hands with the estate. This was a temporary order. The permanent custody hearing will be in February."

■   ■   ■

The following day was my birthday. I turned twenty-three. At the ripe old age of
twenty-three, I felt as though I should already stop celebrating birthdays.
   There didn't seem very much cause for celebration.
   Time ticked on. Only joy stopped.

■　　■　　■

A few days later, I was going through our mail and noticed that a Denial of Benefits notice had arrived for Fred from the Unemployment Compensation office.
He had forgotten to attend the hearing.

   I shook my head in disgust and began the paperwork required to request an
appeal of the denial. Later, I berated Fred for his failure to attend the hearing.

   "To make matters worse, I found all your benefit claim cards piling up on
your desk! All you have to do is fill out those cards on time and mail one out
every week so that it can be processed by the Tuesday of the following week!
This is something you can't procrastinate about. You have to be prompt."

   "Don't nag me about this!" Fred snapped.

   "Fine!" I replied sharply, and left the room.

   Fred came upstairs and tossed his key ring onto the dresser. "When I come
home, all I want to do is relax. I don't want you running up to me and nagging
me about all kinds of shit."

   "Just when do you want to be informed about things?" I asked, hurt by his
accusations. "You run around here and there, and days turn into weeks, and
appointments come and go—forgotten. After I took care of all that paperwork
for you, because you can't even mail anything on time, and then you forget
about that hearing! The hearing was the result of all my efforts!"

   "How could I remember, with all the bullshit going on?"

   "Get yourself a damn calendar or appointment book, then."

   Fred was finally allowed to return to work, assigned to a desk job in the
Detective Clerical Warrant Division. He saw his children every Sunday
between noon and six PM. Barb was ordered to bring Sean and Shannon to
Pewaukee and leave them at Fred's mom and dad's house. The custody order
included these visitation rights. I struggled to occupy my time alone every
weekend; I was not allowed to accompany Fred. I had grown dependent on
him, much to my dismay.

■　　■　　■

The day of my preliminary hearing arrived. It was to last two days. The court-house halls were filled with people. One of my sisters and her boyfriend arrived, taking a seat with my parents and Fred's father. Much to Fred's annoyance, his mother did not show up.

I sat with Eisenberg at a small table, dressed in a gray gabardine suit. It was warm in the room, and I nervously tugged at a wisp of hair that had lost its curl due to the humidity. The judge presiding over the case was Ralph Adam Fine, a young man with dark hair. Police Department witnesses took the stand first and testified about the procedural aspects of the case.

Then the State called Fred's squad partner from the night of the murder. Durfee was as vague and as noncommittal as possible. Eisenberg quietly commented to me on his nervousness. His original report on the events of the night in question had been mysteriously rewritten two weeks later, against Department policy; reports were always required the day of the incident.

Durfee failed to explain why his report was dated two weeks later. It was inconsistent with his first report and conflicted with Fred's. He stuttered and stammered. It was a ludicrous performance. I regretted that a jury was not present to see it.

He denied having ever made any judgment regarding Fred's off-duty revolver. He denied having ever made the statement that it had not been fired, which contradicted his first, written report. He now contended that it would have been impossible to come to any conclusion about the gun, because he was not a ballistics expert.

He did admit that he failed to record the serial number of the revolver he examined that night.

When Eisenberg requested to see his memo book from that night, Durfee informed the court that he had either lost it or thrown it out. That was also a violation of Department regulations.

The court recessed for several minutes, so I left the courtroom to find the women's room. Judy and her mother were sitting on a bench in the hallway, and as I passed by, Judy said hello.

"Oh, hi," I said, stopping to stand in front of them. "I almost didn't recognize you with your new haircut. Cute."

"Thanks!" Judy smiled. "Do you know how long this is going to take today?"

"I'm not sure."

"Look!" Judy thrust out her left hand to show me an antique ring. "Tom and I got married."

"Really?" I raised my eyebrows, because Tom was in prison. "Where are you living now? The return address on your letter was a post office box."

Judy seemed to have trouble answering. Before she could say any more, Eisenberg came out into the hall and motioned to me.

Fred sat down in the witness box and informed the court that he intended to plead the Fifth. I turned to see Fred's lawyer, Joe Balistreri, approach the bench. Once Fred was granted immunity, he began to testify.

Fred explained that on the night of the shooting my mother had arrived at our apartment to help me pack. He said he'd gone to bed, and when he awoke we had finished packing everything.

Fred stated that it was his understanding that I had intended to go out later with a girlfriend, but had trouble getting in touch with her.

He went on to say that he called me several times once he got to work, and that I told him I was going to sleep because I was tired. He then testified that he got a message to contact his captain, who told him about the murder. Immediately afterwards, he telephoned me and woke me up to tell me the news.

Fred got to the part about examining the gun with Durfee, and I was impressed by his testimony on ballistics; his detailed explanation of the presence of dust on all parts of the gun made him sound like an expert on the subject. He emphasized the absence of blood and the absence of traces of lead or carbon.

Then Fred's testimony led to the part where he had to describe his arrival at the scene of the crime, and he stopped suddenly, too emotional to continue. The court had to recess so Fred could regain his composure.

I looked at Eisenberg. "He can't talk about her death, but to me all he does is criticize Christine horribly—even now! I don't get it!" I wondered if it was an act.

Eisenberg put his hand on my shoulder. "Goddamn it! If I'd known Fred was going to do that, I wouldn't have called him!"

I wandered out of the courtroom, feeling hurt and confused. Fred had just told the whole world that he still loved Christine, completely contradicting what he insisted in private.

Alone in the washroom, I leaned up against the sink as my head spun. Splashing water on my face, I squeezed my eyes shut. I couldn't understand what he was doing.

My mom walked into the washroom and stood next to me.

"What was that all about?" she demanded. "What's wrong with Fred? Does he still love her? It sure looked that way to everyone in the courtroom!"

She was right. My mother was always right.

"Please!" I blurted out. "Just leave me alone for a few minutes."

She turned and left, her heels clicking across the tile floor.

After a few minutes, I headed down the corridor toward the courtroom. Stu Honeck stood in the hall with Alice Pennings. I wanted badly to say something to her, to run to her and beg her to believe that I did not do this to her daughter. I knew that I didn't dare say a word. I glanced at them numbly, but remained silent as I passed by.

"She looks stoned," Stu said, loudly enough for me to hear it.

You should know, I thought bitterly. How swiftly they had turned to playing God! Clearly they'd already passed judgment on me and found me guilty.

Honeck took the stand. He slumped in his chair, chewing a wad of gum. He couldn't recall many of the details of his activities on the night in question, nor his whereabouts at specific times. His testimony differed from what Sean had told us. He testified that he was driven home by Christine that evening. He denied that he had ever had a drinking problem. He did, however, admit to having a key to her house.

Then Stu went into a dramatic rendition of the times Chris told him I hated her. He said that Chris had told him I had made her stand outside in the hallway one evening when she'd brought me a blender as a gift, and that I had refused to invite her in.

"That's not true at all!" I whispered.

Eisenberg shushed me, handing me a yellow legal pad to write my comments on.

"NOT TRUE!" I wrote in large, black letters.

But nothing shocked me and my friends more than the Judas performance of Judy Zess. I sat in stunned disbelief as she took the stand and testified that I had made many verbal threats against Christine. She also claimed that she'd seen a green jogging suit in our apartment when we lived together.

"Did you say that you had occasion to talk with the defendant in the hall outside the courtroom today?" Assistant District Attorney Kraemer asked Zess.

"Yes," she replied.

"What did the defendant say to you, if anything?"

"She told me that her lawyer would probably not call me to testify ... and she said she could not understand where the police got this green jogging suit nonsense."

"I never said that!" I wrote.

Our turn for cross-examination arrived. Eisenberg attacked Judy's testimony without mercy.

"Okay, Miss Zess," he began. "Let's go back to this party where the defendant allegedly made threats against Christine. What month was this party held?"

"February."

"Did Laurie and Fred get married on the last day of January?"

"Yes."

"Then this party was a happy occasion? A celebration?" Eisenberg paced back and forth.

"I don't know," was Judy's answer.

"Well, Miss Zess, was this party a happy occasion or a funeral? Fred and Laurie just back from their honeymoon. You picked them up at O'Hare Airport. Isn't that correct?"

"Yes."

"And you were at this dinner party, laughing and having a good time?"

"Yes."

"And what exactly did Laurie allegedly say?"

"We were talking about the cost of living, and she said that it would pay to have Chris blown away."

"How did you respond?"

"I don't remember."

"Did you call the police? Did you laugh it off? What?"

"I ... we ... the conversation was dropped."

"Did you think she was joking?"

"No."

"Would it refresh your memory to read a report that you gave the police last June, where you told the police then that you thought, 'It was said in jest,' and you thought Laurie was joking?"

Eisenberg walked up to Zess and handed her a copy of the report.

"Yes."

"You thought Laurie was joking?"

"Yes."

"But, for the purposes of this hearing, you decided to say that you thought Laurie was not joking?" he asked.

"Objection!" shouted the prosecutor. "The witness has already answered this question."

"Sustained," Judge Fine said calmly.

"I'll withdraw that last question, Your Honor," Eisenberg said. He then asked Zess to repeat her description of the green jogging suit.

"What exactly was the occasion on which you first became aware of this green jogging suit in the Schultz apartment?"

"It was when Fred and I were loading some boxes into a storage locker in the basement. I saw the pants in a box as I was helping him."

"What color were these pants?"

"Green."

"Was it kelly green? Forest green? Light green?"

"It was dark green."

"Was it a baseball uniform?"

"No."

"How could you be so sure?" Eisenberg pressed on. "You just testified that you only saw a pair of pants folded up in a box. How could you tell what it was?"

"It was a jogging suit," Zess insisted.

"Did you ever see Laurie jog in it?"

"No."

"Did you ever see Fred jog in it?"

"No."

Eisenberg attempted to uncover the reason for Judy's damaging, fabricated testimony, but he was restrained by the State's constant objections. She had caught us all completely by surprise. I just couldn't see why she would stab me in the back like that. She'd sent me a sympathetic letter; she'd chatted with me in the hall only a few minutes before being sworn in.

"The witness may step down."

I stared at Judy from my seat at the defense table, but she would not return my gaze. She sauntered past, avoided my eyes and looked at the floor.

Eisenberg leaned over to whisper to me. "What the hell happened with Zess? I thought you two were friends! She's digging your grave."

"I can't understand it, for the life of me. We had our minor differences in the past—I told you about them—but it wasn't enough to warrant these lies. How could she do this to me?"

"I want a copy of her last letter to you."

"She talks to me out in the hall, and then tells the DA that I made a remark about the jogging suit? What—?"

"You should never have said anything to her. Next time, no conversation in the halls of this courthouse."

"Don, all I said was that her haircut was attractive, and then she showed me her ring and told me that she and Tom got married."

"Married? She just testified that Tom was her fiancé! Now what the hell is he?"

"Who's next?" I asked, referring to the witness list.

"Fred's oldest boy."

Sean answered questions directly and with a brave maturity. He smiled at me and sat up straight, trying to fill in the large chair in the witness box. At one point, he began to cry, and I felt so bad for him. Genuinely moved, I wanted to comfort him but had to remain seated. Eisenberg offered him a cup of water.

Several times, Sean stressed that the person he witnessed could not possibly have been me, because the intruder was too large—the size of a big man, he said.

"It couldn't possibly be Laurie," Sean repeated. "Even if she had been wearing shoulder pads, like a football player—it still couldn't have been her, because then her body would have to form the shape of a 'V.' This body was big and came down straight on the sides." Sean used his hands to illustrate his meaning. "Besides, I know Laurie. Laurie always smells good 'cause she likes to wear perfume, and I didn't smell any perfume."

The direct examination continued as Sean recalled the terrifying events of that night. "He was wearing a green khaki army jacket," he said firmly. "It wasn't a green jogging suit. I know because when he or she ran down the stairs, I saw the sides of it flap. You know—an army jacket without the camouflage."

Kraemer didn't miss the fact that Sean used the phrase "he or she" and jumped on this chance to confuse the child. Fortunately, Sean was bright enough not to be fooled.

"Tell me, Sean," Kraemer asked with a sly smile. "Why did you just say 'he or she'?" Is it because you're not really sure if it was a man or a woman?"

Sean looked thoughtful. "Well, I said 'he or she' because those are the only two sexes there are." A chuckle was heard throughout the courtroom.

"Sean," Kraemer asked, "you know that your daddy loves Laurie very much, right?"

"Yes."

"Isn't it a fact that your daddy told you that Laurie didn't do it?"

"No," Sean answered.

"Did your daddy talk to you at all about it?"

"Yes."

"What did he tell you?" Kraemer beamed.

"He told me just to tell the truth," Sean said firmly.

Frustrated, Kraemer turned away from the witness stand. "No further questions, Your Honor."

Eisenberg approached the child for several more questions.

"Honey, I know this is hard for you. I just want to clear a few things up, okay Sean? There seems to be some question of whether or not someone told you what to say today. Did anyone tell you what to say?"

"No."

"Did I ever tell you what to say, Sean?"

"No."

"Did Laurie ever tell you what to say?"

"No."

"So, what you told the police that night after it happened, is that the truth?"

"Yes."

"You know the difference between the truth and a lie?"

"Yes."

"Right now, are you telling the truth?"

"Yes," Sean replied. "There was one thing I forgot to tell the police that night, and then I remembered, so I told my dad a couple of days later."

"What was that?" Eisenberg asked. I wondered what Sean would say next. I didn't know there was something else.

"I remembered that the man growled that night. He growled at me. That's the only thing I forgot to tell the police."

"Okay. And am I right when I say that you had enough good, common sense that night to try and administer first aid to your mommy to try and stop the bleeding?"

"Yes, I did."

"Sean, did Laurie kill your mommy?"

"No."

"Do you love Laurie?"

"Yes."

After Sean, my mother was called to testify. Unaccustomed to the courtroom atmosphere, she appeared frail and nervous as she took the stand. I felt a rush of compassion and love for her as she testified. She described the events that took place that same evening, explaining that she'd been with me at the apartment.

"How many hours did you spend with your daughter that night?" Eisenberg asked my mother.

"I'd say about four hours, because my husband dropped me off right after supper and I stayed until around ten."

"What did you do while you were there?"

"I helped Laurie pack, because she and Fred were supposed to move that weekend. So I remember asking Laurie if I should start on the spare room. It wasn't exactly a bedroom. It was a room full of Fred's books, extra clothes and sports equipment."

"Did you pack all of that up in boxes?"

"Yes, after wrapping everything in newspaper."

"Objection," Kraemer interrupted. "This is irrelevant."

"Your Honor, I believe in a second you will see the relevance."

"Objection overruled. Proceed."

"Mrs. Bembenek," Eisenberg continued, "do you remember packing Fred's jewelry box that evening?"

"Yes."

"In view of your daughter?"

"No. She was in another room."

"Objection! I fail to understand this line of questioning, Your Honor," Kraemer again interrupted.

"The relevance," Eisenberg explained, "is the fact that a bit of circumstantial evidence in this case is the theory of the State that the defendant had access to the Ramsey Street house by using a key, a key that her husband kept in his jewelry box, of which the defendant denies any knowledge. Mrs. Bembenek just testified that she packed away all of Fred Schultz's belongings that night, including the jewelry box that contained the house key. If the key was packed away in a box, by Mrs. Bembenek, before the murder, and if its whereabouts were unknown to the defendant, and if, as Fred Schultz testified, this same key was found still packed away when he had reason to look for it after the murder, the Court will see the thin line of reasoning used to create this theory. The relevance? No access."

"Proceed," Judge Fine said.

Eisenberg resumed his questioning.

"Had you ever been to your daughter Laurie's apartment before that night?"

"Yes."

"When was that?"

"On April 14."

"For what reason were you there?"

"Laurie and Fred invited me and my husband over for dinner."

"Did you notice anything unusual about the plumbing then?"

"Yes. I asked Laurie if I could use the bathroom, and she warned me not to use Judy's bathroom, because the toilet was overflowing."

"So am I correct in saying that this apartment had plumbing problems as early as April 14?"

"Yes."

"Okay. Let's talk about your daughter. You know her as well as any mother knows her daughter, isn't that a fact?"

"Yes."

"On the evening of May 27, when you spent four hours with Laurie ... Strike that. Incidentally, do you know where Fred and Laurie were going to move?"

"Yes. They were moving into an apartment closer to our house, across from a park."

"Did you know why they were intending to move?"

"Because Judy Zess broke the lease."

"Okay, Mrs. Bembenek. Now, going back to that night, was Laurie acting strange?"

"No."

"Was she acting nervous?"

"No."

"Was she acting like a girl who was planning on committing a murder that night?"

"Objection! Speculation!" Kraemer shouted.

"Overruled. You may answer the question." The judge looked at me, as if to analyze me thoughtfully.

"Would you repeat the question?" my mother asked Eisenberg.

"Sure. Knowing your daughter as well as you do, did she, that night, seem like a girl who was planning on committing a murder?"

"Of course not."

"Was she drunk?"

"No."

"Was she on any drugs that you know of?"

"No."

"Did she have any plans for that night, that you knew of?"

"She said—"

"Objection! Hearsay!" Kraemer shouted.

"Overruled. Hearsay from the defendant is admissible."

My mother looked at the judge to see if she should answer.

"You may answer the question."

"Laurie mentioned that she was planning on going out with a girlfriend from work. She was waiting for the girl to call, but she said she might not go, because she was getting tired."

In cross-examination, Kraemer badgered my mother about her testimony. He hauled his heavy body out of his chair and lumbered toward the witness stand in his Hush Puppies.

"Mrs. Bembenek, would you lie for your daughter?"

"No."

"Have you rehearsed your testimony?"

"No.

"Mrs. Bembenek, I find it rather odd that you recall the exact date of the dinner at the Bembenek-Schultz apartment. How do you happen to know it was April 14 when you had dinner there?"

"Because that is the date of my wedding anniversary."

"No further questions, Your Honor."

At long last, the hearing was over. But instead of announcing a decision on whether or not to bind me over for a jury trial, the judge informed us that he wanted both attorneys to file briefs.

My parents and Eisenberg and I left together to have a drink. Fred needed to attend an important engagement elsewhere and told me he'd see me later at home. I was still brooding over his emotional display during his testimony.

"I feel it's important that you at least had plans to go to a bar the evening of the shooting," Eisenberg said. "I mean, it makes no sense. Who would say, 'I can't go out, so what the hell—I'll go out and kill somebody instead'?"

We ordered a round of drinks.

"Don't be too cross with Fred because of his emotional performance," Eisenberg told me. "Ex-wives have a unique way of throwing an enormous amount of guilt on men. I should know—I have two of them!"

"How soon will we be informed of the outcome?" my dad asked.

"In October," Eisenberg replied. "I'm optimistic. It's somewhat unusual for a judge to request additional time to decide on a bind-over. He could dismiss the charges."

"What do you think will happen?" I asked, sipping my Scotch.

"The only thing that the State had to prove at that hearing was probable cause for arrest. It's a probability issue. It's nowhere near as tough to prove as in a jury trial, where the State has to prove guilt beyond a reasonable doubt. The burden of proof is different at the prelim. Here all they had to prove was that it would be reasonable to assume that the defendant 'probably' did it—you know about probable cause?"

I nodded.

"I think we did a hell of a job!" Eisenberg beamed. "We exposed a number of different suspects. The children insisted it wasn't you."

"Honeck denied that he had a drinking problem."

"Simple," Eisenberg said. "All we do is subpoena his employment records with the MPD."

"That suspect that lives across the street from the house on Ramsey—whatever happened to him?" my mom asked.

"He refused to testify. I think he's a fruitcake," Eisenberg said.

"I still can't believe what Judy did," I said sadly.

"I wonder what makes her tick," Eisenberg said. "Somebody must be playing games. The biggest piece of evidence that the State has is the ballistics report on the off-duty gun. I objected to that being submitted, because I didn't have the opportunity to cross-examine the Crime Lab technician, but Fine let it in anyway."

"Do you think it will be dismissed?" I asked again, hoping against hope.

"Don't be devastated if it's not. Of course I hope it will be. It should be! But a lot of judges allow politics to influence their decisions. They have to worry about re-election. You've had an enormous amount of publicity. Fine might just bind you over, to let a jury decide."

The Scotch had relaxed me. I pushed off my tight gray pumps and let them dangle from my toes underneath the glass-topped table.

"I just thought of something," I told Eisenberg. "Judy claims that she saw a green jogging suit in a box when she and Fred were loading some boxes into the storage space? She's the only one who had keys to that locker! She had promised to make copies of the key for both of us but there was no great rush because the boxes were full of seasonal items. She never did give us a key. I remember Fred saying that he had to break the lock on that door when we were ready to move."

"Do you think Fred owns a green baseball or football uniform?"

"No. Not to my knowledge. The pants to his team uniforms are white. I always think it's absurd to wear white since they get so filthy. I have to soak them in bleach for days after a game. His jerseys are maroon and I think he has a yellow one with black letters, but not green."

I paused and then continued talking. "That's just it, Don! I don't own any-thing green. Not a thing! I just don't like the color. My clothes are either purple or lilac or fuschia, with some blue jeans and three-piece suits that are brown or blue. This is so unreal!"

"I know." Eisenberg nodded. "We've been over all of this before. It wouldn't make much sense for a murderer to wear something so unique. I mean, the guy might as well have worn a yellow chicken suit! The army jacket sounds more realistic.

"Well, let's be on our way. You've had a few tough days."

■　　■　　■

Too right, I thought. But worse—much worse—was to come.

13

THE APPROACH OF WINTER

O nce home, I fell prey to serious doubts about Fred and what I really meant to him. There was such a contrast between what he would say one day and what he would do the next. He kept me hopelessly confused and longing for reassurance.

What was I to do? How was I to deal with this? I couldn't begin to believe then that Fred was devious enough to frame his wife for murder. How could I believe that? I wanted reassurances, not further anxiety. It's hard to remember now how confused I was—now that there is no more confusion, only anger; now that I know what the lies were, and who the liars are; now that my life has become a simple thing, a drive to Get Out into the free air.

But in those bad days I was young and confused and didn't know where to turn.

■   ■   ■

I picked up a pile of letters for mailing and I told Fred I was going to walk to the drugstore. I left the house wearing a plaid blouse and cotton shorts. The temperature had dropped several degrees since the afternoon, but I paid no attention to the weather. In my depression, the chill seemed only natural.

Too many people in Fred's world and in my world liked to lie and stab and hurt. It was more than I could bear. I hadn't led a sheltered life—I thought I was wise, streetwise—but nothing had prepared me for this. I thought of calling a women's crisis line for advice, but when I reached the drugstore, someone was using the pay phone. I looked down the street and saw an open tavern. Almost half an hour had passed since I'd left the house. It was getting dark outside.

There was only one customer behind the bar. The bartender was a heavy man with thick glasses and lambchop sideburns. I asked him for change as I put a dollar bill on the bar and ordered a glass of beer.

The phone was in a dark corner of the tavern. As I dialed the number of the crisis line, I realized I didn't even know what I planned to say, or why I was calling. All I knew is that I needed someone to talk to. A woman answered and explained that all the lines were busy at that moment. They would call me back in ten minutes. I returned to my seat at the bar and sipped my beer. I wanted to run away.

But where to?

The streetlights blinked on, glowing greenish yellow against the eerie color of the sky. On top of the bar, the television blasted the news of my hearing.

"Hey!" the bartender exclaimed, walking toward me. "I knew I seen you someplace before! That's you on TV—ain't it?"

Wincing, I nodded silently. My expression made the bartender apologize.

"Gosh, I'm sorry. I never seen such a bullshit case in my life. They gotta let you go. I can't understand it! At first, the cops were asking citizens to help them find the murderer, and they was looking for a man! Then they arrested you? That don't make no sense."

I smiled a weak smile and shrugged. I couldn't escape it.

"You don't look like no man," he continued. "Besides, that little boy seen who done it, and he said it wasn't you."

The door opened and in walked Fred.

I'm being followed like a child, I thought angrily.

Fred sat down next to me as the pay phone began to ring, unanswered. I fought a choking sensation in my throat.

"Laurie—your dad started to worry about you when you were gone over half an hour. You left in those shorts and it got cold out. It started to get dark—"

"I just wanted to be alone for a while! I just wanted forty-five minutes to myself! I just wanted to mail my letters and go for a damn walk!" I tore apart my cocktail napkin. I was near hysteria.

"Well ..."

"You followed me! I'm a grown woman and I can't even go somewhere by myself! You spoil everything! Do I follow you?"

"What were you going to do? Sit in this gin-mill all night?"

"No!" I was practically hissing.

"Look. Your dad started to put on his coat to look for you. I thought it would be better if I went instead. So I took your car." I found out later, dad wasn't involved at all.

"How did you know I was in here? I just stopped in to use the phone."

"I drove past the drugstore and I saw your blond head in the window. Look, I knew you'd be pissed, but I couldn't let your dad run off looking for you," Fred said.

I gulped the remainder of my beer and held the empty glass tightly.

"By the way, who were you trying to call that you couldn't call from home?" Fred asked suspiciously.

"That's my business," I replied, heading for the door.

"I know why you're mad," Fred said, as we got to my car. "I saw your face after I testified about Chris. It was a very emotional incident!"

"How strange! And after such an emotionless marriage, according to you!" I blinked angrily. "Where was the emotion the night it happened? You didn't cry at the morgue. You didn't cry at the funeral. Did you have to wait to cry on cue in the courtroom for the whole world to see? You claim repeatedly that you never loved Chris. You say one thing and do another."

"I'm not going to try and explain it to you," Fred said.

Because you can't even explain it to yourself, I thought.

For the next few weeks, I clung to the hope that the judge would dismiss the charges for lack of probable cause. Eisenberg had always said that the complaint was no good. They didn't even have a warrant for my arrest.

My mother left for the west coast. We'd been arguing, squabbling over trivia; the tension in the house had spilled over to this most secure of relationships, and I felt a mixture of guilt and relief at seeing her go. I didn't blame her for needing to get away from the tension—I wished I could have gone. I knew it wasn't rational to resent her leaving, because I practically drove her out of her own house, but at the same time I missed her and felt abandoned. I was acting like an emotional infant, so I merely feigned indifference.

Boredom consumed me. I had nothing but housework to occupy my time, and the less I did, the less I wanted to do. I lost weight, had trouble sleeping and stopped exercising at the gym.

Fred and I stopped discussing my case altogether.

He would return home after work tense and irritable, claiming his commanding officers were harassing him: people in the office had been ordered not to talk to him; he was constantly reprimanded and spied on.

One night he was sitting at the kitchen table, with his tie loosened and his vest unbuttoned, busily wolfing down a cold beef sandwich. I had my feet up on another chair and picked at the sandwich on my plate, having lost interest in food. I asked him a question, but he didn't answer.

I thought he was in another of his moods. I was almost afraid to talk to him. I felt resentful.

Then there was a noise in the hallway. I glanced up.

A small, furry, adorable puppy crept cautiously around the corner of the kitchen cabinets. It stopped in fear when it saw me.

I shrieked. "Freddy!" I leapt from my chair and got down on my hands and knees to approach the little rascal. He was a German Shepherd about six weeks old. I scooped his tiny body into my arms and hugged him tightly.

"Do you like him?" Fred smiled. "I bought him for you."

I started to cry as the dog's trusting eyes looked up at the sound of our voices. A tiny, pink tongue licked the skin on my bare arm.

"He's so cute! Look at these huge paws! Where did you get him?"

"A breeder on the North Side."

Once again Fred had spent money we didn't have, once again on me. I couldn't be angry. I so needed someone, something, to love me!

I named the puppy "Sergeant."

■　　■　　■

For the next few weeks, Sergeant was all I clung to. After years of disagreeing with my mother over my habit of sleeping late in the mornings, I began to wake up early. Each day at sunrise, I was unable to do anything but toss and turn restlessly, and I had no choice but to get out of bed as early as 5:30 AM.

I'd make a pot of coffee, let Sergeant outside and read the morning paper until Fred and my father got up to get ready for work. I scanned the want ads and ached to find some kind of employment, but it was useless. I was beginning to feel as though no one in Milwaukee would ever hire me again. My time was occupied with training the dog and getting a few projects around the house finished, but my life felt pinched and mean. Without a job, I felt I was without value. Some days were so bad, I could barely get up enough strength to get myself dressed. When Fred asked me why I didn't change out of my nightgown and robe, I asked, "Why should I?" and really meant it.

My artwork lay untouched. My notebook of free verse was stored on a shelf in my closet, forgotten. I stopped jogging and weight lifting. As my depression grew worse, attacks of wrenching anxiety began to hit me.

I was twenty-three. I desperately needed help.

I went to a psychiatric clinic to find a friend.

■　　■　　■

I remember a sparrow circling a slice of sky as I walked through scattered leaves down an East Side street. I remember the noise of my high heels clicking against the pavement. I remember the massive front door. I remember pushing open the door, folding my coat carefully so its tattered inner lining wouldn't show. I remember a brief encounter with the receptionist and some brightly colored chairs, and a handful of other people, *normal* people, sitting quietly and waiting. I don't remember what I told the receptionist, but I remember being ushered into the counselor's office.

I had pictured some bearded Freudian. I got Joan.

Her office was dimly lit, comfortable and warm. Lush plants filled the corners.

She was a small woman with a kind face behind large eyeglasses. She made me feel ... comfortable.

"First of all," she said, "I'd like you to know that we deal with everyone here on a first-name basis and keep conversations completely confidential."

"All right," I said. "Thank you. I'm pleased to meet you."

After I'd answered some preliminary questions, Joan told me to relax and untie my fingers. I guess my nervousness was obvious.

"I'd like to start by asking you why you've come here today," she inquired softly.

"Well, I guess I don't want to end up in a rubber room somewhere," I answered facetiously. As usual, I used my sense of humor as a buffer, a defense mechanism. "Honestly though," I added, "I'm struggling with depression."

"Do you know why?"

"What do you mean?"

"Have you been depressed for a long period of time or has some recent tragedy caused you to experience this?" Joan asked carefully.

I had trouble replying at first. "Recent tragedy? No. Not really. I mean, sort of ..."

"Okay. Back to my original question. Why did you come here today?"

"Because I'm afraid—" I suddenly said, biting my lower lip. Tears filled my eyes and I lowered my gaze to my lap. Crying always embarrassed me.

She moved her chair a bit closer to mine and bent toward me. "What are you afraid of, Laurie?"

I started to speak but failed to finish, my throat closing like a vise. I began again. "I'm afraid that someday soon I'll start screaming and never stop."

"You feel overwhelmed?"

I nodded.

"What has led to this?"

"The past few years ... my life ..." my voice trailed off again.

"Begin anywhere you'd like," Joan said.

I thought for a moment. Begin? Where? My experiences as a police officer? My difficult marriage? The arrest?

"I think I know who you are," Joan said. "And believe me, what you tell me won't leave this room. So you can relax and begin when you're ready. Okay? Take a deep breath."

I started in 1976, the happy summer I graduated from high school. And somehow I never stopped talking.

■　　■　　■

In time, counseling helped. I learned to accept the emotional help I needed instead of hiding all the pain I felt.

Joan was a warm, empathetic, middle-aged woman who listened to my problems and taught me to seek answers to difficult questions. I was harboring a great deal of anger, a consequence of the injustices that I couldn't fight—the negative publicity, the regret after rushing into a marriage that had more than its share of problems. She taught me that the depression that strangled me was a delayed reaction to the traumatic experience of the arrest, coupled with a lingering fear that remained as a result of the continuing legal process. I felt guilty for feeling resentment after my mother left. It was crazy. I had no right to feel forsaken. I knew these feelings were unjustifiable, but I could not change.

"Your biggest problem," Joan told me, "is that you insist on being independent and bearing this burden alone. You never talk to Fred about your feelings. You never let your dad know what's bothering you. You just try to keep up appearances, keep a stiff upper lip. Your load is too heavy. You must learn to lean on someone.

"My God—look what's happened to your life in less than a year! You got sucked into a whirlwind romance, because everything else in your life was a mess at that time. Your marriage is one that Fred's family won't accept, you had to move from apartment to apartment, and now you've been forced to live in your parents' house. Then you get two small children dumped in your lap and everyone expects you to welcome them with open arms. There are estate problems, custody problems, and then you get arrested for a murder you didn't commit. You've had best friends turn on you, lie about you and stab you in the back. And you wonder why you're depressed? Laurie! Give yourself a break!

"You've had to sit back and watch all of Milwaukee read and believe the worst publicity I've ever seen on TV, radio stations and newspapers, you lost two jobs that you enjoyed, and now you're home, waiting for a decision from a judge. It's like watching your future dangle by a thread. There's a limit to what anyone can take. Can't you let Fred share some of these burdens?"

"He's got enough to worry about. I have to do everything, or he'd never get anything done."

"You might be surprised to find out that, if he had to do certain things, he could. With you doing everything for him, why should he even try?"

I explained the incident involving the unemployment claim cards that I found piling up on Fred's desk.

"I swear that Fred intentionally refuses to do a lot of things that I remind him about—as if to spite me. The trouble is, how do you find the happy medium between a simple reminder and downright nagging?"

"Through communication," Joan replied. "Before you leave today, I'm going to show you some small ways to communicate more effectively."

I looked down and nervously chipped the fingernail polish off my thumbnail.

"When you first met Fred, you admired him, and now that that illusion has worn off, you're pretty disappointed, am I right? Do you still love him?"

"I think so. But I don't like him very much," I said.

"That's probably the best thing you've admitted all day."

Walking from the center to where my car was parked down the street, I pulled my jacket closed against the wind. Bare, spindly tree branches were silhouettes against the dreary, gray sky. I dreaded the approach of winter, and considered the fall season a gloomy prelude to the cold.

■　　■　　■

I received several cards from my mother, who explained that she was too despondent to write letters. My father missed her very much, biding his time until his retirement date when he could fly out west to join her.

Troubles came in bunches for my friends, as well. My former employer from the gym told us that his father was in critical condition with a serious heart ailment. My friend Ginger's ex-husband put a gun in his mouth and committed suicide over financial difficulties and some bad investments. Other friends were out of work or laid off from their jobs. Another friend of ours, a veteran, found it necessary to commit himself to a hospital for depression. He asked Fred to hold onto a suitcase that held his gun collection.

The night Chris was shot, I was supposed to go out with a friend from the gym, Marylisa. She had started dating one of Freddy's brothers, Billy, after I introduced them at a football game. She told me that her father had been convicted of embezzling a large amount of money and was being sent to a federal penitentiary. Her ex-boyfriend, Jeff, had been involved in a drunk driving accident while leaving a wine convention in Lake Geneva. Jeff was in a coma. A female friend who accompanied him was killed in the accident. Marylisa had almost accepted Jeff's invitation to go along. Jeff was given five years' probation for homicide by intoxicated use of a motor vehicle.

Fred appeared at his unemployment compensation hearing, after he was granted a new date. He won, was reinstated and received compensation. Small victories like that were dear to us at a time when everything else was going wrong.

The real estate market continued not to favor us, however, and the house on Ramsey Street remained empty. Fred decided then to rent it out.

■   ■   ■

It's pointless to recall all the fights I had with Fred, all the disagreements, all the times I couldn't understand him. Twice, at home, Fred became so threatening that I called the police, but, as I knew, they could not make him leave the house. That was the law. Once, however, our dispute was violent enough to make the newspapers.

It started because of a football game. Fred had bruised his ribs rather badly in the first game of the season, and I suggested that he sit out a few games, since he had no sick days left to pay for an absence from work. He'd fought so hard to get reinstated in his job—it would be foolish to lose it over a stupid game.

Even though he was hurt badly and winced every time I hugged him or even touched his ribs, he insisted he'd continue to play.

"Don't worry about it," Fred said.

The next game turned out to be a wet, cold, muddy event. Afterwards, Fred ran through the thundershowers back to the van, where I sat watching the teams play. He was irritated not to find me sitting in the bleachers.

"That dedicated I'm not," I told him. "I'm not going to sit there in the rain!"

Fred stripped off his soaked football pants and pulled on a pair of dry jeans. The humidity in the van made the windows cloud with steam.

"Billy and Marylisa want to shoot some pool. Do you want to go? Have a few beers?"

"Okay. Sergeant can sleep on his blanket here in the van."

We found a table at the tavern and began drinking as the rest of the football team walked in, covered in mud and soaking wet. A pool table was free so we started a game. I won twice in a row. Fred became frustrated.

As a joke, he bumped my pool cue just as I started to shoot. I tolerated his mischief at first. The second time was not so funny. After the third time, some balls moved on the table and I became angry.

"You don't know when to quit," I said, putting my pool cue back on the rack. "Cheater."

"So what?" Fred laughed. "Let's just play."

"No. It's almost midnight anyway. Let's go."

We left the bar and began walking to the van. We were drunk and we started fooling around, pushing each other back and forth, like we usually did. It was all in fun, and we were feeling our beers.

"Cheater! Cheater!" I teased, lightly punching Fred's shoulder.

"Quitter!" he sang back.

The horseplay suddenly lost its humor when Fred came around with a flying side kick that knocked me clear off my feet and into a rain-filled gutter on my tailbone. Before I knew what had happened, I was sitting in water and pain shot up my spine.

Fred was grasping my hand and trying to pull me up. I wanted to sit for a few seconds while the pain subsided. As Fred tugged at my arm, I burst out crying.

"Come on! Get up before somebody sees you!" he said.

"Wait!" I screamed. "Are you nuts?"

"The sidewalks are wet. You must have slipped."

"Leave me alone! You kicked me too hard!"

Fred pulled me up as we argued, and we struggled. He tried pushing me into the van.

"Shut the fuck up and get into the goddamn van! You'll wake the whole neighborhood."

I was angry and my back hurt. "I'm not getting into the van!" I cried, shocked because Fred was suddenly acting like a stranger. "I'm not going home with you!" I kicked him in the groin.

An old man walking by tried to break up the fight, but Fred told him it was none of his business. "I'm calling the police," the elderly man said, walking away.

Within minutes, a squad arrived. Since we were outside the city limits, it was not a Milwaukee car, but one from the suburb. I sat down in the back seat of the squad while the cops talked to Fred for a few minutes. I couldn't hear what was being said, but the first question that the police asked me when they got back into the car was, "Are you presently seeing a psychiatrist?"

"No," I lied, sobbing. I felt totally betrayed. How could Freddy tell them that? He's trying to get out of this by telling them that I'm crazy or something!

"Take a deep breath and try to stop crying," one cop told me. "Do you want to file a battery complaint?"

"No. But I want to go to a women's shelter."

In the morning, I thought about what had happened the night before, and I was confused about whether or not to return home. The sobering light of day suggested that I should consider it a drunken scuffle that got out of hand. I wondered if I had reason to believe that it was more. I'd promised myself long ago not to put up with any violence or physical dominance. Yet, if we split up, it would be in the newspapers and that would have a negative effect on my case. I didn't know what to think.

I stepped inside the telephone booth in the hallway of the shelter and made a long-distance phone call to my mom.

■   ■   ■

My mom. Always as calm and fresh as the rain-drenched peonies by the back-yard swing—her skin cool and clean. She would tell me what to do, and then everything would be all right again. I could picture her at the park, in her sleeve-less '50s blouse, the wind swaying the tree branches above her. Safe arms to come home to.

How I missed her!

■   ■   ■

When she answered, I was overcome with emotion, once more a child. My throat closed tightly as my hand gripped the receiver. It was difficult even to get two words out.

"Where are you, baby?" my mom asked, her voice as comforting as an embrace.

A few hours later, my dad picked me up about two blocks away from the shelter. I got into the front seat of his car, forgetting about the bruise on my back, until I winced and shifted my weight. My father was anxious to hear my side of the story, since Fred had already given his version, which of course was completely different. Fred told my dad that I was so drunk that I passed out and fell down. I was disappointed that he had lied to my father.

When I walked into the house, Fred begged tearfully for my forgiveness.

My dad stood by. "I may be sixty-one years old, but I'll be the equalizer the next time you pull this," my dad said. "I have two other daughters that had abusive husbands, and I won't stand for it a third time."

Fred humbly nodded in silence.

Later, I received a call from Don Eisenberg.

"How are you?"

"Okay," I replied, acting cheerful, "except I feel as though I've already been sentenced to six months of daytime television. What's up?"

"You had an altercation with Fred. Anything I should know about?"

"Boy, you don't miss a thing in Madison. No. It's all just about settled now."

"Okay. Anything else?"

"No. Why?"

"Well, Judge Fine wants to see both me and Kraemer about something and I just thought you might know what it's about."

"No."

"Look, as soon as I know anything, I'll call you," Eisenberg promised.

I hung up and watched the yellow phone cord twirl back into the usual tangled mess. Now what? Was the judge going to let me go?

I couldn't have been further from the truth. Judge Fine did not have good news to announce.

Fred's brother, John, had written to the judge, who was obligated to make both the defense and the prosecution aware of the letter. As usual, it caught the attention of the local newspapers, and again a sickening headline appeared.

In the letter, John described his feelings of certainty, saying that he "knew" I was guilty. He had of course no evidence to offer. Somehow he worked in that Fred had been "forced" to marry Chris because of the illegitimate pregnancy; he failed to explain why that was relevant, or had anything to do with me.

The letter alleged that Sean and Shannon had not seen the intruder, as they had told police that night, and said Sean had been "brainwashed" by Fred and me. It said that Sean told John that he did not see the murderer because he ran and hid, too scared to see anything.

He then brought up the incident at the Ramsey house when the Pennings had arrived to collect Christine's personal belongings. Fred had interfered and treated them all "like grave-robbers," he said. And he hadn't even been there!

Later that day, Fred's three other brothers apologized for John and offered their support.

■　　　■　　　■

Before the decision on my preliminary hearing was reached, Eisenberg asked me to drive over to Madison to see him; he had something he wanted to discuss with me. When I arrived, he told me the DA was willing to accept a plea bargain. Kraemer didn't want to try the case. He seemed to believe either that Fred had hired someone to kill Christine, or that Fred and I together had conspired in some way to do it. The prosecution was willing to knock my charge down if I would give them a statement telling them "what I knew."

I was insulted. "Are they crazy? Why should I make up some ridiculous story? Why should I admit to something I didn't do? Do they actually think I would cover up something for Fred?"

"Obviously, Kraemer can't figure this case out, and would be delighted with an explanation from you."

"Don," I protested, "no way would I be stupid enough to be a party to a murder. If Fred hired someone to do it, don't you think he would have had the murderer use a different gun? Or don't you think Fred would have gotten rid of it? He had over two weeks to lose it or report it stolen! Whatever!"

"I'm in the process of talking to my own ballistics expert about this whole thing. A gunshot wound like the one that killed Christine was so close to the skin that the barrel of the muzzle actually penetrated the tissue. According to my expert, both blood and tissue would definitely have blown back into the barrel of the gun. You would have had to clean that gun before Durfee and Fred looked at it. And, if you had cleaned it ..."

"There would have been no dust," I said.

Eisenberg nodded. "Especially since the gun was placed in a holster, back into a closed duffel bag. It doesn't make sense. Well ... this all may be premature. Meanwhile, I should tell Kraemer no plea bargain?"

"No plea bargain," I replied firmly. "I'm not pleading guilty to something I didn't do!"

■　　■　　■

But I'd be out by now, wouldn't I? That's the justice system for you. Stand up for your rights and lose. Cop a plea and win.

If I'd lied and said I did it, I'd be a free woman today.

I'd be sleeping in my own bed now.

I could lock the door from the inside, and keep Them all out.

If I'd known then what I know now, what would I have done?

What should I have done?

What would you have had me do?

I'm thirty-three now, and I've spent a third of my life in a place where guards can strip-search me any time they want to. What would you have done?

■   ■   ■

The day arrived when I was to report to Judge Fine's courtroom for his decision. I wore a brown suit and leather pumps.

A friend rushed up to me as I stepped off the elevator.

"Hi! My—you're dressed to kill. Oops. Wrong choice of words."

"You can't quote sarcasm," I warned.

Judge Fine began reading a prepared statement to a hushed courtroom. He began by saying that the evidence he reviewed was both "questionable" and "contradictory," and that this was the most circumstantial case he had ever seen. I held my breath.

"However ..." He paused, and my heart fell. "I see fit to bind the defendant over for a jury trial, finding probable cause for arrest since the defendant was the only one to have access to the murder weapon the night of the homicide."

Leaving the courtroom, I tugged at Eisenberg's sleeve.

"That's not true!" I whispered hoarsely. "I'm not the only one who had access to that gun! And how do we know that the gun they have now is even the same gun that was in our apartment the night of the murder?"

"Take it easy," Eisenberg told me. "Let's go someplace where we can talk."

I was bound over by Judge Fine because he'd decided that I was the only person who had access to the gun. Yet many months later, at my jury trial, Assistant District Attorney Kraemer would stand up in front of a blackboard and write:

ACCESS TO MURDER WEAPON?
1. Bembenek
2. Schultz
3. Zess
4. Gaertner

The defense party dodged the barrage of cameras and reporters and left the courthouse.

14

A NET OF LIES

In the early part of November, I had a short appearance before a new judge, Michael Skwierawski. Because it was a brief matter, I intended to go alone, but my father insisted on taking me there.

■ ■ ■

I stood before the bench in a plain dress with a drawstring waist. The judge was a young, small man with carrot-red hair and a serious face behind wire-framed glasses. He arranged a trial date for the end of February, leaving three weeks open on his court calendar.

The usual number of cameras and reporters were present at the back of the courtroom. They seemed almost disappointed when the whole affair lasted only a few minutes.

"Much ado about nothing," Eisenberg whispered as we scurried past the press. I nodded.

The following day I finally heard from the Department of Labor, Industry and Human Relations on my sex discrimination complaint. They said they found no cause for a complaint, which meant they weren't going to follow up for me. They said I could go ahead with a case, but with my own lawyer and at my own expense. Thanks.

I had other things on my mind right then, so all I did was mail the information to one of Eisenberg's partners.

After getting the letter, Eisenberg phoned me. He had another subject he wanted to discuss with me.

"Where did you get married to Fred?" he asked when I went to see him.

"Before a judge," I answered.

"What county?"

"It must have been Waukegan County, I think. Anyway, it was in Illinois. Why do you want to know?"

"What was that date?" Eisenberg asked.

"January 31, 1981."

"I think we have a problem. Why did you get married there?"

"Because Fred suggested it—I don't know. We eloped. It seemed romantic, I guess. Why all the questions?"

"I'll have to do some checking, but I don't think you two are legally married," Eisenberg told me.

"I don't understand. That can't be. We have a marriage certificate. We had blood tests done and everything!"

"Right. And it may be that your marriage is recognized in the state of Illinois, but it's not legal in Wisconsin. This state has laws restricting people from remarrying less than six months after their final divorce hearing. When was Fred divorced?"

"I was under the impression that it was in 1979. I'm not really sure because Fred mentioned something about getting a 'bifurcated' divorce—whatever that means. So which hearing would you start counting the six-month period from?"

"He may have been separated from Christine in 1979, but perhaps the divorce wasn't final until much later. It takes a long time. There are property settlements and numerous appearances. Have Fred call me so I can get the facts straight. If your marriage hasn't been legal, the DA will swoop right down on that fact and accuse you of cohabiting. I don't want your credibility attacked."

"What on earth do we do, if it's not legal?" I asked.

"Get remarried in Wisconsin."

When I spoke to Fred about the possibility of our marriage being invalid, I received the usual screwy Fred explanation. He claimed that he had specifically phoned Reilly for advice on the matter of getting remarried and was assured that it would be a legal marriage. He said Reilly told him it might not be recognized in Wisconsin, but that it would be a legal marriage. I stared at Fred in disbelief as he led me through all this.

We planned to remarry in Madison at the end of the month.

■　　■　　■

I was doing my best to pull myself together. I felt I needed a library book, a "How To," maybe "How To Fight Depression While Waiting To Be Tried For First-Degree Murder!" There were certainly no fairy godmothers or ruby slippers to save me.

Maybe the solution was to return to school. Registering at the University of Wisconsin–Milwaukee for the spring semester to study art was my next brave plan. I'd already cleaned and organized every closet, attic and basement space in the house and needed something to occupy my mind.

I'd also lost interest in sex, which didn't help. I guess it went along with my lack of enthusiasm for life in general. I tried to shrug it off as a passing mood, but Fred was not as patient. One night, he and I were upstairs in bed, watching reruns of "The Odd Couple" on TV when my eyelids grew heavy and I found myself fighting sleep. I turned on my side with my back to Fred.

"Are you going to sleep?" Fred asked with irritation. "This is the third night in a row!"

"So?" was my tired response. "I'm falling asleep."

"You don't love me anymore," Fred insisted.

"Don't be ridiculous. I just don't feel like making love. That doesn't mean that I don't love you. Go to sleep."

"No, damn it! Sex was the first thing that went to hell in my last marriage, and I'm not going to let it happen again!"

"Why must you constantly compare me with Chris? You're overreacting."

"No, I'm not!" Fred raised his voice. "You've been so callous these past few months, I don't think you even love me anymore! And now this!"

"Would you be quiet?" I asked Fred. "My dad went to bed a long time ago and he's right beneath us, downstairs. You'll wake him up if you don't lower your voice, and he has to work tomorrow." My temper was rising, and I whispered harshly, sitting up in bed. My father's rhythmic snoring had stopped.

"No! No! I won't be quiet!" Fred said. "It's always the same thing, over and over, living in this house! 'Be quiet or you'll wake up my dad! Don't do this! Don't do that'!" He mimicked me savagely. "Well, I'm sick of it! You always refer to everything as yours. It's your house, your bedroom—"

"This is my mom and dad's house. They are nice enough to let us live here. Now will you shut up?"

"I'm not going to shut up! Living in this house is like living in prison!" Fred snapped.

I threw back the covers and scrambled out of bed, whirling around to look at Fred in the light of the small television screen.

"That's a terrible thing to say! How ungrateful can you get? If you think that living in this house is like living in a prison, then get the fuck out."

"Fine!" Fred bellowed, stomping over to the closet and turning on the overhead light. I watched with anger as he pulled on a pair of jeans and hard-heeled Frye boots, stomping across the polished wooden floor.

"Will you stop making so much noise?" I asked again. Fred ignored me and continued gathering his clothes. I got back into bed and pulled the blanket over my head. As I lay there, I heard his footsteps clatter across the bedroom and go downstairs.

To my dismay, I heard my father get up and open his door, which is just what Fred wanted. He wanted my dad to beg him to stay.

"Freddy? What on earth is going on?" I heard my dad say. "Oh no. Don't do this. Talk things out." My dad suddenly called up the stairs. "Laurie?"

I hopped out of bed and hung over the balcony, shouting, "Let him go! You can't talk to that man. He's crazy!"

■   ■   ■

And so it went. Fights all the time, fights over little things and fights over nothing at all. Fred left, and came back, and left again. Back again, back and forth— but who is to say if he really ever came back?

■   ■   ■

One morning, while Sergeant was preoccupied with his food bowl, I went to the front door to see if there was any mail from my mother. Instead, there was a letter from my attorney, enclosing a statement he'd received from a witness who was willing to testify that Judy Zess had committed perjury.

The house was silent, except for the sound of the wind in the trees outside. I sat down with the papers in my hand, staring at the words, and my mouth fell open as I read it.

This is what it said:

Sometime during the last two weeks of the month of June, I came to know Judy Zess. I had been introduced to her by a mutual friend of her boyfriend and myself. One night in June (I don't know the exact date right now) I had called Ms. Zess and asked her if I could come over to look at a car that she was selling for her boyfriend. Ms. Zess said I should come over around 8:00. I had been to her house a previous night

166

for a short while to view the car, also. This particular night, I arrived about 8:30 or 9:00 PM. Ms. Zess invited me into the apartment again. She escorted me into her dining room and offered me a drink. We talked about Tom Gaertner at great length. I told her about myself and she knew that I was a friend of Tom's. Some time into the conversation, I was told by Ms. Zess that Tom G. was to call her about 9:45 PM or so, as this was a practice of his. That night at approximately 9:45 Tom did call collect from the Federal Jail in Chicago. Ms. Zess and myself went into the bedroom—her and Tom's bedroom. She cautioned me to be quiet while she talked with him. According to the first part of the conversation, they were discussing what Zess had accomplished that day. Zess reported that she had done what he had instructed her to do and went down to the detective bureau and viewed several items that were in evidence in the Schultz murder case.

Of course, this was of considerable interest to me. Judy said, "Yes, I did. Yes, I did," several times, responding to Tom G. After several minutes into the conversation, Zess asked me to listen in on the conversation. Zess asked Tom about the car they were selling and several other items that included jewelry, some dope, etc. Tom was talking about the car. The rest of the conversation centered on his property and romantic concerns. After Zess hung up the phone, we both returned to the dining room and continued to discuss Tom G. and several other topics fell into place. Of course, I during this conversation asked her how she was involved with the Schultz murder case. Zess at this time said: "I guess you are a close friend of Joey and Tom, so I guess I can trust you." She told me that she was going to be a witness in the murder trial of Schultz. She told me and demonstrated how the police had given her a phone tape recorder in case she had any threatening phone calls. Several times when the phone rang, she picked up a device and attached it to the end of the phone, saying later that it recorded what the person was saying on the other line, depending if the caller was friend or foe. Incidentally, she did the demonstration when Tom first called her. She went on to say that she and Tom had been working on some sort of an agreement with the local authorities and federal authorities, whereby they could exchange information about Elfred Schultz's present wife, Lawrencia Bembenek. At that time, apparently the investigation was being centered around Bembenek. I asked her what she might be able to say to them that could possibly help Tom. She said she had that afternoon been down to the

167

Detective Bureau, concerning the identification of articles that Police said were used in the murder. Zess told me that they showed her a wig and a length of cord to identify. She said that the police told her that these items were used and found at the scene. Zess said again that if she cooperated, that this could have a positive effect in Tom's case, according to the police. At this time, I believe she smiled at me and got up from the couch to pour us some wine. She returned and continued to talk about the Schultz case. I asked her about the identification itself. I asked if she could identify these things. She said that as far as she was concerned, the wig could have belonged to her mother. (In jest.) What mattered was if she was willing to say it was in the shared apartment before she moved out. She went on to say that she really didn't remember any wig like this one, but that she had remembered seeing a blond wig or other wigs when the three were living together. I said: "In other words, you are not sure of the wig?" Her reply was: "What do you think, dummy? Saying that it was in the apartment was far more helpful than telling them I never saw it before. I told them that it was the wig." At that time, I said: "Don't you think it is being a little bold to make that identification when there could be a lot of problems with lying and following through?" She said: "Honey, I'm good at it, and other things as well." We later went to the bedroom and while in bed, she received another phone call. She attached the gadget that Frank Cole gave her, and answered the phone. I don't recall who was on the other end, and in fact, the conversation was not the sort that I attempted to remember. She told me she was having sex with Frank Cole because Tom G. had told her to do anything to cooperate and do anything for the police. The next morning, Zess and myself woke up and took a shower together. She received another phone call from Tom G. that I overheard because I was nibbling on her ear. As I recall, they were again talking about Tom's situation, and also how Zess might help him get a deal from the federal authorities. After the conversation was over, I asked Judy what was up. She said Tom had been working on another story that could be what the police want in the Schultz case. Judy told me that she was thinking that if she would say that Bembenek had been asking her to ask Tom about having Schultz's wife taken off, meaning bumped off. She went on to say that they (her and Tom) wouldn't really do anything firm until Tom's trial or after he's tried on the drugs. She said: "Then if he's acquitted, and found not guilty, then we won't have to do shit for the police." She said that they wanted to at least have a story together in case they needed it. I said again: "Aren't you getting a little bold?" She said: "I'm doing it for Tom! Wouldn't you do the same?" I said: "I suppose I would." I again asked Judy if she seriously thought that this would get Tom off the hook with the Feds. She said she thought so. I told her: "What if the Feds want to prosecute a convicted dope pusher more than the State wants a police officer?" She said the bitch probably did it anyway. Tom never killed anyone, and that she loved him. She said: "Don't think I don't love Tom because I slept with you." I said: "I never asked for your love." We both smiled and went back to bed. We were getting dressed and the discussion continued. We talked about several things, but again, the subject that had paramount consideration was the issue of Tom G. and how they could bargain for his release. I said several times to her that I thought that this Federal case had more thrust than the State case, or more importance, and that I didn't think the Feds would let Tom go for the shit that her and Tom were putting together. She appeared to get upset at this time. She said angrily: "Look. The bitch is probably guilty and as far as I am concerned, she's no good. If I have to think up something else, then I will. I want to see them nail her ass to the wall." She then said: "Whatever it takes, Freddy, whatever it takes. Tom never killed anyone." I said: "How do you know she did?" She said: "I don't have to know. I just have to figure out a way to help them prove it." I said: "Damn, what if she really didn't do it?" She said: "Who gives a fuck?" I said: "Maybe Elfred Schultz cares."

She said that Elfred is just as guilty as her or his wife. She then asked: "Whose side are you on?" I told her that going to jail for murder was different than going for dope. That night I again stayed with Judy overnight. While in bed, Judy and I talked about more of her relationship with Bembenek. Just prior to her talking of Bembenek, we were discussing sexual fantasies. I had disclosed to Judy that I didn't mind if two women "got it on" at one time and that I would enjoy going to bed with two such women. Then Judy said one night she had been sleeping in the same bed with Bembenek, just sleeping. Judy admitted that she had always had strong homosexual desires for other women of course to her taste. She said that Bembenek was a very beautiful woman. Judy went on to say that while Bembenek was sleeping, Judy tried to go down on her and when Bembenek woke up, she said she was shocked to find Judy doing what she was doing. Judy told me that after that night, the friendship was not the same and very soon after both Elfred and Bembenek ordered Judy to move out. There are other things that were said, but these things I believe are more relevant to the reason for this statement.

Signed, Frederick Horenberger Dated the 27th day of October, 1981. 6 pages; subscribed and sworn before me on this date 10/27/81, Brian H. Blacker, Notary Public, State of Wisconsin Permanent Commission.

Everything fell into place. Things I was unable to understand before now rang clear. Zess's sudden about-face on the witness stand, her lies—it had all been planned ahead of time, in cooperation with the cops. She'd been waiting for me to call her, to see if she could tape our conversation, hoping I'd say something incriminating.

The impact of the statement was paralyzing.

Even the letter that I received from Zess after my arrest, wishing me the best of luck—it was all part of her game, watching for my next move. If I'd sent her a card in return, she would have turned it over to Frank Cole, the detective who arrested me. I cringed at the thought of her sleeping with Cole. It was despicable—sex as a simple fringe benefit. Horenberger had attached a letter to his affidavit, which described the time he'd bumped into Cole on the way out of Judy's apartment. Cole had been alone, on duty, and arrived in an unmarked car. Horenberger said Cole was not pleased to see him there, and threatened to have his parole revoked.

Waves of sadness washed over me. Parts of the statement echoed inside my head. What had I ever done to Judy? Had she wanted a lesbian relationship with me? If so, I never knew it. She was lying to Horenberger about making a pass at me. It was just one of her fantasies. She never tried anything with me or did anything out of the ordinary.

■　　■　　■

Of course, I could say she did and so help discredit the prosecution's star witness, couldn't I? I could admit to what she had already told Horenberger ... that I woke up in bed with her squirming against me? But it would be a lie. I wasn't going to start lying now.

■　　■　　■

The more I thought it over, the more certain unexplained occurrences acquired new meaning and began to make sense. Certain incidents played in my memory

170

like frames of film, fragmented and out of sequence: Judy's mysterious anger when she found out that I'd married Fred; her over-demonstrative, physical mannerisms; the way she'd collected pictures of me; the way she'd always insisted on wearing my clothes, until she gained too much weight and couldn't get into them.

There was also that first vacation we'd taken together, when a male acquaintance of hers told me that she'd confided in him about her lesbian desires. I'd thought he was joking. True, a lot of cops I knew called her a "dyke," but then they called all the females that, especially those who wouldn't sleep with them.

The thought that someone could feign friendship in hopes of acquiring evidence was sickening. It was also sinister—I even started to suspect that the police were in on her plan. I wished Fred would hurry home so I could tell him about it.

After supper, I filled him in.

"You were so suspicious of Honeck? Take a look at this."

Fred read silently for a few minutes, occasionally raising an eyebrow. When he was done reading, I told him: "There's a transcript even more detailed than the written statement. It says that Horenberger tried contacting several different lawyers with this information, but nobody wanted to have a thing to do with it! One lawyer told Horenberger, 'I don't want to touch it!' I'm just so angry that they knew about it and didn't want to help!"

"That's because it's a heavy thing. The authorities are involved. Nobody wants to get mixed up in it. How did Don finally get hold of it?" Fred asked.

"I guess Horenberger tracked him down. Don told me he plans on subpoenaing Horenberger to the trial, to expose Zess's perjury. The only thing he's worried about is that Horenberger's affidavit involves hearsay, so it might be inadmissible.

"This explains everything, Freddy! For months, it's all been like some impossible puzzle. I couldn't understand why Judy was saying those things! I kept racking my brain, trying to remember if I actually said the things she claimed I did. You know what I mean? I thought that maybe I was drunk so I didn't remember, or that I was joking around—I felt like I was losing my mind!"

Fred nodded. "I know. If people keep insisting that you did something you know you didn't do, there's always that tiny doubt that perhaps you have forgotten, that you're wrong, that it's all a misunderstanding. But these issues are too crucial. They spell intent. They spell motive. Either you had that frame of mind, or you didn't. Now—you see? You weren't going crazy. It was all a preplanned story, testimony that the police could use, in exchange for a deal Gaertner would be interested in. I knew Zess was no good."

A few days later, Fred and I drove to Madison in my car, to get remarried in Eisenberg's office. We had applied for the new marriage license in Milwaukee County Courthouse, and we were somewhat unenthusiastic about the second ceremony. I felt that the first time we married was our real wedding, and that this event was just a legal requirement forced on us by the system. I'd not even bothered to buy fresh flowers or a new dress for the occasion; I wore the same outfit I'd worn for Thanksgiving. There was a brief ceremony—just enough to catch the attention of the newspapers—and we were on our way out the door. Fred suggested that we go to Lake Geneva for lunch, since it was a pleasant drive.

"You said some type of good seafood was served at the Playboy Club's café?" Fred asked.

"It's a seafood quiche," I replied. "It's about four inches high and stuffed with scallops, shrimp, crabmeat and tiny mushroom caps. Very, very good!"

We arrived at the Club, only to discover that there was a convention in progress and the dining rooms were crowded. So we were seated at a bar to wait for a table. I ordered Scotch and watched Fred drink his whiskey too fast. Glancing around uneasily, I thought about the police having been there, questioning my former co-workers. I knew that I'd probably been a major topic of gossip here, like everywhere else.

Fortunately, no one recognized me. Employee turnover at the Club was high. A year had passed, and I had changed.

Midway through lunch Fred told our waitress I'd once worked there.

"Oh, we were just talking about Laurie's days here at the Club!" Fred said as she returned with our check. She didn't seem to make much of his comment, and I quickly changed the subject. She walked away.

"I wish you hadn't said anything about me working here," I said.

"Then you should have said something before we got here!"

"I thought you'd have more common sense."

"Do you have something to be ashamed of?" Fred asked.

"No! I'm not ashamed that I worked here, although I wouldn't put it on my resumé. It was something I had to resort to for a few weeks. I'm ashamed that the police were here, questioning everyone about me!" My quiche lay half-eaten on my plate, turning cold.

The argument went on, circular, useless, depressing. I tuned him out.

■   ■   ■

It seemed to us then that nothing was going to work. Fred was still holding a desk job and feeling harassed at work, so he filled out an application for a job with a suburban police department that had several openings. The next day, an article appeared in the newspapers noting that Fred had applied. Subsequently, he was not hired.

"Damn it!" Fred swore, throwing the *Journal* to the floor. "We can't do anything without it appearing in the paper! Do they have to report everything I do?"

I agreed. "What makes us so important or interesting? They've been on our backs for months."

The following day, I'd just finished a load of laundry and fed Sergeant his supper when Fred walked in. He was early, and clearly upset.

"Sit down. We've got to talk."

I pulled one of the wooden chairs away from the kitchen table. Fred didn't bother to take his coat off.

"If I don't resign tonight, Laurie, they're going to fire me. I knew it was coming. I just didn't know when." Fred pulled on his gloves nervously. "I wanted to come home and talk to you about it first. What do you think?"

"What are the charges?"

"Cohabitation," he claimed. I took his word for it.

"You've got to be kidding."

"It was no secret when we got remarried, thanks to the *Journal*. I can do carpentry work until I get something else. Plus, they're giving me hell because of your pending case ..."

"All those years, and they just kick you out, as if you're nothing but a rookie."

"But if they fire me, they'll have to pay me unemployment," Fred said.

"No way. Look at the fight you had just getting compensation out of them for those few weeks! You spent more money on shrink bills for evaluations than it was all worth."

Fred said he'd resign. He said he felt as though a huge load had been lifted from his shoulders.

Around that time, my dad took his well-earned retirement. I threw a small, inexpensive party for him at a local tavern. His friends, co-workers and brothers came. There was a sandwich buffet, and a cake in the shape of a hammer.

The next morning, while I was still nursing a hangover, the phone rang. It was a friend, with interesting news.

"That Zess character is going out with Stu Honeck now. I saw them at a restaurant last night."

"Were they alone?" I asked.

"No. They doubled with another couple."

173

"I'll tell my lawyer about it," I said. I hung up the phone and pulled my blanket up around my chin, closing my eyes.

When the time came for my dad to leave for the coast to join my mom, Fred and I dropped him off at the airport. He packed a large suitcase and wore a big, quilted jacket. We parked the car in the lot and accompanied him to the gate. I fought back tears—I didn't want to make a scene as he was leaving. He hugged me, picked up his suitcase and disappeared through the door that led to the ramp. As I started to walk away, I glanced at Fred and saw that tears were streaming down his cheeks, too. I was surprised to see that he was as moved as I was.

"Aren't airports terrible places?" he asked.

I was unable to answer and my chin trembled. I had an irrational fear that my dad was leaving, never to return. I knew it was silly, and I tried to ignore my anxiety. I knew my mom and dad would fly back for my jury trial.

During this time I suffered from disturbing, recurring dreams. In one such dream, I was in Florida, moving boxes and furniture into a beach house with several friends. I was embarrassed in the dream, because several of my chairs were tattered and shabby. I joined a crowd of people at a picnic area by the shoreline, when suddenly the tide began to advance rapidly, with great speed and frightening power. The crowd ran up the hill, away from the water, and I ran after them, alarmed because I can't swim. When I reached the top of the hill, I was stopped by a chain-link fence. I was about to hurl myself over it, but it was electrified and the shock threw my hands off. I looked over my shoulder, panic-stricken at being cut off. The waves approached, faster and faster.

I would suddenly wake up, drenched in sweat and gasping for breath, Fred lying next to me asleep, undisturbed.

In another dream, I was in a strange city, applying for unknown jobs and climbing dirty stairways that led into small, old offices. After a short while, I became confused and lost. I walked down the street, searching for a phone, when I heard an ugly, mechanical noise behind me. It was a terrifying grinding, a horrid, rhythmic clicking. When I turned, I saw a robot-like creature following me, with the head of a skull, wearing an Uncle Sam hat. Its jaw opened and closed jerkily. I ran. I found a telephone in a hallway, but before I could call, strange people were strapping me down on a stretcher and injecting something into my arm. I struggled with them, pleading and begging to be allowed to call my husband.

I would wake up, clutching the bed covers and too scared to move an inch or even open my eyes.

Life went on. The days passed. Fred suggested we go to Vegas, and we did. We visited our friends in Florida. But none of it meant anything, not really.

■　■　■

I remember a woman we met in Vegas, who recognized me. "I'm so glad your case is over," she said. "I always thought it was bullshit."

"But it isn't," I said.

"Oh," she said, "but I thought the little boy, the eyewitness, said it wasn't you?"

"He did," I said, "but they don't seem to care."

"I'm so sorry," she said. "I think you're adorable."

I didn't know what to say. I never know how to take compliments like that.

And of course it wasn't over, not by a long shot.

■　■　■

After we'd returned from Florida, I casually glanced through the Sunday paper and saw a piece about Fred Horenberger, who'd sent Eisenberg the statement about Zess. He and two other men, Danny Gilbert and Mark Eckert, had been convicted of armed robbery against Judy Zess. I was distraught. Horenberger had pleaded not guilty but was convicted by testimony from Zess, who maintained that, since he'd been to Gaertner's apartment several times, he'd had plenty of opportunity to arrange the robbery. I grabbed a pair of scissors and cut out the article.

"Convicted?" I said. "Tied in to that robbery and convicted! My God—there goes my witness! He knew too much. That's why he's gone. He saw Frank Cole at Judy's. She told him about the deal she and Tom were making with the cops. She told him about her plans to lie on the witness stand. She told him about her affair with Cole. Now Horenberger's gone!"

I showed the article to Fred. "Now that he's in prison, he can't testify for me—can he?"

"Sure he can. But his credibility is shot. Now it'll look like he's just testifying against Zess to get even with her."

"But Horenberger gave us the information *before* all of this!" I said. "I've got to call Don, first thing in the morning."

■　■　■

My confidence deteriorated. First, my counselor Joan's husband had a heart attack and she had to leave the center, canceling our weekly sessions. I never saw her again. Then my mother phoned to break the news that she was going into the hospital for an emergency hysterectomy. Her doctor said she would not be allowed to travel for at least eight weeks after the operation, which meant that she couldn't be home for my trial. The tidal wave dream occurred more often. I grew afraid to fall asleep, knowing that I'd only have another nightmare. I had spells of overpowering anxiety.

One morning I was sitting in a drawing class at the university, completing an assignment. When I was done, I was allowed to take a break. As I left the room to buy a cup of coffee from the machine in the hall, a terrible feeling washed over me. I felt frightened, but I didn't know why. I didn't want to be where I was, yet I had no idea where I wanted to go.

I had to talk to someone. I almost ran down the hallway between the rows of green lockers. When I reached the pay phone on the first floor, I dialed home and prayed Fred would answer.

He was home! Thank God!

"Fred?" I began to cry and could barely talk.

"What's wrong?"

"I don't know." I tried to explain what I was experiencing, without sounding like I was losing my mind. I didn't understand it myself.

"Do you want me to pick you up?"

"Yes ... no! I've got to try to make it through the rest of my classes, otherwise I'll never be able to come back. Let me try."

I made it through the day.

For days, I felt like a child, afraid to be alone. I stayed awake all night, unable to sleep. At last, a doctor prescribed an anti-depressant drug for me; he assured me it was non-addictive, because I was afraid of drugs.

One by one, I dropped my university classes. My days were colorless, endless.

I got very drunk one night and burned three books of my poems in the incinerator, my tears sizzling and hissing in the fire. I tried to burn the pain, but it wouldn't go away.

The bad news kept coming. One morning a headline on the front page of the morning paper caught my eye. At first reading it seemed meaningless. I read it again: "JUDGE ORDERS SCHULTZ TO PAY $6,600 TO SONS."

Wincing, I read over the article. A hearing had just been held in front of Judge Curley, who had ordered Fred to hand over half of his pension money to the children.

According to the original divorce stipulation, Christine was entitled to half of Fred's pension when he retired from his job on the police force, whether or not she remarried. As a result of her death, the boys inherited this money. The

176

Pennings petitioned the court for the money, and they got it. The court was told by Kershek that Fred was also delinquent in his child-support payments. Child support? Fred wasn't required to pay the Pennings or Barb and Bruce Christ child support. Or was he?

The article reported that Fred was shirking his visitation rights, since the guardians had dutifully brought the children from out of state to see their father, only to be told he was vacationing in Florida. I wanted to scream.

Vacationing in Florida? *They* had failed to bring Sean and Shannon down for three or four weeks in a row—including the week Fred and I were in Florida! I felt the lies strangling me. I called Fred over.

"Look at this! Look at the way they make it sound!"

He just tossed it to the floor.

"How can they print any of this, without bothering to verify it?"

"We can't fight it," Fred said calmly.

"We have to!" I cried.

"No."

A few days later, I lost my wedding band at the health club. I'd been working with Fred, who was installing a sauna. We had already arrived home when I noticed it was gone. Although we made every effort to recover it, it seemed to have vanished. I guessed it had gone down the drain when I washed my hands.

Our anniversary arrived. Fred and I had been married only one year. It was overcast and reasonably warm outside for the end of January. We went shopping on the East Side and ended our afternoon with a tour of an art gallery. I didn't feel much like celebrating.

■　　■　　■

The trial was drawing nearer. A letter from my mom arrived. Her doctor was impressed with her recovery and was willing to allow her to travel. I smiled at the good news, knowing that she'd return with my dad for my trial.

I drove through the snow to the airport to meet them. Their flight had been delayed because of the weather. Fred waited in the car while I walked through the sliding glass doors of the terminal.

As soon as I spotted my parents, I broke into a run to embrace them, my face wet with tears.

"Don't cry. We're home now," my mom said softly.

■　　■　　■

Within a few days, Eisenberg called. He'd filed a Motion for Discovery and was given copies of all the police reports. He was finally able to review everything the prosecution was planning to use against me. The trial was one month away.

The police had turned over stacks of reports that filled four huge boxes. The subject matter varied from the utterly irrelevant to statements given by potential witnesses.

There was a report from a member of my Police Academy class, Boville, who told them that I once said I felt I could do anything a man could do. Another report simply confirmed that Fred and I had gone to Florida in May. There were various interviews and interrogations with about twenty different suspects, their mug shots included—all of them male.

Many reports were from concerned citizens, who called to say that they had seen a male jogger in that neighborhood on Ramsey Street. Another pile of reports made up the Judy Zess statements. Some reports were from the Crime Lab. The stack of paper was enormous.

Then Eisenberg pulled out a report involving a woman named Kathryn Morgan. "Where was your mother on June 18?" he asked.

Quickly I looked at my pocket calendar and flipped to the month of June. "It was a Thursday ... were my parents on vacation that week?"

"I hope so. The State has a witness named Mrs. Morgan who claims that she saw your mother going through the garbage at your old apartment complex. She says your mother took something home with her in a garbage bag."

"What!"

"Morgan says that on June 18 she was sitting outside her apartment across the yard from your old place when a woman pulled up in a car. She said the woman was about five feet, seven inches tall, forty-five years old, about 130 pounds, with brown hair. Wearing shorts and a tank top. Morgan claims the woman got out of her car and approached her to inquire if the green bins were the trash containers for the apartments. She then claims the woman went to the garbage bin, pulled out a bag, put it in her car and left."

Eisenberg looked up from the report. "How tall is your mother?"

"Don—no way. She's five-seven, but she's fifty-eight-years old! Impossible. Morgan's either crazy or a liar. If my mom and dad weren't on vacation, then my mom must have been babysitting for Sean and Shannon, because I used to work every Thursday until 3:00 PM."

"Does Virginia drive?" Eisenberg asked, using my mother's first name.

"Not much anymore ..."

"What color is your dad's car?"

"Metallic gold or bronze."

178

"Is it new?"

"Yes."

"Four-door?"

"Two-door. But Don! My dad always takes the car to work! My mom wouldn't have the car at 2:30 on a weekday. Did Morgan get a license number?"

Eisenberg showed me the report.

"Well! The license number is wrong! My God! I can't believe this! Do you know how huge those garbage bins are? I'm tall, but I could never reach into the bin outside the building. The opening was just high enough for me to flip the door open and toss the garbage bag in. My mother wouldn't be tall enough to reach down inside it."

"The State is probably trying to prove that you threw out some evidence and had your mother retrieve it for you," Eisenberg mused. "Is there any way we can prove your dad had the car that day?"

"I'll find out. Maybe his boss can remember. It's all so ..." I paused as something struck my memory. "Remember when my mother testified at my preliminary? Something happened that was strange. Just before Kraemer was finished with his cross-examination, he asked my mom to remove her glasses. Obviously, she complied, and then he told her to put them back on. Let me see that report again."

I scanned the typewritten lines with the aid of my fingernail.

"Here! It says that Mrs. Morgan identified Virginia Bembenek on September 2, 1981, as the woman she saw on June 18, 1981. Morgan identified my mother only after she removed her glasses! The description Morgan gave the police does not include glasses. My mom can't drive without her glasses. She can barely see without them. Her eyes are so bad that she doesn't dare drive at night or on the freeway anymore."

"This is good," Eisenberg agreed. "We're going to have to bring all of this up at your trial. If by chance your parents were on vacation that week, then we're safe."

"I find it so incredible that all these crazy people come forward with all of this bullshit!"

"I know," Eisenberg agreed. "It always happens with a widely publicized case such as yours. People are thrill-seekers. They want to get in on the act. Bored housewife plays detective. And who knows? Maybe there was some loony digging around in the garbage that day. Cities are full of bag ladies."

"Not bag ladies driving new cars, Don! It's an absurd lie, I'm sure! Would someone who wanted to remove evidence go up to a local resident, chat in broad daylight, the car sitting right there?" I was disgusted.

"Well, Mrs. Morgan certainly doesn't help us. Circumstantial evidence by itself is nothing, but it's like little building blocks. You have this witness, and that statement, and this, and that, and pretty soon you build yourself a case."

"But none of it is true!" I protested.

"There are many reports about Fred in here. Many of Christine's friends told the police that Fred physically abused her. There's one from Jo Anne Delikat."

"Dennis's ex-wife. Dennis who now lives in Florida."

"And one from a woman named Polka, and a report from Attorney Kershek. He says Fred threatened Chris the last time they argued. He claims that Fred stopped paying her alimony."

"That's not true. Kershek represents the Pennings."

I flipped through another stack of reports. "Most of these statements were taken in July, after my arrest."

"When did you last see Christine's babysitter?" Eisenberg asked.

"At the funeral. She's about fourteen or fifteen."

"This report says that she claims you and Fred were at the house on Ramsey sometime in May, to pick up Sean for a game, and Fred gave you a tour of the house. She says you talked to the children in front of her—what's her name? Tammy. Tammy says she heard you ask where the dog was."

"No way. Fred never gave me a tour. Plus, I knew that dog was gone in February. Why would I ask about the dog in May?"

"May seems to be the month of interest, obviously. Were you ever at the house before the murder?" Eisenberg asked.

"Yes, but I never went through the house. Once I waited in Fred's van, and once I waited in the entranceway at the front door."

I carted the remainder of the reports home with me. Eisenberg told me to read them all carefully—an exhausting job.

My mother was appalled when I told her about the Morgan woman's allegations. The vacation she and my dad took was ill-timed—the week following June 18.

I sat down in a chair to read the rest of the reports. Then I came across Fred's statement from that night. Fred wrote that after the shooting, he and Durfee arrived at our apartment, and Fred felt the hood of my car, to determine whether it had been driven recently, but it was cold. I thought that was an extremely odd thing to do.

Another report in the pile was written by Fred's lieutenant, Ruscitti, who said Fred had approached him to report finding some of his bullets out of place—again, conveniently, in May.

The report said that Fred claimed to have questioned me about the bullets, but I denied knowing anything about it. The style in which the report was written gave the impression that I had clearly been tampering with Fred's ammunition. I leaped from my chair and stomped into the kitchen, where Fred was eating a sandwich at the table. Dropping the page in front of him, I stood with my arms folded.

He read the report and looked up at me, blank-faced. I stared back silently.

"What?" he asked.

"What on earth did you tell your lieutenant?"

"I didn't tell Ruscitti anything! I mean, what I told him isn't written down here. It was misconstrued."

"Why would you tell him something like that? It's not true! I feel so betrayed! What are you trying to do to me?"

"Laurie, I was telling him about the time when I found that bullet on the floor by my clothes tree."

"By your clothes tree, in your corner of the bedroom, where you used to hang your ammo belt and gun and everything else! I remember the incident! We already had the boys, Fred! Sean and Shannon were right there. And you accused them of playing with your bullets, when the damn bullet probably just fell out of your pouch to the floor. That happened in June! After Christine's death!"

"So?"

"So the report says May. And it says that you claimed to question me about it. This report wouldn't exist if you hadn't gone to Ruscitti about it in the first place! A bullet falls out of your ammo pouch, amidst all of your junk in the corner, and the next thing I know, my husband runs to his commanding officer about it!"

"What I told Ruscitti was that it would have been possible for Judy Zess to have been looking over my ammunition. That's what I told him. I don't know why he wrote that other shit."

"You turned an innocent incident into a condemning one!" I said. "You of all people should know how the police misconstrue reports. And you felt the hood of my car that night? Why, for God's sake?"

"I did that in front of Durfee on purpose! I did it to show him that it was cold! That way, they couldn't turn around and—"

"But Fred! Why would you do that? Why would you even *do* something like that, unless you were suspicious? How could you?"

Then I mentioned the police reports that alleged Fred had physically abused Christine.

"Those people have as much credibility as Mrs. Morgan!" Fred argued. "They're lies! Just like the report about your mother is a lie. Just like the reports about you are lies. Did I ever doubt you for even one second? I don't believe any of the lies about you—why should you believe the reports about me?"

There was something to that.

■   ■   ■

Something, but not everything. So many little lies, so many "innocent mistakes," misconceptions, misconstruings. Was I being paranoid when I wondered, miserably, why people never misconstrued anything my way?

I could feel the net of lies tightening about me.

Left: Taylor Avenue, Milwaukee, 1961. I was three.
My sister Colette took the picture.

Right: First communion, 1966. I was ten, in the second grade.
My mother took this one.

I was twelve or thirteen here, I think.
I know my mother made this outfit—she was always making me clothes.

Both of these pictures were taken when I was
seventeen, for a portfolio I was putting together to
launch a modeling career.
The photographer, I remember, wanted a rural
setting to set off some of the other, more elegant
clothes that I wore.

Above: In my Milwaukee Police
Department uniform at Taylor Avenue.

Right: Fred Schultz at the infamous
Tracks picnic. How I wish I'd never
seen those pictures!

MILWAUKEE JOURNAL PHOTO

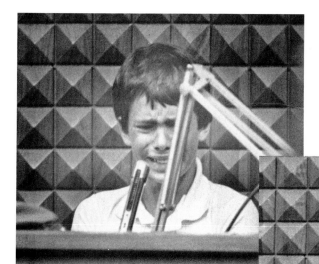

MILWAUKEE SENTINEL PHOTO

Above: In my Marquette
uniform, just after
my arrest.

Below: Judy Zess, the
prosecution's star witness, who
later recanted what she said,
claiming she'd
been bullied into it.

Above: Young Sean Schultz
crying on the witness stand at my
preliminary hearing.
He said very clearly that the
person he'd seen
was not me. I was greatly
moved by his strength and his bravery.

MILWAUKEE JOURNAL PHOTO

Here I am with Don Eisenberg. This was when we returned to court after the preliminary hearing and the judge bound me over for trial.

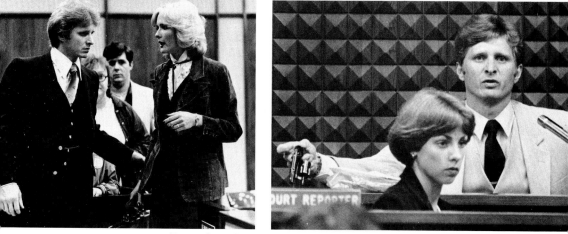

Left: Here I am with Fred at my preliminary hearing. This was before he accepted immunity from prosecution and testified against me.

Right: Fred Schultz on the witness stand at my trial. He is holding the gun—the one that was "proved" to be the murder weapon.

MILWAUKEE JOURNAL PHOTO

Above: Judge Michael Skwierawski,
the trial judge.

Left: Mug shot of Frederick Horenberger.
There is considerable reason to think
that he might have been the
one to have pulled the trigger.
He committed suicide in
Milwaukee late in 1991.

AP/WIDE WORLD PHOTOS

This is one of the many pictures of me in court. This one isn't from my trial
but from a later appearance, I think about 1986.

Above: This was a meeting of the
Inmate Output "editorial board."
It was held in the Home Ec room at
Taycheedah, for lack of any other
space. That's Kathy Braun on the right,
and Judy in the background.

Left: This is my mom's favorite. She has
it hanging on the wall in her home
in Milwaukee.

Left: A group of friends in Taycheedah. We all won trophies for something.
Mine was for poetry, I think, though Kathy Braun entered me as a joke in a spelling bee
and, to her surprise, I actually won! As you can plainly see, we're not all hard cases and
crazies. Actually, we look rather ordinary, don't you think?

Center: This was my graduation day. I received an Associate of Arts degree from the
University of Wisconsin at Fond du Lac. The ceremony was held at a men's prison called
Kettle Moraine, in 1986.

Right: This picture was taken in the visitors' room at Taycheedah. It was just after the
"cosmetology department" was closed, and all the bottle-blonds were going "Eeek." I cut
my hair short—didn't want to look like a calico cat.

Left: Taycheedah, 1990.

Above: This was a wonderful moment during my brief months of freedom in Canada. It was taken in September 1991 in a park just outside Thunder Bay, Ontario. The Kentucky Fried Chicken bag is full of popcorn— one of the forgotten little pleasures of freedom.

Right: My Thunder Bay counsel. Dave Dubinsky was doing pro bono work the day I needed a lawyer. His partner, Ron Lester (now a judge), picked out a refugee claim as a possible defense.

Left: With my mom and dad at a Canadian immigration hearing, 1991.

Below: Ira Robins, my very own personal pitbull.

PHOTO BY NIGEL DICKSON

Above: Here I am with my Canadian attorney, Frank Marrocco, at an immigration hearing. I've learned to trust his judgment —he's always thinking four moves ahead, like a chess player.

15

WOMAN ON TRIAL

The first few days of my trial were uneventful, even boring. There was a lot of legal mumbo jumbo. Most of the time was spent picking a jury, an intricate process full of challenges, counter-challenges and eliminations. Finally, a jury was chosen. Two alternates were added in case of illness. Seven women and five men held my fate in their hands.

Few of the prospective jurors cared to do more than glance furtively at me as we sat in the small annex room adjacent to the judge's chambers. I studied them intently. A retired, old black man with an extreme underbite who wrapped himself in a gray cardigan sweater sat next to a large, solemn woman with a double chin. She said she was a homemaker, sitting erect and folding her hands in her lap. Another woman had the appearance of a schoolteacher as she squinted through thick eyeglasses. There was one young woman, who wore jeans and a simple hairstyle. The male jurors were all older men.

Eisenberg whispered to me during the lengthy process, "By the way, on several occasions now, I've attempted to contact the Pennings or the Christs through Calvey. I wanted to interview Sean Schultz before he testifies again, but I think there is going to be a problem. I sense some resistance on their part."

Before the jury was allowed into the courtroom, the court dealt with several motions Eisenberg had filed, and held a "suppression hearing."

The issue at hand was the legality of the warrantless search of my locker at Marquette. Long after my arrest, two detectives had confiscated my purse from my locker, later contending that hairs from my hairbrush matched a hair found on Chris's body at the morgue.

183

"This evidence was seized after a warrantless search, and so should be ruled inadmissible," Eisenberg told me.

He began to flip rapidly through the heavy stacks of folders on the table. All the police reports had been arranged and bound alphabetically.

He found a page that listed Crime Lab findings and underlined a section that referred to hair and fiber analysis. Several blond hairs were found that "presumedly" matched Shannon Schultz's hair, but samples from his head were never obtained to verify this assumption. Other hair discovered on Christine's bed was unidentified and ignored. Eisenberg underlined the sentence that listed "one color-processed blond hair" that was found "consistent in characteristics" with the hairs from my hairbrush and "could be from the same source."

"This is the sloppiest police work I've ever seen!" Eisenberg said to me. "Could be? Could be? You might be convicted on 'could be's or could not be's?' Jesus Christ! And to top it off, it was an unconstitutional search!"

Thomas Conway, who'd been my sergeant at Marquette, took the stand. He was at that time unemployed. He testified that after my arrest I gave him my locker combination so he could retrieve my extra uniforms. The police had then removed me from the premises.

As he'd opened the locker, two detectives had appeared and asked if they could be present during the examination of the locker contents. Conway had found a variety of items inside—personal articles and Marquette property. As he began lining them up on a bench, the police snatched up my purse and told him, "We'll need this."

To my surprise, Eisenberg informed me that he wanted me to testify briefly about these events in Conway's office.

I walked to the witness stand, nervous and self-conscious. I was overly warm in the sweater dress I wore, and my slip clung to my stockings from static electricity.

A few minutes later, it was over. I had explained that I gave Conway permission to collect the extra uniforms, but not my personal property. I thought I did all right. I was glad of the chance to testify so briefly. It was good practice for the lengthy testimony I would give at the end of the trial.

■　　■　　■

The court recessed and I wandered out into the hall. When I returned, the judge, Michael Skwierawski, ruled on several of the motions that Eisenberg had filed.

"Motion to dismiss this case due to lack of probable cause: denied. The issue of probable cause was dealt with at the defendant's preliminary hearing before the Honorable Ralph Adam Fine, and I don't choose to usurp another judge's decision," Skwierawski began.

"Why even file a motion if you know it will only be denied?" I asked Eisenberg. It seemed foolish to me.

"For the record," he whispered.

"Likewise," the judge continued, "motion to dismiss due to the inadequacy of the complaint is denied. Motion to suppress the hair evidence, seized from the defendant's locker, is also denied. Although the police did not secure a warrant for this seizure, I don't feel that one was necessary in this situation, because it is my opinion that the police were not there acting as a governmental body."

The police were not there acting as a governmental body? What were they? A glee club?

Skwierawski droned on in the esoteric jargon of judicial decisions, quoting several state statutes. I wondered why judges and lawyers couldn't use plain English. Eisenberg argued and made his objections, and I listened to the proceedings until I heard a noise in the back of the courtroom. Turning my head slightly, I saw the District Attorney, E. Michael McCann, walking next to Police Chief Harold Breier.

Eisenberg had subpoenaed the Chief of Police, along with an order for discovery that included access to Department records on Stu Honeck and Judy Zess.

Kraemer immediately objected. "Your Honor! I must object to the defense's request for these records! I also object to Mr. Eisenberg's strategy. His intentions are focused upon pointing the finger at other suspects, and that is not his job! His job is to defend Miss Bembenek, not identify other possible defendants!"

"Your Honor," Eisenberg protested, "may it please the court to understand that the defense's sole purpose in subpoenaing this information is to inform the court that previous testimony by these witnesses was perjury. At the preliminary hearing, Mr. Honeck denied having any problem with alcoholism, and I believe these records will show that he does indeed have a problem, which may be relevant to his recollection of the events on the night of the murder. If he consumed a great deal of alcohol that same night—"

"Your Honor!" Kraemer interrupted. "Whether Mr. Honeck is an alcoholic or not bears absolutely no relevance whatsoever to this case, and I see no reason why it should be admissible!"

"Gentlemen!" the judge finally exclaimed. "If you'll stop for a moment, I'll tell you that I intend to review the records of both Miss Zess and Mr. Honeck in the privacy of my chambers, and decide whether or not they in fact have any relevance to this case. I will announce whether or not I shall deem them admissible. The court will recess approximately one half hour."

While we waited, Eisenberg asked, "Did Fred see Sean and Shannon this past Sunday?"

"No. There was a hassle. Fred tried to see the boys after their appointment with the child psychologist, but he said he fought with Barb. So he called a police sergeant and showed him a copy of the visitation stipulation, but even that didn't work. Fred says the Pennings are afraid that if he has the boys for the afternoon, he'll meet with you and let you talk to them."

"What the hell are they afraid of?" Eisenberg grumbled. "I talked to those children before, and they had no objection. I have every right to talk to witnesses before they testify. It makes them less nervous because it prepares them for the types of questions that will be asked."

"All stand," the bailiff commanded as the judge returned.

Skwierawski, consistent with his pattern of denying all our motions, announced that he chose to suppress the records of both Zess and Honeck.

Half the week had already slipped by.

Kraemer's opening argument, in which he began to lay out the framework of the State's case, was enough to warrant an Emmy award. Solemnly he asked the jury to think of him as Christine Schultz's lawyer. He spoke with a false piety that was dismaying in its transparent pretense.

The jury listened intently as Kraemer laid out his bizarre theory. Apparently, money had been the motive. We hadn't wanted to kill Christine, not really. We just wanted to scare her out of her house, "so that the defendant and her husband, Fred, could move in."

I was sitting next to Eisenberg at the wooden table behind the prosecution. I crossed my legs and couldn't help fidgeting. Finally, I pulled the cap off a felt-tipped pen and began scribbling on a long, yellow pad of paper Eisenberg had again provided for my comments.

"If Kraemer says there was no intent to kill, then why was I charged with first-degree murder?"

For the rest, I couldn't even comment. How idiotic to think a grown woman could be scared out of her own house! How farfetched! Why wouldn't she just change the locks or buy a guard dog or have someone stay with her? Why would she just move out? Christine's boyfriend was a cop, after all. Besides, Fred and I had had a terrible fight over moving into that house. The theory struck me as a patchwork, pieced together for lack of anything credible.

Kraemer's little drama continued. "Ladies and gentlemen of the jury, I believe the evidence will prove that once Christine Schultz heard the cries of her children, her maternal instinct told her to fight for those children—even if it meant she would risk her own life, which she did. The defendant realized she would have to shoot Christine, when Christine got up, turned around and recognized that it was, in fact, Lawrencia Bembenek who was in her house that night ...”

I was supposedly disguised in a wig and whatever else. How would Chris recognize me? She got up and turned around—yet she was shot in the back? How could he say these things without blushing?

"You see," Kraemer continued, "Ms. Bembenek likes to live life in the fast lane. She wears designer clothes, likes expensive vacations, and has even said that she married Fred for his vasectomy, since children would only burden her extravagant lifestyle.

"Another burden for Ms. Bembenek was the amount of money her husband Fred was forced to pay his ex-wife: in excess of seven hundred dollars a month! Allowing Christine Schultz to live in the luxurious tri-level house on Ramsey, rent-free. A house that Ms. Bembenek wanted to live in desperately. A house that Elfred Schultz built with his own two hands and then was forced to give up—to a woman he no longer loved."

My lawyer made several objections to the style in which Kraemer's argument was delivered. Skwierawski was seemingly already so irritated by Eisenberg's objections that he called them improper. However, he did advise the jury that the statements being made by the District Attorney were not to be considered "evidence"; they were to be considered theory only, which Kraemer would try to prove.

Kraemer continued: "If only Christine Schultz had had her head down, like a good girl, I think Ms. Bembenek would have grabbed the jewelry box and fled. But Christine didn't. She didn't because of the screams she heard emanating from the bedroom shared by her two little boys. Sean and Shannon are attacked by the defendant, and Shannon begins to kick about at the person who is on top of his brother. You can just imagine, ladies and gentlemen, what went through Christine's mind when she heard her children calling for help. You can imagine the sound emanating from that bedroom—"

"Well, now, Your Honor! I object to this! This is not an opening statement!" Eisenberg exclaimed.

"Sustained," the judge said dryly.

"Would the court instruct the jury to disregard Mr. Kraemer's last two or three sentences? There is no way for Mr. Kraemer to know if the children screamed, or if Christine heard screams. There is no evidence of that. There is no evidence that anything went through Christine Schultz's mind!"

"Just proceed, Mr. Kraemer," the judge commanded. "Sit down, Mr. Eisenberg."

He sighed and returned to his seat, shaking his head.

"There were screams coming from that bedroom," Kraemer said. "Screams heard across the hall by Christine Schultz, the mother of those two children."

"I object!" Eisenberg said again. "If it please the court, there is no way in the world that this man can prove that Christine Schultz heard anything!"

"Overruled."

He refused to be silenced. "Also, Your Honor, I believe it is prejudicial and I'd like to approach the bench."

"Request denied," Skwierawski replied.

What was going on? I felt that Skwierawski was acting more like a prosecutor than a judge! If this continued, it would be impossible for the jury not to be influenced by it. I threw a puzzled glance Eisenberg's way.

After my lawyer's opening argument, the State announced its intention to call Sean Schultz to the stand first—obviously to minimize his testimony. Eisenberg explained that Kraemer remembered how strong Sean had been at the preliminary, and wanted to weaken the impact he'd have on the jury. The jury would be ultimately less affected by Sean's testimony if it was heard first and several weeks of testimony followed it. It's only human nature to remember what one hears last with more intensity.

I realized for the first time that a trial was like a poker game. Because Eisenberg had insisted on having witnesses testify at the prelim, perhaps we had shown too much of our "hand."

Before the bailiff was instructed to summon the jury back into the courtroom, Eisenberg informed the court that he had not been allowed to interview Sean since the previous August.

"Your Honor, it has been about five months since the child last testified. Because of his age, his memory is bound to fade faster than an adult's. I have requested several times of the temporary guardians to interview Sean, and have subsequently been faced with blatant opposition."

Kraemer quickly stood up. "Your Honor! The grandparents of Sean have told me that Mr. Eisenberg has influenced the boy's testimony, and that the last time he was allowed to question Sean, the child became extremely upset and cried all the way home."

"Your Honor!" Eisenberg's voice angrily boomed throughout the courtroom. "Please excuse my choice of words, but the grandparents are nothing but liars! At no time would I stoop to something as despicable and unethical as to attempt to influence a child's testimony! I'll stake my professional reputation on it! I talked to Sean last August at my office in Madison, in the presence of the guardian ad litem! Where's Lee Calvey?" Eisenberg turned to see if Calvey was still in the courtroom. "He will vouch for me. Subpoena him if you wish. I object to Mr. Kraemer repeating such slanderous accusations in open court and I maintain that I have every right to talk with Sean Schultz before he testifies! The children have asked if they could talk to me. They want to talk to me. I attempted to communicate with Barb Christ on a conference call, and she ended our conversation by hanging up on me!"

Kraemer said nothing further. Maybe he realized that the Pennings had exaggerated. Perhaps, in their grief, they viewed all of us with suspicion and hate, which I guess was understandable.

Judge Skwierawski paused and blinked his eyes. "Let me advise both counsel that it is neither a right, nor a violation of any kind to interview a witness prior to testifying. If the children do indeed wish to speak with Mr. Eisenberg, but have been prevented from doing so, then I think it is the court's obligation to intervene. I will allow the interview to take place. However, I think it is necessary to ask the children again, before any decision is made regarding this matter. The court will recess. Mr. Kraemer and Mr. Eisenberg will meet me in my chambers in twenty minutes, if all parties can be contacted."

While the court was in recess, I made for the restroom in the hallway. I was followed by my sister-in-law, Bob's wife Chris. As we went in, Judy Zess came out, and although I glared at her, she refused to return my gaze and passed by me in silence.

"She'll probably run to Kraemer and tell him that I threatened her in the bathroom," I told Chris. "You're my witness that nothing was said."

Fred's brothers were in the courthouse hallway, with his father and uncle, talking to my mom and dad. All potential witnesses had to remain outside the courtroom because of the sequestration ruling. I could tell that my mother was already exhausted.

"You won't be called to testify, mom," I said. "Why don't you go home and lie down?" She was still recuperating.

"I don't understand why we can't go inside," my mom said, with emotion in her voice. "It's driving me to distraction to sit out here and wonder what's going on in the courtroom!"

"I know." I nodded, feeling helpless. "Are you going home?"

"No," she said. "We're not leaving you."

I returned to the courtroom and followed my lawyer into the judge's chambers. Fred and I sat down on a couch against the wall as reporters filled the hallway that led into the annex and the offices of the court reporters.

A scraggly plant sat on the windowsill, its dry branches tumbling down toward the floor. Kraemer and Eisenberg discussed something off to the side. Skwierawski sat back in his chair, waiting. Several pictures, drawn in crayon by children, were taped to the paneled wall behind the judge.

Barb Christ entered the room with Sean and Shannon, her husband Bruce following her. I looked at her, seeing the resemblance she bore to her sister Christine, but her eyes avoided me entirely. Her bleached hair hung thin and straight, framing her jawline. Hovering over the boys, she instructed them to sit down in front of the judge.

"Hello, Sean. Hello, Shannon," Skwierawski said, trying to ease their nervousness in a room full of strangers. "I have a few questions to ask you today. The first question is whether or not you want to talk to Mr. Eisenberg today, before you testify. You can talk to him, if you want to. Or you don't have to talk to him, if you don't want to.

"The second question is whether or not you want to talk to Mr. Eisenberg alone, or in front of anybody. Do you understand?"

Both boys nodded. Shannon glanced at his father.

"Okay." The judge nodded back. "Would you like to talk to Mr. Eisenberg? You don't have to if you don't want to."

"Yes," Sean replied. "I want to talk to Mr. Eisenberg."

"Would you mind talking to him in front of your aunt and uncle?"

"That won't be necessary," Sean responded.

Suddenly Barb asked, "Don't I have any say so in this matter? I'm the guardian, and I think that if Mr. Eisenberg has anything to ask them, he can do so in front of my lawyer and me."

The judge paused after this abrupt comment. "Taking into account the fact that these boys are still just children, I have decided that if the defense counsel still wishes to interview them, he will do so in the presence of Mr. Kraemer and the temporary guardian."

Fred and I left the courtroom. "Barb should talk about influencing the boys!" Fred said heatedly. "Sean said that every time he refers to the murderer as 'he,' Barb always corrects him by saying, 'You mean, she.' Now what kind of shit is that?"

Eisenberg came out of the judge's chambers and I returned to the defense table. "That kid is super," he told me. "I asked him right in front of those assholes if at any time I ever told him what to say, or if I made him cry, and he said 'NO.' Then I said, 'Did I question you the last time just the way I'm talking to you now?' and Sean said, 'YES.' I can't believe those Pennings!"

"I told you they were difficult."

Skwierawski returned and told the courtroom that since it was late in the day, the court would recess until the following morning.

After dinner with Eisenberg and his wife, Sandy, I drove home.

■   ■   ■

The days of my trial were merging together like waves on a shoreline. The whole affair had a strange, unreal feeling about it. I felt detached, as though I was merely standing in the wings of a theater stage, viewing a play, watching myself perform, unable to move or shout or cry out against those who were hurting me intentionally, against those who were lying viciously, for reasons unknown to me.

In the evenings, my parents and I would play a game of cards or Scrabble, look at photographs or watch a movie. Sergeant would lie on the floor in the middle of the room and demand everyone's attention, tail wagging furiously. Fred would usually read in another room or do paperwork.

Every morning, I awoke long before the sound of the digital alarm clock. Its red numbers glowed in the gray light of dawn. Then it would be a hurried scramble to get dressed and ready to leave—sleepily standing in front of my closet, trying to find something clean to wear, finding a run in my stockings just before leaving the house.

■   ■   ■

But nothing prepared me for the press coverage of the trial. If I didn't break down and cry, they said I was an ice maiden, cold and unemotional, a hard woman from the fast track. If I sniveled at all they accused me of playing to the gallery. If I answered in monosyllables (which I did a lot, out of fear and nervousness and ignorance), they said I was unhelpful and uncommunicative. If I rambled they said I was trying to confuse the court. They wrote about my "style," about my hair, about my looks, about my clothes ... oh, how they wrote about my clothes! They covered the trial like a Paris runway fashion show. No matter what I wore, they crucified me. One day I wore a frilly blouse, and they sneered that it was my "Little House on the Prairie" look, and said I was dressing for acquittal. If I wore something less conservative they accused me of sexual manipulation, and revived the "Playboy bunny" label. On one of the many days I arrived in a three-piece suit, a Chicago Tribune *reporter, angry because my mom and dad had declined a courthouse hallway interview, wrote that I wore "see-through dresses with no slip underneath" and titled his muck "Beauty or Beast?" If my clothes had style they said I'd always been obsessed with fashion.*

191

No one asked me why I wore what I wore. (I had no time to clean or press anything, and I wore whatever was on the next hanger in my closet, until the closet was empty—but that was too simple a truth for them.) The only thing they didn't write were the unadorned facts. They didn't write about the leaps of faith and logic the State was asking the jury to make. They didn't even try to write about what was going on in that courtroom.

I was always the bitch, cold and emotionless—but how could they see the pain?

■ ■ ■

At the courthouse, I saw the crowds of excited onlookers push their way in, trampling others to get to a seat. The minute the courtroom doors opened, they gathered like vultures. Every chair in the spectator section of the courtroom was always filled.

I watched them in disbelief. Once, numbly, I dreamed I could make them all go away—I would tap my heels together three times and they'd vanish. I was nervous and sweaty, sitting through day after day of testimony, objections, motions and recesses. The jury rarely looked at me, fixing their gaze instead upon the judge or the witnesses.

The elderly black juror dozed off occasionally.

Courtroom bailiffs were kept busy with a mentally disturbed woman named Mrs. Bursar who constantly interrupted the proceedings. She wandered in from the street, cried out loud during questioning and demanded to be allowed to approach the bench, to file her motions. I wondered if she had gone mad during a stint at law school, it wouldn't have surprised me. She was physically restrained and removed from the courtroom more than once. On one occasion, as she was being escorted away from the bench, she stole my purse off the defense table and its contents went flying across the floor. The judge threw her in jail.

I wished we could have videotaped Sean's testimony at the preliminary, because the children, as expected, remembered far less now than they did then. Sean was still firm, but his testimony was not as detailed at my trial as it had been the previous September. Kraemer didn't seem to pressure Sean much, but he brought up the fact that my mom and dad took Sean to Great America Park for his birthday. Kraemer insinuated that my mom and dad did this to bribe Sean. The boy denied this. The same line of questioning followed regarding Fred and me. Kraemer asked Sean if we had influenced his testimony, which Sean refuted. My heart went out to him, and I wanted to hug him for being so brave, but I had to remain seated, less than ten feet away from the child.

Judy Zess approached the witness stand, unusually meek. Her bold mood from the prelim had disappeared. Her testimony varied yet again, not only from the police reports, but even further from the story she'd told in September. So far, she'd returned her apartment key to the landlord on three different dates. When Eisenberg made her aware of this, she became confused and wasn't even able to recall the correct month, if indeed she'd turned the key in at all.

She claimed she could recognize Fred's handgun by some grooves or scratches in the handle. I'd seen the gun more than she had, but even I didn't know what she was talking about.

Christine's babysitter, Tammy, faltered in her story about my alleged question regarding the dog in May. She was a shy teenager. Clearly the police report had colored her story.

Kershek testified that before Christine was murdered, she had complained to him that Fred had stopped paying his alimony—again in the month of May. Eisenberg objected, saying that Kershek's testimony was hearsay. It could not possibly be verified because she was dead. The objection was overruled.

"Your Honor," Eisenberg began, "I would like a clarification, if I so strenuously disagree with one of your rulings, may I ask for a clarification or at least ... I don't mean more argument, but—"

"Well, apparently you do mean more argument, Mr. Eisenberg," said Skwierawski. "And you have a habit of objecting after I make a ruling. You also object after you have previously objected on a point and made your argument. I am advising you, now, what the appropriate procedures are in this branch of this court and I expect that counsel will conduct themselves accordingly."

Eisenberg then mentioned that two uncashed alimony checks had been found in Christine's purse after the homicide.

Kershek went on to testify that Christine had complained to him that Fred threatened her in May, saying that he would "blow her fucking head off" if she continued to argue with him. Again, this could not possibly be verified since Kershek had not reported it to the police at that time.

The Milwaukee County Forensic Pathologist (or coroner) took the stand and testified that she had performed the autopsy. Dr. Elaine Samuels was a very precise, intelligent woman, and she explained that the bullet, which she referred to as "the missile," had entered the back of the right shoulder and made a direct, diagonal path to the center of the heart.

Eisenberg asked her opinion of the "blow back" issue, when Kraemer objected.

" 'Blow back' is a subject meant for a ballistics expert. I don't think Dr. Samuels is qualified to testify about that subject."

"Your Honor, would the court ask Dr. Samuels if she thinks she is qualified, and not depend on Mr. Kraemer's assumption that she is not?" Eisenberg suggested.

"Dr. Samuels?" the judge asked.

"I think it is directly within the realm of forensic pathology," Elaine Samuels stated, enunciating every word very clearly.

I was irritated by the prevailing attitude that Elaine Samuels was "strange," not so much because she worked in the morgue, but because of her appearance. She didn't meet the socially defined standards of what doctors are supposed to look like, primarily because of her sex, and secondly because she had short hair and wore no make-up. She was heavy and wore black-rimmed glasses, giving her a masculine appearance. For such shallow reasons, her credibility was apparently questionable. But she was obviously competent enough to work for the County Medical Examiner's Office!

"Then allow me to continue with my line of questioning, Your Honor," Eisenberg said, glancing at me. "Dr. Samuels, would you explain 'blow back' please? For the jury."

"'Blow back' is an event that takes place when a gun is fired at close range to the body. Blood and tissue explode from the missile entering the body, and splash back into the barrel of the gun." She frowned in intense concentration. Usually, she explained, microscopic traces of blood or tissue were found, even if no visible traces were discovered. Tiny striations inside the barrel of a gun spun the bullets from the barrel, and it was these striations that held blood residue.

"Did you observe the bullet wound on the body of Christine Schultz?"

"I did."

"Would you describe that bullet wound?"

"The wound itself was quite large. The skin around the wound held the impression of the gun's muzzle in a visible, circular pattern."

"Would you say the gun was at close range?"

"Yes. It had to have been touching the skin."

"Dr. Samuels, to a degree of medical, scientific certainty, would it be your opinion that 'blow back' would have occurred?"

"Yes."

Eisenberg made a point of tediously repeating this to the jury, because the gun that the Crime Lab identified as the murder weapon had no traces of blood or tissue inside the muzzle or the barrel, nor traces of cleaning solvent. Just traces of dust.

Fred's brother John arrived as a witness for the prosecution. Under direct examination by Kraemer, John maintained that Sean hadn't, after all, seen the intruder. John said Sean told him he was so frightened by the event that night that he ran and hid. It was only because Fred and I had influenced him that he said he'd seen someone, John said. After all, I had sent the boys several photographs in the mail.

Under cross-examination, he grew emotional.

Eisenberg asked, "Isn't it a fact that you took it upon yourself to write a letter to the judge who presided over the defendant's preliminary hearing, the Honorable Ralph Adam Fine, in hopes that it would influence his decision to bind the defendant over for jury trial?"

"Yes."

"And isn't it a fact that you state in this letter that you know Lawrencia Bembenek is guilty of murdering Christine Schultz, when in fact you have absolutely no evidence to support this opinion?"

"I ..."

"Do you have any evidence?"

"No."

"It's opinion?"

"Yes," John meekly replied.

"Yet you took it upon yourself to write a damaging, accusatory letter that received considerable publicity, ending up on the front page of the *Milwaukee Journal*?"

"Yes."

"John Schultz, are you aware that your whole family is present today in support of the defendant?"

"Yes."

"Out of five brothers, you are the only one who has a different opinion about the defendant?"

"Yes." John's face turned blotchy and he nervously folded his hands over and over.

"Tell me," Eisenberg continued. "Isn't it a fact that your wife, Kathy, and the deceased were like sisters, they were so close?"

"Yes."

"And isn't it also a fact that your wife hated Laurie because of the fact that Fred remarried Laurie?"

"Well ... we were trying to work that out."

"But, at the most, your wife merely tolerated Laurie?"

"That's true," mumbled John.

"I'm sorry, I didn't hear you."

"I said, that's true," John repeated.

"If the court would allow me to show the jury the photographs that the State has introduced into evidence, in trying to insinuate that the defendant tried to influence the children," Eisenberg asked. He picked up a small pile of pictures. There was one of Fred, a few of the boys at the apartment, and one picture of the four of us at the Brady Street Festival. One picture of me was included, wearing the blouse that Sean and Shannon had bought me for my birthday.

"Now, I'm assuming that either you or your wife, Kathy, turned these photographs over to the District Attorney?"

"Yes."

"There's a small notecard that the snapshots were enclosed in, with a short letter printed inside from the defendant. Would you read out loud, to the jury, what that letter says?"

John opened the card as tears filled his eyes. He began reading with a weak voice. "It says: 'Dear Sean and Shannon, I am enclosing some pictures of you and your daddy and me. Don't lose these. There is one of Shannon, with a noodle hanging down his chin, and one of your silly daddy, who put popcorn up his nose. Remember'?"

John's voice broke, but he continued. " 'In the picture of me, I am wearing the shirt you bought me for my birthday. Thank you! I like it a lot. The dog too! I wish I could thank you in person. Remember Stan and Suzy from the gym? They went to California on vacation. They have a lot of nice pictures. I love you, Laurie.' "

"Now," Eisenberg said, his hands clasped behind his back, "is there anything in that letter that you would consider unduly influencing?"

"No."

"Did Laurie say, 'Please lie for me'?"

"No."

"Did Laurie say, 'Say I didn't do it'?"

"No."

"Does that letter sound like it came from a woman who hates children?" Eisenberg shouted.

"Objection!" Kraemer interrupted.

"Sustained."

"I'll withdraw the question, Your Honor. Just a few more questions, Mr. Schultz. You lived with Sean for a period of time, did you not?"

"Yes."

"Do you know him to be an extremely bright child?"

"I'm not sure what you mean."

"You have a son who is Sean's age, do you not?"

"Yes. Marshall."

"Well, would you say that they are equal in intelligence, or is Sean a little more advanced than Marshall?"

"I'd have to say that Sean is more advanced."

"Are you aware of the fact that Sean was bright enough, considering the circumstances, to attempt to administer first aid to his mother, while she lay dying?"

"Yes."

"Do you mean to tell this court, then, that a child who had enough composure to administer first aid after the shooting occurred was the very same young man who allegedly told you that he was 'so scared that he ran and hid and that he didn't see the intruder'?"

"Objection!"

"Your Honor," Eisenberg asked, "I'd like this witness to answer the question, please?"

"Sustained," the judge replied.

"Then answer me this, John Schultz," Eisenberg countered. "How do you explain the original reports that Sean gave to the police, immediately after it happened, if Sean, like he told you, didn't see anything?"

"Objection!" Kraemer announced again. "Your Honor, Mr. Eisenberg is obviously asking the same question in a different form. It calls for speculation! And he's badgering the witness."

"I have no further questions," Eisenberg quickly interjected.

"Sustained! Obviously improper," the judge insisted. "The jury is instructed to—"

"No further questions, Your Honor," Eisenberg repeated.

"—to disregard the remarks of Mr. Eisenberg again!"

Eisenberg sizzled with irritation. "If it please the court, I would like to make a comment for the record. I object to the court. I have no problem with the court saying to the jury that they should disregard a statement of mine, but I do object to the court adding the word 'again.' If I make a mistake, I am entitled to have it disregarded by the jury without the court implying that I am repeatedly at fault. I think the court's word 'again' is highly improper, and I object to it."

Skwierawski sighed. "You may object to it. Your objection is overruled. When counsel continuously pushes the limits of admissibility, in terms of questions being asked of witnesses, bordering on and verging on improper conduct in front of the jury, I will take every step necessary to stop it and I will continue to stop it throughout this trial, regardless of how often it happens! And if it happens again and again, then you will be stopped again and again. I don't need any further argument on the issue! The issue is closed!" The judge turned to the Assistant District Attorney. "Wish to redirect?"

"No, Your Honor."

"The witness may step down."

■　　■　　■

It was Friday evening. Eisenberg asked me to meet with him—one of the few "attorney-client privilege" meetings I had with him without Fred being present.

"What I have to show you is very important," he said. We were at a downtown restaurant, in a secluded booth. We always seemed to meet in restaurants or bars. His office was in Madison and he didn't want to come to my house. Maybe he thought it would seem improper.

"What is it?"

We ordered drinks and waited until the waitress left our table. The large diamonds on his cufflinks, rings and tie tack glittered in the candle light.

"This is serious." He was solemn. "I've been investigating this case for about nine months now. In the beginning, I made you realize how important it is for you to be completely honest with me, because I have to defend you. I know you have been. Like I told you before—I don't care what you've done. I wouldn't care if you did commit the murder, because it's not my job to pass moral judgment on you. I've defended people for every crime you can imagine.

"Okay, we've gone over this before several times and you have told me that you didn't do it and I believe you."

"So, what did you want to show me?" I asked, impatient.

"First, I want to ask you something. This is very important. Is there anything you're not telling me?"

"No! What do you mean?"

"About Fred. Are you covering up for him in any way?"

"No!"

"Are you afraid of Fred?"

"No!"

"You've told me everything?"

"Yes! Why?"

"I have some information from my investigators. This guy may be a quack, but I'm not so sure. I can't leave any stone unturned. I have the transcript here.

While you're looking it over, I'll summarize. It says Fred hired a hit man out of Chicago to kill Christine. A lot of what he says jibes with the case, but then again, he may have been able to piece it together from the newspapers.

"He says one thing that makes a lot of sense. That there were actually two guys in the house that night. I've always wondered how one person could tie Christine up and hold a gun on her at the same time—or why she didn't resist at all against only one man. There were no signs of a struggle. She was a good sized woman—not some weak female.

"Also, it says one of the men woke up the kids on purpose so that Sean would see it wasn't his father."

I read the transcript as fast as I could. "This guy that gave us this statement is a convict?" I asked, noticing the address.

"Yes."

"But I thought someone incarcerated has little or no credibility in court ..."

"Do you have any idea what this could be about?" Eisenberg interrupted. "If you do—please, tell me right now. We're talking about a life sentence now. We're not talking about going away for a few months."

"I don't have any idea. I don't know what this is all about. Honest to God! I wouldn't cover up for a murder ..."

"Are you positive? If this is true, Fred is using you."

"I don't know what to think," I said. "I find it hard to believe that some guy sitting in prison calls you out of a clear, blue sky ..."

"All I'm saying is ..."

"All you're saying is that either I could crucify Fred to save my own neck, or keep things the way they are and take my chances?" I looked at him. "It's either Fred or me? This evidence is so shoddy to risk all that! What if I tell you to use this guy, and it turns the jury against me? What if it makes them think Oh wow—now she's even trying to pin it on her own husband?"

I stopped talking as the menus were placed on our table. Fred? Was it possible? I recalled that Fred had said I had a key to the Ramsey house, when I didn't even know he had a key. How did blood get on his on-duty revolver? Why did he burst into tears at the Prelim? Why didn't he write the times that he called me that night in his damned report? Why did he want to move into that house?

I ordered an appetizer, since I wasn't very hungry, and asked for another drink.

"I don't know what to do," I said. "I have to think about this. If we had better proof that Fred hired someone ... but it's such a big risk to take, considering how flimsy the evidence is. Can't we verify this somehow?"

"Speaking of flimsy evidence, I don't see how we can lose this case," Eisenberg assured me. "It's nothing but a collection of contradictory facts, and speculative theory!"

Soon our lunch ended, he climbed into his Jaguar and I drove home. I didn't want to believe Fred hired someone to kill Christine and then made it appear as if I did it. How could I believe that? This was the man I had chosen to marry!

What was I to do? This was Friday and Fred was due to testify on Monday morning!

Fred had the perfect alibi—he was on duty that night. Maybe, I thought, he expected me to keep my date with Marylisa? That way, I would have had an alibi, too ... But there was no *time*! No time to even attempt to verify this statement—a statement from a convict, no less ... I didn't want to think about it anymore. I believed in Fred, still. He'd stuck by me through this whole thing. He lost his house, his job, and his children. No ... I couldn't turn on him. If I did, I wouldn't be able to live with myself.

I called Eisenberg. I told him I didn't want to use the convict's statement.

■   ■   ■

As he did at the prelim, Fred's former squad partner, Durfee, arrived to testify as a witness for the prosecution. His story had changed a bit. This time he included a part where he said Fred and I talked for a few minutes after they arrived at our apartment. He said Fred and I were alone, and he could not hear what was said.

I wondered why Durfee would add this part to his version of what transpired on the night in question. It certainly cast a note of suspicion our way, but it wasn't logical. If Fred and I had had a moment or two alone, like Durfee said, and if I were guilty, I would have told Fred to do anything but examine the gun! Fred could have said it was lost or stolen. Instead, the two of them entered the apartment and walked directly to the bedroom to examine the gun.

Durfee admitted that he failed to record the serial number of the gun he examined that night, a bizarre piece of misprocedure. He said he'd lost or thrown out his memo book from that night. He responded vaguely when Eisenberg questioned him about the Department policy to save all memo books and about the date of his second report.

But at least Durfee maintained that the revolver he examined that night could not possibly have been fired.

I'd supplied Eisenberg with a list of my Police Academy class members to prepare him for the next witness. An officer with tinted glasses and a trim mustache named Keith Faubel was the only one out of over fifty people who claimed to remember that I wore a green jogging suit at the Police Academy.

Faubel admitted that he'd come forward with his story just before my preliminary hearing. When Eisenberg asked why he waited so long to tell the DA about his recollection, Faubel claimed that just after the murder he'd informed his sergeant.

"When did you go to your sergeant?"

"In May or June," Faubel said. "Of last year."

"Who was the sergeant?"

"I don't know his name."

I stifled a groan. Being aware of your sergeant's name was not only mandatory, it was a basic survival tactic. Needless to say, the "mystery sergeant" was never found.

Eisenberg asked Faubel another question. "What shade of green was the jogging suit?"

"Forest green."

"Interesting, Mr. Faubel. You are sure of this?"

"Yes."

"Okay. I'm going to read a list of names to you, and you tell me if these people were your classmates at the Police Academy. Ready? Darlene Anderson, Douglas Boville, Michael Koszuta, Jackie Hawkins—"

"Objection!" Kraemer said.

"—Linda Palese, Michael Stoychavich, Linda Reeves, Samuel Thomas, Robert White—"

"Objection! Your Honor, what is the purpose of this?"

"—Klug, Bradford, Duffee, Wedemeyer—"

Losing his temper, Kraemer flew at Eisenberg, pointing to him and thrashing the other arm about. "Objection!"

Eisenberg calmly lowered the paper from his eyes.

"Mr. Eisenberg?" the judge asked.

"Your Honor, my intention is to ask this witness if he is aware of the fact that out of all these people, out of over fifty people, he is the only one who seems to remember the defendant in a green jogging suit at the Police Academy."

The State subpoenaed a firearms instructor from the Police Academy. I remembered him. He'd always talk and joke with me at the firing range. "That's right, Bembenek!" Marcellus Cieslik would say. "Get 'em right in the ten ring!" He'd been on the police force long enough to remember when my dad was a cop. I was polite to him and he in turn was pleasant, quick with a joke.

Cieslik testified that I was a good marksman. What was the point? Christine was shot at point-blank range.

Eisenberg asked him about the cleaning of revolvers.

"What do you train your recruits to clean their handguns with?"

"We have an oily substance that is standard gun-cleaning solvent."

"Does it have an odor?"

"Yes. A distinct odor."

"Do traces of this fluid remain on guns for long periods of time?"

"Yes, I suppose that inside the barrel, in the striations, traces of this fluid would remain."

I found it odd that answers from a State witness were advantageous to the defense. I turned to look behind me, but realized Fred was still sequestered from the courtroom.

"Now, Sergeant Cieslik—the prosecution has inferred that a gun could possibly be cleaned with soap and water. Is that possible?"

"Yes."

"But, as an instructor, wouldn't you be upset with one of your recruits if you found them cleaning their service revolver with soap and water?"

"I suppose."

"In fact, wouldn't it cause a gun to rust?" Eisenberg asked.

"Not this gun," Cieslik said suddenly, holding Fred's snub-nosed Smith and Wesson.

"Why not?" Eisenberg asked.

"Because this gun is aluminum, sir," Cieslik replied. There was a chuckle throughout the courtroom, yet the judge did nothing to maintain order. I thought he would be pounding his gavel, like judges do on television, but he remained motionless. I was embarrassed for Eisenberg, and of course the *Milwaukee Sentinel* reported the "aluminum" testimony word for word.

Eisenberg remained calm and acted as though nothing had happened.

"All right. Would it be reasonable to conclude that if a person used a gun to kill someone, and if that person had been one of your recruits, and if that person knew that bullets can be traced back to guns, which is what you teach your recruits—would it be reasonable to conclude that that person would want to get rid of the murder weapon?"

"Objection!" Kraemer stood up. "I ask that the court instruct the jury that the comments and statements made by Mr. Eisenberg are not evidence in this case!"

"I haven't made any comments or statements, Your Honor."

The judge stared at both lawyers grimly, saying, "The jury has been so instructed on several occasions throughout this trial, and is again instructed to disregard the last question asked by defense counsel."

When I told Fred about Cieslik's answer, he was furious.

"Why the hell would Cieslik say that? Tell Don that the only aluminum part on that gun is the frame! The rest of that gun sure as hell *would* rust if someone cleaned it with soap and water! Especially the barrel! Jesus! Tell Don to ask the ballistics expert when he's called."

Fred's turn on the witness stand was similar to his testimony at the prelim, except that this time, he didn't lose his composure.

Kraemer spent considerable time belaboring the Waukegan marriage license. He went so far as to bring in a transcript of Fred's divorce hearing. I couldn't see the point.

Fred claimed that he was unaware of the fact that he couldn't by law remarry at the time he married me. Kraemer contradicted Fred by saying that explicit instructions were given to Fred by Judge Curley regarding the issue of remarrying. I began to wonder who was on trial.

Then Kraemer questioned Fred about his finances. Fred told Kraemer that the amount earned from the carpentry work we did in our spare time supplemented Fred's regular salary and my wages. The prosecution's painting of bleak financial despair began to brighten considerably.

In an attempt to support his "life in the fast lane" theory, Kraemer asked Fred about our "exotic" vacations, which ended up sounding like nothing more than a honeymoon and a Florida visit with friends.

Fred explained that it was a Police Department regulation to save memo books, and produced an entire briefcase full of books dating back to 1970. This made Durfee's testimony about losing his memo book sound negligent at best.

Kraemer asked Fred to produce the memo book that held the serial number of his off-duty revolver. After hunting through the briefcase, Fred found the memo book from the year when he purchased the gun.

Kraemer was trying to confuse our "switched gun" theory by asking Fred to verify the serial number, which he did. Of course, it was identical to the handgun in evidence. That wasn't the point. Eisenberg was putting forward the theory that, because Fred and Durfee neglected to record the serial number of the gun they examined that night, the gun they examined might or might not be the same gun that the Crime Lab identified as the murder weapon. Along with the physical appearance of the gun that indicated it had not been fired, there was also the fact that Fred's guns had been confiscated so many weeks later. Some time in between, the gun Fred and Durfee examined that night was taken and replaced with Fred's gun. That was the only logical explanation, because the gun Fred and Durfee had looked at that night had not been fired, and Fred's gun had. As usual, the newspapers confused this issue.

Fred's description of the gun's appearance that night was detailed, and his knowledge of ballistics sounded impressive, but his testimony turned into what Eisenberg called a "two-edged sword" when Kraemer used his knowledge against him.

"So, Mr. Schultz, what you're telling this court is that, even with your extensive familiarity with handguns, you weren't even sure that the gun you and your partner examined that night was yours?"

"No. Not without checking the serial number. The gun itself has quite a common appearance. The grips were standard. I thought it was my gun. But I can't be sure."

Eisenberg surprised everyone when he presented his own snub-nosed revolver. He wanted to show the jury how similar guns appear. Later, at the defense table behind Kraemer, Eisenberg began clicking the barrel release nervously. Kraemer again lost his temper and angrily instructed him to "stop playing with that gun behind my back!"

Eisenberg just chuckled. Kraemer then requested that the court order him to remove his revolver from the jury's view, and Skwierawski complied, adding:

"Well Mr. Kraemer, you probably ought to take the same self-help action that Mr. Eisenberg has taken in this case about four or five times, in terms of just getting up and grabbing onto the exhibits and waltzing them over and putting them in a box somewhere, getting them out of sight. I am not going to let this case be resolved by self-help."

Detective Ronald Krusek had been seated at Kraemer's left throughout the trial. He began testifying about the day Kathryn Morgan identified my parents' car.

"What did you observe Mrs. Morgan do?" Kraemer asked.

"She proceeded east on Ramsey."

"And how long was she gone?"

"Three to four minutes."

"When she returned, did Mrs. Morgan tell you anything about an automobile?"

"Yes. She said—"

"Hearsay objection!" Eisenberg quickly interrupted. Even I knew by then that a witness was not allowed to testify as to what someone else said. The only hearsay that was allowed was when a witness testified as to what the defendant said. The judge, however, disregarded the rules of evidence.

"Overruled."

I gave Eisenberg a worried look. When Conway from Marquette had wanted to tell the court that he heard me call the murder of Christine Schultz a "tragic, unfortunate event," Kraemer raised a hearsay objection and it was sustained, which I didn't understand, because hearsay from the defendant is admissible. Now this detective wanted to testify about what Mrs. Morgan told him, my lawyer raised a hearsay objection, and he was overruled? Not for the first (or last) time, I wondered what was going on.

The notorious Kathryn Morgan finally told the court her fairy tale about my mother digging through garbage bins. Eisenberg's cross-examination was fierce.

"Isn't it a fact that you identified Mrs. Bembenek at Lawrencia Bembenek's preliminary hearing?"

"Yes."

"After requesting that Mrs. Bembenek remove her glasses?"

"Yes."

"The woman you saw on June 18 was not wearing glasses?"

"No."

"Are you aware of the fact that Virginia Bembenek is almost blind without her glasses?"

"No."

"Are you aware of the fact that Virginia Bembenek cannot drive without her glasses?"

"No."

The prosecution had done its homework. They introduced into evidence a copy of my mother's driver's license, but it was to our advantage, since it listed a restriction for correctional lenses.

"Mrs. Morgan," Eisenberg asked, "are you telling this court that you saw a woman once in June of 1981 and identified this woman four months later?"

"Yes." Morgan was in her thirties, with shoulder-length dark hair. She had a cleft chin and a bad underbite, so when she talked I became aware of her "S's." I wondered what made her go to the police with such a story. I had never seen her before.

"Would you like to review the police report to refresh your memory?" Eisenberg walked up to her and handed her the white copy. "Now, you describe the woman you saw as being about forty-five years of age, according to this report?"

"Yes."

"Are you aware of the fact that Mrs. Bembenek is almost sixty?"

"No."

"Are you also aware of the fact that Virginia Bembenek almost never wears shorts, because she's embarrassed about her varicose veins?"

"No."

"Do you really expect this court to believe, Mrs. Morgan, that a woman who was allegedly trying to recover murder evidence from a large trash container would come up to a perfect stranger in broad daylight, ask you about the trash containers, and then take a bag out of them and drive away?"

"Objection!" Kraemer said in a tired voice.

"Sustained! Sustained! We don't need any more of Mr. Eisenberg's editorializing. Defense counsel is instructed just to ask questions the witness can answer."

"All right, let's use this blackboard behind you, Mrs. Morgan," Eisenberg continued. "And write the license number you gave the police. Next to that, I'm going to write the license number of the Bembenek family car."

Mrs. Morgan turned in her chair to see the blackboard.

"Not the same number, is it, Mrs. Morgan?"

"No."

"Are you aware of the fact that the Bembenek family only has one family car and that Mr. Bembenek uses it to drive to work, where he works until 4:00 PM?"

"No."

"You said that you saw the woman digging through the garbage at 2:00 PM on June 18?"

"Um."

"Well, that's what you told the police, Mrs. Morgan. It says so right here in this report. Let's talk about the car you saw on June 18. How did you come to identify this car?"

Eisenberg paced back and forth in front of the witness box. The witness swallowed hard.

"A detective came to my house," Kathryn Morgan replied, "and asked me if I would go with him to identify the car."

"When did this take place?"

"About a month later."

"Who was the detective?"

"He's right there." She pointed at Krusek.

"What exactly happened?"

"Well, I got in his police car and we drove to that house on Ramsey Street, where I saw a brown automobile in the driveway."

"And then what?"

"I told him that it was the car."

"Mrs. Morgan, it says in this report that your exact words were, 'It looks similar to the car I saw on June 18.' Now, I hope you're not getting confused in the excitement of the trial and the TV cameras and everything. Didn't you say that the car looked similar?"

"Yes."

"Not that it was the same car?"

"No."

"How many other cars were parked at the house?"

"I think another car and a van. I think."

I remembered a police car watching the Ramsey Street house when my parents and Fred and I were cleaning. It was either that time, or when we moved our boxes into the house to store them there.

"Were any other cars parked on that street?"

"No."

"On that block?"

"No."

"Mrs. Morgan, do you mean to tell me that Detective Krusek took you to a house that had exactly two cars parked in its driveway, plus one blue van, and asked you to identify the car you saw on June 18?"

"Yes."

"What did he say? Isn't it a fact that he took you over there and said, 'That's the car, isn't it'?"

"Objection! Leading the witness!" Kraemer bellowed.

"Sustained," Skwierawski said firmly. "Argumentative. The jury is instructed to disregard the last several questions."

"The last two questions?" Eisenberg asked.

"That's right. Two is several," the judge replied.

"Two is several?" Eisenberg asked again.

"Yes." Skwierawski nodded. I could see Kraemer shaking his head.

The next trick the prosecution pulled was a fast one indeed. The State claimed to have four witnesses—two cops and their wives—who said they remembered bumping into me and Fred at a movie the previous winter, in 1981. They said I was wearing the infamous green jogging suit, of course.

All four were on the witness list, but when it came time to call them to the stand, Kraemer informed the court that one couple was in Colorado and would not be available to testify. The other cop had since been promoted to detective.

"This is so they don't all have to corroborate their damn story," Eisenberg whispered. "What the hell is this one about? You were at some movie with Fred?"

"Yeah. It was a cop movie, too! Good grief—*Fort Apache: The Bronx*, with Paul Newman."

"Forget Paul Newman, Laurie. What were you wearing?"

"Probably jeans and my ski jacket, as usual. I remember Fred talking to two couples in the lobby. Isn't winter a cold time of year to be wearing a jogging suit?"

"They've already covered that argument," Eisenberg said. "This report says that that's the reason they remember the green jogging suit so vividly—because it was so cold to wear something like that."

"Tricky."

"We'll see how tricky they are when I cross-examine them."

As it turned out, the detective and his wife disagreed about what I was allegedly wearing a year previous to their testimony. The husband, Gary, said it was a green jogging jacket with stripes on the side. His wife, Darlene, said it was a whole jogging suit, including jogging pants. They both disagreed about what type of jacket Fred was wearing.

But they were sure about the date. After the show, they'd dined at the Captain's Steak Joynt and charged the meal on a credit card, which recorded the date.

The whole subject of the green jogging suit had been blown totally out of proportion. The police had neither confiscated this nonexistent suit, nor submitted one into evidence.

Of course, the State was hand-picking its evidence. Fred's younger boy, Shannon, who by now admitted that he remembered absolutely nothing, was the one who originally claimed he saw a green jogging suit. This was the boy who also claimed to have seen a silver revolver with pearl grips.

Sean, on the other hand, was an older and more credible witness, and he said the intruder had worn a green khaki army jacket.

Two young women from the apartment across the hall from where we had lived were subpoenaed by the State. They testified about the plumber finding the wig in their toilet. They also told the court that they'd twice let Zess into the building when she pressed the buzzer. They saw her open our apartment while we weren't home and go in for some time. Those dates were in May, right before the murder and right after.

Whenever the court recessed, I managed to spend a few minutes in the hallway with my mother, who kept her vigil with my dad on the wooden bench. It must have been nearly unbearable to spend all those hours in such an uncomfortable place after an operation. The pace of the trial was hard to judge, and I wasn't sure when she would be called to testify.

The State then summoned a photographer from the *Milwaukee Journal*, Robert Goessner. He claimed to have remembered me from two years before— December 1980. That was the month the paper took a picture to print with a piece about my sex discrimination complaint. Goessner admitted he himself did not take the picture—he only passed me in the hall as I walked to the photo department. It was pretty hard to believe that anyone would remember such a fleeting glance, but he said he remembered me because I was "so beautiful."

Kraemer then produced the black-and-white photograph from the *Journal*, and Goessner testified that it was a picture of me in the green jogging suit he remembered me wearing that day. What I remembered having worn was a red warm-up jacket!

I began writing furiously on my legal pad as Kraemer questioned his witness.

A friend of mine had worked at a photo lab, and had once explained how to tell the color of objects in black-and-white photographs. Through spectroscopy, she'd said, you could determine which end of the spectrum an object was in. Green would be on the opposite side of the spectrum from red. I had no idea if this was true, but I passed it on to Eisenberg.

So he asked Goessner about the process. Fortunately, the witness admitted that such a process, and other tests, could have been used to prove the color of the jacket. No such tests had been done.

"Of course the police didn't test the negative," I scribbled to Eisenberg, "because it would have proved that the jacket I am wearing in the photograph is red!"

Eisenberg nodded, whispering, "If I was Kraemer, I would be ashamed to introduce such cheap, ridiculous evidence."

"Did you ever attempt to test the negative of this photograph to determine the color?" my lawyer asked Goessner.

"I don't have that equipment."

"But that type of equipment is available, isn't it?"

"It might be," Goessner nodded reluctantly.

"And it is available to the County of Milwaukee and to the District Attorney of this city, isn't it?" Eisenberg persisted.

"Objection!" Kraemer shouted.

"Sustained."

"No further questions," Eisenberg added.

Two officers from Marquette arrived to testify. Conway returned, followed by Lieutenant Pileggi. They rehashed the events that led up to my arrest.

When Conway had testified at the suppression hearing concerning the evidence taken without a warrant from my locker, Eisenberg had tried to question him about statements I'd made that referred to the murder in a sympathetic manner. Kraemer raised a hearsay objection, and it was sustained—even though much of the State's case was hearsay.

Now that Pileggi was on the stand, Eisenberg again tried to ask questions about my statements describing the murder as unfortunate. This was perfectly admissible, ordinarily. But Kraemer again objected and was again sustained.

Eisenberg was outraged. "Your Honor! This testimony is hearsay evidence from the defendant, and therefore should be admissible."

"Mr. Kraemer's objection is sustained. Mr. Eisenberg—"

"Your Honor, with all due respect, I must say for the record that I feel justice has done an about-face in this courtroom!" Eisenberg said in frustration.

"One more comment like that, Mr. Eisenberg, and you will be found in contempt of court."

Armed with a thick textbook by Charles O'Hara, Eisenberg began cross-examining Arthur Varriale, a fiber analyst. O'Hara's book was a fundamental text and was on the required reading list for the Milwaukee Police Department Detective Exam. Varriale wouldn't dare quarrel with it.

The expert was forced to admit that fiber analysis was not a science. The closest analysis he said he'd be able to make between two synthetic wig fibers would be "similarity in characteristics," not positive identification. He tended to use the word "consistent" in his analysis, and referred to characteristics like color, chemical composition and structure. Eisenberg raised the issue of the millions of wigs throughout the world that are all composed of the same material. Varriale admitted there was considerable doubt in his "identifications."

"So what you are now telling this jury is that the fiber you examined, found on the leg of Christine Schultz, and the fiber that made up the wig taken from the drain pipe could be the same, or they could not be the same. Isn't that correct?" Eisenberg asked Varriale.

"Would you repeat the question?"

"The two fibers you examined. You cannot tell this jury that, beyond a reasonable doubt, with a degree of scientific certainty, those fibers are identical, can you?"

"No, sir."

"You are only able to tell us that they could be the same, or they could not be the same?" Eisenberg repeated, emphasizing every word.

"That's correct," was the reply.

The next witness for the prosecution was an alleged "expert" in hair analysis named Diane Hanson. In his examination, Eisenberg forced her to admit that her Bachelor's degree was in the field of bacteriology—totally removed from the study of hair analysis. Her knowledge of hair was gained piecemeal, in six weeks at various seminars.

The reluctant admission of her true field of study and the usurpation of her authority upset Hanson. She became evasive and uncooperative. Eisenberg's cross-examination lasted two hours. As he led her into disagreeing with the facts written by O'Hara, she began to appear confused and unsure of herself.

Hanson admitted that hair analysis was even less accurate than fiber analysis, which Eisenberg had already reduced to nothing more than a guessing game. Hanson's temper finally overwhelmed her common sense when she slipped and revealed that she had violated the court's sequestration order. She had discussed Varriale's testimony with him.

This is how she came to admit it:

"So, what you are saying, Miss Hanson, is that you disagree with the statement that I have just read?" Eisenberg asked, an incredulous look on his face. "You disagree with O'Hara?"

"You're not reading the whole paragraph!" she retorted. "That's only part of the paragraph that you've just read!"

Eisenberg's eyes narrowed. "How do you know that, Miss Hanson?" A hush fell over the courtroom.

"Um, is it a part of the paragraph, I'm asking?" She flushed.

"I'm asking you, when did you read this paragraph in O'Hara's book? Today?" Eisenberg asked.

"Today," Hanson quietly squeaked.

"I suppose Mr. Kraemer told you about this? When? Over lunch?"

"No."

"Did any member of the Milwaukee Police Department advise you to look over Charles O'Hara's book today?"

"No, they did not."

"How did you come to know about it today?" Eisenberg refused to back down, as Hanson's reluctance increased.

"I knew that you had asked Mr. Varriale a question," she mumbled.

"How did you know that?"

"He mentioned that you had referred to O'Hara's book."

"Gentlemen," the judge interrupted, "I feel that it is in order at the moment to excuse the jury and look into this matter."

Hanson remained seated, her hands in her lap. Embarrassed, she only glanced at the judge. After further questioning by both counsel, the court found that Hanson had violated the sequestration order by discussing Varriale's testimony while driving him back to the Crime Lab. Eisenberg made a motion to strike Hanson's testimony because of this.

"Denied," the judge said. "It is not substantial. And let me advise you that you are also denied any further argument, Mr. Eisenberg."

"Your Honor, I think Mr. Varriale should be recalled to find out what he will testify to, regarding his conversation with Miss Hanson."

"No. Request denied. All right—I don't require any further argument on this issue. There has been a violation of the court order. The request made by defense counsel to strike this witness's testimony is denied."

"Your Honor—"

"No further argument, Mr. Eisenberg."

"I'm not—"

"I have made my decision."

"I want a request, if it please the court."

"What is it, Mr. Eisenberg?" the judge hissed.

"I would request that you instruct the jury as to what you have just said," Eisenberg asked finally.

"I'm going to ... I object!" Kraemer stammered.

"No! No!" Skwierawski said vehemently. "Request denied!"

■　　■　　■

I remembered what our instructors at the Police Academy had drummed into us: the law protects the criminal. Any tiny technical flaw in an investigation would void a prosecution. Civil libertarians were everywhere, with power to throw out any case on any minute error, no matter how harmless.

It was all nonsense, paranoid nonsense, and I'd known that even then.

I was even more sure now.

16

THE SKYLINE DARKENS

The end of the list of State witnesses was drawing near. Finally I'd be able to see some allies on the witness stand.

The last person to testify for the prosecution was Monty Lutz, the New Berlin Crime Lab's ballistics expert. As we expected, he testified that the bullet removed from the body of Christine Schultz came from Fred's off-duty gun. During cross-examination, however, my lawyer used Mr. Lutz to our advantage, by inquiring whether or not Fred's revolver was made of aluminum, as Sergeant Cieslik had testified.

"No. Just the frame is aluminum. The barrel, and the other parts of the gun, are not. I don't know how detailed you would like me to get ..."

"Thank you, Mr. Lutz. If soap and water were used to clean the gun, would rust appear over a period of time?"

"Definitely."

"If cleaning fluid or solvent was used, would the lab detect traces of it?" Eisenberg asked.

"Yes."

"If cleaning fluid or solvent was used, would dust be present?"

"I suppose over a period of time."

"Over a period of a few hours?"

"It depends where the gun was stored."

"If it was in a holster, stored in a closed compartment, like a gym bag with a zipper?"

"Oh. Then I'd have to say no. Dust would not be present if the gun had been cleaned and then put away."

Eisenberg emphasized this line of questioning because we already knew that Fred's gun had not been cleaned. So if that were the murder weapon, where was the blood? The carbon?

The first six witnesses the defense subpoenaed were former members of my Police Academy class. They testified briefly, as character witnesses, and also to say that they never once saw me in a green jogging suit. I appreciated their cooperation and support, especially since I had not seen any of them in such a long time.

After two weeks of being restricted to the hallway of the courthouse, my parents were finally allowed into the courtroom to testify.

My mom raised her right hand, her face pale and tired. I crossed my fingers and hoped Kraemer wouldn't upset her. Her testimony hadn't changed from the preliminary hearing. She talked about helping me pack on the night of the murder. She denied Morgan's allegations that she had been digging through the garbage bins at the apartment complex.

I knew that her every word meant the world to her, and she was trying painfully to answer every question with care. I had cautioned her that Kraemer found it easy to turn around an honest word to suit the State, and she was more scared than I was. After her testimony, the court recessed and I found her in the hallway, crying.

"Don't, mom!" I said, hugging her. "You were fine. It's over."

"I was so scared that I'd say something wrong! You know how those police can confuse a person who is just trying to tell the truth! So much depended on my testimony today. I'm so afraid for you!"

"I know," I said. "Don't worry."

When we returned, my father's testimony was brief. I'd been even more apprehensive about his testifying, because he had difficulty hearing. But he was fine. He simply explained that he was using the family car the day Morgan claimed she saw my mom pull up in a car. The cross-examination by Kraemer was not rigorous.

Afterward, my parents found a place to stand at the back of the courtroom, since all of the seats were taken. At last they were able to listen and watch the proceedings. Typically, The *Milwaukee Sentinel* suggested that they hadn't cared enough to arrive until the very end, not explaining that they actually hadn't been allowed in.

Fred's father, Elfred Schultz, Sr., testified about the incident that took place the day Fred uncovered the custody conspiracy. He's a highly emotional man, like the rest of his family, and he burst into sobs in mid-sentence. The court had to recess. Afterwards, he contradicted his son John's innuendo about the incident in which John had called the police. John had tried to maintain that Fred had been calling to bully Sean about his testimony in the murder. Not at all, Fred's dad said. The incident was related to the custody battle. Fred's father also served as a character witness for me.

Fred's mother never testified. She never even came to the trial.

It was so easy for the State to make insinuations! For example, while the defense was subpoenaing some last-minute witnesses, Fred had stopped at Marquette's Public Safety office to return my uniforms. He'd talked to Carol Kurdziel, who'd asked him if there was anything she could do. Fred asked her if she'd be a character witness for me. She agreed. He had a few blank subpoenas in his pocket and handed her one. This is common practice. Anyone, with the exception of the defendant, can serve subpoenas.

Fred returned home and told me that Kurdziel would testify. But a few days later, Kraemer began, "Before we proceed, I would just like to inform the court that I have gotten several complaints from people who have called my office, informing me that Elfred Schultz, Jr., is running around delivering subpoenas. One woman from Marquette University in particular does not want to testify."

Eisenberg looked at me curiously, checking the last page of the witness list. "Who is he referring to? Carol Kurdziel? I thought she was a friend?"

"I thought so, too."

"Your Honor." Eisenberg stood. "It is not unlawful for Fred Schultz to serve subpoenas. In any event, the defense has not intended to subpoena someone against their will. We do not want a hostile witness, as I'm sure you realize."

Another witness lost.

The next day, we called three people to the stand. A former neighbor with two children testified that she'd known me for more than ten years; I used to babysit for her son and daughter. She believed in my innocence.

My friend Joanne, who lived in Stevens Point, Wisconsin, told the jury about the phone conversation I'd had with her the night of the murder. She and I had attended the same grade school and high school. We were in the band together and on the track team. We had belonged to the same parish. She had moved away from Milwaukee to go to college, but I drove up north to visit her about once a month. She, too, had known me for over ten years. She believed in my innocence.

My former employer from the gym testified that I had worked for him for about four years. I'd been employed there at the time of the homicide. He praised my work and said he would hire me back if he could. He was someone else who believed in my innocence.

■   ■   ■

The next day, I was to take the stand.

It was a snowy morning as Fred and I drove to the courthouse in his van. Movement was slow in the street because it was so slippery.

Eisenberg opened the proceedings: "The first witness we intend to call this morning is the defendant, Lawrencia Bembenek."

"Bring in the jury." Skwierawski nodded to the bailiff.

"Just a minute," Kraemer said. "There is another matter, Your Honor. There are names on the defense witness list that I object to, and I move that they be stricken from testifying based on their irrelevance to the case." He paused. "One of these names is Frederick Horenberger."

I froze. The DA was attempting to prohibit the testimony of the one person who could discredit the statements of Judy Zess, the prosecution's star! Zess had simply verified anything the State wanted her to. Now her testimony would go unchallenged.

"If Mr. Eisenberg insists on calling this witness to the stand—I understand Mr. Horenberger has been transported from Waupun Correctional Institution to the Milwaukee County Jail—then he should be willing to tell us why his testimony is relevant," Kraemer said.

"Mr. Eisenberg? Would you care to give me an offer of proof?" asked the judge.

"Your Honor," Eisenberg said slowly, "I cannot tell you the relevance of Horenberger's testimony without giving away my whole defense to Mr. Kraemer."

Several minutes of arguing continued, until Skwierawski was able to establish that Horenberger's testimony was hearsay evidence. Subsequently, it was suppressed as inadmissible, despite Eisenberg's objections.

"Even if it's evidence of perjury?" I wrote on the pad.

Eisenberg shrugged. The last speck of optimism that remained inside of me shriveled.

"Bring in the jury," Skwierawski said again.

"Are you ready?" Eisenberg asked me.

"Yes. I think, I'm a bit scared of Kraemer."

"Don't be." Eisenberg grinned. "You're smarter than he is! Laurie, if you're scared, don't be afraid to show it. You usually appear a bit too calm. Probably your police training."

"I'm not an actress."

"Then be yourself."

In total, I spent five hours on the witness stand. The cameras that had stared at my back for over two weeks now faced me like cannons. Beads of sweat rolled down my back.

Eisenberg asked me about my experiences as a female police officer, and the reasons for the complaint I'd filed against the department. He asked about my schooling, my childhood and my ambitions. I told the jury about the details of my marriage to Fred, and the problems we'd had with Judy Zess. The members of the jury stared back at me, expressionless. I looked into their faces for some sign of their reactions, but they were as stoical as the mannequins I used to dress at the Boston Store.

The court recessed occasionally, and I was keeping a fairly stiff upper lip, until my testimony reached the part about Fred's diamond ring. Eisenberg asked me about it to illustrate the point that, if we were as financially devastated as the State contended, I certainly would not have spent fifteen hundred dollars on a ring for Fred. For some reason unknown to me, the subject made me want to cry.

"I understand that in May of last year you took your tax return and bought your husband an expensive diamond ring, did you not?"

"Yes."

"Why did you buy that for him?"

"Because he never had anything like that ..." I said, my throat closing. I was unable to say any more. I didn't burst into sobs but tears filled my eyes. The bailiff brought me a paper cup of water.

I wrung my handkerchief and allowed the emotion to pass.

"How do you feel right now?" Eisenberg asked.

"Scared to death," I replied.

After lunch, Kraemer was scheduled to begin his cross-examination. I nervously tossed down three glasses of wine, remembering how throughout Eisenberg's direct examination Kraemer had sat next to Krusek, smiling and shaking his pudgy head. He acted as if my testimony was so unbelievable it was funny, scoffing at my replies. If I saw his body language, surely the jury did, too? I had to remind myself not to lose my temper with Kraemer and be sarcastic or flippant. He was so easy to dislike.

Kraemer immediately attacked my description of my Police Department experiences. "Miss Bembenek—does the alleged harassment you encountered on the Milwaukee Police Department have anything to do with this trial?"

"I don't know."

"And do any of the things you have just spent the entire morning telling this jury have anything at all to do with this trial?"

"I don't know," I repeated, wanting to say, "You tell me!"

"Ms. Bembenek, let's go into the reason why you were dismissed from the Police Department. Isn't it a fact that you were seen by Milwaukee Vice Squad officers smoking a marijuana cigarette at a rock concert?"

"I object!" Eisenberg shouted. "The subject of Ms. Bembenek's dismissal is not supported by any evidence from the State, and is immaterial."

"Well, Mr. Eisenberg," Skwierawski smiled, "the State was planning on restricting mention of that particular subject, but you are the one who opened that door, during direct examination. Overruled."

I could see Eisenberg scowl.

"Wasn't this concert the one you attended with your former roommate, Judy Zess?" Kraemer asked.

"Judy Zess was arrested for marijuana, but I was not present."

"You were required to file a report about that incident?"

"Yes."

"And isn't it a fact that the report you filed was false?"

"No. It was the truth."

"Weren't you identified by a Milwaukee Vice Squad officer, arrested and then released?"

"No! I was not! Another friend of Judy's was."

"Who?"

"Her name was Jan something. She was Judy's friend, not mine." I looked at Eisenberg. He winked at me and smiled. I knew that I had the statement from Judy Zess, sitting on the table next to my lawyer, if the issue went any further.

Kraemer caught me off guard by changing the subject.

"Let's talk about the marriage license that you and Fred signed in Waukegan. Isn't it a fact that you knew Fred was not allowed to remarry?"

"No. I had no idea."

"Then why did you leave the state of Wisconsin in order to get married? Wasn't it because you could not obtain a license in this state?"

"No. Not at all. I went to Waukegan to get married because Fred suggested it. We eloped."

"That's the only reason?"

"And I thought it was romantic."

"Oh. You thought it was romantic," Kraemer said sarcastically. "But isn't it a fact that you signed that marriage license, knowing that you two were not free and clear, by law, to marry?"

"No! I was free and clear to marry."

"You didn't know Fred wasn't?"

"No. How could I know?"

"Didn't you discuss his divorce?"

"No."

"Oh. Okay. Did you discuss money?"

"In regards to what?"

"Money. You know—what his salary was, what his alimony payments were, his child support, his house payments. Did you discuss that?"

"No."

"Before you were married, you had no discussions about money?"

"No. We were in love. We talked about what we had in common. We didn't discuss money."

The questioning continued. Then Kraemer got to the subject of Chris.

"Ms. Bembenek, isn't it a fact that you hated Christine?"

"No!"

"You didn't have any problems with her at all?"

"No."

"Did you ever talk to Christine Schultz?"

"Yes. A few times. Over the phone and in person."

"Where?"

"One night she came over to pick up the children ..."

"Were you ever inside the Ramsey Street house before May 28?"

"Yes."

"Isn't it a fact that Fred gave you a tour of that house?"

"No."

"But you were inside?"

"I stood in the front hallway by the door on the landing. I did not go in any farther," I explained. "Fred was picking up Sean."

"Was Fred proud of that house?"

"Yes."

"Fred built that house?"

"Yes."

"Fred built that house, but he didn't want to show it off to you?"

"Objection. That question has been asked and answered," Eisenberg said.
"Sustained."

"Ms. Bembenek, did you know that the Schultz family owned a dog?"

"Yes."

"Isn't it a fact that, in May, you asked Shannon, in front of his babysitter, where that dog was?"

"I had no reason to. I knew the dog was sold in February."

"How do you know the month it was sold?"

"It was around Valentine's Day. Fred was angry about it."

Eventually, the subject of my clothes was introduced by Kraemer.

"Ms. Bembenek, how many diamond rings do you own?"

"Objection!"

"Overruled."

"I own facsimile rings. But it's cosmetic jewelry, not genuine."

"I noticed you wore your rings every day, throughout this trial. Yet you're not wearing them to testify. Did you just decide to leave them at home today?"

"Yes."

"You just decided not to wear them today?" Kraemer smiled that same cynical smile.

"That's right," I said. I wanted to explain that my fingers were swollen, and that actually my mother suggested I not wear them, but I failed to elaborate. I was afraid the judge would say, "The witness is instructed to answer the question *yes* or *no*." I wondered why Kraemer was making a federal case out of my rings, anyway.

"Do you own any designer clothes?" he asked.

"Not originals."

"Originals?"

"Nancy Reagan wears originals."

"You don't own any originals?"

"Your Honor," Eisenberg interrupted, "would the court please instruct Mr. Kraemer to ask the defendant to explain what 'originals' are?"

The judge nodded.

"Originals are somewhere in the neighborhood of five thousand dollars apiece. But take designer jeans. Everyone wears those nowadays."

"Did you tell John Schultz to be careful when he helped you and Fred move, because you had 'designer' dresses that you wanted to move yourself?"

"Not exactly. I said that I would not want my dresses to be piled on the floor of John's van. I said I'd carry them myself."

"Did you make the statement at a dinner party in February that 'I would pay to have Christine Schultz blown away'?"

"No."

"You never said that?"

"No!"

"How tall are you, Ms. Bembenek?"

"Five feet, nine or ten inches."

"Would you step down from the witness stand and put this on for me please?" Kraemer held up the red warm-up jacket that I'd brought to match with the jacket in the black-and-white photograph.

"I object!" Eisenberg said.

"Objection overruled. Proceed."

I looked at my lawyer, then slipped on the jacket. Kraemer instructed me to stand next to him, in front of the jury. He was barely six feet.

"I object!" Eisenberg shouted again. "What is Mr. Kraemer attempting to prove? That he's a small man?"

There was a quiet chuckle, and Kraemer glared at my lawyer as he walked toward us.

"I have three-inch heels on, too," I said loudly.

"Take them off," Eisenberg told me. "Or is the State now suggesting that the defendant jogs in high heels?"

"What exactly are you trying to show, Mr. Kraemer?" the judge asked.

"Your Honor, I am illustrating how easily the defendant could have been mistaken for a man, because of her height. As the jury can plainly see, she is not much shorter than I am."

"Your Honor!" Eisenberg moaned.

"You'll have your chance if you choose to redirect," Skwierawski told Eisenberg.

Toward the end of the day, Kraemer seemed to be at the end of his list of questions. His previous calm attitude, by this time, seemed to swell to a thirst for conviction. This angry frame of mind, which he made no effort to conceal, finally consumed his better judgment as he launched into a line of questioning which seemed improper to me.

Producing the snapshot that showed me with Fred and the boys at the Brady Street Festival, Kraemer asked me about the restrictions of my bail conditions.

"Isn't it a fact that upon your release on bail you were to have no physical contact with Sean or Shannon Schultz?"

"That's correct."

He handed me the photo. "Do you recognize this picture?"

"Yes."

"Isn't it a fact that you knowingly violated the restrictions of your bail by seeing the children at the Brady Street Festival, as evidenced by this photograph?"

"No!" I cried. Kraemer was dead wrong.

"Objection!" Eisenberg shouted.

"What was the date you were arrested?" Kraemer asked, ignoring him.

"Answer the question," the judge told me.

"June 24."

"What was the date of the Brady Street Festival?"

"In June," I replied, trying to remember the exact date. I knew off the top of my head that it was in the second week of June, but could not recall the exact date.

"When in June?" Kraemer persisted.

"Um ..." I looked at Eisenberg, hoping he could help. I needed to look at my engagement calendar from the previous summer, which was on the table where Eisenberg was sitting, poised to spring like a tiger. He was obviously furious with Kraemer. I looked at my calendar and then back at Eisenberg.

"Was the Brady Street Festival before your arrest or after?"

"Before my arrest—the first or second week in June."

"Are you telling me that you never saw the children after your arrest, in an attempt to influence their testimony?"

"No!"

"You never saw them?"

"I never saw them!" I answered angrily.

"Your Honor!" Eisenberg hollered. "I object to this entire line of questioning on the grounds that the State has presented no proof as to the date of the festival, when it would be easy for them to verify the date of such a large city event. Mr. Kraemer is inferring that the defendant violated the conditions of her bail. He is insinuating that she saw the children to influence their testimony and stipulates that the photograph proves that she did.

"It proves no such thing, Your Honor! Laurie Bembenek was arrested on June 24 and the Brady Street Festival was in fact held on June 17!" Eisenberg waved his hand in the air as he spoke, holding my calendar in his hand. "I request that the jury be instructed to disregard—"

"Mr. Eisenberg, you are out of order. Your objection was overruled and I suggest that you refrain from further argument."

"Mr. Kraemer cannot support his accusations!"

"Sit down, Mr. Eisenberg."

Kraemer smiled and continued down the path of referring to matters not in evidence.

"Do you know a girl named Laurie Futh?"

I thought for a second. "She is a friend of Judy Zess."

"Isn't it a fact that you once showed Miss Futh pictures from your honeymoon?"

"No." I frowned, wondering what Kraemer was talking about.

"No? Well then, are you aware that Miss Futh told the police that she saw photographs of your honeymoon in Jamaica, and that in one of those photographs she remembers the travel clothesline that you denied owning? A clothesline similar to the one used in the murder of Christine Schultz?"

"I never showed Futh any pictures! My honeymoon pictures do not include any with a clothesline! I don't own a clothesline!"

"Your Honor!" Eisenberg interrupted. "Laurie Futh has not testified in this courtroom! The State has not admitted the defendant's honeymoon photographs into evidence! These innuendoes and inferences that are not supported by evidence should be considered inadmissible and I object to them!"

"Objection overruled."

During the recess, Eisenberg informed me that he planned to use redirect examination to clear up some of the implications Kraemer had tried to use.

"I'll bring in all of my photos from Jamaica. That's how positive I am that no such picture exists!" I told my lawyer.

After answering the last few questions Eisenberg asked, I stepped wearily down from the witness stand, expecting the State to rest its case. But once I had returned to my seat at the defense table, Kraemer stood and informed the court that he intended to call two additional rebuttal witnesses. The names were unfamiliar to me.

Eisenberg turned to me in surprise, and I shrugged.

A middle-aged woman took the stand. She wore a vinyl jacket and nervously picked at her hair, teased to resemble Tammy Wynette's.

She identified herself as Madeline Gehrt, and she testified that she owned a wig store on Twenty-seventh Street, called Olde Wig World. She went on to say that I'd bought a wig from her the previous spring.

With this, the prosecution tried to link me to the wig at the last minute. I was appalled at this preposterous testimony. The prosecution had handed Eisenberg Gehrt's business card, and I stared at it. I'd never been in the store! I'd bought my short, blond wig at Gimbels, and eventually sold it to Suzy.

"Can you believe this cheap shot?" Eisenberg whispered. "Watch this."

"Miss Gehrt." He addressed her sharply, stalking up to the witness stand. "When did you come forward with this information?"

"Yesterday."

"Yesterday?" he shouted. "Yesterday?" He paused, glaring at the pitiful witness with apparent disgust. "The day before the last day of the trial? This highly publicized case has continuously hit the media for the last nine months!"

Intimidated, Gehrt glanced furtively at Kraemer.

"Just what inspired you to come forward at this time?"

"It just dawned on me," she replied lamely.

I began writing down some points on my legal pad, hoping Eisenberg would see them in time.

"It just dawned on you. How convenient. Do you deny that you've read about this case in the paper or have heard it on television or radio?"

"I've ... read about it," she said, in a voice that was barely audible.

"You said the defendant walked into your shop last spring and bought a wig from you?"

"Yes."

"Do you know the date this occurred?"

"One afternoon."

"Do you recall what day it was?"

"No."

"Can you at least tell me what month it was?"

"I don't recall."

"How is it, then, that you can come into this courtroom and identify this young girl as the one who allegedly bought a wig from you?"

"When she paid for the wig, I noticed her name on the check."

Eisenberg strolled over to the defense table to see what I had written.

"Are you aware of the fact that the defendant has not had a checking account since 1977?"

"Um, no."

"Then, Miss Gehrt, wouldn't it have been impossible for you to have seen the defendant's name on a check?"

"She—no, um—she paid for the wig in cash. I remember because she said the wig wasn't for her. It was for a man, she said, for a joke."

"If you now say that the defendant paid for the wig with cash, then where did you see her name?" Eisenberg grew sardonic. "She didn't by any chance have on a green jogging suit, with the name BEMBENEK written across the back, did she?"

"When I asked for identification, I saw the name."

"Do you always ask cash-paying customers for identification?"

"No." Gehrt stumbled in her story. "When she paid in cash. I mean, I saw her name on her billfold."

"And you just remembered the name?"

"I remembered the name, because my girlfriend Maria has the same maiden name."

Maria? I thought. My cousin, Maria?

"I called Maria afterwards," Gehrt went on, "and Maria told me that it was probably her cousin, Laurie."

"Do you have a sales slip for this purchase?" Eisenberg asked.

"No."

"A canceled check or carbon copy?"

"No."

"A receipt?"

"No."

"In fact, Miss Gehrt, you have no physical evidence or record of this alleged transaction with the defendant at all, do you?"

"No."

Eisenberg shook his head and sat down next to me.

"Isn't it a fact that you just wanted to be on television?"

"No."

"No further questions, Your Honor."

As if the Marilyn Gehrt performance wasn't bad enough, I was shocked to see that the State's next witness was a Boston Store employee. Her name was Annette Wilson, and she worked as a store security guard nabbing shoplifters.

She was never very friendly with me, unlike the other employees at the store. When she learned that I'd turned in my resignation, she'd seemed resentful. I remembered the conversation in the cluttered coffee lounge.

"So, I hear you're leaving us," she'd said coyly.

I nodded. My friends had thrown me a going-away party in one of the stock rooms, with a cake and punch, and word got around.

"I'm going to be a police officer."

"If you make it," she sniffed.

"I hope to. I don't see why not. My dad was a cop and he has been encouraging me."

"So? My dad is a cop and he thinks women have no business on the Police Department! You'll see."

I watched her now as she stepped up onto the witness stand. She told the court that in 1979 she'd seen me leaving the store after work in none other than a green jogging suit.

"Laurie used to play tennis after work with a stock boy," Wilson said. "We carried the jogging suit she was leaving in. It was priced at sixty-eight dollars. Naturally suspicious, I checked with our Sporting Goods department to see if Laurie had purchased the suit."

I scribbled to Eisenberg: "Jogging suits not popular back in 1979. Don't think Boston Store carried anything other than some tennis dresses and racquetball shorts. Not any for sixty-eight dollars! The Athlete's Foot carried jogging suits—only about thirty-five dollars in 1978 or '79. No way!"

And I added: "I did play tennis after work, true—but in a white T-shirt and white shorts I bought from Boston Store. Stockboy's name is John Mavis. We could subpoena him! He'd stick up for me!"

The witness said, "So I made my report, for security reasons, and I remembered this whole incident because it was so suspicious."

"What was the color of the jogging suit?" Kraemer asked.

"Forest kelly green. It was made out of velour."

I went back to my scribbling: "Forest? Kelly? Which? Same words as last night's paper! Who'd play tennis in velour? She could never stand me! Her dad is a cop!"

Eisenberg nodded, and arose to approach the witness for cross-examination.

"Annette Wilson, do you read the *Milwaukee Journal* or *Sentinel*?"

"Yes."

"Are you aware of the fact that the news media has referred to my cross-examination of the witnesses, regarding the green jogging suit and in particular that my questions were about the shade of green this mysterious jogging suit is?"

"Would you repeat the question?"

"The shade, Miss Wilson. I'm talking about the shade of green that was printed in the newspaper. I had asked previous witnesses about the shade of green that they allegedly saw, and I mentioned forest green and I mentioned kelly green. Did you say it was both, just to be on the safe side?"

"No."

"Are you telling me that you did not read that in the newspaper?"

"I did not."

"You say you remember this so clearly. What year did this occur?"

"I don't know."

"Would it be 1978?"

"I don't know."

"1979?"

"I don't know."

"Do you remember what years Ms. Bembenek was employed by Boston Store at Southridge?"

"No."

"Miss Wilson, isn't it a fact that your father is a police officer?"

"Thirty years!" Wilson said proudly, nodding.

"Isn't it also a fact that you never liked Laurie?"

"On the contrary, we got along well," she said.

Eisenberg stared at her, paused, and his eyes narrowed. I came so close to shouting "Liar!" that I mouthed the word silently.

"You told the court a few minutes ago that you made a report regarding the incident. Do you have a copy of that report?"

"It was a verbal report."

"A verbal report? Oh—I see. Now, Miss Wilson, since you have inferred that Ms. Bembenek was stealing this 'forest kelly green velour jogging suit' from the store, one—I might add—valued at sixty-eight dollars did you attempt to apprehend Ms. Bembenek as she left the store?"

"No."

"Your job is security guard? Store detective?"

"Yes."

"Did you tell your supervisor?"

"No."

"Was anyone else aware of this?"

"I don't know."

"Miss Wilson, did you ever catch Miss Bembenek shoplifting or stealing anything from the store?"

"No, sir. We weren't that fortunate!" Wilson replied, with the surprise of a sniper.

My mouth fell open in shock. She was implying I'd been stealing from the store!

Eisenberg, who had been pacing back and forth, whirled around to face her. "Weren't that fortunate?" he repeated. "Weren't that fortunate?" His voice rose in disbelief. It was so brazen, so outrageous that he lost his temper. I couldn't blame him; it had been a frustrating two and a half weeks.

"Isn't it a fact, Miss Wilson, that you don't like Laurie because she's prettier than you are?"

Spectators in the courtroom gasped and several boos were heard. Annette's face took on a startled look. Skwierawski simply grinned slightly, his eyes down.

I cringed. It was true, but he was wrong to have said it. It hurt us, and played to all the old prejudices.

As Kraemer stood to raise his objection, Eisenberg quickly offered, "I'll withdraw the question, Your Honor."

"One more thing, Miss Wilson," Eisenberg then continued. "When, may I ask, did you come forward with this information?"

"The day before yesterday," Wilson said, sounding like Marilyn Gehrt.

"The day before yesterday? Why?"

"Because I read that she denied owning a green jogging suit."

Eisenberg informed the court that he wanted to recall me to the witness stand so I could refute the testimony of the rebuttal witnesses. I was sworn in for the third time, and explained that I'd never bought a wig from Marilyn Gehrt because I had never even heard of her store. I told the jury what I wore when I played tennis outside after work. Again, I denied ever owning a green jogging suit.

"How do you feel now?" Eisenberg asked.

"Angry," was my honest answer.

"Did you kill Christine Schultz?"

"No! I did not!"

"The witness may step down," the judge said.

Kraemer announced, "Your Honor, the State rests its case."

Court was adjourned until the following day, when closing arguments would begin. I felt like collapsing.

Once I arrived home, I peeled off clothes wet from nervous perspiration. A pile of my dresses had accumulated because I did not have time to take them to the dry cleaners, and I had exhausted my closet.

A real trial is nothing like the courtrooms depicted on TV, I thought, pulling on a robe. No hysterical outbursts allowed. No dramatic scenes or Perry Mason badgering the butler into admitting his guilt. I wanted so badly to jump up and call some of those witnesses liars at the top of my lungs—but I didn't dare. The bailiffs would have hauled me out of there, and I would be sitting in the slammer, with my bail revoked.

The telephone rang, and the floor felt cold on my bare feet as I hurried across the room to pick up the extension.

"Hi. This is Maria," a timid voice said. "Can I talk to your ... can I talk to Uncle Joe?"

"Maria, this is Laurie. Is it about the Gehrt woman?"

"I'd really like to talk to your dad."

"Please ..." I picked up an apple I'd intended to snack on and nervously dug my thumbnail into it, making small, half-moon indentations. "I'm the one who's on trial. If you have something to tell me ..."

Her voice was shaky. "What I want to know is, do I have to testify if I don't want to?"

"Did the police subpoena you?"

"They said they were going to. Let me start at the beginning. This silly girlfriend of mine—Maddy Gehrt—she owns a wig shop, and the other night she was gossiping to some of her customers that she saw you on TV and I was your cousin. She told them that she knew me.

"Well, a cop was in her store and overheard her conversation, and took her to the DA's office that same day. Two detectives were over at my house today. It was all a big mistake, really. I mean—"

"Who was the cop?"

"Alan Miller. He used to be Maddy's boyfriend. Maddy's husband is causing such a stink, because he doesn't want to pay child support on one of his sons that he says is Alan's kid. It's—"

"Miller? How convenient for him to drop in on a girlfriend who just happens to own a wig shop, of all things."

"Well, I told these two detectives just what I told you now, and they said that they were going to subpoena me because they said maybe I could help you."

"No detectives want to help me!" I argued.

"I'm so shook up. I really don't think I could testify—and you know, my sister was just in a car accident and, and—all I want to know is if they can make me come to court?" Maria whined.

"Calm down," I said, irritated. "First of all, you can relax, because the State rested its case today. That means that no more witnesses can be called to testify. The two cops who talked to you today probably didn't realize it was over. But Maria! I should think you'd want to help me! After all—my life is at stake!"

"I'm sorry ..."

■　　■　　■

The following day—the last day of the trial—was a Friday. Kraemer's closing argument was what I expected, but he changed his theory about the Ramsey Street house. He told the jury that I'd killed Christine so that Fred and I could sell the house.

"Isn't it odd, ladies and gentlemen of the jury," Kraemer crooned sarcastically, "that Lawrencia Bembenek has been able to explain away every minute detail of this case?"

If I couldn't explain some of these things, I'd be guilty! What could be odd about the truth? What did Kraemer expect me to do? Not tell my side of the story and go like a lamb to his slaughter? I was filled with resentment.

"It's as if she and her attorney stayed awake nights, working out every last detail of this case, and presented it to you, the jury, with remarkable smoothness! But that's the worst part of this whole case, ladies and gentlemen.

"The fact that this young lady planned and plotted and manipulated innocent people like those poor, helpless children, to believe her incredible story, and subtly brainwashed them to testify that she was not the intruder who entered their house that night and killed their mother. That is what I find deplorable beyond words."

"How can he say such horrible things?" I whispered to Eisenberg, who rolled his eyes.

"You see?" Kraemer continued. "That is why the defendant took the stand in a last-minute effort ..."

"He should talk about last-minute efforts!" I said, referring to the rebuttal witnesses. Eisenberg hushed me.

"... and told this courtroom that she was now angry! Angry, ladies and gentlemen, because the last two witnesses that I called did not fit into her plan. She was not prepared for them. They were a surprise. She didn't have time to prepare her defense against them or her explanation for their allegations."

"I was angry because it was so unfair! We weren't even allowed to prove they were liars!" I whispered. Eisenberg nodded. I cupped my chin in my hand and leaned on my elbow, letting Kraemer's voice trail off. I couldn't listen to another word.

My lawyer's closing argument lasted five hours. He reiterated the reasonable doubt in every piece of evidence the prosecution presented. He was thorough and direct. He stressed the numerous inconsistencies as he systematically took the jury through the testimony of every major witness for the State. He repeated the fact that the only witnesses to the murder testified that the murderer wasn't me, explaining that I had had no time to "brainwash" the children before the police talked to them.

The skyline outside the windows grew steadily darker. Later, I clawed my way through the mob of spectators and cameramen. Eisenberg shielded me from the hungry throng of reporters. My head ached unmercifully from the strain of the days, the weeks, the months of persecution.

The jury was out.

Unable to do anything else, we could only wait.

17

A WORLD WITHOUT COLOR

It was Saturday, March 6, 1982. The weekend was a devastating combination of anxious speculation and pessimistic expectation that made my heart pound every time the phone rang.

I forced myself to avoid thinking about being convicted; I couldn't bring myself to consider it realistically.

I tried to dull my overwhelming fear with the Scotch left over from Christmas, avoiding the disapproving eye of my mother. I thought, often, about suicide.

Fred and I met Don Eisenberg and his wife Sandy at an East Side restaurant. We sat at the bar, still discussing the trial and the jury and the performance of "Perry Kraemer."

The place filled with customers as we sat at the bar. Suddenly a loud, boorish man loomed up behind us.

"Hey, Tony!" he shouted in the direction of the bartender. Our backs were still to him. "Did anybody hear if Bembenek got burned yet?"

I almost choked on my drink, and I looked at Sandy, who gasped. We all turned to stare at this person. I shook a few wisps of hair out of my eyes and watched as the man noticed me. His smile faded.

I was thinking, You arrogant, ignorant slob ...! I spoke calmly, I think.

"You could be the father of someone my age. Would you say such a thing if I was your daughter?"

He mumbled something I didn't catch. "Bartender?" he called suddenly. "A round of drinks here, on me!"

It grew late, and the judge announced he'd no longer accept a verdict that day. The announcement was televised on every channel. The bartender turned off the TV.

We stepped outside. Don and Sandy went to a hotel, and Fred went to fetch the car. I waited under the large canopy.

A couple approached me on the sidewalk, arm in arm against the cold. As they passed me, they paused and said, "Good luck," reaching out to shake my hand. I thanked them, and they disappeared into the restaurant. It was still disconcerting to have strangers recognize me. If I'd chosen to thrust myself into the public eye, like a politician or an actress, I guess I might have been better prepared.

When we got home, my mother got up from the couch in the den and hugged me.

"I'm so proud of you, Laurie."

"Why?"

"You're so brave. My God, I don't know how you can stand it."

Fred walked in, fed Sarge some scraps from a doggy bag, and went upstairs.

The kitchen lamp had a warm glow. I untied the knot in the belt of my dress and leaned against the counter. There was an awkward silence. None of us knew what to say, feeling that any conversation would seem trivial.

■　　■　　■

The following morning, I was sipping coffee and reading the newspaper when the phone rang. I rushed to answer it.

It was Eisenberg. No decision had been reached yet, but he invited us to join him and Sandy for brunch, if we wanted to get out of the house. I went with Fred and one of his brothers.

It was bright and clear out, but the temperature was below zero.

Eisenberg was tense. He wore jeans and a thick, white sweater and drank a Bloody Mary while Sandy read the menu. He explained that the jury's long deliberation could be interpreted as a good sign.

"I've seen juries take less than twenty minutes to return a verdict of guilty," he said. "We may have a hung jury."

"Then what happens?" I asked.

"Then it's like Judy Zess's trial, remember? She had a hung jury, and they dropped the charges."

"But they wouldn't do that with a murder charge, surely?" Fred asked. "Just drop it, if the jury can't reach a decision?"

"Well, they could re-try the case, but I doubt that."

As we were eating, Eisenberg received word that he was wanted on the phone. I glanced at Fred anxiously as my lawyer left the booth.

Eisenberg sat down. The jury had requested to see the apartment complex where Fred and I last lived. Eisenberg said the defense had no objection to the request, but Kraemer had refused. Since both counsel had to agree, the judge had to deny the jury's request.

"Does the judge tell the jurors which side opposed the idea? Did he tell them it was Kraemer?" Fred asked.

"No," Eisenberg said.

"But that's not fair! The jury might think we didn't want them to see the apartment! They might think we have something to hide," I said.

"I wonder why they wanted to see the place," Eisenberg said. "Damn! I wish I knew what was going through their heads."

"So do I. I wish they could see the size of those garbage bins my mother was accused of digging through. We should have taken a photograph of them, with a person as tall as my mother standing next to them."

"They've been replaced with a different kind. The owners contracted with a different disposal company, and they use another type of bin. They aren't the same bins."

By evening, the judge again announced that he'd no longer accept a verdict that day. He refused to declare a hung jury.

"How are you holding up, Laurie?" Eisenberg asked.

"I guess ... I'm okay."

"I know it's tough. Hang in there. If you aren't acquitted, at least we can hope the jury is deadlocked."

I stayed up late and watched a movie on TV with my mom and dad. Fred sat on the couch, with Sergeant at his feet. Even then, a part of me continued to deny what was happening.

The next morning, Monday, I was told to meet Eisenberg at the courthouse because the jury had requested that portions of the transcripts be read back to them. They were still unable to reach a decision, after deliberating since Friday.

"They want to hear Durfee's testimony again, part of yours and part of Fred's," Eisenberg explained. "Obviously, I'm going to object. It's not fair to take testimony out of context."

"Well, if Kraemer didn't want the jury to see the apartments, then we should be able to refuse this request," I said.

As usual, Skwierawski had other ideas. Despite Eisenberg's objections, he said that, though he'd normally deny such a request, this time he'd break with tradition and allow portions of the transcripts to be read back to the jury.

Again, we were overruled.

By the end of another agonizing day, still no verdict had been reached.

Tuesday, March 9, 1982. I was so depressed I could barely get out of bed. It was a dreary, freezing day. The sky was the color of gray flannel.

I took a warm shower, trying to relax the tension in my muscles by letting the water beat on my shoulders. My mom asked my dad to pick up some sandwiches, and then she paced anxiously, in an aimless stroll about the house. We decided to play a game of Scrabble to pass the time. I wrapped my hair in a towel and sat down at the table. It was almost noon.

The extension phone rang softly. I held my breath and picked up the receiver.

"The jury has reached a verdict," Eisenberg said. "Cross your fingers and see you downtown."

My heart pounded wildly and the color left my face. From my expression, my mother knew that the end to the waiting had arrived. My dad returned with the sandwiches, and his eyes showed concern when he saw my face. An intense feeling of dread washed over me.

My mom walked up to me and held my shoulders. "It's going to be all right, Laurie. It has to be."

"But we thought it would be a hung jury," I said, trembling.

"No jury in their right mind could find you guilty."

"Mom! You just don't know! You weren't there for all of it, because you were sequestered. It was so unfair! I have this awful feeling ..."

"Here," she said, handing me her gold wedding band. "Wear it for good luck."

When we arrived at the courtroom, the cameras and reporters were there, but the place was strangely silent. Eisenberg was there. He wrung his hands as I hung my wool coat over the chair at the defense table.

"How are you?" he asked.

I felt as though I'd been suffering from a terminal illness for a very long time, and was about to die.

"I feel like I'm at my own funeral. Why is it so quiet in here?"

"A better question is why are so many sheriff's deputies in here?" Eisenberg asked. "Do they expect a riot?" Officers from the Sheriff's Department lined the walls like trees.

"I don't know what to think," Eisenberg told me. "I've talked to the bailiffs and they claim the jury took several different votes. They kept coming up with different answers. I just don't know."

234

"Is Skwierawski here?" I asked.

"He will be in a minute. I'll tell you one thing, Laurie. When the jury comes in, if they're looking at you, you're safe. If none of them looks at you, it's time to appeal."

I turned around to see Fred's dad walk in with my parents. They sat down just as the judge appeared, with Kraemer at his side.

"All rise."

The jury walked in.

None of them looked at me.

And then I knew.

■   ■   ■

He sentenced me to life imprisonment.

The rest of my life.

He took my life away.

My life!

My head filled with fog, with gray fog for a gray half-life, gray walls, gray cells, gray places, gray people, gray hours, years of living without life.

A scream rose in my throat, but smothered in the gray, gray fog.

Then they came, and took me away to jail.

■   ■   ■

"Oh!" I heard a male voice say just around the corner. "The new prisoner is here! I didn't recognize her with her clothes on!"

I was taken to another room, where I signed papers I didn't even read. "My purse and my coat," I mumbled, in a stupor. I was in a thin County Jail gown once again.

"You better make any phone call you need to now, because you'll be taken to Taycheedah Correctional Institute tomorrow," the deputy said.

A door opened and I was pointed in the direction of a cellblock. I walked straight to a phone on the wall and tried dialing Fred, twice, but I kept getting a recording. I wondered if my mom and dad were home yet. I realized I had been staring at the phone, unable to use it. The other inmates sat around a table, watching me.

I went to a cot in my cell and burst into heavy sobs. A matron walked in and put a supper tray on the shelf attached to the wall. It looked like dog food with a spoon in it.

I walked back to the phone, and got through to Fred, who was also crying. I told him that I needed a coat and the case for my contact lenses. He said they'd be right down.

The matron walked back in. "Channel four wants an interview."

"No," I said, trying to control my shaking.

I took my contact lenses out and put them in a paper cup with water. Just as I lay down on my cot, a sheriff's deputy came to get me.

"Get dressed," she said.

"Excuse me?"

"Come with me. I'll get your clothes. You're going to Taycheedah right now."

I followed her out, knowing that there was no time to contact my family, who were on their way with my coat. Why did the authorities suddenly feel compelled to rush me out of the Milwaukee County Jail? Some prisoners sat downtown for weeks before being transported in the van to jail.

It was dark outside. I sat shivering in handcuffs and chains that left greasy smudges on my white pullover. I was in the back of a Sheriff's Department squad car, with three officers. The dim countryside along the highway appeared blurry; I had forgotten my contact lenses.

Somehow, though, the blurred world was appropriate, marking a passage from one world to another, far grimmer. A world without any color.

■   ■   ■

So this is what the case against me amounted to:

- A woman whose credibility was suspect, at best, said she'd overheard me saying I wanted to have Christine Schultz "blown away."

- The "motive" was that child-support payments and mortgage payments had put a crimp in our lifestyle, and either I wanted to frighten Christine out of her house in some manner that had gone wrong, or I wanted to kill her so I could move in myself.

- On the night of the murder, a girlfriend of mine luckily canceled a date. Early in the morning, in my heavy police shoes and a green jogging suit, a wig and a mask, I jogged the eighteen or so blocks over to the house. No one saw me. I entered with a key I hadn't known we had, effortlessly bound and gagged Christine, tried to smother the boys, killed Christine and jogged back to the apartment, holding on to the gun. The man the boys saw was a phantom of their imagination, though the jogging suit only one of them had seen wasn't. It wasn't a man at all. It was me, whom the boys had known for some time.

236

- After I got to my apartment, I cleaned the gun and put it away and got into bed and fell asleep, just in time for a call from Fred.
- I was able to do this because I was a cold-hearted bitch (a former Playboy bunny, after all!) who would stop at nothing to continue living life in the fast lane (like working at Vic Tanny's and as a security guard on campus). The thing is a joke.

  A very sick joke.

The motive:

There is a considerable amount of evidence to suggest that Christine feared someone other than me. Her own attorney, Kershek, told the police shortly after her murder that Fred had threatened to kill her and that she thought she was being followed. She believed Fred was angry over her relationship with Honeck; he had already blown the whistle on Honeck for sleeping with Christine, thereby getting him into trouble at work. He'd then let Honeck believe I'd done the fingering.

Two other friends of Christine's, Dorothy Polka and Joanne Delikat, also said Fred had threatened Christine, and both said he'd beaten her severely several times. Joanne said Christine was afraid of Fred.

It wouldn't be hard to establish that I didn't want that house and never had. Too many people had heard me complaining about it. Nor did I want kids—everyone knew that. It's worth noting that I called Josephine Osuchowski only a few hours after the murder, worrying about having to take the kids.

Fred may have had a motive, but I didn't.

And bear in mind this:

- I was suing the Milwaukee Police Department for sexual discrimination, was to be the star witness in a federal investigation, and had been the target of reprisals;
- I had made public, in the anti-discrimination suit, the very unpopular connections between the cops and the drug dealers who ran the Tracks bar;
- I had opened the can of worms that had some officers dealing drugs, running hookers and selling pornography from their cruisers;
- High officials of the Milwaukee Police Department were involved.

  You tell me if you still think this was a clean investigation.

The hairs found at the scene:

The prosecution claimed that a hair found by the medical examiner was retrieved from the bandanna around Christine's mouth. This was compared to hairs from my hairbrush and found to be compatible.

What to say about this?

It was stipulated at the trial that "a hair of light tint" was found on the bandanna. Eisenberg accepted this as fact. In reality, there was no such hair. Dr. Samuels wrote in a letter, after I was found guilty: "... at the time of the unwitnessed autopsy I recovered many brown hairs, along with numerous fibers of non-human origin.... I recovered no blond or red hairs of any texture or length, nor did I recover any hair grossly compatible with fibers from a red or blond wig. All the hairs I recovered were brown and grossly identical to the hair of the victim."

Still, one blond hair, "color-processed," "consistent" with mine mysteriously made its way into the police inventory. Here's the chronology surrounding the hair:

1. The bandanna goes to the Crime Lab.
2. The Crime Lab numbers the hairs one through twenty, *all* of which are consistent with Christine's hair.
3. The bandanna is checked *out* of the Crime Lab by the cops.
4. The bandanna is returned by the cops.
5. The lab discovers additional hairs, which they number twenty-one through twenty-five and Eureka! *one* matches the blond, color-processed hair of Lawrencia Bembenek.

Was it just a coincidence that this happened right after they'd seized my hairbrush and security guard uniform from my locker on campus? It was these phantom hairs that Diane Hanson analyzed and found to be compatible with mine. The jury never knew the stipulation about the hair was false. If they'd known, they might have questioned whether the hair really did come from Christine Schultz's body.

The gun:

Ah, the gun!

The jury said afterwards that the gun was the one compelling piece of evidence that they used to ignore the boys' testimony and convict me. The gun did it for them.

Fred's was the only testimony that connected me to the gun. If he hadn't testified, there would have been no case. If he'd said there was a third gun, and that third gun had been the one in the apartment, there would have been no case either.

I was a cop. I knew about police procedure. I was familiar with guns. Yet the prosecution was asking everyone to believe that I killed Christine with

Fred's off-duty gun, and simply returned it to Fred. If I had killed someone with a gun, would I be dumb enough to hang on to it, even after the murder, when throwing it away would have precluded a case against me?

The State's ballistics guy, Monty Lutz, said the bullet, which the jury was led to believe came from Christine's body, was fired by Fred's off-duty gun. That gun was then identified as "the murder weapon."

But was it?

On the night of the murder, Durfee and Fred came home. Their stories about what they then did differ in some respects. Fred said he and Durfee went straight to the off-duty gun. Durfee said Fred and I disappeared for a while, and after that they went for the gun. Durfee did say he examined the gun and it hadn't been fired, but he could not later identify the murder weapon as the gun he inspected, because he never wrote down its serial number. The notebook in which he made this glaring omission was mysteriously missing—he'd lost it or thrown it out.

Others examined that gun, too. There was a meeting in the inspector's conference room at police headquarters, to which Fred had been summoned. They presumably examined it (why else ask for it?) but presumably concluded, too, that it hadn't been fired. They gave it back to Fred to keep, which he did.

Fred didn't turn the gun in until twenty-two days after the murder. No evidence says that the gun shown to Durfee was the gun later given to Monty Lutz. Fred could have changed it. Anyone could have, in those twenty-two days.

And the bullets? Lutz was given a collection of bullets from Fred. Some of them couldn't be fired from either of his two official guns. At no time was anyone questioned about what missing gun these bullets could have come from. If the jury had known about these bullets, and about the procedures involved in handling the gun, they could reasonably have concluded that there'd been a third gun—after all, Fred at one time testified he owned five. They might have concluded that it was this third gun Durfee inspected, and that this was not the murder weapon. I know now that there are significant differences between the autopsy protocol sheet and the Crime Lab sheet descriptions of the bullet. Not only the sets of initials, but the weight of the bullet differs from sheet to sheet and on one sheet it is described as having a damaged nose. But, no damage to the bullet is listed on the other sheet. This means that somewhere between the morgue and the Crime Lab, the bullet underwent a miraculous physical transformation! Who transports the evidence from the morgue to the Crime Lab? Who else? The police!

The bullet Elaine Samuels released for evidence carried three initials. The bullet introduced in evidence carried six initials. Who knows whether this was the same bullet? Just as with the gun, the chain of continuity is broken. The evidence is, at best, suspect.

Was there some other way of verifying whether this gun was the murder weapon, apart from the ballistics, which were not reliable anymore? Could the gun be matched to the wound? It was a contact wound, and a muzzle imprint was left on the body. When you compare the muzzle imprint with the murder weapon, so called, there is a 250 percent discrepancy.

I have support for these suspicions from, among other people, Werner Spitz, the former medical examiner from Detroit, who knows something about guns; and from Dr. Michael Baden, a top forensic guy from the New York State police; and from Dr. John Hillsdon-Smith, the top Canadian expert, a man who usually testifies for the prosecution.

Said Hillsdon-Smith, Ontario's Director of Forensic Pathology: "It's difficult not to conclude that this woman has been railroaded." His own view was that "autopsy records indicated that the impression left on the victim's back by the rim of a gun muzzle was two and a half times as large as the muzzle of the alleged murder weapon."

The discrepancy is so great that it cannot be accounted for—therefore that gun did not leave that mark. Either there was a switch in the guns, in which case Fred did it, or there was a switch of the bullet. In either case, the basis on which I was prosecuted was false.

Further, what about the blood on Fred's own service revolver?

The green jogging suit:

The only person who ever saw this phantom jogging suit was the younger boy, Shannon. Sean, the older boy, who gave the more complete description, called it a green canvas army jacket. He never mentioned anything about a jogging suit. He also quite clearly stated that it wasn't me, and that the person he'd seen was far too big.

So who said there was a jogging suit?

Zess, of course. At the prelim, she said she saw only sweat pants with tight elastic ankles and couldn't say if it was a jogging suit. At the trial she changed her mind. It was now definitely a jogging suit. Years later (as we will see) she changed her mind again. She said she'd been induced to change her evidence by police promises that they'd do everything they could to help Tom Gaertner, in prison on drug-trafficking charges.

Shannon, who first described this suit, said it was dark green. Detective Shaw said he couldn't place the color exactly. His wife said it was lighter than forest green. Officer Faubel called it kelly green, but no one else ever saw me in it. Faubel and his family were known to one of the jurors.

There was Annette Wilson, of course. But her superior, the chief investigator for the Boston Store, went on television to say she was lying when she said she'd reported me stealing a green jogging suit, kelly or forest or any other green and she was *fired* from her job because of it.

And something else: there had been several sightings—six or more—in the neighborhood on the night in question of a male jogger fitting the description given by Sean. This evidence was never introduced at trial, not even by Don Eisenberg. The most significant sighting was probably that of Nurse Barbara Sarenac, who spotted him that night around the time Fred was calling me. She was never called as a witness. None of this was ever mentioned at my trial.

The key to the Ramsey house:

The key I was supposed to have was never introduced in evidence. It had been packed away somewhere in Fred's jewelry box, I was told, but where my mother had packed it I didn't know. Fred had gone looking for it afterwards, I'd thought. But could he have been replacing it? I was confused. In any case, in a police report on May 29 it was said that Fred handed one key over to the investigating detectives the night of the murder, and then opened the doors to the Ramsey house a few hours later. That would seem to account for both keys.

The clothesline:

Throughout the trial it was suggested that Christine's hands were bound with a clear plastic cord. However, the initial report simply states that Christine had it around her wrist and through the fingers of her left hand. The photographs taken at the medical examination support this.

Zess—of course!—said Fred and I owned such a cord. We, in turn, both said the only cord we knew of belonged to Judy. This cord was supposed to appear in photographs taken on our honeymoon in Jamaica, since it was a traveling clothesline. No such photograph exists.

The wig:

Both kids said their assailant was a man with reddish-brown hair in a six-to eight-inch ponytail. Since I was a blond, with hair too short for the kind of ponytail they described, perforce it must have been a wig for me to have been present. (Later I found out that the wig they found was a cascade—a small hair piece—not long enough to be pulled into a six- to eight-inch ponytail.)

On the night of the crime, the police report indicates that a fiber was found on Christine's thigh after the police turned the body over.

It wasn't until a few weeks later, on June 15, that there was any indication a wig was involved. At that time, our landlady, Frances Ritter, told two detectives that a wig had been retrieved from the plumbing drains that were shared by our apartment and another, occupied by Mr. and Mrs. Niswonger and Judy Nitchka. Sharon Niswonger had called the landlady to complain of an overflowing toilet, and a plumber had fished out this wig. The landlady kept it for a while (hoping she could charge someone for the cost of the plumber) but then threw it into a dumpster. The cops retrieved it on June 15.

Yes, but ... what was never placed in evidence was that the last person to use the toilet in the Niswonger-Nitchka apartment before it backed up was Judy Zess! She had visited the apartment unexpectedly and asked to use the toilet. Sharon Niswonger told Kraemer about this, but he never raised it while she was on the witness stand. Of course not—it would have cast doubt on his nice theory. Again, I remind you that Zess later recanted and deposed that she'd been asked to change her testimony as a reward for help for Tom Gaertner.

One more point about this wig. It's hard to believe that some human hair wouldn't adhere to the inside of a wig. Did they ever examine this wig for such evidence? No! Why not? Because they wouldn't have found any of mine.

If the fiber on the leg could have come from the wig, the fact that Zess might have had the thing in her possession and tried to flush it down the toilet was certainly exculpatory evidence. Surely it might have made the jury think?

And the woman who said I bought a wig from her shop? No one now believes her. I bet her own mother doesn't even believe her.

The fingerprints:

Fingerprints *were* found on the bedpost and window frame of Christine's bedroom. They were compared to the fingerprints of six other people, but not to mine. Nor were they compared to the fingerprints of Frederick Horenberger or those of Danny L. Gilbert, of whom more later ... At the time of the trial, I only saw one MPD Homicide Index Report that stated: "Number of fingerprints found at the scene: none." But other reports later found by Ira Robins made references to prints! Fancy that. Conflicting information about something as crucial as fingerprints at a murder scene!

Me and my movements the night of the murder:

My mom and I were packing on the night of the murder, as I've said. Fred slept until about eleven, when he went to work. He phoned at midnight, and again half an hour later.

Stu Honeck logged the call from Sean at 2:26 AM. Before Sean called, he saw the murderer leave, tried to stem his mother's bleeding with gauze, tried to call the operator, and then called Stu.

Fred called me at 2:40.

The house is eighteen blocks away.

Fred and Durfee checked my car when they came by, and its motor was cold. I had no bike. I would have had to jog over.

Nurse Sarenac saw a man matching the description of the murderer shortly after 2:40. An hour later, Fred called again. Shortly after that I called my friend Josephine Osuchowski.

Another thing. On the Memorial Day weekend, our building's front door lock was changed. The landlady, Mrs. Ritter, confirms it. Neither Fred nor I had a key. If I'd jogged over to kill Christine, I'd either have had to buzz someone to get back in—suuuure!—or somehow propped a door open.

And Fred that night?

Fred's and Durfee's reports differ considerably. Fred said he was never out of Durfee's sight. Durfee said it wasn't so. Both of them said they'd worked the whole time. Others admitted to having seen them both out drinking at Georgie's Pub. If they are inconsistent in this, why not in other things?

So we have Fred on the record as lying. Transcripts we received ten years later from Police Department records show that two detectives, Craig Hastings and James Kelley, caught Fred perjuring himself. They recommended proceeding against him—four counts of perjury at unrelated hearings.

They told McCann.

"Do you want Bembenek or do you want Schultz?" McCann asked.

"He's violating the law," Kelley said, stubbornly.

McCann of course ignored him. He wanted me, not Fred.

But *why*?

Without Fred, of course, there was absolutely no link between me and the crime.

None. Not one.

What about my good friend Judy Zess?

Let's recap the main events: she admitted lying about the concert where she was arrested for having marijuana, and lying about me. But she quit the police force. In 1981, she shared our apartment. She then became involved with Tom Gaertner, a good friend of Sasson, an off-duty cop killed by Fred.

July 2, 1981, Zess was robbed by Frederick Horenberger and Danny L. Gilbert. Both men were convicted and sentenced to prison. Both had long records. The owner of Georgie's Pub has testified he introduced Fred Schultz to Horenberger (though Fred has denied knowing Horenberger); they worked together on construction projects. On the night Christine was murdered, one Danny L. Gilbert was found by the police in a truck at the side of the roadway overlooking Christine's home. He told police he was tired and stopped to rest. It's possible this was another Danny L. Gilbert (they have different birth dates according to their IDs) but it's a neat coincidence, isn't it?

The last person to use the toilet before it backed up with the wig was Judy Zess.

Judy Zess told Horenberger she wanted to get me to help Tom.

And another thing. Who took the bullet to the Crime Lab? Detective Frank Cole. Who was hot on my trail? Frank Cole. Who was the prosecution's star witness? Judy Zess. Who was in Judy's bed? Frank Cole.

And Stu Honeck?

Stu was a cop who lived with Fred between his break-up with Christine and his marriage to me. He said he was engaged to Christine, though no one could prove it. He left Christine's house around 10:50 PM, he said. Honeck was the one who got Sean's call and was one of the first cops there. Sean and Shannon both said a strongbox in the house had been tampered with and was open.

In 1986 my mom and dad got a call from Stu. During that call, Honeck mentioned some three hundred thousand dollars worth of drugs that had gone missing from Christine's house the night of the murder. Honeck claimed Fred took them. Drugs were never mentioned during my trial.

What about Frederick Horenberger?

He's dead now—committed suicide after taking hostages during an armed robbery in 1991. The evidence that he knew Fred is pretty compelling. He was convicted of robbing Zess, using pretty much the same MO [modus operandi] Christine's killer had used. He had a long record of violent crime. He could have been the one who pulled the trigger that night. I just don't know.

The murder scene:

The first cops on the scene found Christine face down. Thomas Hanratty, the medical examiner, found her face up when he arrived. Someone had turned her over.

There were bloodstains on the wall at the scene of the murder. Fred told the cops it was probably from the Great Dane that had been in heat. But Christine had got rid of the dog months earlier. The bloodstains were taken to the police lab. Diane Hanson said she was never asked to do an analysis of the blood, not even to see if it was dog blood.

The medical examiner wasn't called until two hours after the detectives arrived, and it wasn't until several hours afterwards that Elaine Samuels, the assistant, performed an autopsy. No police officers were present at the autopsy, in violation of state law. Further, Fred, who was clearly a suspect at this time, went to the morgue with me to identify Christine, and even turned the body over while he was there. Stu Honeck could have made the identification easily enough.

And Judge Skwierawski?

At the start of the trial, he advised both counsel that he'd once acted as a lawyer for Tom Gaertner. No one objected, not even Don Eisenberg. At the time, Gaertner was in prison awaiting trial on his trafficking charges. Zess, who would later marry him, was the State's star witness.

The jurors, too:

Two of the jurors might have been predisposed. One was a friend of Officer Faubel, the one recruit who believed I'd owned a green jogging suit. The other knew Judy Zess (as a "party friend").

Not to mention my attorney, Don Eisenberg:

Later he was suspended indefinitely from the Wisconsin bar for conflict of interest in another murder trial. My mom and dad paid most of his fees, but Fred chipped in five thousand dollars and signed over his share in the house on Ramsey. He was paid by Fred. Fred was another suspect. Eisenberg had Fred sit in on most of the meetings he had with me. He later appeared on TV with Fred, where both of them said I was guilty.

Great case, right?

18

THE PRISONER

I'd never been to Taycheedah, or even to the County of Fond du Lac, where it is situated. When we arrived at the gatehouse, the deputies were told to remove their gunbelts. I strained my eyes to get a look at the compound but could only make out blobs of light that resembled hungry eyes in the darkness.

"Good luck, Lawrencia," one of the female deputies said.

The next thing I knew, I was in a small room with two shower stalls and a wall lined with shelves that held supplies. I'd been escorted to a large building that was referred to as a "housing unit"—a nice college-dorm euphemism if ever there was one. They made it sound like a condo. A large, male lieutenant named Wood informed me that I would stay in "R&O" (Receiving and Orientation) until I was medically cleared.

The jingle of many keys and locked doors greeted me.

"It's up to you how you want to do your time," Wood said, in a kind of baritone bark. "You can keep your mouth shut, and have it pretty easy—or you can do hard time. It's all up to you."

Hard time? Was there anything else? It had all happened so incredibly fast. One minute I was enjoying the company of my family, playing Scrabble at the kitchen table—and then the metal door of my cell was locking behind me, shutting me in. I knew I'd never forget that iron clang as long as I lived.

I heard the approach of walkie-talkies. Two female prison guards, or "correctional officers," ordered me to remove all my clothes for a strip-search.

Humiliated beyond words, I stood there naked, attempting to lessen my embarrassment by staring at the tile floor. I was still crying.

"Turn around, bend over and spread your cheeks."

After the guards watched me shower with a lice shampoo called "Kwell," I was given a thin gown and a cotton robe that smelled of body odor. I wondered who had worn it before me. Then they took me to my cell. My "room," they called it.

I sat on my bed, staring at walls closing in on me. I could still hear the judge's words echoing in my mind, see his mouth moving. I worried about my family, remembering the sobs I'd heard behind me in the courtroom.

My head ached from crying.

Thoughts of God and Hell swirled in my mind. There were no innocent souls in Hell, were there? Not in any theology they taught at St. Mary's. Perhaps they'd got it all screwed up and the universe was run by malevolent devils? I thought of the eternity to come, the years of iron doors and prurient guards stretching into the future, and considered suicide. It would have been so easy! Easy right then to tear strips from my bedsheets and construct a rope long enough to tie to the pipe, hanging there until blessed oblivion came.... It would have been a relief, finally something constructive to do. It was the thought of my mom and dad that stopped me. They'd had enough pain.

■　　■　　■

I found a passage in Nietzsche, years later: "Everything can be acquired in solitude, except sanity." A melancholy truth. The boredom of the days left me with nothing to do but dwell on my misery. I couldn't touch the food that was brought to my cell. I couldn't sleep at night—I didn't even have control over the large overhead light above my bed. I could only guess what time it was.

The same routine woke me every morning. Keys in the lock on the cell door preceded the voice of the sergeant on duty.

"Six AM. Do you want a breakfast tray, Bembenek?"

"No, thank you," I would answer from my bed, turning over and falling back to sleep. The cell door would close and the lock would turn noisily. After about twenty minutes, the door would wake me a second time, with officers collecting the dishes.

"Tray, please."

"I don't have a tray," I would explain every day. "I refused breakfast."

Just about the time I got back to sleep, the cell door would open for a third time, and the guard would announce, "Shower."

No matter how hard I wished for it, I was never lucky enough to find warm water issuing from the battered old shower faucet in the bathroom. None of the old buildings, I learned, had warm water. Every morning, I would cringe under an icy shower, unable to withstand the cold shock for more than a minute or so. Afterwards, I'd get back into bed, my teeth chattering. I'd curl into a fetal position, pull the cotton blanket up to my chin and shiver until I fell back to sleep.

The next event on the unvarying morning agenda was to supply each cell with a mop and bucket. Cleaning was top priority every morning. By that time, I would usually acquiesce and change into the "state-issue" clothing, which consisted of baggy denim pants and a gray sweatshirt. Old white tennis shoes were provided, and white cotton socks.

One morning, after a heavy snowfall, I was lying in bed, listening to some black women shovel the snow just outside my window. I was on the first floor of the building, and my window was at ground level. It was quiet outside, the snow muffling sound. I could hear the women easily, over the rhythmic scrape of the shovels.

"I seen 'dem bring in a whole lot of womens. I bet R'n'O is full."

"That the poh-lice in that room," one said.

I knew they were referring to me, and I wondered what inmates did to former cops in prison.

So many different guards opened my door over the next few days that I felt like a freak on exhibition. I later found out that they were unprofessional enough to parade to my cell, eager to get a look at the "infamous" Bembenek.

It was the sheer arbitrariness of it all that bothered me most at first, the careless inconsistencies between officers. I was given a huge stack of rules and policies that I was instructed to read. Some of the material was outdated. Some of it was just ignored. Contradictions were everywhere. No one would provide clear answers.

I scanned the regulations concerning visitors. The prison struck me as a virtual paper factory. There were hundreds of memorandums, written policies and procedures, regulations and addendums to the memorandums. There were forms to fill out for visiting privileges, with those approved comprising a prisoner's official Visitors List. Only persons on that list were allowed to visit. After I filled out a request for visiting privileges with a particular person, the Social Services Department mailed that person a form to complete. If my social worker approved the person, the name was added to my list, and could not be removed for six months.

There were request forms for writing privileges that had to be completed in triplicate for all correspondence to another institution. There were forms to request phone calls. We were allowed two ten-minute calls per month, and we could call only a person whose name appeared on our approved Visitors List. The call would be placed by the housing unit sergeant, at the sergeant's convenience.

There were forms to request canteen privileges, medical attention and everything imaginable—a world so foreign to me then. I was confused and fearful, aching to know how soon I would be able to see my family.

I read in the stack of policies that "new commitments" (that was me) were allowed to see immediate family after seventy-two hours. I asked a guard at my cell door about this rule, and she verified it.

Another section of the rules stated that inmates in R&O were allowed to mail seven letters a week without stamps on the envelope called "free stamp letters." I used the pencil and lined paper I was provided and wrote to my parents, asking them please to visit as soon as possible. I also wrote to Don Eisenberg, and to Fred.

When my pencil became too worn down, I had to stop. I had to slip the pencil under the door and wait until an officer noticed it and sharpened it for me. I also slid my letters under the cell door for the guards to pick up. Of course, they read everything.

I looked out my window. It was reinforced on the inside with wire mesh and would only open about two inches. I felt claustrophobic. I could see a farmhouse and a barn past the prison fence, about a mile away in the darkness. The blinking lights in town lined the horizon like fallen stars, a constant reminder of another life, another world. I could run that far, if it meant my life, I thought. I'd done it once, years before. When I was thirteen, I ran away from home. I literally ran, cutting my feet on sharp stones, unseen in dimly lit alleyways. I'd give my right arm to be able to run back home now.

Another guard opened the lock on my door. It was mealtime. Biting into a sandwich, my front tooth broke. When the meal trays were being collected, I asked the officer for a Dental Request form and chatted with him, desperate for conversation.

"I can't wait until I see my family," I said. "They'll be here tomorrow."

"You can't have any visitors until you're medically cleared," he said, shifting his weight in his cowboy boots (only the lieutenants wore uniforms). "That probably won't be for another week or so."

"But the other guard, the female at night, said they could see me after seventy-two hours!" I told him tearfully.

"I'm sorry. That's an old policy. She gave you the wrong info."

"I wrote home and told my mom and dad that they could visit! Now they'll drive here from Milwaukee for nothing!" I cried. "It says in these rules—seventy-two hours!" I pointed to the papers I'd been given.

"Those must be outdated manuals. I also have some letters to return to you. You're only allowed to write five free letters a week."

"But the rules say seven!"

"The rule now is five per week, per prisoner, for the first thirty days of incarceration. Then it drops to one per week."

Later, I found out that five was not the correct number either; it was three.

Every shift of guards did things a different way. I was in their hands now, and totally dependent upon them. From their decisions, large and small, there was no appeal.

It seemed to take forever to get medically cleared. The institution's medical staff and equipment were inadequate, and the tests and "bloodwork" had to be mailed to Madison.

I was aware of the new "commitments" being brought in. There were cells on either side of me. I wondered what day it was, because I had lost track. Black women walked in groups on the sidewalk outside, returning to the building. Some shouted "I love you!" up to prisoners on the second and third floors, so I thought, naively, that there must be male inmates in the building. I wondered why some inmates were allowed outside, and for what purpose.

The following week, I began to receive hundreds of letters and donations from people across the state who supported me. All the envelopes had been opened by the prison before I received them. Fred wrote that a defense fund had been established, and it lifted my spirits to learn that strangers cared about me and were outraged at the verdict.

My mom and dad wrote as soon as they were allowed to. On the night that I was convicted, they said, by the time they'd reached the County Jail, I was already gone. I started to cry again, and cried each time I saw their familiar handwriting.

"They couldn't wait to take you from us, my darling daughter," my dad wrote.

I cried again.

Even as I slept, I clutched my father's letter close to my heart, the writing blurred from the tears.

In the morning, I wandered over to the mirror on the wall and stared at myself. My skin looked bloated, pale and unhealthy from crying. Because I couldn't use a cream rinse or conditioner on my hair, the hard water turned it into a cotton-candy frizzle. My eyebrows were growing in. I ran a hand across my face. My fingernails were chewed down to ugly stubs.

I was moved to another floor in the same building. The third-floor cell wasn't much different, except it faced the woods behind the "housing unit." I was finally medically cleared.

The same day, Don Eisenberg arrived, with my family. Escorted by a guard, I walked to another building in the shabby white tennis shoes that were labeled "R&O" in black magic marker. There was snow on the ground.

I was directed down a hallway to an office. Expecting to see my family, I walked in eagerly. Instead, a woman sitting behind a large desk greeted me. She said she was the warden, Nona Switala.

"Well? Is it as bad as you thought it would be?" she asked.

"Yes," I replied honestly.

"You're still adjusting." She was slender and had straight, brown hair. Explaining that she was concerned about the amount of publicity I had received, she informed me that newspaper and television reporters had been flooding her office with phone calls ever since I arrived.

The media circus was continuing.

"They're anxious to interview you, Laurie," she said. "If you don't wish to be bothered, I will do everything in my power to see that they leave you alone. They've just about been camped out at that gate, waiting to get a picture of you. I don't know what they expect! They were asking me if your window had bars on it! You should have heard them."

The jackals, I thought, still feeding on the carrion. But I kept that to myself. I told the warden politely that I preferred to avoid reporters for the time being, and thanked her for her concern.

I was at last allowed to see my family. Everyone was crying, except Eisenberg, who stood by solemnly as I embraced my mom and my dad. Fred rushed toward me and tried to kiss me passionately, but I pulled away, embarrassed.

"It seems as though the jury was highly undecided," Eisenberg said. "I found out the results of the first vote they took: six women voted guilty, and one woman and all five men found you not guilty."

My dad offered me his handkerchief.

"Apparently, that forewoman was extremely aggressive in arguing her viewpoint while the jury was deliberating, and she swayed many to the guilty side. She really wanted to hang you."

We discussed the appeal, and the length of time it would take. Eisenberg explained that he'd already filed the Notice of Appeal. The next step would be to have the transcripts typed from the trial—a lengthy and expensive process.

"How long will this take?" I asked.

"It's hard to estimate. The Appellate Court has six months to reply. They can decide to confirm the conviction, reverse the conviction or order a new trial. At least you'd be released pending the new trial if that was the decision. Skwierawski denied your appeal bond, you know."

"Is this appeal going to a state court?"

"Yes. We have to exhaust all steps before moving on to the federal court system."

"If I can just hang on for six months ..." I said.

"Guess what," Eisenberg said. "There is a God! Annette Wilson was fired from her job at Boston Store. Her supervisor, Scott Nicholson, called me and said she was lying. He offered to give us an affidavit."

Now he tells me.

"We brought you clothes and things, but the prison refused to let it come in," Fred told me. "We got a copy of the property list. I think there are some things we can bring in, but some items have to be mailed."

"There are limits to what we can have," I said. "I believe it's five tops and five pants. I've got State-issue right now. I just spent two days sewing name tags into everything I own."

"No stamps are allowed?" my mom asked. "I brought a book of stamps."

"No. Stamped envelopes, but no loose stamps," I said.

My family promised to visit me again as soon as they could, without a lawyer in tow. They were given a sheet listing the visiting days and hours. Then they left, after tearful hugs and kisses.

I could see the parking lot as I stared out a hallway window while I waited for the guard to unlock a door. I peered out, my face close to the glass. I raised my hand to wave, hoping my family could see me.

"That's unauthorized communication," the guard said. "Stop it."

The car lights drove away into the distance, glowing, receding, dimmer, taking my beloved family with them.

■　　■　　■

Once I was allowed out "in population," as it was called, I could walk to the building where meals were served. Inmates were not allowed to stop, loiter or change the direction we were walking in while going to meals. Following a line with our trays cafeteria style, we were limited to single portions of everything. We were to be seated, filling up the tables from left to right, and we were restricted from talking to any of the women at other tables.

After my arrest, I'd had to learn legal jargon. Now I was confronted with prison slang. During my first meal, I sat at a table with three black women. I listened to their conversation. It seemed to make no sense.

"And whenever he be checkin' his trap, he beats 'doz hoes asses," one was saying.

"He do?" another asked.

A small woman with skin the color of chocolate pudding suddenly looked at me. "You ear hustling?" She sucked her teeth loudly.

"Excuse me?" I said. Whatever that was, I was sure I wasn't doing it.

"Dippin'."

"No," I said.

"You gone to A'n'E yet?" She was referring to Assessment and Evaluation.

"What's that?"

"That board thing. It's like PRC."

"No. Have you?" I wouldn't see the Program Review Committee for several weeks.

"No. I jus' got out of R'n'O, too."

"What are you in for?" I asked, trying not to sound like the late show.

"Aggravatin' a battery," she replied with a smile.

"Aggravating a battery?" I thought to myself, stifling a hysterical laugh.

She turned back to the other inmates at the table. They were talking about things like "MR" (mandatory release dates) and "kites" (illegal letters passed from inmate to inmate). "TLU" stood for Temporary Lock Up. "Seg" was short for Adjustment Segregation. The jargon reminded me of *Clockwork Orange*.

My cell on the third floor of the Addams Housing Unit was small, with a desk and a metal bed and a bulletin board on the wall. The old radiator was warm. A switch inside the room controled a radio speaker that played country and western music.

"I fought the law and the law won ..." someone sang. I turned it off.

The guards enforced a rule that restricted inmates from sitting on their beds with the bedspread on. If you wanted to sit on your bed, you'd have to unmake it first. But there was another rule that prevented you from leaving your cell without the bed made. We made and unmade the beds all day.

A small, porcelain pot, sort of like an old-fashioned chamber pot, with a lid served as a toilet inside the cell, but I could not force myself to use it. It was unconstitutional to lock us down without a real toilet and sink, but that didn't stop anyone. The only alternative was to pound on the cell door and ask to use the main bathroom. Usually, an irritated guard would shout, "Just a minute!" My digestive system was rather consistent, and after I ate a meal, I'd have to use the toilet. However, knocking on your cell door during meals was not allowed. Since the inmates would eat in shifts, that meant that I had to wait until the second meal was over with, and those inmates were back in their cells, before I could knock. We were given twenty minutes to eat. Still, I could no more use the porcelain kettle (which everyone called a "jitney") than I'd been able to use a hospital bedpan in the past.

Sometimes the guard never came to let me out at all.

It didn't take long for the vast amount of lesbian activity at the prison to become obvious. Some of the women, I guess, were always that way, but some had husbands at home and converted either out of loneliness or just to play the game. "Sexual conduct" was against the written rules, of course, but they were rarely enforced, which only encouraged the hesitant. It hardly mattered, when so many of the female guards were also gay. I found myself part of a small, repulsed minority. At first I was shocked at the lesbian activity. Now I view it as commonplace.

The trickle of hot water on the third floor at Addams was so meager that it was ludicrous to expect us to take a bath in the fifteen minutes allotted, because we also had to clean the tub in that time. On our floor there were no showers, so the one antiquated tub was our only choice. Cool water would initially drip out and gradually accelerate into a pathetic, lukewarm dribble. I thought something was wrong with the faucet the first time, and summoned the guard. She assured me the faucets had always been like that. The water was very hard and the pipes were choked with lime deposits.

Five of us were allowed to watch television in a room at the end of the hall-way. I looked forward to any type of distraction, even an inane sitcom. We sat on stiff chairs facing the television set, but I could barely hear the program over the commands of the guard.

"Sit with both feet on the floor, ladies! You can't put one foot up like that! No talking! Face the front." She sat at a desk, a few feet away. "Turn the TV down! Who turned that volume up?" Despite her determined vigil, two of the women managed to kiss whenever she turned to answer the phone.

Just as I grew interested in a movie, television time was over and we were ordered to return to our cells.

Several women out "in population" looked as though they belonged at a mental institution. One walked around talking to herself and laughing at nothing. Another was so high on Thorazine that she drooled on herself, staggering like a zombie. They frightened me. I was afraid I'd get to be like that.

There were small fights between inmates occasionally, but most were easily suppressed due to the threat of "Program Segregation," or solitary confinement.

The population was a cross-section of society. There were massive, mascu-line women and some who resembled lost little girls. Some were handicapped, on crutches or in wheelchairs; some had missing limbs. Most inmates I talked to were serving short sentences for forgery or theft, or were drug cases, but the institution also had its share of lifers, like me. There were those convicted of violent crimes, arson, sexual assault, sex crimes against children, and women who'd killed infants. The sentence disparity was unbelievable; some inmates were serving five years for the same crime others got twenty-five years for. It was an appalling environment.

Many of the inmates made continuous efforts to get high, despite the consequences if they were caught. They smuggled in drugs, using every available body cavity, only to be sent to lock up for "dirty urine" later. (One enterprising inmate tied drugs into a balloon, tied string to the balloon and the other end to a tooth, and swallowed the thing, hauling it up safely later.) We were requested to "drop" urine at random, but if an inmate was suspected of contraband, a urine analysis was requested frequently. At that time, the penalty for dirty urine was 360 days in Program Segregation.

Not all women were lucky enough to get visits. The prison was out in the country, and most of the families were too poor to own a car. I was thankful that my family lived only sixty-five miles away, as they were my support system, and in the beginning, I willed myself to live from visit to visit. One woman I knew never got visits, because her parents lived out of state. She was convicted of "homicide by intoxicated use of a motor vehicle," and was given five years. I remembered Marylisa's former boyfriend, Jeff, who'd received probation for the same offense.

It was an early spring, unusually warm. I was moved into an eight-by-fourteen-foot cell in the maximum security building called Neprud Housing Unit, where I was lucky enough to be blessed with a heterosexual roommate named Laura Zunker. We discovered we were from the same neighborhood, and a friendship developed quickly. Because we were convicted at the same time and we had never been incarcerated before, we shared the same feelings—the horror, the regret, the despair and the anger.

It was wonderful to talk to someone intelligent again. Her childhood experiences were similar to mine, and she empathized with the "culture shock" I was trying to deal with. We were both exhausted. She was serving a three-year sentence for embezzlement.

Three years! It seemed like a day.

The cell we shared was equipped with a toilet—the prison had started to install them after several inmates filed a lawsuit—but I still found it difficult to use one in such close quarters. I was especially self-conscious about the odor, since the cell was so tiny that it was immediately noticeable. Ventilation was inadequate, because the windows were barred on the outside and almost inaccessible due to a locked, mesh grate on the inside. The same stops prevented us from opening the window more than a few inches, even after tediously picking them open with a pair of tweezers pushed through the grate. Greasy smells from the prison kitchen directly below us routinely wafted in. Our only view was a patch of scraggly apple trees, leafless and skeletal.

Room searches and inspection made it mandatory to maintain order and cleanliness in the tiny cell. Cleaning was stressed obsessively, which seemed to indicate that either the female domestic role was being inculcated or the prison staff was anal-compulsive.

One afternoon, Laura and I returned to our cell to find all our drawers overturned. The two boxes we were allowed to store under the bunk beds had also been emptied. It looked like a tornado had struck the room. I was hurt to see that most of the lead in my pencils was broken. Our bedding was undone and thrown about. My clothes were scattered.

The sergeant had left us a note designed to make us feel like naughty children: "You should know better than to have nametags missing from your clothes and dustballs under your bed! Consider this a warning. The next time, you'll both receive Conduct Reports." A Conduct Report results in loss of privileges, or even in banishment to the hole, to segregation. Later, I found out that she had bragged to the other guards about her room search, saying that she intended to show me how "celebrities" were treated at Taycheedah.

Visits were unbearably painful. It was wonderful to see my parents and Fred for the allotted time, but brutal when they had to leave. In those years, visits were held in the prison gym on weekends, and in a classroom and the Harris Housing Unit card room during the week.

I finally got my chance to appear before the Program Review Committee, and I was asked how I wanted to spend my time at the institution. Why did they bother to ask? Lifers weren't allowed anything interesting. I'd heard about several school programs from my social worker and asked if I could take some classes. I was told, in typical corrections jargon, "Based on your sentence structure, you are not an appropriate candidate for educational rehabilitation." One of the committee members said it would be pointless to take a two-year school program and then "sit around for ten years." What was I supposed to do instead? I was told that I could work in the prison kitchen, the laundry, or in cleaning, called "Homecare." Homecare inmates were called "Environmental Specialists."

Cleaning, cooking or doing laundry? Couldn't they get a little more "female"? The prisons for men had programs like welding, woodworking, metal furniture, industries, auto-body work and mechanics.

I wound up in the steamy prison kitchen, peeling potatoes and scrubbing pots and pans for fourteen cents an hour.

Laura and I talked one night, both of us in our beds, in the dark. I had the top bunk.

"It's the strangest thing," I said wistfully, "but I was peeling potatoes over some newspapers today, and the smell of that suddenly reminded me of home so much. Does that happen to you?"

"Of course," she said. "I really miss the simple things. Being able to answer a telephone ..."

"Driving a car."

"Raiding a refrigerator!"

"Or sitting outside at night. I used to love sitting on the front porch on a fragrant summer night ... lilacs. The wind chimes singing in the breeze, the crickets ..."

"Or the feel of money in your hand!" Any cash we received was deposited directly into our accounts by the Business Office. Money transactions were completed with the use of "money transmittals" written in triplicate.

■   ■   ■

But those things weren't the worst. Sure, we missed them. We missed them, and love and sex and walking to the corner store to buy a popsicle. But as I told you at the start of my story, it was the utter lack of privacy that hurt the most. Privacy! To hold some thing, some thought, private! To be utterly vulnerable to the pettiest bureaucrats—that's what hurt most. To have our love letters read, our every moment "authorized," our property and our bodies open to inspection and scrutiny. God! A world without strip-searches, walkie-talkies blaring in the night, the heavy footsteps of the guards, the hourly flash of light through the bars. Privacy! Without it there is nothing, no person, no individual, no Me.

■   ■   ■

One night I was watching the news from a nearby town and heard that a triple murder and suicide had occurred. A man had shot and killed his wife and children, and then himself. There were problems with a pending divorce action and the visitation rights were said to have upset him greatly. There was a time when I found stories like that mind-boggling. Now, after so many months of persecution, I could understand at least the intensity, if not the action.

I thought of suicide again, often.

I think it was only Mike Levine, the psychologist at Taycheedah, who got me through it. Once he said to me, "I will take you and put you under a cold shower until you change your mind and keep you there, keep you there forever if I have to. I'll hold you there until you change your mind!" He would have, too.

Well, after three years Mike Levine left too. Pressure got to him. But I'll always be grateful for his help.

I was given my first Conduct Report from a female guard. I was in the main building, called Simpson Hall, when I received a "white pass" from the Education Office, summoning me to the other side of the building. An enclosed breezeway separated the two halves of the building. I was required, I learned later, to report to the Control Center with my white pass and obtain a blue pass. Instead, I arrived at my destination with the white pass, and was promptly charged with Unauthorized Movement Within the Institution.

A verbal reprimand was given to me by one Lieutenant Sheridan. She was aunt to Officer Sheridan, one of the guards. Her ex-husband was the Recreation Director. Nepotism among state employees was common, and almost always worked to the inmate's disadvantage. For example, if Officer Kahill "wrote me up," the Conduct Report would be reviewed, for its validity, by a lieutenant. But that might be Lieutenant Kahill, her sister.

Laura and I were both moved to the medium security housing unit, named Harris. We shared a cell with two other women, both black. One suffered from epilepsy, and the other was very pregnant.

There was racial tension everywhere. In the prison kitchens it hung over everyone like a death threat. The other inmates turned simple personality conflicts into an issue of color. Tempers were quick in the steamy heat of the work area, and I kept a worried eye on the paring knives and vegetable peelers. We had only one supervisor in a four-room work area. I left work each day exhausted from the tension and stress. We were strip-searched occasionally, to control food theft, or if a knife was missing. Eight hours usually passed like twenty-four.

I always remained silent, even when anger swelled up in me, even when a co-worker yelled at me, "Honky white trash bitch!" I had a rack of cups thrown at me once. I was constantly sick, sick of the purposeless hate and resentment.

In my cell, I would read or sketch, to relax. I read Marx, Lenin, Dosto-evsky, Hobbes and Paine. I read Quine, Nietzsche and Freud. Women escaped, went to lock-up for contraband, and were moved in and out of that cell. It felt like living in Grand Central Station. I never knew when some of my stamps or instant coffee would be stolen, as they often were. With three cellmates, one can always blame the others. More than once, a gay inmate was moved into the cell, which made me very uncomfortable because of their aggressive attitude. They were nothing like my gay friends on the street, but along the same vein, the black inmates were nothing like my black friends in Milwaukee, either.

Emotions that I had bottled up inside me for years now flowed uncontrollably. I began to burst into tears at the least little thing. With three cellmates, privacy was impossible.

I tried to be brave, knowing that people in the past had survived worse fates, but I was terrified that I would die and be buried in Taycheedah. I had never experienced anything like it in my life.

■   ■   ■

A friend had mailed me a collection of *Milwaukee Journal* articles describing Taycheedah when I was convicted. They portrayed the place to which I was sent (the place that strip-searched its inmates, that had stinking buckets instead of toilets, that was riddled with racial hatred, violence, madness and petty vindictiveness among the guards) as akin to a "country club or small, private college," because of the "quaint old buildings that housed the residents, with beautiful, manicured lawns and luscious surroundings." The college image was furthered by the names of the housing units—Addams, Harris and Neprud Halls—and the administrative building, named Simpson Hall after a former warden. In a system literally riddled with euphemisms, cells were called "rooms," prisoners were called "residents," and the mess hall was called a "dining room." Staff always addressed a group of inmates as "ladies," which I bitterly resented.

In some of these pieces the warden emphasized the wonderful programs and explained that the inmates had their choice of jobs or free college courses. She was quoted as saying that an inmate's security classification had absolutely no bearing on the programs available to them, and that Lawrencia Bembenek would be able to participate in anything she was interested in.

Like the descriptions of the "campus," this was far from reality. At that time, lifers weren't allowed off-grounds school, off-grounds work, outdoor maintenance jobs or even college courses. The newspapers might just as well have told their readers that inmates were given free trips to Florida. In any case, their readers seemed to believe all this crap. Citizens wrote angry letters, which were duly printed. Outraged taxpayers complained that convicted felons were coddled and provided with every luxury. One nice woman wrote that she had sympathized with my life sentence, until she saw the photographs of Taycheedah (which of course showed the portico, not the cells). Another young woman wrote to say that it was so hard for her to work her way through college that she was considering robbing a bank, so that she, too, could go to school free.

I was—again—appalled.

No reporter visited the Segregation Unit on the third floor of Addams; no one ever wrote about the "Adjustment Seg" cages, which were nothing but a metal platform bolted to the gray floor to which women were shackled. There were never photos of the "jitneys." They just showed the pillars in front of Harris, the exercise yard with its birdbath that was named The Sunken Garden and the lush lawns where the inmates were forbidden to go (unless they wanted to be charged with Being In An Unauthorized Area). They wrote about the fucking *flowers*, for God's sake! (Sorry.) And, of course, it's tough to photograph intangibles. You can't photograph the sexism, the inconsistencies, the inequities or the pain of separation from loved ones. That would take imagination on the part of the press.

Norman Mailer said of Jack Henry Abbott: "He even writes, 'It has been my experience that injustice is perhaps the only ... cause of insanity behind bars.'" So much truth! But injustice is another thing you cannot photograph.

Consider the lifer. Lifers have no mandatory release date—unlike other inmates—which means lifers earn no "good time." Good time can be earned by every other inmate, and if nothing else is a convenient management device. For lifers, however, good behavior is a meaningless incentive. At the time, lifers had to remain in maximum security for seven and a half years, which means no furloughs, no early release program, no off-grounds work or school, no halfway house and no work programs—like inmate driver or outdoor maintenance. At other institutions, male lifers could earn a transfer to the camp system—but there wasn't one for women, naturally!

All of this, because we had exercised our right to a jury trial. Because we believed ourselves not guilty (or, in my case, because I *knew* I wasn't guilty). But we had to live side by side with inmates who had committed the exact same crime, or worse, as what they had accused us of—inmates who had declared themselves guilty in order to plea bargain. Those who plea bargained, by virtue of their shorter sentences, were quickly assigned to medium or minimum security and afforded all the benefits denied lifers.

The jurors from my trial were interviewed afterward, and I read how they complained about the long sequestration order that kept them confined to a hotel. It prevented any contact with their families and friends. One woman commented that she had missed her cat terribly over the three weeks.

■   ■   ■

She missed her cat! I flung the paper into the trash. She missed her poor little pussycat.

And she had taken away my life.

19

THE END OF FRED

Let me dispose now of Fred. In a manner of speaking.

I thought about him a lot those first few months in jail. His behavior, always erratic, began to veer off into the pathological. I was the one in jail, I was the one in that world of long gray corridors, the world governed by the clang of iron gates, but Fred behaved as if he were the one imprisoned, as if his life was the one stolen away.

We seemed to spend most of his visits arguing.

One evening, he told me he'd bought two more stereo speakers for his van.

"Fred! Two speakers weren't good enough? You have to have four?"

"Music is all I have!" he whined. "Everything else has been taken from me—my wife, my kids, my job, my house ... Would you really deny that little bit of enjoyment that music brings me?"

And I used to be swayed by this sort of thing!

"How much did they cost? Probably worth more than your van is worth! What if somebody breaks in again and steals them?"

"No. I bought an alarm."

"How much was that?" I asked, frustrated. I was wearing state-issue clothing to save money, using the toothpaste, tampons and other low-quality supplies that the prison dispensed, while Fred wanted to soothe his aching breast with music.

"Eighty-five dollars," he replied.

I rolled my eyes. "Eighty-five dollars for a car alarm? I'm using a deodorant soap on my face, when I could buy a gentle soap at the canteen, because we agreed to save money! Fred, how could you? How much were the stereo speakers?"

"I need something for myself once in a while!" he argued. "I have to think of myself! After all—I'm in prison, too!"

To this outrageous remark, the only appropriate comment was silence. My parents, who were there, simply stared in disbelief.

■　　■　　■

It wasn't long before my parents suggested that we split up the visits, so that Fred could see me alone. They were becoming uncomfortable with the frequency of our disagreements. But this only presented a new problem.

As I suspected, the three of them were not living together under the most harmonious conditions. Whenever my parents came to see me without Fred, I would hear about his misdeeds. He was spending money on other frivolities—personalized stationery, new business cards. He'd hired a new lawyer to represent him in the custody matter. He subscribed to several needless magazines and papers.

Both my friends and my parents described Fred using identical adjectives: evasive, inconsistent, unreasonable, erratic. Everyone said he eavesdropped. He interrupted. He demanded to be the center of attention, and ended up being obnoxious.

I really needed this.

And they didn't tell me everything—how he was staying out all night with the family car, running up huge phone bills by calling Florida and charging all his building materials to my dad's account. They kept this from me initially, feeling that I had enough stress to deal with.

Fred came to visit one afternoon with news that he'd been accepted in Florida for a police job. He said it would solve the problem of trying to live with my parents. He considered it a "fresh start."

"I've got to build a secure future for us, so that when you win your appeal and get out, we'll be together and you won't have a thing to worry about," he said.

"What about your children?" I asked.

"I can get an extension on the joint custody so we can deal with that litigation later when we're better able to."

Reluctantly, I agreed. Maybe it was a good idea for him to go.

After much bickering about what to take—my stereo, my waterbed, my dog—he finally left. I felt nothing but relief.

Of course, nothing worked. A few days later, I asked him to send me some money—ten or twenty dollars—but none came. His letters were short and sounded forced. When I was finally able to call him, he was drunk. The next time I talked to him, he said he wasn't working at all. He was bored beyond belief and passing the time playing tennis and swimming. I could hardly feel sorry for him.

"What happened to the work you said you had all lined up?" I asked.

"The bottom fell out," he simply said. I was about to demand more explicit details when the officer ordered me to hang up the phone. My ten minutes were up.

Then, despite the promise to wait until fall to visit because of the expense involved, Fred impulsively hopped a plane and appeared at the prison one afternoon.

I stared at him in shock as he entered the visiting room wearing a red T-shirt and a tiny pair of red, satin shorts. His dark tan was intensified by his blond hair, which had grown shaggy and was bleached by the sun. A gold bracelet I'd never seen before glistened on his arm, and he wore new sandals, strolling in as if he'd just walked off the beach with sand still between his toes. I was angry that he'd spent money on a plane ticket after telling me that he wasn't even working in Florida. He had only been gone three weeks.

Of course, he acted crushed that I didn't welcome him with open arms.

This was another of our memorable conversations.

"This is a waste of money," I said.

"I don't think you love me anymore."

"I write to you every single day. Isn't that enough?"

"It's the quality, not the quantity!" Fred said.

"You mean the context?" I asked, unable to follow his thinking.

"Stop trying to use big words with me! I'm not a little kid!"

"What are you talking about? I write to you every day on my break. Still you're not satisfied! What do you want? A sonnet?"

"Don't be sarcastic. You don't give a shit!" he wailed.

"You're insecure and demanding," I said.

"Don't use that cop-out."

"It's not a cop-out. I just don't know what more you want from me."

"It's tough on me out there." He began to snivel. "If I didn't love you," he cried, "I would have divorced you the day you were charged!"

I refused to reply.

"I have to say something to get a response from you," Fred protested. "I don't feel appreciated. You say you write every day but I don't get a letter every day."

"That's because our mail only goes out Monday through Thursday," I said. "I've told you that a million times."

"Are you trying to drive me out of your life? Is that it? Look at me when I'm talking to you."

"Where did you get that gold bracelet?" I asked suddenly.

"It was a gift ..." Fred sputtered. "Laurie! Don't let this place do this to you! Don't let it turn you into a cold person. If this isn't resolved this afternoon, I'm coming back tonight."

"No, you're not. I don't want you using up all my allotted visits for the whole week. My mom and dad are supposed to see me tomorrow."

"Who means more to you? Your parents or me?"

"Don't ask me that, because you won't like the answer," I replied.

"Then give me that wedding band, right now."

"No!" I said, jerking my hand away. "I honestly don't know what you want from me."

"So you're saying that the responsibility of this marriage is all mine? That none of this is your fault?"

"Fault and responsibility are two different issues," I said.

"Don't split hairs!"

"Fuck this! I don't even want to argue anymore."

There was a silence. Tears rolled down my face. The visiting-room guard was getting an earful. The officer sipped her coffee.

"It's too bad," Fred said dramatically. "I could have loved you so much." He stood up, kissed the side of my head and walked out.

A month later, more problems developed. Fred began to lie to me about our savings. I thought he had half of his pension—about six thousand dollars—in the bank. In addition to that, he told me that he and I had made about five thousand dollars from the remodeling jobs. He'd even shown my dad one of the checks he received. He told my mom one of his life insurance policies had matured to the tune of over ten grand. He had also organized a benefit marathon run after I was convicted, from Milwaukee to Taycheedah, where he'd collected several thousand, according to a newspaper article. My dad had worked with him on several different jobs. I talked to Fred one last time on the telephone and asked him to send my mom and dad some money for their hospital bills.

Fred told me he had no money.

"I'm sorry, but I'm not going to send your mom and dad my last fifty dollars."

"What? What happened to all of our money?"

"Bills."

"What bills?"

"Oh, you know—phone bills, electricity, gas, food."

"What about that insurance policy you told me about? You said you were going to get twelve thousand dollars from that."

"Oh, that! That was all a big mistake! That was my father's policy! The company made a mistake, because I'm a Junior. The wrong birth date showed up on the printout and they realized their mistake." I hung up on him.

My parents recounted more money troubles. "When he left for Florida, Fred signed a few of his personal checks and told us to pay for the lumber bills and the phone calls to Florida he made on our phone," my dad told me. "Then the checks started to bounce. I wrote him a letter, and he replied, saying that he had closed that account at the bank! I don't understand!"

"I do," I sighed. "I just realized he forged my name on our income tax forms, and the refund check. He filed jointly. That required my signature! I'm also getting bills because he's using my credit card and not paying."

My mom and dad looked at one another.

"We didn't want to tell you this," my mother said. "We felt you had enough to deal with. But when Fred was living with us, he was borrowing our car frequently, and staying out all night. We think he has a girlfriend." She paused. "There's something else. A friend of yours named Ken called me. Fred bought a handgun from him for three hundred dollars. Fred promised to pay him as soon as he could, but four months went by. Ken wrote Fred, but he never wrote back. I guess Ken is thinking of reporting that gun as stolen."

"Fred should be able to pay Ken now. He got that new job ..."

"What new job? He told your father and me that he didn't get the job!"

The guard announced that visiting time was over.

It wasn't long before the man with "no money" spent another three hundred dollars and flew to Milwaukee again. His brother's girlfriend, Marylisa, wrote to me and told me that he'd stopped by. Later, he met them at a bar with an eighteen-year-old girl on his arm.

He moved all of his belongings out of my mom and dad's house and told them he was staying with his parents. When I placed a phone call to his father's house, his dad didn't even know Fred was in town.

The guard distributed the mail. A letter from my husband simply read: "Good luck. Goodbye."

The man who told the newspapers, radio and television stations that he would "wait for me forever" couldn't even wait six months. I was numb. I felt nothing. I tore up his letters, one by one, scattering the pieces. His smell lingered on my fingers.

I sat down at my small desk and began to write to my lawyer. Then I saw that in the upper left-hand corner of the envelope, instead of writing my correct return address, the prison, I'd written my old home address on Taylor Avenue.

That was when I started to weep in earnest.

■　　■　　■

Fred was gone. I'd met him and married him in a time of despair. I thought I loved him, once—I did love him, once. Then his jealousies and his lies enmeshed me.

He went on national television not long ago to say he was convinced I had, indeed, committed the murder. I was a cold, hard bitch, he said.

I thought of the tears that had fallen, the many, many tears, and felt only sadness.

I couldn't forget, in the end, that it was his testimony that put me here.

20

A NATION OF INMATES

When I first got to Taycheedah I was depressed, but I was also scared, freaked out. As a result, I became totally obsequious, fawningly servile, super-obedient. So, if I eventually became a super-litigious jailhouse superlawyer, they had it coming. They made me what I am today, and I hope they're happy.

As the years passed, I got more and more angry, and more determined to force them to comply with their own regulations. They were breaking so many rules and laws, so many federal standards! There was so much illegal inequity that often I used to think, Wait a minute, they've got the wrong people behind bars! In the end, it was the only sense of autonomy I could find anywhere, having that little bit of legal leverage, the authority to make them comply with their own directives and force them to court.

As the years passed, I grew more mature and more angry, and my anger had to be channeled into constructive causes, positive outlets. It's interesting how people's responses to incarceration will differ. You get radical. You find your best friends sometimes doing some really weird things. In my case, I became a little obsessive about things like exercise, which I suppose was relatively harmless. I also moved about as far left politically as I could. Eventually, though, I found out there's no black and white in the real world. In prison, you don't know that. In that artificial world, everything is black and white, and extreme positions are normal.

Taycheedah was in many ways an archaic facility when I first got there. There was no running water or plumbing in the cells. All this was quite unconstitutional. But the female prison population is more passive than the male—it's their socialization, I guess—and there are fewer of them. In any case, they don't often riot and aren't as violent, so of course they aren't taken seriously.

The women seemed to me to be living under eighteenth-century conditions.

For years the prison had been under a federal court order to install toilets, and they'd just ignored it. No money, they said. Eventually they were installed, in 1984, and they shuffled us about from cell to cell while they put them in.

When I got there, we were allowed only two ten-minute phone calls a month. Requests for calls had to be submitted seventy-two hours in advance, on paper, and we could only call people who were on our Visitors List. Calls had to be made from the sergeant's office, and the guards would insist on doing the dialing themselves. What a waste of time! It was preposterous! In any case, you didn't want to talk to people you got visits from; you wanted to talk to your sister in California, people you never saw in person. Our Visitors List was limited to twelve adults, and we didn't dare waste spaces on people who wouldn't visit.

Well, when I found out that the men had phones in their prison—phones they could use themselves whenever they wanted—you never saw a complaint written up so fast! It was such a blatant inequity that they didn't even want to risk a judicial review, so they simply installed them. In the meantime, though, I'd lost contact with many people, many good friends.

At that time I had made one really good friend—I guess she's still my best friend—named Kathy Braun. Kathy and I were lifers who shared the same socio-economic background. She's ten years older than me, but she's from Milwaukee, so we had a few people in common and I felt comfortable with her. I always felt she was an island of sanity in a sea of madness.

Hers was a typical Milwaukee case. She got a life sentence for being party to a crime, first-degree murder. She'd merely been standing in the room with her husband and the actual killer, the man who pulled the trigger. This man, who later dumped the body in the Milwaukee River, turned State's Evidence against both of them and didn't do a single day in jail. He was given immunity in exchange for his testimony. And his was a premeditated first-degree murder! Kathy was defended by the best Milwaukee talent, James Shellow, and her parents had money, but it didn't help.

Kathy's husband plea bargained and is now out on the streets with their kids. She got life.

Is it any wonder that we lifers are cynical about the justice system?

We tried for a long time to share a cell. There is a long and tedious process you have to go through to get the cellmate you want. You fill out a request form, and then the other person fills one out. Eventually, if you're lucky, you get put on a list to be moved. But of course no one can be moved until there's an empty bed. So it took a while.

While we were waiting, we were both living in the Neprud Housing Unit. My cellmate at the time was finishing a drug treatment program ... I think. As I've said, it's like Grand Central Station in there. All these inmates with piddly little eighteen-month sentences come and go and they use your things and break your stuff and steal from you—of course, they don't want to *buy* anything because they're not going to be there long enough to really justify spending the money. Whenever one of these people moves in with a lifer, it's always, "Can I watch your TV? Use your blow-dryer and your typewriter?" They break things and then they leave. That's why lifers like to share cells.

Kathy had been convicted in the '70s. She escaped for seven and a half years and got brought back to Taycheedah in 1983. We met in one of the classes—we were both taking a program they called PREP, which led to university credit associate degrees. I was the first lifer to get approved for that, after a struggle.

Finally, my cellmate was transferred to a halfway house, and Kathy and I moved in together.

Our cell, our "room," was tiny. One corner was sectioned off for a sink and a toilet. Radiators and other hot pipes prevented furniture placement in some areas. There were bunk beds and two desks crammed into sixty square feet, but we were happy. We didn't have to worry anymore about roommates coming and going.

We thought.

One day maintenance people knocked on the door. They had instructions to move a third bed in. They agreed it looked screwy, but they had their orders. They put a third bed in there, and in came a third body.

I was convinced there was something wrong. Federal standards require so many square feet per prisoner. I wrote to the superintendent, the warden. I pointed out that the cell next door was much bigger yet contained only two people. I thought perhaps they'd got the two cells switched on some list.

But, of course, authority hates to admit error. The superintendent wrote back: No, you're wrong and we're right.

Kathy used the Inmate Complaint System. This provides a sort of ombudsman, who can deal with less important complaints, so that the superintendent doesn't have to suffer through too many judicial reviews.

The Inmate Complaint Investigator had a neutral party re-measure the room, and found, of course, that we were right.

The superintendent wrote back, acknowledging the mistake but refusing to move the bed out. It was a somewhat hollow victory.

That was the superintendent's worst mistake. As a result of her being stubborn over this square-foot issue, we started what I think is the biggest women's class-action in the history of Wisconsin—and it's still going on.

I went to the prison's meager library and read up on as much case law on overcrowding as I could. I didn't want to do anything unless it was well researched. I was looking for federally mandated standards. I found there were many; a number of federal cases had been decided. The most liberal judge decreed that 120 feet per inmate was the minimum acceptable standard. The strictest judge required at least 60 square feet per person. We had three people in 60 square feet! Taycheedah had a rated capacity of 126 inmates, but of course they paid no attention to the legal limits. The population went up to 287; we were being stacked up like sardines.

I found out how to file a federal class-action suit from "guerrilla law manuals," more or less like self-help litigation manuals. And of course you network with other inmates and learn what you have to learn. We had a great case. They couldn't lie about the number of bodies or the number of cells, and so it was obvious they had a population way over the rated limit. Kathy and I and one other person got affidavits from everybody we could. We talked about the plumbing breaking down because of overuse, about the problems of second-hand smoke, about the violence levels going up because of the overcrowding.

Prisoners don't have a constitutional right to rehabilitation, but they do have a right to live in conditions that are not "degenerative." Eventually I filed a motion for court-appointed counsel with a brief in support, and we got lucky. The Federal Court gave us a wonderful lawyer named Diane Sykes. She was a godsend, a feminist, interested in the case and a total professional.

It felt so good to force them to grit their teeth and lose. It was therapeutic for me to direct my anger toward something productive.

This is one of the things outsiders can't understand about prison, this tightly wound anger. It's one of the great dangers of being locked up. When you're in a tiny cell like that, twenty-four hours a day, with total strangers coming from opposite backgrounds, the result can be bloodshed.

People read in the papers how one inmate killed another because he used his toothbrush, and they write these people off as animals, as violent crazies. They don't understand the long history of petty aggravations that took this person to the breaking point. I felt myself on the edge many times. Your self-control has to be phenomenal; you have to keep in mind always that you're only hurting yourself by reacting.

A prison is like a little community in itself; the jail has its own little jail, and if you commit an offense, fighting or whatever, the police come and they handcuff you and they take you to the hole, down to this building called Program Segregation. You can go to Seg for 360 days. This means a year of total isolation, twenty-three-hour-a-day cell time, one visit a week, no property. They hold that over your head all the time, until the threat of going to Seg is worse than the actuality of it. I did go to Seg lockup once, for refusing to shovel snow at 5:00 AM, and when I got there I thought, well, this isn't so bad! It wasn't that much worse than being in jail in the first place!

This was a bleak period for me. I was between lawyers then. I didn't have any appeals going. And then there came another setback.

I was studying in the Pilot Re-Entry Program, needing only six credits to graduate and get my associate of arts degree, when they took the program "off grounds," meaning they would henceforth hold classes elsewhere. There are fewer women inmates in the prison system, and they decided to hold classes in the men's institution. Because I was a lifer and wasn't allowed off grounds, I was cut off from my courses. The program review committee wouldn't approve me or Kathy.

Two full semesters went by before I was able to win a fight to get classes back. During that time I plugged into a data-entry program that was in reality nothing more than a secretarial course, learning to be a typist ... A typical female kind of thing, though better than peeling potatoes.

Eventually, they brought the classes back, and I graduated with a degree from the University of Wisconsin–Fond du Lac.

My mom and dad have a picture of me in my cap and gown. I'm standing with them, and they look so proud! I was the first lifer to be approved for the program, and the first to graduate.

This is what I said in my graduation speech, on July 31, 1986:

"PREP gave me goals, when being warehoused seemed real useless. It changed my focus and allowed me to survive. The very process by which I was able to respond to the challenge of the program constituted an exercise in freedom. I had to take responsibility—responsibility for interpreting, analyzing and studying. Like all of us here today, I had to practice self-discipline in meeting deadlines, completing assignments, accepting views different from mine.

"Accepting that responsibility is a choice. Because it's a choice, it's also an exercise in freedom. There is virtually no other aspect of our lives in prison where we are required, much less permitted, to assume such responsibility ...

"... Every semester was interrupted by bad news: either an appeal getting denied, or a family member in the hospital, or another appeal being denied. Not that 'free' students don't have problems, but I believe they have many more alternatives than inmate students. Come on! They aren't strip searched on the way to graduation! And they aren't discouraged by the prevailing attitude that inmates don't deserve a free college education—especially women! Especially lifers!

"... With all that to cope with, PREP was the only way for me to keep my sanity. It provided pathways to the power of knowledge that everyone wants—self-awareness, greater clarity, a sense of place in life. PREP offers the opportunity to realize that you can abandon negative patterns for positive choices! Embrace the risk of self-change! Comprehension is satisfaction ..."

All this seems hopelessly naive now. But I meant it. PREP helped me keep sane.

After PREP I went into a program called ACCESS and worked towards a Bachelor of Arts degree in humanities from the University of Wisconsin–Parkside. ACCESS is a quasi correspondence-course arrangement. It's not for prisoners only, but any non-traditional students. It's a four-year program. You must already have sixty credits to be eligible for ACCESS.

The co-ordinator was a terrific woman named Frances Kavenik, who actually came out to the prison once every six weeks, all the way from Kenosha. In my senior year I wrote papers ranging from an extensive analysis of perestroika, through toxic tort litigation and marine pollution to—my best project—a huge paper on recidivism. After all, I had the perfect opportunity to do primary research!

A cellmate, Sherry, and I started a prison newspaper for inmates called *Inmate Output*. The first issue came out in November 1983. It looked amateur, but I hope its standard of journalism was better than I'd been used to seeing in the metropolitan papers.

I was also a very active member of the Task Force on Women in the Criminal Justice System for almost nine years. The Task Force made recommendations to the Governor's Advisory Council on the Female Offender and was chaired by an extremely dedicated, competent and intelligent lawyer named Victoria McCandless. Vicky is a super person that I admire.

So I survived. After a few years we got several lifers interested in the battered old tennis court on the grounds. We weren't Wimbleton, but a group of us got really serious about tennis, playing as often as we could.

Keep in mind the insurmountable odds you have to go through just to get from point A to point B in prison, the small things most people take for granted. We had to fight for everything. We were given privileges little by little, and given them only because we raised parity issues, because we made— quite literally—a federal case out of it.

Lifers have to work hard for everything. And we get angry when some little clown walks in with a two-year sentence and ruins everything. It happens over and over.

An example: we fought for months for the simple privilege of being allowed fresh fruit from our visitors (if I ever see another can of fruit cocktail again I'll scream). We were *starved* for fresh fruit. Finally, we were grudgingly given permission. But some short-term idiot got the bright idea of injecting oranges with vodka. They thought it was so funny! Of course, the warden's response was to cancel the privilege. They messed it up for everybody, as usual.

We lifers felt the need to make the place as tolerable as we could. Kathy had two kids from a previous marriage, and two other little boys while she was on the run. So she became involved in a program to cheer up the playground where the kids played during visits. Some inmates volunteered countless hours to sit behind the concession stand in the visitors area selling snacks and chips; they bought playground equipment with the proceeds. True, all the profits essentially went back into the institution, and we took some flak for that, but it was for the children we did it. I painted some wall murals for the kids, and I don't regret it. The concession stand project, incidentally, was dissolved when a short-timer was busted stealing from the profits. Yet another example of one person ruining it for everyone.

■   ■   ■

I used poetry as a release. When every aspect of your life is open to scrutiny, you can't keep a diary—it would just get stolen or confiscated. Cellmates are probably going to read it and the guards certainly will. I loved the obliqueness of poetry, the way images could be powerful and allusive and hidden all at the same time. The real meaning would be known only to me. So if there was an issue that wouldn't let go, I'd open the chambers of my heart a little and let the anger simmer in my head for a while until I could sit down and put it down on paper, and then I'd feel better.

This is one of my poems, written in late 1987.

October

It now takes more than one hand

to count all the birthdays I've spent here
Waiting in a dark office one cold morning
I glanced up at tree branches outside
noticing that already they look like
veins stretched skyward
and realized
I can no longer live like this

You would think
that after years of being subjected
to so much dehumanizing
degradation and intrusion, after being
strip-searched while menstruating
    (to the obvious delight of two lesbian guards)
after being forced to use the toilet
in front of many strangers,
after being seized in the middle of the night
to shovel snow or to urinate into a cup—on command

after year upon year of sensory deprivation
    of mental sodomy
of being harassed
blamed
controlled
embarrassed
segregated
confined
humiliated
put-down
accused
criticized
discouraged
threatened and interrogated

you would think
the small punishments could be ignored—
when we are loudly warned
not to let a visitor kiss us again
when we are ordered to do meaningless work
and then lose two days' pay for being late,
when we are helplessly moved from place to place,
when we are denied a package of cookies from home;

but this deathless oppression only grows worse—
becomes more unbearable

I'm tired of wondering
how many fascist assholes read my letters
(and then wonder if they will reach their destination)
of being monitored by cameras
deprived of sex
ruled by a lack of alternatives and the
sound of bells, keys and walkie-talkies.

I can no longer watch the children
outside the fence, crying: "But mommy!
I don't want to say goodbye!"
I have no children, but I feel like that child.
I look quickly away
from the red-eyed women I
don't want to see anymore.
I can't stand the paranoia, the worry and despair.

Sometimes of late
it feels as though I could explode;
but then They would win.
I would trade only my poignant reality
for psychotropic drugs and paper gowns.
So I gather up another armful of resistance
and go on
for now.

■   ■   ■

ally which was necessary to win the peace, but few British officials understood how GCHQ shaped the process. GCHQ's role in the Cuban missile crisis was not an anomaly, but rather an illustration of that during the air atomic era as a whole. In any movement towards war, much intelligence would be British, but all command would be American, though GCHQ's reporting offered a means to moderate the risk by providing evidence to shape that strategy. Between GCHQ and Prime Minister Harold Macmillan's relationship with President Kennedy, Britain influenced the key decisions of that crisis, but did not make them.

From 1961, however, American strategy adopted the ideas of 'mutually assured destruction', and 'flexible response'. The central purpose of nuclear forces became deterrence, because their unrestricted use meant mutual suicide. Both sides had large numbers of nuclear weapons, which remained the greatest target of intelligence. Western strategists, however, emphasised conventional forces and thought that war might be prolonged. With both sides increasingly reliant on reserves based outside Europe, Western strategists needed more warning of war in order to fight one. These changes in strategic circumstances and attitudes transformed the role of military intelligence and Sigint. NATO no longer planned an offensive to break a Soviet attack as it began. Its stance was defensive, but preparation for conventional war became more serious than before. The elimination of the hair trigger eased problems of intelligence and analysis. More time was available to think and act, and also to exploit a broader and more interactive base of sources. UKUSA and Allied Sigint both grew in power and ability, because their work was more important and difficult than before. Satellite imagery expanded even more in strength, offering overwhelming amounts of data, too much for analysts to handle at the time. American, British and French liaison missions (such as BRIXMIS – the British Commanders-in-Chief Mission to the Group of Soviet Forces in Germany) in Berlin travelled with fewer constraints than the Soviets would have liked in the GDR, providing physical observation.

These changes complicated the politics of intelligence and decision-making. American presidents and their advisors made the key decisions, but the European members of NATO rose in power. NATO, while politically cohesive, was incoherent on many military matters, because national interests conflicted frequently, especially between the United

States and its European allies, including Britain. Following the Berlin crisis of 1961, the United States aimed to have its European allies increase their forces, to make a conventional war possible. Precisely to avoid that fate, they refused to do so, which in turn increased the likelihood that any conflict would become nuclear. Many states contributed to NATO decisions on strategy, especially as it approached any threshold to war. Each might trip another up. NATO command was convoluted and fragile, and elements of its strategy were often intended just to camouflage disagreements. No one really thought that war was imminent or could stay conventional for long if one began. Some warning was necessary to mobilise reinforcements, while strategy required accepted and accurate facts. Yet intelligence which convinced one group might not do so with another. The criteria for 'Indicators & Warnings' (I&Ws) and warning periods were therefore often arbitrary; none could cover all cases and organisations within NATO, and its individual members differed over them.

The politics of NATO Sigint drove GCHQ to be independent, able and persuasive. GCHQ, like Britain as a whole, emphasised its relationship with the United States as its best means to influence NATO policy, while using its European allies to influence Washington. Britain used its almost primary role in intelligence to strengthen its far-more-than-secondary position as a power. This process was messy and easy to miss, because the evidence remains closed. In order to be politically effective, GCHQ had to provide accurate intelligence which would aid NATO policy. American, British and Canadian authorities could see the evidence unvarnished; Europeans heard just an echo of it. Intelligence could not end uncertainty, but GCHQ could increase certainty, and hope, at national levels of decision-making and at the top of NATO commands.

Sanitisation and Strategy

Only sanitised Sigint could be used for all-source assessments sent outside indoctrinated circles, including key headquarters such as the British Army of the Rhine (BAOR), Fleet Command and Strike Command. During the 1960s, 350 copies of the annual estimates of United States Army Headquarters, Europe were distributed to American planners and commanders.[19] Sanitised appreciations aimed to preserve as many key facts as possible, and to avoid any error and needless specificity, which might make readers wonder whence such knowledge came. A yearly assessment need not say that a unit arrived on 11:32, 7 March 1965: 'March' would do. In sanitised reports, Sigint was not described as such, but silently checked other sources, steered all-source assessments, prevented error and added truth.

Sanitisation led 'unwashed' consumers to underestimate the centrality of Sigint to intelligence, which caused shock in the hour when first they were baptised and finally could see. It also enabled the UKUSA officers who controlled the machinery of force down to unit level, but saw nothing above Secret intelligence, to plan and act in ways congruent with top-secret material. This process best balanced the value and security of Sigint, and eliminated the impact of erroneous material from other sources within UKUSA. Commands outside UKUSA received none of these gains and suffered other losses. Even after the Sigint reforms around 1978, these commands did not receive such material thoroughly or directly, but just through cleared CANUKUS personnel. Probably non-UKUSA commands learned what they needed to know, which would matter most during crises. Category 2 material, moreover – the meat and potatoes of military Sigint – was traded to individual NATO countries. They could interpret that material themselves, and disseminate it to their national forces, though without the context available to UKUSA. It rarely gave allies any Category 3 material – the steak and lobster of military Sigint – and only if it was vital to understanding, and then by taking precautions to prevent them from guessing the source and thus UKUSA's power. UKUSA commands without access to top secret material were still better informed than any non-UKUSA ones with their own national Sigint.

None of this would help NATO in a conventional war, which it increasingly emphasised. From 1980, for the first time in twenty-five years, Britain systematically honed Sigint for conventional operations during 'tension and war between NATO and the Warsaw Pact'. GCHQ, backed by service opinion, drove these proposals, which were congruent to and necessary for NATO's adoption of Air/Land Battle, in which long-range air interdiction and mobile defence would stall any assault by the Warsaw Pact. GCHQ's proposals emphasised that Sigint must maximise warning of attack, strengthen all services just before war broke out, and survive if war started. Operations needed to be dynamic, not defensive. Warning and collection could no longer be passive and isolated: they needed to be integrated with operational preparations just before war. These proposals would redefine the strategic and tactical use of Sigint and their relationship with Elint and electronic warfare (EW). They would force major expenses and changes in Sigint and command, sanitisation and strategy, and relations within UKUSA, and with third parties in NATO.[20]

These proposals were enacted – slowly, incompletely, but significantly – over the next decade. For the first time in a generation, the British military boosted its Sigint forces. RAF Siginters moved from Digby, Lincolnshire, to Germany, augmenting Sigint in the forward area. BAOR received the 14th Signals Regiment for EW in war, the Royal Navy boosted its shipboard Sigint, which was integrated with data links on the 'Outboard' system, while the Royal Marines created their first Sigint unit. The only test of these developments occurred just as they began, in the Falklands conflict. Supporting forces that were inexperienced with these practices and out of area, GCHQ reduced sanitisation to the lowest possible level consistent with IRSIG, yet still the integration of Sigint with tactics was poor. Probably British forces would have used Sigint better in war against the Warsaw Pact, and abandoned sanitisation even more, but how far cannot be known.

Meanwhile, UKUSA became more flexible in circulating Sigint, especially Category 2, to NATO. The heads and officers of NATO Sigint agencies met often, lubricating their relations, institutionally and personally. The 'Wintex' command post exercises schooled theatre and national leaders across NATO in crises and the start of a war with the Warsaw Pact in real time. These exercises helped authorities to test their machinery for decision-making, and their own mettle. They also helped authorities in UKUSA, though not third parties, to overcome some of the problems caused by sanitisation and to understand how Sigint would work during crisis and war. From 1981, Britain integrated Sigint into the British parts of Wintex. One group within GCHQ generated thousands of imaginary reports to reflect the material which Sigint should provide in circumstances like the exercise scenarios. This material was released realistically within GCHQ and to decision-makers, including the JIC, MOD, commanders and politicians. All participants received an opportunity to learn interactively. GCHQ personnel analysed all of this exercise information for consumers, interpreting 'Indicators & Warnings' for Whitehall in the early stages of the crisis, and later guiding BAOR, RAF Germany and the fleet. Authorities peppered GCHQ with questions like: 'We are getting reports of BACKFIRE bombers deploying to CUBA? Can you confirm this please?' The exercise also practised personnel in passing sanitised Sigint to other NATO forces.[21]

Formal and Informal Estimates

In order to plan forces, deployments, and war, strategists required an idea of the warning they could expect of Soviet attack. As the COS wrote: 'All Global war planning must to a greater or lesser degree depend upon agreed assumptions about the warning likely to be available.'[22] Alas, several problems dogged the use of 'warning periods'. The JIC and COS concluded that basic 'differences of opinion ... based on opinions as to the lines on which the Soviets might think, rather than on concrete evidence', must hamper any assessment of war with the USSR.[23] Kenneth Strong, for the JIB, saw 'scarcely any evidence as to how their leaders think or would act in given circumstances'.[24] Soviet attack might take many forms. 'No single period of warning ... can be assumed as valid to cover the different possible methods of attack with which NATO may be faced and which would be applicable to all types of force throughout the NATO commands.' Soviet planners 'might well catalogue targets in a different manner' than British ones might expect. The COS rejected attempts to have NATO define more thorough and longer periods of warning, because these might reduce the incentive of its allies to maintain their forces, though Whitehall privately made such calculations for precisely that purpose. British strategists used arbitrary rules of thumb about warning periods, which governed forces in different ways. Many of its nuclear and conventional units must always be ready for surprise attack, without warning. All other conventional forces, including BAOR and RAF Germany, the crown jewels of Britain's commitment to NATO, should be mobilised within seven days, but many of their support elements might not be ready for a month.[25] All of its allies followed similar procedures, often with less attention to forces able to fight without warning of attack.

Ideally, estimates compare problems and intelligence and then guide actions. At worst, they become parts of checklists for planning, or compromises to conceal chasms between views. Formal estimates always reflect a political relationship between the interests of organisations, and differ from informal ones – what decision-makers really expect. Routinely, informal estimates cause leaders to disregard expertise without engaging it – to unfortunate effect. NATO followed the first part of this pattern, but not the second. Warning periods always involve forms of worst- (or worse-) case planning. In this instance, they reflected real but remote dangers. Soviet conventional or nuclear forces might attack by surprise from their standing position, while full mobilisation would increase their superiority in numbers over NATO. Soviet leaders controlled these decisions; Western intelligence and statesmen had to guess about them, which they did through a range of assessments.

From 1954, British strategic decision-makers simultaneously assumed warning periods ranging from 0 to 4 hours against a bolt from the blue – provided only by radar detection of enemy aircraft as they struck – to perhaps seven (and, implicitly, even twenty-eight) days if the Soviets mobilised in order to increase the weight of attack. American forces in Europe adopted a similar formula of 0 to 4 hours, to four to nine days.[26] These formulae were partly political, aimed at making NATO allies increase their conventional strength. Had NATO leaders really believed these formal estimates of warning periods, they would have had to maintain far larger forces, on a hair-trigger basis, which would have alarmed the Warsaw Pact, which exaggerated Western aggression and power. These warning periods also contradicted the possibility of reinforcing forces in Europe, which underlay American, British and Canadian planning for war, especially after 1970. Here, as often, NATO planning aimed simply to complete a paper record. NATO was politically cohesive, but operationally fragmented. National forces and commanders were poorly coordinated, while modes for mobilisation of forces were optimistic. Throughout NATO's history, especially during the Berlin crises between 1958 and 1962, the United States wished its allies would strengthen their conventional forces so that a non-nuclear war might be fought in Europe. For precisely that reason, they refused to do so.

Judged strictly, NATO's warning periods failed to achieve their ends, being both vague and ignored, which should have crippled its capabilities for deterrence and defence. That outcome did not happen because of the way that politicians treated the problem, and intelligence, especially Sigint, filled the gap. NATO leaders ignored these formal warning periods. Informally, they thought that war was possible, but not imminent, nor likely to occur suddenly. In 1959–61, the JIC agreed that 'we have virtually no chance of intercepting either the policy decision to go to war or the operational orders for the attack', yet also did 'not expect an attack whilst there is no exceptional political tension'.[27] Political developments, which they could detect, probably would precede steps towards danger. NATO responded tolerably well to such signs, as in the Berlin crises. Hydrogen weapons would explode when shots were fired, eliminating victory, but also deterring war. These informal estimates enabled NATO members to cap their conventional forces and states of readiness, and reduced the chance that uncertainty and fear about ever-imminent danger would paralyse decisions, or provoke the Warsaw Pact into undesired escalations.

These steps also increased the Warsaw Pact's chances for victory in war, if it was lucky (and NATO blind), but Western eyes were sharp. These challenges with warning periods caused intelligence providers, especially GCHQ, to adopt roles which no one fully understood at the time. I&W emerged to increase the real likelihood of detecting signs of Soviet preparation for war, days or months before they started one. Good models of I&W were successful in measuring changes in danger. Even when overly schematic and bureaucratised, they aided assessments and actions with a timeframe of weeks or months. Most sets of I&W were formulated through debate between institutions and intelligence services. Siginters devised their own sets, based on experience and technical factors which no outsider could understand or challenge. These models had to be trusted on faith alone, or else all hope be abandoned. Given Sigint's centrality to intelligence, these were the dominant elements of I&W, though they were never discussed or authorised by superiors, or by the JIC – just taken on trust.

These Sigint models covered periods ranging from hours, to months, but usually days and weeks. Siginters had to provide the best real warnings possible, based on their own sets of I&W, rather than fit the artificial deadlines of warning periods, which were arbitrary. The questions were, 'Will World War Three start today? Or in a week, or a month, from now?' Siginters steadily improved their answers, thereby reshaping the balance of deterrence and defence. Sigint was one of the few sources both of illumination for warning and of encouragement for the decision-makers confronting that bleak picture. The daily empirical success of Siginters thus built the confidence of NATO leaders in the stability of the military balance, and their ability to understand it. That confidence served to reduce the effect of fear and uncertainty in planning, and stabilised one side of the Cold War. Nor was it unreasonable. This defensive effort could have no deterrent effect, because neither side could know in advance how it would work. One hidden problem in deterrence during the Cold War was that neither side could know how far its intelligence, and that of its foe, would shape the balance of certainty and uncertainty which guided actions. Perhaps a sense of that ignorance reinforced caution for both sides.

Strategic Forces

Relations between American and British airmen and Siginters in 1945 drove their cooperation in nuclear intelligence until 1992. During the Combined Bomber Offensive, British and American air forces quarrelled but cooperated. In particular, the USAAF, weak in intelligence, relied on British Sigint and photographic interpretation.[28] After 1945, both air forces aimed to win an air atomic war, through atomic bombs delivered by bombers.[29] They made that an UKUSA of their own, exchanging all aerial photographs, including those each had seized from the Luftwaffe. Their relationship was looser than the UKUSA in Sigint. The McMahon Act limited American ability to work in atomic weapons with any foreign state, the core of air atomic power, until Britain independently built its own weapons. The USAF outweighed the RAF in size, and hoped not to depend on British intelligence. Yet by 1952, after years of effort, the USAF remained weak in collection and analysis.[30] It went backwards, while the RAF and GCHQ honed their craft and power. They outweighed their American counterparts in intelligence, while British aircraft, especially the English Electric Canberra bomber, matched American ones as platforms for aerial photography and Sigint.

Knowing its inadequacies and respecting British prowess, the USAF intensified cooperation in intelligence. Each boosted the other, with effects that lingered through the Cold War. British Sigint was central to American intelligence for nuclear war between 1950 and 1962, and important until 1992.

For years, the RAF conducted hair-raising overflights of eastern Europe and the western USSR. They provided useful imagery of most major LRAF bases at a time when this knowledge was essential and available through no other means.[31] By 1956, Lockheed U-2s succeeded Canberras as deep intruders, yet British crews still flew U-2 missions under the Union Jack. President Eisenhower and the USAF happily let allies share the risks and rewards of this game.[32]

Sigint probably gave SAC and Bomber Command the intelligence they needed to blunt enemy forces and defeat the USSR during the air atomic age. Certainly, it built their confidence in the likelihood of that prospect. Yet the process and outcome were never simple. The division between NSA and the Air Force Security Service hampered the quality of American airborne Sigint, which was shaky throughout the 1950s.

Between 1960 and 1966, the air-atomic age ended. Ballistic missiles replaced bombers as the main delivery component of nuclear strength, with the aim of deterrence through mutually assured destruction, rather than victory. GCHQ carried some strengths into this new age. Soviet strategic forces remained a preeminent target. When American satellites became the main platform to collect imagery from inside the USSR, and significant to Sigint, Britain continued to receive and analyse the data. It also was fundamental to the one area where Sigint flights on the Soviet periphery remained vital.

From 1960 to 1990, pairs of modified Canberras and de Havilland Comets, formidable aircraft for the task, flew low and fast over the Baltic Sea towards Soviet airspace. Suddenly, one climbed sharply while the other loitered to watch the fun. The Soviets scrambled their air defence, using radars and plain-language commands freely, thereby exposing sensors, command and communications systems and, often, their incompetence. These missions revealed not just local matters, but far better than any other means tested the working of the PVO, the air defence shield around the USSR. They aided planning for the air strikes which remained central to Western strategy, whether nuclear or conventional in composition, especially under the concept of Air–Land Battle. Not surprisingly, the Foreign Office insisted on approving each of these politically risky missions beforehand. When, in 1989, it challenged all of them as being unnecessarily provocative, the end of the Cold War, and of that particular age of Sigint, was at hand.

Meanwhile, Sigint built power against another Soviet delivery system. By 1955, an AN/FPS-17 radar system was installed at an American base in Turkey. It initially aimed just to trace Soviet missile launches from their bases in Kapustin Yar, in Central Asia, but soon collected data which could betray key intelligence on Soviet nuclear power, if analysed well.[33] GCHQ and the best analytical agency of the era, the JIB, showed how to do so, by unifying an effort which was divided between far larger American agencies. British Siginters, in Cyprus and elsewhere, collected Sigint from these tests at Kapustin Yar, as did the advanced British radar systems, Chaplain, Sandra and Zinnia.[34] Soviet telemetry signals were transmitted on multichannel radio systems, which inadvertently hindered encryption and helped attack.[35] Whereas the Soviets never appreciated that technical weakness, GCHQ discovered and exploited it. British authorities created telemetry intelligence by combining radar, Elint and Sigint in an excruciating analysis of an unknown problem, with two parts. In order to acquire data from signals, and then intelligence from the data, British authorities tapped their best civilian and governmental scientists, including world authorities at Jodrell Bank Observatory such as Sir Bernard Lovell. After a ten-man cell in GCHQ solved the signals problem, Air Intelligence and the JIB tackled the difficulties with data. They differed over their significance and the process. RAF intelligence thought that its 'opinion, experience and judgment' mattered most, and more than the method of scientists. The JIB credited the success to the method and organisation of its group of scientists, who also integrated assessment of nuclear missiles, warheads, and sites.[36] The Templer Report, which assessed these issues and evidence thoroughly, firmly supported the JIB and rejected the RAF's position.[37] Probably the JIB mattered more than Air Intelligence, but no matter the truth, all of these Sigint attacks required craftsmanship, experience and flair. Once Britain succeeded, for decades it kept that preeminent place on fundamental issues regarding nuclear intelligence for UKUSA, at a small cost in personnel or money. Against this, NSA and the USAF separately processed Sigint; NSA had no role against Elint, while Lockheed Missile Systems Division and the Stanford Research Institute analysed radar intelligence. These American organisations were excellent, but none had full access to all the relevant material. Difficult tasks, with high priorities, overwhelmed them, as did their rivalries. Nothing else in the record of Cold War intelligence better illustrated the virtues of Britain's small but unified Sigint and intelligence systems, compared to a larger but diffuse American effort.

GCHQ also survived another characteristic American problem: lack of security. On 21 October 1957, the periodical *Aviation News* exposed every American element of the programme, but none of the British ones. Robert Cutler, Eisenhower's Special Assistant for National Security Affairs, called this action 'treason'. Fortunately, it inflicted little damage.[38] The Soviets failed to overcome the problem because missile tests were necessarily exposed to radar and needed communications links, and the Soviets misunderstood the vulnerability of their multichannel radio systems. *Aviation News* did not compromise GCHQ's mode of attack, which worked effectively for another two decades, boosted by additional muscle from American radar. Telemetry matched imagery as a source on Soviet ballistic missiles, becoming the foundation upon which UKUSA built its intelligence against Soviet nuclear capabilities, and stood to watch the horizon for signs of war. Between 1974 and 1977, however, what GCHQ called 'traditional missile telemetry analysis' declined in value. Though Strategic Arms Limitation Talks (SALT) prevented the encipherment of missile telemetry, that of associated traffic – especially from satellite communications (Satcom) and spacecraft – became enciphered, which, GCHQ warned, 'affects exploitation for warning and indicator purposes'.[39] Meanwhile, signals became increasing complex. Against this, the expansion of the Soviet enterprise – the need for range control, security, and chase aircraft, among other things – increased the number of targets to attack. As ever in Sigint, any chain of security is as strong as its weakest link. Until 1992, GCHQ remained a useful partner to NSA in telemetry, though the latter waned in value as a source.

Sigint and imagery were the two great sources of Western intelligence on Soviet nuclear capabilities during the Cold War. Even combined, their power had great limits. Between 1955 and 1962, Western military institutions grossly overrated Soviet strength in bombers and missiles, as the US later underestimated the construction of Soviet nuclear forces. These failures primarily reflect the power of institutional perceptions and self-interest in analysis, but also the limits to the intelligence at hand. Imagery and Sigint counted deployed forces fairly well, but were weak in predicting their rates of expansion and their strength in the years ahead. GCHQ and the JIC were better at assessing these issues than most other intelligence organisations, partly because they had less self-interest in the issues than American agencies.[40] Again, UKUSA leaders such as Eisenhower often hoped that Sigint could reliably warn of Soviet nuclear attack; these hopes drove the creation of Criticomm, a fast-moving C3I system which aimed to warn a president within ten minutes of danger being discerned.[41] Their subordinates downplayed some of these hopes. After the Czech crisis of 1968, the British Minister of Defence, Denis Healey, asked 'whether it would be possible to deduce, from the patterns of Soviet exercise activity (and especially Strategic Strike exercises) what would be the main targets of the Soviet nuclear delivery systems in war. DIS Colonel thought not, and pointed out gently that no nation would be so foolish as to disclose its targeting plans in this way.' For GCHQ, Tovey wrote: 'I agree entirely with DIS on this point; we can deduce a great deal from LRAF/SNF [Long Range Air Force/Soviet Nuclear Forces] behaviour, both in exercises and at other times, but would not expect precise targeting data to emerge.'[42]

These caveats were powerful in general; yet in practice, Sigint and imagery provided powerful and precise warning intelligence on nuclear matters, every day. LRAF, SNF and PVO would take part in any dangerous Soviet activity, and reveal major intentions. GCHQ remained active against all of these targets throughout the Cold War, to aid war-fighting, but especially deterrence. GCHQ consistently contained alarmism on nuclear issues throughout the Cold War, especially during crises.

Economic and Technological Intelligence

Economic and technological prowess were fundamental to the Cold War, and to net estimates of Western and Soviet power. Intelligence on these matters was unbalanced. Western states publicly provided accurate economic statistics and open access to many leading matters of technology. They were also more exposed to espionage than communist states. The latter could gain most of the knowledge they needed through subscriptions to statistical digests, and periodicals such as *Aviation News*. They also collected technological material through an admirably effective campaign of espionage, the most successful branch of Eastern bloc intelligence activity during the Cold War. Meanwhile, especially before the Khrushchev thaw, the USSR hid basic data on all of these issues, while its public statistics were always incomplete and of dubious accuracy. Only good collection and analysis of intelligence could penetrate that shield. The best intelligence possible could not match the adversary in attack or defence, but merely staunch the bleeding. The USSR sought to blind the West to Soviet strengths and weaknesses, causing confusion and uncertainty, while stealing as much Western technology as possible. Western states aimed to minimise confusion and uncertainty, illuminate the struggle to determine and counter emerging threats, and guide offensive actions, such as controls over technology exports to the Eastern bloc, which contained these dangers in a cost-effective fashion.

These issues have received less attention than they merit, while much of the evidence about intelligence remains secret. Neither of the two histories of the leading British analytic organisation, the JIB, had much access to GCHQ records.[43] These problems obscure a central element of the Cold War. Soviet intelligence on technology was excellent in collection, decent when analysing technical issues, but incompetent on broader ones. Western intelligence on economic, scientific and technological matters behind the Iron Curtain was far from perfect, yet better than supposed. The key was excellent analysis of volumes of fragmentary data, building on a British method stemming straight from the War Trade Intelligence Department (WTID) in 1915. Western intelligence always had enough good sources, varying in significance by time and issue, to sustain such analysis. From 1956, imagery and open sources dominated that process. Sigint was overwhelmingly the primary source during 1946–56, when the task began; accurate evidence was fundamental and hard to find. Interception of civil text provided accurate intelligence, and a trusted means to judge the quality of other sources, including official Soviet statistics, which prepared analysts well for the moment when Sigint waned on the matter. British consumers expected GCHQ to analyse this kind of material, which its Commercial Section had done capably with economic intelligence since 1938. GCHQ and its main consumer, the JIB, simply continued work which their predecessors had done in economic warfare during 1939–45.

Between 1946 and 1956, GCHQ published probably several hundred thousand summaries and translations of civil text messages which, cross-indexed with each other and sometimes with reliable material from other sources, entered thousands of Sigint assessments. These messages had little value until they were collated, processed and analysed by experts both in Sigint and economic intelligence. GCHQ, sometimes aided by experts from other military or technical organisations, maximised the power of one source, while the JIB and military analytic units assessed material from all of them. These Sigint reports reproduced every relevant message, either verbatim or summarised. Their data was analysed painstakingly in diagrams, tables and text for the purposes of understanding and presentation. Reports illuminated many industrial, technological and military–economic issues, but were too fragmentary to do so with the Soviet economy as a whole. They included material on shortages of labour or raw materials, such as oil or coke, at factories or across the country; or on the links between Soviet establishments and the 'personalities' (names and work of individuals) within them. During the famine of 1946–47, civil text tracked grain requisitions across the USSR, demonstrating the scale of the catastrophe, and the state's ability to meet its needs, if not those of a million dead.[44] Civil text aided assessment of Soviet aircraft capacity, by tracing the work of aircraft plants, the Soviet electronic industry, and the provision of kit to the air forces. It provided many otherwise unavailable facts on key issues, such as political dissidence within the USSR, serial estimates of Soviet aircraft production, the capacity of munitions factories, specific areas of technology, including atomic research, and the poor quality of manufactured kit.[45] Civil text illustrated the confusion and friction within a command economy spread across Eurasia and the shoddy workmanship of manufactured goods in many emerging areas of technology, which was important to know and also reinforced underestimates of Soviet quality at its best.

From 1956, Comint on most economic issues vanished. During 1968, amidst a major rationalisation of analytic resources, GCHQ 'drastically' reduced its section addressing these matters, which 'had lost their importance', while 'the material was progressively becoming poorer'.[46] Still, from 1975, Sigint significantly penetrated Soviet defence economics by tracking raw material allocations, food production and new weapons, including warships, but especially those using communications at high altitudes, such as aircraft and ballistic and cruise missiles. Sigint was particularly useful in identifying research and development programmes, and the testing of prototypes. In 1979–83, GCHQ monitored the development of anti-tank guided weapons, the construction of major warships, submarine navigation and fire control systems, airborne anti-submarine kit and Soviet spacecraft.[47] Sigint bolstered a defensive campaign of economic warfare in peacetime, which contained Soviet strengths in intelligence and security and exposed its weaknesses in economics and technology. This was the area where Eastern bloc intelligence most beat Western, but to little avail. Western analysts misconstrued the Soviet economy, but overall their errors were too small to matter. Intelligence and the tighter security it led to impeded the Soviet acquisition of Western technology, despite the power of Eastern bloc espionage. Ignorance of its own economic position compared to Western states crippled Soviet understanding of and the ability to wage the Cold War. Ultimately, and ironically, lack of true data on their own economies led Eastern bloc authorities to rely on published CIA estimates of their economies. As usual in the history of intelligence, wisdom was to data as three is to one.

The Early Cold War: Challenge and Response

British Sigint against the USSR developed several layers between 1945 and 1970. In 1945, organisations hitherto focused on Germany immediately turned to attack similar targets in the Soviet Union, reflecting the realism of Siginters. GCHQ stations across the world followed Soviet targets. Cheadle continued to collect intelligence for defensive and offensive strategic air warfare, until air defence became impossible and the V-bombers declined in value. Then, converted to civilian status, Cheadle and other air-focused stations covered all Soviet Air Force traffic in western Russia, providing deep coverage beyond East Germany.[48] Scarborough, originally a Royal Navy base but converted to civilian status, remained Britain's main naval Sigint station, covering naval and mercantile traffic of the Warsaw Pact; and the alliance between the USSR and its satellites in eastern Europe in the Baltic Sea and the Atlantic Ocean. The station's reporting went to GCHQ and the Royal Navy, continuing old traditions of naval Sigint. Scarborough also loosely controlled the East Atlantic Direction-Finding network of NATO.[49] Culmhead, inheritor of the old GC&CS stations, used the most advanced techniques to attack the hardest targets in the Warsaw Pact.[50]

Surface warships collected Sigint, as did submarines, through intrusive missions deep in Soviet waters, among them some of the most sensitive and courageous acts of intelligence-gathering during the Cold War.[51] Radio Proving Flights, or 'ferret' flights, tested Soviet air defences, especially over the Baltic Sea. Bases in West Germany – mostly Army but also RAF, reflecting the traditions of field Y – focused on targets within East Germany. Western Sigint in Berlin was most visibly based at Teufelsberg, an 80-metre mound of rubble constructed after 1945, and more discreetly at RAF Gatow. Located in the heart of the Group of Soviet Forces Germany (GSFG), the greatest conventional formation in the world, Gatow was ideally placed to collect Sigint, especially voice, in 'a Sigint gold mine, a window into the heart of the Communist Bloc military system'.[52] The Army and the RAF concentrated much of their effort in Berlin, because Sigint would matter greatly in any period before war. Any units based there, however, would probably be lost when war began, and have only a degraded value in defence elsewhere even if successfully withdrawn in time of war. Elaborate plans for this process were drawn up at the peak of the Berlin crisis in 1959–61, but otherwise ignored.[53] Parochial concerns multiplied these strategic contradictions: Britain's reluctance to base units in Germany, which cost more than at home, and the physical limits to Gatow itself. The Army kept a large detachment at Gatow, for voice collection, but held most of its capabilities at Langeleben, balanced to provide intelligence in peace and war and to serve BAOR. The RAF concentrated its forward efforts at Gatow. It rated Sigint in deterrence, or in any period leading to war, above any aid for defence during battle or the needs of RAF Germany. These hard choices each met the needs of their masters and Britain.

GSFG stood on a peninsula assaulted by Siginters from three sides, simultaneously the most exposed and significant territory of the Cold War. UKUSA had great Sigint capabilities against enemy units in East Germany, its leading priority for conventional forces. They were reinforced by Sigint from third parties, and an interactive and inter-Allied combination of other sources. Through Allied arrangements in 1945–46, American, British and French ground and air forces were legally allowed to monitor East German and Soviet forces in the GDR. A few soldiers in Commanders-in-Chief Missions, including BRIXMIS and its American, French and Soviet counterparts, travelled in each other's zones. American, British and French military aircraft also collected imagery when using three twenty-mile-wide air routes from West Germany to West Berlin. These American and French flights collected some Sigint, but not British ones.[54] This was one of the few means for France to gather Sigint on Soviet forces in Germany, while the United States picked up everything it could. Britain had better and cheaper means to acquire Sigint. Meanwhile, under the guise of maintaining aircrew proficiency, personnel (nicknamed 'Biggles' and 'Algy', after famous fictional British aviators) in RAF Chipmunks based at Gatow conducted low-level air missions across the GDR, including imagery taken from hand-held cameras through open windows in freezing weather.[55] Through Chipmunks and BRIXMIS, Britain maintained greater air and ground reconnaissance capabilities than its allies were allowed. Each source could corroborate anything reported by another. Ideally, BRIXMIS and Chipmunks would shadow a Soviet exercise, and Sigint monitor all traffic to and from it. Chipmunk personnel were trained on BRIXMIS missions before flying, to ensure knowledge of the ground and kit. The Allied air and ground missions interacted loosely, but were insulated from Sigint – in theory. During 1978, one incoming head of 26 SU, Tony Cunnane, was introduced to BRIXMIS and its American and French counterparts by his predecessor. Next morning, Cunnane was ordered onto the first flight west to meet the senior RAF intelligence officer in Germany, who warned him never to repeat the exercise.[56] Reports from these air and ground sources flowed back to UKUSA intelligence authorities in Germany, who integrated the information to help guide future missions. Siginters independently added to that pot, and took from it, to guide their own activity.

American and British Sigint sought to monitor all Soviet targets, certainly the most central of them, with the aim of identifying every anomaly, and warning their masters of any signs of danger. Ultimately Siginters achieved these ends by living within the net of Soviet signals by monitoring the same command links for decades and developing anthropological skills based on a finely granulated attention to detail. This skill and success were not easy to achieve.

GCHQ and Crises in the Early Cold War

During the autumn of 1956, GCHQ confronted two unexpected crises at once – its greatest challenge of the Cold War. Throughout 1956, Egypt subverted and aimed to overthrow Britain's position in the Middle East. In particular, Egypt nationalised the Suez Canal, which Britain and France owned. British forces planned for war, which GCHQ supported by penetrating diplomatic and military systems of the Middle East, especially Egyptian ones. GCHQ also prepared against an Israeli attack on Britain's Arab allies, which might have the potential to involve Britain in war, by aiming to provide 'a reasonable chance of detecting signs of aggressive intentions and of making a rapid change-over to a wartime degree of exploitation', without damaging collection on Russia.[57] Force alone could stop Nasser's threat to vital British interests, but only with difficulty, which Eden's government multiplied. Trapped in the world politics of anti-imperialism, and leading a state uncertain whether it was or was not a great power, Eden declined to use force directly. Instead, he did so through a conspiracy with France and Israel, which Britain hid from its allies and officials. Israel would attack Egyptian forces in Sinai, without provocation, and drive for the Suez Canal. Britain and France would use this event to justify occupation of the Canal Zone, and Egypt. Even a determined and able government would have found this plan hard to execute. Britain lacked such a government.[58] Even worse, Eden launched the conspiracy without fully consulting his strategic advisors or intelligence agencies, which crippled Britain's ability to execute his aims. As GCHQ noted right after the crisis: 'We were alerted 4 days before HMG's ultimatum … and, one day before, by gaining unofficial knowledge … but the public news was the first that GCHQ officially gained about HMG's intentions. (MI6 clearly knew a little more)… Even after operations had started we had to rely for briefing about operational plans on a black-market service from Admiralty. An official service from the Ministry of Defence would have been preferable but, in the event, perhaps less efficient.'[59]

That four days of warning and 'black-market service' enabled GCHQ to focus its resources against Egypt during the intervention of 1–7 November. GCHQ effectively aided an operation on which it was barely briefed and created means to deliver its product to decision-makers, including Eden.[60] The effect was futile. Good intelligence could not save incompetent policy.

Suez was a big crisis, yet precisely as GCHQ improvised its way through it, a greater one emerged in Europe. During October 1956, political unrest in Hungary sparked a revolution, and a Soviet onslaught during 1–11 November. These events coincided with the Suez crisis, increasingly bad Anglo-American relations, the last days of an American presidential election, and great tensions between the USSR and Poland, where popular anti-Soviet unrest was manifest. The Hungarian crisis surprised everyone. This sudden and large use of force raised the issue of where the Soviets would stop and tested the rules for order in Europe. Soviet panic proved contagious. The DIRNSA, General Canine, thought 'drastic changes' were needed in American decision-making. 'Worst thing in a crisis is a jittery G2 [military intelligence] and that we have had.'[61] Sigint did not predict the crisis and could not have done so, but the Five Eyes response was confused and mediocre, for political and organisational reasons. Britain and the United States were unready for such a crisis; NSA was a new organisation with fragile control over US Sigint agencies and uncertain contacts with American headquarters. After the crisis, NSA commented that it 'received very little information on U.S. plans, intentions, and operations during the crisis', with 'painfully obvious' damage to its work.[62] American Sigint was confused in structure and had never confronted a crisis of this nature and magnitude. Whitehall and GCHQ had more experience of such matters, but lacked procedures or preparations to handle the crisis. GCHQ, concentrated on war in the Middle East, was not a twenty-four-hour organisation. British Sigint was uncoordinated: GCHQ did not control army Sigint in Europe, while the latter was technically mixed in quality and reported to Army headquarters, which could not direct these units, or even know that they should.

UKUSA was even more uncoordinated. British Siginters believed that they were good, while their American colleagues often were not. US Siginters made alarmist – and alarming – claims, which British Siginters rejected. One of GCHQ's aims became to minimise alarmism in American reporting and among American consumers. One senior British Army Sigint officer 'thought US military reports in the crisis were "rubbish"', and disregarded by NORTHAG, the British headquarters which commanded NATO in northern Germany – a frightening commentary.[63] Sigint communications were clogged perhaps more than ever during the Cold War. For the first time, amidst crisis, UKUSA confronted the unintended consequences of its standard operating procedures for reporting and dissemination. US Siginters transmitted only spot reports, but did so immediately, which at this stage NSA could not properly collate. Their widespread and instantaneous dissemination spread alarm and error as reports ricocheted across the Five Eyes: as

Francis Raven, a leading NSA official told Palmer: 'Basic problem is U.S. consumer demand for everything from everywhere to everyone at top priority.'[64]

These problems were serious, doubly so because leaders in Britain, NATO and the United States feared extreme Soviet actions: military intervention in Poland, the dispatch of 'volunteers' to Egypt, and possibly more. Here, GCHQ played its greatest role of the Cold War, and a unique one, which combined a professional focus on accuracy with an openly political campaign to contain alarmism across UKUSA. That aim was easy to achieve in Whitehall, where intelligence and military authorities accepted GCHQ's evidence calmly. The JIC, for example, held that Soviet mobilisation against Poland was small in scale, indicating 'that the Russians are placing themselves in a state of complete readiness to strike at once if any trouble should develop in POLAND, but there is no evidence that they are preparing to strike now'.[65] GCHQ's aim was much harder in Washington, where events in Suez caused American authorities and Siginters to suspect British motives, precisely at the peak of the Hungarian crisis. Americans were particularly sensitive to British manipulation, precisely as GCHQ manipulated them more than at any other moment of the Cold War. Though Suez blindsided GCHQ, Americans were right to wonder whether it was lying to them over the Middle East; and if so, why not in Europe too? Here, fortunately, the personal trust between Director Jones and DIRNSA Canine, and the latter's friendship with the SUKLO, Palmer, reduced tensions.

GCHQ focused all of its resources on quality control, addressing the fears of Soviet intentions and correcting mistakes among American Siginters which might cause errors in action. Internally, GCHQ established a large section to study 'Russian intentions' and report on them daily. GCHQ's judgements rested on positive and negative intelligence about matters which changed and remained the same. They were expressed in detailed reports and broad appreciations, despite the supposed ban on that practice. For example, GCHQ told NSA:

1. ...Latest Sigint information as of 1600 8/11 gives no indication of Soviet preparation for global war or of intention to intervene with force in the Middle East. Soviet Air, Naval and Merchant Shipping activity appears normal, subject to Hungarian situation.

The only other communications activity which appear at all unusual is in the Group of Soviet Forces in Germany where cumulative evidence from 30 October to 8 November suggests a general state of readiness. The evidence is that military practice traffic has virtually disappeared from the main networks of the Mech Armies in GSFG since 4 November; that there has been a silence on certain links from HQ to Armies from about 1350 on 6 November; and that there was on 7 November (Soviet holiday) a small amount of fighter code in an Air Army in Germany which is unusual during a holiday.

2. With present intercept resources it is virtually certain that Sigint would detect Soviet preparations for global war or any large scale preparation to intervene in force in the Middle East. The scale of Sigint resources and their state of alert is such that negative evidence in these contexts is considered reliable.

3. Sigint could not however be guaranteed to detect small-scale Soviet moves in connection with the Middle East situation. The movement of technicians, small supplies or small amounts of aircraft to the Arab countries would not necessarily be detected by Sigint, though there is a reasonable chance that aircraft movements would be observed.[66]

GCHQ traced the Soviet suppression of the Hungarian revolution in detail, as Soviet forces abandoned signals security in combat. This material illuminated current events and, later, underwrote exhaustive analyses of the operations and command and control of all Soviet formations involved in this campaign, from divisions to army groups, airborne to air forces – all priceless information for any military officer considering how their enemy would actually fight.[67] GCHQ contained fears of Soviet mobilisation against Poland or Egypt, Turkish accounts of Soviet air mobilisation in the Caucasus and Black Sea, and reports of LRAF flights to the Arctic Ocean, which would have been an alarming signal.[68] It compiled original evidence that the LRAF was about to begin flights in the Arctic, but offered a counter-intuitive reading of that evidence: 'It is however considered most unlikely that such a movement (which would almost certainly be detected) of LRAF aircraft would be connected with present international situation.' GCHQ defined the LRAF's real states of alert, which were high but not warlike. That a

Soviet atomic test was proceeding normally suggested a similar pattern.[69] J division 'is keeping an eye on Kapustin Yar range to see if any evidence of weapons being transferred westward', and found none.[70] Despite constant harassment and tension, GCHQ was remarkably calm and stoical. It rarely issued alerts to military Sigint units, which it thought able to understand their situation without direction.[71]

The Cuban missile crisis occurred because American intelligence, at almost the last moment possible to act, detected a covert Soviet attempt to deploy medium-range ballistic missiles (MRBM) to Cuba, which would have weakened the United States in political and strategic terms. Had this action been discovered earlier, the United States could easily have blocked it without crisis; weeks later, it would have been a fait accompli. The American problem combined a lack of intelligence, the power of Soviet security and the weight of preconception. The seeming unlikelihood of the Soviet action kept suspicions which bubbled deep in the bowels of many agencies from reaching the brain of all-source analysis. *Maskirovka* security and deception covered the loading of missiles and warheads onto merchantmen in Soviet ports, the middle passage to Cuba, and their conveyance to bases.[72] Soviet ships' crews were denied knowledge of their cargoes. When they approached Cuba, their captains, alongside their KGB minders, opened written orders telling them their next actions. No wireless signals mentioned their task. This *maskirovka*, basic but competent, failed in the end, but prevented GCHQ or NSA from sounding an alarm that Siginters yearned to ring earlier.

Experience of the Hungarian crisis taught GCHQ that Soviet mercantile shipping was 'an entity to be watched as an indicator (positive or negative) of war', through 'the sudden increase in cypher traffic to and from ships, orders to ships concerning dangerous areas, re-routing of tankers and other ships and the apparent decrease in the numbers of positions reports sent in the clear'.[73] Siginters routinely covered Soviet mercantile traffic by reading open reports from Lloyd's of London and newspapers, foreign port officials and plain-language messages, and noting the use of cypher. In the months before the crisis broke, a sharp rise in Soviet shipping to Cuba caught the attention of Siginters. Every report emphasised that Sigint had no idea of the cargoes. Any unusual reports were marked 'Priority', and distributed to the JIC, the Foreign Office, DIRNSA, and sometimes MI6 and

American and British naval intelligence, along with usual consumers. On 20 July, for example, GCHQ's outstation at Scarborough noted that two Soviet passenger and cargo ships, ostensibly bound for Vladivostok, had mentioned positions which 'would normally indicate' they 'were possibly en route Cuba', and that they had received enciphered messages which might suggest 'that their voyages are other than routine'.[74] Ultimately, these two vessels did not sail to Cuba; many Soviet merchantmen leaving the Baltic turned north towards Murmansk, where they loaded 'military associated cargoes to Cuba' (which many sources also reported was occurring). GCHQ monitored an unusual 'large-scale communications exercise' between all Soviet merchantmen at sea and their controllers in the USSR, and an unusual wireless transmitter on board a Soviet tanker on a 'routine' trip to Cuba.[75] Probably GCHQ and NSA read all messages to and from Soviet merchantmen bound for Cuba. None seemed alarming, even in hindsight, while Soviet conventional and nuclear forces worldwide avoided abnormal behaviour. When collated, the Sigint evidence simply showed that the USSR was shipping some conventional weapons to Cuba, and aiding the development of its military and air defences. Soviet Comsec blocked UKUSA from offering any evidence, and also restrained potential fear.

Instead, the crisis broke just before Soviet actions were complete, in the explosive circumstances of an American Congressional election. By early October 1962, other sources provided enough evidence to raise suspicions: some emigré reports about Soviet deployments in Cuba proved accurate while buried within a spoilheap of rumour; imagery suggested that some of the deck cargo on some Soviet merchantmen fitted the profile of the standard Soviet medium bomber of the day, the Ilyushin IL-28; while Soviet surface-to-air missile (SAM) sites on Cuba were deployed like those found around Soviet ICBM bases. Contrary to popular legend, John McCone, head of the CIA, was not the only intelligence chief worried about Soviet shipments to Cuba: the US Defence Intelligence Agency, GCHQ and NSA had equal concerns, as did junior officials in many agencies. McCone and the Pentagon, however, could bring another source to bear. On 14 October, a U-2 spyplane caught the first proof that Soviet missiles were on Cuba, setting UKUSA, and the crisis, into motion. NSA and GCHQ promulgated Sigint alerts on 23 October.

GCHQ's normal work in monitoring Soviet nuclear forces and conventional formations in Europe illuminated matters which were fundamental to the crisis. So too, Scarborough's daily toil in following Soviet mercantile traffic proved fundamental to watching merchantmen carrying nuclear warheads to Cuba, until they gradually turned about, and the sudden flurry of urgent enciphered messages from Moscow to its transport ships after President Kennedy announced a pacific blockade of Cuba – the moment when the fever broke.[76]

GCHQ spoke with credibility and intimacy to its American counterparts. They appreciated its performance. GCHQ worked well because it needed only to service its standard links to British forces and NSA. However, the chaotic command system of American forces during the crisis would have determined the impact of this intelligence, had war occurred. In particular, Sigint would have provided excellent intelligence to guide NATO nuclear strikes. Had war broken out, however, the US Secretary for Defense, Robert McNamara, planned to abandon plans for that campaign and improvise his way to victory, as he later did so well in Vietnam.[77]

GCHQ and the Middle Cold War

By 1964, when GCHQ absorbed the individual service Sigint organisations, it had become the sole national organisation responsible for Sigint on the Warsaw Pact. Its military and intelligence consumers also became more unified as the MOD grew in power over the services. Some problems declined, while others rose.

Warsaw Pact manoeuvres became large and constant. Exercises produced more traffic, along with uncertainty and 'noise'. The Pact did not intend exercises to pose an intelligence problem for NATO, but they had that effect. The actions of exercises were hard to distinguish from those which marked the start of a crisis. As the MOD's Defence Intelligence Service (DIS) noted in 1968:

> It will always be difficult to make a timely, correct and definite interpretation of the significance of Russian activities. Individual indicators could have alternative explanations, for example: as reflecting a military exercise. A combination would clearly be of more significance; indeed it might only be by shrewd study

of a number of concurrent indicators, some of them small in themselves, that we could hope to arrive at a true interpretation of Soviet activities. Such a combination could be interpreted as indicating that an attack was being planned. But if each side was alerted and reacting to the other's successive moves, it might well be wrong to deduce warning of impending attack from the enemy's preparations, which might only be designed to intimidate, or to demonstrate to the West that the Union could not be intimidated. Indeed, the precautionary measures could reach a stage at which the Soviet Union was fully mobilised but had no intention of initiating general war.[78]

Errors of analysis might expose NATO to surprise attack, or spur the USSR to start one. Only hard and able work could prevent these dangers. The 'generally increased and more realist Soviet Armed Forces' activity', J division warned, caused an 'atmosphere of high activity and greater realism', which produced welcome 'stimulation', but added 'strains and stresses on an already over-stretched Division'.[79] That stress became the norm. Twenty-one major exercises occurred in 1967. From 1970, Warsaw Pact manoeuvres occurred almost every day.

UKUSA's reliance on traffic analysis would have appalled Bletchley. Historically, traffic analysis was a good source, especially for order of battle, but weaker about enemy intentions and vulnerable to signals deception. It worked best, as with 'Sixta' at Bletchley, when combined with good Comint. That component was absent against the USSR, which had demonstrated competence in signals deception. In 1945, Soviet *maskirovka*, including wireless deception, matched the Western Allies' in operations, though not in strategy.[80] Western analysts misunderstood Soviet quality in that sphere at this time. Excessive secrecy over the historical record damaged UKUSA's general understanding of wireless deception while, misled by the conspiracy theories of the KGB defector Anatoly Golitsyn, some intelligence officers and politicians distorted *maskirovka*'s general power to deceive Western strategy.[81] Soviet security was good, but its deception less so. Mediocre executions of field *maskirovka* could too easily be mistaken for a KGB masterplan. Elementary *maskirovka* covered the Soviet deployments to Cuba before the missile crisis.[82] A few Siginters thought they observed Soviet wireless deception during the Czech crisis of 1968.[83] The JIC accepted

GCHQ's view that wireless deception had not occurred, but demanded a 'record' – that is, justification – of its views.[84] The intelligence coordinator, the admired veteran Dick White, still insisted that 'the KGB's Disinformation Section was well capable of carrying out a first-class deception operation through secret agents'.[85]

In its post-mortems of that crisis, DIS, anticipating consumers' questions, asked whether wireless silence would handicap predictions, 'since almost all of our current intelligence comes from Sigint sources'. If so, that danger could cripple every assessment of Soviet preparations for attack and diminish the power of Sigint, thereby multiplying the effect of fear, uncertainty and alarmism on Western strategy. DIS concluded that the danger was small: the Soviets could not avoid using radio, while wireless silence would betray that something unusual was afoot. GCHQ wished to refute this danger in even firmer terms. Any 'evidence' of large-scale wireless deception 'would clearly be a discovery of considerable importance'. GCHQ searched for signs of it in vain. The evidence was 'blatantly incompatible' with that idea, as 'the behaviour of the General Staff communications provided the clearest possible indicator of what was really happening'.[86] Britain 'must put this whole business of "radio silence" in context. Frankly – so far as the Soviet Army is concerned – we have no real evidence of any attempts to put such a concept into practice.' Whether because of that practice or 'more likely' through 'technical SIGINT difficulties not primarily of the Russians' own making, moves of one or two Divisions into the Forward Area could go undetected by us until a few days after arrival ... We must honestly confess to some degree of doubt about our ability to discern, or at least, to identify as such, Rear Service exercises, mobilisation measures, and the like.' Still, Sigint observations, especially of General Staff traffic, would detect 'any <u>major</u> reinforcement of the Forward Area', that is, of more than a few divisions.[87]

As with Cuba in 1962, Soviet secrecy on political matters aided tactical surprise for the invasion of Czechoslovakia. Again, signals deception did not aid that outcome, which Soviet signals insecurity compromised, this time damaging *maskirovka* as a whole. GCHQ's critique helped to inoculate Western strategy from Golitsyn's conspiracy theories, which infected only Western Humint. A foe able in wireless deception might have fooled UKUSA. The Soviets were not that foe – their wireless operators were sloppy and their command and communications cumbersome, though NATO was no exemplar. Soviet signals insecurity also crippled its ability to conduct wireless deception. UKUSA, meanwhile, developed traffic analysis of unparalleled skill and experience in the radio age, which, from 1955, probably could have contained *maskirovka*.

UKUSA's central task was to be an intelligence tripwire: to calculate order of battle and thus infer capabilities and intentions. Any sign that Warsaw Pact forces were improving their ability to attack sounded a warning. Little sound was needed for NATO states to adopt their only possible response, which was to reinforce their cover, and stand for war. UKUSA's ability to follow enemy movements, and crucially to know when it lost track of any formation, eliminated the danger of a surprise attack followed up by a secret mobilisation, which many other sources would be able to monitor too. The narrow space of the Central Front also denied the Soviets the bewildering range of alternative prospects which best aids deception.

Still, the Soviets could launch a conventional or nuclear strike without any background of political tension, or military mobilisation. In that case, they might conceal concentrations of standing forces at select points, if they were skilled or lucky enough to execute the efforts. Any systematic efforts at wireless silence to cover any other eventuality would backfire, however, by drawing attention to deception, especially if applied for the first time by inexperienced practitioners. *Maskirovka* might marginally have reinforced Soviet tactical surprise at the start of a war, but little else, and equally, might have eliminated it altogether. We shall never know, fortunately.

The Test of Czechoslovakia

During the Cold War, the Soviet Union often considered whether it must forcibly prevent the defection of an ally: with Yugoslavia in 1948, Hungary in 1956, Czechoslovakia in 1968, Afghanistan in 1979, and Poland in 1980–84. Ultimately, the USSR invaded three of these countries. For observers in Britain and the USA, the military concentrations needed to achieve these ends might enable the USSR to pursue greater ambitions. These examples demonstrated the problems in predicting any Soviet attack on NATO. They, and the Soviet efforts to intimidate NATO into abandoning West Berlin between 1958 and

1962, ranked among the Five Eyes' greatest challenges of the Cold War. These challenges also gave GCHQ and NSA opportunities to measure and improve their skill.

During the 1960s, American Sigint rose sharply in quality and quantity. GCHQ's analytic capabilities were great, and matched those of NSA. But during the Czechoslovak crisis of 1968, American Sigint provided most of the relevant coverage while transitional problems reduced British power. GCHQ relied on semi-processed American material, which it could challenge only carefully: 'this process inevitably involves a certain element of inspired guesswork and is barely a substitute for an adequate study of one's own intercept'. Also, J division was part-way through the process of changing from a reliance on hand logs of intercepts to automatic semi-processed material. 'Analysis thus tended to have the worst of both worlds, having lost both the facility and the habit of studying raw logs, but being unable to take full advantage of the machinable semi-processed material by which logs had been replaced.'[88] These problems reduced GCHQ's characteristic strengths. GCHQ made a 'significant contribution' in 'interpretation', through 'presenting in a reasonably digestible form (the daily ARU-H reports) what otherwise would have been a mass of paper well beyond our customers' power of assimilation'.[89] Fifty ARU-Hs, which compiled and analysed reports received over one to three days, were released between 11 August and 24 September 1968, more than one per day.[90] Hooper, Director of GCHQ, later praised its 'rapid and readable end-product' despite the 'steady drain of manpower and teamage' in recent years, but this statement perhaps gilded the lily.[91]

The crisis demonstrated UKUSA's power in determining order of battle, and its weakness over intentions and the politics of policy.[92] Sigint demonstrated that the Soviets could overwhelm Czechoslovakia, but did not penetrate the intentions on either side, except to show that Czech military traffic was 'deliberately passive and non-provocative'. In order to overawe a major ally on the frontier with NATO, the USSR had to transform its command and deployments. These actions gave NATO ample time to prepare as it wished. From 7–9 May, a major and unexpected Command Post Exercise occurred. GSFG command links were extended to the GDR–Czech border, to where the 20th Guards Army advanced from Berlin. On 10 May, Soviet airborne and general staff command links escalated in unusual ways. GDR officials discussed the movement of Soviet troops towards the Czech border. A GDR soldier warned his wife that he soon would leave East Germany. From 11 to 30 May, Soviet troops advanced from one of their two main feeders into central Europe, the Carpathian Military District, towards Czechoslovakia, as did Soviet and Polish aircraft. In June, manoeuvres mobilised the Warsaw Pact against Czechoslovakia, and left Soviet forces in the country. Around 7 July, exercises and command links produced a 'distinctly suspicious appearance', though GCHQ recognised that many actions that the press thought dangerous stemmed simply from logistical exercises. Then, tension declined.[93] The military standstill suggested that the crisis had abated, reinforced by the withdrawal of Soviet forces from the country after exercises, and public negotiations between Czechoslovakia and the Warsaw Pact. Beneath this surface calm lay agitation within the capitals of the Warsaw Pact, and a decision to solve this problem by force.[94] These states hid signs of this agitation, which no Western source penetrated.

GCHQ showed that Soviet forces could strike from out of the blue, but it did not predict an invasion and ended its emergency staffing. Soviet movements had been aimed to lull suspicions in Prague, and also did so with NATO and GCHQ. On 20–21 August, forces from the Warsaw Pact struck Czechoslovakia with tactical surprise and quickly subdued the country. Over the next tense month, GCHQ watched the movements of all Warsaw Pact forces and allayed fears that the USSR would strike elsewhere. Analysis of this traffic honed GCHQ's baseline for assessing the nature and intentions of Warsaw Pact redeployments and preparations for major attack, which may have guided its acute reading of Soviet movements during the Polish crisis of 1980–81.

This performance, Tovey noted, produced an 'almost euphoric adulation of SIGINT ... at the height of the crisis', replaced by a 'rather more sober appraisal' when other sources emerged and analysis of the event as a whole become possible.[95] He thought this change was good for GCHQ, as it also was for judging the performance of intelligence against the main enemy. Czechoslovakia was a success for Sigint, but not a triumph; had this mobilisation been directed westward, NATO would have had ample time to counter-mobilise its full strength. It would have confronted only the smallest and unavoidable forms of tactical surprise, at a time when it would already have suspected danger, and been able to assess Soviet intentions, if only from diplomatic contacts. DIS credited

Sigint with providing 90 per cent of its material.[96] Military attaché and press reports delivered the rest. GCHQ enabled its consumers to understand Soviet capabilities and its ability to act as and when it wished, though Cheltenham could not precisely predict the attack. As Tovey said: 'until AFABF aircraft were actually flying over Poland en route to Czechoslovakia none of us could point to any firm SIGINT indication of imminent invasion. Even then there could have been other indications, right up to the time when the aircraft approached the Czech frontier.'[97] These errors, and uncertainties, demonstrated what the best traffic analysis on earth could not deliver, which an Ultra might have done.

This mixed success led GCHQ and DIS to reconsider how well they could detect a Soviet attack on NATO. During the lull in the crisis, DIS concluded that experience confirmed their pre-existing views. In November 1966, the JIC had concluded that the Warsaw Pact could launch a surprise attack from a standstill, but if it deployed the LRAF and naval air forces, NATO would have forty-eight hours' warning – four to nine days if the enemy entirely abandoned 'strategic surprise'. Military movements might be exercises, defence against expected NATO actions, or 'measures intended to intimidate the West or the prelude to Soviet attack'. Yet GCHQ had traced every indicator which the JIC emphasised: the extension of GSFG communications, westward movements of Soviet forces, staff and logistics exercises and troop concentrations. 'Our experience here,' DIS wrote:

> shows that we were able to detect the military warning indicators
> of the move of Soviet troops in the Carpathian Military District
> on to the Polish/Czech border. This warning was received very
> shortly after the troops had started to move and therefore should
> strengthen our confidence that similar indicators would be detected
> if such large scale movement appropriate to an attack on NATO
> should begin ... we were able to detect air deployments very soon
> after they had occurred. All this information should enable us to
> build up an accurate intelligence picture of Soviet deployments
> from Western Russia in sufficient time to be able to warn NATO.[98]

That confidence waned after the surprise Soviet move on 21 August. DIS concluded that it could not predict intentions purely by military preparations divorced from political ones. The Warsaw Pact could launch a successful surprise attack from a standstill, while NATO could expect three to eight days' warning if the Soviets mobilised in order to multiply their 'weight of attack ... In either case the Russians could achieve tactical surprise in terms of the moment of attack.' Meanwhile, Soviet power was strengthened by its constant improvements in Comsec and communications.[99] GCHQ was even more disconcerted, reflecting its discovery of unexpected technical problems. As Tovey wrote:

> Immediately before the invasion we were faced with the apparent contradiction of a situation of seemingly lowered political tension accompanied by a military posture indicating immediate readiness for intervention. Therefore, when the Russians assessed (unknown to us) that they were not going to achieve their aims as a result of the Cierna–Bratislava discussions, they were able to achieve tactical surprise by their political decision to intervene ... the lesson for the future is clear. A period in which both the political and military indicators are 'red' can be followed, as they were in this instance, by a situation in which the political situation shows itself as 'green' while the military situation obstinately remains at 'red' – in such circumstances in future we cannot (as we and our consumers have tended to do in the past) gloss over the military indicators by, for example, attributing them to exercise activity or the like, but must continue to take them very much to heart.[100]

Ultimately, GCHQ concluded that the problem was just marginally worse than before: GCHQ could provide the three to eight days' warning which DIS wanted of major movements, say of several divisions from several Military Districts, but not necessarily just one division from a single Military District.[101] To do so would require greater resources and heightened procedures, every day.

GCHQ set out to provide just that. For years beforehand, GCHQ had readjusted its resources, reducing J division and Siginters in Europe marginally, so that K division could go forth and multiply. GCHQ wished to avoid becoming mired in tasks involving Cold War Europe, which had inexhaustible calls for resources, in order to maximise its chances for original work elsewhere. Partly as a result, in 1968, British Sigint did not collect much material relevant to the greatest crisis in Europe for a decade. GCHQ's reliance on semi-processed American material undercut its claims for 'that independent British contribution which is a primary justification of J division's existence'. It had sufficient resources to handle the crisis, but only barely. As Tovey wrote: 'the Soviet invasion, including the manner of its preparation and the way it was actually carried out, can leave us in no doubt that the situation confronting J division today is fundamentally different from that of a year ago. What we cannot do, therefore, is to revert simply to the policy and procedures which were in vogue before the crisis supervened.'[102] Equally significant were revelations about morale within GCHQ:

> Virtually all staff, irrespective of level, obviously derived a sense
> of stimulus and satisfaction from the realisation that J Division's
> product was now at the forefront of Whitehall's thinking; these
> considerations far outweighed any inconvenience in the working of
> extended hours. Similarly, the almost neurotic belief that 'nobody
> really cares about the Soviet bloc anymore', the chilling sensation
> that there was no point in producing intelligence quickly ('the
> Americans will get it out first anyhow') – these undesirable if
> understandable concomitants of the reduction of J manpower over
> the past few years evaporated over night as the Czech crisis gained
> pace.[103]

The Czech crisis exposed GCHQ's limits as a worldwide organisation, just as Indonesian Konfrontasi did in 1964–65. Afterwards, GCHQ stopped its reductions of J division and military Sigint in Europe, which threatened 'the maintenance and development of that sound technical understanding of the Soviet problem in depth on which all our work, whether in crisis reporting, routine reporting, or long-term studies, ultimately depends'.[104] It steadily boosted the capabilities of J division.[105] These steps significantly increased GCHQ's capabilities in Europe, while diminishing those elsewhere. The end of empire and the Czechoslovak crisis led GCHQ to reverse its strategy of the previous decade, and to concentrate its resources in Western Europe, thereby maintaining a flagship position in the greatest theatre, while declining elsewhere across the world. This policy was telling, yet mirrored the main trends in British strategic policy. It also achieved its end.

Living in the Force: the High Cold War

GCHQ produced intelligence on an industrial scale, which its consumers processed in the same way. Together, they drove a flood of data through the mill of analysis to produce Sigint, the most powerful form of military intelligence during the Cold War. GCHQ assessed British material and everything it received from second and third parties.

Assessment always had a political dimension. Multiple and overlapping consumers were driven by different interest and concerns. 'For Distribution to Sigint Producers Only', GCHQ issued 'Technical Supplements' on matters such as the frequencies and call signs of signals entities.[106] Another great set of consumers were British intelligence assessment bodies, of which the JIC was not the largest. In the early Cold War, the JIB was GCHQ's main consumer for strategic intelligence, especially on economic issues. The JIB's successor, the more military-focused DIS, became the main consumer for GCHQ's material on the main enemy. Many DIS reports were sanitised Sigint. None directly contradicted the Sigint record; most were confirmed by it, in various ways, and some stemmed from the source. The structural problems which dogged British analysis – bad liaison between DIS and the JIC, or officers swamped with responsibilities – were largely absent in assessing the Soviet problem in the Cold War, because Britain created analytic capabilities fit to handle it. Even on peripheral issues such as Soviet relations with, say, Afghanistan, GCHQ and DIS analysts constantly addressed intelligence and demanded and provided constant warning about minor matters.

More than in wartime, military consumers were usually staff and analysts rather than commanders. The security procedures within Sigint – the distinctions between Categories 2 and 3, or of Special Compartmented Intelligence (SCIs) and their British equivalents, Very Restricted Knowledge (VRK), differentiated military consumers into different groups. Reading folders kept Sigint distinct from everything else: analysts across the desk from each other might have different categories of access. Security procedures blocked these reports from NATO third parties, who received sanitised versions or none at all. From 1970, UKUSA gave much Category 2 material to NATO third parties, in sanitised forms, as 'NATO Secret'. Security also limited the combination of Sigint and non-Sigint sources for any consumer. Every year, GCHQ produced a few finely granulated assessments which compared the Sigint record with other sources. It lacked the analysts to do so often, while DIS and the BAOR lacked the staff and the clearances needed for the purpose. Security restrictions limited their distribution. BRIXMIS never received a copy of an excellent 1981 report on Soviet armoured tactics, for which its personnel provided key material.[107]

GCHQ was not supposed to offer appreciations unless consumers requested them, but in military intelligence it could encourage such queries, or convey the answers unasked. Most military Sigint reports were factual narratives, but many were organised analytically – appreciations in all but name. GCHQ presented data in powerful and sophisticated graphic forms. Analysts loved nothing more than to squeeze yet another drop of data from a report and to represent it in even more complicated graphs. Regular reports addressed specific issues at the same level of analysis, categorisation and audience. Individual specialists, or dozens of them, produced special reports, each tailored to distinct readerships. Some special reports, reflecting secrecy or narrowness, had tiny distributions. Others were downgraded from Category 3 to 2 by removing individual items of Comint from the text, which, against the Warsaw Pact, rarely damaged comprehension. This step allowed wide distribution among anglophone military commands and enabled the technically most qualified officers to consider the best evidence on enemy practices alongside that from other sources. One such report, 'was intended to convey, in a timely manner, short items of original and noteworthy information' about narrow matters; others provided broad and detailed accounts of everything known about great topics.[108] Many special reports were Sigint analyses of the order of battle of Warsaw Pact forces, intelligence fundamental to assessing their numbers and organisation, though inadequate to define capabilities.[109] Other GCHQ reports illuminated capabilities insofar as they could be judged outside war.

GCHQ did not give consumers the raw intercepts which it received, nor did it show how the sausages were made within the factory of analysis: they were generally incomprehensible to outsiders. Daily and weekly summaries were hard enough to follow; spot reports were even worse. GCHQ issued two genres of weekly reports – one detailed, the other a synopsis – on matters such as 'Soviet Air Force and Air Defence',

'Eurcom Activity' and 'Soviet Bloc Political and Military Activity Abroad', within GCHQ and to NSA and major British intelligence and military agencies. GCHQ provided detailed observations and notes on abnormalities. It had enough analysts to handle the work, as could specialists in other departments. Britain allocated enough resources in collection and analysis to squeeze juice from low-level sources and to make rye whiskey from strong but crude ones.

GCHQ and Crises during the Later Cold War

Between 1976 and 1985 the Cold War intensified. Both sides became more fearful, angry and confrontational. Western countries thought their position across the world was challenged and that hard responses were necessary. Soviet leaders feared decline, the loss of allies and, perhaps, a pre-emptive strike by NATO. Crises and exercises were constant. The old problems remained: how to discern the unusual detail taken from a host of routine reports and to determine whether an exercise marked the opening of a crisis. GCHQ's track record on these matters was good – powerful in technique and effective on policy, yet limited by its inability to determine Soviet intentions directly. Those mixed characteristics marked its performance during two great crises which set the end game of the later Cold War, when the USSR invaded Afghanistan, but not Poland.

GCHQ monitored Soviet intentions through their reflections within links for command, control and communications, especially airborne warning and control aircraft (AWACS) aircraft or those platforms 'associated' with specific commanders, and of Soviet organisations central to emergencies, such as nuclear or airborne forces.[110] Two of these links shaped GCHQ's work during the Afghan crisis, though in both cases past practices changed.

During 1979, the communist regime of Afghanistan imploded. Soviet leaders, fearing that the Afghan dictator, Hafizullah Amin, might betray them and align with the United States, decided to overthrow him with 700 special forces and paratroopers, occupy the country with 50,000 soldiers, and reform the regime. This issue is usually seen as an intelligence failure for Western countries.[111] In fact, the USSR – grossly distorting Amin's ties with the United States and underestimating the difficulty of controlling Afghanistan – made far greater errors of intelligence. The role of intelligence during the invasion of Afghanistan was diametrically opposite from that in the Cuban missile crisis.

Throughout 1979, GCHQ looked for signs of Soviet aggression by searching the signals of those forces which would support it. Originally, this issue was on the periphery of British concerns, but GCHQ and DIS had enough analysts to handle it well, probably just a few in each case. GCHQ's professional performance aimed to avoid alarmism while pinpointing danger. GCHQ was preadapted to assess events in Afghanistan, where open sources revealed crises between Soviets and their clients. For one thing, Amin's murder of his rivals was a hard signal to miss. GCHQ associated changes in communications between Soviet headquarters and their offices in Kabul with 'unrest in Afghanistan'. This attention exploded in September 1979 when Amin overthrew his rivals. Painstaking review of every Soviet communication with its offices in Kabul and airborne forces showed anomalies: codeword messages from the airborne command in Moscow to formations in Asia 'of a type not seen before', their meaning unknown, but probably taken 'from a list which includes codewords raising and lowering readiness status'. Yet there was 'no repeat no evidence of preparations on the Soviet side for intervention … no repeat no evidence of any state of heightened readiness on the part of Soviet forces such as might have been expected if there was an intention to intervene militarily'. By October, everything returned to routine, including minor abnormalities. Just before December, anomalies slowly swelled again. GCHQ noted a 'slight increase' in enciphered text and voice between general staff Moscow and stations in the Military Districts of Turkestan, Central Asia and Transbaikal. Its 'significance … is not known, but the fact that the communications have involved probably the Military Districts Head Quarters and have not been continuous suggests that it is not exercise related'.[112]

This traffic turned to a flood, as the USSR positioned itself to pre-empt a problem abroad rather than react to it. Increasing numbers of transport aircraft landed at the Soviet airbase at Bagram, near Kabul, while airborne forces across Russia flocked to Central Asia. On 12 December 1979, GCHQ warned that these developments might be 'related to events' in Afghanistan or Iran. Quickly, the target became more precise. The Soviet invasion did not surprise GCHQ, though it did Amin, who experienced the KGB's favourite form of overkill: poison followed by gunshots.[113] In coming years, GCHQ monitored the Soviet campaign in Afghanistan, its failure, and major political developments, like truces with and attacks upon the resistance leader Achmed Shah Masoud, in the Panjshir valley – first-rate information on a major theatre of the late Cold War. [114]

GCHQ viewed its own performance as a success, rightly. It warned accurately, without alarmism, that the USSR was creating capabilities to enter Afghanistan. GCHQ revealed Soviet intentions and gave a week's warning that intervention was imminent. This was all the information Whitehall needed to know, on an issue where Britain had major concerns but no plans to act. It also illuminated an issue that concerned the United States rather more, though NSA probably drew parallel conclusions from the same evidence and cared more about it because its consumers did so.

The limits to such intelligence emerged a year later in Iran, a country with which the USSR had mixed relations. In August 1980, military exercises in Transcaucasia and Turkestan, adjacent to Iran, led GCHQ to give consumers a special report with a rare warning, a 'Summary and GCHQ Comment'. 'Live play' by air and ground forces in these areas was low. Soviet signals followed routine hours, but they

> are in their scope and capability much in excess of what would be required for exercises involving a single front, and are clearly being practised to control both the Transcaucasus and Turkestan fronts … the evidence at present is insufficient to suggest that any assault on Iran is imminent. On past experience a build up of ground forces and transport aircraft in the border areas would be expected: none has so far been seen, in many areas e.g. Eastern Europe normal training appears to be in full swing. But CPX [Command Post Exercise] in the Transcausasus in July, together with the capacity of the Communications being exercise[d] from Baku, suggest that the Russians are setting themselves to acquire the competence to conduct an operation against Iran in the future if they chose to do so.[115]

Throughout autumn 1980, GCHQ followed these developments, which waned and then vanished.[116] GCHQ tracked changing Soviet capabilities, which suggested concern over conflict with Iran, yet could not indicate what these actions actually meant. Ultimately, they led nowhere, and may just have reflected the faintest form of Soviet contingency planning. These reports reflected GCHQ's close attention to any signs of Soviet aggression, aided British policy, and encouraged analysts to think about possibilities.

They also show how other developments affected British analyses of Soviet actions in Poland during 1980. Sigint showed that explosives were piling up, and then had been decommissioned without exploding, but remained in place and could easily be rearmed. Were the Warsaw Pact to attack Warsaw, it would need massive forces, which would force redeployments of divisions and the development of new systems of command, control and communications. Such actions would surely echo elsewhere. On 22 August, ten days after the crisis became obvious, GCHQ gave its consumers an unusual report, which prepared them for an unexpected development. GCHQ offered two pages of commentary about the situation in Poland based on open sources, for context, followed by a long record of all relevant Sigint, including material which might have been noted before, but was now being applied to this situation. Then, during September 1980, GCHQ detected the creation of a Comsat link between the general staff in Moscow, subscribers in western Russia and an unidentified 'high-level authority in the Warsaw area'. The latter, perhaps 'a communications centre for a General Staff operations group acting as a theatre level authority', was little used, 'which suggests that the network is in the early stages of setting up and is not being used for actual command and control purposes'. The 'precise nature' of this system 'is as yet unclear', but it may 'represent the initial testing of communications facilities required for contingency operations. No Sigint reflections of troop deployments have been noted.'[117] In the coming months, GCHQ carefully monitored this system, which became linked first to the general staff's command train and finally to the headquarters of the Soviet Northern Group of Forces at Legnica, the USSR's main base for influence throughout the Polish crisis. By December 1980, GCHQ noted, this system remained in being, but quiet: a latent rather than a live capability. So it stayed for years.

Almost certainly, GCHQ had caught the Soviet command, control and communications system which was being developed for an invasion of Poland, just as it was being established. Such new links often emerged within the Warsaw Pact. This news was useful, but otherwise GCHQ's surveys of Sigint offered little on the crisis. For example: 'The recently announced closure of the Polish/GDR border to persons not possessing a visa has been widely discussed by staff in many WBKs (*Wohnungsbaukombinant*, the state construction enterprises in each state of East Germany, which combined political and paramilitary activities) and an apparently directed sounding out of local opinion has produced an almost universal favourable reaction. Such a reaction seems to be due at least equally to the stopping of Polish shopping trips to buy consumer goods in GDR as to any condemnation of political events in Poland.'[118] In 1981, GCHQ noted that: 'Fears of strikes occurring in the GDR are increasing. Any hints of such troubles will be dealt with severely as official opinion towards Poland remains hard-line,' while the 'combined forces (WP) HF (Warsaw Pact High Frequency) comms network in the GDR' continued in being, and the Polish general staff developed a military communications link seemingly intended to sidestep problems posed by the Solidarity movement.[119] Sigint lacked the precision to follow such events in Poland, but, fortunately, other sources carried this burden.

At the Cold War's End

GCHQ and NSA played many parts in the struggle with the main enemy. Any conclusion about their effect requires an averaging out of many loosely connected cases. British and American Sigint had three main tasks: to trace the Eastern bloc order of battle, warn of war, and help to fight one. Its performance for the first task was excellent, for the second tolerable, outweighing any other source, but only weak for the last. Overall that record is imperfect, but good, and better than conventionally understood. The failures of Western intelligence, and its debates over the biggest of uncertainties such as the bomber and missile gaps, and the Soviet economy, do not demonstrate incompetence, but rather the irreducible problems in interpretation which remained after a good attempt at a hard pitch. These debates reflect UKUSA's success in containing confusion and uncertainty.

Still, their limits left ample room for uncertainty and error on military matters, especially given the confused politics of Sigint and decision-making within NATO. These dangers were contained because Western statesmen doubted that Soviet counterparts would risk mutual extermination, while intelligence remained sufficiently credible and powerful to warn of real threats, stop the distortion of imaginary ones, and to indicate that war was not quite at hand, even in the worst moments of the Berlin and Cuban crises.

Sigint was one part of a global competition against able enemies in many areas. Soviet Humint crippled UKUSA Sigint. Western Humint never returned the favour against the Warsaw Pact, though Western Sigint hurt Soviet spies. The Eastern bloc won the Humint struggle against UKUSA, though not by much after 1960, partly because of a renaissance in the power of MI5 and MI6. Britain is often seen as being uniquely vulnerable to penetration by foreign espionage during the Cold War, in part because British writers export the *vice anglais* into the history of espionage, searching for any excuse to flagellate themselves. In fact, Warsaw Pact Humint penetrated Britain far less than it did France, Germany and the United States.[120] American Sigint lost more to spies and traitors than did GCHQ. The Soviets and their allies, good in many areas of Sigint, struck UKUSA directly and indirectly. UKUSA regarded Soviet Sigint with respect but not the cryptosystems of its NATO allies. The USSR gained from material on members of NATO, even if it could not penetrate UKUSA. Knowledge of Soviet successes in Comint is sparse, but the KGB told its masters that it devoured the communications of foreign embassies in Moscow, including those from NATO countries.[121] While these claims perhaps were exaggerated, no doubt the USSR exploited the weak security in NATO embassies, including those of Britain and the USA, and intercepted plain-language traffic in foreign capitals, especially that carried by microwave. The huge forces of Warsaw Pact military Sigint undoubtedly picked up much of the same material acquired by the UKUSA system, but probably mined it less well.

One cannot yet determine the relative quality of both sides in this struggle, nor who won it. Yet these questions of quality and victory are secondary in significance. In the struggle with the Warsaw Pact, NATO wanted Soviet Sigint to be decent or good, because that status helped to achieve its strategic aim: deterrence. For the enemy to know that NATO was politically unified, militarily formidable, but not preparing an offensive war, was good. Soviet leaders found those points hard to believe. Since so many NATO decisions were made openly, espionage declined in value as a source against them. Yet Soviet espionage wormed deep into the secrets of NATO, which still never neared defeat in the Cold War, and won it. Equally, the secrecy around decisions within the Pact maximised the value of high-level penetration by any Western source. By eliminating this danger, the greatest Soviet victories in intelligence during the Cold War were defensive in effect, not offensive.

NATO did not need intelligence to answer the biggest questions of the Cold War: how would its political cohesion and economic health compare to that of the Warsaw Pact? Who was winning this struggle of attrition? NATO did need intelligence to address the military aspects of these issues, but these were secondary in importance, unless the Cold War turned hot. Here, GCHQ and NSA sustained confidence in London and Washington, which flowed to other NATO capitals, that at any given time the Warsaw Pact was unlikely to launch a surprise attack while such an assault could be predicted. Better intelligence on Soviet intentions would have helped achieve this outcome, but proved unnecessary to it. UKUSA reinforced the many factors which enabled the members of NATO to pursue a reasoned policy with calm, especially by capping uncertainty and alarm. UKUSA was thus an unsung element in the success of deterrence. Without UKUSA, NATO would have done less well, but probably still have won the Cold War. UKUSA was a useful secondary factor behind Western victory in the Cold War, yet two weaknesses remained: UKUSA could not have predicted a Soviet surprise attack launched from a standing position, which would have boosted an already powerful stance, while the NATO Sigint system would have collapsed in a hot war, without providing a force multiplier. The factors which helped NATO to win the Cold War might not have done so in a hot one.

Comint and the End of Empire, 1945–82: Palestine, Konfrontasi and the Falkland Islands

In 1930, Britain was the foremost power on earth. Its prestige and power deterred threat. It could guarantee commitments across the globe without having to defend them physically, a resort which rarely happened more than one case at a time. After 1945, British power shrank steadily towards that of a great secondary power. It faced a succession of economic problems, imperial overstretch and commitments across the world which were beyond its strength to maintain; political challenges within its colonies, and painful decolonisation. Britain made concessions to its colonies, including the granting of independence while pursuing a hegemonic status over them, in order to try to preserve its status as a global power. After the Suez crisis of 1956, British elites increasingly came to see world power as impossible to maintain, and the attempts to do so as damaging their country. Britain abandoned inconvenient colonies on the best terms possible and retained some possessions, such as Gibraltar, Hong Kong and the Falkland Islands, where conflict with neighbours remained a possibility.

Decolonisation was accompanied by armed struggles between Britain, challengers within colonies and imperial neighbours. Britain's decline in power and prestige increased the number of these challenges, including those from protectorates which it had lost, such as Egypt. Deterrence became harder to maintain and wars more difficult to win. Britain had to defend many colonies against challenge, often by force, and sometimes several at once. The conventional armies of non-Western countries improved. Between 1815 and 1939, Britain's ability to deny modern weapons to its subjects and imperial neighbours had let small home and colonial forces manage large enemies. This edge ended from 1955, as rival states offered Britain's imperial neighbours significant supplies of modern arms. By 1960, only major British forces could protect clients like Kuwait from powers such as Iraq. Yet sustained commitments hampered the handling of other problems, in particular economic ones. This contradiction drove Britain to abandon empire, though a degree of world power remained.

This chapter studies three instances of this phenomenon, and how Comint affected it: in the Palestine Mandate, 1945–48, the confrontation with Indonesia, 1962–66, and the Falklands conflict of 1982. This history has complete access to the record of military Comint in these cases and to many secret British policy records, but none to the diplomatic and civil traffic of the key players or of other states. It does, however, make use of such material where it is in the public domain. This account of how Sigint affected these cases is accurate as far as it goes, but necessarily incomplete. It will note how documents which are withheld might affect these stories when they are released.

These cases and others, such as the Suez crisis of 1956, share characteristics. Britain confronted the international politics of anti-colonialism and challengers driven by differing fusions of mass politics, nationalism, religious conviction and revolutionary ardour. Increasingly, international opinion saw empires as fundamentally bad, their cases as inferior to nationalist ones when these clashed, and the first use of conventional force as automatically wrong. Britain's enemies adopted practices such as terrorism or covert action, which challenged older ideas of the legal use of force and harassed Britain. Response through the deployment of conventional arms was delegitimised, unless managed carefully. When the British embassy in Jakarta was ransacked in 1963, Prime Minister Harold Macmillan told the Cabinet: 'Palmerston no good anymore.' The need to avoid looking 'Neo-Colonialist' dogged British policy in Asia throughout the 1960s.[1] All of these cases involved threats to British prestige and power and struggles of political attrition short or long in duration. Britain militarily outmatched its challengers: the problem was how to make this superiority serve politics. The balance of intelligence affected that of power. A second-rate power possessing first-rate Sigint confronted third- or fourth-rate powers possessing usually poor Comint and Comsec.

These cases have commonalities but also differences. For Britain, the Falklands conflict was a political and strategic crisis involving the fate of states. The other issues were major but secondary. One of these case studies involved action aimed at preventing decolonisation, another to manage it, the last to survive the process. In Palestine, Britain's foe fought to live; in the other instances, imperial neighbours threatened British interests for reasons of internal politics and to achieve limited diplomatic ends. In the event, Jewish success enabled the State of Israel; Indonesian and Argentine failure wrecked their regimes. The attitudes of the United States, Britain's chief partner for strategy and intelligence, varied in each case, and so too the value of other sources of intelligence and the balance between them.

One case featured major conventional operations. Two involved guerrillas, terrorists, counter-insurgency and counter-terrorism, where Britain's enemies found it rational to murder civilians, British personnel or their families. Broadly, these cases illuminate the relationship between force, politics and Comint during the age of decolonisation and the Cold War. They also illustrate the technical side of Sigint mobilisation, communications and their relationship to command. Sigint was so good that it enabled much more to be done than could be acted on in political or operational terms. The limit was political – what Britain was willing and able to do with its power and intelligence. Even in the Falklands conflict, Britain held its military hand, fearing that to use British power fully would impede victory.

Sigint and the End of the Palestine Mandate, 1944–48

The Anglo-Zionist Divorce

Between 1944 and 1948, GCHQ worked well on the Palestine question, but power and politics limited its effect.[2] British authorities misconstrued how their power compared to that of the Yishuv – the Jewish population of Palestine – and their Arab counterparts. Authorities assumed that the Yishuv needed British support to swim in an Arab sea. It must know that fact and follow Britain. The Yishuv had different views, and many of them at that. Most Palestinian Jews would have followed Britain had it accepted their demands, but since Whitehall could not do so,

Jews chose to survive through their own strength, which was greater than they originally knew. Zionist propaganda painted Britain as anti-Semitic; Britain was the only state of the time which was willing to protect Jews on its terms, which Zionists rejected. Conflict flashed over how to replace the Mandate, the borders between Jewish and Arab populations in Palestine, and emigration. After the Nazi holocaust, 600,000 Jewish survivors needed a new home – old ones were no more. They happily would have gone to Canada or stayed in France, but no Western state wanted them. Gentiles found Palestine the simplest solution to the Jewish problem, which they threw at Britain and the Arabs. US President Harry Truman was a Zionist from conviction and calculation: he knew Americans favoured Jewish immigration to Palestine but not to the United States.

Holocaust survivors needed succour: the Yishuv alone offered it. Only by letting them into Palestine and expanding the area of Jewish settlement would the Yishuv support Britain. British intelligence, military and political authorities thought, rightly, that to do so would wreck British politics among Arab countries.[3] As British power in India evaporated, the Middle East rose in importance as a base for influence.[4] The Anglo-Zionist alliance foundered on the rock of immigration. Without the prospect of almost doubling the Jewish population of Palestine, the Yishuv would probably have continued to shelter behind Britain. An existential issue for the Yishuv clashed with a great British interest – a clash that caused a revolution in Anglo-Zionist relations, which no one understood. Each side stumbled as they entered a new game, where no one knew the rules, the moves, the next step, or the final one. Neither side understood the true balance of power between them.

Britain had lost control of Palestine. It could be restored only by conquest, which Britain could not stomach. In 1937, the leading Arab politician in Palestine, the Grand Mufti of Jerusalem Amin al-Husseini, led an Arab revolt against Britain. A tough colonial policeman, Charles Tegart, broke Arab power, almost as much as did their internecine feuding. By neutering one community in Palestine, Britain destroyed the opportunity to balance between them. Meanwhile, in order to withstand threats from Arabs and Germans, Britain strengthened the Yishuv. The Jewish Agency, a state within a state, administered the Yishuv. It had a large army, the Haganah, which was poor compared to the British and Transjordanian ones, but better than other Arab forces.

Britain trained the Palmach, the competent core of Haganah, and Jewish intelligence services. Haganah hid within the Jewish Settlement Police, a British-subsidised paramilitary force formed to protect kibbutzim, which included at its peak 3,000 permanent and 16,000 temporary personnel. Britain trained the core of Palmach, expected it to prepare others in order to resist potential German occupation of Palestine, and helped it to build a fallback wireless network to aid resistance. Britain gave battlefield experience to the Jewish Brigade of 5,000 Palestinian Jews, drawn from Haganah and Palmach, as were some members of the Special Operations Executive (SOE) who served in the Balkans. British intelligence at its peak trained those of two peoples, Americans and Israelis; both students took firsts.

Many British military intelligence officers were Zionists; consequently, British experts on the Yishuv were not employed during the Palestine campaign. They helped Jews develop military and intelligence organisations and, during 1944–48, were kept from service against the Yishuv, probably because their loyalties seemed uncertain. Meanwhile, the fascist terrorist group Lehi, which Britons called the Stern gang, assassinated the experts on the Yishuv within the Criminal Intelligence Department (CID), the political police force in Palestine. Imperial police forces, managed by a few British officials, who kept their files in their heads, were particularly vulnerable to assassination. In 1945, British intelligence relied on advice about problems and solutions in Palestine from the intelligence services of the Jewish Agency more than from the CID. With the best of British understatement, MI5's authority on the Middle East, A. J. Kellar, called this position 'embarrassing'.[5]

British politicians assumed that Jews and Arabs would recognise their wisdom and accept their solutions as being the best compromise for all; soldiers thought their bayonets could shape politics like scalpels. Both were hubristic. Britain could control Palestine only through one of the largest commitments ever made in peacetime across its empire. It lacked the will and power to rule Palestine purely by force, against four simultaneous threats. The Yishuv and its central institutions, the Jewish Agency and Haganah, resisted British policy by all means short of war. After a ceasefire between both sides during 1940–44, the Revisionist Zionist movement, Irgun zvai Leumi, also sought to overthrow British rule by violence. It demanded treatment as a legitimate belligerent. When Britain treated Irgun's actions as criminal, and executed some of its members, Irgun hanged captured British soldiers. Lehi murdered any British policeman, soldier or official it could find whose back was turned. Thus any British action was vulnerable to one or another of these threats: non-cooperation by the Yishuv and Haganah, armed resistance by Irgun (and some elements of Haganah) and terrorism by Lehi, and sometimes also by Irgun. Ultimately, the Yishuv beat Britain because it was more determined, powerful and ruthless. Meanwhile, Arab power and resistance to both Britons and Jews grew. Militants on both sides rejected compromise and pressed for maximal aims, taking them towards war. For Britain to appease one side would enrage the other. Alan Cunningham, the High Commissioner of Palestine, saw powder keg and sparks: the reviving power among Arabs of a 'war criminal', the Mufti, who had allied with Germany during the war, and 'the unbalanced emotionalism' of the Yishuv which its leaders 'constantly whipped up'.[6] He warned that 'temporary expedients in the absence of an imposed solution' would only 'lead us deeper into the mire'.[7] Yet Britain could neither avoid expedients nor impose solutions. In 1948, when it realised that Jewish and Arab populations would not accept its rule – nor its rules – Britain abandoned Palestine, leaving these peoples to fight each other.

An Intelligence Struggle

Fundamentally, superiority in intelligence could not have overcome these weaknesses. Quite apart from that fact, it also did not exist. Jews beat Britain in Humint, which was central to campaigns of subversion and terrorism. Britain was superior in Comint against a competent foe. Haganah Sigint monitored Coast Guard radio nets, which helped it to aid ships carrying emigrants towards the Palestine coast. Jewish operators ran the civil telephone network of Palestine. In February 1945, Kellar found that Jews 'entirely manned' military and secretariat switchboards at the King David Hotel in Jerusalem, the centre of British administration in Palestine. 'Police monitoring was operated by Jewish personnel with every possibility that the latter doctored what they handed in.' Jewish cleaners freely entered offices where official documents could easily be stolen.[8] Haganah's intelligence service, Shai, devoured the messages of Arabs and rival Jewish organisations alike. Jewish superiority in Sigint and Humint aided them against Arabs during the Mandate, as well as after it. Shai also acquired much intelligence from the British military and occasionally the CID, but the latter threat was contained through British use of veiled language and scrambler telephones.

When British and Jewish forces worked together against the Mufti, the Zionist leader Moshe Shertok warned Tegart that the King David Hotel was insecure. 'There should be a sort of "Holy of Holies" in the CID where information would only be seen by British personnel.'[9] Britain duly created a tabernacle for Sigint between 1944 and 1948. Through elaborate protocols, Comint personnel hid the receipt of communications to the 'OATS block', sometimes called the 'SIME (Security Intelligence Middle East) unit' and 'L.S.S.L.U.', the title for the Sigint communications unit in Jerusalem. The term 'FOG unit' meant both the 'OATS block' or just its members indoctrinated in FOG, within 'the FOG cage'. Similar protocols covered the dissemination of intelligence to indoctrinated – 'Oated' or 'Fogged' – personnel. Sigint Liaison Unit links carried all Comint traffic between Jerusalem, Cairo, Cyprus and London. Direction-finding reports from Cyprus were routed through No. 2 Wireless Regiment at Sarafand and then to the Oats block via a secret, dedicated and rarely used telephone, 'led into FOG Unit by BUTTERCUP Section'. The phrase, 'I have a message for you' was followed by a verbal dictation of Typex groups, which simply covered bearings.[10]

Between 1939 and 1945, Britain developed capabilities against Jewish traffic, driven by the combined threats of Haganah, Irgun and Lehi. The Radio Security Service (RSS) monitored communications within Britain and the empire, searching for signs of subversion and espionage. Its branch in Egypt, the Middle East Radio Security (MERS) group, followed all Haganah and Palmach radio networks within Palestine. The latter used simple procedures and cyphers, subdivided into just a few different superencipherment systems, which changed infrequently. Jewish soldiers and politicians signalled rather more than necessary. A commercial codebook, *Bentley's Second Phrase Code* (1929), which used simple superencipherment, covered Jewish Agency traffic on cable.[11] Codebreakers found that these systems were easy meat.

Reading the meaning of traffic proved harder than breaking it. The greater problems were linguistic and political, reflecting the complex relations between British Gentiles and Jews about Palestine. Few British subjects except Jews understood modern Hebrew. Only those with Zionist affiliations really understood the colloquial language, which raised questions of loyalty. Until 1945, Britain and Zionism had been allies. GC&CS could trust British Jews to work against Irgun and Lehi, as the Yishuv's intelligence authorities did, but some went further. In 1943–44, at Berkeley Street, ISPAL (Illicit Signals Palestine) attacked traffic from the Yishuv. Initially, Haganah cable and radio traffic – codenamed Ispal I and, from 1944, Isoats – was the main target, while that of the Jewish Agency – first called Ispal II and later Istria – was a secondary one. Ispal I/Isoats provided military intelligence, with Ispal II/Istria tracing the political and diplomatic activities of the Jewish Agency. By November 1945, Isoats 37,220 was produced and Istria 110.[12] Ultimately, around 50,000 Isoats and 5,000 Fog messages were published, and an unknown number of Istria and Buttercup ones.

In 1944, an academic at London's School of Oriental and African Studies (SOAS), James Heyworth-Dunn, warned that one of ISPAL's members, Bernard Lewis, later a renowned scholar, was a Zionist, and thus untrustworthy to handle ISPAL messages. That the Foreign Office liaison officer to the intelligence services raised this issue, and the head of MI6 and GCHQ replied to it, shows its significance and complexity. Menzies wrote:

> LEWIS has been engaged on his present work with us in ISPAL II for a year or more, and it is clear that if he had been responsible for any leakage, this would have been reflected in the material itself. It would clearly be preferable not to employ a Jew on this particular work, but the language difficulties make it virtually impossible to employ anyone else. DENNISTON is entirely satisfied of LEWIS's reliability and I understand that KELLAR of MI5 who has lately worked with LEWIS on ISPAL II shares this favourable opinion of him.
>
> Heyworth DUNN himself must be regarded as a very tainted source of information. He has an Egyptian wife and is known to be violently anti-Semitic.[13]

When MI5's Director of Counter-Espionage, Guy Liddell, asked Denniston if Lewis and his colleague Samuel Stalbow would 'read back some Hebrew reports for us relating to the activities of Shertok and others, Denniston was quite prepared that they should do this work, and regarded them as 100 per cent reliable'.[14] Stalbow, born in

Hackney in 1916 to a Jewish family of eastern European origin which ran firms in the rag trade, became an artillery captain in 1943 and was seconded to Berkeley Street. Lewis and Stalbow translated material on the Jewish Agency for Britain without feeling that they were betraying 'their' side. Neither Lewis, Stalbow, nor any of the many Jews who worked at Bletchley, such as Walter Ettinghausen (later, Walter Eytan, the professional head of the Israeli foreign ministry), betrayed their trust, though experience in Hut 3 perhaps inspired Israeli diplomatic Comsec. His brother, Ernest, another Bletchley veteran, ran GCHQ's library until 1956, when he resigned and returned to the brighter lights of London. Postwar, Siginters showed no signs of anti-Semitism towards their colleagues, whom they treated as exactly that (though the same was not always true at Bletchey Park). British intelligence trusted these British Jews with Yishuv traffic more than they did Englishmen in Palestine with Jewish 'mistresses' or wives.

However, the divorce between Britain and Zionism caused ruptures in many unions of dual loyalties. From 1945, intelligence and military authorities eased Jews from work with Palestine. To make them work against their kin raised questions of fairness and security. New recruits attacked Jewish codes in a unit directed by Captain Hastings, the Deputy Director for diplomatic intelligence (DD 2, and later DD 3). When Berkeley Street operations moved to Eastcote in 1946, the unit took an office at Chesterfield Street in London, isolated from other elements of GCHQ. Though no hard evidence survives, probably one or two members of the Commercial Section stayed to handle cryptanalysis. Stalbow remained the core of its translating effort through 1945, perhaps longer, while Lewis returned to academe.[15] The records suggest a churn in personnel, which cannot be traced in detail. Probably new entrants were Englishman who knew biblical Hebrew and/or Arabic, which eased entry to modern Hebrew, though causing occasional misidentifications. Until 1948, Siginters and their consumers found translation from Hebrew a real test, eased because the Jewish Agency sent much of its traffic in English. Their targets and procedures were unique; the unit attacked commercial codes for diplomatic purposes. In 1944, Hastings's unit had peculiar communications characteristics.[16] It retained them and an SLU structure – even when GCHQ generally abandoned these practices – simply because they worked and the task was urgent. Like RSS, but generally unlike GCHQ, the unit intercepted the messages of British subjects for purposes of security and counter-terrorism. In the special circumstances of Palestine, GCHQ was granted a special warrant to intercept and read the traffic of British subjects. Initially, MERS and No. 2 Wireless Company in Sarafand intercepted radio traffic. In 1946, however, MERS shifted to Cyprus; its personnel were slowly replaced during that year and it was replaced by a direction-finding station in Egypt.

Material was signalled from Palestine to London, where codebreakers broke, translated and returned it by wireless and Typex. When Comint was first introduced for operational purposes, processing 'special messages' took eight to twenty-four hours, and normal ones three to four days. Soldiers thought the 'operational value of these messages would increase tremendously' if major messages were returned within eight hours, and average ones within twenty-four.[17] Soon, this process worked with blinding speed: priority messages intercepted in Palestine were read and returned from Britain within four hours, routine ones in sixteen to thirty-one hours.[18]

In 1944, the Foreign Office had rated among its three intelligence priorities in the Middle East the 'prime importance' of obtaining 'reliable secret intelligence about Zionist activities', especially 'the Jewish Agency's contacts with foreign Governments', and its 'efforts (if any) to establish good relations with the Arabs'.[19] Ispal was carefully restricted. Only four diplomats, 'all permanents' and 'the Departmental lady', received it. From 1945, as the system became mature, the Defence Security Officer disseminated material to consumers and summarised every 1,000 messages for all major ones, including the Secretary of State at the Colonial Office. Officials noted that DD 3 'are daily telephoning Colonial Office with most important' Oats messages. Key authorities in London read Oats and Istria.[20] The Defence Security Officer (DSO) reported that General Barker, the General Office Commanding Palestine, said: 'We are entirely dependent for our only absolutely reliable information' on Oats.[21] Comint channels carried messages on high policy, such as those entered in the 'TOP SECRET NIGHTCAP' series, which were destroyed when the task to which they referred ended. Their loss affects the record.[22]

In 1944, the main consumer of Comint was a cell at SIME in Cairo, a quasi-autonomous British military agency which ultimately was incorporated within MI5. In 1945, the SIME cell was placed under the

DSO, a military intelligence position which was just becoming MI5's station chief in Jerusalem. Though Comint was his central source, the DSO had others, along with many tasks. Quickly, Comint became a source for operations as well as counter-intelligence. So much material was produced that SIME asked to receive only parts of it.[23] Even so, in June 1946, Kellar claimed that SIME 'is almost entirely concentrated on Jewish affairs. Arab matters are sadly neglected.'[24] An attempt to maximise security intelligence against Jews may have damaged that against Arabs. By 1947, as Director General of GCHQ, C made the DSO, Gyles Isham, his personal representative for Sigint in the Middle East. MI5 and MI6 also had an unusually harmonious relationship in Palestine. The DSO had remarkable, perhaps unique, powers for any authority in British intelligence. He was the main analyst of Comint and Humint, including material from the CID and military intelligence; he advised British political and military authorities on matters of intelligence, security and counter-terrorism, and directed British warships and aircraft to intercept immigrants' ships.

Just a few people ran this system. The unit in London had perhaps five cryptanalysts and translators, a small and highly specialised group with limited surge capacity. In Palestine, nine cypher and wireless operators handled all Comint traffic in and out. Probably similar numbers served in London. The MERS party had thirty-five personnel when it reached Cyprus. In April 1947, probably a representative date, the 'SIME party' in the DSO's office had ten members indoctrinated in Fog: four officers, a corporal and 'five women', who processed data and analysed intelligence. These officers, three of the women and five other Sigint personnel were indoctrinated in the broader Comint category, 'Cream'.[25] The Fog unit consisted of an officer and two to three women. The former oversaw intelligence production and the latter handled intelligence, 'case work', a combination of data retrieval and intelligence and, during 1947–48, probably aided bookbuilding of new Haganah systems. The other two to three secretaries managed the Registry of Comint traffic, the less secret Comint material, and other secret material.[26] These women were trained MI5 secretaries, or the wives of British servicemen in Palestine. J. C. Robertson, an inspector from MI5 visiting around April 1947, had reservations about the quality of the DSO's personnel, but not the DSO himself, Colonel Magan: 'In this atmosphere of continuous monotony (interrupted only occasionally by real danger), it is much to the credit of Magan that the morale of his staff, especially among the women, is so high' – probably referring to their response to the terrorist bombing of the King David Hotel on 22 July 1946. In particular, Robertson noted:

> The FOG Unit is in a class apart from the rest of the office. Captain Burbidge, who is responsible for its organisation, is a first-class intelligence officer whom Magan has praised very highly. He receives useful assistance from Mrs. Sales and Miss Ann Clerk (who however left for Singapore just before my return to the U.K.). The FOG records and situation map are a model of precision and clarity. This assists materially in maintaining the prestige of the D.S.O., since the most important part of the service he provides is derived from CREAM. It is in the 'FOG cage' that the daily G.O.C.'s meeting is held.[27]

The FOG unit created an efficient Registry of traffic and a card index system listing proper names of people, units, ships and places. It was the main source for a 'Black List' which traced the loyalties of Palestinian Jews, in order to guide British authorities working with them.

Security against Jewish espionage in Jerusalem drove these processes. When Britain first considered sending ISPAL to Jerusalem in 1943, Liddell warned the Director of Military Intelligence (DMI) that 'it was extremely important to ensure that the material was properly handled at the other end. We knew that most offices in Palestine were penetrated.' In 1944, the DMI and C refused to send ISPAL to the DSO Jerusalem, Henry Hunloke, until he was 'completely white-washed' from allegations of having a 'Jewish mistress'.[28] The DSO hid Comint from most British personnel. Only top civil and military authorities and key staff members were indoctrinated. In April 1947, these included the High Commissioner, the Chief Secretary of the Mandate government and the general officer commanding (GOC) Palestine and five of their staff officers, the air officer commanding (AOC) Levant and two RAF officers, three officers in the Palestine Police, and the naval liaison officer (NLO).[29] Some of them had ample experience with Sigint, especially the High Commissioner, Cunningham, who had been a major recipient of Ultra in 1941.

Comint was concealed from most analysts, including those working with other sources on issues which Comint affected and who received it in sanitised forms. The monitoring of individuals shows how any mistake or misfortune complicated indoctrination and confused intelligence. Lieutenant Hodge from the Royal Navy's Mediterranean Fleet hinted about Comint to his brethren and was admonished. To transfer an indoctrinated officer from Jerusalem to the cage at SIME might raise suspicions in Lieutenant Roberts, who worked on illegal immigration, but was not indoctrinated. 'There have, as you know, been signs from time to time of his suspicion that he has been excluded from some available intelligence on shipping. He has also shown some curiosity on occasion about the function of the cage.'[30] To make matters even more confusing, Roberts actually had been indoctrinated in FOG several months prior, which the DSO might not have known.[31] When captured documents referred to Mossad wireless nets, a Palestine police officer, John Briance, and a government official, G. G. Grimwood – neither indoctrinated – suggested that they be monitored. The DSO's office mounted elaborate discussions to convince them that the idea had been tested, but proved impossible to execute.[32] In November 1947, without warning, the NLO brought Commander Stannard, communications officer for C-in-C Mediterranean, to visit the assistant DSO, Captain Wright. Hastings himself had indoctrinated Stannard, of which Wright had not been informed. Stannard aimed to ensure that the Royal Navy received adequate Comint to handle illegal immigration, but did not know that the NLO was initiated. The NLO later informed Stannard that his relations with the DSO's office were good. Wright declined to address the issue until Stannard 'revealed so much knowledge of FOG set-up and officers employed in it that I decided to take him at face value'. Wright implored that he 'not be placed in this invidious and insecure position again owing to failure to keep us informed of changes in initiates' list'.[33]

Comint in Palestine

GCHQ acquired diplomatic Comint on Palestine from Arab and European states, which shaped the key international dimension of British policy, but it is unavailable to this history. Comint provided many thousands of reports between 1944 and 1948, through four means. By telephone taps in Palestine, run through an office technically linked to the SIME cell, Buttercup, penetrated Arab politics, especially the revival of jihadist and nationalist resistance, and gained some information on the Yishuv. From 1945 British personnel managed much of Buttercup, though probably some operators remained Jewish. Via Isoats, Istria and Fog, GCHQ attacked the codes of Haganah and Palmach, the Jewish Agency, and Mossad Le'aliyah Bet, which ran illegal emigration to Palestine (not to be confused with the later intelligence service Mossad). Isoats traced in detail the order of battle and personalities of Haganah and Palmach, and their policies and preparations. It monitored constant concerns – whether Haganah was preparing an insurrection, or supporting sabotage. Isoats probably inspired many or most of the arms raids on kibbutzim, which met with mixed success. It constantly provided guidance for plans by British military authorities to seize important targets, such as Kol Israel, Haganah's radio propaganda station, and Palmach headquarters.[34]

Isfog replaced Isoats as a codename in February 1947, and divided its work almost equally against Haganah and Mossad Le'aliyah Bet – for intelligence on military and emigration matters. Istria illuminated the complex politics within the Yishuv and the work of the Jewish Agency, especially its manoeuvres abroad. The Yishuv was an amalgam of peoples from many countries, marked by political traditions, including conspiratorial and revolutionary ones, from central and eastern Europe. The Jewish Agency was not a party, movement or government; it represented the Zionist movement and world Jewry to the British Mandate, especially on issues of immigration and security, and was elected from all Jewish parties in Palestine. Secretly, it was led by conspirators who controlled an army which its executive funded, often without understanding that fact. British authorities found these matters even harder to understand.

The sheer mass of sources and reportage obscured the useful material on the leaders who most drove the Yishuv, including David Ben-Gurion and Moshe Shertok. Reports were easy to misconstrue. Thus, Lehi's assassination of Lord Moyne, British Resident Minister in the Middle East, on 6 November 1944, drove Haganah to help Britain stop Jewish attacks on its officials. In December 1944, Liddell noted, Istria showed that: 'SNAKE has given the Palestine Police over 500 names and addresses of terrorists and dumps of arms.

The police have already made over 250 arrests. There is no doubt, I think, that the more moderate elements in the Zionist Movement are afraid that the actions of the extremists may jeopardise the whole future of Zionism.'[35] These points were true, but not the whole truth. Haganah aimed to protect Jewish interests, if possible with – but if necessary, against – Britain. It guided British intelligence to arrest its rivals in the Yishuv, Irgun, and the murderers of Lord Moyne. Otherwise, Haganah detained some members of Irgun and most of Lehi in its secret prisons, preventing them from terrorism and British punishment – albeit momentarily: Haganah released them all when it turned against Britain in autumn 1945.

British Comint never touched Irgun and Lehi, which did not use radio. It could not overcome what Cunningham thought the greatest limit of intelligence: 'the lack of information available regarding the terrorist organisations and individuals and the small success we have had in tracking them down', which he blamed on the Jewish Agency and CID.[36] Initially, soldiers, Cunningham and the DSO mistrusted CID, partly for reasons of class and ethnicity. Kellar called its head, Arthur Giles, 'a difficult personality ... Of Cypriot origin and married to a Maltese, he suffers from a noticeable inferiority complex and is unnecessarily sensitive to any suspected slight.'[37] These attitudes had one unfortunate consequence. CID did not receive access to Isoats or Istria until 1946, damaging its revival and the union of Comint and Humint. Even in 1947, the two bureaus worked at some distance, if in the same direction. Still, MI5's inspector Robertson regarded CID as a 'high-grade intelligence organisation' and respected 'the extent and power of the C.I.D., and ... the calibre of its senior officers', including Giles.[38]

By 1946, CID covered the Yishuv well, with two sources at high levels in the Jewish Agency, and others beneath. Combined with Buttercup, Oats and Istria, Britain briefly had good and multisource material on politics in Palestine, enabling each to augment or check the other. Oats, Isham noted, showed 'the Hagana source at CID HAIFA sometimes misleads them'.[39] This material illuminated the views and actions of Britain's main challengers, Ben-Gurion, Haganah and the Mufti. The news was gloomy. Perhaps for that reason, British authorities misinterpreted it. Comint provided much neutral evidence, which supported all interpretations without challenging prevailing views. It illuminated bureaucracies, but not the conspirators who nudged them from the shadows. These limits, combined with the weight of preconceptions about Jewish dependence on Britain, led British authorities to error. Even more than usual, authorities exaggerated the significance of reports supporting their preconceptions, and resisted those that challenged them. In particular, from autumn 1945, Haganah, Lehi and Irgun loosely cooperated in sabotage against Britain, which revealed the radicalisation and resolution of the mainstream leaders of the Yishuv. Isoats and the CID each accurately noted this cooperation, but their masters were slow to appreciate its significance.[40] British authorities thought the Jewish Agency should, and could, abolish Haganah and suppress Irgun and Lehi. They overestimated Jewish leaders such as Chaim Weizmann, who favoured cooperation and compromise with Britain, and underrated their hostility to British policy. Authorities misunderstood the power of Ben-Gurion, though they knew he was predominant.

As hostilities intensified, on 18 June 1946 an indoctrinated member of DSO's staff, Owen Chadwick, was among five British officers kidnapped by Irgun in Jerusalem. SIME doubted that Irgun knew of his role, but if so, 'we must expect third degree and consequent danger to OATS material, personnel and installations. Request closest scrutiny all messages for indications uneasiness or possible change to use OATS for GALVESTON purposes.' SIME concluded that Haganah had not known of this act in advance, minimising the danger to Oats, but since it 'probably' knew Chadwick worked with the DSO, it 'may therefore attempt [to] arrange interrogation'. Irgun, 'through [a] series of cut-outs', told British authorities that the officers were being treated well, and would remain so, if a sentence of death passed on two of its members was not carried out. Then, Chadwick managed to escape, returning 'cheerful but dirty'. He reported that the real target of the kidnappers was General Barker, whom Irgun was 'determined repeat determined to "get"'. Chadwick had been well treated, fed with white bread and propaganda, and had escaped when his guards fell asleep, fleeing to safety on a bus with Irgun gunmen in hot pursuit.[41] Chadwick was immediately moved to MI5 in London while, pressed by Haganah, Irgun released the other kidnapped officers. This episode was a foretaste of tragedies in store for British personnel in Palestine.

Operation Agatha

During 1945–46, officials experienced a frustrating stalemate, what MI5 called 'the practice of a well-nigh intolerable restraint to preserve conditions in which a just and lasting settlement might be found'.[42] Arabs and Jews were atomised. Each atom had a veto, every action a perverse consequence. Delicate calculations tripped over each other, especially as Britain negotiated with the United States to solve the problem of Palestine. The extraordinary complications of the internal and international politics of Palestine deterred action. Holding Palestine had heavy diplomatic, financial and military costs for Britain. The Colonial Office, the Foreign Office and the Army split over policy in Palestine, which further impeded action. So did faith that conferences between British and American authorities, or Arab and Jewish ones, could somehow end the political stalemate.

The difficulties of action, and in using intelligence, were illustrated in the summer of 1946. British authorities finally understood the cooperation between Haganah, Irgun and Lehi, the political and military power of the Yishuv, and its refusal to accept British terms. Attacks on British personnel and installations escalated, enraging Britons and eroding their will to hold on. Comint and human sources showed that Ben-Gurion and Haganah aimed to challenge British policy in cooperation with Irgun and Lehi – through confrontation, and perhaps insurrection.[43] Yet Moishe Sneh, the head of Haganah and of its most militant section, warned Ben-Gurion of its 'catastrophic financial position', suggesting Haganah's power was fragile.[44]

British authorities sought to break the stalemate through the precise use of force. Guided by intelligence from Comint and the CID, Operation Agatha aimed to arrest the Jewish politicians who opposed British policy, paralyse Haganah, intimidate all players, and force Arabs and Jews to accept British terms.[45] Authorities understood that this effort was a gamble against the odds. Cunningham warned the Colonial Secretary, George Hall:

> with all the force I can that BEN-GURION and SHERTOK should be detained if the operation is to have more than a limited success.

(2) We have unimpeachable evidence that they direct the Hagana as witness ISOATS message 37793 which I have just seen from BEN-GURION to the Chief of Staff HAGANA and SHERTOK.

(3) To allow them to remain at large will leave leaders who are in position to sway YISHUV against us and to coordinate the broken armies in a manner that no one else can.[46]

Ironically, Isoats 37,793 may have been Ben-Gurion's order of 25 June that Sneh and Shertok force Irgun to release the kidnapped British officers, without giving it any concessions.[47] Cunningham's message effectively admitted defeat before Agatha even began, because Ben-Gurion was already out of British hands, in France.

Britain's efforts under Operation Agatha failed mainly due to its limits in intelligence, power and ruthlessness – but only barely. Shai Comint compromised Britain's first attempt to move. Knowing action was imminent, some Jewish leaders hid their papers. On 29 June 1946, with tactical surprise, British authorities arrested half of Palmach and many Jewish politicians whom they wished to detain, including Shertok and hardliners such as Rabbi Abba Hillel Silver, head of the Zionist Organisation of America. However, several key targets were missed, especially Sneh, the head of Palmach, Yigal Allon, and some unit commanders. Haganah's chain of command survived intact, but its relations with politicians and control over units were disrupted. Documents seized from Jewish leaders, including Sneh, and from Haganah and Palmach headquarters, shed light on the Jewish Agency's support for stealing arms and sabotage, which enlightened and shocked British authorities. Borrowing words from Cunningham, the Colonial Secretary described Haganah espionage against Britain as 'a vast system for the theft of Top Secret' documents, which 'could have been obtained only by means of a wide-spread system of corruption and espionage'.[48] These seizures stunned Shai, surprised by British intelligence superiority for the only time in the Palestine troubles. If British authorities could launch one bolt from the blue, why not another – especially given the intelligence they just had gained.

Until Agatha, Jewish leaders outside Irgun and Lehi did not know how they would react if Britain forced them to submit. Agatha made them ask: what did they want? Dare they break with Britain? Agatha also exposed the conspiracies of Ben-Gurion and his lieutenants. Many, perhaps most, moderate leaders, and possibly the majority in the Yishuv, wanted to restrain Ben-Gurion and negotiate the best deal possible with Britain. The leader of Irgun, Menachem Begin, later conceded that 'defeatism raised its deadly head. People began to question our ability to fight the British regime'. This drove him to escalate the crisis.[49] Britain's inability to penetrate Irgun proved fatal to many of its servicemen and officials, and its policy.

British authorities thought they had succeeded in killing a conspiracy. They overestimated the effect of Operation Agatha and over-interpreted the evidence behind it, including Comint. Sneh signalled Ben-Gurion (and, unknowingly, Britain):

> The internal situation is steadily deteriorating. Hayyim is gathering a collection of personal friends and has passed an ultimatum that all activities must cease. Hayyim has invited Shaw to his house to have a cup of tea. Nobody knows who is the Executive. The detainees are kept silent as are Rcksch and Yemin. I am excommunicated and banned by the Jerusalem Executive. Let me have a clear answer as to what I am to do and please give me specific instructions.[50]

That message inspired British authorities. Cunningham signalled Hall that this 'deterioration … refers to the position of the more extreme Jews, and the advocates and perpetrators of violence, and not to the more stable elements represented by Weizmann, nor the Government's position. Connection of Ben-Gurion with extreme elements is sufficiently clear from this message.'[51] The DSO's office agreed that Sneh's message showed a weakening of the extremists, a rise of moderates and confusion in Jewish politics, though Ben-Gurion had power to play in a Zionist conference convening in Paris.[52] Isham noted Weizmann's 'present self-assurance and particularly conviction that [he] could control more extremist members of Agency'.[53] Yet the situation was volatile: certainly some Jews would retaliate, the only questions being who, when and where. On 3 July 1946, Sigint showed that Haganah communications and command were broken. 'Morale. Impression from traffic is that organisations are stunned and PALMACH temporarily disrupted.' Remaining commanders could 'do high-level planning', which units might be unable to execute. However, 'violent reaction' against British forces or to free detainees was inevitable.[54] 'All overt sources suggest violent reaction will not be long delayed but its most likely forms are (a) mob violence and (b) IRGUN operations.'[55] On 8 July, Isham reported that Palmach and Haganah were reorganising slowly, and 'there is nothing in OATS traffic to show that Hagana realise Army operations resulted from interception of their W/T traffic and breaking of their ciphers'. However, 'Hagana, like British authorities, suspect right wing terrorist reaction forthcoming.'[56] Both were right.

Attlee and Irgun

The Cabinet hoped to exploit Operation Agatha by doing 'everything possible' to 'strengthen the hand of Dr Weizmann and his associates'.[57] They all overrated their power. Britain quickly pledged to release most detainees, including Palmach members, in order to enable negotiations with the Jewish Agency as a whole and representatives of the Palestinian Arabs at a new conference in London. That aim immediately stalled, as the collision of atoms produced an explosion. On 22 July, exploiting dismal British security, Irgun terrorists bombed the King David Hotel at a time when they knew it would be most crowded. Through incompetence or cynicism, Irgun provided warnings which could never reach British authorities in time. Later, Irgun tried to blame the victims for having murdered them.

Haganah's role in this action remains uncertain. Decisions were made by a few conspirators, who purposely did not record them well. Then, driven by subsequent conflicts between Irgun and Haganah, they offered conflicting accounts of what they had said and done at the time. The evidence is contradictory. Agatha incapacitated Haganah's body, but not its will. Haganah had previously destroyed British government property, but attempted to avoid killing Britons. It also tried to prevent Irgun and Lehi from doing so until autumn 1945, when it loosely cooperated with them in actions where the latter spilled blood. After Agatha, Sneh – wishing to retaliate but lacking the means – asked Irgun to attack the King David Hotel, allegedly at a time when it would be most empty, but still with the aim of killing Britons. Then, according to Haganah accounts, Sneh asked Irgun to abandon the attack and give time for civilian resistance to grow instead. If so, Irgun rejected this advice, which would have served to strengthen its rivals, Haganah and Ben-Gurion. Irgun thus used its strengths to achieve its aims, simultaneously attacking both its British and Jewish rivals. Haganah and Ben-Gurion then disassociated themselves from terrorism, while still exploiting it.

Irgun killed ninety-one people at the King David Hotel, including British clerical staff and officials, and civilians of many nationalities. Among them were eleven of the thirteen clerks and the cypher operator who handled OATS from the DSO's office. This strike was a human tragedy for British Comint, however it missed its centre of power. The Registry of Comint traffic was a 'total loss': a number of other papers were destroyed, but most of them, above all the card index and the reports, and all intelligence personnel, survived unscathed. Fluke drove this outcome.[58] On the day of the bombing on 22 July, the leading British intelligence authorities in the Mandate, Giles and Isham, had driven to Beirut to investigate stories that Irgun aimed to bomb the British legation there. The traitor in SIS, Kim Philby, distorted and disseminated these stories so to confuse British intelligence. Accidentally, he spared it harm.[59]

By bombing the King David Hotel, Begin created a victory – for Ben-Gurion. This act finalised and embittered the Anglo-Zionist divorce. Not surprisingly, British intelligence failed to report precisely what the conspirators had done. Two top CID agents – its best one in the Jewish Agency, 'Circus', and another 'independent high-grade' source – stated that Haganah knew of the attack in advance, and did not stop it. Isoats 38,465, sent thirty minutes before the explosion, 'shows that Haganah may have been anticipating a large scale curfew'. Many sources warned that Haganah and Irgun had cooperated in the affair, but offered alarmist and perhaps inaccurate details. Begin and Sneh had drawn lots on who would conduct the bombing. Haganah, Irgun, and Lehi would soon assault many other British installations.[60]

The hotel bombing aroused horror and anger in the Yishuv, first against the perpetrators, then the occupiers. Intelligence and outrage sparked a British crackdown. Operation Shark, enforcing harsh martial law through troops on the street, served to bolster the civilian resistance which was Haganah's strength and Ben-Gurion's hope. Operation Agatha evaporated, and terrorism triumphed. Yet a more tepid British response also would probably have sapped its position. Isham reported that the Yishuv was unified against Britain, awaiting decisions from the Zionist conference in Paris. 'Moderate Jewish elements here unlikely exert any influence.' Haganah would cease restraining Irgun and Lehi, which would strike, while Palmach perhaps would 'go over to sabotage and Hagana cause crowd nuisance'. 'Consider possible H.M.G.'s actions may strengthen hand of BEN-GURION, SILVER and SNEH. Impossible forecast exact shape of events to come.'[61] When Dr Arie Altman, leader of the Revisionist Zionist movement, the political parent of Irgun, asked, 'What did I think the Jews should do now?' Isham replied, 'Stamp out terrorism. He said terrorism is futile if the British Government have really got a policy. But some people argue that they have not got one and bombs may make them think quickly.'[62] That comment cut to the quick. Britain could handle Jewish resistance, if it wished to rule by force, but lacked the stamina to do so. It could not find Jewish terrorists, would not match their attacks on civilians, and could not stop the Yishuv's turn against Britain.

In September 1946, Circus reported that since Operation Agatha, a struggle between moderates and hardliners had dominated politics in the Yishuv. 'BEN-GURION and his clique' had outmanoeuvred Weizmann and his allies, and seized power over the Yishuv, by playing 'Haganah and the youth of the country against the moderate elements'. Ben-Gurion 'always' supported 'exaggerated reports of British brutality during searches of Jewish colonies, etc ... and has steadily built up that feeling of enmity and hatred towards the British'. Thus, he and his friends could 'call any Jewish leader willing to cooperate with Gt. Britain, a Quisling. Threats were also issued against the Moderates' who 'were without any power in the Yishuv'. At Paris, Ben-Gurion overrode moderate views, claiming that he represented the Yishuv.[63] He was right. Jewish parties boycotted the British conference intended to exploit Agatha, meaning that Britain freed most of the opponents it had captured in Agatha for nothing. Shortly, Britain started down the slippery slope to failure when it accepted that Palestine had to be partitioned and the United Nations (UN) given responsibility for the matter.

By October 1946, the DSO in Jersualem concluded that Haganah was assassinating specific police officers for alleged misdeeds, showing the personalisation of the campaign and the superiority of Jewish intelligence.[64] In 1929, when handling subversion in Bengal, Tegart had emphasised that his men could succeed only if they thought themselves on top of the terrorists.[65] That sense of confidence did not exist in

Palestine during 1946. Even worse, Britain inadvertently boosted Jewish intelligence by wrecking its own. In August 1946, Britain published a White Paper which included intelligence that showed the links between the Jewish Agency and Haganah, and the latter with Irgun and Lehi. At its core were eight messages from Oats and Istria, which the paper implied were just part of Britain's collection. MI5 briefed ministers not to say anything more than the White Paper about the source of these messages, 'which was prepared with the most scrupulous attention to the protection of our sources of information and further comment is liable to destroy those sources' – but the damage was done.[66] After all, some Jews could read English.

Operation Agatha became politicised in Britain and the United States, where Whitehall was negotiating for support over Palestine and a loan. The Attlee government correctly regarded these negotiations as important. Much of the Labour Party opposed official policy, supported Zionism and condemned Agatha. Its leaders felt personal betrayal and irritation at having been fooled by Zionists. Naively, they thought that to prove that the Jewish Agency controlled Haganah and cooperated with terrorists would be enough to embarrass it into cooperation and justify Agatha to Parliament and the world. British officials in Palestine, Whitehall and within the Cabinet believed that to publish this material might even 'ruin the Jewish Agency in its present form', and thus Zionism.[67] Attlee, stung by criticism, justified Operation Agatha to Parliament by noting that 'some' but not all leaders of the Jewish Agency directed Haganah, which was linked to terrorists. When challenged to prove the point, he promised to do so after papers seized from the Agency were inspected. Later, he agreed to provide the material which had inspired Agatha, rather than anything gathered through it.

When asked in turn what evidence was available for the purpose, Cunningham erroneously replied that Attlee had overstated anything sent to him from Palestine. Comint alone proved these points, yet to publish it would be a disaster.

> The compromising of these sources will result in the loss of all
> incontrovertible information available to us about the illegal
> activities of the Jews. These sources are within the sphere of
> activities of the Chiefs of Staff with whom the matter would require
> to be discussed. I would most strongly urge that the security of

this information be not compromised unless overriding political considerations render this absolutely unavoidable. I hope means may be devised that if the information has to be utilised its source may be disguised. If in spite of all objections it is found politically necessary to use this information I feel it is essential that an intelligence officer from this country should proceed home to discuss possibility of providing cover.[68]

Hall retorted: regarding the 'vital necessity for producing as convincing a statement of evidence as possible. We shall have to consider disclosure of evidence from top secret sources if such a statement cannot be based on other sources.'[69] Hall told Attlee that the Cabinet 'faced the difficult choice between declining to reveal documentary evidence in support of the statement we have made or "blowing" our sources', which would 'have a most disadvantageous [effect] on immediate military operations', and 'wider repercussions, in view of the use made of similar means of interception in other spheres'.[70] Cunningham attempted to solve this dilemma by formulating a case without involving Comint, but it was weak, if one excluded material seized during Agatha. Lord Jowitt, the Lord Chancellor, who assessed the evidence for the Cabinet, noted that documents seized through Agatha were useless as a means of justifying it. 'We must, as it seems to me, give some strong and clear indication that we had knowledge before acting which compelled us to act; or at least strong grounds for suspicion which have now been confirmed.'[71]

Authorities in Jerusalem sought desperately to save Comint. Barker warned 'that if he is required to deal with internal security situation in future and armed violence of HAGANA and PALMACH he will be virtually without necessary operational intelligence should CREAM sources be divulged. This will involve him in possible mistakes which may have serious political consequences.' Comint enabled Agatha to seize the 'right' targets. 'Without OATS he would have had to risk more wrongful arrests and possible failure of operations owing to the lack of intelligence. Owing to his knowledge he was able to avoid casualties. This might not have been possible without his CREAM sources.' Meanwhile, Haganah and Palmach were reorganising; without Comint, future operations might involve casualties. 'We may be ignorant of the operational set-up of the Jews and be with the same difficulties as confront us when dealing with IZL and STERN group who we are unable to neutralise owing to lack of precise intelligence.' Cunningham, Isham, Shaw and the DMI shared these prophetic views.[72]

Reluctantly, Cunningham accepted publication of Comint, as did C and MI5.[73] MI5 preferred that the paper be based 'on evidence not derived from wireless interception. If this source of intelligence were destroyed, the General Officer Commanding in Palestine would be deprived of information without which recent operations would have been impossible, and future operations would have to be carried out in the dark and with much greater risk of casualties.' Attlee retorted that 'his undertaking was to produce the evidence on which action was authorised and therefore any post hoc evidence secured from examination of Jewish Agency documents was only of value as confirmatory. By revealing our interception of wireless traffic we were not revealing our methods of breaking cyphers. The task would be to overcome a change of cypher on the part of the Zionists, which was no novel problem.' The powerful minister, and Labour Leader of the House of Commons, Herbert Morrison, added: 'The Parliamentary statement on the complicity of the Zionist leaders must sweep public opinion both here and in the United States and might have a salutary effect on those whose contributions to the Zionist cause had been misappropriated by the leaders to finance violence in Palestine. A revelation of the extent of our knowledge might shake the nerves of the organisers of these activities.'[74]

Given two chances to make an effective White Paper without Sigint, MI5 could not do so. MI5 also perhaps preferred to use Sigint because the only other good evidence would endanger the CID's sources within the Yishuv, who 'must be protected, since disclosure would imperil the lives of those on whose testimony some of the evidence is based'.[75] This position was humane and rational. Other authorities failed both these tests. Admittedly after the terrorist outrage of 22 July, the Chief Secretary's Office in Palestine advocated publishing portions of a CID report, even though if the source's '"high treason" were divulged, he would not be likely to survive for long'.[76] British officials were willing to risk burning all of their intelligence to bolster this propaganda. Despite the unfortunate consequences of releasing Comint to justify Operation Agatha, in the spring of 1947 Whitehall considered burning what remained of Britain Sigint capabilities to provide evidence to the UN Commission. Fortunately it abandoned that effort.[77]

After the Fall

Attlee achieved what Irgun could not: decapitating British Comint in Palestine. When Britain had compromised its grasp of foreign cryptosystems to score political points in the 1920s, the causes were trivial; not so in 1946, however much legalism and party considerations distorted ministers' minds. The publication of Istria and Oats reduced unofficial American and British public attacks on British policy, and angered moderate political leaders in the Yishuv, suddenly aware of how Ben-Gurion had gulled them.

This action had some political gains, but greater cryptanalytical costs. The Jewish Agency quickly adopted better cryptosystems and ended the operators' errors which had helped to compromise the old ones. It retained Bentley's codebook, but adopted a better, though still simple, subtractor system, and changed it frequently. Britain found it unbreakable.[78] Jewish leaders avoided discussions by cable and wireless and moved to the cumbersome yet secure method of face-to-face meetings. Haganah's wireless operators improved, probably through training by veterans of the Jewish Brigade and SOE.

From 15 September 1946, months after the White Paper was published, two GCHQ successes against Haganah traffic collapsed. Haganah and Palmach units adopted new cyphers on 1 November which proved time-consuming to break, and massively increased the number of distinct superencipherment systems in use, and their rate of change. These units transmitted less material by wireless, while codewords covered proper nouns.[79] Britain's difficulty in overcoming simple improvements in cryptography reveals this Palestine-based unit's isolation from the mainstream of GCHQ (though Tiltman offered assistance) and the increasing indifference towards its work by Whitehall. Had this traffic remained a high priority, it would have been broken.

Britain lost its best source during a critical period, but Comint had always missed key matters, while other sources continued to provide insight. CID and Buttercup remained excellent on politics in Palestine. Abroad, liaison relations with foreign services, and British and foreign intercepts of cables and telephone calls by Jewish leaders, provided many useful fragments on Zionist politics.[80] From autumn 1946, Britain lost this battle of intelligence, but as ever, the key problems were weaknesses in policy and power. The Attlee compromise cost Britain precision, power, thoroughness and certainty, in two areas. Istria and Isoats alone had penetrated the conspirators around Ben-Gurion. That capability was wrecked. Its loss also eliminated a useful means of validatory checks on CID information, which came from people in direct or indirect contact with that inner circle. Isoats alone had illuminated the policy and intentions of Haganah and Palmach, and, better than any other source, the activities of Irgun and Lehi. That power withered, but did not quite die.

Thus, by late 1946, British Comint in Palestine faced disaster. It read no current Jewish military traffic, nor did it know where Haganah's headquarters were. Britain was exposed to Palmach, the 'prime threat to security after terrorists', and also vulnerable to the greatest danger: full mobilisation by Haganah 'in event unfavourable turn Palestine situation' (i.e. if Britain turned decisively against the Yishuv). The need to suppress both bodies 'may arise at any moment'.[81] Precisely as the Jewish threat rose, intelligence on it declined, eroding the value and raising the cost of the use of force. Improved direction-finding soon tracked some Haganah headquarters. Perhaps exploiting the poor practices of specific operators, British codebreakers cracked the cryptosystems of Haganah's northern Galilee district, and occasionally those of other groups, such as Unit 2 of Palmach, one of its four battalions, in Negev. The Galilee traffic may include a series of messages entitled 'DAN', perhaps referring to Dan settlement in the area, traditionally associated with the eponymous Hebrew tribe.

Isoats once covered all of Palestine, from Dan to Bersheeba. In 1947, it covered only those towns. Still, this intelligence from the ends of the Mandate enabled the British to draw cautious, but accurate and useful, inferences that Haganah and Irgun were feuding, Palmach was not conducting terrorism and perhaps trying to impede it, while insurrection was not imminent.[82] From current and back traffic, analysts steadily reconstructed internal codewords and book values, group by weary group. By June 1947, Comint enabled a detailed order of battle for Haganah and Palmach, and operational intelligence, albeit more speculative than certain.[83] As usual when attacking back traffic after current accesses had vanished, success declined on major issues, but rose against minor tasks, such as comparing the card index to names in a CID report or the Jewish press. The *Palestine Post* became a major source. Britain monitored 'typical Palmach punitive expedition[s]' against Arabs, or assassinations of Hungarians or Germans interned in Palestine and suspected of involvement in the Holocaust.[84] As Comint ceased to indicate major issues, the DSO abandoned the 1,000-message summaries, and focused on consumers' requirements in Palestine, rather than London.[85] From October 1947, the DSO again derived significant intelligence from Haganah traffic. The latter's reports 'on Arab activities which might affect the Yishuv' were often dubious or alarmist, but sparked military preparations in Galilee.[86] Even so, only in December 1947 – after Britain ended the Mandate, and war began between Jews and Arabs, forcing Haganah into long and often emergency communications – did Britain again routinely penetrate Haganah communications.[87]

GCHQ's greatest success in Palestine during 1945–48 – and its only one after September 1946 – was against 'illegal' emigration, carried over what it called the Diaspora network, from across Europe to Tel Aviv. Military authorities wished to 'attempt intercept every ship no matter what size carrying illegal immigrants to PALESTINE', though, SIME noted, 'need not be unduly disturbed however if small ship succeeds in running gauntlet as this provides degree of cover for OATS'.[88] In this campaign many British intelligence sources overlapped. Comint – as Oats and later Fog – assisted by other intelligence sources, accurately tracked the preparation of every shipment of immigrants. Fog, and Y, especially MERS, tracked ships through European waters. Inefficiencies in collection and reportage by the direction-finding station at Abu Sukir in Egypt, however, compromised coverage on the important southern approach to Palestine.[89] 'It is vital repeat absolutely vital that we receive bearings on ships as soon as you can despatch them,' the DSO warned the intercept organisation in Cyprus – which was efficient but badly placed to pick up traffic from the southern approach. 'RAF aircraft hours here is extremely critical and there is a limited number of search days each month. Most careful calculations have therefore to be made in order to avoid running out of aircraft during searches,' including time for maintenance and stand-downs.[90] Firm but factual admonishments spurred improvements of interception in Egypt and Cyprus.

Good camouflage and signals security covered the identity of immigrant ships in the waters between Egypt and Cyprus, from which they could lunge towards Palestine. Without Fog, many or most of these ships might have reached their destination, reshaping the politics of the Mandate.[91] However, Fog – camouflaged as 'reliable intelligence' to hide the involvement of Comint from British personnel (the DSO once noted 'complete absence overt information to serve as cover for search is most embarrassing') – guided reconnaissance aircraft and warships to locations well suited to intercepting these inbound vessels.[92] Almost all of these ships were stopped and their passengers interned in Cyprus. In this, Comint best aided an aim of British policy for Palestine and pleased its consumers. Internment of refugees in Palestine would have overwhelmed the police, at barely 50 per cent of their authorised strength.[93] Control of immigration was a powerful card for Britain to play with Jews and Arabs. Intelligence and military authorities agreed, as one head of SIME wrote: 'Occasion of any PALESTINE disturbance will almost certainly be illegal immigration.'[94] Cunningham feared that an inability to control incoming migrant ships 'would unquestionably produce an immediate and hysterical Jewish reaction' and Arab counter-reaction, wrecking any hope for negotiations.[95] Comint helped to avoid that risk, and to press Ben-Gurion; yet control of immigration remained a public relations disaster for Britain and an unpleasant practice.

In Palestine, GCHQ was one of Britain's two main sources, matched by CID. All forms of Comint strengthened Britain's policy, but could not save one so weak as this. Ultimately, Comint sustained a stalemate but could not end it. Even if British authorities had understood the truth, which only a combination of Comint and CID at their best could have provided, they would have been reluctant to believe it. The truth simply would have made Britain surrender faster than it did.

Konfrontasi: Living Dangerously

The Suez crisis of 1956 shook British power over its colonies and its will to hold them and encouraged all local competitors to challenge it at once. Against this, over the next decade, Britain sought to preserve its economic interests within and influence over these colonies via indirect rule: by giving independence to the best-disposed of local leaders while maintaining regional hegemony through an effective but affordable military presence in the Indian Ocean. In particular, Britain sought to combine all of its colonies and protectorates in southeast Asia (Singapore; and Sabah, Sarawak and Brunei, on the northern coast of Borneo) with the already independent state of Malaya. This 'Malaysia' would give strategic depth to a base in Singapore, which might enable a cheap but strong presence to sustain Britain's friends in east Africa, the Persian Gulf and southeast Asia.[96] To fuse such a federation around a Muslim and Malay state was not easy. Most people in Sabah and Sarawak, neither Muslim nor Malay, were no more attracted to Malaysia than Indonesia, and indifferent to either. Some preferred Indonesia to Malaysia. Brunei was an independent principality, Singapore a Chinese city. Politicians in all these regions pursued competing interests. None were puppets, although Britain influenced them all.

Indonesia exacerbated these problems. Its nationalist and irredentist leaders had won independence through war. They believed in their own power and Western weakness. Their chief, 'Achmad' Sukarno (born Kusno Sosrodihardjo), wanted to lead African and Asian states to overthrow a Western-dominated order and to have Indonesia match the USSR and China as a revolutionary power. However unrealistic, these ambitions drove his actions. Sukarno also pursued revolution at home, aiming to weaken the political positions of the strongest factions outside his control – Muslims and the military – by working with the Indonesian Communist Party, the Partai Komunis Indonesia (PKI). The PKI became the strongest political force in Indonesia, organised but unarmed. Sukarno's policies created political and economic crisis in Indonesia. All of these forces drove Indonesia to challenge Britain.[97] Sukarno and his generals viewed Malaysia as a creature of neo-colonialism, which bolstered imperialism in Asia. For Sukarno, confrontation – Konfrontasi – with Britain simultaneously served prestige politics and his internal and external aims. It diverted his army towards shared aims abroad and away from differences at home, turning their guns at Britain rather than the PKI – or himself. Sukarno proclaimed Konfrontasi 'a year of living dangerously'. He was more prophetic than he knew.

Through politics and force, Indonesia sought to splinter Malaysia and to control Sabah, Sarawak and Brunei. Though it borrowed from Maoist and Vietnamese theory and practice, Indonesian strategy was innovative. An unconventional campaign aimed to pin large British forces in perpetual check, erode Britain's patience and to multiply political divisions in Malaysia. To prove Indonesia's power and shake local nerve, terrorists, moving by ship or parachute, attacked targets in Singapore and Malaya across the 550-mile long Straits of Malacca, augmented by black radio broadcasts, propaganda letters sent to individuals and the pasting of posters or slogans on walls. Soldiers infiltrated the 1,000-mile frontier between Indonesia, Sabah and Sarawak, terrain dominated by hill and jungle. A few lateral roads approached both sides of the frontier, where they became trails. Indonesian volunteers, regular forces and local supporters pursued indigenous political influence, attacked Commonwealth and Malaysian positions, and pursued 'liberated zones' where armed men might build popular support and subvert Malaysia. The purpose of military activity in zones inside Malaysia was to carry out sabotage and illegal political activities in order to radicalise politically peoples and leaders.[98] These zones were located in areas where the local population was thought to be hostile to Malaysia, generally among Chinese settlers. British authorities regarded liberated zones as their greatest danger; Indonesia's failure to create them drove its defeat. Indonesia could escalate these practices at will, but fear of British conventional power capped its actions at the level of systematic infiltration. These Indonesian raids usually involved forces of ten to a hundred men. During 1963, Indonesia committed some 2,000 irregulars to the frontier with northern Borneo, which reached 12,000 irregular and regular personnel by 1965.[99]

This pocket version of the Suez crisis divided British authorities. Calculations were delicate. Authorities wanted to defeat Indonesia's policy without alienating it. Politicians did not want to lose a contest over prestige, but wobbled over the details of policy. They paid much to avoid defeat, yet considered compromise about Malaysia and wanted good relations with Indonesia, especially on economic issues. Conservative governments took a harder line than their Labour successor, but valued sales to Indonesia; Harold Wilson's government, while more open to compromise, refused to be bullied.[100] Meanwhile, British military leaders confronted a threat at the peak of imperial overstretch, in a time of economic and military crisis, which threatened their strategic effort to manage decline. Containing Konfrontasi required a military commitment approaching that to NATO, 56,000 soldiers and large naval and air forces, with no end in sight. In order to break Konfrontasi, during 1964–65 military leaders advocated major acts of retaliation, including covert raids on Sumatra, and open maritime and air war. Indonesian authorities feared them, but British politicians rejected these ideas.[101] Britain's allies – Australia, New Zealand and the United States – wished it well but kept aloof. Too much cooperation with Malaysia might make Sukarno confront their own interests too, like American firms in Indonesia, or the Australian protectorate of Papua New Guinea.

Sukarno was right to think that a prolonged war of political attrition would damage Britain, but wrong about its power and policy. Britain defeated every level of Konfrontasi, if sometimes at frustrating cost. It let Malaysian leaders take their own political decisions, demonstrating their independence, which also undermined British policy. British diplomats defeated Indonesia in international fora, building legitimacy for Malaysia and driving Sukarno to stupid responses. Britain won the battle of infiltration and deterred Indonesia from escalating, while showing the power and capability to do so itself. British and Malaysian police and regular forces defended Singapore and Malaya and the interior of Sabah and Sarawak. The Australian and British special air services (SAS), and Australian, British and Gurkha infantry dominated war on the frontiers, supported by artillery and mortars. Helicopters aided logistics, mobility and medical evacuation. In order to break infiltration, from 1964 Britain secretly authorised its forces to operate up to 3,000 yards, and then 10,000 yards, within Indonesian territory on Borneo, sometimes informally extended to 20,000 yards, thereby enabling ambushes on the lateral roads to the front and attacks against forward Indonesian positions. These British operations, codenamed Claret, were politically risky and tactically difficult. For Indonesia to capture any Commonwealth prisoners or bodies in its territory would prove that Britain was doing something that it publicly denied was happening. To kill fifty Indonesian soldiers but leave two Commonwealth casualties behind might lose a battle. The few soldiers available for these operations – in a vast and difficult area, with astonishingly low force-to-space ratios – could easily be worn out by the need to return casualties or by employment in blind searches, through rough country, always vulnerable to accident or counter-ambush.[102]

Under these circumstances one would expect a hard and long campaign of counterinsurgency, but this was not such a case. Britain confronted an irregular war, not a guerrilla one: constant small raids across a frontier by conventional units or 'volunteers'. In conceptual terms, the campaign was more like strategic air defence than counter-insurgency – which explains its success. Indonesian forces stood or moved behind the frontier and the Straits of Malacca, or raided across it, with no secure insurgency base within Malaysia. They could be ambushed where they stood or moved, especially through the able use of intelligence. A shot of Comint served to fortify the Claret.

Sigint Preparation of the Battlefield

The first step towards Konfrontasi surprised Britain. The Brunei revolt of December 1962 shook its colonial structure, briefly, in part from misjudgements by MI5's outpost, Security Intelligence Far East (SIFE) and poor coordination between intelligence and security agencies. Brunei police officers anticipated the revolt and prepared for it. Indeed, their arrests of revolutionaries precipitated the revolt. Meanwhile, SIFE and Special Branch in Borneo denied the danger, which kept military reinforcements from being deployed to Brunei before the revolt, and confused their response to a rising by 4,000 rebels.[103] This failure enraged both the Malaysian prime minister, Tunku Abdul Rahman, whose warnings had been ignored, and British political authorities in Singapore.[104]

GCHQ's local representative, the Government Communications Officer (Singapore), (GCO(S)), Harold Fletcher, asked it and the Australian Defence Signals Bureau (DSB) to 'examine their conscience' self-critically. They must test their competence and prepare for politics. Fletcher, warning that 'a storm might eventually brew' over the intelligence failure at Brunei, gathered 'evidence of Sigint's prescience and alertness while subject still fresh, in case witch hunt develops'.[105] Comint cleared their conscience: it had uncovered Indonesian contacts with politicians in Brunei but not evidence for the coming revolt, which no one expected it to have done. Fletcher held that 'all consumers are satisfied that Sigint has done and is doing all it can'.[106] He soon noted 'the almost childlike faith in the miraculous powers of Sigint in these parts'.[107] DSB warned that 'the stakes are large for Malaysia and for Sigint and want to be sure that we are all "on net" to produce fullest intelligence for consumers'.[108] Throughout Konfrontasi, Siginters remained sensitive to their reputation among intelligence consumers. For GCHQ, this crisis was a test of the Hampshire Report's recommendation to increase spending and of the Treasury's counter-attack. Its success in this theatre paid dividends elsewhere.

How far Indonesia inspired the Brunei revolt was unclear. The Far East Sector Heads of intelligence in London saw 'no evidence of direct Indonesian involvement'.[109] Apparently, Sigint could not answer the question. British authorities, however, expected Indonesia to act against Malaysia as it had just done successfully against the Dutch in New Guinea: through confrontation, combining constant pinprick raids, cooperation with local rebels, the creation of liberated zones and vehement diplomacy and propaganda. Unlike the case of Suez, GCHQ had time to plan a measured response to the threat. Australia and Britain could work on Indonesian communication systems, because of Indonesia's reliance on radio for communications with scattered forces. From Australian stations, DSB dominated this coverage, its main mission under UKUSA. Civil links were not covered, but DSB held that military nets would carry all 'worthwhile intelligence', while 'anything of any importance or value' would pass through Jakarta.[110] 'It is Ninety per cent probable that indications of Indonesian intentions would be available from present strategic intercept (since policy messages are habitually referred to Jakarta on currently exploitable links),' though neither this coverage nor additional tactical intercept might give 'exact areas of e.g. planned operations'.[111] Britain and Australia realigned collection from existing resources, sacrificing coverage of other southeast Asian military targets. Diplomats in Jakarta also provided strategic intelligence on Indonesia, but Comint dominated collection on Konfrontasi. Though Indonesia had decent human sources, the Commonwealth outweighed it in intelligence.

Despite the differences between Australian and British policies over Malaysia, DSB oversaw operations there, including control of targets, which it had to justify to a senior partner with changing demands. DSB told Fletcher: 'It is essential that we know of "wind-changes" or of approaching high/low pressures which may affect winds of consumer requirements.' DSB's normal processing of Indonesian traffic assumed a two- to seven-day time lag in translation and distribution; for consumers to demand reports in four to twenty-four hours would cripple other efforts.[112]

That problem soon emerged, as DSB adopted a seven-day-a-week effort against urgent messages.[113] For UKF 200 during Konfrontasi, 'urgency' became the 'prime consideration', forcing more ' "T" (translation of individual message) reporting' as against ' "C" (collated or round-up) reporting', and thus the dissemination of more messages, often minor in nature.[114] The GCO(S)s, Fletcher (1962–64) and Brian Tovey (1964–66), commanded British Sigint resources in Malaysia, as well as Australian ones, subject to decisions in Australia. They dealt separately with DSB and GCHQ, while connecting the two. GCHQ worked closely with the services in London, as the GCO(S)s – based in a two-room office within British headquarters at Phoenix Park – did with local British commanders. Britain, Tovey noted, was so reliant on Comint that GCHQ communications channels carried key British military communications, especially during periods when Indonesia escalated its actions.[115] SK2's large Comcen, of fourteen British and fourteen Australian personnel, including several women, handled these swollen signals well. NSA was not much involved. The Commonwealth could handle its own problems, while Americans had more than enough of their own in the region.

Konfrontasi marked GCHQ's last hurrah of the radio age. Its resources were stretched to their maximum: there was no fat left, as GCHQ insisted to PSIS, but thankfully enough bone and muscle remained to sustain it and to find new operators and train linguists. GCHQ was not just an intelligence agency, but an executive one, with microscopic control over the resources needed to create intelligence across the world, which it did with informality, professionalism, self-criticism, and a focus on problem-solving. Communications with officers abroad were frank, and fast, including details about individual operators and pieces of kit. Errors were admitted by apology, and acknowledged without elimination. GCHQ negotiated directly with sister agencies in the Five Eyes, and British military services. Its few administrators minuted incoming messages by hand with ballpoint pen and passed them to others with advice or queries, to streamline and speed up decisions. Pneumatic Lamson tubes moved information by paper within GCHQ in seconds, not much slower than the speed of email. Signals carried messages across the globe from desk to desk in hours. Messages were divided into letters, and especially cables in categories of Flash, Operational Immediate, Priority and Routine. The need to transmit so much material so urgently crushed signals and cypher resources on Comint links between London and Singapore, and Singapore and Borneo; yet still they moved.

During Konfrontasi, as Brian Tovey later noted: 'Basic principle was to retain normal peacetime Sigint structure and to modify this only to extent dictated by genuine operational necessity.'[116] In 1963, that structure was sound. The main problem was the provision of too many 'innocuous' messages to consumers, and too few synthetic or compilation reports, due to the lack of 'good C Report writers'.[117] Fletcher thought 'the coverage of main lines ... is just about the maximum that can be done, and is very efficient'.[118]

The challenge was tactical Y in Borneo, especially against low-frequency traffic which could not easily be intercepted outside the island. This need required the formation of a new unit, which DSB estimated would require five teams, and GCHQ four, about the number of intercept operators in UKF 200 or 121 Signals Squadron.[119] The great administrative and political problems involved in creating units of twenty to forty men reflect the limits to GCHQ's resources, confronting financial pressure at home and growing problems abroad, and the undeveloped state of Borneo at the time. GCHQ faced global limits on interceptors, and of personnel able to read Indonesian languages, and above all, to understand voice. It could reinforce UKF 200 only by cannibalising units handling important missions against the USSR and China, and by retraining two local British interpreters of Malay in the related Indonesian language. It hoped that DSD would solve the problem by providing a tactical unit. DSD would have done so but, to GCHQ's annoyance, could not until the Australian government chose to confront Sukarno openly. Nonetheless, Australian Siginters offered much technical assistance. In 1963, the services assembled 14 men with experience in the Malay or Indonesian languages for training as Morse and voice operators, for service in Singapore.[120] UKF 200 temporarily based a forward team in Borneo, which was withdrawn when a team and a half of nine British intercept operators and analysts from Germany – later doubling in size and augmented by an Australian interpreter of Indonesian – moved there.[121] By June 1964, as Konfrontasi intensified, GCHQ sent twenty civilian wireless operators to Singapore, replacing 121 Australian Signals Squadron. The latter moved to Borneo, providing the bulk of the Indonesian linguists there. Two British and Australian tactical units, each around twenty-men strong and based in Labuan and Kuching, handled the task, using substantial amounts of kit like amplifiers and tape recorders to maximise voice interception. To find even three more cypher operators for Singapore to cover traffic to London was hard, yet just about possible.

Two problems emerged on Borneo. If unusual languages carried Indonesian voice, new translators needed to be found. Initially, British authorities thought Indonesians might use Dayak, the language of the majority population of northern Borneo, for voice. Britain could cover it only by recruiting Dayaks from the paramilitary Sarawak Rangers, and training them in interception. While this problem did not emerge, during 1965–66 some Indonesian operators used Javanese, which Britain covered by retraining four local interpreters.[122] More ominous was the question of what Comint could enable. The UKLO in Melbourne noted that Sigint might fail to track 'in advance exact areas, or even timing of operations ... though the build up of forces (and their location) and the fact that something was planned usually became very clear'.[123] Commonwealth forces improved on this performance, because they had more intelligence and power than the Dutch, and better opportunities for offensive rather than defensive action.

Scattered across wide territory, Indonesian forces signalled mostly by radio via voice and Morse, augmented by field telephones. Some traffic went in plain language, and operators were generally inefficient. They used fixed call-signs, frequencies and skeds, simplifying interception, and communicated primarily during office hours, enabling SK2 to focus on those periods and minimise personnel for other shifts.[124] Comint was the dominant British tactical and operational source during Konfrontasi, married to eyeballs on the ground for tactical purposes. The tertiary sources – aerial or photo reconnaissance, agents, prisoners and the local population – determined some enemy positions and penetrations, and provided cover for Comint. Simultaneously, Comint removed the errors of these sources, and revealed their truths. The most fruitful communications links were within Indonesian units on Borneo, and between the authorities in Jakarta and Indonesian Special Services (which combined political subversion units and commandos) and military commanders in Borneo and Sumatra. In organisational terms, Special Services was highly personalised, while the army was hyper-bureaucratic. Both worked via micromanagement, handling subordinates through an odd combination of detailed orders and political exhortation. Comint mastered the intentions, plans, operations and after-action assessments of Indonesian Special Services and army battalions on the front. Those Comint successes wrecked enemy operations, and eased British fears that action might compromise intelligence sources. A massive quantity of details about the Indonesian army, often from logistical and administrative traffic, and occasional revelations of plans and intentions, exposed any planned escalation of its strength or operations in Borneo.

These reports illuminated Indonesian attacks, but less so its underlying policy. Comint defined the convoluted Indonesian chain of command, and the role of each link in Konfrontasi. It enabled sophisticated British analysis of Indonesian decision-making, which allowed Britain to avoid elementary errors, but not to overcome more significant ones. In particular, Comint revealed that Special Services, the most aggressive Indonesian agency, reported directly to Sukarno.[125] This knowledge perhaps led British analysts to overstate the significance of Special Services as an indicator of Indonesian policy, and to oversimplify the latter's nature. In fact, Indonesian policy was formulated in a chaotic and personalised fashion. The head of Special Services, Colonel Magenda, and his deputy, Colonel Rujito, were belligerent partly in order to maintain their status in Jakarta. They had bad relations with every conventional arm. Military Comint revealed those ruptures and hinted at disputes in Jakarta over the execution of policy. However, it rarely penetrated the plans of top leaders, but did so just enough to show that the latter supported Konfrontasi with Britain, and its escalation, precisely as other secret, official or public sources suggested. Diplomatic Comint probably provided more material in this sphere.

Comint and Claret

Konfrontasi escalated the more that Malaysia integrated. From April 1963, Indonesian forces, mostly Special Services, began shallow incursions – codenamed in their messages as 'A' operations – into Borneo. They failed to prevent integration or to build liberated zones. By early 1964, Comint was able to show that Indonesia aimed to intensify the pressure, by combining force, subversion and a diplomatic effort to delegitimise Malaysia across Asia. Several organisations prepared independently to launch deeper penetrations across Malaysia. They strove to destabilise all of its parts and to build liberated zones, which would demonstrate opposition to Malaysia and subvert it during national elections and international conferences. Special Services moved to Sumatra, to begin a campaign of terrorism in Malaya and Singapore, working with the Indonesian Air Force, Marines, Navy, and allied Chinese and Malay political parties. Two Indonesian army battalions reinforced the strength of 3,500 volunteers and irregulars in Borneo. Comint illuminated the strength of a number of smaller units, and then showed that 5,000 to 10,000 volunteers would reach Borneo with plans to attack on specific dates.[126]

The slow development of Indonesian actions let Commonwealth forces prepare an effective counter. They did not want to move faster and further than necessary. Too eager action might antagonise decision-makers in Canberra and Washington, who hoped for a diplomatic solution. Any action required the development of elementary infrastructure. Merely to build or rent houses for Siginters and to find locations to deploy aerials – and to do so while achieving effect, security, and plausible cover – proved to be daunting tasks. Comint followed these developments. This period of operational warning enabled a military and Sigint build-up which eventually provided a tactical triumph.

By January 1964, GCHQ and the Australian Defence Signals Division (DSD), the renamed DSB, recognised that Indonesian actions made an escalation of their own effort 'inescapable'. Thirty-one Australian and British teams covered 'high-level links from which intentions and O.B. [order of battle] can normally be recovered', plus tactical links in Borneo. The rise in Indonesian forces and ambitions created more links and traffic to monitor, needing another five intercept teams in general and three in Borneo, expanded Sigint communications, and requiring a reorganisation of processing and distribution.[127] As the crisis grew in mid-1964, experience guided recalibration of effort.[128] A card index enabled intelligence to exploit every name of individuals or units mentioned in an Indonesian message. It enabled astonishing granularity of commentary, which was printed neatly in black pen on printed messages. Comint penetrated Indonesian efforts at deception – including its public claims to be withdrawing forces from Borneo – as part of international efforts to end the crisis.[129] Instead, as Indonesians purported to negotiate a ceasefire to Konfrontasi, they prepared to intensify the war of nerves. They aimed to send large forces into Borneo for just a few days, in order to evacuate them immediately in front of international observers, purporting to come from long-standing liberated zones.[130]

This material drove Australia to back Britain in Borneo and Whitehall to increase intelligence and military resources there. Commonwealth forces deployed four brigades in Borneo, reaching 17,000 soldiers, controlled by a Joint Force Headquarters (JFHQ) under DOBOPS (Director of Borneo Operations), Generals William Walker (1963–65) and George Lea (1965–67). In 1964, DSD reported the 'unanimous opinion of all intelligence authorities ... that without Comint, Australia would have been in dark concerning Indonesian planning and implementation of "A" operations against Malaysia'. Stations should be thanked for their 'excellent service of timely voluminous and meaningful Sigint'. Via the GCO(S), 'the intelligence community of Singapore' echoed this praise.[131] The C-in-C Far East pressed MOD to support GCHQ's expansion in Malaysia, given 'how dependent we are on Sigint for the successful prosecution of operations'.[132] Statesmen in Canberra and London frequently read Comint, which illuminated issues about which they cared.

Relevant staffs and commanders in London, and in Malaysia down to brigade level, were indoctrinated to receive Comint. In Singapore, conventional practices continued. Comint was disseminated rapidly to consumers during the day, but between 2015 and 0730 hours they had to visit UKF 200 to see any emergency messages.[133] On Borneo, the aims were speedy and thorough dissemination, which did not always follow standard practices. Initially, one-time pad-encrypted messages sent by radio, and cleared officers conveying top secret material by hand, carried Comint to DOBOPS. It was handled and transmitted by his intelligence chief, who also served as an SLO. Intercepts from local sources were returned to Singapore by Top Secret bag. In June 1964, a more orthodox organisation emerged. A 'secure Comint cell' was established at JFHQ. Raw and finished Sigint was carried between it and Singapore on two radio lines, serviced by cypher machines.[134] An officer at JFHQ, GS (Int) (S), received Comint and disseminated it to DOBOPS and his senior intelligence officer, who verbally briefed British brigade commanders. Many lower ranks involved in moving Comint at JFHQ also were indoctrinated.

GCHQ considered limited cooperation on Sigint with Malaysian officers, but rejected the idea. JICFE was authorised to brief them with sanitised material from Comint.[135] Otherwise, Britain aimed to keep knowledge of Comint from Malaysian officers, who commanded many forces in Malaya, one of the brigades in Borneo, a fleet, the police and especially Special Branch. Walker thought 'half' the intelligence 'value' of a policeman 'is lost if he has not access to club's material'.[136] That comment was an understatement. Indonesian messages routinely discussed their collaborators in Sarawak and Singapore, often including names and addresses and negotiations with dissident politicians and parties within Malaysia. This material enabled any competent security organisation, like Malaysian ones, to disrupt or control internal subversives working with an external enemy. Comint shaped an important but hidden dimension of Konfrontasi – political warfare, defensive and offensive – on both sides at once. It explains Indonesian failure in that campaign.

So to assist these Malaysian forces, and to gain corroborating material from them, Britain indoctrinated a few 'expats' – retired British officers serving as deputies within Malaysian organisations – to ensure their quality while Malaysian officers gained experience. Since this process was unusual under the rules of UKUSA, GCHQ asked NSA to present it to the United States Communications Intelligence Board. GCHQ emphasised that only a few men, previously indoctrinated, would be involved. USCIB approved the request albeit, as SUKLO soon discovered, with major reservations, especially about the numbers of expats. To raise the number would anger the US services and embarrass NSA, which privately tolerated a rise from six to eight expats, and later 10, without informing USCIB. Hooper, emphasising 'we must be very careful not to abuse General Blake's confidence or trust!', insisted on authorising every additional indoctrination.[137] Keeping the number of indoctrinated expats to ten men remained a headache.

Expats were briefed orally by visiting intelligence officers. They never saw end product and rarely saw appreciations based on Comint, which they could read but not retain. This process enabled Comint loosely to guide and to gain cooperation from Malaysian organisations.[138] Claude Fenner, the Inspector General of Police of Malaysia, was authorised in an emergency to give material from Comint described as such to the Tunku. If their Malaysian superior officers questioned proposals based on Comint, expats were to reply that they rested on intelligence which British authorities thought reliable, leaving the impression that they stemmed from MI6. Expats could not be vetted normally. Their past police or military service was usually sufficient to solve the problem. Britain also found means to send Comint during emergencies direct to the officer commanding the British battalion under Malaysian command in Borneo. He received Comint only if it could be used 'in such a way as to not arouse suspicion on the part <u>either</u> of the enemy <u>or</u> the Malaysian Bde Cmd and his staff'. He was briefed verbally, either from DOBOPs or his chief intelligence officer, who also 'indicates how it can be safely used (info not given unless safely usable)'.[139] In return, the Tunku probably had better human intelligence on Indonesia than Britain did, but did not share it, save when it suited his interests.

GCHQ wished to prevent Commonwealth and Malaysian military units from practising Sigint for fear this would compromise its work. It briefed the British Chief Signals Officer of the Malaysian Army to keep his men quietly from the practice.[140] When DOBOPS authorised the SAS to tap an Indonesian field telephone line across the border, Tovey sternly warned him from repeating the action.[141] GCHQ insisted that Comint be concealed from the personnel who acted on it: battalion, company and platoon officers, section or patrol leaders. The army accomplished this well: soldiers did not understand how Comint guided them; in fact, many thought intelligence better served the Indonesians than their own side. The dissemination of Comint to these levels was effective, though deliberately imperfect. Orders followed principles such as: 'translate SIGINT into operational orders. It is better to say to a Bn Cmd "Watch your left flank" than "We think an attack on your left flank is imminent".'

> [If] <u>compelled</u> to make an intelligence statement to Bn Cmds ... the information MUST be suitably generalised. Thus, to say 'A very good source shows that the enemy is planning to mount recce patrols against the following places (X, Y and Z)' is WRONG; to say 'We are inclined to think that the enemy may be planning to deploy patrols in the general area Q' (this area would incorporate the particular places X, Y and Z) is MUCH BETTER ... The invention of spurious sources (JAMES BOND etc) is to be avoided and should NEVER be done without consulting GCO through GCO (Int) (S) ... The use of collateral (ground sources etc.) – being guided by Sigint in selecting the 'right' collateral item – is by far the BEST method whenever possible ... any action taken by our forces as a result of SIGINT information should be so carried out as NOT to arouse enemy suspicion of our extraordinary percipience. One good way of achieving this effect is to 'generalise' such action: for

example, to bring down mortar fire on <u>one</u> jungle trail (known
from SIGINT as a likely enemy approach/withdrawal route) is
RISKY; to mortar several jungle-trails (<u>one</u> of which is known as a
good likely target from SIGINT) is MUCH SAFER.[142]

Reconsidering Konfrontasi

Tovey emphasised that Comint provided 'impetus and direction to
search for relevant ground source intelligence on which military action
could then be taken', especially by police and Special Branch.[143] This
camouflaging of Comint distorts official documents on Konfrontasi,
and previous accounts of it, through no fault of the authors. Some of
them, such as Nick van der Bijl, David Easter and Jeffrey Grey, used
the Sigint records they found in open documents well.[144] Any reference
in records to accurate foreknowledge of Indonesian intentions almost
certainly stems from Comint, as do all physical interceptions of their
forces. GCHQ's records force a reconsideration of a campaign where
Britain had military advantages, problems and opportunities.

Regular and irregular Indonesian forces and commanders were largely
mediocre. Malaysian units were inexperienced, though Indonesians
respected their security services. Gurkha and other Commonwealth
forces were excellent and also outnumbered their foes. They followed
doctrines and trained for jungle warfare and the 'hearts and minds'
school of counter-insurgency, which suited this campaign. Indonesian
forces conceded that Commonwealth counter-insurgency denied them
any local support save among the Chinese population in Sarawak and
ensured toleration of Malaysian rule through most of that country.

Commonwealth forces could crush any enemy attack they might
predict and any Indonesian unit found on the frontier. Surprise was
therefore essential to Indonesian success. The more it happened, the
greater their effect, and vice versa. Walker, a veteran of the Burma
campaign of 1944–45 and the Malayan emergency, was a master of
jungle operations, counter-insurgency and the use of intelligence. So
was his successor, Lea, commander of 22 SAS during the Malayan
emergency. Translating operational knowledge into tactical success
was easy against maritime and air insertions on Malaya, but harder in
Borneo. Movement was slow. Ambushers advanced perhaps 1,000 yards
per day. One snapped twig might lose the element of surprise for a
company. Routine movements were tough and tedious, punctuated by

fear, stink, and occasional action, mostly involving a few men across metres and minutes.

During the first phase of Konfrontasi, in Borneo during 1963, several attacks by Chinese or Malay volunteers overseen by Indonesian Special Services surprised small police or military posts. Oddly enough, large Commonwealth forces were always in the vicinity. They quickly destroyed or expelled these infiltrators – killing far more men than they lost – and denied them local support. Probably Comint inspired these deployments by showing that attacks were imminent in specific areas, without precisely indicating where and when, as with the Dutch experience a few years before.

In 1964, Comint helped to wreck two campaigns with precision. Special Services and the Indonesian air force, marines and navy undertook the maritime or airborne insertion of volunteers and irregulars from Sumatra to Malaya, while the Indonesian Army raided Borneo with regulars and irregulars. These efforts required surprise for success – all were vulnerable to interception or pre-emption. In Borneo, Britain poured Claret, maximising its strengths by using a blend of Comint and seasoned soldiers offensively against the crust of Indonesian forces on the Borneo frontier. Sukarno's means to threaten Britain became hostages to fortune. Indonesian attacks declined; regularly ambushed, their forces on the frontier began to move over to the defensive and towards demoralisation. Commonwealth mortars and artillery hit men moving to forward positions and aided ambushes. Indonesian units were ordered to halt every British incursion, while being careful to avoid enemy tricks; indeed.[145]

Britain wrecked attacks on Malaya and Singapore in one of the best-recorded campaigns of counter-terrorism. Indonesian Special Services ordered infiltrators to build liberated zones in Malaya and terrorists to strike Kuala Lumpur and Singapore. It did not foment the race riots between Chinese and Malay peoples which shook Singapore during 1964, but immediately strove to exploit and deepen divisions between the two communities.[146] Infiltrators, acting as though disaffected members of the population, should target both economic targets and the authority of the government of Malaysia itself.[147] Instead, during 1964, British forces intercepted Indonesian forces in international waters or airspace. Warships blocked infiltrations, capturing forty-one sampans running guns and carrying infiltrators, and deterred many more. The RAF intercepted aircraft, causing some to crash in the Straits of Malacca and killing their cargo of parachutists, and others to abort missions. The few infiltrators who landed were surrounded immediately by Commonwealth and Malaysian forces and crushed. Malaysian security caught ships at sea and infiltrators at customs posts and wrecked subversive 'reception committees' which were expected to guide infiltrators to safety.

As its efforts and allies failed, Indonesian Special Services looked desperately for further friends, such as triads from Hong Kong. It strove to contact the Malayan Communist Party, crushed in the Malayan emergency and now becalmed in southern Thailand.[148] Infiltrators tasked with disposing of enemy leaders were able to conscript anyone they came across who might be useful, though, in the event of doubts about their loyalty, the conscripts might be killed.[149] Recriminations arose from the rot. The Indonesian navy refused to support Indonesian Special Services.[150] The latter believed that criticism of their lack of success 'might be motivated by enemies within' or rivals in Jakarta who were, consciously or unconsciously, obstructing 'A' operations.[151]

Comint drove the greatest Indonesian defeats in this campaign, as when a hundred Indonesian soldiers and infiltrators landing at Pontian in Malaya were captured in August 1964, and when the British frigate HMS *Ajax* seized sixty-one infiltrators on Christmas Eve 1964.[152] Indonesia's only intelligence on these disasters were reports from the BBC, Malaysian newspapers, or the few survivors who returned. Morale among infiltrators-to-be crashed. One Indonesian Special Services officer noted that his men were affected by Radio Malaysia broadcasting an interrogation of a captured Indonesian Lieutenant Sutikno.[153] Sutikno's messages, believed by some Indonesian officers to be a shameful betrayal, became central to Malaysian propaganda.

By January 1965, realising that every raid of recent months had failed, Special Services abandoned large ones. It returned to small attacks, which faded to nothing.[154] Comint let Commonwealth and Malaysian forces crush all major operations, but not all small ones, including the murder of three civilians at MacDonald House in Singapore on 10 March 1965. These attacks, while personal tragedies, were politically irrelevant. They did not affect Indonesian aims to split Singapore from Malaysia – not that this trend needed reinforcement. The difficulty of attacking Singapore and Malaya, and the disasters that Indonesians tolerated before abandoning their efforts to do so, show the significance which they placed on these targets, and of British success against them.

Meanwhile, focused by Comint, Commonwealth and Malaysian forces punctured all Indonesian-liberated zones like balloons. Indonesians preferred that large forces establish such zones, but also sought to do so through small bodies which tried to regularise supplies and intelligence before embarking on combat.[155] Special Services and the army routinely reported that local populations refused to cooperate with them due to fear of Britain and opposition to Indonesia. For example, one Indonesian raid failed because it could not find a target. At least some of the local population was suspected of active help to 'the enemy' while among the rest there was no willingness to provide any support at all.[156] Britain's tactical ability to destroy pockets of men and wreck small operations crippled Indonesian strategy.

These failures weakened Sukarno and his allies in Jakarta and intimidated his generals and admirals. During the Sunda Straits incident of September 1964, a small Royal Navy force deliberately crossed international waters bisecting Indonesia to symbolise the country's vulnerability. Indonesian forces issued a war alert and considered the danger of hostilities.[157] One provincial military command warned that Britain might launch Gulf of Tonkin-like raids without declaring war.[158] Special Services insisted that its operations must not give Britain a pretext for war. Tovey later noted that Comint revealed Indonesian reluctance to risk escalation.[159] When the British read communications between Sukarno and his ambassadors about Britain, the JIC noted: 'Our recent actions impressed them far more than any word could have done.'[160] The deputy Chief of the Defence Staff, Vice Admiral Norman Denning, said that 'the principal Indonesian fear in recent weeks had been that we might mount an attack upon them and Sukarno was known to have asked his attachés in Western Capitals to report on our intentions'. Yet Sukarno still might escalate the crisis. Denning recommended diplomatic means to press Sukarno towards de-escalation, which the Foreign Office thought unlikely. The interdepartmental 'Joint Confrontation Department' noted 'the large number of peace feelers being put out by the Indonesians in almost every quarter of the globe', yet warned that 'we must retain the military deterrent which had in itself been the cause of these peace feelers, which were really nothing more than probes to detect cracks in the deterrent. None had apparently been detected so far and it was therefore a nice question of judgement as to whether it would be desirable to increase this deterrent at this particular moment, and run the risk of being considered provocative. It was primarily a question of timing.'[161] The British Ambassador to Indonesia, Andrew Gilchrist, agreed that Indonesian leaders, 'now visualised as a distinct possibility offensive action by the United Kingdom if there were a repetition of Indonesian operations such as the recent air drops into Malaya', but still 'would continue covert subversive and infiltration activities, which cost them comparatively little, since they believed that in the longer term the United Kingdom would wish to liquidate their expensive commitments in the Far East'. Britain had no means to avoid a long stalemate. British military and political authorities accepted this hard logic.[162]

Britain and Malaysia outmanoeuvred Sukarno in diplomacy, overcoming the international politics of anti-colonialism and delegitimising Konfrontasi in Asian and international politics. Yet still Indonesia escalated. Sukarno ordered Special Services to increase the level of confrontation effort in Malaysia and Singapore, and the army to do likewise in Borneo.[163] Between October 1964 and January 1965, Comint noted a national intensification of Konfrontasi, the intentions to send 16,000 volunteers and three brigades (12,000 soldiers) to Borneo, and the actual deployment of formations and units. These forces practised airborne and amphibious assaults and developed the infrastructure necessary for major attacks. Special Services and the army warned units that British forces might attack them and raised the prospect of direct contact, though generally emphasising the need to avoid that threshold. Major conferences in Borneo and Jakarta discussed how to use these forces.[164] Operations by Special Services reached their peak while the army seemed to be readying itself for unprecedented actions. They pursued liberated zones both in Malaya and Sarawak. Commonwealth intelligence foresaw a crisis. DSD concluded that: 'Though Indonesian intentions have frequently run ahead of their capacity for fulfilment, there is body of opinion that present build-up will cause logistic problems forcing either early attack or withdrawal of forces. All evidence points to intention to attack in some form. We therefore have to cover next six months period on assumption that we shall have short (we hope) limited war within that period.'[165]

Tovey warned that current Indonesian strength against north Borneo equalled three to four battalions, or 2,000 men. Indonesia planned to add another twelve to fourteen battalions, to 12,000 men. Precise Indonesian intentions were unknown, but this expansion would let them 'increase the scale and depth of their cross-border incursions', create a 'psychological weapon against Malaysia and her allies', and even to launch a major incursion into Borneo.[166]

These British expectations reflected Sukarno's hopes. In an unpredictable turn, however, the Indonesian army refused to act fully on them. It feared British power and the danger of war, especially as Britain escalated its actions. Instead, Comint showed that, rather than exploiting enemy losses on Claret operations for propaganda purposes, Indonesian units rarely mentioned Claret attacks, and reported imaginary actions in which British units had been annihilated.[167] Indonesian forces buried Gurkha dead outside their own military cemeteries without military honours. In February 1965, Britain authorised attacks up to 10,000 yards across the Indonesian border, and reinforced Walker's command. These developments had consequences for Sigint. Tovey reported that when he and Director DSD visited Borneo, 'with a singular but none the less refreshing lack of inhibitions, Commander West Brigade, GSO 1 (Int), DOBOPS and COMLANDBOR all referred to the vital need for Sigint, both before and after the event in the context of their greatly expanded scope for cross-border operations'.[168] Tovey held that: 'the struggle in BORNEO is being very largely fought (and so far contained) on the basis of the sound, rapid intelligence which SIGINT alone provides. Unless SIGINT can provide an efficient service, of the same kind as it is providing now, on the vastly larger complex of communications targets presented by the build-up of Indonesian forces troops in KALIMANTAN, the military consequences – and indeed the political implications – could be extremely serious.'[169]

Commonwealth Sigint on Borneo had ten Morse and two voice positions. They needed to immediately receive four more Morse and one voice position. If Indonesian forces developed more sophisticated command and control for a force approaching a division in size, another four Morse stations would be needed.[170] DOBOPS would provide weekly reports to commanders and Siginters at Singapore on Claret and Comint, including Indonesian reactions to attack. He would warn of every proposed mission, so DSD and UKF 200 could provide 'any relevant intelligence on the strength, dispositions, etc. of enemy forces in the target area … without delay … at

suitable precedence to DOBOPS/JFHQ'.[171] These actions enabled the
Commonwealth successes of 1965, which wrecked Indonesian forces on
the frontier, broke their nerve and deterred attacks on Malaya. British
intimidation of Indonesia shaped the revolution which occurred in
Jakarta in autumn 1965. Against this, the prospect that Singapore and
Brunei might join Malaysia collapsed.

The Wilson government reacted rationally to these developments.
It understood that Britain's initial strategic aims were impossible,
yet defined victory of a sort. 'Our long-term aim is a reasonably
non-aligned, stable and viable Indonesia, with which Malaysia and
Singapore can live peacefully. Any tolerable approximation to this ideal
requires an end to confrontation, other than by surrender.'[172] Britain
achieved this end. After negotiations in 1966, Indonesia abandoned
Konfrontasi and recognised Malaysia. In turn, Britain withdrew
from Borneo. Tovey warned that Britain could not rebuild its Sigint
capabilities there easily, or at all.[173] Britain promised to defend Malaya
from attack, but not necessarily Borneo, where elections would
determine if the population wished to join Malaysia. Britain took a
calculated gamble, which accepted an outside prospect that Malaysia
might collapse. Indonesian intentions and actions were unpredictable.
As DOBOPS intelligence noted, 'all Indonesians tend to allow their
emotions to overcome their reason', while 'the Eastern mind' worked
unlike the Western one.[174] The JICFE held that Indonesia wished
'to disrupt Malaysia, or at least to bring its government into a state
of subservience to Indonesian wishes, using chiefly political and
subversive means'. Indonesians dreamed of conquering north Borneo,
but probably in vain. The JIC in London varied from believing
Indonesia does 'not intend to indulge in external adventures for a
long time to come', to holding:

> that the Indonesians have called off military operations for the
> moment; that they are more likely to use propaganda and bribery
> than sabotage or attacks on security forces in order to influence the
> forthcoming elections; and that as long as the present Indonesian
> Government remains in control and their economic difficulties
> persist, they are unlikely to use military force on a large scale either
> in a direct attack or as the last phase of a long term plan to separate
> the Borneo territories from Malaysia.[175]

Tovey called Konfrontasi, a 'classic example of safe but effective use of Sigint', with 'superb service' in processing, 'efficient welding' with other sources, and 'admirable caution and readiness to abide strictly by our action-on rules in use of our material'.[176] Examples from the campaign illustrate this fusion, which did not entirely follow Tovey's formulation. During 1964–65, Special Services supported local Chinese communists to infiltrate the western corner of Sarawak, where much of the population was Chinese and communist organisation was powerful. This combination continued into 1966, even though the Indonesian army was slaughtering the largely Chinese PKI in Java. Indonesia pressed Malaysia militarily as the two states negotiated an end to Konfrontasi and communists hoped to establish a liberated zone. In February 1966, guided by intelligence, 600 Commonwealth and Gurkha soldiers waited in depth along the Serian Road, in the Tebedu region, where Indonesians planned to pass three platoons in sequence. When the first echelon was crushed, Indonesia abandoned its plan and formulated another. In later months, human intelligence, especially Special Branch, reported an imminent incursion to Bau district. Sigint identified the time, extent and range of these operations, their armament, approach routes and orders. That military authorities in Jakarta planned these operations showed their political significance. DOBOPS analysed this evidence well. Deployment of forces to the anticipated approach routes faced no 'action-on' problem; Humint provided adequate plausible cover. Even more, the commander of West Brigade noted, his men lived in an atmosphere of war. 'No one here is the least suspicious if I make plans against their use anywhere on my front. I have even been accused recently by Police and my COs of being smug about this threat.' Eight hundred Commonwealth soldiers covered every expected approach route in depth. Thirty-six infiltrators in two groups crossed the border on 4 June, almost exactly to the day and within the area DOBOPS expected. One group, claiming to have been hit on the frontier, and perhaps struck by mortars or artillery, withdrew immediately. Between 15 and 24 June, Australians thrice ambushed the other group. Most were killed and captured, the rest chivvied back to Indonesia. Many Chinese civilians, perhaps communist cadres, were arrested alongside infiltrators.[177]

Comint has driven few campaigns so much as Konfrontasi. Lea held that without Comint he would have needed another twenty to thirty battalions to succeed in Borneo – triple the size of his command, which would have been impossible for Britain to provide.[178] Comint increased certainty about enemy operations and its immediate to medium-term intentions. This knowledge let Britain deploy its forces effectively, especially by pre-empting the Indonesian expansions in Borneo during 1964 and 1965. By monitoring the state of readiness and movements of Indonesian ships and aircraft – just like the British Grand Fleet had with the German fleet in the First World War – Comint eased the wear on the RAF and Royal Navy. In tactical terms, Comint increased the ratio of successful contacts and reduced risk and wasted effort. Tiny forces acted surgically on the basis of accurate Sigint, inflicting massively one-sided damage, stalling any enemy successes and crippling the morale of Indonesian units and commanders. This, the most remarkable success of Claret, feels strikingly modern – like the use of unmanned aerial vehicles (UAVs) and special forces against mobile insurgents over the past decade.

Yet Comint had its limits. It could not reveal Indonesian strategic intentions, which turned on a political struggle. Comint could not reveal Sukarno's intentions directly, though it did so in effect by following military orders or his messages with ambassadors. No intelligence source could penetrate the convoluted high politics in Jakarta, especially when British actions contributed to a revolution there. As the JIC Far East noted: 'Even the more practicable Indonesian plans have an element of fantasy: they normally plan for operations on a lavish scale, but only a small proportion are actually put into effect.'[179] Konfrontasi was more bluster than force: a puppet show. The Commonwealth build-up of 1965 rested on a worst-case idea of Indonesian intentions, though British actions frightened the Indonesian army into rejecting its orders. British authorities did not understand what the Indonesian army intended in 1966. They always overestimated the unity of Indonesian decision-makers and the coherence of their strategy.

Any interpretation of the evidence, including orders to conduct 'terrorism', is conjectural to some degree. Translations can be tested only against the original messages in Indonesian archives, which may not be possible for decades, if ever. IRSIG prevented thorough documentation on how Comint was interpreted. Enough evidence remains to solve that general problem, but some matters are still unclear. Indonesian officials certainly feared internal security problems and thought Britain or Malaysia manipulated them that way. These states may have done so, perhaps guided by Comint, which showed that Indonesia was feeling the strain. Indonesian operational reports were generally factual and honest. They reported Indonesian casualties with detail, which aided battle damage assessment for Britain. When compared with the reports from their own units, British commanders understood the attritional exchange well, unlike Americans in Vietnam. Reports often mentioned the morale of attackers in positive and negative terms, and suggested problems among the Chinese and Malay allies which Indonesians sought to move across the frontier. However, some Indonesian reports from the front lines, and many which commanders in Borneo sent to Jakarta or to their subordinates, reported imaginary actions or distorted British losses in real ones. They rated Commonwealth forces as mediocre, with poor morale. British analysts and commanders had to guess why such reports were issued and whether they were believed. Perhaps Indonesian authorities exaggerated their actions? Did they feel that lies alone could maintain the morale of their subordinates, and the trust of their superiors? In a prolonged struggle of political and military attrition, these questions mattered. Comint could not answer them.

So What?

The Labour Minister for Defence during Konfrontasi, Denis Healey, rightly called it 'a textbook demonstration of how to apply economy of force, under political guidance for political ends'.[180] In particular, 'the CLARET operations were highly successful from all points of view. They were indeed most carefully planned and reflect the greatest credit on all those who carried them out both on the staff and in the field'. John Grandy, Commander-in-Chief Far East between 1965 and 1967, thought 'the whole 900 mile border area was totally and completely dominated by our forces and that Indonesia had a very great fear of the border. All operations were proceeded by meticulous and most careful planning, training and practice. Hazardous operations in appalling conditions of terrain, jungle and climate were successfully carried through not only by SAS specialists but by many line British regiments and Marines Commandos, as well as Ghurkhas. These operations provided a tremendous fillip to morale and there were countless examples of heroism, tenacity, courage, and fine junior leadership.'[181]

This campaign was marvellous, and myth-making. Healey and Walker held that Britain conducted counterinsurgency far better than did the United States in the Vietnam war, which would have gained (and perhaps won) by adopting British practices.[182] Indeed, here, as in the Malayan emergency, British intelligence and counterinsurgency were excellent, and better than American practices in Vietnam. However, the North Vietnamese Army was stronger and better than the Indonesian one. It would have smashed efforts based on these British models and force levels, and would have turned low-level insurgency into high-intensity battle. Nor could Claret have been poured in Vietnam. NSA provided little help to American attacks (larger, but less precise and successful than those of Claret) on the Ho Chi Minh trail – the supply conduit from North to South Vietnam, via Laos and Cambodia.[183] Superiority in Comint would have strengthened these attacks, but not enough to win the war.

Again, Healey, Walker and other authorities held that Claret sparked the collapse of Sukarno and Konfrontasi. These claims have some truth, but require perspective. During 1964–65, Claret and British diplomacy stalled Indonesia in a losing position, which it dared not escalate. Britain's escalations of summer 1964 and spring 1965 intimidated the Indonesian army. The latter also began negotiations for compromise with Malaysian leaders, which both sides hid from Sukarno and Britain.[184] The PKI used the stalemate to challenge the army, and demand arms for a militia under its control. These developments ratcheted the strains which wrecked Sukarno's regime: they drove him to the PKI, and the latter to demands which frightened the generals, who would strike only if struck. When the generals did strike, they killed hundreds of thousands of PKI members and civilians, abetted to some degree by Britain and the United States, though this game was bound to end in blood, no matter who won the throne.

Yet the effect of any penultimate cause on an event is easy to overestimate. For Britain and Indonesia, Konfrontasi simply intensified strains which stemmed from other matters, rather than created new ones. An incompetent coup on 1 October 1965 by some communist leaders and officers triggered the implosion. Had the coup not happened or been competent, Sukarno might have won the internal struggle and thus his external one. In prolonged wars of attrition, victory goes to he who lasts the final quarter of an hour. During 1965, as Britain contained

Konfrontasi, relations between Singapore and Malaya collapsed, and with them the strategic value of Malaysia to Britain. Singapore could no longer be a cheap and secure base. When Singapore left Malaysia in August 1965, Sukarno proclaimed victory; he might have secured one had his regime lasted another year. Britain considered abandoning its policy towards Indonesia, constrained only by the need not to lose prestige, nor to antagonise Australia, New Zealand and the United States. Six weeks later, the tables turned, and blood was spilled.

The battlefield successes of Comint and Claret shaped the near-run power politics of Konfrontasi. They ensured that strains intensified on Indonesia more than Britain, by calming British fears, and raising those in Jakarta. Comint and Claret bought time to contain the contradictions between American and British policy, and British politicians and generals; and to lead elements within the PKI and military to believe they must strike the generals; and to drive Sukarno against his soldiers and the United States, while unifying the latter. Konfrontasi was a case of the dog which did not bark in the night: something which mattered less than it might have done. Comint and Claret silenced the dog.

For Britain, Konfrontasi was a tactical triumph with mixed strategic results: a failure, but not a disaster, for its power, and a success for decolonisation. The real confrontation was not between Britain and Indonesia but, rather, factions in 'Indonesia' and 'Malaysia', imagined countries struggling to be born. 'Malaysia' won because the Tunku outmanoeuvred his rivals abroad. A subalterns' revolt against Britain and Sukarno drove the outcome. Comint and Claret enabled Britain secretly, and cheaply, to defeat Indonesian policy without alienating Indonesia, but not to achieve the victory it pursued. Malaysia could be created only through a shotgun marriage between Malaya and four brides. Two blushed, and two refused the veil. Differences between politicians and peoples, not Konfrontasi, pushed Singapore and Brunei away from Malaysia and drove a stake into the heart of British strategy. Indonesian generals and Malaysian leaders outflanked Britain and Sukarno through secret negotiations. They could find a modus vivendi, so long as both their masters were eliminated.

These defections led Britain to conclude that a cheap and secure presence at Singapore was untenable. That conclusion shaped the abandonment of Britain's greatest aim in the campaign: the maintenance of its position east of Suez and its status as a world power, though economic, political and military trends really drove that outcome. When imperialism became philanthropy, Britain counted its change. Defeat in Konfrontasi helped the generals to seize Indonesia, but not the adjacent ex-colonies of Britain, which secured Britain's secondary aim: a peaceful and stable transfer of power. The consequence of Konfrontasi is the success of Brunei, Malaysia, Singapore and Papua New Guinea. That this last battle of the British empire in Asia was a brilliant victory obscures its significance. Failure at Suez hastened the end of empire perhaps by a year. Victory in Konfrontasi lengthened it by not one day.

Sigint and the Falklands Conflict

Origins and Impulse

The Falklands conflict was the last British imperial campaign and the first battle in a new age of Sigint. For both Argentina and Britain, the Falkland Islands were a minor issue involving major principles. Argentina claimed sovereignty over the islands. Britain maintained that 1,820 anglophone islanders had rights to national self-determination. The resulting war began by fluke, and was dominated by it. Margaret Thatcher's government bungled its policy towards the matter, partly because the Argentine junta also did so. In 1981, Britain told Argentina that only if the Falklands population accepted rule by Buenos Aires – which all thought unlikely – could Britain accept that outcome. The JIC concluded that Argentina might respond by invading the islands. Argentine armed forces were large and competent; 'Fortress Falklands', a British garrison able to withstand them, was almost impossible to maintain, given other British commitments.[185]

During early 1982, the junta publicly demanded that it gain sovereignty over the islands. Whitehall dithered and increased the problem by planning to slash the British sea power assets which defended the islands. Nor did the JIC raise Argentina's low place on its priorities. These decisions tempted fate, and disaster. In April 1982, the Argentine junta seized the Falkland Islands impulsively, to score a victory which would stabilise its political position at home. The junta assumed that Britain could not and would not retaliate. That assumption would have been true within a few months, had Britain carried out its plans to sell the ships which became essential to victory. In 1982, however,

Britain still had the power needed to retake the islands, and a prime minister determined and desperate enough to use it. Failure to retake the Falklands would wreck Britain's status as a power and Thatcher's as a politician.[186]

In simple terms, had the Falkland Islands been a hundred miles closer to the South American mainland, they would have become Las Malvinas. Britain would have lost the war and probably not even attempted it in the first place. In contrast, had the islands been a hundred miles further offshore, Britain could have won almost bloodlessly. One-sided superiority in Sigint was fundamental to British success in this war, which was a more close-run thing in general than most realise. Without Sigint, Britain might have lost, though many other factors also might have caused defeat. Argentina might have won the war had its air forces possessed twenty Exocet anti-ship missiles instead of five – and trained with them; or primed their iron bombs to detonate properly during attacks on Royal Navy ships at San Carlos Sound – instead of failing to explode or passing through ships before they did. The main causes of British victory were the quality of British forces and, once the conflict started, of its military and political leaders.

Argentina had no rational plans for war against Britain in 1982. Though its air force was decent in quality, it had never prepared to fight warships. Its initial attacks were its first tests in the area. Argentine air force and navy aircraft lacked the infrastructure needed to attack warships effectively, having few air tankers to extend the range of attacking aircraft, or reconnaissance platforms to guide them onto targets. This inexperience caused the bad priming of bombs which lost the fruits of self-sacrifice at San Carlos Sound. The Argentine army was poor and those on the Falklands among the worst. They were unready for battle, raw recruits missing massive amounts of necessary kit. The Argentine navy, its warships half obsolete, half modern, was also unprepared for war. A few weeks at sea in a South Atlantic autumn eroded its quality, as mechanical failures sent one warship after another back to port for repairs. Perhaps these failures of their own led Argentine admirals to underestimate how a well-prepared navy could handle such conditions.

The Argentine admirals wanted war. They pursued aggressive, ambitious and unachievable plans. British strategists too were stunned; they had thought little about to how to fight such a war, for which Britain had decided no longer to prepare. In the event, Britain conducted a campaign at the extreme level of possibility, which only one other country – the United States – could have mounted, though more easily.

Britain sent Task Force 317 (TF 317) south in several echelons. Two nuclear and four conventionally powered submarines took the lead, followed by eight destroyers, fifteen frigates and two aircraft carriers, *Hermes* and *Invincible*. This Carrier Battle Group had few escorts, which also had to defend other valuable units. It was unusually vulnerable to all forms of assault in ways which British planners both understood and misconstrued. Behind them, amphibious groups carried two brigades on transports, accompanied by landing assault ships and flotillas of supply and auxiliary vessels. In blue water, this fleet would have overwhelmed the Argentine navy. In green and brown water it was vulnerable to airstrikes. British authorities anticipated '25 per cent battle attrition of naval, and maritime air forces', including ten Sea Harrier fighter aircraft, twenty-two to twenty-seven other aircraft, an aircraft carrier, a nuclear submarine, four destroyers and frigates, and eight support vessels. Of these losses, the carrier, two surface warships and five support vessels nominally could be repaired.[187]

These academic and worse-case calculations were accurate about aircraft, but overstated the losses to warships and misunderstood the menace. Britain preserved its greatest assets, the carriers, by minimising their exposure to attack – and so reducing their use to the minimum necessary for victory. Submarines achieved their missions without loss. However, any warships exposed to aircraft suffered greater losses than expected. Argentine aircraft and warships had ship-killing weapons; British warships had weaknesses. Air and naval data links unified the sensor feeds from all parts of a unit – say, every radar on all ships in TF 317 – and gave each part the same overall sensor picture. No Western force had used data links in war, and much remained uncertain about their working. RAF and Royal Navy officers were inexperienced with data links; their failures to marry data links and properly organised radar to defensive weaponry aided Argentine air strikes. The RAF quickly overcame its mistakes by refitting platforms based in Britain, but warships deployed thousands of miles from home had to suffer until war was done. Inexperience with data links shaped the destruction of the Type 42 destroyer, HMS *Sheffield*, on 4 May 1982. In order to protect flotillas at sea, the Royal Navy made individual ships serve as radar pickets, acquiring data for the whole force, while advertising themselves to Argentine detection. Failures to coordinate radar collection to guide surface-to-air missiles crippled British anti-aircraft defence.[188]

Ethnocentrism affected assessments and estimates, albeit marginally. Tovey, by now Director of GCHQ, removed the phrase 'typically Latin' from one JIC assessment.[189] Nonetheless, British intelligence analysed Argentine capabilities well, if anything overstating them, save in one area: air attack at sea. That failure occurred because of divided responsibilities in green water, a tendency to overrate British capabilities in defence electronics and data links, and the focus on the threat posed by Argentine surface and submarine forces. Some British observers viewed Argentine air forces using a car-racing analogy: good drivers and mediocre pit crews. As a widely disseminated analysis noted in 1970: 'In general flying skill is of a good standard. Airmanship, however, could certainly be better if a high degree of self-discipline could be imposed. Patriotism, national spirit and bravery are undoubtedly marked in most officers and NCOs,' and concluding: 'The standard of training is relatively high both on the ground and in the air.'[190] The RAF assessed the Argentine air force well on issues of strength, quality of personnel, surge capacity, sortie rates and ability to handle attrition. It gained from the willingness of the French air force to let Harriers practise dogfights against Mirage fighters, learning lessons for free. French authorities also prevented the export of a key weapon to Argentine air forces, the Exocet anti-ship missile. The RAF, however, did not ask what would happen when Argentine aircraft struck British warships, other than to raise two key points: Argentine aircraft had not prepared for such actions; their quality here was unclear.[191]

Not unreasonably, the Royal Navy focused on blue water operations more than green. It thought the two modern Argentine submarines could endanger its carriers and nuclear-powered attack submarines (SSNs), as its four veteran ones also might do. British surface vessels were prepared for older Soviet missiles, but not the Exocet missiles based on Argentine (and British) aircraft and warships.[192] The Royal Navy boosted defences against Exocets for HMS *Illustrious*, the carrier under completion, the only platform it could materially upgrade and strengthen for war.[193] British planners understood that they were unprepared against Exocets, but misconstrued their menace. Exocet missiles, whether mounted on Super Etendard aircraft flying from aircraft carriers, or on surface warships, were dangerous, but electronic countermeasures (ECM) such as chaff could (and did) degrade their power. British planners addressed well how these technical and tactical issues would work in a fleet battle scenario. The one threat which the naval staff did not examine in detail was that which most inflicted harm during the war: opportunistic raids from land-based aircraft, whether Super Etendard or older Skyhawk, Dagger and Mirage aircraft, in green water close to shore. These older aircraft could be 'dealt with adequately' unless they were operating within 350 miles of their bases – as, unfortunately, occurred during the British landings.

These technical and interservice issues were multiplied because the military intelligence chief, the Deputy Chief of the Defence Staff (Intelligence) – DCDS (I) – was a soldier. General James Glover said that Argentine air forces 'have only an outside chance of inflicting severe damage' on the Task Force 317.[194] The naval staff thought Argentine radar 'generally poor', while that on the Task Force was good, though it 'may suffer from jamming'. It was 'well balanced' in anti-aircraft capability – 'Provided the Task Force is not too widely scattered, it has a very adequate AA defence capability.'

TF 317, alas, was extraordinarily scattered. The threat of Argentine aircraft was 'negligible' 700 nautical miles from any air base, but 'much greater' at 300 miles.[195] The RAF and Royal Navy each misunderstood tactical and technical capabilities in an area where neither service was the sole authority – how land-based Argentine aircraft and weapons systems would fare against British warships. They continued to underrate that danger until HMS Sheffield was sunk. Even when planning the invasion two days later, the worst-case view was that Britain might lose two or three warships.[196] Instead, Britain lost four warships – with many more crippled and only prevented from destruction by Argentine inexperience – along with several assault and supply ships.

TF 317 avoided the worst consequences of this situation by keeping its carriers far east of the islands, save when launching an attack. Had Argentina crippled one of the carriers before the British landing, the counter-invasion probably would have failed. Only the twenty Sea Harrier 'jump jets' initially carried by the British fleet (joined by eight more by mid-May) could defend it and the amphibious force and, along with fourteen other RAF Harriers, hope to achieve air superiority. The Argentine air force and navy had 130 fighters and bombers able to attack the fleet from the mainland and operate over the Falklands, and a dozen less effective Pucará ground-attack aircraft based on the islands. These aircraft were badly maintained, ground crew made errors, and aircrew could operate for just a few minutes over targets – yet every ship in TF 317 was at risk within their reach. To get men and supplies ashore and forwards was a difficult task for the British. After these perils had been surmounted, invading ground forces must cross arduous terrain and defeat an enemy numerically equal and dug in, albeit an enemy correctly presumed to be inferior in quality. As Glover said, 'aggressive attrition' could wreck 'the crucial and most vulnerable element in the Argentine defence': the morale of untrained conscripts, marooned far from home.[197] This best part of British analysis was the key to its desperate victory.

GCHQ records, and its history of the Falklands conflict, frequently mention diplomatic intelligence, though often in vague terms – such as 'a message which reflected the Junta's thinking on future UK action' which had fifty words redacted.[198] The GCHQ history of the Falklands conflict frequently mentions diplomatic intelligence, especially about British efforts to block armss shipments to Argentina. Politicians and diplomats carefully followed intelligence reports as a key part of the broad war effort.[199] Initially, this Comint overwhelmed the FCO which, GCHQ thought, 'were not equipped to deal with such volumes'. By May, the FCO received 'about 1,100 items of SIGINT a week on the Falklands crisis'.[200]

Diplomacy was central to this war. To enable TF 317 to sail, and to keep that support as war began, Britain needed to convince other states that Argentina was in the wrong. Unprovoked Argentine aggression alone let Britain overcome the politics of anti-imperialism and achieve these ends. That the local population wanted rescue affected public views in the Five Eyes, but nowhere else. UN Security Council Resolution 502 demanded that Argentina evacuate the Falkland Islands and negotiate with Britain over their status, while avoiding hostilities. Britain, invoking Article 51 of the UN Charter, then dispatched the Task Force in self-defence. Yet this diplomatic success was fragile and became eroded once the Argentine cruiser *General Belgrano* was sunk and Argentina finally took diplomacy seriously. The JIC warned that 'intelligence was needed on the positions, secret and public, of foreign governments. In this context, public positions might be the more important.' GCHQ produced 'evidence that Argentineans are keen to present a more favourable image in W. European nations', while 'the Argentines were considering whether to call a meeting of the Security Council'.[201]

The more militarily successful Britain was, the more even its friends wanted it to negotiate on unfavourable terms. That diplomatic tension drove the need for speed in operations felt by the War Cabinet and all senior commanders, especially two politically desperate actors: Prime Minister Thatcher and the Royal Navy. Diplomatic Comint mattered as much as its military counterpart to Thatcher's strategy, and more tempered her will. As the Foreign Secretary, Francis Pym, wrote to GCHQ: 'Timely intelligence has been of the essence during the past few weeks, and I have been deeply impressed by the speed and efficiency with which you have responded to the demands placed upon you to provide us with comprehensive signals intelligence coverage of all aspects of the dispute ... The overall contribution you have made to our efforts ... has been very substantial indeed, and I know the Prime Minister shares my gratitude.'[202]

But in diplomatic terms, even Britain's allies were lukewarm. Without the personal support of a few statesmen, particularly François Mitterrand, Ronald Reagan and Caspar Weinberger, their countries might have offered Britain little help. Many American agencies kept their distance from Britain, save those which mattered: those under the military, particularly the US Navy. American agencies cultivated good relations with Argentina as part of its struggle for influence in Latin America, especially against Cuba and Nicaragua. Aid to Britain would wreck those relations, and damage those in Latin America. GCHQ was reluctant to press NSA for support, not wishing to cause 'political embarrassment', or make it refuse a request because of politics in Washington.

Wrong-footing to War
The invasion, as Britain's able ambassador to the UN, Anthony Parsons, said, wrong-footed Britain. Argentina held the islands – it could lose them only by leaving, voluntarily or otherwise; Britain could win only by making Argentines leave through threat or violence. Miscomprehension shaped actions. Each side pursued credibility; neither had it at the outbreak of war. The COS did not understand how much force was needed to retake the islands – in part because that

was not Britain's initial aim – and barely reached a minimum strength for success. Britain had to build credibility and take belligerent actions, which would both strengthen and weaken its diplomatic position. Soon after the crisis began, Defence Secretary John Nott said: 'Our submarines were now committed to the blockade. We should soon have to consider whether it was right to allow Argentinean naval vessels to leave port. [The American Secretary of State] Mr. Haig commented that if Argentinean ships did leave port, and nothing happened, British credibility would suffer. He had already received some information suggesting that the Argentinians did not believe that we meant to fight.'[203] In addition, Thatcher was warned that Argentine counsels were divided: 'The Navy were looking for a fight. The Air Force did not want a war. The Army were somewhere in between.'[204] Sigint shaped some of the interminable debates, such as whether Argentine submarines had entered the Exclusion Zone.[205]

Though war was the most likely outcome, Britain preferred a negotiated settlement, on humanitarian and realist grounds. In the first week after invasion, military planning centred on re-establishing posture and presence. A beachhead in the Falklands would strengthen Britain's hand in the negotiations which external pressure would surely make Argentina entertain. These attitudes changed only when Thatcher decided that if Argentine forces did not withdraw, Britain must force them out. Yet the Iron Lady was no desiccated calculating machine: after *Sheffield* and *Belgrano* were sunk, Thatcher wept for the dead, whose ends she had shaped. She deplored, she said, the:

> most awful waste of young life if we really have to go and take those
> islands … We have more respect for young life than they do. But
> the resolve will still be there but I just feel that absolutely everything
> should be done to make it absolutely clear that in the end it is they
> who have no respect for young life … and they have to matter.
> And in the end they'll fight for ideals … I will do everything before
> the final decision has to be taken to see if we can uphold the rule
> of international law and the liberty and justice in which I believe
> passionately for our people to see if we can stop a final battle.[206]

Spooked by memories of Suez, civil servants and admirals warned of Britain's tenuous diplomatic and military position. Frank Cooper (PUS to the Minister of Defence) emphasised that unconsidered actions, perhaps involving a few deaths among Falkland civilians, 'might create such a backlash that Ministers might feel unable subsequently to authorise a landing ... the worst outcome would be for Ministers to have to stop the operation after it had started but before it was completed'. Armstrong warned of an even worse case: for Britain 'to be held responsible for the failure of diplomatic efforts to get a ceasefire and withdrawal agreement now and then not to be able to repossess the Falkland Islands: to end up either in a stalemate with continuing casualties and attrition ("Gallipoli") or in a withdrawal'. The First Sea Lord and Chief of the Naval Staff (CNS), Admiral Henry Leach; Admiral John Fieldhouse, Commander-in-Chief Fleet; and General Edwin Bramall, the Chief of the General Staff, also feared stalemate.[207]

Intelligence built certainty against fear. Antony Duff, the coordinator of the intelligence services for the Cabinet, told GCHQ: 'At this time, with the prospect of diplomatic negotiations continuing for at least a week or two, it is particularly important to obtain every scrap of intelligence we can about the advice, counsel and information being given to the Argentine government. In collection terms this means, I think ... issuing a very large proportion of relevant traffic ...'[208] Britain bent further in diplomacy than Argentina, accepting forms of words which could place the islands under temporary international control and might eventually give Argentina sovereignty over them, against the inhabitants' will. Ultimately, neither side would abandon its case in advance. Argentine diplomacy was mendacious, aimed to hamper British operations, and stubborn – it would only accept a settlement which guaranteed its sovereignty over the islands, rapidly. This diplomatic intransigence legitimised warlike British actions. British diplomats at the top of their game prevented Argentina from wrong-footing Britain again, as their countries waltzed to war.

GCHQ and the Outbreak of the Falklands Conflict
During 1976–77, Argentina had challenged Britain's claims to the Falkland Islands. The Labour government had responded with firm diplomacy, silently backed by deploying a nuclear-powered attack submarine and a ten-man GCHQ team to the area. This combination of force and intelligence trumped any likely Argentine attack, but Argentina did not know of their presence, and folded in the face of

British determination, rather than through deterrence. After these events, GCHQ declined to leave a permanent presence on the islands, which would have been difficult and expensive to deploy and maintain, and vulnerable to capture in case of invasion.[209] It also would not have shaped the outbreak of war in 1982 at all.

Before the 1982 crisis, the JIC had placed the Falkland Islands in 'Priority 4', the lowest group of intelligence priorities, alongside Brunei and below Belize, Gibraltar or Hong Kong. Among these dependencies, the Falklands were the least defended; indeed, defenceless. In 1981, the MOD's Defence Intelligence Service (DIS) tried to place the islands in Priority 2, without noticeable effect on what the DCDS(I) later described as a 'complacent' level of collection and analysis effort.[210] These decisions were wrong, so too was GCHQ's belief that it would predict hostility in time to deter Argentine action. The 1982 crisis astonished GCHQ. Because of delays in receiving routine messages about the Falklands, it misconstrued the first signal received on the issue, on 20 March, from the only Royal Navy vessel in the South Atlantic.[211] HMS *Endurance*, with a small but unique Sigint capability, helped monitor the crisis from start to finish.[212] Just after the invasion, Tovey 'exploded' on hearing that *Endurance* would return for refuelling to Ascension Island. Glover, 'very apologetic', offered to find alternatives, the JIC adopted a 'no gap' policy, and a refuelling vessel was sent to *Endurance*.[213] For several weeks, unsupported by other British forces, it hid among icebergs from Argentine warships while intercepting unique elements of their traffic and sending it home. When, as war waned, Whitehall wished to withdraw *Endurance*, morale crashed among its crew, until GCHQ sent them well-deserved thanks for their work, and let them finish it.[214]

The crisis began on 19 March. Scrap-metal dealers from Buenos Aires, ostensibly searching for salvage but in truth looking to undermine British rule in the Falkland Islands, visited one of its uninhabited dependencies, South Georgia Island. There they raised an Argentine flag. For the next fortnight, matters escalated in a complex fashion. An Argentine vessel reached that island and withdrew most of the civilians. Secretly it left a dozen men behind, as Britain discovered through observation and Comint. British authorities accepted that they must tolerate Argentine force against islands associated with the Falklands, having allowed an Argentine presence on Southern Thule since 1977. Following a decade-old reflex regarding the Falklands, and fashionable ideas about rationality and 'escalation ladders' during crises, Britain reacted cautiously in order to avoid provocation and to buy time. Whitehall thought that crisis loomed, but it was months away – likely after a slow and rational process of escalation, focused first on negotiations, then on economic and diplomatic coercion from Argentina, but possibly reaching war within the year. Whitehall disassociated the flashpoint of South Georgia Island from the Falkland Islands. It overestimated the rationality of the Argentine junta and the pace of the unfolding crisis. Thatcher later said: 'It seemed utterly ridiculous to contemplate an invasion of the Falklands then.'[215] British diplomatic, military and political decision-makers were capable, and took good note of signals, but they fell victim to a classic failure of intelligence. Authorities saw what they expected to see, interpreting intelligence and actions within a schematic framework of how they thought a competitor must move. They overthought the game and misunderstood their rival. Whitehall thought the Argentines were climbing a ladder. The Argentines preferred to dance the tango.

Several factors bolstered these preconceptions until late in the day. Whitehall generally did not assess outbreaks of war well – except regarding the Warsaw Pact where its performance was decent. British authorities, ethnocentric and overly rational, projected their logic onto foreigners. In particular, reflecting the impact of nuclear deterrence, and the politics which impeded British use of force during decolonisation, authorities believed that states would start wars only with reluctance and when risks were low. They forgot their experiences with Hitler, Mussolini, Nasser and Sukarno when analysing the assessments and actions of foreigners. If authorities saw a threat, they assessed evidence on it well. If not, they were slow to see danger or to change preconceptions. The JIC buried evidence of specific threats in broad discussions of many issues, and monitored them badly. Outside priority areas, no JIC officer and few DIS officers were assigned to assess all the cumulative evidence on emerging problems. Only a startling piece of intelligence, or an alert analyst, could shake this complacency. A senior Siginter, Doug Nicoll, warned the JIC of these flaws, just as it repeated them in the Falklands crisis.[216] This failure was an extreme example of general problems.

Few people handled intelligence on the Falkland Islands, which slowed its processing and impact. Busy people not already focused on the area found the reportage hard to follow. Everyone was busy, nobody specialised. Most Argentine signals were opaque or minor, and many were garbled – incomprehensible until corrected days later. DIS, charged with basic analysis, had no specialist on the Falklands and only two officers tasked to handle Latin America, meaning one person at a time.[217] Ministers and senior officials were swamped with other important matters, including renegotiating the terms of Britain's nuclear deterrent with the United States. Often they were out of Britain and rarely in direct touch, hampering the personal liaison which dominated decision-making under Thatcher. Meanwhile, Argentine counsels remained divided. Their decision to invade the Falklands was impulsive and irrational, driven by factional rivalry and internal politics. The signals acquired by GCHQ reflected these ambiguities. British decision-makers reacted well to the first public statements which clearly contradicted their assumptions – but these were late in the day. Had Argentine leaders followed more conventional modes of aggression, nuclear-powered submarines might have reached the Falklands before the invasion, perhaps enabling it to be deterred.

GCHQ provided Whitehall's first and best warnings of Argentine intentions, and of changes in them, though diplomats provided useful and parallel analyses. GCHQ monitored Argentine signals, initially without concern. Naval exercises explained Argentine actions. On 25 March, however, GCHQ distributed a day-old message from the Argentine naval commander, Admiral Jorge Anaya. He reported that Britain wanted the scrap merchants removed from South Georgia, but that Britain recognised that to do so via force and HMS *Endurance* might inflame the Argentine public. Argentina agreed to withdraw them, but secretly intended to leave some civilians behind 'on the South Georgias. The MFA's objective is to exert pressure for an urgent meeting (on) the Falklands Group.' That message, GCHQ's only reflection of Argentine intentions before the invasion, suggested that Argentina would intensify pressure on South Georgia Island to break the diplomatic stalemate over the Falkland Islands. An Argentine naval message distributed alongside it described in detail British forces across the South Atlantic and Caribbean Sea, concluding: 'If there is any information, I shall give a daily routine 20 hours, update or when possible.'[218]

Scenting a crisis, GCHQ's Latin American codebreakers and traffic analysts immediately adopted twenty-four-hour shift work in order to solve and distribute signals quickly. This surge in procedure reduced the time required to process intercepts, from an average of forty-eight hours down to eighteen. It also led to frustratingly incomplete record-keeping about the times when GCHQ reports were distributed, which hampers analysis of how Sigint affected British actions on 31 March. Between 26 and 30 March, GCHQ reported Argentine naval preparations and assessments of British forces across the Atlantic. These messages could be explained as part of pressure on South Georgia Island. Quite which authorities saw what GCHQ reports, and precisely when, is impossible to know. Thus, the Anaya message immediately prompted analyses by DIS and the Foreign Office, but took days to reach the top. Thatcher probably saw only the most important of reports – as did the two ministers most involved with intelligence. Nott and Foreign Secretary Lord Carrington were caught with pressing and complex concerns, and were often travelling away from Britain. Nott's staff overlooked the evidence until it became unambiguous; so too did military and diplomatic subordinates. Referring to the Anaya signal, Fieldhouse later said, 'there was a rather more sensitive [message], it was a code word signal which I did not see at the time, and arguably need not have done, and I think that it had a strictly limited distribution and was somewhat later'.[219]

Each worrying GCHQ report caused authorities to think that Argentina had advanced one step up the escalatory ladder, until suddenly it leapt almost to the top. The signals showed Whitehall that a crisis was at hand, but reinforced the usual reflex to avoid provocation. By 24 March, Carrington told Thatcher that further negotiations over the Falkland Islands were 'unlikely'. A GCHQ solution of diplomatic traffic indicated 'that the Argentines may be prepared to take early actions to withdraw Argentine services to the islands' – that is, Argentina would take the first step on its escalatory ladder, to cut the commercial and air links which connected the islands with the world; and then follow each schematic stage of confrontation in sequence.[220] In the face of this danger, Carrington advocated only cautious and preparatory action. By 26 March, probably reflecting the Anaya message of two days prior, the Foreign Office told ministers that negotiations on the issue would be fraught, probably impossible. The MOD warned that to deter Argentina, possessing 'some of the most efficient armed forces in South America', would be expensive. To reconquer the Falkland Islands would be difficult or impossible. Thatcher underlined a minute written on this paper: 'Very gloomy.'[221]

On Sunday 28 March, politicians suddenly took alarm. The cumulative effect of reports, perhaps including the Anaya message, led Thatcher to telephone Carrington at home and warn that the Argentine junta aimed to provoke a 'confrontation' over South Georgia Island. Around 7 a.m. on Monday 29 March, as Carrington and Thatcher met to fly from RAF Northolt, they concluded that Argentina would attempt to seize the island. In order to start building a negotiating position, they immediately asked Nott to send a nuclear-powered attack submarine to the region. He sent two, while Carrington asked for a third. The Royal Navy rejected that request, which would disrupt prior commitments to NATO. These submarines would not reach the theatre for two weeks. By 30 March, the MOD and FCO saw 'at present no sign' that Argentina intended to invade the Falkland Islands. The JIC doubted that it would do so imminently.[222] None thought an emergency was at hand. The naval attaché in Buenos Aires warned that a small Argentine invasion of East Falkland Island was possible, and asked GCHQ for any indicators of that issue. GCHQ could not confirm that danger, because no evidence supported it.[223] A matter of hours later, GCHQ was able to show that Argentine forces were bound for Port Stanley, the capital of the Falkland Islands.

The central intelligence at this point – Anaya's message – was high-level, self-evident and reflected Argentine views – but of the previous week. Carrington, Nott and Thatcher thought their actions were prudent and timely. DIS and the JIC felt no need for new estimates. Events were moving as the last estimate predicted. Unfortunately, the junta changed its mind. Again, GCHQ was the first to detect the truth. At some time on 30 March, GCHQ distributed an Argentine order that the Type 209 diesel-electric submarine *Santa Fe* sail with remarkable caution, launch a 'reconnaissance of the beach and/or disembarkation (word garbled)', and then move twenty miles east of the San Felipe (or Pembroke) lighthouse, just off Port Stanley. Obviously, the beach being reconnoitred was in the Falkland Islands.[224] This remarkable message might not have arrived until late evening on 30 March, but it would have been on a DIS desk at 0900, 31 March, alongside another one: the Argentine aircraft carrier, *Veinticinco de Mayo*, would receive special meteorological reports. On this basis, an alert DIS officer might have called the alarm several hours faster than actually occurred, though taking that action would not have changed the situation. No doubt desks were already inundated with paper. The 'beach reconnaissance' message did not mention Pembroke lighthouse: perhaps no one enquired where San Felipe was.

No one raised an alarm until late in the afternoon of 31 March, when GCHQ began a drumroll of alarming messages, collectively showing that Argentine warships would concentrate around Port Stanley on 2 April. The precise nature and sequence of reportage and analysis cannot be reconstructed. Only one, or perhaps two, messages, along with the 'beach reconnaissance' and the meteorological reports, can certainly be shown to have triggered the alarm. At 1436, GCHQ distributed a message showing that an Argentine auxiliary vessel was to take 'a position south of the Falkland Islands' and, at 1738, that 2 Marine Infantry Brigade would soon land somewhere. In the evening, but too late to shape British decisions, a cacophony of messages demonstrated that Argentina would invade the Falklands, and suggested details of the time and organisation of attack. Several messages on 31 March which cannot be timed also made that point; possibly some of these also shaped the first DIS warning, though probably not, so finely poised is the evidence.

That defence intelligence warning and key GCHQ reports reached military and diplomatic consumers just after 1800 on Wednesday 31 March. These messages, too obvious to need analysis, and strong enough to overcome the prospect of error, had among the most instantaneous and electric effects of any reports GCHQ has ever issued. While Nott was preparing a speech for the House of Commons on Britain's nuclear deterrent, aided by his Private Secretary, David Omand, DIS delivered two (or, just perhaps, three) reports from GCHQ about the Falklands, one of which was the 'beach reconnaissance' message.[225] The two men immediately recognised its meaning. They rushed to Mrs Thatcher's office at the House of Commons, followed by a stampede of ministers, officials and messengers carrying leather pouches with GCHQ reports, to discuss what she called 'this appalling piece of information'.[226]

All British calculations to date had been wrong. Argentina would seize the Falklands immediately. British authorities attempted to deter the threat, by raising the issue at the UN and asking President Reagan to warn off the leader of the Argentine junta, General Galtieri, but it was too late to matter. Britain was confronted with a choice between humiliation or war. As Thatcher recalled: 'That night no one could tell me whether we could retake the Falklands – no one. We did not know – we did not know.'[227] Nott and the DIS believed that Argentina had achieved a fait accompli to which Britain could not even respond. Ministers knew that inaction would create humiliation at home and abroad. Then, the First Sea Lord, Admiral Henry Leach – in full dress uniform – arrived in Thatcher's office unbidden, after having been detained and almost arrested by security in Parliament. He told Thatcher that Britain could send a large force to the islands quickly – and must do so, or suffer a decline in status. His assessment, drawn from instinct not intelligence – and Thatcher's nerve, spurred by outrage – drove another Reconquista.

GCHQ and the Falklands Conflict

Many decision-makers blamed Britain's inability to forestall invasion, in the words of Rear Admiral D. W. Brown, Assistant Chief of the Defence Staff (Operations), on 'an intelligence failure of the first order'. Beacham said, 'here we were badly let down'.[228] They were wrong. This was a failure of policy: neither to make the Falklands Islands population join Argentina, nor to deploy a permanent garrison able to deter attack and enable help to arrive. Neither approach was palatable before the invasion. Instead, Britain adopted a magical policy which assumed perfection both in operations and intelligence – the ability always to predict Argentine intentions in time to deploy a deterrent from the North Atlantic. Any mistake in timing could wreck this delicate hair-trigger policy. Britain made many mistakes, all of them minor. JIC's failures merely exemplified those of policy and decision-makers. On the other hand, GCHQ's performance during the crisis suggests that it would have enabled an effective response to anything but an impulsive action by Argentina, especially since ministers considered redeployment of sizable forces to the islands from the moment that they knew a crisis had opened. Only by 30 March did intelligence suggest imminent action against the Falkland Islands. Argentine authorities probably did not make that decision until then. If so, GCHQ detected that intention hours after it emerged, when Britain already was dispatching a deterrent. Conversely, even had Britain dispatched nuclear-powered attack submarines right after receiving the first *Endurance* signal, they could not have reached Stanley by 2 April. This gap was the fatal error in British assessment, foolhardy in so many ways. GCHQ performed well, and many other authorities tolerably, during the crisis. They could not save an incompetent policy.

GCHQ adjusted to these events with speed, turning *Titanic* on a tuppence, a practice in which it specialises. Before the crisis, 'good housekeeping' ensured that it was abreast of all major Argentine systems, which two linguists and traffic analysts kept on a 'care and maintenance' basis alongside other duties.[229] GCHQ did its job about Argentina better than any institution in Britain. Soon after Stanley fell, GCHQ circulated floods of deciphered Argentine traffic from high-frequency Morse, mainly naval, with less from the army and little from the air force. That pattern reflects the nature of Argentine communications which Britain could intercept, more than British success in cryptanalysis, with exceptions. Britain intercepted but could not break the communications between the garrison commander at Stanley, General Menendez, and his commanders at home. Though Argentine commands on the mainland signalled by landline, radio carried significant operational and strategic messages to forces in the Falklands, and at sea. Many of these messages – especially those of the Argentine Navy – unnecessarily addressed war plans and intentions. During the first month of the crisis, Argentine communications security was dismal. Argentine forces did not think about security until disaster struck, and then could not improve it. For Britain, the take matched Ultra at its best. Solutions were fast: during much of the crisis, on average the time between interception of encrypted traffic and dispatch to TF 317 of translated solutions was just three to eight hours.[230] As the Task Force advanced, its Sigint components intercepted voice from the islands, where, again, Argentine commanders and personnel were indiscreet. The naval Siginters received some keys to Argentine systems, but probably focused on direction-finding Argentine stations, where no other sources existed; on Argentine submarines, which were seen as a particular threat; and electronic warfare.[231]

During the campaign, DIS synthesised and distributed material under its own name. Much of it was sanitised Sigint, which decision-makers did not know. They relied more on GCHQ than they knew, which multiplies the force of their praise for it. This material reached three classes of consumer: politicians and officials; diplomats; and military and naval officers. Thatcher took her key decision – to make Argentina leave the islands through compulsion or war – without considering intelligence. Thereafter, Comint shaped the War Cabinet's diplomacy, its demands for speed in operations and its self-confidence in strategy. Politicians praised GCHQ's performance. Though most of its product came sanitised by the DIS, Carrington, Nott, Pym and Thatcher received much GCHQ material direct. Diplomats acted in the context of Comint, guided by a special series of daily highlights which the FCO had GCHQ prepare. Sigint drove the plans and actions of staff officers, military intelligence and commanders. Much Comint also went straight to SAS headquarters at Hereford, to guide its missions, which were strategic and independent, intended to cripple Argentine air power and to aid deception – successfully in both cases. GCHQ, however, provided little help for SAS attacks against Argentine aircraft on the mainland.[232]

The political significance of the crisis was obvious within GCHQ and Whitehall. Tovey noted that the special JIC meeting of 4 April was drafting a 'full blown JIC note. Its purpose is to defend ministers and indeed the intelligence community, against far-fetched accusations of "an intelligence failure"'.[233] Tovey and his colleagues thought they deserved no blame, though Z noted that questions concerning the low priority the JIC had attached to the Falkland Islands 'may be asked by those not well-disposed to it'.[234] When Thatcher established the Nicoll committee to assess British intelligence before the invasion, Tovey warned that 'repeated investigations into the efficiency of our intelligence arrangements were liable to be construed as insulting and could be highly damaging to morale'. Nicoll should 'confine himself as far as possible to looking at our end-product and to refrain from lengthy interrogations of staff who are already very hard pressed ... I have no doubt we shall emerge from this investigation with our credit if anything enhanced.'[235]

Partly for this reason, GCHQ maintained close touch with consumers, to determine their needs and to meet them. As consumers suddenly witnessed its success in achieving that aim they replied effusively. A witness of the War Cabinet meeting on 29 April told Tovey that 'all those present from the Prime Minister downwards spoke in glowing terms of the value of the Sigint contribution'. Others praised GCHQ to Tovey's face. Glover, the DCDS (I) described GCHQ as 'a service beyond all possible praise'. He had been an ardent fan of GCHQ for some time.

> But even I was amazed by the speed and remarkable efficiency
> with which you honed in on the Argentine target when the crisis
> broke. From a standing start you developed an operation whose
> breadth, relevance and immediacy was extraordinarily impressive.
> Certainly it provided me with the material I needed to brief
> both the Chiefs of Staff, and John Nott. And I believe that the
> intelligence you provided formed the base line for some of the
> most difficult decisions taken during the campaign. Without it we
> would have been blind and without it the outcome might have been
> very different. Such, if I might say so, is the measure of GCHQ's
> achievements ... Day in, day out, night in, night out, queries and
> requests were invariably received – often no doubt by tired men
> (and women), with wonderful patience and understanding.[236]

The Director General Intelligence, head of the DIS, thought Sigint was 'virtually the only hard operational intelligence that we have'. The Chief of the Defence Staff, Admiral Terence Lewin, called it '500 per cent marvellous'. Tovey noted: 'Anything I can add is liable to verge on the superfluous but this much I can say: in over thirty years' service in GCHQ I have never known us do a more thoroughly professional job or receive more well-earned compliments from those whom we serve.'[237] The Commander-in-Chief Fleet, Admiral John Fieldhouse, praised 'the tremendous value of Sigint' as a 'revelation', and recognised GCHQ's 'tremendous service' and 'priceless information'.[238]

Crisis and Recalibration

As the crisis began, Thatcher opened the vaults. GCHQ, like the fighting services, abandoned cash limits, spending whatever victory required.[239] On 5–6 April, it moved to 'get its own house in order' in order to handle 'future intercept'. GCHQ created a fusion centre, which combined sub-units from its codebreaking, intelligence and Elint sections to attack the new target: H74X, K25X and V2X. GCHQ expanded its personnel and considered how and where they should work. Z liaison must attach personnel to intelligence bodies in London and support 'an action-on component'. K might handle 'additional crisis-related in-depth analysis (up to now the main effort has been on decrypts)'; outside of periodical summaries of messages, however, this recommendation was not exercised. GCHQ must build 'some knowledge of a technical base of Argentine communications – there is little knowledge either in UK or U.S.'. Cheltenham calculated how to liaise with allies and third parties.[240] J division outlined GCHQ's technical aims:

> Our interests are two-fold. First is the need to fill out the strategic intelligence picture, both now and for the crisis period two–three weeks hence. Second (and in a way more pressing) is to provide a technical base of Comint and Elint target data on which the Navy can start to plan their tactical Sigint efforts afloat. On this they are starting almost from scratch on this target. A third consideration is that we can easily saturate transcription and processing resources if we adopted a mass vacuum cleaner approach. It all points to an intelligent and discriminating search and development effort, and this takes time, of which (despite the apparently leisurely pace of the Fleet) we may not have too much.[241]

Since this was one crisis in a minor area, resources could be borrowed from others, especially J. Ultimately, K25X, V2X and H74X had around a hundred Siginters and Elinters, and perhaps as many typists and messengers. They would 'handle' around 5,900 Comint and 900 Elint reports during the war, with other sections perhaps producing as much diplomatic intelligence.[242] GCHQ, pressed to its limits, might not have done so well during a greater crisis. The head of K division praised H's 'usual outstanding cooperation', and prior success against Argentine systems.[243] Yet H barely handled the strain, and only did so by abandoning computer and cryptanalytic work against other targets. GCHQ's product then overwhelmed the FCO. Spanish linguists were in short supply, above all in TF 317, which may have cost ships and lives. K division's experience with crisis management spurred success, alongside problems. K noted that: 'Starting from almost virtually nowhere, we built up a very creditable effort which provided a very good quick comprehensive service which received bouquets from all directions.' However, in Cheltenham's version of Maoist self-criticism, he noted, regarding himself: 'K Management ... was too slow to realise that this was, in important respects, much more like a J than a K crisis (requiring fusion and short/medium-term analysis, T/A etc, with backup overseeing distribution, clearing up loose ends, etc). We started with things K traditionally does well (quick textual reporting, essentially without (and without need of) comment or fusion), and only came to others later if at all.'[244]

As the card index and computerised ages of cryptology collided, GCHQ faced technical and organisational problems in every atom of its organisation simultaneously. A nine-to-five agency focused on eastern Europe and the Warsaw Pact – in which translators and analysts wrote reports by hand, passed them to typing pools or the Comcentre, usually for transmission within days – now confronted a war in the South Atlantic and the urgent need for speed and mass. Immediately, GCHQ communications warned: 'An Achilles Heel is signals output.' Normally, every day, the Comcentre – manned by five shifts each of thirty-eight officers and operators – rapidly transmitted large volumes of traffic, some marked 'Flash' for immediate signalling. However, the duty signals officer had to read all manuscript messages to assess legibility and action-on. The simultaneous receipt of nineteen handwritten messages in crisis overwhelmed him.

Soon, however, such loads became routine and manageable because GCHQ already had the knowledge and resources to strengthen its surge capacity, while ensuring the accuracy of every character in any message. Shifts of several officers took over action-on. Material moved through a tough system of priorities. The Comcentre rejected any manuscript reports, except on emergency issues. An improvised section of touch-typists on twenty-four-hour shifts, using IBM Selectric typewriters, put handwritten messages onto special forms, returning them to translators to ensure accuracy, and if necessary retyping them. The Comcentre fed these forms physically into an Optical Character Recognition mechanism, producing punched tape to be put into teleprinters, which obviated the need for further typing or encipherment.[245]

The sections attacking Argentine traffic boomed in size and moved to twenty-four-hour shifts. Initially swamped by reports, the newly created Elint section V2X first adopted two eight-hour shifts, and then three on 18 April, when acquisition reached maturity and the Task Force entered dangerous waters. V2X developed an 'Elint/EW data base', which automatically identified and collated all reports on every source of emission. Cryptanalysts spent much time 'answering a deluge of questions from an assortment of LONDON customers'. They mastered changes in cryptosystems, new computer programmes for cryptanalysis, and frequent 'hardware/software faults', one caused by torrential rain in Cheltenham. On 28–29 April, as fleets clashed in the South Atlantic, the Hectra decryption programme crashed, eliminating Comint; heroic efforts created an entirely new database, focused purely on the Falklands, within eight hours.[246]

A secondment of most Spanish linguists in GCHQ, originally over twenty but perhaps rising past thirty, handled the explosion in Comint. Intercept operators and traffic analysts switched from other targets, and learned new ones. They reconstructed Argentine radio networks, determined the most valuable and vulnerable links, and attacked them. Locations were represented on a paper map – not very different to those paper plots used by the London Air Defence Area in 1917–18 – yet this was the first Sigint war fought without card indices. No index existed when the crisis began. Material was entered on an electronic database. This 'data-base interrogation system known as FINDERS KEEPERS' – by implication more powerful than any GCHQ had used before and perhaps its first – enabled analysts to enter search terms for given periods into perhaps the first widespread production-branch IT collaboration system used by GCHQ. The Time Sharing Option (TSO) enabled multiple users to interrogate the Sigint database. 'This helped greatly to save time when answering customer queries, and remained in use for some years after the crisis was over.'[247]

Production was automatic and industrialised. At the time, Michael Herman, head of J and V at various stages of the war, wrote that:

> crisis analysis and reporting is a difficult, worrying and exhausting
> activity. Part of the key to doing it well is the right balance
> between seeking perfection (which we must strive towards …), and
> recognising that we can never achieve it. We must guard against
> mistakes but they are going to happen; the important thing is to
> learn from them and not be rattled; the only inadmissible error is
> to play safe and do nothing … it seems to pay to spend a lot of time
> getting the paper handling and record keeping routing as good as
> possible, simply to reduce the chances of error when people are
> keeping watches and are tired and under stress.[248]

Later, Herman recollected that Siginters had 'no real idea of priorities' for consumers, who never defined them. 'You have a certain amount of material, you whizz it through to [RN Headquarters] Northwood as fast as you can' without spending time on analysis, which personnel had no time to do. Codebreakers followed the principle of 'doing the plain things well as the priority, not trying to be too clever'. GCHQ 'rediscovered' the methods of Bletchley's Hut 8, producing verbatim translations of text and sending them straight to consumers, with the usual annotations as in any textual report. 'K Division product was largely though not entirely a decrypt reporter.'[249]

Morale – a 'Falklands Spirit' – was high. At GCHQ, as across the country as a whole, people thought this a 'good' war, where Britain rescued Britons from aggression. When Herman 'asked an elderly lady in V why she was still sorting signals late after normal closing', she replied, 'I'm doing it for my son – he's in the Task Force.'[250] Another veteran remembers a cryppie running into the codebreaking office, H74X, during the early hours, bicycle clips on trousers, to test an idea that arrived in his sleep. That spirit eased organisational frictions. Initially, night shifts were established in H offices, because cryptanalysts could not walk down the Oakley hill constantly with solutions. Instead, linguists crawled up and down at dusk and dawn from their offices, working aids in hand. Messengers carried incoming signals up the hill. The 'crisis crypt/reporting party' was based in Spur 9 of C Annexe, an H space, 'because of the proximity of machines for H usage and the convenience for K reporters'. Pole Star terminals were added to enable the use of Hectra. Spur 9, initially without secure links outside the building, was soon connected with SUKLO Washington by STS, Northwood and the National Security Operations Center (NSOC) at NSA by Brahms. H74X, K25X and the T/A and map-plotting staff shared an open-plan office. Because of inadequate space, the Elint office, V2X, and a reading room stood across the hall.[251] Even that small split damaged liaison, preventing Elint from being automatically displayed on the map serviced by T/A and Comint, but rather first on a separate map of its own. Since Spur 9 was outside the pneumatic tube system, messengers ferried signals between the shift party and the W Comcentre. Basic kit stood in offices working on a nine-to-five basis. Triumph occurred when the night shift gained access to the library and a photocopier in KHQ, the main intelligence office. Typists and messengers also adopted twenty-four-hour shifts. Initially, eleven personnel from H division worked the shifts, soon reaching thirty after volunteers were trained 'in the systems pertinent to the crisis'. The intelligence section, K25X, had five shifts each of four people, some temporarily seconded from J, which also handled ancillary tasks. Eight sailors were seconded as transcribers and analysts.

The T/A party, initially four, reached six. Its work was aided by material seized from the Argentine submarine *Santa Fe*, captured when Britain retook South Georgia Island on 25 April. After a missile launched from a Wasp helicopter carried by HMS *Endurance* penetrated its conning tower, the crew raced to beach the *Santa Fe*, which lay ashore for a day. Its cryptosystems were ditched at sea but British forces captured many 'valuable documents', including recent operational messages and technical and procedural signals matters, valuable at a time when the Argentine navy's 'call signs were [sic] not understood'.[252] As Royal Navy officers noted sniffily, the boat was 'in poor condition before attack, dirty, scruffy, haphazardly stowed'.[253]

An around-the-clock effort between intercept and cryptanalytic units, and military headquarters, caused surges in new forms of traffic, and changes in processes and communications. GCHQ filtered transmission of irrelevant Comint and Elint to Northwood, which did the same for TF 317. Northwood communicated with TF 317 via a tight bottleneck of off-line cypher systems and narrow bandwidths. At one point, GCHQ feared that TF 317 might receive just 600–1,000 groups an hour, though that level rose enough to enable effective operational and intelligence communications.[254] Fortunately, when testing the shipborne intercept/DF system Outboard in 1981, HMS *Hermes* received an RN INTEL set, a dedicated Comint channel on the ship's Satcom system, which, the Fleet Comint officer said, 'is like having Christmas every day'.[255] Every other British vessel except *Hermes*, however, transmitted intercepted Argentine material back to GCHQ through extraordinarily cumbersome procedures, further slowed by the focus on radio silence. Improperly transmitted traffic produced a 'black hole' with Hectra.[256]

Intercepts from high-frequency stations moved through normal channels to GCHQ. There, H division attacked the traffic and sent messages to analysts, which were worked on and forwarded to consumers. Each message was recopied and resent at every link. Comint and T/A reports at GCHQ were written by hand, typewritten, proofed and walked down the hill to the Comcentre, where they were sent to Northwood, which retyped the messages it sent to the fleet by satellite. Northwood, suddenly GCHQ's main consumer, received and assessed all political and military intelligence, becoming the operational interface between the JIC and military operations. Northwood directly gave TF 317 all tactical material, including 'positional info. What where whither when of Arg naval forces', while sanitising all strategic and political intelligence.[257] Intercepts from the Task Force were returned by satellite to Northwood, sent to GCHQ, and returned as intelligence. Midway through the war, GCHQ adopted the computerised system, New Moon, by which dedicated typists released reports from K to customers including Northwood, overcoming bottlenecks at the Comcentre by enabling the elimination of one repetition of reportage. New Moon sped the delivery of messages by some ninety minutes, and eased the overload, especially for priority items.[258] GCHQ officers deployed to Northwood – GCO (N) – worked shifts to liaise between these organisations and handled the key questions of 'action-on': another twenty-four-hour rota of officers at K handled queries from Whitehall. Task Force commander Admiral Sandy Woodward and selected officers on *Hermes* and *Fearless* received Comint up to Category 3, selected by Northwood and signalled over Comint channels.[259]

Meanwhile, the Task Force received a capability to pick up signals in-theatre. The Royal Navy provided three sets of printer equipment and five 'Chandos packages' – Sigint suites, with two HF and two VHF receivers and an Elint position. *Hermes*, *Fearless* and *Coventry* were the main platforms, *Sheffield* and *Endurance* secondary ones. *Hermes* carried five communications technicians, two interpreters, a Chandos suite and an intercept equipment tailored to a specific Argentine system, plus a teleprinter facility to send and receive Sigint information securely. *Fearless* and *Coventry* each carried four communication technicians, one interpreter and a Chandos set.

Sigint proved a jinx for ships. *Coventry*, *Sheffield* and the supply ship *Atlantic Conveyor* were all sunk carrying GCHQ kit. In fact, Argentine forces destroyed 20 per cent of the Sigint equipment sent to TF 317, without killing any personnel.[260] The Task Force had sixteen naval Siginters, including four RAF Spanish linguists, ten army Siginters, aided by RAF linguists. Unfortunately, many of these linguists were rusty, or worse. Few could handle tactical voice communications – astonishingly, given the services' focus on the medium. Even worse, perhaps, the eight best RAF translators, originally assigned to Gibraltar by the Chief of the Air Staff (CAS) despite protests from RAF Sigint authorities, reached TF 317 only on 25 May.[261] Collectively, these personnel provided useful material for the fleet, but little material for land forces, or against air forces.

Approaching a New Age of Sigint
GCHQ was the first codebreaking agency to confront a seismic shift in public attitudes towards secrecy in war. During a parliamentary debate after the Argentine invasion, Ted Rowlands, the Labour spokesman for Foreign Affairs, said:

> I have great difficulty in understanding how the intelligence failed.
> Our intelligence in Argentina was extremely good. That is why
> we took action in 1977. We found out that certain attitudes and
> approaches were being formed. I cannot believe that the quality
> of our intelligence has changed. Last night the Secretary of State
> for Defence asked 'How can we read the mind of the enemy?'
> I shall make a disclosure. As well as trying to read the mind of the
> enemy, we have been reading its telegrams for many years. I am sure
> that many sources are available to the Government, and I do not
> understand how they failed to anticipate some of the dangers that
> suddenly loomed on the horizon.[262]

What Rowlands called 'a very personal emotional statement' shattered prior standards of discretion about Comint by politicians.[263] Rowlands' loathing of the government's failures to deter Argentine aggression – which he believed a Labour government had managed successfully during the crisis of 1976–77 – dovetailed with the Labour Party's partisan assault on the Iron Lady. He compromised British intelligence at a time when war was likely: perhaps not the best moment to remind foreign states, especially one's enemy, to mind their codes and cyphers.

Rowlands' statement might be expected to alarm Argentine diplomatic and military authorities, yet he was not publicly admonished for the act. Meanwhile, during the campaign, the press published accurate accounts of military planning. The problem was not so much leaks as reporters adding facts one by one, and using their presence in the MOD to squeeze confirmation. Retired officers, commenting on television and in the press, analysed issues precisely as the MOD did; some of that speculation was bound to be accurate. Leading British and American newspapers published several stories which either revealed GCHQ's capabilities against Argentine cryptosystems, hinted at them, or even cited its reports. The veteran A. R. V. Cooper called these actions 'putting good copy before the national interest, which is irresponsible at best and treasonable at worst'.[264] The British Defence Staff Washington emphasised, 'how Americans in positions of responsibility speak with the most remarkable freedom to press enquiries even on sensitive subjects. Thus investigative reporting on intelligence activities and cooperation is not likely to be damped down.'[265] Nor did this occur in Britain. Robert Armstrong feared that articles in the *Sunday Times* on 18 April 1982 'enable the Argentines to speculate knowledgably about our intentions and possibly to take deceptive measures themselves. In so far as methods are concerned the damage to our capabilities, though possibly not immediate, is likely to be widespread and long lasting.' These stories included material that must have come from officials, whom he asked 'to deal with all questions on intelligence matters in the only approved manner: that is, by refusing to comment'.[266] The Chief of the Defence Staff (CDS), Terence Lewin, told the Chiefs of Staff: 'If DCDS (I) is to give us a worthwhile intelligence brief, he must continue to quote from intercepts,' which must not be leaked.[267] Some members of the MOD accused Defence Secretary Nott of leaking material when he briefed backbenchers, though Lewin exonerated him.[268] Whitehall pressed media outlets to avoid 'speculation about future operational plans and interception of Argentine communications'.[269] Neither effort met with success.

GCHQ believed that Argentina could easily change its procedures in order to block penetration. Argentina 'applied greatly increased protective COMSEC procedures' which caused 'some delay in our ability to exploit their traffic', yet these changes failed to achieve that end. On 22 April, H division reported that 'difficult' problems affected some material, but 'there was no specific move by AR to change their procedures in reaction to press reports etc'. In any case, a new age dawned in the relationship between Sigint, state and society. Journalists had broad access to Comint from many officials. They and politicians felt free to discuss it in war and were not stopped from doing so, despite the risk to lives. Crypto went public amidst a war. And there it has stayed ever since.

Nor was this the only change in the practices of Sigint. During 1982, that art stood at the dawn of a revolution which converted C3I (command, control, communications and intelligence) into C4ISR (command, control, communications, computers, intelligence, surveillance and reconnaissance), and enabled the second age of Sigint. Britain was the first nation to enter this new world in warfare, largely through aid from the United States which was far further ahead in technical terms. New forms of fusion between sensors and Sigint from across the world, and within warships, reshaped combinations of intelligence, electronic counter measures (ECM), electronic warfare (EW) and operations. Data link systems gave every ship within a fleet the material from all sensors on every other one, and let national intelligence agencies automatically service fleets at sea. In 1982, however, Royal Navy equipment could not exploit most of the latter opportunities, nor all of the former ones. Consideration was given to the use of a pioneering concept and system, Special Support Activity (SSA), which gave commanders 'precisely tailored real time intelligence support to a tactical operation', through powerful modes of data retrieval and display, and 'careful' and centralised selection and synthesis of reports, transmitted through special kit and personnel. This would 'ensure that the intelligence support to the Task Force Commander was not only timely but was adequately packaged and tailored to meet his needs, and that as early as possible the controlling headquarters should somehow simultaneously be able to "see" the information that was available to the task force, given particularly the close control that was likely to be exercised by London over this operation'.[270]

GCHQ longed to use SSA but decided not to, because of its lack of experience with it, inadequate time to install the system on TF 317 and train personnel, and fears that SSA would swamp the Royal Navy's C3I, which 'are not accustomed to full service of relatively raw Sigint'.[271] This calculation was correct: the Royal Navy could not use SSA during 1982. Had it tried, any attempt to suddenly incorporate such a new system in communication, organisation and command would have degraded intelligence, which worked well enough in any case. In 1982, a C3I system more like that of 1916 perhaps worked better than the

1982 versions of C4ISR could have done. As K division noted, a crisis was not 'the time to create (or even use in hot blood for the first time) new channels of command and consultation ... we need to use the existing channels with which people are familiar, with reinforcement if necessary'.[272]

During the war, consumers were positive about Elint, but less so afterwards.[273] Thus, perhaps referring to occasional pieces of Elint suggesting that Argentine submarines might be out at sea, Glover held that 'on balance ELINT was for the DIS something of a mixed blessing, producing almost as many spurious reports as it did reliable ones'.[274] Fieldhouse thought Elint 'relatively minor' as a source compared to Comint.[275] These criticisms have force, but the critics still placed Elint second as a source, overshadowed only by Comint, which Herman described as being of 'marvellous value'. He emphasised how V, handling 'tactical real-time Elint' for the first time, conducted 'a tremendous feat of improvisation' that achieved 'colossal success'. Elint provided much valuable material on Argentina, without 'detailed steerage and feedback; and no one is going to be able to write thank-you letters. In the fog of war we are never going to know in advance what are the vital items. We just have to proceed largely on a basis of reporting everything that we think may be useful, as quickly and accurately as possible, in the conviction that it may be quite vital to someone.'[276] This approach was defensible. None was better at the time, but for consumers encountering Elint for the first time it may have been confusing.

These developments in Elint favoured Britain, but also gave Argentina its greatest intelligence successes against Britain, and significant ones at that. By tracking the feed from British satellite communications to TF 317, the Argentine air force guided its sole long-range reconnaissance asset, a Boeing 707 aircraft without Sigint capability, to follow the Royal Navy south. That knowledge was unactionable, though the Task Force monitored the menace of ambush posed by submarines. The Argentines abandoned these missions after abortive attacks by Harriers. More significantly, by detecting the take-offs and landings of Harriers, Argentine radars at Port Stanley located *Hermes* and *Invincible*. Thus, Argentine aircraft, either land- or sea-based, could theoretically hit British carriers even 700 miles from the mainland. Britain understood this vulnerability, which forced caution on carriers and restricted the time Harriers could spend on missions – so making Argentine airstrikes easier on British warships to the westward. These radars also provided the only early warning of airborne Harriers to Argentine aircraft attacking around the islands. British V-bombers – based on Ascension Island and flying 'Black Buck' missions over distances of 7,000 miles, which required refuelling eleven different times – sought to destroy this radar system with missiles homing in on radar signals, but failed. The Argentines detected these flights, probably through Elint or traffic analysis, understood their aim, and simply closed down their radar during the period of operations, which aided Britain marginally. This radar system, Argentina's greatest strength in intelligence, cramped British sea power as much as Argentine warships.

The General Belgrano

Initially, Comint was the only source on the Falklands crisis, and remained the main one for operations. Eventually, other sources provided key material. GCHQ guided SSNs onto Argentine warships, which they shadowed through sonar and observation. RAF imagery and Sigint flights around the islands occasionally covered most areas. Harriers provided tactical intelligence. The SAS and Special Boat Squadron – good consumers of Sigint and Britain's best national source for intelligence collection after Sigint – provided superb material from the islands, including around Port Stanley.

The British campaign had two phases: southward deployment of warships and aircraft, mostly based at or supplied through Ascension Island; and invasion of the Falkland Islands by ground forces, aided by aircraft and warships. The Royal Navy headquarters at Northwood and its adjunct, the RAF's 18 Air Group, commanded all warships and aircraft assigned to the fleet. In order to use intelligence effectively, the navy and RAF had to cooperate – which historically they had often found difficult – and to pass reports and orders forward over thin communications links. Fortunately, long experience at Northwood and friendship between commanders eased relations between the two services; their standard procedures for reporting forward met operational needs, and signals proved able to carry that material. Military customers received masses of Sigint, which aided war at sea, and invasion of an island – but not its conquest.

Meanwhile, Britain warned that it would sink any Argentine warship within an Exclusion Zone, 200 miles in radius, around the Falkland Islands. Initially, British military intelligence thought the Argentine navy competent but since 'many ships, particularly the aircraft carrier, have serviceability problems', it would behave cautiously. 'National pride' would drive the navy to keep a 'substantial' fleet at sea, on the 'pretext' of defending the mainland, but it would avoid the Exclusion Zone and, implicitly, conflict with British adversaries.[277] Though some later assessments admitted that the Argentine navy might fight, most concluded, in Glover's words, 'they would be unlikely to risk their surface fleet in a match which they must reckon they must lose'.[278] National chauvinism affected these assessments; Sigint corrected this view, and showed that Argentine forces, especially the navy, grossly overestimated their position. They misconstrued British professionalism and determination and their own capabilities. Argentine forces did not believe that Britain could retake the Falklands. The Argentine navy told commanders that the international political situation was 'becoming complicated', yet 'the British force is neither ready nor trained for crossing the South Atlantic'; while Thatcher's opponents 'are still reacting strongly'. Even if 'an armed clash occurred, the balance would weigh in our favour'. Argentine naval officers reported an 'extremely effective' performance in their first ever naval/air exercise, which somehow they imagined would translate to success in war, and outlined their tactical preparations in detail. After a visit to the Falklands, the Argentine air force commander found morale of 'all personnel … of great comfort'.[279] Argentine commanders misunderstood how a good fleet could handle the South Atlantic, and how the Royal Marines might conduct amphibious assault. The Argentine army thought that its defences were good, but they collapsed immediately when hit. Only as TF 317 neared the islands did the Argentines begin to exhibit alarm and understand the true military balance. Once the shooting started, Argentine forces rapidly improved the quality of their system for intelligence and operations, especially in the air, but too late to matter.

GCHQ also showed that the Argentine navy aimed to fight aggressively, if naively. The Royal Navy grasped enemy intentions and deployments perfectly, and its capabilities just well enough. It used knowledge effectively against an enemy inferior in power and intelligence, yet still dangerous. This pre-landings phase perhaps led

British admirals to overestimate their invulnerability and the power of their intelligence – both matters that would be shaken with the loss of HMS *Sheffield.*

By 22 April, GCHQ thought 'as yet there was no indication of the AR battle plan or indeed their intentions'.[280] The situation quickly changed. Solutions of Argentine naval traffic illustrated that it aimed to fight the Royal Navy. None suggested any intention for compromise or to avoid action.[281] GCHQ also penetrated the Argentine plan of attack. Argentine forces fell into three groups: the aged aircraft carrier *Veinticinco de Mayo* and three destroyers to the north; a body of three corvettes; and the *General Belgrano* and two destroyers to the south. A fourth loose collection of spy ships disguised as fishing vessels, including the *Narwal,* sailed to the east of the islands to locate the Task Force. Destroyers and corvettes carried Exocet missiles, able to sink a carrier. When Argentine warships moved to meet the Royal Navy on 24 April, their orders were alarming: to advance on the Exclusion Zone without entering it, in 'a "wait and see" attitude' to threaten the navy, 'assess the situation before the decision to use force' and 'to make it difficult for the opponent to act by dividing his effort by means of a threat from different directions'. They should prepare an ambush. Warships must maintain tight communications and full fuel loads, 'the concept being to use them to the maximum of their ability with the minimum of forewarning'. Argentine forces should 'operate as a dissuasive element in the region'. However, 'if an escalation of the situation leads to a generalised conflict', warships and land-based aviation must 'intercept and/or neutralise' the Task Force through 'the mission of force as a whole, by acting in as coordinated a way as possible with the other groups' – a coordinated assault by land- and sea-based aircraft, followed closely by warships carrying Exocet missles, from many vectors at once.[282]

Between 28 April and 2 May, just before the attack on *Belgrano,* GCHQ gave its consumers interceptions of increasingly warlike Argentine orders. On 29 April, the Argentine naval command told commanders: 'The lack of progress in the diplomatic negotiations does not permit any expectation of immediate change in the existing situation' while 'a continuation of British offensive action is foreseeable'. Argentine ships would penetrate the Exclusion Zone in order to test British responses, following its prior offensive plans, 'use of arms without restriction'. On 1 May, the Argentine command gave all warships 'freedom of action', and ordered 'commencement of offensive operations'. *Veinticinco de Mayo* would 'deploy by night to a favourable position in order to launch a daytime air attack on units detected' through its own air reconnaissance. 'This movement will be carried out during the night, keeping one's distance from the enemy in order to minimise risks of a night air attack, in order to subsequently initiate an attack at first light.' The corvette group would assault 'units damaged by the air attack and any other dispersed units'. The *Belgrano* group would hit British warships with missiles. 'Attacks should only be made on targets when conditions are favourable, taking into account the threat from the air.' Every Argentine warship must launch an early reconnaissance and unleash 'a massive attack on the surface units before they withdraw'.[283] These plans were academic, but not unachievable. If they worked, Argentina would win the war, and Britain cease to be a reckonable power.

As the fleets closed, this knowledge of Argentine plans alarmed as well as assisted the Royal Navy. Intelligence focused on finding 'the Argentinean Aircraft Carrier Group' so British SSNs could locate and, if necessary, destroy it.[284] Although GCHQ and Royal Navy submarines frequently tracked *Veinticinco de Mayo*, often its position, course and speed were unknown. The combination of its speed, the range of its aircraft, and the guidance of Neptune tracking aircraft endangered British carriers. On 27–28 April, the CNS Admiral Leach warned Chiefs of Staff that *Veinticinco de Mayo* had mounted five Super Etendard aircraft with Exocet missiles. 'The 500 nautical miles operating range of Super Etendards would, once they were embarked, make it very difficult to determine when the threat would materialise; it was therefore essential to neutralise that threat from the outset. The safety of our own ships required the ability for immediate pre-emptive action once attack was threatened.' *Veinticinco de Mayo* had to be destroyed whenever possible at sea, or warned of this potential fate if it left port.[285]

Leach marginally overstated the danger. Argentine Neptune aircraft did guide the attack on *Sheffield*, but then became unoperational, replaced by C-130 Hercules with unsatisfactory performance. Limited catapult capability had prevented the placing of Super Etendards on *Veinticinco de Mayo*, which were replaced by seven A-4Q Skyhawks with half the range and less punch. Against this, the Royal Navy was not yet aware of how detectable it was at range. Harriers had to fly combat air patrols to protect the fleet. The Argentine radars at Port Stanley regularly located British carriers by picking up the aircraft operating from them, though perhaps their reports were poorly integrated with Argentine naval intelligence. Yet if these radars found the Task Force 200 miles to the east, while *Veinticinco de Mayo* was 200 miles offshore, its aircraft might strike British carriers within ninety minutes. One lucky hit could deliver Argentine victory.

Leach was correct to claim that *Veinticinco de Mayo* gave Argentina a small but real chance of victory. He understood the danger of underestimating an enemy: Leach had served in the Royal Navy's Force Z during 1941, where his father had died on the new battleship, HMS *Prince of Wales*, sunk by Japanese bombers. His warning clears the Royal Navy from any charge of underestimating the foe: its errors of assessment, however great, were on the complex interaction between several untested weapons systems.

The Chiefs of Staff split over Leach's demands, but the War Cabinet authorised it, driven by Comint and a sense of danger. This debate and Sigint both shaped British decisions during the abortive Argentine ambush of 30 April–2 May. Early on 2 May, the Royal Navy lost contact with *Veinticinco de Mayo*, which Woodward feared had penetrated the submarine screen. He was right – it had. Following its orders precisely, the *Veinticinco de Mayo* prepared a Skyhawk strike on British carriers, which weather conditions prevented. When detected by a Harrier, the Argentine carrier withdrew temporarily towards the mainland. Meanwhile, to the south, the British SSN HMS *Conqueror* had the *General Belgrano* in sight, but believed it might easily lose her. Like the northern half of the pincer, the *Belgrano* was withdrawing temporarily, albeit in order to strike again. Given the risk, and after consulting the War Cabinet, Fieldhouse ordered *Conqueror* to sink *Belgrano*, which it did with two Second World War-vintage Mark 8 torpedoes. Tragically, while *Conqueror* was ordered to withdraw, and did so, *Belgrano*'s destroyer escorts not unreasonably assumed that *Conqueror* was still nearby and could sink any vessels attempting rescue. The escorts thus refused to try, which magnified the loss of life from *Belgrano*. Probably they could have rescued most if not all of those who died.

These reports justified the attack on the *Belgrano*, a classic counter-ambush of an ambush. Good Sigint well used, however, had perverse consequences. Without wider knowledge of this source, the attack seemed fishy – anyone hostile to British policy could claim it stank. Britain had warned that it would attack any Argentine warship threatening its forces, and also any entering the Exclusion Zone. *Belgrano* entered that zone to ambush the Task Force, commanding destroyers mounting Exocet missiles, but was sunk outside that zone as it withdrew to prepare another attack. That fact complicated public understanding of events. Britain had overemphasised the issue of the Exclusion Zone compared to that of the general threat posed by the Argentine fleet wherever it might be. Indeed, on 27–28 April, General Bramall rejected a pre-emptive strike on *Veinticinco de Mayo* at sea without prior, specific and public warning that it would be sunk on sight. On 1 May, the Foreign Secretary, Francis Pym, warned that such an immediate public warning would 'immeasurably' strengthen such an action'.[286] Civilians and opinion-formers across the world also underrated the Argentine navy, and therefore the warlike necessity of British action. The action could easily be presented as an unnecessary and unprovoked assault, with nefarious motives – to scupper a compromise pursued by Peru. Yet any such military action must necessarily disrupt diplomacy, since these spheres intersected. Both sides made diplomacy an adjunct to war, and display of force a tool of policy. Many people sought to mediate; the Peruvian proposal arrived after the fleet engagement began, and Britain took it more seriously than Argentina did. Any British response to danger must seem bad when based on intelligence it could not report without losing the source.

The British government declined to justify this act by publishing Sigint – it understood very well the centrality of the source. Indeed, the first official statement on the topic was intended precisely to draw attention away from the role of Sigint in the sinking of the *Belgrano*.[287] Nott claimed that it was sunk while advancing to attack Task Force 317, and because that act had been detected. Unfortunately, because the MOD did not know what had happened, Nott's statement was erroneous. After the war, these errors became public, through leaks by the civil servant Clive Ponting. He knew about the role of Sigint in the sinking of the *Belgrano*, but did not leak material on it, presumably to protect the source. Together, these actions enabled conspiracy theories to flourish, crippling understanding of these issues for thirty years, until Lawrence Freedman published parts of the Sigint record in his official history of the Falklands conflict.

This action was justifiable but eroded support abroad, except in the key quarter: Washington. After the *Belgrano* was sunk, Alexander Haig said that if any further British attacks occurred, 'US opinion, and for that matter Western opinion more generally, might become less favourable toward [the UK]. People might say we were overreacting.' Nicholas Henderson, the British ambassador, retorted that, 'according to information he [Haig] would have seen, the Argentineans had ordered three frigates to attack the *Hermes* and the carrier had been given instructions to attack British ships. It could not therefore be said that the Argentineans were behaving peacefully and that it was only us who were prepared for continued action.'[288]

GCHQ Comint prevented members of the Reagan administration from trying to use the sinking of the *Belgrano* to discredit Britain, or micromanage its policy – rather, the reverse. Similarly, GCHQ Sigint sapped Haig's attempts to convince Whitehall of 'a degree of Soviet involvement and/or interest' above that accepted by American or British analysts, or his 'claims to have evidence (known to no one else) of the emergence of a 'moderate centre' in Argentine politics'.[289]

To San Carlos Sound

The sinking of the *General Belgrano* transformed the war. Thereafter, the Argentine navy specialised in study of the mainland shore. The Royal Navy stood off the Falklands, guarding against attack and preparing for amphibious assault. GCHQ shaped its success in both areas. Yet until the end of the war, the MOD feared that the Argentine navy might come out and somehow win. On 11 May, the CDS was informed: 'Argentine Appreciation?? Time beginning to run out to attack UK amphibious/logistic group before it RVs with main task force – must commence attacks shortly?'[290] This risk was overstated, but not impossible. By any conventional standard, TF 317 had far too few aircraft and surface warships to defend two carriers or an amphibious assault from Argentine air and submarine attack, let alone these three tasks at once. GCHQ simplified the problem. As Fieldhouse wrote after the war:

Exploitation at the strategic level was of the utmost value to me personally and to the Task Group Commanders, revealing the changing political and military attitudes of the Junta and of senior Argentine commanders, their frustrations, dwindling morale, internal dissent and most importantly their will to fight. It revealed a very different story to that being broadcast to the world from Buenos Aires, and gave a vital insight into the likely intentions of the forces they commanded. It was also invaluable in our assessment of the Argentine ORBAT and of the effectiveness of their efforts to buy more military equipment. With the benefit of this wide ranging information, I and my subordinate commanders were able to plan with increased confidence ... At the tactical level, COMINT on slow moving targets such as ships and of the Argentine Fleet and Submarine Broadcasts, in particular, allowed CTG 317.8 [task force commander] to conserve assets, bias his disposition towards AAW (anti-aircraft warfare), rather than ASW (anti-submarine warfare) at a vital time, and was a highly important compensator for his lack of surveillance assets. It also was a key factor in the dispositions of our submarines.[291]

In other words, GCHQ guided the posture of TF 317 and overcame its lack of warships and aircraft. It prevented waste of TF 317's scarce escorts, and heightened the certainty that British SSNs would kill enemy warships which attempted to sail. At the end of the war, the Task Force's commander, Sandy Woodward, valued Sigint as equivalent to two SSNs and six frigates – almost 20 per cent of his fleet – without which invasion would have failed.[292] Meanwhile, Sigint guided the destruction of Argentine assets at sea, especially Elint surveillance ships such as *Narwal*, which might aid air strikes. Northwood constantly had specific requests for GCHQ. For example, on 14 May, during an SAS raid against Pebble Island which might have caused a major reaction, Northwood tasked GCHQ 'for signs of air attack being prepared/launched at first light assumption that *Hermes* etc are still in same area. Note that details of Skyhawk attack were noted in material from this source.' Two weeks later, Northwood asked GCHQ to study 'patterns of activity' of the Argentine radars at Stanley, to determine the best 'time frame' for a Black Buck attack.[293] GCHQ derived its own priorities – for example, making submarine broadcasts 'flash priority'.[294]

Military planners emphasised the need to collect 'tactical intelligence' for invasion.[295] 'It goes without saying, also, that intelligence on Argentinean equipment, strength, activity and disposition of forces will be a high priority requirement for the commander of the Task Force in planning his options ... especially ... in preparing for the insertion of Special Forces.'[296] Planners assumed that SAS, SBS or aerial reconnaissance would meet this need. Though they provided useful material, the best source was Comint. It captured all elements of the Argentine order of battle on the islands and it provided an excellent grasp of Argentine perceptions, including its rank-ordered views of likely British actions and the danger they posed.[297] Panicked by a growing sense of their own vulnerability, Argentine commanders on the Falklands demanded help.[298] The Argentine air force would intervene, but not the navy. Argentine forces were absent from San Carlos Sound (where military logic suggested Britain should land), and were instead divided into immobile pockets, unable to effectively counter-attack or cooperate.

Any sign of special forces or RAF raids on mainland airbases alarmed Argentina.[299] Here Comint may have shaped action and effect. Britain considered but abandoned an elaborate global deception plan aimed at passing material to Argentine intelligence in order to draw aircraft and warships away from the Falklands.[300] Still, it sought to divert forces from the target, through leaks to diplomats or journalists. This campaign shaped press reports and SAS actions, suggesting that Britain might attack other parts of the islands, or the northern or southern edges of the Argentine mainland, and mentioning every possible target save San Carlos Sound. In particular, during the nine days before the counter-invasion, actions by helicopter, special forces, electronic emissions and the 'leak[ing of] spoof area of operations to locals' in Port Stanley built the credibility of a 'spoof beach'. On D-Day, 'dummy para drop and radar echo multiplication to simulate helo assault' occurred there.

As ever, judging the effect of deception is hard because it works by reinforcing perceptions rather than creating them. In this case, perhaps the best judgement is that deception was effective, but unnecessary. Comint, aided by the SAS and SBS, shaped the selection of the target by showing that few Argentine forces stood at San Carlos Sound, or were likely to move there. As in the fight against Nazi Germany during 1943–44, Comint enabled Britain to monitor the effect of this campaign, and learn enemy intentions. On 16 May, GCU Northwood noted: 'Mention of San Carlos in 3/AA/98444 caused problems today. MGRM [Major General Royal Marines, the commander of the land element, Jeremy Moore] believes that although something has aroused ARG suspicions there does not appear to be evidence of detection of patrols. 2. Pending discussions, planned insertions/extractions were postponed in the Ajax and San Carlos areas but decision has been taken to go ahead with plan laid down. Useful info contained in above report will obviously be now be taken into account.'[301]

More broadly, Comint showed that Argentine commanders had no idea where Britain would land. It also noted that many Mirage aircraft, a large part of a declining fleet, were committed to territories too far away to interfere in the Falklands theatre. Most or all of this deployment, however, reflected an effort by the Argentine air force to conserve and salvage its scarce assets, paralleled by the Argentine navy's concern with Chilean forces and concentration around Tierra del Fuego. Though Chile was a rival, this focus conveniently saved the Argentine fleet from destruction and left the air force to defend the Falklands. As the British embassy in Chile noted: 'everything has to be seen against background that as a traditionally peacetime force, each of armed forces has regarded the others as rivals for slice of annual budgetary financial cake in order to keep up amount of men equipment and thus share of influence of balance in military/political power play. Each service is thus desperate to avoid loss of equipment in current conflict knowing how difficult it may subsequently be to regain former position of influence for lack of ability to resupply, and each is ready to launch accusations at any moment of being forced to lose e.g. aircraft or ships so to benefit the other.'[302]

On 20 May, GCU Northwood reported:

> 1. H Hour was formally announced as 210630Z. Support vessels will start moving into Falkland Sound from 202359Z onwards and various direct actions by SAS/SBS already on Falklands will take place over next 24 hours to create confusion/diversions. Main amphibious landing will take place from 211130Z onwards in the San Carlos area.

2. For the first few hours after the landing it will be important still to disguise from the Args the scale of the operation. It has been agreed that key personnel may be told the full story but that they should be asked to treat the release of any information in the same manner as embarked press, i.e. that initial reports should indicate another series of softening-up landings (like Pebble Island) with suggestions that what started as a raid is developing into a major assault when it has become obvious.

3. As far as tasking is concerned main priorities are:

A. Any Elint indications of impending air attack (this I believe will be confined to detections of Neptune and poss C130 surveillance activity) which may be used to direct attack A/C onto Blue targets.

B. Any Comint reflections of A/C movements real or intended into or within the operational area.

C. Any Comint or Elint reflections of movements of major surface or submarine forces.[303]

As Britain landed men and kit, Sigint could not help against air attack which, after the sinking of HMS *Sheffield*, GCHQ called 'our single biggest intelligence gap'.[304] Glover later noted: 'Air to air, air to ground and Air Force command communications remained a closed book.'[305] Planners knew that invasion would cost ships and lives; Britain could not stop air attack, merely try to contain damage and beat the threat slowly. Argentine aircraft did not need elaborate communications to attack targets in a known location, but as ever, stereotyped signals accompanied air strikes, and opened opportunities for Sigint. GCHQ worked fast, but any problem with processing hampered its use for tactical purposes.

On 8 June 1982, GCHQ produced much material about the Argentine attack on British landing ships *Sir Galahad* and *Sir Tristram* offloading infantry at Bluff Cove near Port Stanley, which was processed far faster than was usual for Ultra, yet still too late to save fifty-one British lives.[306] Errors by Siginters and about Sigint shaped this failure. Siginters on TF 317, inexperienced against the danger, took time to pick up indications of attack. A Flash message from Rio Grande naval base in Tierra del

Fuego to Port Stanley preceded many attacks, which even unread still enabled warning of their time, though not place. Such information could have enabled concentrations of Sea Harriers to loiter over targets, but still perhaps not have saved even one ship. On 9 May, Siginters at GCHQ and TF 317 discovered this pattern, but failed to exploit it, or cooperate against this threat.[307] This discovery and its exploitation might have been made faster had superior officers outside the Sigint chain of command not seized Sigint resources for other purposes. The Chief of Air Staff, against warnings from his Siginters, sent a tactical Sigint unit elsewhere, with seemingly its best Spanish speakers, while RAF Sigint linguists later were landed to be interpreters during the interrogation of prisoners.[308] The failure with voice interception was astonishing, given Britain's focus on the medium against the Warsaw Pact. A greater number of experienced traffic analysts, or voice interceptors, might have discovered more radio indicators of air attack, which could have minimised unnecessary deployments, maximised concentrations and saved warships.

British sensors could not easily detect Argentine aircraft skimming the sea, climbing for an updated radar fix and then diving again to run against warships. This tactic prevented Britain from concentrating aircraft for defence, instead forcing constant combat air patrols by just a few Sea Harriers at the extreme edge of their operating radius. Instead, the Royal Navy saved supply and landing ships by standing on Calvary. Warships sited at the mouth of San Carlos Sound, and radar pickets covering flotillas further out, attracted Argentine attack, sacrificing themselves to save others while enabling attrition by Sea Harriers and anti-aircraft missiles. Argentina sank or damaged warships and the supply ship *Atlantic Conveyor* – carrying much kit essential to supporting the land operations, such as heavy-lift helicopters and GCHQ material for the army section – but still British forces moved. The desperate expedient of unloading troops from the requisitioned P&O liner *Canberra* directly in San Carlos Sound succeeded – as did its flight away – yet it risked annihilation had Argentine forces attacked the ship, as they later did other British forces in Bluff Cove.

If slightly better, or luckier, Argentina could have crippled British forces as they landed, like a Gallipoli. Instead, Argentina scored tactical successes without strategic effect. Rather like Admiral Beatty, as battlecruisers blew up before his eyes at Jutland sixty-six years prior, when Argentine aircraft hammered his surface fleet, Admiral Woodward wrote: 'There is something wrong with our ships again.' A few days after the landing, Woodward pulled the carriers back to sea, crippling British air defences at San Carlos Sound. 'Convoys will be run in and out by night' only, Woodward commanded, limiting transshipment to a few hours per day, so slowing the logistical build-up needed to advance, and feeding the vicious circle.[309]

Soon, on 27 May, Fieldhouse reminded his subordinates that even American support for Britain was wobbling. Despite 'world wide calls for ceasefire and a degree of uncertainty in her own team, PM has held out resolutely for victory not ceasefire. The one thing which could undermine her position and could lead to complete about-turn in public opinion in UK, which at present strongly supports her, is catastrophe at sea with large loss of life.'[310] His fears illustrate how commanders balanced tactical, strategic, diplomatic and political concerns during this near-run battle.

To Port Stanley

Once forces were ashore, Comint instantly became less useful. High-level Argentine assessments still drove Whitehall's confidence and demands for speed in attack and concerns for its carriers. Just after the invasion, GCU Northwood noted: 'Northwood assesses threat of Argentine air attack on Blue Force carriers, particularly *Hermes*, to be probable during 23 May. This based on CDR Falklands (Arg) insistence and poss indications of planning for such an attack (Comint).'[311] On 1 June, intercepts of Argentine naval orders for operations around the islands, combined with ambivalent material from traffic analysis that the modern submarine *San Luis* was at sea, caused a temporary 'furore in London'.[312] This lack of certainty and accuracy about the location of one Argentine submarine reflects how intelligence on them minimised waste. GCHQ perfectly determined enemy losses and sometimes illuminated enemy morale. Argentine commanders grossly overstated British aircraft losses, and often underestimated Harrier strength by 100 to 300 per cent.[313]

Traffic showing that the Argentine navy preferred port to combat no doubt pleased Admirals Fieldhouse and Woodward. The British assault at Goose Green on 28–29 May stunned Argentine officers, who reported receiving 'intense naval and mortar fire' and a 'rapid (British) advance in the face of all supporting fire and deterrent, and even deployed whilst receiving (possibly recoilless) rifle fire, automatic fire and under air attack'. They overestimated the British forces by 300 per cent, as three battalions, who 'attacked through the weakest position'.

Hours after Goose Green fell, the Argentine air commander in Port Stanley praised the British airmen, sailors, squaddies, marines and special forces who bled for their victory. Britain maintained 'absolute supremacy at sea, with all the operational and logistical consequences which this implies'. British 'absolute air superiority ... allows him to develop air and helicopter transport operations with absolute freedom of action' and to erode Argentine power. At Goose Green, 'the enemy demonstrated great mobility through [the use of] helicopters, overwhelming fire power and anti-air [fire power] through the use of portable missiles, acting in exact coordination with supporting naval fire, employing it as back-up and relief for the troops engaged in the front line'. These advantages in material and training 'became decisive' in the battle, and 'represent the most important differences with our own troops' capabilities'. Argentine forces 'offered strenuous resistance', but were badly trained and led. Their defence relied utterly on air support, which Harriers wrecked. Britain had 'unsurpassable conditions to extend the occupation of the islands ... When the enemy decides to operate again against our positions, he will find a defence lacking in mobility and with relatively less fire power and training, which ... will previously have been softened up by intense naval, fire and air support ... a modification of this situation is not anticipated because of the total absence of our own naval resources. This message is top secret.'[314] Northwood received the commander's missive, headlined 'Commander Falklands Group Laments the Inferiority of the Argentine Forces', at about the same time that authorities in Buenos Aires did.

GCHQ's success was reflected in MOD and FCO requests for material they understood it could not provide, based on the likelihood that the regime would collapse: 'We could do with more on the Argentine internal situation, the impact of our landing on the Junta's standing/ popular support, the reported tensions between the Argentine navy and air force and other potential indicators of Argentine will to continue fighting or to negotiate. But those needs are already recognised and for obvious reasons we cannot expect a great deal in those directions.'[315]

Yet Sigint gave little help to land forces at the kill, because disorganisation distorted supply, demand and command. Initially, when the Falklands crisis began, the JIC and DIS made errors aplenty. DIS complained of a twenty-four-hour delay in receiving one Elint report from a partner organisation. GCHQ investigated and found that claim to be a 'complete mare's nest': DIS had 'had the info but did not know it exclam'.[316] Despite infighting and crossed wires, ultimately JIC and DIS handled the problems well for their consumers in Whitehall.[317]

The difficulties lay elsewhere. The Falklands conflict occurred just after Britain changed its military command system, by boosting the power of the Chief of the Defence Staff over the Chiefs of Staff. The CDS, Admiral Lewin, was in New Zealand when the crisis broke. By the time he returned, he claimed 'things were almost out of control'.[318] He found a way to exercise his power as the government's chief military advisor. Beneath the strategic level, command and intelligence followed traditional patterns which, as an old salt, perhaps Lewin found natural. Established modes of command and intelligence, designed for the different circumstances of NATO, were unsuited to this crisis. When the JIC proposed to create 'a JIC Military Working Group to produce rapid tactical assessments of military-related int', Lewin rejected 'any additional machinery which might slow down the existing service to the Chiefs of Staff', from DIS and GCHQ.[319] Northwood dominated operations, more than even the Royal Navy at its peak had done. Only Northwood could integrate British operations with the War Cabinet's strategy. Lewin and Fieldhouse were friends, from a fraternity of submariners more experienced in intelligence than any other British sailors or any decision-makers, save a few diplomats; they were accustomed to acting independently, striking silently, and explaining afterwards. Worried by leaks, and the dangers confronting Task Force 317, they restricted the amount of operationally sensitive information given to the MOD to the minimum needed to support operations. Consequently, senior levels of Whitehall understood the intentions of Argentine forces better than their own.

This approach short-circuited normal strategic decision-making in Whitehall, which was designed for NATO matters. However, although the usual middlemen were shut out, the proper chain of command was maintained in an undocumented fashion. Every evening during the key moments of the campaign, Nott, Thatcher and their private secretaries drove to Northwood to be briefed by Fieldhouse and Lewin on the logistical and operational circumstances and dangers. They carried this knowledge to decisions by the War Cabinet.[320] This approach may have been better suited to circumstances than the standard British model; it certainly fitted Thatcher's preference for small and flexible groups for decision-making. The arrangement shaped loyalties towards Prime Minister Thatcher – and facilitated an understanding of her fragile political position – leading Lewin and Fieldhouse to press ground commanders on the Falklands to win quickly once they landed.

Northwood received all relevant Comint and Elint straight from GCHQ, rather than through DIS. GCHQ swung into action to support the Royal Navy as it had in 1940, tailoring its production to military needs. Even officers who disparaged intelligence during the crisis praised that support. Glover, the DCDS (I) said: 'SIGINT was the fundamental ingredient of almost all our assessment effort, and COMINT and ELINT provided as much as ninety per cent of all our raw intelligence. It was this input that enabled us to keep S of S [Secretaries of State], CDS and the Chiefs of Staff well briefed, not only on the interplay (at UN headquarters) in NEW YORK, but also on the tactical intentions of the Argentine Service commanders, the relationships between them, their individual grip on their units, and even on the strategy of the Junta itself.'[321] British land forces praised GCHQ for its 'very great assistance ... This most excellent service has been our greatest single source of reliable intelligence, indeed for much of the time our only one,' which gave General Bramall 'accurate and timely briefing[s] which [have] been vital to the host of decisions he has had to make'.[322] Unfortunately, the system created to give intelligence about Argentina to Northwood and TF 317 rode roughshod over standard modes of dissemination to organisations outside that chain of command. As RAF intelligence complained: 'the "need to know" principle was applied so vigorously that it became counter-productive and divisive', failing 'to keep essential personnel informed of future intentions'. If 'a non-standard command and control system is to be established in time of tension or war, than the peacetime structure must be modified to mirror that system', backed by 'a fusion centre where all source intelligence could be analysed and properly distributed to all concerned'.[323]

Nor did that standard system work. By 1982, British military intelligence had shrunk to two good organisations: for forces in NATO, and GCHQ. Britain fought in an area where it was unprepared and intelligence was fragile, inflexible and weak. Every element of British intelligence failed in the Falklands conflict, except those which could be refocused on the South Atlantic: GCHQ and Northwood. These organisations had capacity enough to enable victory at sea, but nowhere else, where many problems combined. Once ashore, the key nodes of command were at levels which were not supposed to receive Sigint. Command was loose – almost tribal – over elite formations such as the Royal Marines Commandos and the Parachute Regiment, who preferred to fight as separate brigades or battalions. In the first week after landing a Royal Marines general commanded his brigade and, allegedly, two paratroop battalions one hundred miles away, who pursued a plan he thought pointless. Days before the assault on Stanley, the Royal Marines Major General Jeremy Moore took command while a third brigade of Guards and Gurkhas entered the fray. Furthermore, planning was initially dominated by Royal Marines officers, used to seizing and securing bridgeheads rather than driving deep and fast. This produced the seeming stalemate in the week after the British landing which alarmed Northwood and Thatcher. These improvised arrangements did not make for effective command. Soldiers won this war, not generals, which in turn undermined the value of Siginters.

By 1982, beyond forces committed against the USSR, military Sigint was decadent. Neither GCHQ nor the MOD controlled these resources: they were the small and separate property of each service, without senior and experienced leaders, or 'an identifiable MOD co-ordinating authority'.[324] GCHQ and the services issued conflicting orders to military Sigint. Siginters on board Task Force 317 did not cooperate between them, weakening their already limited capabilities; they did not even know others were present, until they met accidentally. At the last minute, the Royal Navy appointed a 'Force Comint Officer' to the fleet, without any experience in the field. He did not even visit GCHQ before he sailed. Not one Sigint unit in TF 317 accepted his command.[325]

Once landed, fighting units had little sense of what Sigint could offer. For example, 3 Commando Brigade headquarters was inexperienced and incompetent regarding any form of intelligence, let alone Sigint. As the Army Sigint commander, Major Thorp, reported: 'having a person with experience of our product collocated at the Bde HQ int cell would have made a big difference'. Noting that another brigade and perhaps a divisional headquarters soon would reach the island, Thorp asked: 'Please advise soonest chain of command for this det and to whom we should provide our product. This information essential to plan future intentions.'[326] This question never received an adequate reply.

Comint confirmed the planning assumptions for the land campaign and every order or appreciation from Northwood until the kill. In particular, high-level Argentine assessments drove Whitehall's confidence and demands for speed in attack. On 14 May, Fieldhouse told Woodward and the ground commander, Royal Marines Brigadier General Julian Thompson, that 'a relatively calm overview of the last few days of battle' indicated 'despite some severe pain we are winning and furthermore clearly hold the initiative. Increasing signs of desperation from your local enemy all serve to confirm.' Britain must 'take full and early advantage of this situation before the international call for ceasefire becomes unbearable' and strike for Stanley.[327] Royal Marines General Jeremy Moore, land commander at Northwood, emphasised that 'the enemy possesses neither will nor means to mount effective offensive ground operations, and that rapid and powerful action will bring about speedy resolution of overall situation'.[328] Thompson must 'push forward from the bridgehead area, so far as the maintenance of security allows'.[329]

That situation was far from pleasant. Thompson's forces faced harrowing air attack, with only two helicopters to support the advance in a large area vulnerable to counter-attacks. Following Royal Marines doctrine designed to seize Norwegian fjords during war with Warsaw Pact countries, Thompson wanted to secure bridgeheads, not drive deep and fast. His focus on building supplies, security, air superiority and certainty – reinforced by intelligence on the enemy – before launching an open-ended attack, produced the seeming stalemate which alarmed Northwood and Thatcher. 'Info aval here on en determination is thin but performance so far and questioning of PW tends to show that he must be expected to fight.'[330] Thompson had 'so far seen no sign of imminent enemy collapse and therefore consider we must plan on defeating him in the conventional sense', while being ready to exploit 'any signs of collapse which might appear'.[331] Northwood replied with estimates, drawn from Comint, that few Argentine aircraft could attack his forces, but had no intelligence to shake his strategy.[332]

Whitehall's confidence in Thompson was shaken, unfairly. However cautious, he faced an unpleasant variant of a difficult task – amphibious assault against defended positions. Judging enemy willpower is hard, while he and Northwood had divergent intelligence pictures, one drawn from Sigint and the other from battle. When Moore superseded Thompson as commander on the islands, he asked his own successor at Northwood, Richard Trant, 'to do all you can to keep instant strategists off my back'.[333] Moore knew the Sigint record to 26 May. For the first time since the landing, a general combined both Sigint and local knowledge. Yet after the first major engagement on land, a stunning British victory, Moore still adopted Thompsonian views. 'The final defeat of the enemy is dependent on his will to fight. At Darwin/Goose Green our intelligence assessments underestimated both his strength and the fervour with which the more fanatical core fought. We must be prepared for this to occur again at Port Stanley leading to a protracted battle.'[334] Moore and Thompson both overated the enemy – a Victorian general would have estimated the odds better. This mistake stemmed from experience in preparing for difficult operations against a serious foe, and had no cost, save a few days in time.

Siginters had little to offer on land and failed to cooperate with each other and their customers. Partly because of the loss of kit on *Atlantic Conveyor*, military Sigint units failed to advance, or to aid the new consumer. The Royal Marines' Sigint unit, just established, collapsed in its first use. The beach swallowed its vehicles. Its RAF linguists were conscripted to interrogate Argentine prisoners, which Royal Marines officers thought more valuable than Sigint, which produced useful material. GCHQ insisted that Thorp exercise control 'with particular emphasis on restricting' the distribution even of sanitised Comint to the brigades on the islands. When Thorp followed these instructions, an Army officer who knew his function physically assaulted him. Thorp then disobeyed his orders by briefing straight from Sigint Colonel 'H' Jones – soon to lead 2 Para's assault at Goose Green – with the objective of protecting the base at San Carlos Sound while the main force assaulted Port Stanley. Thorp claimed, plausibly, that he reversed an incompetent briefing to Jones by 3 Commando Brigade. In any case, Sigint provided excellent material about Argentine forces at Goose Green. Jones was among the British deaths for a victory in which 600 British paratroopers killed or captured 1,000 Argentine soldiers and broke their nerve across the islands.[335] Other superiors ignored Thorp and his intelligence that Argentine forces might counter-attack British positions in San Carlos Sound. He provided no intelligence for the assault on Stanley. The main source became tactical intelligence from troops, who also jury-rigged Sigint of their own.[336] An indoctrinated officer, Major Dawkins, was attached to the staff of General Moore to handle Comint, but he received little from the source.

In terms of its direct contribution to battle on the Falkland Islands, British Sigint failed. On 13–14 June, Argentine air forces at Stanley reported: 'Their strategy is clear and they are probably planning to move in late evening or tomorrow morning. Their fire power has complete dominance over ours.' Argentine forces would collapse 'in 24 to 48 hours'.[337] British forces could observe these same facts themselves. Fortunately, intelligence was unnecessary for the victory on land. The men proved themselves enough.

Professional Deformations

Comint and Comsec were GCHQ's stock-in-trade, honed against excellent adversaries. As a result, GCHQ was predisposed to overrate Argentine Comint. However, reinforced by an assessment that Argentine Comint was effective only against internal opponents, GCHQ correctly told the JIC 'that the Argentinians would not be able to break British cyphers provided that these were properly used'.[338] Argentine practices, however, initially rudimentary, improved rapidly. Their national effort produced decent traffic analysis by 14 June. GCHQ easily traced this rise.[339] GCHQ's conclusions about Argentine Comint were alarmist, but its actions were reasonable; it devoted no more effort to the Argentine threat than was justified, and perhaps contained its growth. However, this exaggeration shaped a greater issue: GCHQ's effort to follow IRSIG.

Siginters and their consumers had little experience with Sigint in war. They followed rules written by those who had done so: folk memories of what was supposed to happen confronted startling instances of Comsec incompetence. RAF security noted 'the extremely amateur attempt to "make safe" an operational topic through open reference to *Jane's Fighting Ships* is a classic and appalling breach of security'.[340] Actors wished to use intelligence that addressed their problems, which, in the Falklands conflict, were among the greatest they had known. Given the nature of this crisis, the power of GCHQ and its use by the FCO, non-codeword diplomatic telegrams often mentioned material generated from Comint – even worse, exclusively from that source. GCHQ could not prevent this spread of knowledge, but did contain action taken on it. In particular, diplomats wanted to act on intelligence to stop Argentine arms purchases, say, by warning foreign governments off actions they were known to be considering. One diplomat complained that 'over-strict adherence to the letter of the rule book may prevent ... tactical advantage of fresh COMINT reports that is their only real value'.[341] GCHQ retorted that warning foreigners 'we were reading their international commercial traffic' was dangerous, let alone hinting at compromises of their diplomatic cyphers.[342] It controlled such actions, often small in significance and liable to compromise the source, but sometimes imperative. Britain might have gained from burning its coverage of diplomatic and commercial targets in order to stop the sale of ten Exocet anti-ship missiles, though that dilemma never emerged.

GCHQ never challenged how senior commanders acted on Sigint. Why not? Victory was at stake, few actions could really endanger the source, while imagery could be used plausibly to cover British actions. GCHQ authorised Fieldhouse to use Sigint as he wished, so long as the source was not mentioned outside Comint channels or in orders. Its material for Northwood aimed for 'packaging and tailoring ... in best Savile Row style – neat smart and pertinent'.[343] Much friction, however, arose from efforts to provide Sigint to staff officers, or to give predictive intelligence – where enemy ships might move, or the strength of enemy garrisons two days away – to the commanders of ships or battalions, who often acted independently, far from superior officers. To pass predictive intelligence from Category 3 Comint to recipients outside Sigint channels, such as junior commanders – when by definition 'there is no real cover (real or notional)' – only endangered the source.[344] GCHQ resisted this pressure, particularly after the Ted Rowlands compromise led Argentina to improve its cryptosystems. Junior officers had less need for Comint than senior ones, and standard procedures to sanitise information seemed sufficient.

Still, this friction caused pain. On 23 April, Fieldhouse informed many ships that 'intercepts' showed *Santa Fe* was near South Georgia. GCHQ had just shown that Argentine forces anticipated a British attack in the area.[345] This timely warning to a command 1,000 miles away from TF 317 that was about to attack the island shocked GCHQ, primarily because the submarine was named. The liaison officer at Northwood, GCO (N), reported this event secretly to Z in a teleconference, because 'it is totally informal with only the one paper record which I can destroy, whereas a formal signal is kept here on file and our STS phone is in the middle of the working area surrounded by all ranks, etc'. GCHQ representatives fought to keep Fieldhouse 'on the even keel of asking permission for action, taking advice on rules etc, but our success was not total'. Z replied: 'Only you [GCO(N)] at NORTHWOOD have power to take codeword off. The RN has to accept that or get a hell of a rocket from enormous height. If you can give evidence of flagrant abuse we can and will take up the cudgels but I guess that it's mainly a case of creeping sin which is harder to stop.'[346]

In signals copied to DGI and DCDS (I), GCHQ soon reminded Fieldhouse of the rules, and its flexibility with them. He promised to behave well, and to have Woodward do so: but a war was on. GCHQ tolerated this situation, concluding that 'whilst the matter had not been handled correctly, no harm had been done to Sigint', especially after documents captured from the *Santa Fe* showed Argentine confusion and ignorance.[347] Still, it warned Fieldhouse that if Argentina concluded:

> the UK is intercepting important traffic (which we are) they can
> easily stop us doing so by some quite simple procedural changes
> … GCHQ has given to authorities at Northwood blanket
> authorisation for action-on (if downgrading to secret level) only
> for actual or past locations of Argentinean or Soviet military units.
> All other requests for action-on must be taken in consultation
> with GCHQ and we have posted GCHQ officers to Northwood
> with delegated authority to take action-on decisions to make this
> as swift and efficient a process as possible. These officers are under
> strict instructions to report after the fact to GCHQ, all cases
> where action-on has been taken, including those cases where Sigint
> security rules have been breached by action being taken without
> prior consultation with GCHQ.[348]

As the war became hot, GCHQ authorised the downgrading of Category 2 Comint to secret levels, but not of 3, which Fieldhouse and Woodward received in floods. Ultimately, Siginters met military needs, enabling the use of actionable Sigint without compromising security. GCHQ was more concerned with its rules on secure handling and Comsec than absolutely required, but only at miniscule cost.

The Falklands conflict was the first of a series of cases, which continue today, where GCHQ aided expeditionary forces which suddenly fought in unexpected areas. To get national level or tactical Sigint to forces of divisional strength or below in size proved hard in Kuwait in 1991, Bosnia in 1992, and Iraq and Afghanistan after 2001. GCHQ was good at sudden crises, but better at set pieces. GCHQ worked best where it had more time for preparation and to work with larger forces. Time and experience was needed to deliver Sigint to small forces, as the mixed records of the cases of Konfrontasi and the Falklands conflict illuminate; even so, GCHQ's performance in these cases was excellent, and it handled these emergencies better than its enemies.

Secrecy, Translucency and Oversight, 1830–2019

Comsec and Communications-Electronic Security, 1945–92

In 1939, British – and American – Comsec was mediocre. Hostile Sigint agencies compromised many British systems. Only Ultra ensured British and American victory in the wireless war, which demonstrates the poverty of their cryptography. Allied forces did not understand their failures until after Germany surrendered and Axis Siginters outlined their successes. These failures affected British policy only years after the war. GCHQ always believed that Sigint and Comsec should be unified. Many Comsec authorities countered that if so, as before 1939, the needs for attack would always overwhelm those for defence. In 1945, GCHQ planned to control cryptography which, it claimed, needed to be combined with cryptanalysis. Initially, no one challenged GCHQ's view, since Britain had moved to the top of the world in Comsec and cypher machines.[1] However, by 1952, no new online systems had been completed since the war's end.

The most ambitious of the crypto projects pursued by GCHQ – designed by cryptanalytic machine experts such as Pat Bayley and Welchman – failed partly because GCHQ managed them poorly. GCHQ's work with all forms of technical research and development hit its nadir perhaps due to a failure to appreciate the significance and complexity of these matters, leaving other institutions to lead them.[2] GCHQ was led by the man most responsible for the prewar failures in cryptography, Travis. Its personnel had little or no responsibility for Britain's best crypto machines – for example Typex, Typex Mercury, UCO (Secretype) and Rockex II – which outsiders designed and other institutions, such as the Army, RAF and SIS, carried through initial development. GCHQ worked with only one of these developments, the later stages of Rockex II.³ GCHQ's great success in Comsec kit – Tiltman's Stencil Subtractor Frame – was not a machine. Experts in Comsec, especially in the military services, and some civil servants, particularly Edward Bridges, who had handled policy towards cypher machines for fifteen years, discerned a connection between past and present failures. In 1953, they concluded that the Comsec elements of GCHQ had to become independent, in what ultimately was named the Communications-Electronics Security Department (CESD). That GCHQ did not challenge this approach, nor anyone else, shows that its competence in cryptography was questioned. In any case, GCHQ had work enough elsewhere to absorb its attention.⁴

Though the leaders of CESD reflected signs of empire-building and an allergic reaction to cooperation with GCHQ, this division was justified. CESD and GCHQ maintained the necessary links between Comsec and cryptanalysis. CESD did better in developing cypher machines than GC&CS and GCHQ had done. CESD unified the efforts of the technical teams working on cypher machines in many units and brought them into one. It established sound means for research and development and production based on the models of military work with signals. CESD bequeathed good systems which saw British cryptography through to 1980, though few prototypes entered standard use. Mistakes were made and recovery from major ones was slow and hard. CESD had to work with every technical research group in Whitehall that handled signals security, which sometimes overwhelmed it. Ultimately, CESD died as a separate organisation because the need was no longer clear, partly because of its own success, while the costs were obvious – not financial, but human. The greatest limit for British Sigint was in procuring scientists and technicians. CESD needed far more of them per capita than GCHQ – indeed, absolutely almost as many as Cheltenham required – yet found them even harder to hire because it was a small and isolated unit and essentially military in character. CESD's solution to these shortages – to hire retired officers – solved problems of quantity and quality only in the short term, and perhaps reinforced the unwillingness of young scientists to join CESD. The fighting services refused to cooperate as CESD needed them to, as they moved away from leadership in Sigint and the expertise of retired personnel became obsolete. Though no one fully appreciated the fact, CESD fell behind in technical areas involving cryptography.

GCHQ had greater skills than any other government organisation for the new age of digitisation.[5] GCHQ became competent in managing research and development and production for technical equipment, and in acquiring scientists and technicians. CESD leaders served far longer than those of GCHQ, because they ran a technical unit, where leaders were few. By 1969, when Captain Stannard, RN, the second head of CESD, died, seventy-three of its complement of 310 were vacant (including 30 per cent of its research and development staff) with no likelihood of improvement in sight. GCHQ's complement of scientists, conversely, at last was complete.[6] No one questioned the quality of CESD's work, but all doubted its viability as an independent institution. After an investigation led by the intelligence coordinator Dick White, Whitehall abolished CESD as an independent unit and returned it to GCHQ as a distinct division named the Communications-Electronics Security Group (CESG).[7] The abolition of CESD was as justifiable as its creation had been. CESG remained quasi-independent until two decades after the Cold War ended, with enough resources to handle its task.

The experiences of CESD and CESG provide a useful mirror for GCHQ. Politically, CESD was weaker compared to American organisations than GCHQ. The United States service Sigint agencies controlled cryptography, where NSA was weak, the opposite situation to Sigint. CESD bargained from an inferior political and technical position with its American counterparts. It defended core British interests in cryptography, but had little effect on American decisions or modes of decision-making. This weakness particularly shaped 'equities' – the need to balance the conflicting interests of security and intelligence such as the classic question affecting all decisions about cryptography with third parties: would spreading awareness of a Comsec vulnerability reduce Siginters' capability to exploit it? American Siginters were unwilling to let any ally, including Britain, near their best cryptographic equipment. American and British Comsec authorities routinely bickered, and sometimes fought, over the level of aid they should give NATO. In 1962, shortly before aiding GCHQ during the Hampshire Report, Tordella warned that if Britain were to challenge American policy over marketing cypher machines to NATO it would cause 'quite serious strain in U.K./U.S. dealings'.[8] UKUSA also hampered British firms from exploiting fully the possibilities for sales of cryptographic machines to Commonwealth countries, where substantial interest existed.[9] Whether independent, or subordinate, CESD and CESG also distanced GCHQ from some outside organisations. They worked better with British industry than GCHQ did. CESD ensured that British defence electronics firms benefitted as much from contracts for cypher machines as any other Western country and financed technological and commercial developments, whereas GCHQ did little to help the British computer industry.

New problems emerged in Comsec. Between 1945 and 1980, the use of telephones rose more than any other form of communication, yet speech security initially was primitive. Creating secure speech systems became essential, and difficult. Consumers disliked the first generation of speech encryption kit, the American Sigsaly, which they said made them sound like Donald Duck.[10] Those factors, and clumsy protocols, caused irritations among consumers throughout the Cold War. The first decade of British work in the field failed because direction was weak. In 1958, high-level telephone conversations between Eisenhower and Harold Macmillan were covered only by scrambler systems, which provided no security.[11] Then, however, Britain regularly developed sound secure speech systems, moving from Pickwick in 1958 to Brent in the mid-1990s. Brent machines became the most familiar cryptographic items in Whitehall. Thousands of copies sat on official desks in the UK and its establishments abroad.

The discovery around 1956 of the phenomenon of Tempest, which enabled emissions from electronic equipment to be intercepted from hundreds of yards away, threatened any electronic system of cryptography by compromising layers of encryption. Overcoming Tempest imposed a huge burden on machine design to minimise radiation, and an even greater cost for physical infrastructure – such as shielded rooms – in locales where they were based. No crypto machine designed before Tempest was prepared to handle it, which crippled many of them – particularly the standard system for the Foreign Office, Rockex II. The problem was both the machine and the many areas where it was deployed, Eastern bloc and third-world countries where Soviet intelligence might intercept traffic from British embassies. Earlier versions of Rockex II could not be used securely for teleprinter traffic except on circuits where remarkably shielded areas protected both points – as on the most important links, like London to Moscow.[12] A later version of Rockex II, Mk IV-BID/08/07, produced in small numbers, was 'Tempest compliant', as were later online machines like Noreen. In any case, for a decade, suddenly British diplomatic systems returned almost to the stone age. Rockex II was used in manual format in a stripped-down version, which eliminated its main value – rapid one-time pad security for teleprinter traffic – and exposed its weak point: the reliance on expensive and fragile one-time tape. Diplomats returned to books, covered by manual one-time pads.[13] These problems were smaller for military Comsec, where machines were not used in vulnerable areas. Typex Mercury and 5 UCO were used for top secret traffic until 1965. By the 1980s, further problems emerged for Comsec with digitisation and then with the advent of personal computers – where encryption increasingly was baked into the body of the cake, rather than being added on later as a layer of icing.

More than perhaps any other Western country except the United States, Britain produced good and cost-effective cypher machines during the Cold War. Its best kit outmatched anything produced by European members of NATO. CESD and British industry developed better and cheaper cypher machines than any of these competitors. In a cut-throat battle of the 1960s, NATO adopted the British system, Alvis, to cover high-level communications. This success helped the British economy, exports in defence electronics and Western cryptography.[14] Yet many CESD programmes failed. Its problem was standard for the British defence industrial sector: the pursuit of too many prototypes simultaneously, overstretched the limited strength in engineers, increased costs and extended the time for completion. The loss of time led to missed opportunities and exposed programmes to continual upgrades while still under design, which produced further delays or made machines obsolete before completion. In the 1960s, it took seven years to move cryptographic machines from a statement of requirements to production – assuming they ever reached that stage.[15] Soon, seven years was seen as a remarkably fast time to finish that process.

The system worked as it was supposed to on many good British cryptosystems, such as Alvis. Yet almost equally often, only emergencies or a high priority could provide enough pressure to overcome the problem of time. Small teams, with able leadership, which pursued unorthodox solutions to problems best exploited such opportunities. Problems and solutions varied, however, and not every unorthodox approach succeeded; just as not every orthodox one failed. In every success, skilled and visionary technicians treated these projects as their main work, and controlled research and development up to the moment of production, rather than passing the project over to others halfway through. These characteristics marked the development of about half of the best British cryptosystems of the twentieth century, such as Typex, Rockex II and 5 UCO between 1934 and 1945. Experienced signals personnel independently pursued innovative approaches, which their institutions backed as soon as the first signs emerged of success. So too, in the later 1950s, when military authorities demanded immediate secure speech, CESD rapidly converted a prototype scrambler telephone system, Pickwick, into a good system for secure speech. Pickwick was then applied across British commands, overcoming a decade of CESD's failure to produce such a system.[16]

Some of these characteristics continued after the Cold War. Between 1988 and 1995, CESG developed Brent, 'the first UK desktop High Grade fully Tempest-approved secure telephone', designed to be user-friendly, with 'true-to-person speech quality'. CESG did so by giving a small team control over design and development to the production stage, rather than passing the system over to a civilian contractor when development began, so to control events, minimise bureaucratisation and exploit advanced commercial practices. The team rejected older procedures, and '1950s to 1970s ironmongery'. Instead, they combined the aims of state security with the convenience of the best civilian kit, substituting public key cryptography for old labour-intensive means. Brent pleased a generation of Whitehall users and became a commercial success. A few years later, however, while attempting to follow this model, CESG handled another secure speech system, Pippa, as clumsily as any other project in the history of British cryptosystems.[17] These patterns of success and failure are not British, but universal. Designing effective cryptosystems is hard. Protecting them is even harder.

CESD and CESG produced equipment for defensive purposes and manuals on how to use it, not intelligence. CESG handled distinct customers, on the long timescales that characterised procurement rather than on the short ones for the consumption of intelligence; its successes were seldom dramatic or even knowable. Furthermore it was remote from GCHQ, geographically from Cheltenham and psychologically from Oakley or Benhall. Comsec was outside the mainstream of GCHQ, but close enough to enable technical cooperation and the exchange of knowledge and people. Cryptosystems were developed rationally and avoided the errors of the interwar period. The wastage, and the number of failed or abandoned projects, fell within the normal range for British defence electronics. The successes kept Britain at the upper end of a competitive market in encryption. One cannot know the success of British Comsec until the records of the other side are released. The success of the Walker family of spies in penetrating US Navy cryptosystems demonstrates the costs of slips in Comsec, and the range of enemies it confronts.

The Contradictions of Secrecy

For Siginters, secrecy was more than just a means for security; it was almost an aim in itself: part of their being – membership in a cult involving honour and doctrine. When their secrecy was violated, Siginters felt disgust, like Malcolm Kennedy when the US Congressional committee on Pearl Harbor released Magic, and Tiltman when Frederick Winterbotham published *The Ultra Secret*.[18] Even in 2020, Siginters feel disquiet when they see the name GCHQ, in press headlines.

Whitehall had equally intense views on the secrecy of Sigint, but focused on security. All of Whitehall was secret, but GCHQ was its quintessence. Whitehall oversaw GCHQ in a unique and unorthodox fashion, treating it both as a normal department and a secret service. MI5 and MI6 were open secrets; Whitehall sought to keep GCHQ a real secret. GCHQ reported to the Foreign Secretary and acted only on principles approved and monitored by LSIC and PSIS, while the Treasury audited its finances, loosely. Whitehall felt that any closer management might endanger GCHQ's work or political neutrality and expose politicians to embarrassment. One Foreign Secretary, Austen Chamberlain, expressed this traditional view in 1924: 'It is of the essence of a secret service that it must be secret, and if you once begin disclosure … there is no longer any Secret Service and … you must do without it.'[19]

For secret services, secrecy was paramount, and parliamentary control impossible. This situation was tolerable constitutionally, because Britons could trust honourable men to guard the guardians. For anyone who knew the facts, these arguments about GCHQ had force and those arrangements arguably were proper. Whitehall, however, kept these facts from the public, where from 1960 faith eroded in honourable men. Since GCHQ was an unavowed institution, any of its actions, if known, must raise suspicion, as would the secrecy around it. Since GCHQ was a large department, which interacted openly with tens of thousands of people, such suspicions were hard to avoid. GCHQ knew that material already in the public domain would reveal its existence and work and believed that the story of Ultra, and hence its existence, would become public. Changes in public and official attitudes towards privacy, secrecy and security soon exacerbated these contradictions in the secrecy around Sigint. They emerged particularly in law and history.

Between 1844 and 1914, officials and politicians disliked intercepting communications outside of war, and thought the British public had similar views. During the Great War, it was noted how censors working in postal censorship felt 'an involuntary and deep-seated disgust when (they) first broke the seal of an unknown person's correspondence, a natural sentiment which indicates how profound was the confidence men had in the posts and how inconsistent with liberty and with good faith it appeared to invade the rights of private correspondence which ought to be held peculiarly sacred'.[20] Yet such experiences taught Whitehall that Sigint – and secrecy about it – was essential in peacetime. These ends required the legal ability to intercept diplomatic cables in times of peace, which did not exist in Britain. Intelligence authorities, fearing public opposition to that power, handled it gingerly.[21] Section Four of the Official Secrets Act (1920) ordered cable and wireless operators to give the government, under the warrant of any Secretary of State, 'all telegrams, or of telegrams of any specified class or description, or of telegrams sent from or addressed to any specified person or place, sent or received to or from any place out of the United Kingdom'.[22] This section openly changed prior practice, yet received little public criticism, unlike other clauses in the legislation, which suggests that experiences with censorship and war had changed public attitudes towards the interception of communications. In any case, this section was moderate, compared to the censorship regime between 1914 and 1919, and seemed simply to extend agreed rules for postal censorship to telegrams.

In fact, bulk intercept became more common with telegrams than post. Under a rolling warrant, automatically renewed each year, cable companies give GC&CS drop copies of the telegrams of all foreign governments which passed through British territory. Any further intercepts required a special warrant, which might be substantial. The Home Office warrant during the General Strike of 1926, for example, covered 'all telegrams into and out of Great Britain containing messages directed to impeding necessary action, or to procuring undesirable action in the present emergency ... one of the main objects ... is to prevent the transmission of messages directing payment of large sums of money to persons and bodies acting in defiance of Emergency provisions'.[23] Companies could not scrutinise every cable entering or leaving Britain on such a broad range of issues, which emphasised communists and some trade unionists: they simply would have examined the telegrams of specific individuals or organisations named on a list, or those sent to and from specific addresses. Though contemporaries would have considered this warrant, and the rolling one, to be general warrants, in modern terms they warranted bulk collection.

For thirty-five years, that rolling warrant regulated the collection of telegrams, which fell in significance. Procedures were taken for granted as experiences in a second total war reinforced those from the first. By 1955, however, legal authorities in the Foreign Office questioned this approach, because the Official Secrets Act aimed to prevent espionage, not to collect intelligence on foreign states.[24] No one had raised this objection before, or acted on it, but it signalled changing attitudes towards law and Sigint. The Vienna Convention on Diplomatic Relations of 1961, and the British Diplomatic Privileges Act of 1964, raised questions about the legality of intercepting foreign traffic, though these instruments legitimately could be read to mean that diplomatic messages might be copied so long as they were delivered.

Nonetheless, changes in attitudes, and technology, and the sting of scandals, made legal issues matter to GCHQ. Public debates emerged over the danger of the interception of telephone conversations – forms of industrial or personal espionage which were often called 'eavesdropping'. Though these fears overstated the danger, foreign states, and criminals at home and abroad, became able to intercept communications within Britain – as could, of course, British authorities. Several scandals drew public attention to the issue. In 1956, for example, authorities publicly used telephone taps against a criminal, Billy Hill, in a successful effort to disbar his barrister, Patrick Marrinan. A decade later, Chapman Pincher, a journalist with the *Daily Express*, disclosed the rolling warrant, while naming the MOD (rather than GCHQ) as the recipient. That Pincher failed to discover GCHQ's role reflects the effect of security procedures around it. This story provoked the D-notice affair, a major scandal in British politics during the 1960s.[25]

Though these scandals, with the exception of the D-notice affair, were unrelated to GCHQ, they sometimes produced public statements or legal rulings which affected its work. Matters involving Sigint were discussed openly in the press. Through backstairs work, GCHQ kept itself and Sigint from these public discussions, even over the D-notice affair, which quickly turned to personal scandal and abuse. GCHQ representatives met the Birkett and Radcliffe committees, which examined these two scandals, and explained GCHQ's involvement in these issues or how they might damage British security. These committees kept GCHQ from their reports and safe from their proposed legislation.[26] The Birkett Committee of 1957, which examined the Hill case and more broadly 'the interception of communications', did not even mention GCHQ or the interception of foreign communications, Instead, in sections nominally dedicated to MI5, but extendable to GCHQ, the committee stated obliquely that 'the problems of national security are such that no reasonable weapon should be taken from the hands of those whose duty it is to watch over all subversive activities in the safeguarding of British interests ... the methods of interception hitherto employed are necessary, and have been productive of important results which could not have been obtained in any other way'.[27] In particular, the committee approved the interception of communications between a British subject in Britain and any entity based abroad. Viscount Radcliffe originally aimed to discuss interception practices thoroughly, but first requested briefings from the intelligence agencies. After hearing the accounts of GCHQ, JIC, MI5 and MI6, the Radcliffe Committee instead focused on D-notices rather than drop copies, though it gave the government a 'Confidential Annexe' on Sigint.[28]

These issues caused GCHQ and the government to consider more thoroughly than ever since 1920 the legality of their practices of interception, and to institute regular reviews which continue to the present day. After both the Birkett and Radcliffe reports, the prime minister of the day chaired a committee of senior ministers and civil servants which reviewed all practices for interception of communications. These committees tightened procedures without transforming them, while extending practices to cover emerging forms of communication, such as trunk telexes. GCHQ asked the Foreign Office's approval for any changes in practices. It never touched British-to-British communications, unless this accidentally occurred through interception of ILC or Comsat traffic.[29] Due to pressure from the prime minister at the time, Harold Wilson, any foreign communications which mentioned MPs, or the accidental harvesting of their own messages, were treated with special discretion as 'UK Governmental' – which was the same category covering similar practices regarding ministers. When the D-notice affair demonstrated confusion over the practices of interception, Whitehall issued new general warrants in 1969, which thereafter were renewed every six months, and only after an explicit revaluation of their work. The privatisation of the GPO raised questions about whether the government could collect correspondence through warrants, which ministers and officials maintained through brilliant obfuscation. The Post Office Bill of 1969 ordered the private company to obey ministerial orders, 'to secure that a particular thing that it or a subsidiary of its is doing is no longer done or that a particular thing that it has power to do, but is not being done either by it or a subsidiary of its, is so done'. Such orders must remain secret – if anyone could understand their meaning.[30]

The government acted to ensure that Sigint worked legally, yet secretly, with one gap. When capturing ILC and Comsat traffic in international space, GCHQ unavoidably caught the traffic of British people. It simply discarded this traffic unless a special warrant covered the person or content. The dictates of the Birkett Committee, and of two prime ministerial committees, supported this approach, but legally questions might be raised. The issue seemed minor, given GCHQ's focus on military and diplomatic traffic, but its significance swelled after 1990, with the end of the Cold War and the reduction in high-frequency radio, and the rise of the internet.

Meanwhile, history compromised secrecy. Between the wars, British intelligence attempted to prevent any publications about British Sigint, with mixed success. Admiral Sinclair, Denniston and the Cabinet Secretary, Maurice Hankey, held that Britain must hide the existence of the GC&CS so not to have other governments raise their cryptographic standards or alarm the British public. Yet the publication of Soviet telegrams of 1920–23 and 1927 showed everyone these facts, while details of the GC&CS's personnel were published with the Naval Estimates until 1922, and the Foreign Office Vote until 1941.[31]

In 1920, the NID and MID kept Marconi from publishing a monograph about its role in military wireless and Sigint during the Great War. 'Most civilised countries must have realised that we did possess a highly organised Wireless Intelligence and a Cryptographic Bureau, but practically no information has ever been available to them as to the pitch of perfection that these organisations reached, and it is most desirable that this information should still remain unavailable'. So to maintain advantages over any enemy, 'it is most desirable that as little information as possible should be made public either as to the organisations employed, or the nature or method of handling of the information obtained'.[32] Yet the NID and MID simultaneously let the Marconi officer H. J. Round, Britain's leading expert in wireless interception, publish a long technical report on that matter through the Institute for Electrical Engineers, including some discussion of the role of direction-finding against submarines and Zeppelins, and at the battle of Jutland. Conventional scientific considerations motivated Round. He thought that through interception, 'the most amazing developments have taken place, in which I think we may safely say more knowledge has been obtained than in all the years before, since wireless was first thought of', although 'we have all been working under the difficulty that the ordinary safety valve of the scientific man – the ability to show off his stunts and gadgets to an admiring audience is absent due to war secrecy'.[33] In 1921, moreover, several writers who had served in Sigint – Ferdinand Tuohy, Filson Young, and Stephen McKenna – published accurate accounts of Room 40, military wireless intelligence and the WTID. Many veterans, including Churchill and Ewing, later wrote of their experiences with Sigint, without efforts to suppress them. Such publications inspired naval Sigint in Italy, Germany and the United States. From 1932, however, with the trial of Compton MacKenzie over his memoirs as an MI6 officer in Greece during 1916–17, attitudes stiffened towards histories of intelligence. Admiral Hall was soon prevented from publishing a ghostwritten memoir.

Those attitudes escalated after 1945, and prevented any publication to match the most significant of the interwar years. Even so, many official and unofficial histories referred obliquely and sometimes directly to Sigint during the Second World War, enough to point towards truths. GCHQ believed that sufficient evidence was available in the public domain to confirm that it was a Sigint agency.[34] It also thought that public knowledge of Ultra and the breaking of Enigma was just a matter of time.[35] By 1966, the pioneering historian of Sigint, David Kahn, almost discovered the Ultra secret as he researched *The Codebreakers*. GCHQ and NSA regarded Kahn as among the greatest security threats they had yet faced. When he visited Cheltenham in an abortive attempt to interview Hugh Alexander, GCHQ announced uneasily that 'Kahn is at the gate' – as one internal GCHQ history noted, whether Genghis or David was unclear. GCHQ thought that Kahn would discover and describe Ultra. He did not quite seize that prize, although he mentioned that British Sigint centred on Bletchley Park, employed over 30,000 people by 1944, and asked what they might have been doing. In order to ease publication, and perhaps for reasons of patriotism, Kahn and his publishers also agreed not to use much material he had collected about the work of GCHQ and NSA after 1945, which demonstrated the vulnerability of their cover stories.

Soon after these histories, the Polish and French veterans Marian Rejewski and Colonel Bertrand openly described how they and GC&CS had broken Enigma during 1939–40. GCHQ knew that the rest of the story would come out, especially after Britain put its archives open to historical scrutiny and on a thirty-year basis. GCHQ and the JIC discussed these issues every few months between 1966 and 1973, and also the commissioning of an official history of British intelligence during the Second World War. GCHQ prevented writers of the late 1960s, such as Donald McLachlan, from mentioning Ultra, and blocked Patrick Seale from exploiting his privileged access to Denniston's papers. GCHQ, however, decided that it would not oppose the next author who tried simply to publish the story. That the book in question had significant errors eased this decision. During 1974, in *The Ultra Secret*, Winterbotham released the first general account of Ultra. Even so, 'a basic GCHQ aim' remained 'of discouraging further attempts by private individuals, following Frederick Winterbotham's example, to fill gaps in the public history on intelligence subjects, particularly any such attempts which might include information on methods and techniques'. GCHQ hoped to further this aim by announcing that it would publish an official history of the matter, while discouraging competent authors from tackling the topic.[36] The next question obviously would be: what happened to GC&CS at the end of the war? For GCHQ, history was not dead; it was not even known.

Coming Out: Scandal and Avowal

GCHQ managed these challenges quietly and well, behind the scenes. This very success left it unprepared for a public competition over secrecy and openness, which opened suddenly between Whitehall and forces that GCHQ had never faced before: public critics, and a decline in deference towards and trust in government. GCHQ, the most secret agency of a government marked by secrecy, was most exposed to these forces. As this struggle opened, no one knew the rules. It reflected and shaped subliminal changes in public attitudes. The particular way that scandals exploded shaped the relationship between contradictory trends which echo today about the value of intelligence and security against those of privacy and secrecy.

Until 1970, outside Gloucestershire, GCHQ was simply an entry in government directories. GCHQ was not only secret, but anonymous. Between 1945 and 1975, GCHQ appeared in *Hansard* only on lists of departments. *The Times* mentioned GCHQ on just ten occasions: nine were 'situations vacant', while the last repeated the revelations of a former NSA employee about UKUSA and GCHQ, originally published in *Ramparts* magazine across the water. After thirty years of happy obscurity, journalists and events gave GCHQ fifteen years of unsought publicity. Chapman Pincher revealed elements of intelligence, though his work later became peculiar, sometimes conspiratorial. Revelations about GCHQ moved from anti-establishment magazines to the quality press. In 1976, *Time Out* published two articles by Duncan

Campbell and Mark Hosenball, each at the start of outstanding careers as journalists. These articles, well researched and generally accurate, provided the best snapshot of GCHQ on the public record. As GCHQ already knew, much evidence about it was public, including material which Campbell and Hosenball overlooked. Whitehall, believing that politically motivated adversaries were assaulting Western intelligence, launched a heavy-handed counter-attack. Though it was bound to use the Official Secrets Act, the flimsiness of which no one understood, to ignore Campbell would have served the cult of secrecy better. Together, in ways which suited neither of their aims, Whitehall and its opponents drove Britain down a road of scandal, which ultimately made GCHQ a public and trusted institution.

Whitehall deported Hosenball, an American citizen, as a threat to national security, but Campbell remained to torment mandarins for decades. Campbell, an able and courageous man of the left, whose mother had served in Sigint during the Second World War, denounced British foreign and defence policy, and Sigint, as illegal, immoral and unnecessary. 'Why do I keep going?' he wrote in retrospect. 'Because from the beginning, my investigations revealed a once-unimaginable scope of governmental surveillance, collusion, and concealment by the British and U.S. governments – practices that were always as much about domestic spying during times of peace as they were about keeping citizens safe from supposed foreign enemies, thus giving the British government the potential power to become ... a virtual "police state".'[37] His *Time Out* articles led a former Royal Signals NCO, John Berry, to offer further details about GCHQ. Berry and Campbell were arrested, alongside another *Time Out* journalist, Crispin Aubrey. Their subsequent trial under the Official Secrets Act – inevitably the 'ABC trial' after the names of the defendants – generated more publicity than the original article. Although the three were convicted on minor charges, this was a Pyrrhic victory for the government. The Official Secrets Act was discredited, and GCHQ became a target for many journalists and for the three stalwarts of the left-liberal press, the *Guardian*, the *New Statesman*, and the *Observer*. Campbell and the *New Statesman* together published many attacks on British intelligence and security policy.

The ABC affair, GCHQ's equivalent of the Lady Chatterley trial, revealed how old hands misunderstood new attitudes, though the lessons were not learned for another fifteen years until an Australian court embarrassed Robert Armstrong, the Cabinet Secretary, over efforts to censor *Spycatcher*, the memoir of retired MI5 officer Peter Wright. The establishment could no longer manage the press. The Official Secrets Act could no longer block disclosures about intelligence. The press no longer would police itself or be policed. Any evidence about GCHQ attracted attention, like a drop of blood amidst sharks. Anything secret must be scandalous, or bad. The mere existence of secrecy sparked conspiracy theories, which overwhelmed public understanding of intelligence for a generation. With so little evidence in the public domain, any real or alleged fact could be made to fit any case. GCHQ, which really was fixated on the threat from the Eastern bloc, could be described as an agent of 1984. Scandals stemmed simply from reporting basic facts, which often were innocuous. Accounts of GCHQ's successes could not be reported. GCHQ could not defend itself publicly against attacks. Any defence of its actions had to be made by others and taken on trust, which was where the problem began in the first place.

Several scandals struck GCHQ between 1982 and 1986. The first was the trial of Geoffrey Prime, the greatest traitor in the history of GCHQ. During the 1960s, Prime had trained as a Russian linguist with the RAF, and then entered the London Processing Group and GCHQ. Shortly before leaving the RAF, Prime sold himself to the Soviets because of 'a misplaced idealistic view of Soviet socialism which was compounded by basic psychological problems within myself'. He remained undetected throughout his career in GCHQ. His treachery was discovered only in 1982, after he retired, following his arrest for sexual assaults on young girls around Cheltenham.[38] The Prime case, which combined a favourite recipe on Fleet Street – sexual deviance and treachery – attracted sensational press interest. The Security Commission publicly condemned GCHQ and recommended that polygraphs be used for security vetting. This proposal was never adopted, partly because the prime minister, Thatcher, thought it useless, but it drew further unfavourable attention to GCHQ. Simultaneously, the quality newspapers, including teams of the best investigative reporters in Britain, published material which threatened security and victory during the Falklands conflict without being challenged by the Official Secrets Act.

These actions described the details of Sigint during a live crisis more than ever before anywhere, and inflicted far greater damage to British security than Campbell ever did – though they also gave the British public its best view of GCHQ's prowess during the Cold War. Two years later, in 1984, the government banned trade unions at GCHQ, which became a major issue in partisan politics. Annually, for the next twelve years, Labour politicians and trade unionists marched down the streets of Cheltenham, wielding banners and umbrellas. In 1986, Campbell, commissioned by the BBC to develop a six-part TV series entitled *Secret Society*, scored his greatest coup. He revealed the project to develop a British Sigint satellite, Zircon, and that its cost had been concealed from Parliament. The BBC was persuaded not to broadcast the episode on the grounds of national security. The *Observer* publicised this action. Injunctions and/or Special Branch raids struck Campbell, his researchers, the *New Statesman*, and the BBC. Attempts to show the episode to MPs within the House of Commons were thwarted, but samizdat copies were shown elsewhere in the UK. The Attorney General accepted that prosecutions would be inflammatory and probably unsuccessful: government overreaction generated far more publicity for GCHQ than unfavourable journalism. Once ignored, the Zircon affair faded from the headlines. Only the chattering classes cared about scandals over Sigint, and then not much.

GCHQ was not the only part of the secret establishment that was dragged into the open during this period, but it suffered the hardest blows. MI5 had always endured suspicion. GCHQ moved suddenly from anonymity to becoming a favourite target for suspicion on the left of British politics and the media. These events killed the cult of secrecy. From 1975, for administrative and political convenience, GCHQ quietly aimed to move from secrecy towards 'status', or a more conventional position as a department. These aims were enacted slowly. After the Prime case, in 1982 Thatcher avowed that GCHQ was an intelligence agency. The Intelligence Services Act of 1994 gave GCHQ statutory existence, alongside MI5 and MI6. Later, Britain borrowed the idea of parliamentary oversight of agencies from American practices. GCHQ led rather than resisted these developments, in order to disarm attacks based on its secrecy. No one knew, however, what would result. GCHQ did not intend to have its current activities made as public as they are in 2020.

The unexpected driver became the effect of history and myth on public attitudes. With the disclosure of Ultra, some veterans wrote memoirs and historians worked with records and interviews. The multi-volume official history of *British Intelligence in the Second World War* described wartime Sigint in detail. A few academics began to study the history of British intelligence because it was an important and unknown topic. First, without fanfare, and later through the Waldegrave Initiative, authorities declassified most Sigint records before September 1945. Enthusiasts tackled British Sigint during the Second World War. Aided by a substantial donation from British lotteries, they rebuilt Bletchley from a series of dilapidated buildings into a sort of shrine, a locale for pilgrimage, with relics such as working versions of Colossus. These enthusiasts struck a public chord. To the astonishment of Cheltenham, and without much encouragement from it, Bletchley – and by extension, GCHQ – came to symbolise British virtues and survival during its darkest hour. Soon, the cult of Bletchley, its saints and a martyr, protected GCHQ more than the cult of secrecy ever had done.

GCHQ and the Second Age of Sigint, 1990–2020

Coming in from the Cold War

The late Cold War was a marvellous time for GCHQ. Its work was honoured by those who knew of it. GCHQ solved long-standing structural problems, acquired more resources and power, and became an avowed organisation. Despite failing to develop a purely British Sigint satellite in Zircon, GCHQ realised that bold innovation was necessary, which prepared it for the period of transformational change as the Cold War waned.

By 1989, indications abounded that the Cold War was ending. The Foreign Office questioned the need for even routine Radio Proving Flights against the Warsaw Pact, implying that their political risks outweighed their intelligence gains.[1] GCHQ noted increasing signs of erosion within the Warsaw Pact and unprecedented civil unrest in the USSR.[2] The London Signals Intelligence Board (LSIB) linked Sigint closely with military operations. By 1991, however, it expected service Sigint units to evacuate Germany and decline.[3] For the intelligence services which had enabled victory, the consequences were bitter sweet. Many agencies specialised in narrow topics, which soon no one might support or fund. GCHQ ranked high among them. The Soviet threat absorbed most of GCHQ's effort. Ecological change exposed GCHQ – overdeveloped in one niche of Sigint – to disaster, like its greatest consumer. DIS was trapped in specialised analysis of minutiae. It demanded full servicing of its needs – Sigint alone could enable the work and careers of specialists in, say, tugs for the Baltic Fleet. Another danger was that DIS might grip GCHQ like a drowning man. Siginters, however, were agile and suited to many ecosystems, if only they could swim there.

The Director, John Adye, sidestepped disaster through an astute version of GCHQ's standard strategy of the Cold War. Victory was won, but any troops left on the field might die; so he withdrew as many as possible. He abandoned some tasks so to preserve the whole by shifting resources from the Warsaw Pact to broader matters, keeping bodies for trade. That effort began in 1990. It became a flood after the abortive coup in Moscow of 1991 showed the Russian threat was disintegrating. J division moved most of its resources to K, ultimately 90 per cent of them, while still servicing DIS demands. If GCHQ's masters were willing, it might provide great economies in resources, especially intercept operators and stations, to trade for the funding needed to serve new missions, could they be found.

This strategy reduced risk, but could not evade the Treasury's desire for a peace dividend. GCHQ faced demands for cuts like those imposed on all departments involved in hard power – which ultimately ranged between 20 per cent for the services as a whole to 50 per cent for organisations focused on the Warsaw Pact. This fate was avoided through a national, but secret, process, involving external reviews, backstairs manoeuvres, leading civil servants, the membership of GCHQ and a succession of directors able in different ways. This process unfolded through serendipity, without a master plan, or a Svengali. Several groups tackled parts of a problem, without knowing what it was, or the solution would be. As they acted, targets and threats evolved, and changes in communications and computer systems opened a new age of Sigint. No one understood where these developments would lead, until they got there. Only the terrorist outrages of 9/11 and 7/7 crystallised that understanding in Cheltenham, and in NSA.

In 1994, Whitehall began a series of defence reviews. Michael Quinlan, a retired permanent undersecretary from the MOD famed for understanding the theory and practice of strategy, assessed intelligence needs. He and his staff, Treasury and joint intelligence officials, considered all aspects of intelligence. They interrogated GCHQ and its consumers, visited NSA, DGSE (Direction générale de la sécurité extérieure) and BND, and read much Sigint product. Quinlan, grasping what intelligence had done for Britain during the Cold War and might do again, distilled several principles to guide policy. Defining the resources required for intelligence and Sigint rested 'more on judgment than on measurement and calculation; no formula existed … Even with the benefit of hindsight … it was not possible to assess the absolute value of secret intelligence since the difference between "with intelligence" and "without" would be hypothetical and unquantifiable, especially in those circumstances where the benefit was an unwelcome event averted.'[4]

Secret intelligence aimed to 'offset gaps, uncertainties or distortions in overt information in order to advance national interests', especially 'by enabling national forces to prevail in conflict, with minimum loss'. The end of the Cold War reduced 'the direct military threat', but produced 'a world more complex and interdependent, less certain and less stable, with a wider and shifting range of conflict risk'. These circumstances increased the value of secret intelligence, especially Sigint, with its ability 'to build up patterns of understanding over time, especially in military and security fields, and the wide range of targets that were amenable to attack'. The nature of targets and power between attack and defence shifted constantly: 'careful cost/benefit analysis would be needed and … there would remain constant pressure for innovation and investment to maintain capability'. GCHQ's costs had risen since 1984, but it was efficient and economical. Any 'significant' reduction in its budget would cause 'an unacceptable reduction in the provision of intelligence … GCHQ's current level of capability must be maintained'. GCHQ 'provided a national asset of high standard', whose 'capabilities should be maintained at broadly planned levels of cost'. However, its work against Russia should be examined, while an 'outsider, experienced in the high technology private sector', might assess the room for economies and efficiencies.[5] Prime Minister John Major, who proved a friend to GCHQ – critical but judicious – endorsed Quinlan's 1994 report.

These comments whetted the Treasury's appetite for economies and GCHQ's desire to survive. Whitehall had Roger Hurn, chair of Smith's Industries – an industrialist with a national reputation, connections to Cheltenham and a love for hunting, high technology and institutional change – assess GCHQ. All departments hoped he might lean their way, and schemed to shape his terms of reference, and panels of advisors.

GCHQ loaned Hurn a team, led by David Pepper, a rising star, who had executed Adye's strategy, aided by MOD and Treasury officials. Hurn, inexperienced in intelligence, but not in business and industrial management, was a fast learner with some *idees fixes*. He saw how GCHQ functioned as no outsider had done since Evill or Hampshire. Hurn's focus on the idea of charging consumers for intelligence wasted much space, but at this stage he understood the relationship between high technology and institutions well. Hurn illuminated other issues with a power which impressed Pepper. Hurn assessed processes, how value was added in intelligence, and visited the shop floor. He asked units why they worked as they did. Personnel often could answer only that they always had done so, and then rethought their work.

Hurn reported that: 'GCHQ is a very high quality, well-funded organisation employing a large number of talented and committed high quality people, most of whom stay with the organisation for all of their careers. They are justifiably proud of their record and place in the nation's intelligence community. In short, GCHQ is undoubtedly a centre of excellence which responds impressively to the many new challenges it faces in requirements, targets and technology.' Civil service bureaucracy marred GCHQ less than most departments, he found, though every unit still should 'delayer' one level of management. The focus on Russia must end immediately, and planned reductions of staff be completed rapidly. The formulation of policy on all matters, such as intelligence production and human resources, should be more centralised, but its execution more decentralised. He offered proposals which guided GCHQ for a generation. GCHQ officials must work in other departments, and vice versa, to emphasise contacts between consumers and producers. Palmer Street must become a permanent embassy in London to reduce GCGQ's isolation within Whitehall, and a few outsiders should become permanent members of the directorate to reduce the impact of 'inbreeding'. Above all, GCHQ must continue its ongoing 'shifts in behaviour and organisational culture, there is no simple prescription to achieve these things but without them the changes will be piecemeal and will fail to achieve their full effect. This is the biggest part of the challenge for GCHQ's management.'[6]

Much of Hurn's conclusion was implicit, and perhaps expressed verbally to his consumers. GCHQ was a great national asset which must reform to handle changes in consumers, targets, techniques and technology. With DIS and the Soviet threat both waning, GCHQ must find new tasks and consumers. Its strategy for change was broadly right, but must accelerate. Reinvention was necessary, though Hurn did not prescribe its forms. GCHQ's proposed economies were of the right size but he did not mention (or oppose) expansion or recommend any budget for GCHQ. The organisation which had won the Cold War was too slow and hierarchical to handle emerging tasks and needed outside leadership to do so.

This report convinced the civil servants responsible for Sigint. Even the Treasury switched its focus from economy to efficiency. Through a process which is not entirely clear, GCHQ kept most of its share of the peace dividend to reinvent itself – under new management. Again, GCHQ and the deterrent were Britain's priorities in defence. During the Defence Reviews of 1994–95, 50 per cent of the forces under BAOR and RAF Germany were disbanded. Collectively, the services lost 18 per cent of their personnel. DIS became a ghost. Military Siginters declined by 33 per cent in size, precisely as demands for them in conflicts grew. In Germany, No. 26 RAF SU and 13 Signals Regiment were disbanded, though some elements moved to other units; 14 Signals Regiment transferred to Wales, where its aid to the local economy helped it live. Military Sigint bodies in Britain were unified. GCHQ lost many civilian personnel, but reallocated those savings to new tasks, which paid dividends. GCHQ's manpower was cut; and some of the savings from this were reinvested in GCHQ's advanced collection capabilities. Intercept organisations focused on HF radio traffic in Europe were traded for the means to acquire all kinds of traffic across the globe. GCHQ achieved its greatest priority of the late Cold War, rebuilding its collection infrastructure for the digital age, at a price it could pay.

Reinvention

Privately, Hurn recommended that Britain exploit Adye's looming retirement to appoint a director from outside GCHQ. If GCHQ was a national asset, then its control must be nationalised. Prime Minister Major, the Foreign Secretary, the Cabinet Secretary and the Permanent Secretary of the Treasury agreed on this recommendation and a candidate: David Omand, a leading civil servant in the MOD – whose first civil service job, helpfully, had been in GCHQ – and a member of the advisory board on Hurn's report. Whitehall thought well enough of GCHQ to send three high-flyers there in a row. These actions upset a seventy-six-year-old tradition of appointing Sigint leaders from within, and began five years of outside instruction, while people and attitudes changed in Cheltenham.

Omand had joined GCHQ as a cadet but soon moved to the normal civil service, an unusual step at that time. He knew how GCHQ and Whitehall worked and how defence was managed. Omand was a mathematician, Fortran programmer and early adopter, but learned through experience. Clearly, the age of radio interception was ending, while the internet enabled some new era of communication and information. GCHQ could economise further on radio interception, meeting MOD demands with legacy systems, while investing in sources suited to the digital age and new consumers. Omand sought to make GCHQ a 'consumer facing organisation', which cultivated new customers across Whitehall, such as counter-proliferation and counter-narcotics units. GCHQ must give decision-makers 'value added intelligence' through agility and speed, unlike the industrial line production for DIS during the Cold War. The office at Palmer Street was staffed by an undersecretary and a team ordered to act 'more like SIS' – to identify potential consumers, determine their needs and meet them. Whereas DIS had known exactly what it wanted, new consumers might not know what they needed or could receive.

Knowledge of GCHQ, and a feline sense of opportunity, drove the formulation and execution of Omand's campaign. By 1990, reflecting its targets and consumers, GCHQ was a civilianised version of military models, more than at any other time in its history. Omand sidestepped these structures. He gave many employees his email address. If they raised important issues, he visited them directly rather than going through channels, which shocked his subordinates. GCHQ's leaders debated the case for change in informal meetings at Omand's flat in Cheltenham, rather than through directorate meetings with memoranda. Siginters were characterised by analytical ability and preference to work as a team. The leadership group was small, unified and knew each other well. This empirical approach produced consensus and detailed processes and systems for reform. NSA took years more to achieve similar ends because its leadership was larger and scattered across a continent – rather than concentrated at Cheltenham – and embedded within military organisations, where theories of an RMA, imposed top down, drove efforts at reform. When NSA did move, however, the speed and effect were extraordinary.

These developments changed lives. A generation of individuals, many groomed for promotion in a patronage-driven system, were frozen from the highest levels of GCHQ. The value of old technical skills diminished and those of new ones multiplied. Basic competence with PCs and the internet became essential for success, which opened new opportunities below. However, old hands worked loyally, including some who had seen the directorship in their future and now saw it slip from their grasp. All could see that GCHQ had escaped a worse fate and was proceeding on rational lines. The time needed to continue legacy systems and to inaugurate new ones enabled a phased pattern of retirements and dignity to all. Not until after 7/7 did the last of the old hands retire. For younger staff, these decisions were liberating. The old system and the obsolescence of its approach to computers and the internet frustrated many who joined after 1989. Young staff received the chance they wished – to play with the best kit and to match the successes of their parents and grandparents since 1940.

Reform involved re-education. GCHQ did so by hiring a private agency, ITS, which helped firms manage change. The firm educated, first, the upper 200 members of GCHQ, and ultimately the top 30 per cent of them – every manager and worker on any creative coalface. Through this programme, 'Lead 21', several outsiders regularly met small groups of Siginters who were drawn from different parts of GCHQ. These presenters received unparalleled access into Britain's most secret agencies, an indicative change in its own right. They addressed issues such as organisation and psychology, using devices including the Myers-Briggs personality assessments, which illustrated how different groups of people perceived circumstances and acted on them. Despite much academic criticism, these assessments often cause reflection among non-specialists. This approach challenged all the old conditioning of Siginters. They tended to be introspective. They were not encouraged to reflect on their work, but just to do it, generally in self-contained groups, without talking much to others. They had no collective experience of education in their profession or nature. Suddenly, large groups of Siginters went through the same collective psychological experience, talking openly about themselves and their work with others, and discussing, explicitly, issues such as introversion and extraversion, sensing and intuition, thinking and feeling, judging and perceiving, and emotional intelligence. Veterans of Lead 21 and ITS remember the experience as illuminating, causing them to criticise concepts which they had internalised without thought and to change their attitudes and behaviour. Throughout this process, the personal views of people were canvassed on a variety of matters. Many requests were made, not all of which could be honoured, but enough to satisfy people. This process marked the morale and attitudes of an entire generation at GCHQ, overcoming the shock of change and loss of colleagues, and leading people to move happily in new directions.

Success created problems of its own. The technical and cultural transformation at GCHQ caught Whitehall's attention. After eighteen months at GCHQ, Omand became Permanent Undersecretary at the Home Office, which ministers wanted an outsider to reform. He invited Pepper to lead the modernisation programme within the Home Office, including big PFI projects for IT and accommodation. This move aimed to give Pepper experience outside GCHQ, so to make him an effective director there, but it also took the two leading proponents of reform from Cheltenham. Kevin Tebbit, a senior Foreign Office official, replaced Omand. He calmed nerves which were palpitating over transformation, but after only a few months became Permanent Undersecretary at the MOD. In January 1998, after a year of three directors, he was succeeded by Francis Richards, a former military officer turned diplomat. Richards had no hands-on experience of intelligence, but much in an unusual number of other areas, where his hands had always proven safe. He understood consumers, leadership and management. He inherited a reform just beginning and sketchy in many details. Rather than abandon it and pursue a programme named after himself, Richards honed the one he was with. He stayed for five years, long enough to establish the Omand–Richards reforms, and for GCHQ to reinvent itself. When Richards retired, Pepper replaced him, beginning a twelve-year period where GCHQ's directors were Siginters, yet with an understanding of Whitehall which matched that of Cheltenham.

GCHQ adapted itself to the second age of Sigint just as it emerged, but not without error. The construction project that would become 'the Doughnut' – making this most secret of agencies iconic across the earth – illustrates how that process combined success and failure. In 1996, GCHQ launched the initiative 'Sinews' – Sigint's new systems – to define and hone the procedures needed to live in the digital world. This project was pioneering but complicated because the engineers and computer scientists in Benhall were physically and psychologically distinct from the directorate, cryptanalysts, analysts and linguists in other buildings. To coordinate their work, or even converse about it, was difficult. The convoluted organisational and physical structure of GCHQ was well suited to the radio age and the Cold War, but not to answer new questions, let alone to execute solutions or ride a revolution.

Digital technology was hard to introduce in the warren of GCHQ's old, often dilapidated, offices. GCHQ needed new accommodations, which its capital budget could not start, let alone complete. Opportunity emerged when the Treasury asked departments to surrender their capital budgets in favour of public–private partnerships, where private investors would finance the construction of buildings, to be repaid over decades. Omand convinced the Treasury that an ambitious partnership, aiming to bring all of the scattered parts of GCHQ into one building, would heighten its efficiency and effect. An open plan would help Siginters transform their culture to meet a digital environment. The project, for several years the largest construction site in Europe, met that aim, and proved a key to reinvention. It also was far more expensive than predicted: partly because GCHQ lacked the experience needed to manage large programmes, as it ceased to be simply an intelligence agency but also became an executive arm of state, but mostly because Siginters underestimated the scale of change that processing the global packet switched networks of the internet would demand of GCHQ.

As Pepper said, in the early 1990s, GCHQ's information technology:

> was essentially composed of a number of stand-alone systems,
> large systems but they were not interconnected and they were not
> networked because at that stage networking was not the way IT was
> organised ... we began gradually to introduce networking to our
> systems for two reasons: one, because that was the way technology
> was going, but also because we faced a change of circumstances in
> that we had an IT system which had evolved during the Cold War
> when we had very large, monolithic, essentially static targets and we
> were able to operate in effect with stove-piped IT systems. During

the early 1990s the Cold War ended; we were faced with a much more volatile and varied set of targets and it became necessary to make our systems much more flexible and to make the way we used them more flexible.[7]

By 1995, 'there were a lot of networking connections between the systems'. Engineers and cryptanalysts patched together powerful, but disconnected, networks of computers and specialised systems, relying on individual memory rather than documented configuration control. No one recognised 'quite the extent and the full implications of the transition we were going through, the totally new IT world that we were moving into'. Technical personnel did not realise that dismantling each system and reconstructing them in the new building would be difficult. They did so only after a study, involving 150 man years, assessed how all of their networks could handle 'Y2K', the bug which many feared might wreck all computer systems on midnight, 1 January 2000. Engineers, now grasping the greater problem, mapped all the processes needed to install their capabilities in the Doughnut. These unforeseen factors caused a cost overrun, and eventually a much greater cost was incurred than originally announced. Richards had to plead for more resources, which were granted, after an independent report was published. Its author, General Sir Edmund Burton, an experienced manager of major projects, immediately became a non-executive director. The Treasury covered £216 million of this overrun, demonstrating that Whitehall was impressed by GCHQ's work. GCHQ was left responsible for the rest. Ultimately, the NAP costs were underestimated in error but were corrected before the programme was approved, after an encounter with the Public Accounts Committee. Omand, rightly, stated that the Doughnut more than paid its way, but these cost overruns demonstrate elementary flaws in GCHQ's understanding of Sigint in a new age, even as it adapted to them.[8]

Meanwhile, military Sigint paid a heavy peace dividend, for a peace that never came. The cuts in military Sigint temporarily stopped recruitment. Some personnel retired, others retrained in new technologies and languages. Royal Navy Siginters, integrated into communications, command, control and intelligence systems on warships, were least affected, but still faced problems with targets and languages, when operations began in the Balkans during 1996. Army and RAF Sigint units shrank, but their personnel, forced into successive expeditions, served in war zones more than ever since 1945. In a slow and halting fashion, at some cost, these campaigns retaught GCHQ and the services lessons about Sigint they had known well in 1945, but had since forgotten. GCHQ and the military were badly coordinated when wars began in the former Yugoslavia – 'not our finest hour', Adye sighed.[9] During the 1991 Gulf War, Sigint was 'an invaluable source', but many of its problems in tactical use from the Falklands conflict recurred.[10] Siginters bickered over 'jointery' – the need for people with many cap badges to cooperate seamlessly – and over what practices were electronic warfare or Sigint, for either the services or GCHQ to fund and control. GCHQ was tough about funding service Siginters. They usually cost more than civilians but possessed skills the latter lacked and, unlike them, could operate in combat zones. Slowly, however, GCHQ and the MOD improved their coordination and the dissemination of Sigint to commanders. Government Communications Officers (GCOs) already in the MOD, and static commands to coordinate supply and demand in Sigint, became normal in expeditionary headquarters. The Transportable Cryptologic Support Group, borrowing American terminology but following British practices of 1945, gave commanders tailored feeds of Sigint. Though this group originally was intended to support a theatre-level headquarters, its first use was three echelons of command below. It supported a battle group in the Balkans, whose commander praised its 'outstanding source of high-grade intelligence and endless cups of tea'.[11] The MOD established a senior military advisor at Cheltenham, to bring operational experience into Sigint planning for military operations.

GCHQ faced dangers during the 1990s. The end of the Cold War threatened its resources, while the rise of the digital age particularly imperilled Sigint agencies. GCHQ surmounted these challenges rather well. GCHQ transformed itself to fit the digital age because of its small size, unity, its institutional culture of teamwork and agility in action, and reasoned and empirical debate. Unlike many organisations which tried but failed to transform, GCHQ ignored theories of an 'information age', or revolutions in business or military affairs, but focused on real problems and solutions. GCHQ's early exposure to practical issues drove its rapid adaptation to them – transformation was not about theories, but tasks. GCHQ was able to reinvest the peace dividend into new forms of Sigint and to exploit government fashions of economy to finance its reconfiguration. As it shed some of the largest elements of its staff, such as intercept operators and clerical personnel, it received ample opportunity to hire youngsters with different skills. GCHQ developed the kit, personnel and organisation suited to the new targets and threats of the digital age. These developments eliminated GCHQ's main technical weakness of the Cold War – its inability to meet the costs of emerging forms of interception – and returned it to the top table, at an affordable price. GCHQ ceased to decline compared to NSA: for several years after 1995, GCHQ rose sharply in relative quality. It was also the first institution in the world to enter the second age of Sigint. That age had many roots and was driven by unintended and unexpected consequences.

On the Cyber Commons

Between 1945 and 1989, Siginters attacked two communications targets. They aimed to collect as much material as possible from military radio networks protected by specialised personnel and cryptography, and small amounts of traffic – mostly of states, but sometimes foreign individuals or entities – on civilian communications systems, including cable, microwave and satellites. The end of the Cold War accelerated changes in technology that had affected the collection and processing of Sigint for decades. HF radio, and the large conventional sites that collected it, became marginal to communications and Sigint, though Siginters maintained capabilities in these areas, as they did against manual codes – just in case. Satellites, and land and maritime cables, became the mainstays for state and civilian communication and Sigint. GCHQ's targets, whether diplomats, spies or terrorists, no longer used distinct and unique communications systems, but rather civilian ones. Their traffic could not be intercepted unless one also touched that of civilians, including one's own people, because the source and destination of messages could be identified only by checking external features. That characteristic had been true since ILC emerged on radio during the 1920s, swelled through use on satellites and after 1990 became universal across all modes of communication.

Civilian systems also changed. Before the digital age, few countries could intercept any traffic outside of their borders at a time when postal and telegraph services created the first world-wide information commons. Liberal states, above all Britain, were masters of these media. They did not intercept the communications of foreigners because they valued privacy and liberty for themselves and others. Necessity drove Britain to censor all internal and international cable and postal communications during the First and Second World Wars, but these practices ended with those conflicts. Even then, it acquired only private data moving across the waves, not that resting in drawers. Strong boundaries between nations, and media, marked civil communications. The only exception was ILC which, nonetheless, after 1960, became one of its main types, through satellite communication. Different means were needed to garner information resting in drawers, and moving by cable, or post or telephone. Rarely could private parties attack others, or states. The limits of technology and the power of governments kept individuals from intercepting the traffic of other parties. State censorship of information became hard in liberal countries and easy in totalitarian ones. Even when the bars to collection were raised – in fact, precisely for that reason – private material threatened information overload far more than did the traffic of foreign states simply because it was so voluminous and its importance was so difficult to gauge. The problem became one of data storage and retrieval – as letters had to be copied and telephone calls transcribed manually, and their myriad details indexed and filed.

Regular attacks on civilian systems and private messages, outside of war or within one's own state, emerged through a halting process, which was linked to the legal and technical characteristics of telephone and wireless traffic, especially from foreign countries. Radio telephones emerged around 1930. Their traffic easily was intercepted, with effective modes of security for states arriving only in 1942–43. Private shields remained weak. From 1960, private messages were transmitted in large volumes by satellite or wireless media and were easy for all states (liberal or otherwise) to intercept, unlike cable, line telephone or post. Many states began systematically to intercept foreign messages of this sort, especially commercial traffic such as telexes, which gradually expanded to include telephone calls. This expansion was enabled by the absence of legal restraints and the end of taboos about violating individual privacy, coupled with the rise of radical pragmatism. States mired in decades of hot and cold wars learned the value of Comint. Liberals viewed the traffic of foreign states as fair game, and the privacy of foreign individuals as collateral damage. Totalitarian states became even more cynical than before. These processes were driven by the presence of Comint institutions that wanted to exploit all modes of data collection. Even so, the best Sigint agencies on earth could attack only tiny samples of the material carried on Comsat, and never the postal systems of foreign states. No attacker could read every document scattered through millions of drawers – which provided some security to states and far more to individuals.

Increasingly from 1990, communications and information were digitised and joined into one system: the internet. Anyone on the internet was connected to everyone. The internet was jury-rigged, rather than designed, but its prevailing characteristics placed disclosure and surveillance above security or privacy. Electronic mail, dispatched by telephone lines, carried voice and print messages. Data at rest and in motion became unified and digitised, simple to acquire, store, retrieve, analyse – and to intercept. All could be attacked by the same cryptanalytical means. Once state and individual archives went online, documents were exposed to attack, just like email. This step increased the power of sampling. If one could detect a current threat and access its computer, its data-processing system would provide its past records. The rise of mobile wireless devices increased the amount of private communications susceptible to interception. Communications, carried online and through wireless telephones by signals that crossed national boundaries promiscuously, linked to any data stored on computers connected to the internet, became open to interception by all-comers at once – not merely to states with sole control over cables or postal services. This material could be copied as easily as electrons, although retrieval and analysis remained frustrating. Prevalent modes of communications were a cryptanalyst's dream: unprecedented numbers of communications junkies, actively drawing attention to themselves and exposing their secrets with abysmal security. A novel threat emerged: that of a nuclear strike on data. One could not merely read the documents in someone's archive, but write them.

The internet also enabled the rise of an anarchic international order. 'Cyberspace' is not a metaphor, realm or place, but rather a part of many things and of the connections between them – a commons of communication and information. As on other commons, such as markets or the seas, a struggle between many players, states and others defines the practices within overlapping competitions between state and non-state actors. These practices alter with changes to conditions, interests, power and time. They always are in dispute. Those practices which emerged over cyber involved as many actors and interests as ever on any commons: intelligence and security for states, and privacy and surveillance for individuals across the world. A social market emerged on the cyber commons centred on the ability of people to communicate and for messages to be intercepted. This market was marked by the self-interest, cooperation, warfare, intelligence-gathering, deception and security characteristics of the individuals, states and pirates that abound on every commons. In order to maximise their gains from this social market, people simplified the processing of information. They paid for that end with privacy, thus easing piracy. Privacy and surveillance are problematic concepts, as attitudes towards them vary by culture and time. There may have been no more privacy or less surveillance in villages than there is in the global village. Bourgeois forms of privacy and respectability aimed to contain surveillance, which limited one's opportunities on the signals market. Given the mass of other people, one best could find individuals, attract their attention or pursue comparative and mutual advantage, by combining openness with the constant transmission of, and search for, broad and narrow signals. People commodified others, and themselves. Voting with their digits, they assigned privacy a low price, if sometimes pretending that its value was higher. Their modes of communication transformed the relations between their reputations and themselves. New needs to communicate outweighed old modes of privacy, which produced a society based on signals and surveillance, with individuals being simultaneously subject and object.

These developments eased the interception and transmission of signals and dissolved established borders between states and societies, internal and external relations, war and peace, civil and military, security and insecurity, and sovereign and non-state actors. Once Sigint agencies could distinguish between traffic intercepted at home and abroad, it let liberal states combine civil liberties and cryptanalysis. That status no longer was true when messages surged automatically between servers at home and abroad and Sigint agencies had an unparalleled ability to read the mail of private people, as against foreign states. Once, states fought only each other, and alone controlled the highest levels of violence (part of the problem with terrorists was their claim to act like states, and their efforts to do so). Now, non-state actors used the same techniques of Comint as governments and applied them against foreign states, or people. Citizens were threatened by attack from their fellows, foreign governments, firms and criminals. States could not easily protect their people against these threats, and thus failed a fundamental condition of sovereignty.

Privacy and surveillance, intelligence and security, and old distinctions between states and individuals, and their competitions, were transformed. The greatest change was not in the ability of states to attack each other, or their own people, though these capabilities did rise. It was the ability of states to monitor foreign civilians, and above all of private parties to read anyone's mail or memoranda – private or governmental, home or abroad. As ever, states lacked the resources to read all of the traffic they could intercept, but they no longer were the only power on these seas. Individuals were more open to attack from pirates and foreign governments than on any other commons. Pirates attacked from desks, not decks. Individuals relied for security on whatever encryption their computers or cell phones possessed. For most civilians, these levels were higher than possible in the analogue age, but not for states. Cryptanalysts easily broke the basic encryption in most commercial kit. Good encryption, including high-end commercial cryptography, required trained personnel using specialist procedures and cryptosystems. For perhaps the first time in history, anyone could acquire cryptography proof against the best of codebreakers. A few civilians did so, but the overwhelming majority did not, while even many state entities slipped in security. Pirates had unprecedented power, precision and range. States attacked the communications of foreign individuals and corporations far more than ever before in peacetime and faced greater challenges in defending their citizens.

Changes in the characteristics of communication spilling across national borders also affected how liberal states intercepted any traffic of their citizens, home or abroad, or foreign messages passing through their space. In the analogue age, lawyers and Siginters could differentiate between traffic transmitted at home and abroad, and illegal and lawful interception. In the digital age, domestic traffic moved abroad, and foreign messages through one's home. Messages between offices in Cheltenham might pass, say, through Beijing; traffic between Russian intelligence in Moscow and Petersburg move via London. Foreign targets might best be attacked by intercepting communications passing through your home, even though the legal position might be different. Domestic traffic would be acquired through legally acceptable interception abroad. Bulk collection of any internet traffic must include one's citizens, in the first instance. To do otherwise would be to abandon Comint, which one's rivals would not. Yet any analysis of such material, whether intercepted at home or abroad, must touch the envelopes, the metadata, of their citizens' mail without warrant. These procedures were legal, but felt unpleasant.

Cyber Intelligence, Terrorism and Strife

No commons can survive without security. They all feature competing forms of securitisation. The cyber commons was securitised from its birth and then militarised by actors across the earth. The 'weary giants of flesh and steel' never left that commons free from realpolitik, as one internet libertarian prophesied.[12] However, even its practitioners did not fully understand the degree of that militarisation until a decade after it began. The public, even civilian technical experts, took rather longer to appreciate its existence.

GCHQ entered this commons when it was terra incognita, as old practices of Sigint were dying and new ones began. People learned from experience with no idea of the outcome. During the 1990s, GCHQ translated the practices of Sigint from one age to another; it was among the first and biggest institutions to combine technical skills from both sides of the divide, to learn how to attack and defend the new target systems on the cyber commons – the internet, individual computers and cryptosystems. GCHQ hired 'hackers', a different group to cryppies in both technical prowess and intellectual background. Its hackers came from the ethical rather than the malicious branch of that tribe. Together, they created cyber intelligence, a practice distinct from Sigint or Comint. Hackers – whom the Five Eyes termed Computer Network Operators (CNO) – opened doors themselves, or brought cryppies there to do so. Cryptanalysis struck the cryptosystems embedded in computers. Computer network operators carried that success to the heart of computers, then vanished, leaving no signs of their passing – merely hidden payloads to enable later re-entry, or viruses to spread insecurity or chaos across networks. Operators pursued general tasks which earlier auxiliaries to Sigint had handled through human means in unique cases, such as acquiring access to traffic or cryptosystems opportunistically through black bag jobs or suborning telegraph clerks. These tasks simplified the work of cryptanalysis, often to dramatic effect. CNO was divided into several categories, such as: CNE (computer network exploitation) or 'cyber intelligence'; computer network attack (CNA), to incapacitate computers or corrupt the data they contain; and CND, computer network defence, against both threats. CNO became an ally to cryptanalysis, rather than an auxiliary, both working interactively against targets. It was a technical and universal discipline, with the exploitation of human frailty one of its categories, rather than an individual opportunity.

Cyber intelligence became central to GCHQ's repertoire, but was used essentially against traditional targets, until powerful acts of terrorism and long wars in Afghanistan and Iraq drove escalations of that effort. These acts included 9/11 – the largest terrorist attack in history, when on 11 September 2001, hijacked airliners struck buildings in Manhattan and Washington, killing 2,996 people – and 7/7: 7 July 2005, when one of the largest terrorist assaults ever on British soil resulted in the deaths of fifty-two civilians. The Five Eyes confronted loosely organised but persistent foes, mainly groups of Salafi-jihadist terrorists. They had to block attacks by – or kill – motivated individuals. Cyber intelligence became their main source, ahead of Humint and Imint (imagery intelligence).

For GCHQ, the only parallel experiences in these areas were fights against guerrillas or terrorists. Experiences such as Konfrontasi and Palestine demonstrated that success was rewarding, but hard to achieve against adversaries with good Comsec. Siginters had to provide detailed and live intelligence on specific people to other agencies, such as MI5, or to forces in a position to attack enemies, such as deployed aircraft. Intelligence might involve the names of people in Britain who communicated with terrorist recruiters abroad, or, say, the location of Taliban insurgents preparing to ambush British soldiers near the Kajaki dam in Helmand province on 3 September 2008. Such material must be found amidst billions of messages each day crossing civilian systems. Attack and defence also involved third parties, which faced threats from common foes, and had sources of intelligence unavailable to UKUSA. Greater cooperation was necessary with such countries against terrorism than fitted the classic model of relations between the Five Eyes and third parties. States might attack each other's cryptosystems, but cooperate against terrorists.

Achieving any of these objectives was hard. Other issues made it harder. In particular, terrorism is a danger which is easily overrated. Events combining low probability and high costs are difficult to calculate and counter, particularly when the danger is a hidden enemy which might suddenly strike close to home. Terrorists exploit media and attack emotions in order to drag fear and rage onto the scales of calculation. They build an emotional bomb among electorates, which any outrage might detonate at any time. Counter-terrorist personnel often feel personal responsibility for any failure. Treating terrorism as war, and making the prevention of every possible act of terrorism the criterion for competence, distorts all balances between intelligence, security and other objectives. Terrorism, like the cyber commons, dissolved old boundaries: between war and peace, uniformed and non-uniformed belligerents, foreign foes and traitors, and the idea of home and abroad. Like a black hole, terrorism sucked in intelligence agencies. They were pushed to allocate greater attention to terrorism than the danger was probably worth, compared to other enduring interests of state or society. After 7/7, GCHQ made counter-terrorism one of its major concerns for the allocation of resources, but still developed the most rapid and precise means possible to gather Sigint on a host of individuals posing known threats, and to try to detect as-yet unknown ones.

Support for counter-insurgency during wars reinforced that trend. It followed patterns from conventional operations, like Iraq in 2003, where air forces coordinated command and intelligence with unprecedented skill, multiplying all forms of rapid, precise and long-distance weapons. Strikes rose even more in power for special forces or UAVs against insurgents, whether individuals or small groups, in Iraq and Afghanistan. Intelligence and precision weapons enabled exact attacks, by the standards of air power or counter-insurgency, often the equivalent of snipers firing at known individuals. As ever, when force is used near civilians, innocents die – the only question being, how many? Excellent imagery and human and signals intelligence helped to define targets, to execute strikes, and to minimise civilian casualties. Siginters became more entangled in battle than ever before. The decline in service Siginters and the rise of military precision strikes threw civilian officials into kill chains. Military Siginters wanted to be there, but civilians psychologically preferred some means to distance themselves from decisions for death. GCHQ no longer was just an intelligence organisation, but part of executive agencies for the use of force. It was the executive authority for the burgeoning areas of CNA and CND.

Britain's enemies had many targets. GCHQ could not keep every threat at bay. Some would bite Britain. At best, GCHQ could maintain a favourable balance of order on the border and bite back harder; which it did. British civilians and soldiers died. Cybercriminals, some associated with foreign states, pillaged the accounts of private citizens, or stole technology from UKUSA firms. Other states or pirates might match UKUSA in hacking, but none could touch its power in cryptanalysis, cyber intelligence, or bulk collection. GCHQ also minimised interference with the lives of their own people, and civilians in other countries too.

States remained the major target, struck through tailored attacks. Government and public opinion, however, understanding the problems only through their manifestation in murder, drove GCHQ to protect British civilian and military lives from terrorists, insurgents and pirates. Had GCHQ and UKUSA not beaten these threats they would have failed their duty and been reviled. Internal and external threats fused. GCHQ acted as it rarely had before: more like policemen within Britain than soldiers abroad. Such acts stretched its legal mandate against external threats, yet if it did not take the work, who else had the technical capabilities for it? How else could GCHQ prevent agents based abroad from stealing secrets from firms in Glasgow, inspiring terrorism by British subjects in Bradford, or subverting elections across the country?

In order to man British frontiers on the cyber commons, GCHQ adopted a new and unique form of bulk collection. The old warrant to collect diplomatic telegrams worked entirely through cable addresses and caught them all. The WTID and Siginters working against Russian civil text attacked unencrypted traffic. They read every message they intercepted, discarded 95 per cent of them based on a quick scrutiny of content, and analysed the rest. All of these Siginters aimed to intercept 100 per cent of the traffic sent. Workers against ILC, especially satellites, took tiny samples of traffic. They treated plain-language traffic as the

WTID had done, and then used traffic analysis to determine the addressees of encrypted ILC messages and cryptanalysis to attack those which from external features seemed interesting. Traffic analysis was useful essentially to guide cryptanalysis. After 1990, against internet traffic passing through cables or wireless, GCHQ took even tinier samples than that from ILC. If all the world's internet traffic was a billiards table, GCHQ sopped up a beer mat's worth of messages and processed through traffic analysis only a full stop, with far less than that amount attacked and read.

All of this material had some encryption, elementary at lower levels, but often hard at upper ones. As a practice, traffic analysis turned systematically from assessing the external features of signals between HF radio sets, to the IP addresses of computers within networks. This transformation required operators with different skill sets, though they retained the creative and painstaking ability to analyse the external features of communications which drove GCHQ's successes in fusion during the Cold War. This traffic analysis illuminated potential threats or problems long before any content was read, and was the main part of success against bulk traffic. Cryptanalysis provided just the icing on the cake. The metadata of IP addresses was anonymised, stripping all personal details, which simplified Sigint and GCHQ's legal position. Traffic analysis determined which IP addresses communicated with those already under suspicion, so identifying further suspects. Cryptanalysis attacked only messages from suspect addresses. If these addresses involved non-Five Eyes citizens working from non-UKUSA addresses, the decision to attack was purely technical, made by analysts and cryptanalysts. If they touched a Five Eyes citizen, location or address, warrants were needed to justify attacks on the content of messages.

As Iain Lobban, the Director of GCHQ, said in 2013

If you think of the internet as an enormous hay field, what we are trying to do is to collect hay from those parts of the field that we can get access to and which might be lucrative in terms of containing the needles or the fragments of the needles that we might be interested in, that might help our mission. When we gather that haystack, and remember it is not a haystack from the whole field, it is a haystack from a tiny proportion of that field, we are very, very well aware that within that haystack there is going to be plenty of hay which is innocent communications from innocent people, not just British, foreign people as well. And so we design our queries against that data, to draw out the needles and we do not intrude upon, if you like, the surrounding hay. We can only look at the content of communications where there are very specific legal thresholds and requirements which have been met. So that is the reality. We don't want to delve into innocent e-mails and phonecalls … If I have that haystack, I am looking for needles and fragments of needles. That is what my queries pull out. I do not look at the surrounding hay. It may have been intercepted. A small portion of that may apply to British citizens. We will not look at it without a specific authorisation.[13]

The overwhelming number of potential targets, compared to the tiny resources for traffic analysis, cryptanalysis and languages, drove this process. GCHQ lacked the means to attack any message which did not have high priority. Every day it could assess the metadata of billions of messages, yet perhaps touched just tens of thousands of them, and read a small proportion of the traffic of hundreds of new targets. The latter, however, enabled many successes. GCHQ devised efficient means to sample massive quantities of traffic; to hold, examine and, where relevant, retain traffic; and then to flush its databases and repeat the process. As it later wrote: 'GCHQ uses its bulk powers to access the internet at scale so as then to dissect it with surgical precision. By drawing out fragments of intelligence … and fitting them together like a jigsaw,' GCHQ could 'discover new threats', provide 'unique intelligence about the plans and intentions of current targets', and 'protect the UK against cyber-attack from our most savvy adversaries and to track them down in the vast morass of the internet'.[14]

In 2009, 'complex analysis' of bulk data led GCHQ to identify several different terrorists in Britain working with leaders abroad, who were arrested before they struck. During the war in Afghanistan, GCHQ enabled the rescue of kidnapped British nationals without loss of their lives, and the disruption of attacks on its base at Camp Bastion. GCHQ's work in analysis of bulk collection was essential to the work of MI5 and MI6 against threats.[15] These gains were smaller than those acquired through GCHQ's work in war against Germany or Argentina, but they secured Britain's border on the cyber commons and saved British lives.

From Secrecy to Translucency

These developments drove GCHQ into new relationships with some elements of society. GCHQ moved cautiously into the open, especially after 9/11 and 7/7. Restrained by an instinctive focus on secrecy, still GCHQ built contacts with the press, some academics and many firms worried about cybersecurity and cybercrime. It offered assistance, at arm's length, mostly through loans of equipment, to the Bletchley Park Trust, which fostered the memory of British Sigint during the Second World War. GCHQ expanded cooperation with other ministries, which saw its value in aiding Britain against threats which the public thought were existential. GCHQ built good relations with parliamentary oversight authorities, whom it treated with respect. GCHQ became much more open within Whitehall, yet remained weak in areas where other ministries liaised with the public. In particular, its offices for press and public relations and law were tiny, essentially servicing contacts in Cheltenham.

GCHQ did not openly address the operational and legal elements of bulk collection because it did not know how to do so, rather than having anything to hide. Since 1815, British agencies have followed the law about intercepting the communications of British subjects. The few documentable instances of illegal actions are illuminating. During 1914–15, Admiral Hall illegally used powers against suspects which he did not have the right to apply. He and General Cockerill went to the edge of the law, and perhaps just past it, in intercepting letters for blockade – though that mail was foreign, not British, and authorities quickly authorised these actions.[16] Between 1919 and 1936, MI5 routinely and, so it claimed, inadvertently, violated the law when acquiring warrants for telephone tapping, which its Director arranged straight with the GPO, without approval by a Secretary of State.[17] An official in 1930s India illegally intercepted a rival's telegrams for political reasons.[18]

More actions than these probably occurred, but nothing suggests that British authorities often or routinely illegally intercepted private communications. The greater issue, legal but inappropriate monitoring, is a matter of opinion as much as fact. MI5 bugged Communist Party offices in King Street for decades and intercepted the correspondence of left-wing agitators more than that of right-wing ones. Political inclinations shape how far one thinks those actions were legitimate, or not, but certainly they were legal. More broadly, these actions show how the ability to intercept messages increased the power of states against political dissidence during the twentieth century, where Britain fell within the more restrained group of liberal states. GCHQ and MI5 were certainly not like the Stasi, if less restricted than British agencies had been between 1844 and 1914. These agencies did not create the surveillance state in Britain; this stemmed from surveillance capitalism, from private firms deploying CCTV and commercial monitoring of internet data.

Law prevented GCHQ from monitoring the messages of British subjects, which it did in only three cases. First, as in Palestine, when security services required Sigint against internal armed opposition, but could not collect it, GCHQ was warranted to do so, legally. Second, GC&CS executed lawful warrants to intercept telegrams of political agitators and collected them because its work with diplomatic traffic provided the necessary connections with cable companies, which no other department had. In 1925, GC&CS told the Treasury that the number of telegrams to and from Britain which were checked 'depends on the number of Bolshies whom the SOS, in the public interest, decides to keep his eyes on'.[19] These numbers expanded dramatically during and after the General Strike, under a general warrant from the Home Office. This action, incidentally, shows that the warrant for cable intercepts did not cover British civilians, which otherwise would have been unnecessary.[20] Finally, after 1928, GCHQ intercepted civilian wireless traffic on the ether: all of the take was legal and some of it valuable. Sometimes, GC&CS captured messages from British civilians, whether communicating between Britain and another country, or between two foreign states. GC&CS could not know that British subjects were involved until an analyst saw that fact, when they read the message and discarded it. That action contained the potential illegality of the action, which no one really considered. Legal and operational needs supported each other. The interception of ILC aimed to capture espionage or diplomatic traffic. A warrant would already cover any Britons suspected of espionage; GC&CS lacked the personnel to waste time on anyone else. Its procedures for handling bulk traffic always began with purging anything but material on a few topics.

Ample experience since 1928 coloured GCHQ's response to bulk collection and British civilian communications in the digital age. Yet it no longer collected such material from the ether, but often from a legally different space: British subjects in British territory. GCHQ used such material only after anonymising metadata, which hid the identity of British subjects. Little intercepted material was touched. Content was not read without a special warrant. GCHQ believed these procedures were legal. Its personnel knew they were not behaving badly, but rather saving British lives. GCHQ explained these practices and their legal and operational rationale to its ministerial masters, and to the parliamentary oversight committee, which approved them. Yet these practices were unknown to the public, and their possibility buried amongst a host of details in the relevant legislation, the Intelligence Services Act of 1994, and the Regulation of Investigatory Powers Act of 2000 (RIPA). The law for the interception of British traffic was obsolete, and GCHQ alone could not modernise it. Only a government effort could do so, and no one particularly wished to handle the task. GCHQ believed that its work was essential and legal. GCHQ did not consider how the public would react if suddenly, without explanation, it learned of these practices. GCHQ assumed that such an event could not happen, because it could control any movement away from secrecy.

This belief contradicted the record of recent decades and proved optimistic. In 2013, Edward Snowden, a contractor and systems administrator at NSA, copied reams of records about the working of UKUSA, and leaked them to journalists and activists, though GCHQ and NSA neither confirmed nor denied their authenticity. Suddenly, the public and technical specialists confronted the reality of militarisation and Comint on the cyber commons, and were genuinely shocked. Initially, the disclosures were incomprehensible. As every case of traffic analysis against metadata (and sometimes, merely the number of messages collected and anonymised) was taken to mean the reading of mail, people assumed that the Five Eyes read infinitely more messages than was true – confusing the 'full stop' for the 'beer mat' and sometimes even the 'billiards table'. The *Guardian* wrote that authorities had powers 'beyond what Orwell could have imagined'. Privacy International complained that 'while the Stasi had files on one in three East Germans', GCHQ 'intercepted and stored' the 'communications of almost everybody in the UK'.[21]

These disclosures were one-sided and naive. Critics assumed that just a few Western countries conducted Comint on the cyber commons, unlike nice states such as China and Russia, which swore on their word as gentlemen that they never would consider doing such a thing. Critics held that these practices aimed solely to monitor UK and US citizens' lives, ignoring matters such as war, terrorism, cybercrime and hostile state activity. Critics of Sigint – competent or incompetent, principled or hostile – drove the disclosures. A classic press campaign, like Lord Beaverbrook's 'Empire Crusade', aimed to sell newspapers. Internet libertarians, viewing state intelligence and secrecy as evil, purported to defend freedom from the slavery caused by pursuit of security.

These comments had some force, but more melodrama. They ignored the problems of competitions on common ground, and the existence of enemies. The metaphors used to describe this situation – 1984 or the panopticon – were one-dimensional. They considered only peoples being attacked by their own state – not those assaulted by foreign governments or exploited by criminals. Nor was the question simply the gaze of the state. People used this panopticon for their own purposes – to attract attention and display what they wanted to show, rather than to tremble before the unblinking eye. In Western countries, most people would not be assaulted by their own states: more would be attacked by foreign governments and private parties. Fewer people might fear Big Brother than need his help, or want it.

This crisis stunned GCHQ, still more a Cheltonian than a national institution. It did not know what material would be published and lacked a press office with a remit to counter criticism at a national level, though it rapidly developed one. Its representatives could not at the outset clearly explain the legal or technical issues in public, nor how GCHQ had saved British lives. However, GCHQ's record and myth saved it. Leading Conservative and Labour politicians agreed that GCHQ had properly informed them of its actions. The technicalities involved, and the constant drip of information, confused and bored the public. Quickly, evidence emerged that every competent state conducted Sigint, while cybercriminals and terrorists planned to exploit or attack British subjects. The enemies of Sigint overplayed their hands by making statements which obviously they could not substantiate, and which were untrue – such as that bulk collection had not reduced terrorist attacks, or by inflating the number of messages of British citizens which GCHQ read. The debate turned on myths. Critics insinuated that GCHQ was Big Brother or Sauron. Civilians could not easily imagine Bletchley's heirs as Orcs. British people thought they faced existential threats, against which they viewed GCHQ as Gandalf and themselves as Hobbits in need of help. Slowly, the debate became informed and public. Balanced reports by objective experts undercut alarmism.

In 2015 and 2016 the British government commissioned David Anderson, QC to assess the legal and operational aspects of bulk collection Although few knew the fact, Anderson's report followed older genres: the assessments of British intelligence by Evill and Quinlan, and of GCHQ by Evill, Hampshire and Hurn. Their reports were written for mandarins familiar with Sigint product but concerned with cost-effectiveness and value. Anderson wrote for the public, both the knowledgeable and those who did not know what GCHQ did, but all of whom cared about issues of defence, freedom and terrorism. Anderson said nothing about cost or cost-effectiveness. He focused far more than earlier reports had done on the technicalities of collection, and on correlating operational and legal issues. His mandate was unique, public rather than secret. The major political parties cooperated in a bipartisan fashion, on an issue which they understood was complex in many technical areas, was important and required solution. They depoliticised the issue – unusually difficult for politicians of those years to do – in order to ensure the best technical balance between liberty and security.

A wise man must handle this assessment task. Anderson, a leading barrister on matters of national security and civil liberties, and the Independent Reviewer of Terrorism Legislation, was already responsible to the Home Secretary and Parliament. Unlike previous investigations of the intelligence services, departments did not provide his staff. He selected them from outsiders, including leaders in civil liberties and national security law such as Cathryn McGahey, QC; in Sigint collection and security, Dr Bob Nowill, with senior experience from British Telecom and GCHQ; and Gordon Meldrum, a consumer of secret intelligence on organised crime. They, and he, were cleared to see anything relevant to his brief, including material never before viewed by anyone outside the intelligence agencies. Anderson canvassed widely among critics of Sigint, and his staff applied those critiques to the agencies' cases. His position was unique among external assessors of intelligence. He could demand documents from the intelligence agencies, and have them offer their best sixty cases on the issue, for his staff to interrogate in detail. They could check the arguments of critics against the reality of intelligence, and of practitioners against other possibilities, to determine how far bulk collection was useful and necessary. Anderson could publish a sanitised version of the evidence, and a critique of it, to Parliament and the public.

Anderson treated all parties with respect and praised their aims. The sincerity and competence of British intelligence officers, especially from GCHQ, impressed him and his staff. Anderson largely rejected the critics' challenges to the necessity of these procedures or their proposed alternatives and kindly demolished their supposed value or practicability. Many of these critics' proposals were forms of unilateral digital disarmament, which would prevent bulk collection and Sigint more widely, and for Britain but not for anyone else. Britain would walk naked across the cyber commons, where everyone else remained armoured.

Anderson concluded that the agencies had not abused their powers in bulk collection and justified its necessity and utility: bulk collection was essential for British security, and GCHQ had handled it well:

> Much of its work involves analysis based on a fragment of information which forms the crucial lead, or seed, for further work. GCHQ's tradecraft lies in the application of lead-specific analysis to bring together potentially relevant data from diverse data stores in order to prove or disprove a theory or hypothesis … significant analysis of data may be required before any actual name can be identified. This tradecraft requires very high volumes of queries to be run against communications data as results are dynamically tested, refined and further refined. GCHQ runs several thousand such communications data queries every day. One of the benefits of this targeted approach to data mining is that individuals who are innocent or peripheral to an investigation are never looked at, minimising the need for intrusion into their communications.[22]

Nonetheless, Anderson proposed a stricter version of GCHQ's procedures, with much more oversight. 'RIPA, obscure since its inception, has been patched up so many times as to make it incomprehensible

704 BEHIND THE ENIGMA

to all but a tiny band of initiates. A multitude of alternative powers, some of them without statutory safeguards, confuse the picture further. This state of affairs is undemocratic, unnecessary and – in the long run – intolerable.' Instead, 'a comprehensive and comprehensible new law should be drafted from scratch, replacing the multitude of current powers and providing for clear limits and safeguards on any intrusive power that it may be necessary for public authorities to use'.[23] That process must be public and transparent.

In coming years, the issue received much attention from press and Parliament, perhaps more than any other case of intelligence in British history. Anderson's views did not please opponents, who labelled the new law the 'Snooper's Charter', yet even they recognised that their opposition had little public support.[24] Debate turned from the public to the legal sphere, which continued into 2020, on minor issues not involving the intelligence agencies.

GCHQ's relationship with the public, and secrecy, changed more between 2013 and 2020 than ever before in its history. Long before 2013, GCHQ staff knew that their actions on the internet might infringe upon the liberties and privacy of fellow citizens, and themselves. They turned from temptation, guided by an institutional 'Ethical Framework', an 'ethics officer' to hear complaints, and protection for whistle-blowers. After the Snowden disclosures, GCHQ staff internalised the idea of 'a democratic license to operate', as it was named by an independent team of hard-headed and eminent figures whom the government put in place to review the recommendations of Anderson's committee.[25] During the crisis of 2013–15, its level of secrecy exposed GCHQ to accusations of bad behaviour. Iain Lobban did not 'think "secret" means "sinister"', but critics did.[26] Secrecy gave glamour to GCHQ, and inculcated conspiracy theories. This level of secrecy weakened GCHQ's ability to handle public attacks, or to explain its actions; so it took a difficult decision. GCHQ entered the public sphere, discarding the cult of secrecy while looking to maintain operational security.

This decision has transformed public discourse. The more material that has been released about British intelligence, the weaker conspiracy theories about it have become, even when the grounds for criticism have risen. Critics who attacked GCHQ for secrecy lost their best card, the ability to raise suspicion about everything it did, and saw it gain new ones. GCHQ took several steps, each political and principled, aimed to explain itself to the public, consider criticism, and gain informed consent for its actions.

GCHQ behaved like other departments. It increased its press office and engaged with national periodicals. Journalists received tours through the Doughnut, which civilians found attractive, and spoke to analysts, sparking newspaper articles and television programmes. Directors became public figures, discussing their profession, aided by one retired colleague, Omand. Some other Siginters were cleared to speak openly, though most remained bound by old constraints. Support from friendly outsiders, especially the royal family, was gratefully accepted. GCHQ expanded its legal staff, from one part-timer in 1980 to thirty-two full-time personnel by 2020, to handle public debates about law. As critics challenged GCHQ through legal means, it had to explain its views. By forcing Siginters and critics to argue openly, this system aided an elevated public debate, on both sides, and a highest common denominator of liberty and security. GCHQ commissioned an independent account of its history, so readers could understand its roles, failures and successes, and judge its value as they could other civilian and strategic departments. It is in your hands.

The National Cyber Security Centre and the Cyber Commons

GCHQ's greatest challenge lay in adjusting to the cyber commons and the needs of a new consumer – society – alongside its traditional customer in the state. Comsec, a secondary task for GCHQ during the Cold War, handled by a subsidiary element – the Communications-Electronics Security Group (CESG) – became its most public and perhaps greatest job. The new technical world threatened CESG more than any other part of GCHQ. While the skills of radio operators, Russian linguists and traffic analysts of the Warsaw Pact waned in value, legacy requirements and age demographics let careers end gracefully. Senior GCHQ personnel carried principles from their work into new areas. The old skills of linguists and analysts remained useful. Cryppies and CDOs cooperated. The principles of traffic analysis were basic against bulk traffic, even if analysts changed.

CESG had less to bequeath and more to learn. It had focused on setting standards and designing equipment for the Cold War, above all machines to protect communications by radio and cable and, to a lesser degree, telephones. CESG produced technical pamphlets, designs for equipment and masses of ephemeral 'keymat' – the punched tapes, plug settings and other media that provided key settings for cypher devices. As CESG's military consumers declined, so did need for that product, which gradually became obsolete, though some remained useful in 2020. CESG had little expertise with computers and cybersecurity, while its consumers in government were slower to adopt new equipment than firms and individuals – which suddenly it was expected to serve. Traditional Comsec and cybersecurity involved specialised kit and skills, which proved mutually exclusive. The characteristics which suited CESG's long twilight struggle – precision engineering, controlled pursuit of projects to serve for generations, reliance on firms (closely and expertly supervised) to produce designs and equipment – did not suit this revolution. Union between generations proved impossible, compared to the combination of cryppies and CDOs. Nowhere else in GCHQ did the gap between the expertise of old hands, and new, matter more than with CESG.

For a generation after the Cold War ended, CESG approached cybersecurity as it had done Comsec. Like most departments and firms, CESG was slow to understand cybersecurity, seeing it as a problem for IT departments, not as a transformation in work. Businesses with technical expertise would provide advice and equipment about IT. Alas, these firms were often more expensive than they were useful. CESG lacked the expertise to control the quality of their work, or understand it. Most of GCHQ understood that it must change, or die. CESG did not, nor did its masters, until they suddenly demanded that it lead a revolution. CESG embodies what might have happened to GCHQ as a whole, without the Omand–Richards reforms.

The growing need to police the cyber commons posed organisational problems for Siginters. Cybercrime endangered large firms and countries with significant financial sectors, such as Britain. States struggled to organise Sigint and Comsec as they confronted new relationships with military organisations and internal ones. Should Siginters, or soldiers, command Computer Network Attack, where digital and kinetic means combined? Should Siginters or policemen handle cybercrime? These questions raised complex issues of organisation and law. Everywhere, the internal structures of countries drove answers. Some smaller states, especially Israel and Singapore, coordinated cybersecurity years before Britain and the United States, where many agencies confronted larger and more complex versions of these issues.

From 2007, when it stood below American or Israeli standards, a confluence of events pressed Britain to pursue a coherent policy for cybersecurity. Politicians, driven by their own observations, not advice from GCHQ or departments, thought cybersecurity was a great problem which required solution. They treated the issue in a non-partisan fashion, not constantly overturning each other's work. As prime minister, Gordon Brown had Britain define a strategy for cybersecurity. The government produced stirring statements: 'Just as in the 19th century we had to secure the seas for our national safety and prosperity, and in the 20th century we had to secure the air, in the 21st century we also have to secure our advantage in cyber space;' basic principles, especially the need to coordinate state and private actors, but few practical changes. A small central unit monitored developments on the cyber commons. Another at GCHQ handled threats. GCHQ quietly advised firms about cybersecurity. Still, fifteen departments acted as they pleased in the field.[27]

The Conservative–Liberal Democrat coalition of 2010–15 built on Brown's work. Its leading members, including the prime minister, David Cameron, made cybersecurity a national priority. As Robert Hannigan, Director of GCHQ, wrote, ministers sought to make Britain:

> 'the safest place to live and do business online' … It is, of course,
> a relative ambition and does not imply that the UK can be 100
> per cent safe. It was based on the key assessment that the UK
> could harden its defences to the point that cybercrime would be
> displaced elsewhere to easier targets. While this may sound cynical, it
> assumed that an international raising of the baseline would make all
> economies harder targets and encourage others to up their game. The
> long-term bet was that good resilience and security would become
> a market differentiator for UK business and attractive for inward
> investors.[28]

Cybersecurity was a leading priority, among Britain's four 'Tier 1 threats', in a tough national security strategy, which slaughtered many sacred cows.[29] The government defined clear criteria for success on the strategy bridge between policy and action, including coordination between departments, and with private firms. A £650 million programme over four years funded cybersecurity well.[30] GCHQ seized almost 60 per cent of that budget, and responsibility for 'the most sophisticated nation state attacks'. The Computer Emergency Response Team, an open body under the Cabinet Office, handled most assaults on firms.[31]

Directors of GCHQ recognised that the danger existed and must be solved, and offered rewards. They did not understand the technicalities of cybersecurity, but drove subordinates to address them. This sudden shift in demands exposed the generation gap. The older members of CESG were reluctant to handle non-state consumers and relied on IT firms they knew for guidance. The younger generation disliked those producers and procedures and thought many of these firms alarmist and expensive. They wished to revolutionise Comsec to fit the cyber commons, and to lead a national effort in cybersecurity. GCHQ's leaders let old hands at CESG handle its traditional roles, while others controlled policy for cybersecurity. Ciaran Martin, an official with wide experience in Whitehall, including intelligence, but not at GCHQ, became manager of cybersecurity and Comsec at Cheltenham. He worked with the radicals to handle cybersecurity, where they followed original ideas, and studied American and Israeli models.

Between 2011 and 2015, GCHQ worked closely with government agencies and firms, and established offices to assess cyber threats. As Hannigan wrote, assessing threats and risks on the cyber commons:

> is particularly difficult not just because it is a relatively new field but because it requires in-depth technical understanding alongside assessment of other sources ... ministers who had a framework for judging the seriousness of a terrorist threat or incident had no framework against which to measure cyber threats. The figures were always large, because all figures on the internet are, and no one knows what 100 per cent is: internet data is hard to measure and not static. Traditional assessment bodies, notably the venerable UK Joint Intelligence Committee, simply did not have access to the right technical skills to make useful assessments or even to second-guess those made by others.[32]

Even more, policy faltered because 'no one has asked the obvious question of the right experts. Particularly in the UK civil service, which tends to favour generalism over deep and long expertise, there simply were not individuals who could give creative technical advice, or indeed assess suggestions made by others.'[33] Some of these criticisms could also have been applied to GCHQ, at the time.

These successes were dissipated because agencies gave conflicting advice to firms, which could not handle the burden thrust on them. GCHQ gave intelligence, and fought foes on the cyber commons, but firms mostly received advice, not aid, and could not be chivvied into line. State defence for firms was dislocated. Hacking attacks became high grade, sometimes linked to foreign state Sigint agencies. The Bank of England warned that this chaos damaged Britain's economy and softened security enough to attract cyber criminals. The national policy based on coordination had reached its limits. Leadership was needed. After the election of 2015, the Conservative government demanded a national strategy, guided by one public centre for cybersecurity, and led by GCHQ. 'When a cyber incident happened there were lots of departments represented at the table, but most of the questions gravitated to GCHQ,' Cameron told Hannigan. GCHQ, said the Chancellor of the Exchequer, George Osborne, 'is rightly known as equal to the best in the world … It is the point of deep expertise for the UK government. It has an unmatched understanding of the internet and of how to keep information safe.'[34]

Other departments resisted the loss of authority in cybersecurity, until MI5 did so, breaking the logjam. Only law enforcement agencies, responsible for tackling forms of cybercrime, remained independent, though working closely with GCHQ. Many within GCHQ disliked becoming public and taking responsibility for cybersecurity. Senior ministers overcame these reservations and assigned those responsibilities to the 'National Cyber Security Centre, a part of GCHQ'. That body had a unique name, and structure. Its leaders came from the reformed CESG. Martin was the first head of the NCSC, with Ian Levy its Technical Director or, as he said, the government's 'chief cyber security geek'.[35] Five of its leaders were avowed, able to speak and be named openly, more than in the rest of GCHQ. By spring 2019, the NCSC had 740 staff. It had elements within the Doughnut, alongside world leaders in cyber intelligence and CNO, and offices in London, beside private citizens. The NCSC was within the Government Security Zone, outside the Whitehall village, yet close to ministers. During emergencies, the NCSC and GCHQ gave Whitehall real-time knowledge of cyber threats and struck them down where possible as they rose. The NCSC combined two compartments: one working with open cybersecurity communities; the other with secret agencies. Like Bletchley, the NCSC was freewheeling, with many parts. Once the Khyber Rifles defended far-flung British frontiers: now the Cyber Rifles did so, in the far, mid and near space. The NCSC became inspector general for cybersecurity with firms; the mobiliser of civilian resources for that purpose; agony aunt for those suffering digital heartaches; and missionary for social and educational change in the nation.

Once the NCSC was created, it quickly took command of British policy for cyber security, aiming to defend Britain's society and economy. As Martin said: 'We want this digital revolution to succeed. Our job is to help make the digital economy and digital Government work, by making it safer' against 'the three main motivations for systematic cyber attack ... One is power: the traditional "statecraft" just playing out in the digital age. Countries and rogue actors seeking to gain advantage by stealing secrets, or by pre-positioning for a destructive attack in a time of tension. Another one's money: anything from the sophisticated theft of intellectual property to the simple theft of cash from a bank account. Another is propaganda.' Hostile states included 'great powers, using cyber attacks to spy, gain major commercial and economic advantage or to pre-position for destructive attack'. Smaller states exploited 'the relatively immature rules of the road in cyberspace to tweak the nose of those they see as bigger powers in a way they would and could never contemplate by traditional military means'. Some criminals 'operate under the protection or tolerance of uncooperative states, and this is something new about cyber because it makes it much harder to bring them to justice because they don't need to set foot in our jurisdictions or those of our allies to harm us. Some of these gangs are extraordinarily sophisticated. We've seen some of the most MBA-grade management information systems that tell them, in great detail, which lines of attack are profitable and which are not. But not all that much of the crime we see is MBA-grade and too much of it gets through.' The 'world's major terrorist groups have the intent, but not the capability, to launch a destructive cyber attack. Now, that might change.' Meanwhile, Britain must contain 'the horrific misuse of the Internet by terrorists across the globe for the purposes of propaganda and radicalisation'.[36]

The NCSC worked with GCHQ and military cyber forces against attacks by hackers and nation states, including regular forays across the cyber commons to find threats and disable or ambush them. It also followed a deeper strategy, aimed 'to make the UK safer in cyberspace ... put right some of the security flaws built into the internet', and 'change the economic equation for cyber criminals and alter the attacker-defender landscape'. The government moved 'from blaming users and expecting individuals to bear all the strain of security'.[37] Levy formulated this strategy, the Active Cyber Defence programme, which the NCSC published openly. He emphasised 'a common complaint from industry to governments about cyber security. It's generally that governments tell them they're not doing enough and must do more, often without really understanding the real-world impacts or commercial implications of their demands. Well, our strategy is to use government as a guinea pig for all the measures we want to see done at national scale. We'll be eating our own dog food to prove the efficacy (or otherwise) of the measures we're asking for, and to prove they scale sensibly before asking anyone to implement anything.'[38]

The NCSC challenged fundamental principles of the internet, by making security rather than surveillance its base. Working with private firms, the NCSC tackled technical weaknesses within the internet, such as improving standards for email or infrastructure protocols by which internet providers routed messages. The NCSC would 'drive the UK software ecosystem to be better', by warning British entities that communicated with government websites of vulnerabilities in their software. Levy also attacked firms whose sales pitch 'basically says "you lot are too stupid to understand this and only I can possibly help you – buy my magic amulet and you'll be fine." It's medieval witchcraft, it's genuinely medieval witchcraft.'[39] The NCSC also would 'go looking for badness and take it down', disabling websites across the internet which attacked British targets. 'We're still going to do things to demotivate our adversaries in ways that only GCHQ can do.' That statement was 'euphemistic by design'. Levy warned: 'All of this will evolve. Some of it will work: some won't. We'll have to respond to adversaries as they respond to our defences. That's probably the new normal though … It's time to stop talking about what the winged ninja cyber monkeys can do and start countering in an automatic way the stuff we see at massive scale that causes real damage to citizens and businesses alike every day.'[40]

This programme involved many actions which might arouse suspicion of government censorship or surveillance. The NCSC countered that danger by establishing a reputation 'as a trustworthy and transparent organisation', and publicised means for anyone to opt out of its proposals. The public, even seasoned critics of GCHQ, knew that the problem was great and must be solved. They viewed NCSC as a bobby on the beat, rather than a secret policeman. Openness created trust that Siginters worked for the security of the nation, rather than subverting its liberties. The NCSC warnings of threats – and weekly and yearly estimates of security problems, with different versions for technical specialists, businesses, and individuals and families – became a common feature in British media, and reached many audiences. They were an open equivalent of the reports which GCHQ and JIC published throughout the Cold War. NCSC was the first organisation to provide national intelligence assessments to plain folk regularly, providing, for example, 'evidence of Russian pre-positioning on some of our critical sectors, along with detailed technical guidance to business on how to get rid of it from our networks'.[41] Though most of these reports came from open sources, some involved the NCSC's own work. No doubt old practices of sanitisation covered the dissemination of material from more secret sources. That the NCSC and GCHQ both released far more material about their work than ever before, including that against states, was another sign of differences between the first and second ages of Sigint.

Underlying this strategy was a campaign to prepare Britons for life on the cyber commons. Inspired by Israeli models and a desire to increase diversity in business, government and GCHQ, the NCSC spread knowledge of cybersecurity. It expanded GCHQ's traditional recruitment in Cheltenham, to help schools across Britain offer courses in computer science, and universities to develop cybersecurity programmes. 'Cyberists,' the NCSC told candidates, 'are intrigued by unexplored technology. Dedicated to fulfilling a bigger role in society. Keen to protect friends, families, communities and commerce. Determined to make an impact. Eager to learn and never let up. They are our new generation of cyber security experts. As technology enhances more and more of our daily life, cyberists will be the ones who'll safeguard it from all manner of threats. Cyber security roles are constantly evolving, consistently challenging and crammed with potential. They could be anybody – and they could come from anywhere. To help find them, support them and train them, we've created CyberFirst.'[42]

Through CyberFirst Bursaries, hundreds of schoolchildren spent summers working in cybersecurity with firms or government. CyberFirst Degree Apprenticeships let undergraduates 'earn while they learn, ready for a job at GCHQ'. The NCSC particularly addressed schoolgirls through special bursaries and courses: the 'CyberFirst Girls

Competition provides a fun but challenging environment to inspire the next generation of young women to consider a career in cyber security'. Over 800 schools entered that programme in 2019, from Jersey to the Orkneys. The leading ten teams conducted a well-publicised contest in London.[43] GCHQ developed outreach programmes of its own, which combined the glamour of past accomplishments with emerging challenges. GCHQ teams attended national meetings in Science, Technology, Engineering and Mathematics (STEM) disciplines, including of 80,000 students at the Big Bang UK Young Scientists and Engineers Fair. Boys and girls handled Enigma machines, played interactive games on computers made by apprentices at GCHQ, and solved puzzles with cypher wheels, pencils and paper. Earnest adolescents discussed cryptography and careers with Siginters. GCHQ became the school of the cyber nation.

Conclusion

GCHQ began as a secret intelligence organisation, as the first age of Sigint opened. Until 2000, it remained an intelligence agency, marked by the highest levels of secrecy. No other Sigint agency pioneered more advances. Only one, NSA, matched or exceeded GCHQ's level of quality. GCHQ had failures, and Sigint had limits, but it ranked among Britain's most cost-effective investments in power and was a great force multiplier. GCHQ helped to keep Britain a great secondary power until 1992, and to maintain the 'special relationship' with the United States. After the Cold War ended, GCHQ rose in power and quality again.

By 2020, GCHQ was one of the great agencies in the second age of Sigint – but no longer secret, nor simply an intelligence bureau. The NCSC was a public body, shaping discourse across Britain, and guiding individuals and firms; while almost on a routine basis GCHQ was in the news. Both gave the public intelligence estimates. GCHQ was the behemoth among British intelligence agencies, and increasingly a fighting service as well. Jeremy Fleming, the incumbent Director, said that GCHQ had 'responsibility for a major national risk for the first time in our hundred-year history'.[1] It also supported the agencies which handled every other risk. Between 1914 and 2019, states across the advanced world moved from units based on brute force, like infantry divisions, towards those stemming from C4ISR. GCHQ was at the vanguard of this trend, as one crude indicator shows: in 1938, Britain had 200,000 sailors to 1,000 Siginters, a ratio of 200 to one; in 2020, the ratio was more like seven to one. Until 2000, GCHQ supported only actions conducted by other state bodies, mostly military and law enforcement. Afterwards, GCHQ supported many consumers, private ones matching the military in moment, and acted independently on its own product. Its budget rose commensurately. During the Cold War, GCHQ's estimates moved slowly towards 2 per cent of that of the MOD. In 2018, the Single Intelligence Vote, spent mostly on GCHQ, was £2.2 billion, or 7.7 per cent the size of that of the MOD.[2] GCHQ was better funded than core elements of British conventional forces, such as armoured units or the Royal Marines.

GCHQ was not merely public, but also popular. Walter Bagehot emphasised that 'mystery' was the 'life' of the monarchy, which must avoid daily politics so to preserve reverence 'from all combatants' – 'We must not let daylight in upon the magic.' For GCHQ, daylight fell upon magic without destroying reverence or power. GCHQ's public reputation was high. Bletchley Park became a metaphor for British genius, and one of its finest hours – reinforced by memories of sections such as Room 40. Television programmes, popular fiction and films were set at Bletchley almost as often as 221B Baker Street. Journalists and other outsiders were allowed to watch GCHQ analysts track terrorists and drug-trafficking networks, and report on their observations. Leaders of GCHQ and the NCSC became perhaps the most public civil servants in Britain, with a remarkable ability to speak their minds. They were seen as genuine and objective experts on technical issues which few understood, but many needed to know. Controversy continued, but media accounts were far more positive, or neutral, than negative – even among old critics. The *Guardian* found good words for GCHQ.

These developments, of course, were subject to change. Since 1914, any major development in communications and data-processing systems, in power and geopolitics, or social and political mores within polities, has affected Sigint – in some cases transformed it. They would do so again. Lesser things were already changing. GCHQ's expansion occurred mostly outside Cheltenham. While the Doughnut remained its headquarters, large elements of GCHQ emerged or grew in London, Manchester and Scarborough. Changes in locale always altered GCHQ, which surely would happen again. The importance of being Cheltonian would decline, its staff would become more national, and their diversity would rise. The expansion in GCHQ's importance also eroded other ambitions. As one old condition of GCHQ changed – its tight finances – so did its internal autonomy. GCHQ was the first of the intelligence agencies to bring Non-Executive Directors on to the Management Board. Directors were once again drawn from across Whitehall. Would this pattern become normal, with all it entailed for management of GCHQ, and promotion within it? Would greater movement in mid-career between GCHQ and other departments become normal for Siginters and civil servants from elsewhere? If so, might GCHQ's qualities of agility, creativity and technical mastery erode, or perhaps find themselves exported across other sections of the British state?

Politicians openly discussed the value of Sigint, which was described as central to British policy. These discussions were phrased in national terms, with less attention to the Cold War arguments that GCHQ did the most to maintain intelligence relations with the United States. A generational time bomb emerged under UKUSA. Common threats of terrorism, and China and Russia, provided grounds for cooperation, while Americans appreciated the resurgence of GCHQ. Yet the ties provided by cooperation against an existential threat eroded, while new generations in its member states were culturally cooler towards each other. UKUSA, the pillar for Sigint between the Five Eyes for generations, was more shaky than before. It might vanish; if so, all of its members would weaken. That UKUSA might vanish, however, was less surprising than the fact that this improbable alliance had lasted so well for so long.

Meanwhile, changes in technology and targets, such as terrorism, NATO's wars in Asia, bulk collection and the focus on non-state actors, transformed the relationship between second and third parties. Each needed some access to each other's databases and to Comint derived from cryptanalysis. These practices could not easily be placed within UKUSA's old 'Categories'. Whether UKUSA eroded, or cooperated more with Sigint agencies from other Western states, one thing was clear. GCHQ would remain a powerful sword and shield for Britain, and its people, as it had been from its start.

Appendix

GCHQ by the Numbers, 1960–95

Analysing statistics, and drawing inferences from them, illuminates GCHQ as a social organisation, particularly its normal folk. The figures in question come from HR records for GCHQ personnel, taken from snapshots in 1965, 1975, 1985 and 1995. 'Scampi', the database of that era, recorded basic personal information – such as previous employment and education, posts, promotions and training at GCHQ. Scampi was an electronic system but flat, without analytic functionality – like material entered in file cards. Over time, its structure gained extra elements, the significance of others was forgotten, and data entry conventions changed. My research assistant, James (Jock) Bruce, anonymised these figures and converted them to a format which modern IT could search and analyse. He checked this data with a sample of witting individuals, to ascertain the accuracy of Scampi data after conversion.

Jock Bruce then combined these raw figures and organised them into data fields. All material on educational background, for example, was converted into terms such as 'local school leavers' or 'polytechnic graduates'. Career data was gathered into functional fields, such as 'clerical' or 'intercept', to avoid difficulties caused by changes in unit designations. The term 'generalist' describes the standard positions in civil service departments, whereas 'specialist' denotes occupations exclusive to GCHQ, or those requiring particular qualifications, such as engineers, scientists or technicians. This data remains classified. Jock Bruce then turned it into several graphs and charts, published in this book, which illustrate basic issues about GCHQ as a whole: the average age on entry of its members between 1960 and 1995; and the gender, age, and entry as generalists and specialists of entrants into various divisions of GCHQ. Charts and graphs illustrate women's positions in leadership roles at GCHQ between 1972 and 1994. Jock Bruce is the basic analyst of this data, though we discussed his findings at length, and compared them with qualitative evidence on these matters. The two sources generally pointed in similar directions, but the statistical evidence raised nuances and questions which shaped interpretation at many important points, such as career advancement by non-elite members of GCHQ, and the status of women in leadership roles.

This material illustrates social and demographic dynamics inside GCHQ, but with reservations. The outcomes might vary marginally with different snapshots, say 1963, 1973, 1983 and 1993. Since, with Department Specialists (DSs) and some other areas, few people were involved, small changes in absolute numbers may distort their representation as percentiles. The year 1995 had a small intake, and our figures end before their careers did, which prevents complete comparison between these sets of data. The crude terms used in the analysis, such as 'military service' or 'local school leavers', cover many backgrounds – for instance for the latter: the appropriately named Crypt Grammar School in Gloucester; St George's School, Hong Kong; the Army Apprentices College, Harrogate; the Royal School of Needlework, and one alumnus from both the RAF School of Wireless and the Goethe Institute. These figures also exclude the backgrounds of entrants to the service Sigint agencies, which recruited even fewer personnel, almost all male, through military channels – some of whom later entered GCHQ under our category of 'ex-servicemen'.

The number of entrants to GCHQ each year was small, and variable. Absorbing the civilian units from service Sigint created 768 entrants in 1965. The 138 entrants in 1995 reflect the planned rundown of GCHQ personnel. On average, GCHQ, with around 8,000 staff, enrolled about 375 entrants annually, enough to maintain that strength, or to run it down to achieve rationalisation. Superiors and the Apprentice Committee could manage the training of individual Departmental Specialists, and technical specialists, in detail. GCHQ's enrolments aimed to give areas the desired strength five to twenty years ahead. Most notably, a careful rundown tried to reduce the radio grades by 50 per cent between 1970 and 1990. Afterwards, that decline became terminal.

The average age for entrants was surprisingly high, since many were school leavers: around twenty-six years for women and thirty for men.

These averages reflect the large number of males entering GCHQ after military service, and of women returning to work after raising families. The radio grades and communications and cypher officers were almost exclusively male for most of this period, and almost all originally uniformed or civilian members of the services. Otherwise, at GCHQ the two largest sources for male entrants were local school leavers and retired military personnel, with graduates far behind. For women entrants, local school leavers were far and away the dominant source, with graduates also far behind. The groups were perhaps almost different castes. Male entrants usually stayed for life. The proportion of women at GCHQ remained much smaller than their share of entrants, reflecting higher rates of retirement, for which GCHQ planned. The proportion of women among GCHQ personnel declined steadily between 1955 to 1973, from 23 per cent to 18 per cent, but then rose steadily to 28 per cent by 1995. Although the absorption and retirement of members of the services' intercept organisations boosted this decline and fall, still, by 1995, women were a notably larger part of GCHQ than in 1955, or 1973. GCHQ's leaders were civilians, and Siginters, but below that it had a civilianised military atmosphere. Older men with military experience, aided by younger civilian males, dominated collection and technical issues. Females, divided equally between young and fairly transient clerical staff, and older career women, handled administration. Only in intelligence and analysis did men and women normally work side by side.

The smallest group of entrants for both sexes, between 0.5 per cent and 1.5 per per cent, were in the departmental specialist class, where wastage was high. Most entrants, marginally more women than men, resigned or never reached the administrative class. Those who remained had quite a clear run for senior positions. Had Oxbridge graduates recognised how open this field was, they might have found it more attractive.

As the DS scheme sputtered, GCHQ boosted recruitment into the executive class by almost 200 per cent, by directly reducing the prior numbers of personnel taken into the clerical classes. In particular, during each of 1965, 1975 and 1985, around ten male entrants into the executive class were scientists or engineers, a sharply rising percentage of that class, especially if it really represented yearly practices. Male entrants into the clerical classes also increasingly had technical skills, which reinforced this means to augment GCHQ's power among scientists and engineers. GCHQ had non-elite men and women handle middle to senior leadership roles and tasks, and particularly reduce its perennial problems with lack of engineers, scientists and linguists. A large proportion of men, rising from 28 per cent in 1965, to 44–45 per cent in 1975 and 1985, entered the executive class. Most of them, 42 per cent in 1975 and 1985, and 66 per cent in 1965, were in the radio grades. (In 1965 neither radio grades nor communications and cypher operators were rated as 'executive class', but both soon achieved this status under a system of 'unified grading'.) Other entrants to the executive class varied in occupation, every year. In 1965, they primarily were vetting officers, recruited from retired local policemen. In 1975 and 1985, most male entrants to the executive class were university or polytechnic graduates, with the rest being ex-military. Of these graduates, 10 per cent entered as generalists, or executive officers, 30 per cent had science and engineering backgrounds, and 15 per cent, declining to 8 per cent in 1985, were linguists. The clerical class remained almost tied with the executive class as the largest category for male entrants, though falling from 55 per cent in 1965, to 33 per cent in 1975, and 40 per cent in 1985. Men entered equally as general assistants, or in science and engineering grades. Entrants mostly were local school leavers, many with technical degrees from colleges. The rest had military experience, especially communications and cypher personnel.

Far fewer women than men entered the executive class – 5 per cent of female entrants in 1965, rising to 14–16 per cent in 1975 and 1985. This discrepancy was fundamental to the lack of advancement for women, compared to men, in middle management across GCHQ. It may explain most of this difference between genders in advancement. These women were hired primarily as generalists or linguists, in proportions varying each year. From 1975, they overwhelmingly were graduates. Far more than men, women entered the executive class as linguists and generalists, and less often as specialists, scientists or engineers. The largest group of women entered in the clerical class, 90 per cent in 1965, falling to 66–69 per cent in 1975 and 1985. Half of them were recent school leavers, but about 10 per cent were older than thirty-five. In 1965, about 66 per cent of these women entered essentially in secretarial roles, as clerical assistant or clerical officers, or typing staff. About 20 per cent were in technical branches, as laboratory assistants or drafting technicians, and about 15 per cent as CCOs at outstations. Later, almost all female entrants in the clerical class were clerical assistants or officers, with an average age of twenty-two. The lack of substantial further recruitment of women in technical branches or

CCOs suggests that once recruited into these areas, women stayed rather than retired, even after motherhood. Needs in those areas did not decline and males did not take them over. That women selected taxing technical careers suggests more investment in them. CCOs characteristically worked in small provincial towns where other jobs and women with the requisite skills were scarce, and a steady career suited both them and GCHQ.

About 20 per cent of male entrants annually were in the industrial classes, like labour and drivers, declining to 12 per cent in 1995; 5 per cent, rising to 18 per cent, of women entered the industrial classes, as caterers and cleaners, perhaps also being older.

Promotion within a class offered money and status, especially if moving from executive officer to senior principal in the executive class, and even more so, advancement between classes. These advantages drove the ambitious, like many young males originally enrolled in the lowest ranks of the clerical class. In these snapshots, advancement within and between classes was not different between men or women in any given area, but likelier among those who joined young and stayed on, which was more true of men than women, and also in the areas dominated by males. In the largest male groups, however – radio and communication grades – promotion even just within class was almost impossible, and little better within the largest female clerical grades. Advancement within grades, and between clerical and executive classes, was easiest for people classed with scientific and engineering skills, which, however, generalists might acquire, especially in the early days of IT. About 30–35 per cent of clerical entrants in these areas reached the executive classes before retirement, fewer in other areas. C or E grades were not promoted to DS in any of these sample years, although this occurred rarely at other times.

These socio-historical figures describe a dead body. The GCHQ of 2020 is a different beast. Since 1992, two major occupational groups, the radio grades and secretarial branches, have died; military and ex-military personnel fell in significance, while graduates became the core of the organisation. Yet matters which seemingly illustrate change actually show continuity. That 35 per cent of GCHQ's staff in 2018 are female, compared to 28 per cent in 1995, stems partly from the passing of all male groups, such as the radio grades. The rise in their proportionate share between 1995 and 2019 is no greater than between 1973 and 1995. Women are not much larger a proportion of GCHQ in 2019 than in 1992, though they have achieved higher ranks.

1965

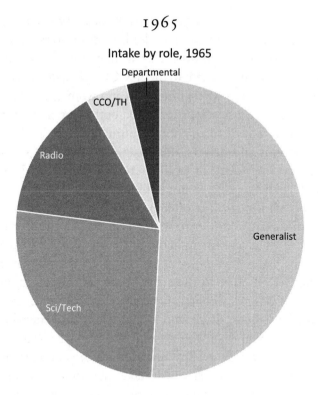

Intake by role, 1965

Departmental

CCO/TH

Radio

Generalist

Sci/Tech

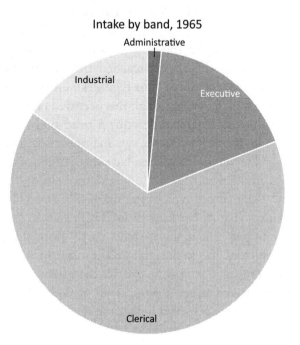

Intake by band, 1965

Administrative

Industrial

Executive

Clerical

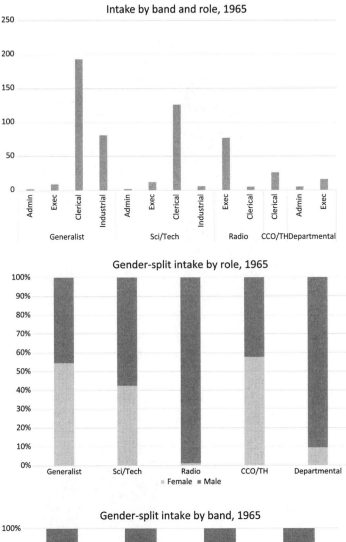

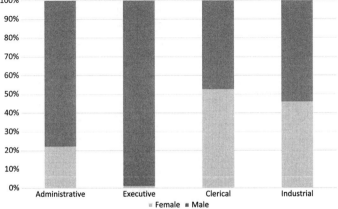

1975

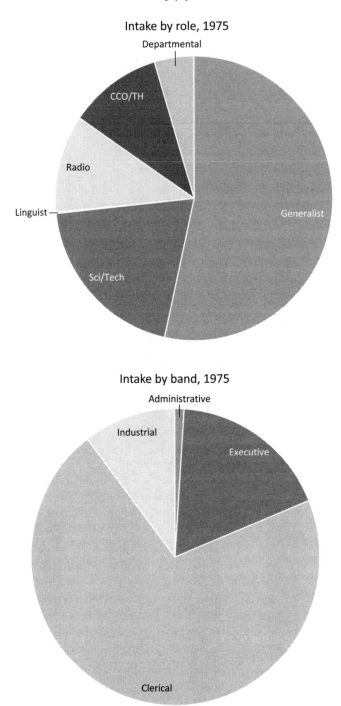

Intake by role, 1975

Departmental

CCO/TH

Radio

Linguist

Sci/Tech

Generalist

Intake by band, 1975

Administrative

Industrial

Executive

Clerical

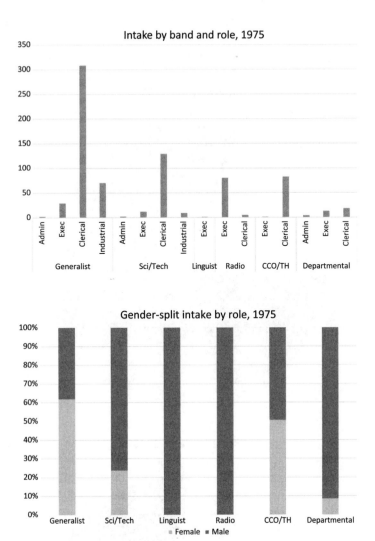

Intake by band and role, 1975

Gender-split intake by role, 1975

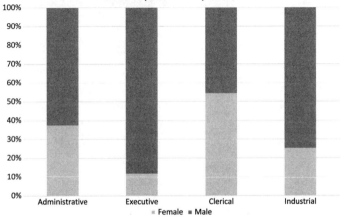

Gender-split intake by band, 1975

1985

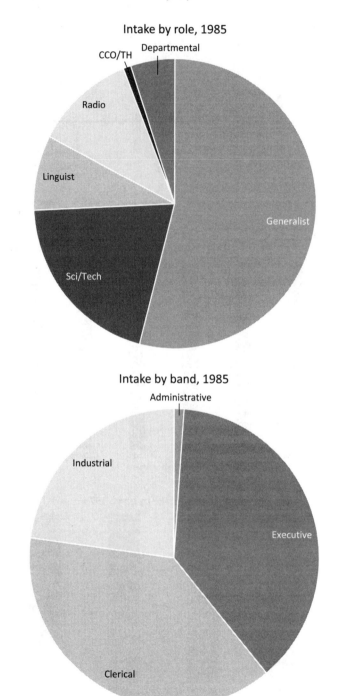

Intake by role, 1985

Intake by band, 1985

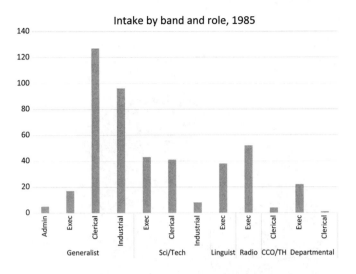

Intake by band and role, 1985

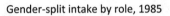

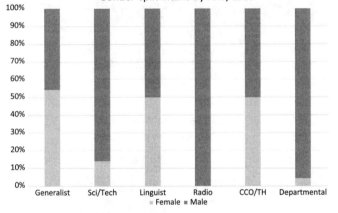

Gender-split intake by role, 1985

Female ■ Male

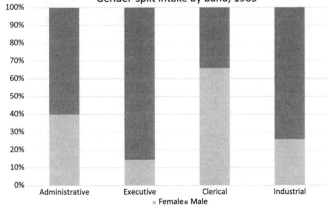

Gender-split intake by band, 1985

Female ■ Male

1995

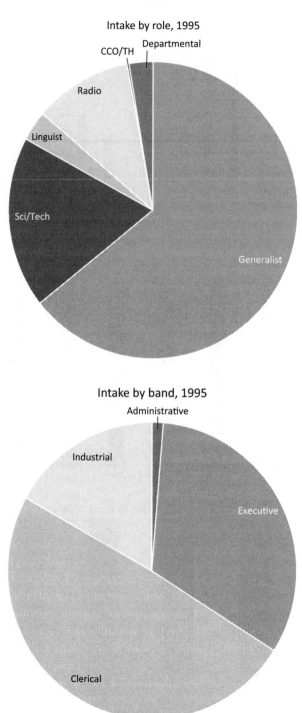

Intake by role, 1995

- CCO/TH
- Departmental
- Radio
- Linguist
- Sci/Tech
- Generalist

Intake by band, 1995

- Administrative
- Industrial
- Executive
- Clerical

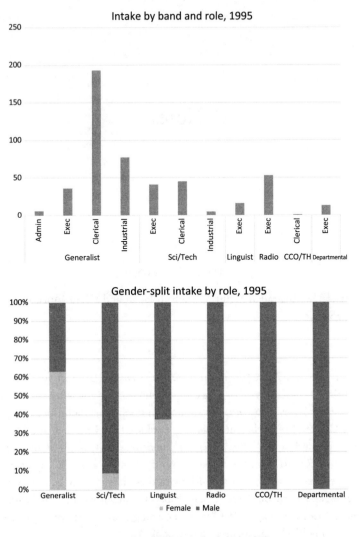

Intake by band and role, 1995

Gender-split intake by role, 1995

■ Female ■ Male

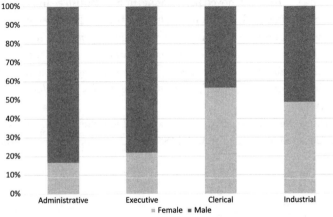

Gender-split intake by band, 1995

■ Female ■ Male

Notes

INTRODUCTION

1 Report of UK/Australian Sigint Mission to Japan and Korea (April to July 1953), 1.7.53, SS/1940.

CHAPTER 1

1 Kenneth Ellis, *The Post Office in the Eighteenth Century* (London, 1958), Chapter 6; David Kahn, *The Codebreakers, The Comprehensive History of Secret Communications from Ancient Times to the Internet* (Simon and Schuster, 1996), pp. 170–74, 187–88; W. Gibson, 'An Eighteenth-Century Paradox: The Career of the Decipherer-Bishop, Edward Willes', *British Journal for Eighteenth-Century Studies*, 12 (1989), pp. 69–76; 'Report from the Select Committee on the Post Office Together with the Appendix', 5.8.1844, HD 3/15. Many of these reports may be found in the SP 107 series, cf. Jeremy Black (ed.), 'State Papers Confidential', in *State Papers Online, Eighteenth Century, 1714–1782*, Cengage Learning 2018, https://www.gale.com/intl/essays/jeremy-black-state-papers-confidential

2 Neil Kent, 'The Hanoverian Connection: British Intelligence and Counterintelligence as Recorded by Spymaster Thomas Pelham-Holles, 1st Duke of Newcastle, Against the Jacobites', *Journal of Intelligence and Terrorism Studies*, 2016, 1; Jeremy Black, 'British Intelligence and the Mid-eighteenth-century Crisis', *Intelligence and National Security*, 2 (1987), pp. 209–16, and 'Eighteenth-century Intercepted Dispatches', *Journal of the Society of Archivists*, 11 (1990), pp. 138–43.

3 Bernstorff to Reventhow, 16.6.1801, marked 'Decyphered', *passim*, Comte de Marcov to Alexander II, 11.3.03, Add. MSS 38237, Liverpool Papers, British Library.

4 Mark Urban, *The Man Who Broke Napoleon's Codes: The Story of George Scovell* (Faber, London, 2001); Huw J. Davies, *Spying for Wellington, British Military Intelligence in the Peninsular War* (University of Oklahoma Press, 2018).

5 Home Office to General Post Office, 7.4.1818, *passim*, HO 79/3; cf. HO 32/20, HO 151/7; Emialiana P. Noether, '"Morally Wrong" or "Politically right"? Espionage in Her Majesty's Post Office, 1844–45', *Canadian Journal of History*, 22 (1987), pp. 73–91; F. B. Smith, 'British Post Office Espionage 1844', *Historical Studies*, 14/54, (1970), pp. 189–203.

6 There is no complete collection of solutions after 1815, but these statements fit the material surviving in the substantial collections of drafts by the Deciphering Branch in the W. A. MacKinnon bequest and the Willes Papers, Add. MS. 32353–32309 and 45518–23, British Library, and those scattered through the papers of recipient, like an Under Secretary at the Foreign Office between 1824–28, Lord Howard de Walden, cf. FO 360/3–5 (e.g. Baron de Mareshal to Metternich, 28.9.25, FO 360/3.

7 Bode to Backhouse, 25.10.28, *passim*, minute by Palmerston, 22.1.31, HD 3/3; Backhouse to Addington, 21.11.43, HD 3/22; cf. HF 3/11, 15, 16, 17, 35.

8 House of Commons Debates (HCD), 24.6.1844, Vol. 75, cc. 1264–305; HCD 18.2.1845, Vol. 77, col. 698. For context, cf. Bernard Porter, *Plots and Paranoia: A History of Political Espionage in Britain, 1790–1900* (London, Unwin Hyman, 1989) and David Vincent, *The Culture of Secrecy: Britain, 1832–1998* (OUP, 1998).

9 Bode to Aberdeen, 21.12.44, *passim*, HD 3/14.

10 Memorandum by Addington, 'Office of Secret Service Decipherer Messrs. Willes and Lovell', 7.8.1844, *passim*, HD 3/16; 'Mem sic on Mr. L. H. Lovell's letter of 5 Jan sic 1846', HD 3/22; HD 3/35, *passim*.

11 John Ferris, 'Before Room 40: The British Empire and Signals Intelligence, 1989–1914', *The Journal of Strategic Studies*, Vol. 12, Number 4, December 1989.

12 Herbert Maxwell, *The Life and Letters of George William Frederick Fourth Earl of Clarendon, Vol. II* (London, Edwin Arnold, 1913), p. 282.

13 Max Jones, '"Measuring the World": Exploration, Empire and the Reform of the Royal Geographical Society, c. 1873–1892', in Martin Daunton (ed.), *The Organisation of Knowledge in Victorian Britain*, OUP, 2005).

14 Ferris, J. R., 'British Intelligence and the Old World Order', in Greg Kennedy (ed.) *Imperial Defence, The Old World Order, 1856–1956* (Routledge Press, 2008), pp.176–96; John Ferris, *Intelligence and Strategy, Selected Essays* (Routledge, 2005), pp. 8–44; William Beaver, *Under Every Leaf, How Britain Played the Greater Game from Afghanistan to Africa* (Biteback Publishing, 2012).

15 Minute by Granville, nd but c. April 1884, FO 83/909; Godley to Burne, 18.2.1885, *passim*, L/PS/8/1.

16 John Ferris, 'Before Room 40: The British Empire and Signals Intelligence, 1989–1914', *The Journal of Strategic Studies*, Vol. 12, Number 4, December 1989.

17 Christopher Andrew, *The Defence of the Realm, The Authorised History of MI5* (Allen Lane, 2009); Keith Jeffery, *MI6: The History of the Secret Intelligence Service, 1909–1949* (Bloomsbury, 2011); Richard Poppelwell, *Intelligence and Imperial Defence, British Intelligence and the Defence of the Indian Empire, 1904–1924* (Routledge, 1995).

18 'Censorship of Submarine Cables in Time of War', 2.10.1898, CAB 17/92; cf. David Paul Nickles, *Under the Wire: How the Telegraph Changed Diplomacy* (Harvard University Press, 2003).

19 High Commissioner for South Africa to Governor, Natal, telegram No. 2, 24.2.1900, DO 119/513; War Office to Kitchener, 6.7.01, WO 108/306; Milner to Colonial Office, 16.5.00, FO 2/441.

20 Ferris, 'Before Room 40'.

21 Report of Censorship of Cable and Wireless Committee, 7.7.1908, CAB 17/92; Admiralty Intelligence Division, 8.11, 'Regulations for the Censorship of Radio-Telegraphy in Time of War', FO 371/ 1283, 38965; Memoranda by General Staff, 1906 and 1907, A 1039, 'Censorship of Submarine Cables in Times of War', and Second Meeting, 'Censorship of Submarine Cables', 26.10.10, L/MIL 7/13581.

22 Memorandum by War Office, ibid., ADM 1/7576; War Office, A 1039, 'Censorship of Submarines Cables in Time of War', 1906 and 1907 versions, L/MIL 7/13581.

23 Admiralty Intelligence Division, 8.11. 1911, 'Regulations for the Censorship of Radio-Telegraphy in Time of War', FO 371/ 1283, 38965.

24 War Office to Foreign Office, 21.2.06, FO 371/165, 6428.

25 First meeting of the Censorship of Cables Committee, 11.7.10, CAB 17/92.

26 Andrew, *Defence*, pp. 37–48.

27 Ferris, 'Before Room 40'.

28 Government of India to Foreign Office, 6.3.13, *passim*, FO 228/2579; cf. FO 228/2581–86, L/PS/11/47, L/PS/10/393.

29 For the background, cf. Thomas G. Fergusson, *British Military Intelligence, The Development of a Modern Intelligence Organisation* (Arms & Armour Press, 1984), pp. 166–236, and Jim Beach, *Haig's Intelligence, GHQ and the German Army, 1916–1918* (CUP, 2015), pp. 1–23.

30 John Ferris, 'Intelligence, Information and the Leverage of Seapower', Daniel Moran and James A. Russell (eds), *Maritime Strategy and Global Order, Resources, Security*, (George Washington University Press, Washington D.C., 2016).

31 Daniel Headrick, *The Invisible Weapon: Telecommunications and International Relations, 1851–1945* (OUP, 1991); Daniel R. Headrick and Pascal Griset,

'Submarine Telegraph Cables, Business and Politics, 1838–1939', *Business History Review*, 75/3, autumn 2001, pp. 543–78; Peter Hugill, *Global Communications since 1844: Geopolitics and Technology* (Johns Hopkins University Press, 1999).

32 Minute by MacDonogh, 11.2.14, WO 32/7048; meeting of Committee on Imperial Wireless Telegraphy, 17.1.12, WO 32/7045.

33 Elizabeth Bruton, 'Beyond Marconi; The Roles of the Admiralty, the Post Office and the Institution of Electrical Engineers in the invention and development of wireless communication up to 2008', University of Leeds PhD diss. 2013); cf. ADM 1/9204, ADM 1/29126.

34 Nicholas Lambert, 'Strategic Command and Control for Maneuver Warfare: Creation of the Royal Navy's "War Room" System, 1905–1915', *The Journal of Military History*, 69/2, April 2005, pp. 361–410.

35 Andrew Gordon, *The Rules of the Game, Jutland and British Naval Command* (John Murray, 2005).

36 Nicholas Black, *The British Naval Staff in the First World War* (Boydell, 2009), pp.1–74.

37 Memorandum by Spring-Rice, 19.2.1898, FO 83/1651.

38 Currie to Rosebery, 28.8.1893, Algernon Thomas (GPO) to 'Eric' (Chief Clerk's Office), 5.4.1894, FO 83/1424.

39 Monson to Sanderson, 18.12.1899, FO 83/1760.

40 Arthur Hardinge to Sanderson, 30.9.1901, FO 83/1883; Langley to Jordan, 6.4.12, FO 350/1.

41 Minute by Currie, 18.2.90, HD 3/80.

42 War Office to India Office, 14.11.11, 14.10.12, L/MIL 7/10223.

43 Ferris, *Intelligence and Strategy*, pp. 139–40.

44 Ferris, 'Before Room 40'; Nicholas Hiley, 'The Strategic Origins of Room 40', *Intelligence and National Security*, 2/3, December 1987.

CHAPTER 2

1 Undated and unsigned memorandum on the origins of Room 40, by Denniston, Denniston Papers, DENN 1/3, Churchill College, Cambridge.

2 Unsigned and undated memorandum, presumably by Sir Ronald Nesbitt Hawes, 'An Intelligence Section of the First World War', Intelligence Corps Museum, Accession No. 198.

3 Undated and unsigned memorandum on the origins of Room 40, by Denniston, Denniston Papers, DENN 1/3.

4 Undated memorandum, c. 1918, George Young, 'Political Branch of Room 40', ADM 223/773.

5 Hall to 'My dear Commander in Chief' (Beatty), 'Personal and Secret', 18.5.17, ADM 223/768.

6 Report of Cypher Conference, 27.2.19, ADM 1/8637.

7 Alice Ivy Hay, *Valiant for Truth, Ian Hay of Seaforth* (London, Spearman, 1971). https://archive.is/20120722130348/http://www.archiveshub.ac.uk/news/0508fraser.html

8 Ferris, *British Army and Signals Intelligence*, pp. 10–11.

9 Clauson to Crocker, 9.10.1917. Clauson papers, Imperial War Museum.

10 Ferris, *British Army and Signals Intelligence*, pp. 241–95.

11 Hay, *Valiant*, p. 78.

12 Young, 'Political Branch of Room 40'.

13 Ibid.

14 Ibid. Walter Bruford,' "Room Forty" in the 1914–1918 War', 23.2.77, BRUF Misc 20, Churchill College Cambridge; Elizabeth Tucker, 'Some Anniversaries and Ceremonies at Christ's Hospital, Hertford', Dr Doris Jones-Bakers (ed.), *Hertfordshire in History*, University of Hertfordshire Press, 2004, p. 296.

15 The works which use the material from Room 40, most thoroughly, Patrick Beesley, *Room 40, British Naval Intelligence, 1914–1918* (London, 1982), and Paul Gannon, *Inside Room 40: The Codebreakers of World War One* (Hersham: Ian Allen, 2010) do not tackle naval records generated from outside the NID. The Room 40 tradition focuses on the NID more than the Royal Navy. Norman Friedman, *Fighting the Great War at Sea: Strategy, Tactics and Technology* (Seaforth Publishing, Barnsley, 2014), pp. 89–97, places Sigint within the context of contemporary seapower.

16 Jellicoe to Beatty, 1.4.16, Beatty Papers, 13/22, National Maritime Museum.

17 W. F. Clarke, *History of Room 40*, 1914–1919, Chapter Two, pp. 1–4, HW 3/3.

18 William Carless Davis, *History of the Blockade Emergency Departments* (1920), p. 8, MUN 5/113.

19 Entry, 5.11.14, Mo5b war diary, ADM 223/767.

20 'English Spy System Said to Excel German', *New York Times*, 3.3.15, p. 3.

21 Filson Young, *With the Battle Cruisers* (1921).

22 W. F. Clarke, *History of Room 40*, 1914–1919, Chapter Two, p. 1–4, HW 3/3.

23 Battlecruiser Force to Grand Fleet, NO SE, 20.1.15, ADM 137/1938.

24 Gustav Kleikamp, 'Der Einfluss der Funkaufklarung auf die Seekriegfuhrung in der Nordsee 1914–1918', Gehiem MDiv. 352, Dientschrift Nr. 13, Leitung der Fuhrergehilfenausbildung der Marine (Berlin, 1934); Keith W. Bird and Jason Hines, 'In the Shadow of Ultra: A Reappraisal of German Naval Communications Intelligence in the First World War', *The Northern Mariner*, XVIII/2 (Spring 2018), pp. 97–117; Hilmar-Detlaf Bruckner, 'Germany's First Cryptanalysis on the Western Front: Decrypting British and French Naval Ciphers in World War

One', *Cryptologia*, 29/1, 9 2005), pp. 1–22; Martin Samuels, 'Ludwig Foppl: A Bavarian Cryptanalyst on the Western Front', *Cryptologia*, 40/4, pp. 355–73.

25 Unsigned letter (but Hall by internal evidence) to Sturdee, 25.5,17, ADM 223/ 768.

26 Gustav Kleikamp, 'Der Einfluss der Funkaufklarung auf die Seekriegfuhrung in der Nordsee 1914–1918', Gehiem MDiv. 352, Dientschrift Nr. 13, Leitung der Fuhrergehilfenausbildung der Marine (Berlin, 1934).

27 Grand Fleet to Admiralty, No. 50/H.F. 0022, 9.1.18, ADM 116/1349.

28 'Conference on Board "Iron Duke", 17 September', Grand Fleet to Admiralty, No. 339/H.F. 0034, 30.10.14, No. 411.H.F. 0034, 12.11.14, *passim*, ADM 137/995.

29 Battlecruiser Squadron to Grand Fleet, 20.1.15, ADM 137/1936.

30 Admiralty Committee Report, 4.2.15, ADM 1/8411.

31 Commander in Chief Grand Fleet to Captains, Grand Fleet, 'Grand Fleet Code 1914', 10.10.14, ADM 137/472; Commander in Chief Grand Fleet to Admiralty, No. 2840/HF 008, 16.12.15, *passim*, ADM 137/1896; Commander in Chief Grand Fleet to Admiralty, 31.1.17, *passim*, ADM 137/1895.

32 Bird and Hines, 'Shadow of Ultra'.

33 Jeffery, *MI6*, pp. 84–5; cf. ADM 223/267.

34 John Ferris, 'The British Army and Signals Intelligence in the Field during the First World War', INS 3/4, 1988, pp. 32–5.

35 Sophie de Lastours, *La France gagne la guerre des codes secrets 1914–18* (Paris, Tallandier, 1998) and Douglas Porch, *The French Secret Services, from the Dreyfus Affair to the Gulf War* (London, MacMillan, 1996), are useful studies. John R. Schindler, 'A Hopeless Struggle: Austro-Hungarian Cryptology during World War I', *Cryptologia*, 24/4 (2000), pp. 1–10, is excellent. The longest account of German military sigint, Wilhelm F. Flicke, *War Secrets in the Ether, Vol. One* (Aegean Park Press, Laguna Hills, Ca., 1977), pp. 1–78, must be used with extreme caution. Yves Gylden, *The Contribution of the Cryptographic Bureaus in the Great War* (Aegean Park Press, 1978: original, Swedish and French, 1931), compiles useful material about signals intelligence from the German army's official histories, and also those of Britain and France.

36 Ferris, 'Signals Intelligence in the Field', pp. 32–44.

37 Ferris, *British Army*, pp. 14–16, 85–114; Ferdinand Tuohy, *The Crater of Mars* (London, 1929), pp. 132–48.

38 Memorandum OAD 314, Kiggell, CGS, GHQ, to Third Army, 17.2.17, AWM 51/ 52, Australian War Memorial, Canberra.

39 Jim Beach and James Bruce, 'British Signals Intelligence in the Trenches, 1915–1918: part one, listening sets', and 'British Signals Intelligence in the Trenches, 1915–1918: part two, interpreter operators', *Journal of Intelligence History*, 19/1, January 2020, pp. 1–23, and pp. 24–50.

40 Ferris, *Signals intelligence*, pp.13–14, 25–54.

41 R. E. Priestley, *The Signal Service in the European War of 1914–1918 (France)* (Chatham, 1920), p. 236.

42 FAIS No. 890, 21.6.17, WO 157/76.

43 Canadian Corps Operations Orders No. 156, 11.7.27, No. 140, 28.7.17, WO 95/1050.

44 2nd Canadian Division, 6.8.17, 'Report on Conversations Picked up by Wireless Intelligence in 2nd. Canadian Division Sector', RG 9/III/C–5/4438, National Archives of Canada.

45 CCIS No. 117, 24.7.17, WO 95/1050, John Ferris, 'Seeing over the hill: the Canadian Corps, intelligence, and the battle of Hill 70, July–August 1917', INS, 32/2, April 2017, pp. 351–64.

46 J. R. Ferris (ed.) *The British Army and Signals Intelligence During the First World War* (Army Records Society, 1992, pp. 297–316). The best accounts of intelligence in these campaigns are Polly Mohs, *British Intelligence and the Arab Revolt: The First Modern Intelligence War* (Routledge, 2008) and Yigal Sheffy, *British Intelligence in the Palestine Campaign, 1914–1918* (Frank Cass, 1997).

47 Ibid. and WO 95/4966.

48 EC 850–51 (GHQ Salonica to DMI, two telegrams, 17.7.18), CAB 27/29; EC 1071, 'The Turco-German Advance into the Caucasus', General Staff, 7.8.18, CAB 7/30.

49 John Ferris, 'Pragmatic Hegemony and British economic warfare, 1900–1918', in Greg Kennedy (ed.), *Britain's War at Sea, 1914–1918: The War They Thought and the War They Fought* (Praeger, 2016).

50 John Ferris, 'The War Trade Intelligence Department and British Economic Warfare during the First World War', in T. G. Otte (ed.), *British World Policy and the Projection of Power, 1830–1960* (CUP, 2019).

51 Undated memorandum, *c.* 1918, George Young, 'Political Branch of Room 40', ADM 223/773.

52 Hardinge to Lloyd George, 14.12.16, 15.12.16, F/3/2, Robertson to Lloyd George, 14.12.16, F/44/3, Lloyd George Papers, House of Lords Record Office.

53 'Note on the division of responsibility between the War Office and the G.C. & C.S. in the event of war', 21.7.32, HW 62/19. Peter Freeman, 'MI1(b) and the Origins of British Diplomatic Cryptanalysis', INS, 22/2, 2007, pp. 206–28; James Bruce, '"A Shadowy Entity": MI1(b) and British Communications Intelligence, 1914–1922', INS, 32/3, 2017, pp. 313–32.

54 Daniel Richard Larsen, Ph.D diss., 'British Intelligence and American Neutrality during the First World War', Cambridge University, 2013.

55 Ibid. and Thomas Boghardt, *The Zimmerman Telegram: Intelligence, Diplomacy and America's Entry into the First World War* (Annapolis: Naval Institute Press, 2012).

56 Washington to Vienna 22.2.17, Vienna to Washington 27.2.17 (Austro-Hungarian decrypts), HW 7/17; cf. HW 7/22; Bullitt Lowry, *Armistice 1918* (Kent State University Press, 1996), pp. 83–4, 126.

57 Captain H. J. Round, 'Direction and Position Finding', *The Journal of the Institution of Electrical Engineer*, Vol. 5 8 (1920).

58 Brian Hall, *British Army Communications on the Western Front, 1914–1918* (CUP 2017).

59 Major W. Arthur Steel, 'Wireless Telegraphy in the Canadian Corps in France', Chapters One–Eleven, *Canadian Defence Quarterly* (Vols 6–9, 1928–31).

60 Undated and untitled memorandum by Denniston on the origins of Room 40, Denniston papers, 1 /2 and 1/3; Ann Powell, 'In Memory of Edward Russell-Clarke', n.d., https://historypoints.org/index.php?page=in-memory-of-edward-russell-clarke; Elizabeth Bruton, 'Hippisley Hut: Wireless Interception at the Outbreak of World War One', 29.3.2015, http://blogs.mhs.ox.ac.uk/innovatingincombat/tag/world-war-one/

61 Beach and Bruce, 'British Signals Intelligence in the Trenches, 1915–1918: part two', *Journal of Intelligence History*, 19/1, January 2020, pp. 24–50.

62 Jim Beach (ed.), *The Diary of Corporal Vince Schürhoff, 1914–1918* (Army Records Society, 2015).

63 Stephen McKenna, *While I Remember* (Thornton Butterworth, London, 1921), pp. 163–65.

64 'Origin and Development of the War Trade Intelligence Department', 'A', by Penson, undated. c/.11.17, BT 61/12/7; Ferris, 'The War Trade Intelligence Department, in Otte (ed.), *Britsh World Policy*, pp. 24–45.

65 Meeting at Trade Clearing House, 11.3.16, ADM 137/2735.

66 Memorandum by Emmott, 27.3.19. CAB 15/6/4

67 Tamson Pietsch, blog, 24.1.17, 'Trixie Whitehead: Intelligence and the First World War', http://expertnation.org/trixie-whitehead-intelligence-and-the-first-world-war/

68 Memorandum by Emmott, 27 March 1919, CAB 15/6/4. 'History of Postal Censorship', pp. 321, 329, 330, DEFE 1/131.

69 Jim Beach, 'The HushWAACS – The secret ladies of St. Omer, September 2017', https://www.gchq.gov.uk/information/hush-waacs

70 Memorandum by G. E. G. Watkins, 'Memoirs of a HushWaac in France', undated, MCN 944, National Army Museum.

71 M. D. Peel, *The Story of the Hush-Waacs* (Newcastle-under-Lyme: Mandley & Unett, 1921).

72 Memorandum by Brooke-Hunt, 'Nominal Roll of M.I.1.b.', 2.8.19', HW 3/35 'History of the Cryptographic and Wireless Intelligence Organisations'; unsigned, *c*. 1.23, HW 3/39.

73 Ivo Juurvee, 'Birth of Russian SIGINT in World War One on the Baltic Sea', INS, 32/3, 1917, pp. 300–12; Admiralty to Foreign Office, 'Urgent and Secret', 7.9.14, *passim*, FO 371/2095.

74 Betsy Smoot, 'Impermanent Alliances: cryptologic cooperation between the United States, Britain and France on the western front, 1917–1918', INS, 32/3, 2017, pp. 365–77.

75 Mediterranean Station W/T Orders, 8.11.16, ADM 137/1603; Commander in Chief Mediterranean Fleet to Admiralty, 14.1.16, *passim,* ADM 137/2171; Commander in Chief Mediterranean Fleet to Adriatic Force, 5.12.17, ADM 137/2125; cf. ADM 116/429.

76 Captain H. J. Round, 'Direction and Position Finding', *The Journal of the Institution of Electrical Engineers,* Vol. 5 8 (1920), p. 238, *passim;* Round to Royal Commission for Awards to Inventors, 20.12.26, War Office to same, 5.1.28, T I73/ 428.

77 Robert M. Grant, U Boat Hunters: Codebreakers, Divers and the Defeat of the B-Boats, 1914–1918 (Annapolis: Naval Institute Press, 2003); cf. ADM 1/8512.

78 J. R. Ferris, "Airbandit":C3 I and Strategic Air Defence During the First Battle of Britain, 1915–1918' in Michael Dockrill and David French, (eds), *Strategy and Intelligence, British Policy During the First World War* (Hambledon, 1996).

CHAPTER 3

1 John Ferris, 'British Intelligence and the Old World Order', in Greg Kennedy (ed.) *Imperial Defence, The Old World Order, 1856–1956* (Routledge Press, 2008), pp.176–96.; J. R. Ferris. '"Now that the Milk is Spilt": Appeasement and the Archive on Intelligence', in B. J. C. McKercher and Michael Roi, (eds), *Appeasement Reappraised* (special issue, *Diplomacy & Statecraft,* 2008).

2 Beesley, Room 40, p. 304; W. F. Clarke, 'The Years Between', Chapter Three, W. F. Clarke Papers, Churchill College, Cambridge.

3 Curzon to Auston Chamberlain, 25.3.19, T 1/12517; conference of ministers, 29.4.29, *passim,* ADM 1/8637.

4 C.P. 3105, July 1921, Lord Curzon Papers, F. 112/302, India Office Records Library.

5 Minute by Waterhouse, 9.5.19, T 1/12517/13418.

6 Ibid.

7 Ibid., 13.12.19, T 1/12517/13418.

8 Bruce, 'Shadowy Entity',; Hay, *Valiant for Truth.*

9 Clarke, 'The Years Between', Chapter Three.

10 Record of Conference held at the Admiralty on 5 August, 1919, HW 3/35.

11 Andrew, *Secret Service,* pp. 262–74; Richard H. Ullman, *Anglo-Soviet Relations, Vol. III, The Anglo-Soviet Accord,* Chapter Nine (Princeton, 1972); minute by Sinclair, March 1921, Lloyd George Papers, F/25/1.

12 Curzon to Lee, 25.4/21, ADM 8637.

13 'Report of the Committee Appointed by the Cabinet on March 22nd', 27.7.21, 15/ B/10, *passim,* KV 4/157.

14 C.P. 3105, July 1921, Lord Curzon Papers, F. 112/302, India Office Records Library.
15 Ibid.
16 Meeting of the Secret Service Committee, 2.3.25, FO 1093/68.
17 Alastair Denniston, 'The Code and Cypher School between the Wars', *INS*, 1/1, January 1986, pp. 48–70.
18 Ullman, *Anglo-Soviet Relations*.
19 Curzon to Lloyd George, 5.10.22, F. 112/224 B, Curzon to Baldwin, 9.11.23, F.112/320, Curzon Papers.
20 Report of the Inter-Service Directorate Committee, 9.4.23, AIR 2/246.
21 Undated memorandum by the GC&CS, July 1923, AIR/2/246.
22 Curzon to Hoare, 20.12.23, AIR 2/246; cf. WO 32/4897
23 'History of the Cryptographic and Wireless Intelligence Organisations', unsigned, *c.* 1.23, HW 3/39.
24 Denniston, 'Code and Cypher School'; Draft memorandum by Loxley, 4.11.44, FO 1093/195.
25 Undated, unsigned memorandum by the Treasury's Finance Branch, probably December 1925, T 160/239.
26 Howard Smith to Denniston, 7.5.37, HW 3/64.
27 For records of these meetings, cf. AIR 2/246 and WO 106/5392.
28 Draft 'History of Sigint Communications', p. 28, HW 3/91.
29 H. F. P. Sinclair's Service Record, ADM 196/43. p. 368. I am indebted to Jock Bruce for his unpublished study of Sinclair's personal background, 'The Secret Admiral: Notes on the Life of Admiral Hugh Sinclair'.
30 'Note on the division of responsibility between the War Office and the G.C. & C.S. in the event of war', 21.7.32, HW 62/19.
31 'History of Naval Section, 1919–1941, Introduction', by W. F. Clarke, undated but c. 1946, HW 3/16.
32 'Inter-Departmental Conference', 8.5.1919, T 1/12517, 'G.C. & C.S. Standing Orders', 1.12.27, HW 62/19.
33 Memorandum by McCormack, 'Berkeley Street', n.d., c 5.43, RG 457/1119, NARA, College Park.
34 Curzon papers, Vol. 302.
35 Foreign Office to Treasury, 13.1. 37, FO 366/978, X. 7105.
36 Memorandum by Kenworthy, 3.5.32, 'Y Station New Scotland Yard', HW 3/81; Minute by Howard Smith, 7.10.37, HW 3/80.
37 'J. E. S. Cooper, 'Air Sections GC and CS and the Approach to the War, 1935–39', June 1975, HW 3/83.
38 'G. C. & C. S. Standing Orders', 1.12.27, HW 62/19.
39 John Tiltman, *DNB*; Peter Freeman and Ralph Erskine, 'Brigadier John Tiltman: One of Britain's Finest Cryptologists', *Cryptologia*, 27/4 (2003), pp. 289–318.

40 'Diplomatic & Commercial History', n.d. *c.* 1946.

41 Ibid.

42 Memorandum by Knox, 1928, HW 3/1.

43 Memorandum by Turner, 1928, HW 3/1.

44 Memorandum by McCormack, 'Berkeley Street', n.d., c 5.43, RG 457/1119, NARA, College Park.

45 Memorandum by Armed Forces Security Agency, 'The Significance of the Archive as an Aid to Cryptanalysis and a Source of Information (Lecture Delivered to the 5th Chi-Meeting, 7.3.1945', RG 457/1313; Memorandum by Aurell, 'Intelligence and Information Section', 1.6.43, RG 457/1009.

46 Diplomatic & Commercial History.

47 Memorandum by McCormack, 'Berkeley Street', n.d., c 5.43, RG 457/1119, NARA.

48 NSA Oral History, Interview with John Tiltman, 11.12.78, 05–7B, https://www.nsa.gov/Portals/70/documents/news-features/declassified-documents/oral-history-interviews/nsa-OH-05-78-tiltman.pdf

49 Memorandum by Travis, 18.2.43, HW 14/67.

50 Undated memorandum by the GC&CS, July 1923, AIR/2/246.

51 Unsigned memorandum by Junior Assistants, 22.1.37, HW 3/64.

52 GC&CS to Chief Clerk's Department, 4.10.27, HW 62/19.

53 Denniston to Creswell, 7.7.38, HW 72/9.

54 Ibid.

55 Denniston to Wilson, 16.5.38, HW 72/9.

56 For regulations for applicants to the GC&CS, cf. FO 366/815, X 8536, FO 366/846, X 3567, CSC/30.

57 Denniston to Guy, 25.2.38, HW 72/9.

58 For regulations for applicants to the GC&CS, cf. FO 366/815, X 8536, FO 366/846, X 3567, CSC/30.

59 Minute by 'B.' (Major Joseph Ball), 19.3.26, KV 2/2317.

60 Denniston to DNI, n.d., *passim,* HW 3/35.

61 Memorandum by Bodsworth, 'Naval Section, 1927–1939', HW 3/1.

62 NSA Oral Interview with John Tiltman, 06–78, 13.12.78, https://www.nsa.gov/Portals/70/documents/news-features/declassified-documents/oral-history-interviews/nsa-OH-06-78-tiltman.pdf

63 Cf. Jacqui, Uí Chionna's forthcoming, *Secrets and Sonatas: The Lives of Emily Anderson.*

64 Denniston Papers. 1/3.

65 Clarke to Denniston, 24.3.31, HW 3/1; Memorandum by Military Section, 14.6.38, HW62/21.

66 Wilson to Wright, 4.1.40, FO 366/2378.

67 Denniston to Robinson, 27.4.36, HW 3/57.

68 'Clerical Staff as authorised by T. L. E. 4278/4 of 7th December 1936', HW 3/39.

69 Robinson to Foyle, 31.7.37, FO 366/1000.

70 Denniston to Wilson, 24.11.39, FO 366/2378.

71 Memorandum by Clarke, 21.10. 35, HW 3/1.

72 Memorandum by McCormack, 'Berkeley Street', n.d., c 5.43, RG 457/1119, NARA.

73 Denniston to Howard Smith, 2.1.36, FO 366/978, X 185.

74 Ferris, 'Whitehall's Black Chamber', pp. 62–3, 89–90.

75 Robinson to Foyle, 31.7.37, FO 366/1000.

76 'G.C. & C.S. Standing Orders', 1.12.27, HW 62/19; Malcolm Kennedy Diary, entries 12 February 1941, 6 December 1941, Sheffield University Library.

77 John Ferris, 'Consistent with an Intention: The Far East Combined Bureau and the Outbreak of the Pacific War, 1940–1941', INS, 27/1, 2012, pp. 5–26; Richard Aldrich, *Intelligence and the War Against Japan: Britain, America and the Politics of Secret Service* (CUP, 2000) pp. 25–45.

78 Minute by Parker, 1 February 1935, T 162/972, E 17426/3.

79 Peter King, 'The Military Career of Freddie Jacob OBE', (Bletchley Park Trust, 2017).

80 Military Secretary's Division, Simla, 'Annual Reports for 1911 on the officers of the British Service serving on the Headquarters of the British Army in India', 2.5.1912, Major G. R. M. Church RA, L/MIL 7/17047.

81 Minute by Dickens, 26.10.33, ADM 116/3114.

82 Memorandum by Jacob, 20.4.26, L/MIL 7/12541. The Indian Army called codebreakers, 'signals computers'. During 1939–45, British Siginters described military personnel trained to decode known systems as 'computers'.

83 Richards to Waterfield, 15.6.28, *passim,* T 162/974/4.

84 Ferris, *Strategy and Intelligence*, pp. 150, 178, 354–5.

85 Report of Cypher Conference, 27.2.19, ADM 1/8637.

86 Foreign Office Circular, 30.1.21, FO 513/1; cf. HW 3/39.

87 'Report of Cypher Conference', 27.2.19, ADM 1/8637.

88 Memorandum by Wright,14.3.29, for DNI, ADM 116/2445; memorandum, undated but circa 1932, 'Battle Code', ADM 116/2978.

89 Minute by Denniston, 19.3.31, HW 3/52; minute by Travis, 12.6.44, FO 850/134.

90 Memorandum by Clarke, 16.9.35, HW 3/1; Cooper to Denniston, 24.4.38, HW 62/21.

91 Denniston to Director, 6.2.39, Denniston to Titterton, 23.6.39, HW 62/21.

92 Memorandum by Tiltman, 3.1.39, Military Section, G.C. and C.S., Progress Report, 15th July, 1939, Tiltman to Page, 16.8.39, HW 62/21.

93 NSA Oral History Interviews, John Tiltman, 13.12.78, 06–78, https://www.nsa.gov/news-features/declassified-documents/oral-history-interviews/

94 Wilson to Davenport, 24.9.79, transcribed by Peter Freeman, original lost.

95   Ibid.

96   'Security of R.A.F. Signal Communications', n.d., and no author cited, but
     c. December 1944 by internal evidence, AIR 20/1531,

97   John Ferris, 'The British Enigma: Britain, Signals Security, and Cypher
     Machines, 1906–1953', Ferris, *Strategy and Intelligence*, pp. 138–80.

98   Southey to Lywood, 17.1.39, AIR 2/1255.

99   Indian War Department, undated draft chapter, 'General Staff and Analogous
     Matters, 1939–1944', L/R/5/278.

100 Memorandum by Turner, 1928, HW 3/1.

101 Memorandum by Alfred McCormack, 'Berkeley Street', n.d., c. 6.43, RG 0457/
     1119.

102 Undated memorandum by the GC&CS, July 1923, AIR/2/246.

103 Undated and unsigned memorandum on diplomatic cryptanalysis in 1940,
     31.1.41, HW 14/11.

104 'Order of Priority of Foreign Countries from S.I.S. Point of View', n.d., c. 1935
     by internal evidence, *passim*, WO 32/5392.

105 Denniston, 'Code and Cypher School'.

106 Memorandum by Turner, 1928, HW 3/1.

107 Second meeting of Colonial Office Code and Cypher Committee, 3.1.1922, CO
     537/625; Inter-Service Directorate Report, op.cit. AIR 2/246.

108 Unsigned memorandum, but probably by Denniston, 29.4.32, HW 62/19.

109 Air Section, Report on Experiment into Decentralisation, 26 March, 1938, to 1
     April 1938, HW 62/21.

110 Unsigned, undated 'Memorandum', c. 1921 by internal evidence,
     HW 3/39.

111 'Order of Priority of Foreign Countries from S.I.S. Point of View', n.d., c. 1935
     by internal evidence, *passim*, WO 32/5392.

112 Ralph E. Weber, *United States Diplomatic Codes and Ciphers, 1775–1938* (Chicago,
     Precedent Publishing, 1979); Daniel Larsen, 'British Codebreaking and American
     Diplomatic Telegrams, 1914–15', INS, 32/2, 2017, pp. 256–63.

113 Memorandum by Clarke, 'Naval Section, Government Code and Cipher
     School', 4.8.37, HW 3/1.

114 Head to Naval Section of Head of GC&CS, 20.1.36, *passim,* HW 3/1.

115 Unsigned, undated, memorandum, but by Jacob and 1938 by internal evidence,
     'Nominal role of officers of the Military Section of the G.C.& C.S. and a
     summary of the work carried out by each officer during the past year', HW 3/88.

116 Undated memorandum by the GC&CS, July 1923, AIR/2/246.

117 Memorandum by Jacob, 14.6.38, Denniston to Jebb, 17,6.38, *passim,* HW 62/21

118 Cooper to Buss, 13.1.38, Air Section, Report for Second and Third Quarters,
     1937, 12.1.38, unsigned memorandum, 'German Air Force', 27.4.38, HW 62/21

119 Coordination of Interception Committee, meeting 7.11.34, HW 42/1.

120 Military Section, G.C. and C.S., Progress Report, 15.7.1939, Tiltman to Page, 16.8.39, HW 62/21.

121 'Directorate-level Overview of GCCS at Bletchley Park with Recommendations for GCHQ in the Future', 1946, HW 3/87.

122 Memorandum by Denniston, AGD 1124, 11.10.44, HW 3/169.

123 Memorandum by Bodsworth, 'Naval Section, 1927–1939', HW 3/1.

124 W. F. Clarke, 'History of Naval Section, 1919–1941, Chapter VI, War, 1939–1941', HW 3/16.

125 G.C. and C.S. Military Section, Monthly Report, No. 1, 1.7.38, HW 62/21.

126 'Emily Anderson and Beethoven's Letters', *The Beethoven Newsletter,* 1/3, Winter 1986, pp. 48–49.

127 Memorandum by Bodsworth, 'Naval Section, 1927–1939', HW 3/1.

128 de Grey to Cavendish-Bentinck, 30.6.45, FO 1093/480.

129 'Diplomatic and Commercial History'.

130 'Mediterranean O.I.C. War Communications', N.I.D. 00714/39, by DNI and D.S.D., 7.39, HW 62/12.

131 Hay to DNI, 11.5.19, HW 3/35; Denniston to Jebb, 18.11.39, FO 1093/106.

CHAPTER 4

1 The standard account of Yardley, his bureau, and its role during 1921–22 is David Kahn, *The Reader of Gentlemen's Mail, The Story of Herbert O. Yardley* (Yale University Press, 2004). Useful studies of naval arms limitation between the wars, and of the Washington Conference, are Emily O. Goldman, *Sunken Treaties: Naval Arms Control between the Wars* (HIA Book Collection, 1994), and Erik Goldstein and John Maurer (eds), *The Washington Conference, 1921–1922: Naval Rivalry, East Asian Stability and the Road to Pearl Harbor* (Routledge, 1994).

2 Director, Naval Communications, to Secretary of the Navy, 21 January 1931, Secret, 'Report on decrypting activities in various branches of the Government', file 'Earliest Naval Comint', and Herbert Yardley Papers, Box 1 / 2, David Kahn Collection, National Cryptologic Museum, Fort Meade.

3 Notes on docket F/1/23, February 1922, FO 371/8042.

4 John Ferris, '"It is our Business in the Navy to Command the Seas": The Last Decade of British Maritime Supremacy, 1919–1929', in Keith Neilson and Greg Kennedy, *Far Flung Lines, Maritime Essays in Honour of Donald Schurman* (Frank Cass, 1996).

5 Tadeshi Kurumatsu, 'The Geneva Naval Conference of 1927: The British Preparation for the Conference, December 1926 to June 1927', *The Journal of Strategic Studies,* 19/1, March 1996, pp. 104–21; Richard Fanning, *Peace and Disarmament: Naval Rivalry and Arms Control, 1922–23* (University Press of Kentucky, 1995).

6 John Ferris, 'British Intelligence and the London Naval Conference, 1919–1930', in Chris Bell and John Maurer, *Crossroads of War and Peace, The London Naval Conference, 1930* (Naval Institute Press, 2014).

7 'London Naval Conference' file, HW 12/126.

8 Gillian Bennett, *The Zinoviev Letter: The Conspiracy That Never Dies* (2018).

9 Ben Pimlott (ed.), *The Political Diary of Hugh Dalton, 1918–1940, 1945–60* (Jonathan Cape, London, 1986), pp. 69–72, 80–81; NC 278, 27.3.30, HW 12/126.

10 Sadeo Asada, 'From Washington to London: The Imperial Japanese Navy and the Politics of Naval Limitation, 1921–1930', *Diplomacy & Statecraft*, 4/3, September 1993, p. 177.

11 Asada, 'Washington to London', pp. 147–91; NC 135, 25.2.30, *passim*, HW 12/126.

12 NC 102, 15.2.30, NC 188, 11.3.30, HW 12/126.

13 NC 112, 18.2.30, NC 247, 22.3.30, HW 12/126; Ferris, 'London Naval Conference'.

14 NC 132, 24.2.30, HW 12/126.

15 NC 299, 31.3.30, HW 12/126.

16 Ferris, 'London Naval Conference'.

17 Minute by Smith, 10.1.36, FO 371/19804, A 279.

18 The best accounts of diplomacy and strategy in the Middle East between 1918–23 are, Zara Steiner, *The Lights that Failed: European International History, 1919–1933* (OUP, 2005), pp. 80–130; David Fromkin, *A peace to end all peace: The fall of the Ottoman Empire and the creation of the modern Middle East* (H. Holt, New York, 2001); Paul C. Helmreich: *From Paris to Sevres: The Partition of the Ottoman Empire at the Paris Peace Conference of 1920* (Ohio State University Press, Columbus, 1974), and Sean McMeekin, *The Ottoman End-Game, War, Revolution and the Making of the Modern Middle East, 1908–1923* (Penguin, 2016). Strong accounts of British policy are, John Darwin, *Britain, Egypt and the Middle East: Imperial policy in the aftermath of war, 1918–1922* (St Martin's Press, New York, 1981); John Fisher, *Curzon and British Policy in the Middle East, 1916–1919* (HIA Book Collection, 1999); and Keith Jeffery, *The British Army and the Crisis of Empire, 1918–1922* (Manchester, Manchester University Press, 1984).

19 John Ferris, 'The Internationalism of Islam: British Perceptions of a Muslim Menace, 1840–1951', *Intelligence and National Security* (24/1, February 2009), pp. 57–77.

20 John Ferris, 'The British empire vs. the "CUP-Jew-German-Bolshevik Combination", 1919–1923', in Greg Kennedy (ed.), *The British Way in Warfare: Power and the International System* (Ashgate, 2010); John Fisher, 'The Interdepartmental Committee on Eastern Unrest and British Responses to Bolshevik and other Intrigues against the British Empire during the 1920s', *Journal of Asian History*, 34/1, 2000; Andrew Orr, "We Call You Now to Holy War": Mustafa Kemal, Communism and Germany in French Intelligence

Nightmares, 1919–1923', *Journal of Military History*, October 2011, Vol. 75 Issue 4, pp. 1095–1123; A. L. Macfie, 'British Intelligence and the Causes of Unrest in Mesopotamia, 1919–21', and 'British Views of the Turkish Nationalist Movement, 1919–22', *Middle Eastern Studies*, 35/1 (1.99) and 38/3 (7.02).

21 War Office to GOC Baghdad, 87609 21.1.21, 15.11, High Commissioner Cairo to Minister Jeddah, 8.2.21, FO 141/433/3.

22 Minute by D. G. Osbourne, 23.9.20, FO 371/4946, E 11702.

23 Bulant Gokay, *A Clash of Empires: Turkey between Russian Bolshevism and British Imperialism, 1918–1923* (I. B. Tauris, London, 1997).

24 Documents on British Foreign Policy (DBFP) xvii, pp. 301, 714; minute by Churchill, 9.12.20, WO 32/5743; minute by Curzon, 10.2.21, FO 371/6265, E 1478.

25 DBFP xvii, pp. 45, 47, 224–27, 242–43, 424

26 Memorandum by Harington, CR/BFT/58410/C.H.H., 'British Forces In Turkey, C-in-C's Dispatch, Period 1920–1923', WO 32/5743.

27 Minute by Osbourne, n.d., March 1921, FO 371/6466, E 2919.

28 Memorandum by Leeper, 19.5.22, 'Anti-British Activities of the Soviet Government', minute by Curzon, 30.5.22, FO 371/8193.

29 Curzon to Austen Chamberlain, 13.5.22, AC 23/6, Austen Chamberlain Papers. Maxim Litvonov was the second-ranking official in the Soviet foreign ministry; the Genoa conference was an abortive effort to settle political and economic problems in Europe.

30 John Ferris, '"Far too dangerous a gamble"?: British Intelligence and Policy during the Chanak Crisis, September–October 1922', *Diplomacy & Statecraft*, 14/2, June 2003, pp. 139–84.

31 DBFP, xviii, p. 25.

32 Ferris, 'Gamble'.

33 Ibid.

34 Curzon to Hardinge, 16.9.22, FO 800/157;

35 S.I.S. No. 887, 22.9.22. Military Intelligence I.C. (i.e. M.I.I.C.) HC/3918, 19.9.22, WO 106/1504; SIS 'Eastern Summary' No. 865, 13.9.22, FO 371/7891.

36 Harington to WO telegram. No. 2509, 29.9.22, FO 371/7897; Harington to WO, No. 2462, 26.9.22, FO 371/7895; Harington to WO, telegram No. 2460, 27.9.22, FO 371/7896.

37 Rumbold to FO, No. 474, 'Private and Secret', 28.9.22, WO 106/1441,

38 Admiralty to Commander in Chief, Mediterranean Fleet, telegram No. 929, 19.9.22, WO 106/1503; Admiralty to Commander in Chief Atlantic Fleet, 24.9.22, 'Appreciation of the Situation in the Near East, a.m., Sunday, 24.9.22, ADM 137/1778.

39 S.I.S. No. 877, 18.9.22, WO 106/1503; Note of telephone message between Tyrell and Curzon, 6.40 p.m. 22.9.22, FO 800/157; record of telephone conversation

between Lloyd George and Hankey, 4.30 p.m., 22.9.22, Cab 21/241; S.I.S. No. 892, 25.9.22, WO 106/1507; SIS CXG.433, 23.9.22, FO 371/7893

40 DBFP, Vol. XVIII, Nos 41–43, 48, 49.

41 Harington to War Office, No. 2516, 29.9.22, FO 371/7897.

42 Harington to WO, telegram No. 2506, 28.9.22, FO 371/7899; Harington to WO telegrams No. 2493, 29.9.22, WO 106/1441; Harington to W.O., telesgrams No. 1222, 27.9.22, No. 1223, 28.9.22, No. 2485, 28.9.22, FO 371/7896.

43 Keith Jeffery and Alan Sharp, 'Lord Curzon and the Use of Secret Intelligence at the Lausanne Conference, 1922–1923', in Christopher Andrew and Jeremy Noakes (eds), *Intelligence and International Relations, 1914–45* (Exeter Studies in History, No. 15, Exeter, 1987), pp.103–26.

44 Sevtap Dimirci, *The Lausanne Conference: The Evolution of Turkish and British Diplomatic Strategies, 1922–23* (PhD diss., London School of Economics, 1998) is the best account of the conference. For British policy there, cf; Erik Goldstein, 'The British "Official Mind" and the Lausanne Conference', *Statecraft & Diplomacy*, 14.2, June 2003, pp. 185–206, and for intelligence, Keith Jeffery and Alan Sharp, 'Lord Curzon and the Use of Secret Intelligence at the Lausanne Conference, 1922–1923', in Christopher Andrew and Jeremy Noakes (eds), *Intelligence and International Relations, 1914–45* (Exeter Studies in History, No. 15, Exeter, 1987), pp.103–26.

45 T. G. Otte, "A Very Internicene Policy": Anglo-Russian Cold Wars before the Cold War', in Christopher Baxter, Michael L. Dockrill and Keith Hamilton, *Britain in Global Politics, From Gladstone to Churchill* (Springer, 2013), pp. 17–49; and Keith Neilson, *Britain, Russia and the Collapse of the Versailles Order, 1919–1939* (CUP, 2006).

46 Neilson, *Versailles Order* is the best account; for an alternative view, cf. Gabriel Goredetsky, *The Precarious Truce: Anglo-Soviet Relations, 1924–1927* (CUP, 1977).

47 Timothy Edward O'Connor, *Diplomacy & Revolution: G. V. Chicherin & Soviet Foreign Affairs, 1918–1930*. 1987); Samuel J. Hirst, 'Transnational Anti-Imperialism and the National Forces: Soviet Diplomacy and Turkey, 1920–1923', *Comparative Studies of South Asia, Africa and the Middle East* 33/2 (2013), pp. 214–26; and Ben Fowkes and Bulant Gokay (eds), special issue of *Journal of Communist Studies and Transition Politics*, 25/1, 2009, 'Unholy Alliance: Muslims and Communists'.

48 Minute by Strang, 13.1.26, FO 371/11775, N 32; Jeffery, *MI 6*, pp. 183–96.

49 Minute by Tyrrell, 4.12.26, FO 371/11787, N 4881.

50 GC&CS No. 003934, 20.8.20, HW 12/13.

51 Andrew, *Defence*, pp. 139–59; Jeffery, *MI6*, pp. 176–209; and Victor Madeira, *Britannia and the Bear: The Anglo-Russian Intelligence Wars, 1917–1929* (Boydell & Brewer, 2014).

52 Ferris, 'CUP-Jew-German-Bolshevik Combination'.

53 Fisher, 'Inter-Departmental Committee on Eastern Unrest'.

54 No. 34377, 8.4.29, HW 12/117.

55 No. 23652, 26.8.26, No. 023660, 27.8.26, No. 023661, 27.8.26, and No. 023663, 27.8.26, HW 12/85.

56 E. S. K. Fung, *The Diplomacy of Imperial Retreat: Britain's South China Policy, 1924–1931* (Oxford, 1991); Bruce A. Elleman, *Diplomacy and Deception: The Secret History of Sino-Soviet Relations, 1917–1927*; M. E. Sharpe, 1997; Alexander Pantsov, *The Bolsheviks and the Chinese Revolution, 1919–1929* (Richmond, 2000); Michael Share, 'Clash of Worlds: The Comintern, British Hong Kong, and Chinese Nationalism, 1921–1929, *Europe-Asia Studies*, 57/4, June 2005, pp. 601–24; and Michael Weiner, 'Comintern in East Asia, 1919–39', in Kevin McDermott and Jeremy Agnew, *The Comintern: A History of International Communism from Lenin to Stalin* (Palgrave Macmillan, 1996), pp. 158–90.

57 Minutes by O'Malley, 2.1.25, Wellesley, 3.1.25, and Austen Chamberlain, 3.1.25, FO 371/10984, N 16.

58 No. 34384, 9.2.24, HW 12/117; No. 24005, 27.9.26, HW 12/86; No. 34315, 4.4.29, HW 12/117; cf. Hasan Ali Karasar, 'Chicherin on the delimitation of Turkestan: native Bolsheviks versus Soviet foreign policy. Seven letters from the Russian archives on razmezhevanie', *Central Asian Survey* (2002), 21 (2), pp. 199–209; Anna di Briago, 'Moscow, The Comintern and the War Scare, 1926–28', in Silvio Pons and Andrea Romano, *Russia in the Age of Wars* (Milano: Feltrinelli, 2000), pp. 83–102.

59 John Ferris, 'Counter-Insurgency and Empire: The British Experience with Afghanistan and the North-West Frontier', Scott Gates and Ray Kaushlik (eds), *Counter-Insurgency in Afghanistan* (Routledge, 2014); and Brandon Marsh, *Ramparts of Empire, British Imperialism and India's Afghan Frontier, 1918–1948* (Palgrave Macmillan, 2014)

60 Stephanie Cronin, *The Army and the Creation of the Pahlavi State in Iran: 1910–1926* (New York and London: Tauris Academic Series, 1997) and Houshang Sabahi, *British Policy in Persia, 1918–1925* (Taylor & Francis, 1990).

61 No. 22197, No. 22242, 26.1.26, HW 12/78; No. 23271, 8.7.26, HW 12/86; Nos 24034, XXX, 023891, 16.9.26, No. 23994, 25.9.26, HW 12/84.

62 Minute by Gregory, 19.8.25, FO 371/10841, E 4803.

63 No. 24005, 27.9.26, HW 12/86

64 Leon B. Poullada, *Reform and Rebellion in Afghanistan, 1919–1929* (Ithaca, NY, Cornell University Press, 1973); Ludwig W. Adamec, *Afghanistan's Foreign Affairs to the Mid Twentieth Century: Relations with the USSR, Germany and Britain* (University of Arizona Press, Tucson, 1074).

65 No. 34443, HW 12/117; Nos 35132, 34998, HW 12/119; No. 023721, 31.8.26, HW 12/85; 34315, 4.4.29, HW 12/117

66 Telegram from Viceroy to India Office, 14.2.29, *passim*, FO 371/13992, N 1037; cf. FO 371/13995, FO 371/14003.

67 Minute by Craigie, 5.10.36, *passim*, FO 371/20094, E 5280

68 This material may be found in the HW 17 series. The best, if brief, account is Andrew, *Defence*, pp. 171–3.

69 'Image and Accident: Intelligence and the Origins of the Second World War, 1933–1941', in John Ferris, *Intelligence and Strategy, Selected Essays* (2005); Neilson, *Versailles Order*, pp. 41–2, and Zara Steiner, *The Triumph of the Dark, European International History, 1933–1939* (OUP, 2011), pp. 1–9, 1036–58.

70 The literature on appeasement is overwhelmingly large. The articles in a special issue of *Diplomacy & Statecraft*, 19/3, 2008, especially Sidney Aster, 'Appeasement: Before and After Revisionism', pp. 443–80, present a balanced account of the topic, with good bibliographies.

71 Though most commentators on Chamberlain's statesmanship remain negative (cf. John Ruggiero, *Hitler's Enabler: Neville Chamberlain and the origins of the Second World War* (Santa Barbara Ca., ABC-Clio, 2015), and Steiner, *Triumph*, pp. 610–59), he has some supporters (cf. John Charmley, *Chamberlain and the Lost Peace* (Chicago: Ivor Dee, 1990). For balanced overviews, cf. R. A. C. Parker, *Chamberlain and Appeasement: British Policy and the Coming of the Second World War* (London, 1993) and David Hucker, 'The Unending Debate: Appeasement, Chamberlain and the Origins of the Second World War', INS, 23/4, 2008, pp. 536–51.

72 Antony Best, *Britain, Japan and Pearl Harbor: Avoiding War in East Asia, 1936–1941* (1995) remains excellent, although published before the release of flimsies in the HW 12 series.

73 No account incorporates the Comint record; Jill Edwards, *The British Government and the Spanish Civil War, 1936–1939* (London, 1979), remains the best study.

74 No. 067433, 14.1.1937; No. 067440, 15.1.1937; No. 067442, 15.1.1937, HW 12/211; Foreign Office to India Office, 'Most Secret', 29.1.1937, Walton (India Office) to Metcalfe (Government of India), 1.2.1937, Foreign Office to India Office, 'Most Secret', 4.5.1937, L PS/12/225, India Office Record Library, British Library.

75 Stephen Wagner, *Statecraft by Stealth, Secret Intelligence and British Rule in Palestine* (Cornell University Press, 2019), Chapter 9.

76 Untitled and unsigned Memorandum, 24.11.38, HW 62/21.

77 Wagner, *Statecraft*.

78 John Ferris, 'Vansittart, Intelligence and Appeasement' and 'Image and Accident: Intelligence and the Origins of the Second World War, 1933–1941', in John Ferris, *Intelligence and Strategy, Selected Essays* (2005).

79 W. C. Mills, 'The Chamberlain–Grandi Conversations of July–August 1937 and the Appeasement of Italy', and 'Sir Joseph Ball, Adrian Dingli, and Neville

Chamberlain's "Secret Channel" to Italy, 1937–40', in *International History Review*, 19/3 (1997), pp. 594–619, and 24/2 (2002), pp. 278–317.

80 GC&CS No. 070481, 1.1.38, No. 070552, 9.2.38, HW 12/224; No. 070729, 8.3.38, No. 070754, 11.3.38, HW 12/225; Andrew, *Defence*, pp. 195–209; Bruce Strang, 'Sir Alexander Cadogan and the Steward–Hesse Affair: Assessments of British Cabinet Politics and Future British Policy, 1938' (forthcoming, *International History Review*).

81 Carl Boyd, 'The Role of Hiroshi Oshima in the Preparation of the Anti-Comintern Pact', *Journal of Asian History*, 11, 1 (1977): pp. 49–71; J. W. M. Chapman, 'A Dance on Eggs: Intelligence and the "Anti-Comintern"', *Journal of Contemporary History*, 22/2, 1987, pp. 333–72; John Fox, *Germany and the Far Eastern Crisis, 1931–1938: A Study in Diplomacy and Ideology* (Oxford, 1982); Wolfgang Michalka, 'From the Anti-Comintern Pact to the Euro-Asiatic Bloc: Ribbentrop's Alternative Concept of Hitler's Foreign Policy Programme', in Koch H. W. (ed.) *Aspects of the Third Reich* (Palgrave, London, 1985; Tajima Nobuo, 'The Berlin–Tokyo Axis Reconsidered: from the Anti-Comintern Pact to the Plot to Assassinate Stalin', in Christian W. Spang and Rolf-Harald Wippich (eds), *Japanese German Relations, 1985–1945, War Diplomacy and Public Opinion* (Routledge, London, 1999), pp. 161–80; Ōhata Tokushirō, 'The Japanese–Soviet Confrontation, 1935–1939', in James Morley (ed.), *Deterrent Diplomacy: Japan, Germany and the USSR, 1935–40, Selections from The Road to the Pacific War* (Columbia University Press, 1976); Neilson, *Versailles, Order*, pp. 191–95.

82 Ferris, *Intelligence and Strategy*, pp. 55–87, 134–5.

83 Gerhard Weinberg, *The Foreign Policy of Hitler's Germany, Vol. II, Starting World War Two* (Chicago, The University of Chicago Press, 1980), pp. 282–83; Steiner.

84 No. 069514, HW 12/220.

85 GC&CS No. 070335, 12.1.38, HW 12/223.

86 Mills, 'Chamberlain-Grandi Conversations', H. Matthew Heffler, "In the Way": Intelligence, Eden and British Foreign Policy Towards Italy, 1937–1938', *Intelligence and National Security*, 33/6, 2018, pp. 875–93.

87 Reynolds M. Salerno, *Vital Crossroads. Mediterranean Origins of the Second World War, 1935–1940* (Ithaca, NY, Cornell University Press, 2002), pp.73–107.

88 GC&CS No. 070335, 12.1.38, No. 070383, 20.1.38, HW 12/223; GC&CS No. 070505, 4.2.38, HW 12/224.

89 GC&CS No. 070755, 11.3.38, HW 12/225.

90 GC&CS No. 070539, 8.2.38, HW 12/224.

91 GC&CS No. 070690, 3.3.38, No. 070830, 19.3.38, HW 12.225; GC&CS No. 071392, 12.5.38, No. 071337, 19.5.38, HW 12/227.

92 GC&CS No. 070829, 19.3.38, No. 070861, 23.3.38, HW 12/225; No. 071026, 6.4.38, HW 12/226; No. 071295, 12.5.38, HW 12/227.

93 Dilks, 'Flashes of Intelligence', pp. 154–8; memorandum by Sargant, 19.11.38, FO 371/21639, C14209.

94 CG&CS No. 073458, 26.1.39, HW 12/235

95 GC&CS No. 073447, 073467, 25.1.39, HW 12/235.

96 GC&CS No. 073585, 28.1.39, HW 12/235.

97 Memorandum by Tiltman, 3.1.39, HW 62/21.

98 GC&CS No. 073729, 20.2.39, HW 12/236

99 GC&CS No. 073921, 9.3.39, HW 12/237; GC&CS, No. 074271, 11.4.71, HW 12/238.

100 Dilks, 'Flashes'; Andrew, *Defence*, pp. 201–8; Andrew, *Secret Service*, pp. 262–9, 537–41; Jeffery, *MI6*, pp. 303–12; Ferris, *Intelligence and Strategy*, pp. 45–137; Steiner, *Triumph*, pp. 671–1058, integrates the intelligence record as it then was known.

101 Lawrence Pratt, *East of Malta, West of Suez, Britain's Mediterranean Crisis, 1936–1939* (CUP, 1975); Christopher Bell, *The Royal Navy, Seapower and Strategy Between the Wars* (Stanford University Press, 2000) pp. 117–25.

102 Neilson, *Versailles Order*, pp. 260–70

103 Hiroaki Kuromiya and Andrzej Peplonski, 'Kozo Izumi and the Soviet Breach of Imperial Japanese Diplomatic Codes', INS, 28/6, 2013, pp. 769–84.

CHAPTER 5

1 Undated and unsigned memorandum on diplomatic cryptanalysis in 1940, 31.1.41, HW 14/11.

2 John Ferris, 'Achieving Air Ascendancy: Challenge and Response in British Strategic Air Defence, 1915–1940', in Sebastian Cox and Peter Gray (eds), *Airpower History: Turning Points from Kitty Hawk to Kosovo*, (London, 2002, Routledge).

3 Report of Admiralty Committee on W/T Organization, ADM 1/8740/69.

4 Meeting of Wireless Interception Committee, 28.4.38, HW 42/1; Minute by Hugh Sinclair, 17.10.38, HW 3/1; Memorandum by Godfrey, 12.47, ADM 223/284.

5 Gordon Welchman, *The Hut Six Story, Breaking the Enigma Codes*, 2nd revised edition (New York, William Morrow and Co., 1997).

6 Stephen Budiansky, *Battle of Wits: The Complete Story of Codebreaking in World War Two* (London, Viking, 2000), pp. 98–102.

7 29.4.32, untitled and unsigned memorandum, but by Sinclair, according to internal evidence, HW 62/19.

8 'History of C.M.Y. Section and The Development of Civil (International) W/T Interception during the War, 1939–1945', HW 3/162.

9 Sinclair to Dill, C/8794, 13.3.34, 'Memorandum on United States Communications Merger, Proposals and Effect', HW 62/19.

10 Minute by Travis to Dennison, 28.12.39, HW 3/81.

11 Sinclair to Walton, WO 208/5063.

12 Ibid.

13 Maine to Wilshaw, 28.9.38, DOC/CW/1/516, Telegraph Museum, Porthcurno.

14 Minute by Howard Smith, 1.5.37, HW 3/79; Sinclair to Howard Smith, 30.9.37, HW 3/80; Sinclair to Jebb, 21.1.39, FO 1093/105.

15 Memorandum by GC&CS, undated, *c.* July 1923, AIR 2/246.

16 Denniston to Sinclair, 21.10.38, HW 3/1.

17 J. E. S. Cooper, 'Air Sections GC and CS and the Approach to the War, 1935–39', June 1975, HW 3/83.

18 Denniston to Peters, 26.4.32, HW 72/9.

19 Memorandum by Temperley, DDMO&I, 3.1.33, HW 62/19

20 Undated memorandum by Kenworthy, HW 3/81; Nigel de Grey, draft 'Allied Sigint Policy and Organisation', *c.* 1946, Chapter 3, p. 29, HW 43/75.

21 NSA Oral History Interviews, John Tiltman, 13.12.78, 06–78, https://www.nsa.gov/news-features/declassified-documents/oral-history-interviews/

22 Tiltman to Menzies, 11.8.40, HW 14/6.

23 Denniston to Sinclair, 21.10.38, HW 3/1.

24 Memorandum by Saunders, 15.2.39, 'Position regarding "Y" Interception of German Naval and Naval Air Traffic'; memorandum by Bodsworth, undated, 'Naval section 1927–1939', HW 3/1; undated memoir by Kenworthy, 'Chapter VI', HW 3/81.

25 Minute by Tiltman, 'Military Section G.C. and C.S., Progress Report: 15th July 1939', HW 62/21.

26 Albert W. Small, 'Special Fish Report', RG 457/ 1417.

27 David Edgerton, *Warfare State, Britain 1920–1970* (CUP, 2006); Paul Kennedy, *Engineers of Victory, The Problem Solvers Who Turned the Tide in the Second World War* (Random House, 2013).

28 'An Interview with Arthur L. C. Humphreys, OH 23, Conducted by Erwin Tomash on 28 February 1981, Los Angeles, CA', Charles Babbage Institute, Center for the History of Information Processing, University of Minnesota.

29 De G, 'Allied Sigint Policy and Organisation', Part 2, pp.148–49, HW 43/77; Memorandum by Travis, 18.2.43, HW 14/67.

30 Eames, Charles and Ray, *A Computer Perspective: Background to the Computer Age* (Harvard University Press, Mass, 1973).

31 Chris Christenson, 'US Navy Cryptologic Mathematicians during World War Two', *Cryptologia*, 35/3, 2011, pp. 267–76.

32 Frode Weierud and Sandy Zabell, 'German mathematicians and cryptology in World War II', *Cryptologia*, 44/2, June 2019, pp. 97–117.

33 Untitled notes by Newman, for Newman to Rendle, undated, but *c.* 1976, f. 32, Max Newman Papers, St John's College, Cambridge, Box 3.

34 Joel Greenberg (ed.), Gordon Welchman, 'Ultra Revisited, A Tale of Two Contributors', INS, March 2017, 32/3. The best accounts of the attack on Enigma are, Nigel de Grey, draft 'Allied Sigint Policy and Organisation', *c.* 1946, HW 43/75–77; Andrew Hodges, *Alan Turing: The Enigma* (Princeton University Press, 1983); Gordon Welchman, *The Hut Six Story, Breaking the Enigma Codes,* 2nd revised edition (New York, William Morrow and Co., 1997); Gordon Welchman, 'From Polish Bomba to British Bombe: The Birth of Uktra', INS, 1/1 (1986), pp. 70–111; Ralph Erskine and Michael Smith (eds), *The Bletchley Park Codebreakers: How Ultra Shortened the War and Led to the Birth of the Computer* (Biteback Publishing 2011); H. H. Hinsley and Allen Stripp (eds), *Codebreakers: The Inside Story of Bletchley Park* (OUP, 2001); Joel Greenberg, *Gordon Welchman: Bletchley Park's Architect of Ultra Intelligence* (Frontline Books, 2014); Hinsley. Et.al, Vol. Three, Part II, pp. 945–61, and R. A. Ratcliff, *Delusions of Intelligence, Enigma, Ultra and the End of Secure Ciphers* (Cambridge, CUP, 2006).

35 Joel Greenberg (ed.), Gordon Welchman, 'Ultra Revisited, A Tale of Two Contributors', INS, March 2017, 32/3.

36 Ibid.

37 Ibid.

38 Tutte, 'FISH and I', pp. 11, https://uwaterloo.ca/combinatorics-and-optimization/sites/ca.combinatorics-and-optimization/files/uploads/files/corr98-39.pdf

39 A. P. Mahon, 'The History of Hut Eight, 1939–1945', p. 14, HW 25/2

40 Ibid., p. 23.

41 Interview with DS, 2.10.18.

42 David Kahn, *Seizing the Enigma, the Race to Break the German U-Boat Codes, 1939–45* (Houghton Mifflin Harcourt, 1991).

43 Memorandum, unsigned, but Travis by internal evidence. 18.11.39, HW 14/2.

44 Unsigned and untitled memorandum, 20.5.40, on GC&CS structure, HW 14/5.

45 Mahon, 'The History of Hut Eight', p. 20.

46 Memorandum by Travis, 18.2.43, HW 14/67.

47 John A. N. Lee and Golde Holtzman, '50 Years After Breaking the Codes: Interviews with Two of the Bletchley Park Scientists', *IEEE Annals of the History of Computing,* 1995, 17/1, p. 37.

48 I. J. Good, 'Early Work on Computers at Bletchley', *Annals of the History of Computing* 1/1, July 1979, p. 43.

49 Lee and Holtzman, '50 Years', *IEEE Annals of the History of Computing,* 1995, 17/1, p. 39

50 The best accounts of the attack on FISH are, Jack Good, Donald Michie and Geoffrey Timms (1945), 'General Report on Tunny, with Emphasis on Statistical Methods', HW 25/4 and 25/5; B. J. Copeland, *Colossus, The secrets of Bletchley's code-breaking computers* (OUP, 2010).

51 Allen W. M. Coombes, 'The Making of Colossus', *Annals of the History of Computing*, 5/3, 7/83, p. 253.

52 Tommy Flowers, 'The Design of Colossus', *Annals of the History of Computing*, 5/3, 7/83, pp. 239–52.

53 Hinsley et al., *British Intelligence*, Vol. Two, Appendix Three, pp. 655–7.

54 Memorandum by Head of Naval Section, 28.3.41, excerpt from 'Rates of Pay for Women', HW 50/18.

55 Menzies to Brittain, 15.10.42, CAB 301/74; Menzies to Waley, 25.8.42, CAB 301/74.

56 De Grey. 'Sigint Policy and Organisation', p. 24, Chapter One, HW 43/75.

57 'Housing of the Commercial Section', 29.9.39, unsigned but Denniston by internal evidence, HW 14/1.

58 W. F. Clarke, 'B.P. Reminiscences', HW 3/16.

59 Ibid.

60 Whiteley to Churchill, 22.12.39, FO 1093/307.

61 Memorandum by Travis, 18.2.43, HW 14/67.

62 Menzies to Brittain, 10.6.42, CAB 301/74.

63 Welchman, *Hut Six Story*, pp. 146–7.

64 Denniston to Director, 16.9.39, HW 14/1.

65 Memorandum by Travis, 18.2.43, HW 14/67.

66 10.6.32, 'Memorandum by the G.C. and C.S.', 13.6.32, 'Memorandum on Wireless Interception in the Event of a National Emergency', HW 62/19.

67 Unsigned note, but Denniston to Menzies by internal evidence, 23.10.40, HW 14/7; Jacob to Arcedeckne-Butler, 28.11.40, HW 14/8.

68 John Ferris, 'FECB'.

69 Godfrey to Hankey, 2.2.40, FO 1093/193.

70 Memorandum by Hankey 11.3.40, 'The Secret Services, Inquiry by the Minister Without Portfolio, First Report', FO 1093/193.

71 Denniston to Blandy, 4.11.39, HW 14/2.

72 Unsigned memorandum, 1.3.40, 'Interception of Enigma Traffic'; Denniston to Menzies, 29.4.40, HW 14/4; 'The History of Military Sigint', pp.193, 206, 214A, 215 A, HW 3/92.

73 John Ferris, 'The "Usual Source": Signals Intelligence and Planning for the Eighth Army "Crusader" Offensive, 1941', in Alvarez, *Allied and Axis Signals Intelligence*, pp. 84–118.

74 Hinsley et al., *British Intelligence*, Vol. Two, p. 22.

75 Denniston to Menzies, 6.2.39, HW 62/21.

76 Clarke, 'History of Naval Section, Chapter IV, Wars and Rumours of Wars, 1944–37', HW 3/16.

77 HW 62/21.

78 Denniston to Saunders, 27.10.39, HW 14/1

79 Denniston to Menzies, 29.4.40, HW 14/4.

80 'The History of Military Sigint', pp.75–76, HW 3/92.

81 Memorandum by Saunders, 'Proposals for G.C.C.S', 15.5.40. *passim,* HW 14/5.

82 Appendix A, Memorandum by de Grey, 17.2.41, HW 3/158.

83 Memorandum by Menzies, 'Special Section, G.C. & C.S', 12.6.40, HW 14/5.

84 Arthur Bonsall, 'Bletchley Park and the RAF Y Service: Some Recollections', INS, 23/6, December 2008, pp. 827–41.

85 Memorandum by David Petrie, 13.2.41, KV 4/88.

86 C Ho D Alexander, 'Cryptographic History of Work on the German Naval Enigma', HW 25/1.

87 Mahon, The History of Hut Eight', p. xx, HW 25/2.

88 Memorandum by Travis, 18.2.43, HW 14/67.

89 Unsigned memorandum to 'Commander Denniston', 18.11.39, with pencil addition from uncertain date, 'Paper ? by EWT', HW 14/2. There is no possible alternative, and the paper reflects Welchman's independent account, written decades later, of his discussion with Travis at this time.

90 Memorandum by Travis, 18.2.43, HW 14/67.

91 'Report on Military Intelligence at the G.C. & C.S.', by W. E. van Cutsem, 30.1.42, WO 208/5070.

92 Sinclair to Davidson, 11.3.42, WO 208/5070.

93 Clarke, 'B.P. Reminiscences 2', HW 3/16.

94 'Meeting held at B.P. on the 27th December 1941', HW 14/25.

95 Memorandum by Travis, 18.2.43, HW 14/67.

96 Ibid.

97 American Embassy London to MILID, No. 4869, 22.5.43, American Embassy London to MILID No. 4869 25.5.43, RG 457/1009.

98 'Appreciation of the "E" Situation June to December 1942', HW 3/164.

99 'Squadron-Leader Jones' Section', n.d., or author, 1945, HW 3/164.

100 'History of Hut 3 at BP, 194–1945, Volume I', pp. 17–18, HW 3/119.

101 'Appreciation of the "E" Situation June to December 1942', HW 3/164

102 'History of Hut 3, Volume I', p. 46, HW 3/119.

103 'History of Hut 3, Volume I', p. 16, HW 3/119.

104 COS to SACSEA, Ultra 196, 'Security of Ultra Intelligence', 9.6.44, WO 203/5157.

105 Ralph Bennett, Ultra and Mediterranean Strategy, pp. 42–5.

106 'History of Hut 3, Volume II', pp. 45–46, HW 3/120.

107 Memorandum by Jones, 'The Value of Ultra – accurately handled', 897 TOPSEC U, 7.3.45, HW 3/127.

CHAPTER 6

1 F. H. Hinsley, E. E. Thomas, C. F. G. Ransom, and R. C. Knight, *British Intelligence in the Second World War, Its Influence on Strategy and Operations, Volumes 1 – 3* (HMSO, London, 1981–88), offers the best account of how Ultra affected battles and campaigns, though many accounts supersede it on special matters. Stephen Budiansky, *Battle of Wits, The Complete Story of Codebreaking in World War II* (Free Press, New York, 2000), is a useful overview.

2 Army Security Agency, *European Axis Signal Intelligence in World War* (Washington, 1946), http://www.nsa.gov/public_info/declass/european_axis_Sigint.shtml.

3 John Ferris, 'Intelligence', in John Ferris and Ewan Mawdsley (eds), *The Cambridge History of the Second World War', Volume One, Fighting the War* (CUP, 2015), pp. 637–63.

4 Alfred Price, *Targeting the Reich, Allied Photographic Reconnaissance over Europe, 1939–1945* (Greenhill Books, 2003); Peter Mead, *The Eye in the Sky, History of Air Observation and Reconnaissance, 1785–1945* (HMSO, London, 1983); Constance Babington-Smith, *Evidence in Camera. The Story of Photographic Reconnaissance in the Second World War* (London: Chatto &Windus, 1958) and Louis Brown, *A Radar History of World War Two, Technical and Military Imperatives* (Bristol, Institute of Physics Publishing, 1999).

5 R. A. Ratcliff, *Delusions of Intelligence, Enigma, Ultra and the End of Secure Ciphers* (Cambridge, CUP, 2006).

6 Cadogan to Radcliffe, 3.2.42, INF 1/380.

7 Ferris, *Intelligence and Strategy*, pp. 138–238.

8 Ibid., pp. 157–9.

9 Hinsley et al., *British Intelligence*, Vol. One, pp. 632–41.

10 Ferris, *Intelligence and Strategy*, pp. 157–9.

11 Eiji Seki, *Mrs. Ferguson's Tea-set, Japan and the Second World War: The Global Consequences Following Germany's Sinking of the SS Automeden in 1940* (Global Oriental, 2007).

12 Memorandum by Bartlett, 1946, ADM 223/184.

13 Cypher Security Committee, 23.3.44, 'Security of British Communications, Notes compiled from Conversation with COMMANDER CIANCHI, Royal Italian Navy on 13th, 15th and 16th February', ADM 223/803. CSDIC/CMF/Y 31, 'Second Detailed Interrogation Report on Two German Prisoners', undated but *c.* May–June 1945 by internal evidence, WO 208/3248.

14 Ferris, *Intelligence and Strategy*, pp. 160–70.

15 Sargent to Markham, 1.9.44, FO 1093/328.

16 CSDIC, 'Report on Interrogation of Thirteen German Intelligence Officers', July 1945, WO 204/11457.

17 David Kahn, *Hitler's Spies, German Military Intelligence in World War Two*, London: Hodder & Stoughton, 1978), is the best work in the English language on German intelligence, augmented by Hans-Otto Behrendt, *Rommel's Intelligence in the Desert Campaign, 1941–1943* (London, Kimber, 1985), United States War Dept. General Staff, *German Military Intelligence, 1939–1945* (University Press of America, 1984), Albert Praun, 'German Radio Intelligence', pp.1–128, in John Mendelsohn (ed.), *Covert Warfare: Intelligence, Counterintelligence and Military Deception in the World War II Era, Volume 6, German Radio Intelligence and the Soldatsender* (Garland Press, New York, 1989.

18 For German intelligence on the Eastern front, cf. Magnus Pahl, *Fremde Heere Ost. Hitlers militärische Feindaufklärung* (Berlin: Christoph Links Verlag 2013); David Thomas, 'Foreign Armies East and German Military Intelligence in Russia 1941–45', *The Journal of Contemporary History*, 1987, Volume 22, pp.261–301; Volker Detlef Heydorn, *Nachrichtennahaufklärung (Ost) und sowjetrussisches Heeresfunkwesen bis 1945*, Freiburg: Rombach Verlag, 1985) and DF–1123, AS–14–TICOM, Survey of Russian Military Systems, 1.4.1948. http://www.scribd.com/paspartoo/d/85583814-DF-112-Dettmann.

19 Barton Whaley, *Codeword Barbarossa (*MIT Press, 1974); John Ferris, 'The Roots of Fortitude: The Evolution of British Deception in The Second World War', in Thomas Mahnken (ed.), *The Paradox of Intelligence: Essays in Memory of Michael Handel* (Frank Cass, 2003).

20 Ferris, *Strategy and Intelligence*, pp. 163–68.

21 David Alvarez, 'Axis Sigint Collaboration: A Limited Partnership', in David Alvarez (ed.), *Allied and Axis Signals Intelligence in World War Two*, Frank Cass and Co., 1999), pp. 1–17); John Chapman, 'Axis Sigint Cooperation among the Tripartite States on the Eve of Pearl Harbor', *Japan Forum*, 3/2, 1991), pp. 231–56; Army Security Agency, *European Axis Signal Intelligence in World War* (Washington, 1946), http://www.nsa.gov/public_info/declass/european_axis_Sigint.shtml

22 Bradley Smith, *The Ultra-Magic Deals and the Most Secret Special Relationship, 1940–1946* (New York, 1993), and pp. below.

23 Bradley Smith, *Sharing Secrets with Stalin, How the Allies Exchanged Intelligence, 1941–1945* (Kansas Modern War Studies, Lawrence, KS, 1995).

24 Ferris, *Intelligence and Strategy*, pp. 164–65.

25 Ferris, 'The "Usual Source"', in Alvarez, *Allied and Axis Signals Intelligence*, pp. 84–118.

26 R. J. Overy, *Why the Allies Won* (W. W. Norton and Co, 1995), pp. 245–81; Alex Danchev, *A Very Special Relationship: Field Marshall Sir John Dill and the Anglo-American Alliance 1941–44*, (London: Brassey's Defence Publishers, 1986).

27 Helmut Heiber and David M. Glantz (eds), *Hitler and His Generals: Military Conferences 1942–1945: The First Complete Stenographic Record of the Military Situation Conferences, from Stalingrad to Berlin*, (English edition, Enigma Books, 2005); *Fuhrer Conferences on Naval Affairs, 1939–1945* (United States Naval Institute Press, 2015); David Irving, *Das Reich Hort Mit* (1989), http://www.fpp.co.uk/books/Forschungsamt/index.html

28 Memorandum by COMNAVFORGER, 21.8.51, 'Historical, Naval Radio Intelligence ("B-Dienst")', by Captain Bonatz, RG 457/604, NARA.

29 Hinsley et.al., *British Intelligence*, Vol. Three, Part 1, pp. 331–45.

30 Brad Gladman, *Intelligence and Anglo-American Air Support in World War Two: The Western Desert and Tunisia, 1940–43*, (London: Palgrave, 2009).

31 Ibid. and Ian Gooderson, *Air power at the Battlefront: Allied close air support in Europe, 1943–45* (Frank Cass, 1998).

32 Carl Boyd, *American Command of the Seas Through Carriers, Codes and the Silent Service: World War II and Beyond* (Maritime Museum, 1995); Christopher A. Ford with David Rosenberg, *The Admiral's Advantage: U.S. Navy Operational Intelligence in World War II and the Cold War* (Naval Institute Press, Annapolis, 2005).

33 John Ferris and Evan Mawdsley, 'The War in the West, 1939–40: The Battle of Britain?' in Ferris and Mawdsley, *Fighting the War*, pp. 315–30; Donald Caldwell and Richard Muller, *The Luftwaffe over Germany: The Defence of the Reich* (Greenhill Books, 2007).

34 Robert Ehlers, *Targeting the Third Reich, Air Intelligence and the Allied Bombing Campaigns* (Kansas Modern War Studies, Lawrence, KS, 2009).

35 The best account of European naval operations is Ewan Mawdsley, *The War for the Seas: A Maritime History of World War Two* (Yale University Press, 2019). Stephen Roskill, *The War at Sea, Volumes One to Three* (HMSO, 1954–61), remains valuable.

36 Hinsley et al., *British Intelligence*, Vol. One, pp. 339–46.

37 Cunningham of Hyndhope, *A Sailor's Odyssey* (London, 1951), pp. 320–37.

38 Hinsley, et al., *British Intelligence*, Vol. One, pp. 403–6; Mavis Batey, *Dilly: The Man Who Broke Enigmas* (Biteback Publishing) is illuminating, but not always reliable.

39 Christina Goulter, *A Forgotten Offensive: Royal Air Force Coastal Command's Anti-Shipping Campaign 1940–1945* (London: Frank Cass, 1995).

40 Hinsley, et.al., *British Intelligence*, Vol. Two, pp. 199–227.

41 Jurgen Rowher, *The Crucial Convoy Battles of March 1943* (Naval Institute Press, Annapolis, 1977); David Syrett, *The Defeat of the German U-Boats, The Battle of the Atlantic* (University of South Carolina Press, Columbia, SC, 1994).

42 The outstanding analysis is W. J. R. Gardner, *Decoding History, The Battle of the Atlantic and Ultra* (Naval Institute Press, Annapolis, 2002). Alan Harris Bath, *Tracking the Axis Enemy: The Triumph of Anglo-American Naval Intelligence* (Lawrence, KS: University Press of Kansas, 1998), is excellent. For B-Dienst, cf. Heinz Bonatz, *Seekrieg im Äther: Die Leistungen der Marin-Funkaufklarung, 1939–1945*, (E. S. Mittler, Herford, 1981) and Jak P. Malmann-Shovell, *German Naval Codebreakers* (Annapolis, Naval Institute Press, 2003); 'German Naval Communications Intelligence', no author cited and undated, but by Op-20-G, *c.* late, 1945, RG 457/625; Memorandum by COMNAVFORGER, 21.8.51, 'Historical, Naval Radio Intelligence ("B-Dienst")', by Captain Bonatz, RG 457/604, NARA.

43 Mark Milner, 'The Atlantic War, 1939–45', in Ferris and Mawdsley, *Fighting the War*, pp. 455–84.

44 Ibid.

45 Simon Ball, *Bitter Sea: The Struggle for mastery in the Mediterranean, 1935–1949* (HarperPress, 2009) and Douglas Porch, *The Path to Victory, The Mediterranean Mediterranean Theater in World War Two* (Farrar, Strauss and Giroux, New York, 2004) are the best modern accounts.

46 Hinsley et al., *British Intelligence*, Vol. One, pp. 210–13, 404–06.

47 Ibid., Vol. Two, pp. 323–30, 346–50.

48 Ibid., Vol. One, pp. 375–403; John Ferris, 'The British Army, Signals and Security in the Desert Campaign, 1940–42', in John Ferris, *Intelligence and Strategy, Selected Essays* (London, Routledge, 2005), pp. 181–238.

49 Hinsley et al., Vol. One, pp. 375–82; Andrew Stewart, *The First Victory, The Second World War and the Ethiopian Campaign* (I.B. Tauris, 2017).

50 Memorandum by Cunningham, 6.6.41, 'East Africa Force, Report on Operation from 1st November, 1940, to 5th April, 1941', Alan Cunningham Papers, 8303104–12-1, NAM.

51 Ferris, *Intelligence and Strategy*, pp. 181–238.

52 Jonathan Fennell, *Combat and Morale in the North African Campaign, The Eighth Army and the Path to El Alamein* (CUP, 2011); Ferris, *Intelligence and Strategy*, pp. 181–238; David French, *Raising Churchill's Army, The British Army and the War Against Germany, 1919–1945* (Oxford, Oxford University Press, 2000).

53 Perhaps the most useful English-language works on Rommel are Ian. F. Beckett, *Rommel, A Reappraisal* (Pen and Sword, 2013) and David Irving, *Rommel, The Trail of the Fox* (Weidenfield and Nicholson, 1977).

54 Otto von Behrendt, *Rommel's Intelligence in the Desert Campaign, 1941–1943* (London, Kimber, 1985).

55 Ferris, *Intelligence and Strategy*, pp. 163–68.

56 Ibid., pp. 181–239; Ferris, 'Crusader'.

57 C. J. Jenner, 'Turning the Hinge of Fate: "Good Source" and the U.S.–U.K. Intelligence Alliance, 1940–2, *Diplomatic History*, 32:2, pp. 165–205.

58 Ferris, 'Crusader', pp. 222–26; Ralph Bennett, *Ultra and Mediterranean Strategy* (William Morrow and Co., 1989).

59 Ibid.

60 Jenner, 'Hinge of Fate'.

61 The best account remains, J. A. I. Agar-Hamilton and L. C. F. Turner, *Crisis in the Desert, May–July 1942, Union War Histories* (New York, Oxford University Press, 1952).

62 Gladman, *Intelligence and Anglo-American Air Support.*

63 F. W. von Mellenthin, *Panzer Battles* (New York, Ballantine Books, 1956), p. 94.

64 'A Force War Diary', entry 2.7.42, CAB 154/1; Maunsell, 'Security Intelligence'; F. H. Hinsley and C. A. G. Simkins, *British Intelligence in the Second World War, Its Influence on Strategy and Operations, Volume IV, Security and Counter-Intelligence* (HMSO, 1990), pp. 166–67; Typescript memoir, nd, Brigadier R. J. Maunsell Papers, Imperial War Museum.

65 Bennett, *Mediterranean Strategy;* Nigel Hamilton, *British Intelligence in the Second World War, Its Influence on Strategy and Operations*

66 Bennett, *Mediterranean Strategy.*

67 Vincent P. O'Hara, *Torch, North Africa and the Allied Path to Victory* (US Naval Institute Press, 2015).

68 David Rolf, *The Bloody Road to Tunis: Destruction of the Axis Forces in North Africa, November 1942–May 1943* (Greenhill Books, Mechanicsburg PA, 2001).

69 For intelligence and operations in the Italian campaign, Carlo D'Este, *World War Two in the Mediterranean, 1942–1945* (Algonquin, Chapel Hill, New York, 1990), Bennett, *Mediterranean Strategy,* and Kevin Jones, *Intelligence and Command at the Operational Level of War: The British Eighth Army in the Italian Campaigns, 1943–1945* (Routledge, 2005).

70 David Kahn, *Hitler's Spies, German Military Intelligence in World War II*, p. 173; Irving, *Das Reich*, pp. 62–70, http://www.fpp.co.uk/books/Forschungsamt/index.html; Percy Scramm, *Kriegestagebuch des Oberkomando der Wehrmacht – 1943, Teilband II, Eine Dokumentation*, pp. 852–54. (Bernhard & Graefe, 1983).

71 Memorandum by Hugh Trevor Roper, 'The German Intelligence Service and the War', 1945, CAB 154/105

72 Katherine Barbier, *D-Day Deception: Operation Fortitude and the Normandy Invasion* (Praeger, 2007); Michael Handel, *Strategic and Operational Deception in the Second World War* (London, Frank Cass, 1987); Roger Hesketh, *Fortitude, The D-Day Deception Campaign* (Overlook Hardcover, 2000) and Thaddeus Holt, *The Deceivers, Allied Military Deception in the Second World War* (London, Weidenfeld & Nicholson, 2004).

73 Memorandum by NID 12, 20.7.45, 'German Appreciation of Allied Intentions', ADM 223/298; for copies of these reports, cf. CAB 154/76, pp. 95–96.

74 Memorandum by Nalder, 'Wireless Cover and Deception in the Italian Campaign', *c.*1945, CAB 154/103; Handel, *Strategic Deception*, pp. 161–62.

75 John Ferris, 'Agreed Texts: Intelligence, Military Rationality and the Planning for Operation Overlord', in John Buckley (ed.) *Overlord Sixty Years Later* (Routledge, 2006), pp. 119–56; Ralph Bennett, *Ultra in the West, The Normandy Campaign of 1944–45,* (Encore, 1980).

76 Williams to Whiteley, 2.2.44, RG 331/12/9, NARA.

77 Ferris, 'Intelligence before Overlord'.

78 JIC (44) 215 (o) 25.5.44, RG 331/3/128, NARA.

79 Nigel Hamilton, *Master of the Battlefield, Monty's War Years, 1942–1944* (New York, McGraw-Hill), pp.582–89.

80 Ferris, 'Intelligence before Overlord'.

81 Smith, *Emperor's Codes, The Thrilling Story of the of the Allied Code Breakers who Turned the Tide of World War II* (Biteback, 2011); John Ferris, '"Consistent with an Intention": The Far East Combined Bureau and the Outbreak of the Pacific War, 1940–1941', INS, 27/1, 2012, pp. 5–26.

82 Ferris, ibid.

83 Smith, *Emperor's Codes;* Alan Stripp, *Codebreaker in the Far East* (Frank Cass, 1989).

84 David Dufty, *The Secret Codebreakers of Central Bureau: how Australia's signals intelligence network helped win the Second World War (Scribe, Melbourne, 2017); Peter Donovan and John Mack, *Codebreaking in the Pacific* (Springer, 2014).

85 Memorandum by Jones, 'Clear Decks' (832 TOPSEC U), 13.11.44, HW 3/127.

86 F. H. Hinsley, 'British Intelligence in the Second World War', in Christopher Andrew and Jeremy Noakes (eds), *Intelligence and International Relations, 1900–1945* (Exeter, 1987), pp. 217–18; Harry Hinsley, 'The Counter-Factual History of No Ultra', *Cryptologia*, XX/4, 1996, pp. 308–24.

87 Eisenhower to Menzies, 12.7.45, HW 3/168.

CHAPTER 7

1 For long-term policy, cf. David French, *The British Way in Warfare, 1688–2000* (Routledge, London, 1990); George Peden, *Arms, Economics and British Strategy: From Dreadnaughts to Hydrogen Bombs* (Cambridge. CUP, 2007) and David Reynolds, *Britannia Overruled: British policy and world power in the twentieth century* (Taylor & Francis, London, 2013). For defence policy after 1945, cf. Michael Carver, *Tightrope Walking: British Defence Policy since 1945* (London, Hutchinson, 1992); Stuart Croft, Andrew Dorman, Wyn Rees and Matthew Uttley, *Britain and Defence, 1945–2000: A policy re-evaluation* (Routledge, 2001); Michael Dockrill, *British Defence since 1945 (Making Contemporary Britain)* (Oxford: Wiley-Blackwell, 1991); Bill Jackson and Edwin Bramall, *The Chiefs: The Story of the United Kingdom Chiefs of Staff* (London: Brassey's, 1992).

2 Richard Aldrich and M. F. Hopkins, *Intelligence, defence and diplomacy: British policy in the postwar world* (Taylor & Francis, London, 2013); D. W. B. Lomas, *Intelligence, security and the Attlee governments, 1945–51, An uneasy relationship?* (Manchester University Press, Manchester, 2016); Michael Goodman, *The Official History of the Joint Intelligence Committee, Volume One: From the Approach of the Second World War to the Suez Crisis* (Taylor & Francis, London, 2015); Calder Walton, *Empire of Secrets: British Intelligence in the Cold War and the Twilight of Empire* (Outlook Press, London, 2015).

3 W. Brian Arthur, *Increasing Returns and Path Dependence in the Economy,* (Ann Arbor, Michigan: University of Michigan Press, 1994); Paul Pierson, *Politics in Time: History, Institutions, and Social Analysis* (Princeton University Press, 2004).

4 John Baylis, *Ambiguity and Deterrence: British Nuclear Strategy, 1945–1964* (Oxford, OUP, 1995), Matthew Jones, *The Official History of the British Nuclear Deterrent, Volume 1: From the V-Bomber Era to the Arrival of Polaris* (Taylor & Francis, London, 2017); Matthew Navias, *Nuclear Weapons and British Strategic Planning, 1955–1958* (Oxford, OUP, 1991).

5 *British Sigint*, Two, pp. 478–534.

6 Ibid., Four, pp. 352–370.

7 Cf. below.

8 Minute by Cadogan, 9.11.44, FO 1093/197.

9 Memorandum, unsigned and undated but *c.* June 1944, 'Re-adjustment in the Functions of M.I. 5 and M.I. 6', CAB 301/11.

10 Memorandum by Norman Brook, 12.5.43, CAB 301/11.

11 'The Intelligence Machine, Report to the Joint Intelligence Sub-Committee', by Victor Cavendish-Bentinck and Denis Capel-Dunn, 10.1.45, CAB 301/11.

12 Memorandum by Cavendish-Bentinck, 27.9.44, FO 1093/195.

13 C to Loxley, 24.4.44, FO 1093/195.

14 Until 31 March 1946, the organisation normally was called GC&CS, though many other titles as well. From 1 April 1946, it was called GCHQ, but until October 1948 also occasionally the London Sigint Centre. The text calls the organisation GC&CS until 1 September 1945, and GCHQ thereafter.

15 'The Intelligence Machine, Report to the Joint Intelligence Sub-Committee', by Victor Cavendish-Bentinck and Denis Capel-Dunn, 10.1.45, CAB 301/11, Report of Bland Committee, 12.10.44, CAB 301/48.

16 ACAS (I) Inglis to Cavendish-Bentinck, 24.4.44, MID to Cavendish-Bentinck, 15.6.44, FO 1093/195.

17 Nigel West, *The Guy Liddell Diaries, Volume Two*, p. 236.

18 Minute by Cavendish-Bentinck, 27.9.44, FO 1093/195; 'The Intelligence Machine', 10.1.45, CAB 301/11; Report of Bland Committee, 12.10.44, CAB 301/48.

19 *British Sigint*, One, pp. 22–30.

20 Ibid., pp. 30–35.

21 Ibid., pp. 35–44.

22 Ibid., pp. 40–44.

23 Ibid., pp.76–77.

24 Loxley to C, 11.11.43, FO 1093/326.

25 Minute by Cavendish-Bentinck, 23.10.44, FO 1093/329

26 *British Sigint*, One, pp. 45–48.

27 Ibid., pp. 48–62.

28 Ibid., pp. 48–62, 534–8.

29 Ibid., pp. 537.

30 Ibid., pp. 539–41.

31 Minute by Drew, 14.2.61, DEFE 23/23; Minute by Whitehead, 11.11.74, ZCZ 1/42.

32 *British Sigint*, One, pp. 232–63.

33 Hooper to Wyatt, 17.4.61, T 296/278

34 *British Sigint*, Three, pp. 178; Field Marshal Sir Gerald Templer, 'Review of Service Intelligence', 16.12.1960, T 296/277; Interception Working Party, first meeting, 9.3.61, AIR 40/2757.

35 *British Sigint*, One, pp. 250–51.

36 Ibid., Two, pp. 84–85, 94.

37 Ibid., pp. 100–3, and Three, p. 302. Richard Aldrich, 'Counting the Cost of Intelligence: The Treasury, National Service and GCHQ', *English Historical Review*, 128/532, June 2013, pp. 602–4.

38 *British Sigint*, Two, pp. 72–5.

39 Ibid., pp. 70–92, and Three, p. 303.

40 Memorandum by Baldwin, 17.2.61, 'Service Intelligence', to Wyatt, Wyatt to Baldwin, 'Templer Report', 21.2.61, T 296/277.

41 *British Sigint*, One, pp. 539–41.

42 Memorandum by Jones, 'Summary of the Career of Mr. E. M. Jones', 12.1.52, FO 1093/96.

43 Ibid. is useful, but the constant references to his career being guided by a search for education are probably a defensive reaction to anticipated criticisms of his lack of a degree.

44 Memorandum by Reilly, 1.1.52, FO 1093/96.

45 Minute by Reilly, 'Sir William Strang', 14.3.52, minute by Strang, FO 1093/96.

46 Memorandum by Reilly, 1.1.52, FO 1093/96.

47 Memorandum by Reilly, 'Top Secret', 11.1.52, FO 1093/96.

48 *British Sigint*, Two, p. 84.

49 Memorandum by Reilly, 'Top Secret'.

50 C to Reilly, 14.1.52, 'Report by Deputy-Director G.C.H.Q.', 11.1.52, containing 11.1.52, underlining probably by Reilly, FO 1093/96.

51 Memorandum by Strang, 'Director of G.C.H.Q.', 24.1.52, Strang to Slim, 30.1.52, FO 1093/96.

52 Minutes by Eden, 25.1.52, FO 1093/96.

53 Memorandum by Menzies, n.d., 'Special Meeting to consider the appointment of Director, G.C.H.Q., 1st January 1952', FO 1093/96.

54 Helen Fulton, Sir Brian Tovey Obituary', *Guardian*, 4.1.2016.

55 *British Sigint*, Four, pp. 53–61; Memorandum by Jones, 'Summary of the Career of Mr. E. M. Jones', 12.1.52, FO 1093/96, 'Jones, Sir Eric Malcolm', DNB; 'Loehnis, Sir Clive', DNB'; 'Hooper, Sir Leonard James', DNB; 'Sir Peter Marychurch Obituary', *Guardian, 1.6.07, Independent*, 25.5.07.

56 *British Sigint*, Two, pp. 71–100, 90–6, and Three, p. 305.

57 Ibid., pp. 85–91.

58 Ibid., Three, pp. 123–24.

59 Ibid., p. 126.

60 Ibid., pp., 123–30.

61 Memorandum by Templer, 'Review of Service Intelligence', 16.12.60, DEFE 23/23.

62 Q/LSIB/58/62, 21.5.62, 'The Cost of Sigint–1962', LSIB 1962.

63 Aldrich, 'Counting the Cost', pp. 608–27.

64 LSIB Z1/63, 19.4.63, 'Hampshire Review of Sigint', LSIB 1963.

65 *British Sigint*, Three, pp. 131–40.

66 Memorandum by S. N. Hampshire, 'Review of Signal Intelligence', 1.2.63, LSIB 1963.

67 Ibid.

68 Ibid.

69 Ibid.

70 Memorandum by S. N. Hampshire, 'Review of Signal Intelligence', 1.2.63, LSIB 1963.

71 Ibid.

72 *British Sigint*, Three, pp. 139–50.

73 Ibid., Four, p. 63.

74 Ibid., pp. 28–29.

75 GCHQ briefing to LSIB/LSIC members, D/0897/1401/4, 14.2.75, 21.1.75, LSIB 1975.

76 Aldrich, 'Counting the Cost'.

77 Minute by Burke Trend to Prime Minister, 13.3.67; Note for the record by Trend, 2.8.67, PREM 13/2688; J. W. Young, 'The Wilson Government's Reform of Intelligence Co-ordination, 1967–67', INS 16/2, pp. 133–151.

78 LSIB (71) 1st Meeting Minutes, 'Minutes of a Meeting held on 17 June 1971', LSIB 1971.

79 LSIB 4/74, 'Five Year Sigint Forecast (1975–1980)', 6.3.74, LSIB 1974.

80 LSIB (71), 1st Meeting Minutes, 'Minutes of a Meeting held on 17 June 1971', LSIB 1971.

81 LSIB (70), 1st Meeting Minutes, 'Minutes of a Meeting held on 11 June 1970', LSIB 1970.

82 LSIB 6/71, 3.6.71, 'Future Sigint Programmes and Costs, 1971', LSIB 1971.

83 LSIB 167/51, 6.9.51, 'List of Persons Indoctrinated in British Government Departments as of 1st July 1951', LSIB 1951; LSIB/20/63, 'Totals of U.K. Comint Indoctrinated Persons as of 1st January, 1963', LSIB 1963.

84 LSIB 1/70, 2.2.70, 'Five-Tear Sigint Programme (1971–1976), LSIB 1970; LSIB (71) 1st Meeting.

85 'Proposal for the Establishment of a Sigint Finance Committee', 19.7.63, LSIB 1963.

86 LSIB meeting, 25.5.65, LSIB (65) 1st Meeting, 25.5.65, LSIB 1065.

87 NEW JIC (66) 5th Meeting, 3.2.66, CAB 159/45.

88 LSIB 11/67, 21.8.67, 'Record of the Meeting of the PSIS (Sigint) Committee on 26th July, 1967', LSIB 1967.

89 LSIB meeting, 26.9.63, LSIB (1963) 4th Meeting (Minutes), LSIB 1963.

90 Aldrich, GCHQ.

91 LSIB meeting, 21.5.64, LSIB (64) 1st Meeting (Minutes), LSIB 1964.

92 Ibid.

93 'Attachment to LSIB/27/65, 'Extract from a letter, Burke Trend to Paul Gore-Booth, on PSIS meeting of 19.7.65', LSIB 1965.

94 LSIB (65) 3rd Meeting (Minutes), 11.11.65, LSIB/52/65, 26.10.65, LSIB/29/68, 3.12.68, 'Report of a Visit to Washington in September/October 1965 by the Director GCHQ', LSIB 1965.

95 LSIB (65) 3rd Meeting (Minutes), 11.11.65, LSIB 1965.

96 LSIB 10/65, 28.6.65, LSIB 1965.

97 LSIB 10/66, 9.8.66, 'Record of the Meeting of the PIS (Sigint) Committee on 12th July, 1966', LSIB 1966.

98 LSIB (68) 3rd and 4th Meeting (Minutes) 25.10.68, 26.1.68, LSIB/19/68, 23.7.1968, PSIS (Sigint) Commtteee meeting, 28.7.68, LSIB 1968.

99 Cost Analysis of Sigint, Annex C to LSIB/3/66, LSIB 1966.

100 LSIB (75) 1st Meeting Minutes, 28.6.75, LSIB 5/75, 'Future Sigint Programmes and Cost: Five-Year Forecast 1976–81', 6.6.75, LSIB 1975.

101 LSIB 6/77, 17.5.77, 'Implications of Cuts of 3.5 per cent and 5 per cent in the Cost of Sigint; 1977 Draft Report by LSIB to PSIS', LSIB 1977.

102 C(75)1, 25.2.75, 'Statement of the Defence Estimates 1975', CAB 129/181.

103 LSIB (71) 1st Meeting.

104 LSIB 3/76, 'Future Sigint Programmes and Cost: Five Year Forecast 1977–1982', 4.6.76, LSIB 1976; LSIB 5/77, 17.5.77, 'Future Sigint Programmes and Cost: Four Year Forecast 1978–1982', LSIB 1977.

105 LSIB (81) 2nd Meeting (Minutes), 27.5.81, 'Minutes of the Meeting held on 21 May 1981', LSIB 1981.

106 LSIB (77) 1st Meeting (Minutes), 21.6.77, 'Minutes of the Meeting held on 25 May 1977', LSIB 1977.

107 LSIB (78) 1st Meeting (Minutes), 8.6.78, 'Record of the Meeting held on 31 May 1978 to Discuss the Report to the PSIS and the Cost of Sigint Four Year Forecast 1978', LSIB 1978.

108 LSIB 5/78, 12.5.78, 'Future Sigint Programmes and Costs', LSIB 1978.

109 LSIB (81) 1st Meeting (Minutes), 'Minutes of the Meeting held on 22 January 1981', 29.1.81, LSIB 1981.

110 LSIB (79) 1st and 2nd Meetings (Minutes), 13.2.79, 'Minutes of the Meeting held on 14 January 1979', 5.6.79, 'Minutes of the Meeting held on 23 May 1979', LSIB 14/1979, 5.4.79, 'The State of Sigint, 1978', LSIB 1979.

111 LSIB (80) 1st Meeting (Minutes), 17.2.80, LSIB 1980.

112 'Ralph Benjamin: An Interview Conducted by Peter C. J. Hill', 16.9.2005, IEEE History Centre, Institute of Electrical and Electronics Engineers, Inc., ethw.org/Oral-History: Ralph_Benjamin.

113 'Visit of the Prime Minister to GCHQ', *Contact* magazine, No. 32, 2nd issue, 1980, pp. 2–3.

114 LSIB 1/81, 30.12.80, 'The State of Sigint 1981', LSIB 1981.

115 LSIB 6/82, 30.6.82, 'The State of Sigint 1982', LSIB 1982.

116 LSIB 9/82, 'Future Sigint Programmes and Costs', LSIB 1982; LSIB 13/82, 30.12.82, 'The Falklands Crisis: Review of Sigint Performance', LSIB 1982.

117 Ralph Benjamin, *Five Lives in One: An Insider's View of the Defence and Intelligence World* (Tunbridge Wells, Parapress, 1996); 'Ralph Benjamin: An Interview'.

CHAPTER 8

1 Desmond Ball and Jeffrey Richelson, *The Ties that Bind: Intelligence Cooperation between the UKUSA Countries* (Allen & Unwin, Sydney, 1985), is the pioneering work on the topic, and excellent given restrictions to the material. However, it and other subsequent works which refer to UKUSA were wrong on many issues, including whether it was a formal treaty. In 2010, British and American authorities released the basic documents on UKUSA: www.nationalarchives.gov.uk/ukusa, and /www.nsa.gov/news-features/declassified-documents/ukusa/). Any modern work must start from that basis.

2 Michael Hayden, *Playing to the Edge, American Intelligence in the Age of Terror* (Penguin, New York, 2017), pp. 41–42.

3 Sigint agencies often changed names. I follow these changes, except that I replace 'GCHQ' for 'GC&CS' from September 1945. The term 'American Sigint' includes the service Sigint elements and NSA. The term 'British Sigint' applies the same to Britain, though from 1964 the term 'GCHQ' really represents the British whole. This usage differentiates the relations between GCHQ and NSA, and of both from the American service Sigint units, matters which drive UKUSA.

4 Mark K. Wells, *Courage and Air Warfare: The Allied Aircrew Experience in the Second World War* (Frank Cass, London, 1996).

5 David Hobbs, *The British Pacific Fleet: The Royal Navy's Most Powerful Fleet Force* (Naval Institute Press, 2017).

6 John Baylis, *Ambiguity and Deterrence: British Nuclear Strategy, 1945–1964* (OUP, Oxford, 1995); Margaret Gowing, *Independence and Deterrence, Britain and Atomic Energy, 1945–52, Volume 1, Policy Making and Volume 2, Policy Execution* (London, Macmillan, 1974); Jones, *The British Nuclear Deterrent, Volume I*; Navias, *Nuclear Weapons*.

7 Bradley Smith, *The Shadow Warriors, O.S.S. and the Origins of the C.I.A.* (Basic Books, 1983).

8 John Ferris, 'Gentlemen's Agreements and Gentlemen's Mail: Communications Intelligence and the Diplomacy of Naval Disarmament, 1921–1930', *Issues in British and American Signals Intelligence, 1919–1932*, Special Series, Volume 11 (Center for Cryptologic History, Fort Meade, 2015), pp. 42–59.

9 Kennedy, *Engineers of Victory,*.

10 Thomas G. Manhken, 'U.S. Grand Strategy, 1939–1945', in Ferris and Mawdsley (eds), *Fighting the War*, pp. 189–212.

11 Smith, *The Ultra-Magic Deals* is the pioneering work in the field, and a brilliant work of intelligence history. Because he could not acquire complete documentation about the access Britain gave the United States on its work against Enigma during spring 1941, some of Smith's judgements are skewed. Later key works include Ralph Erskine, 'Churchill and the Start of the Ultra-Magic Deals', *International Journal of Intelligence and Counter-Intelligence*, 10/1, Spring 1997, pp. 57–74 and David Sherman, 'From Improvisation to Permanence: American perspectives on the U.S. signals relationship, 1940–1950', *Journal of Intelligence History*, 18/2, 2019, pp. 63–85.

12 United States Military Attaché to War Department, telegram No. 401, 5.9.40, 'Early Papers Concerning US–UK Agreement, 1940–1944', https://www.nsa.gov/news-features/declassified-documents/ukusa/.

13 Memorandum by Sherman Miles, Acting Assistant Chief of Staff, G-2, 'Codes and Ciphers', 4.10.40, 'Early Papers Concerning US–UK Agreement, 1940–1944', https://www.nsa.gov/news-features/declassified-documents/ukusa/

14 Menzies to Churchill, 31.1.41, DIR/C.

15 NSA-OH-02-79 Thru 04–79, 'Dr. Abraham Sinkov, May 1979', pp. 3–6, www. nsa.gov/Portals/70/documents/news-features/declassified-documents/oral-history-interviews/nsa-OH-02-79.sinkov.pdf

16 Sherman, 'Improvisation to Permanence'.

17 Ibid.

18 Manhken, 'U.S. Grand Strategy'.

19 *British Sigint*, One, p. 299.

20 Sherman, 'Improvisation to Permanence'.

21 CSS to 48000, 25.8.42, HW 14/50.

22 Tom Johnson, *American Cryptology during the Cold War, 1945–1989: Book One, The Struggle for Centralization, 1945–1960,* Center for Cryptologic History, National Security Agency, 1995, p. 7.

23 Memorandum by Strong, 5.12.42, 'Doctor A.M. Turing', Early Papers Concerning US–UK Agreement, 1940–1944, https://www.nsa.gov/news-features/declassified-documents/ukusa/

24 'Report by Lieut. General J. H. Tiltman on his Visit to North America during March and April 1942', HW 14/46.

25 Hastings to 'Dear John' (Tiltman), 17.8.42, HW 14/49.

26 Stevens to Denniston, 28.9.42, HW 14/53.

27 Ibid.

28 NSA-OH-01-85, Interview with Telford Taylor, 22.1.85, /www.nsa.gov/Portals/70/documents/news-features/declassified-documents/oral-history-interviews/NSA-OH-01-85-Taylor.pdf

29 Stevens to Denniston, 27.10.42, HW 14/56.

30 CSS to 48000, 25.8.42, HW 14/50.

31 Manhken, 'U.S. Grand Strategy'.

32 Dill to Marshall, 7.1.43, containing Tiltman to Strong, 7.1.43, Early Papers Concerning US–UK Agreement, 1940–1944, https://www.nsa.gov/news-features/declassified-documents/ukusa/

33 Sherman, 'Improvisation to Permanence'.

34 'Turing's Report on his Visit to NCR, December 1942', edited by Ralph Erskine, Phillip Marks and Frode Weirud, 9.2000, cryptocellar.org/US Bombe/turncr.pdf (original RG 38/Crane Library, file, CNSG 5750/441, NARA).

35 Noble to King, 19.2 44, RG 38/1038.

36 Sherman, 'Improvisation to Permanence'; Johnson, *American Cryptology: Book One,* pp. 13–15

37 Sherman, 'Improvisation to Permanence'.

38 NSA-OH-01-85. Interview with Telford Taylor, 22.1.85, www.nsa.gov/Portals/70/documents/news-features/declassified-documents/oral-history-interviews/NSA-OH-01-85-Taylor.pdf

39 Telford Taylor, 'Memorandum to Colonel Clarke', 5.4.43, Early Papers Concerning US–UK Agreement, 1940–1944, https://www.nsa.gov/news-features/declassified-documents/ukusa/

40 Ibid.

41 John Ferris, 'The British Enigma', pp. 162, 168–71.

42 Ibid.

43 Personal Minute by Churchill, 27.1.44, Bridge to Churchill, n.d., but January 1944 by internal evidence, and 31.1.44, Stewart Menzies to Bridges, 31.1.44, CAB 21/2519.

44 Ibid.

45 Ferris, 'The British Enigma', pp. 170–76; Christopher Smith, 'Bletchley Park and the Development of the Rockex Cipher Systems: Building a Technocratic Culture, 1941–1945', *War in History*, 24/2, 2017.

46 Minute by Communications Department, 3.8.44, FO 850/134

47 David Alvrez, *Secret Messages, Codebreaking and American Diplomacy, 1930–1945* (University Press of Kansas, 2000).

48 Memorandum by Safford, 15.4.47, 'Administrative History of World War II: Cryptographic Research Section', RG 38/1030/110, NARA.

49 Memorandum by Wenger 15.5.45, 000628220, 'Release of Free French Material to British', RG 38/1030/92, NARA.

50 Jebb to Loxley, 21.4.44, and minute by Bland, 18.7.44, FO 1093/195.

51 Cadogan to C 16.7.43, FO 1093/324; O'Conner to Menzies, HMOC/1486, 6.9.44, FO 1093/329.

52 Memorandum by Telford Taylor, Office of the Military Attaché, American Embassy, London. 8.6.44, FO 1093/329.

53 8th Meeting, Army–Navy Cryptanalytic Research and Development Committee, 21.2.45, RG 38/1030/91, NARA.

54 *British Sigint*, One, pp. 301–3.

55 Johnson, *American Cryptology: Book One*, p. 16.

56 Ibid.

57 Presidential Executive Order, 28.8.45, RG 38/1030/92, NARA.

58 *British Sigint*, One, pp. 299–301.

59 Ibid., pp. 301–8.

60 Ibid., pp. 306–8; Joint Meeting of Army–Navy Communication Intelligence Board, and Army–Navy Communication Intelligence Coordinating Committee, 15 October 1945, 29 October 1945, https://www.nsa.gov/Portals/70/documents/news-features/declassified-documents/ukusa/joint_mtg_15oct45.pdf., https://www.nsa.gov/Portals/70/documents/news-features/declassified-documents/ukusa/joint_mtg_29oct45.pdf

61 Ibid., One, pp. 307–8.

62 Ibid., pp.307–13; Joint Meeting of Army–Navy Communication Intelligence Board, and Army–Navy Communication Intelligence Coordinating Committee, 29 October 1945, https://www.nsa.gov/Portals/70/documents/news-features/declassified-documents/ukusa/joint_mtg_29oct45.pdf

63 Ibid., p. 309.

64 Ibid., Two, pp. 657–9; Joint Meeting of Army–Navy Communication Intelligence Board, and Army–Navy Communication Intelligence Coordinating Committee, 29 October 1945, https://www.nsa.gov/Portals/70/documents/news-features/declassified-documents/ukusa/joint_mtg_29oct45.pdf

65 Ibid., One, pp. 319–20.

66 ANCIB Memorandum for General Marshall and Admiral King, 22.8.45, https://www.nsa.gov/Portals/70/documents/news-features/declassified-documents/ukusa/ancib_22aug45.pdf

67 Memorandum by Smedberg, 19.2.46, 'U.S.–British Agreement', https://www.nsa.gov/Portals/70/documents/news-features/declassified-documents/ukusa/fbi_stancib_19feb46.pdf

68 Henry C. Clausen and Bruce Lee, *Pearl Harbor: Final Judgment* (Crown Publishers, New York, 1992).

69 *British Sigint*, One, pp. 312–19; Joint Meeting of Army–Navy Communication Intelligence Board, and Army–Navy Communication Intelligence Coordinating Committee, 1.11.45, https://www.nsa.gov/Portals/70/documents/news-features/declassified-documents/ukusa/joint_mtg_1nov45.pdf

70 Ibid., pp. 286–98; *British Sigint*, Two, pp. 656–59, 670–84;

71 *Ibid.*, pp. 76–86, 324–29.

72 1951–53, UKUSA Comint Agreement and Appendices Thereto: www.nsa.gov/news-features/declassified-documents/ukusa/

73 *British Sigint*, Two, pp. 669–70.

74 Ibid., Four, p. 857.

75 'Appendix J, Principles of UKUSA Collaboration with Commonwealth Countries Other than the UK', 13.2.61, https://www.nsa.gov/Portals/70/documents/news-features/declassified-documents/ukusa/principles_of_ukusa_collaboration_with_commonwealth_countries_other_than_the_uk_appendix_j_13_february_1961.pdf

76 *British Sigint*, Three, pp. 1107–8.

77 Ibid., Two, pp. 661–64; Three, pp. 1125–30; Four, pp. 208–20.

78 Kaplan, To Kill Nations, pp. 680–81.

79 Farquhar, Need to Know, p 36.

80 *British Sigint*, Two, pp. 680–81.

81 Cf. below.

82 Johnson, *American Cryptology: Book One,* pp.11–12, 26–30, 82–3.

83 *British Sigint*, Two, pp. 664–66; ibid., Three, pp. 399–400; ibid., Four, pp. 167–71; Johnson, *American cryptology, Book One*, pp. 93–101.

84 *British Sigint*, Three, pp. 80–91.

85 *Ibid.*

86 Johnson, *American Cryptology, Book One*, pp. 23–35; Aid, The Secret Sentry, The Untold History of the National Security Agency, pp. 8–25, 41–45.

87 *British Sigint*, Two, pp. 659–63

88 *Ibid.*, p. 661; Johnson, *American Cryptology: Book One*, p. 16.

89 General Ralph Canine USA, OH–2012–81, p. 8 /www.nsa.gov/news-features/declassified-documents/ukusa/

90 Johnson, *American Cryptology: Book One*, p. 229.

91 *British Sigint*, Three, p. 1117.

92 *Ibid.*, Two, pp. 667.

93 *Ibid.*, Three, pp. 1105–7.

94 *Ibid.*, Four, pp. 190–3.

95 *Ibid.*, Three, pp. 1113–15.

96 LSIB/102/56, 30.6.56, 'Reduction in G.C.H.Q. Establishment', 30.5.56, LSIB 1956.

97 LSIB Meeting, 8.12.56, LSIB 1956 (6th Meeting) 15.12.56, LSIB 1956.

98 LSIB (65) 3rd Meeting (Minutes), 11.11.65, LSIB/52/65, 26.10.65, LSIB/29/68, 3.12.68, 'Report of a Visit to Washington in September/October 1965 by the Director GCHQ', LSIB 1965.

99 NSA-OH-02-79, Interview with Dr. Abraham Sinkov, p. 127 /www.nsa.gov/Portals/70/documents/news-features/declassified-documents/oral-history-interviews/nsa-OH-02-79.sinkov. pdf

100 *British Sigint*, Four, pp. 236–37.

101 Richard Goette, *Sovereignty and Command in Canada–US Continental Air Defence, 1940–1957* (University of British Columbia Press, Vancouver, 2018), Joseph. T. Jockel, *Canada in NORAD, 1957–2007, A History* (McGill-Queen's University Press, Kingston, 2007).

102 *British Sigint*, Three, p. 1122.

103 *Ibid.*, Four, p. 159.

104 *Ibid.*, Two, pp. 662–63, 677–83;

105 Ibid., Three, pp. 1117, 1120.

106 Nick Hopkins and Julian Bolger, 'Exclusive: NSA pays £100 million in secret funding for GCHQ', *Guardian*, 1.8.13.

107 'UK intelligence work defends freedom, say spy chiefs', BBC News, 7.11.2013, https://www.bbc.com/news/uk-politics-24847399

108 *British Sigint*, Four, pp. 181–90.

109 Ibid., Two, pp. 666–68, 677–82.

110 Ibid., pp. 679–80.

111 Ibid., Three, pp. 1098–99.

112 Ibid., Four, pp. 49, 133, 672, 1061.

113 Ibid., Three, pp. 1099–1100; Ibid., Four, p. 239.

114 Ibid., Four, pp. 15, 190–3, 198, 237–38, 895–96.

115 Ibid., Two, p. 680.

116 Ibid., Four, p. 171.

117 Ibid., Four, pp. 162–66; Johnson, *American Cryptology: Book Three, Retrenchment and Reform, 1972–1980*, pp. 21–27.

118 *British Sigint*, Four, pp. 190–93.

119 Ibid., p. 196.

120 Joe (Hooper) to White, 3.3.69, CAB 163/119.

121 *British Sigint*, Four, pp. 134–50.

122 LSIB/2/82, 5.3.82, 'The UKUSA Sigint Balance: Fact Sheet', LSIB 1982.

123 Entry, 1.5.87, William Odom Papers, Box 25, Library of Congress.

124 LSIB/14/ 1979, 5.4.79, 'The State of Sigint, 1978', LSIB 1979.

125 SA OH 15–88, 3.10.88, General Marshall Carter, pp. 201–2, 207–8, 305, /www.nsa.gov/Portals/70/documents/news-features/declassified-documents/oral-history-interviews/NSA-OH-15-88-Carter.pdf

126 NSA OH 15–88, 3.10.88, General Marshall Carter, pp. 201–2, 207–8, 305, /www.nsa.gov/Portals/70/documents/news-features/declassified-documents/oral-history-interviews/NSA-OH-15-88-Carter.pdf

127 Johnson, *American Cryptology: Book Three*, pp. 157–59.

128 'Description of Sigint Relations between NSA and GCHQ (U)', 12.85, https://www.documentcloud.org/documents/5759138-2-Description-of-SIGINT-Relations-Between-NSA.html

129 U.S. Cryptologic Partnership with the United Kingdom, 5.97, 'An Assessment of the UKUSA Relationship: Where Do We Go From Here', undated, https://www.documentcloud.org/documents/5759141-5-an-Assessment-of-the-UKUSA-Relationship-Where.html

130 *British Sigint*, One, pp. 41–42, 334–46, 529–30.

131 Kurt Jensen, *Cautious Beginnings: Canadian Foreign Intelligence, 1939–51* (University of British Columbia Press, 2013)

132 Ibid.

133 British Delegation Washington to C.S.S./G.C.C.S., 3XC.317, 4.6.42, HW 14/47.

134 Stevens to Denniston, 2.9.42, HW 14/51.

135 Jensen, *Cautious Beginnings British Sigint*, One, pp. 332–33.

136 Joseph Straczek, 'The Empire is Listening: naval signals intelligence in the Far East to 1942', *Journal of the Australian War Memorial*, 1.12.2001.

137   *British Sigint*, One, p. 333; Edward Drea, *MacArthur's Intelligence, Codebreaking and the War Against Japan, 1942–1945* (University Press of Kansas, 1991)

138   *British Sigint*, One, pp. 321–24, 352–58.

139   Evatt and the Petrov Affair are among the most divisive issues in Australian political history. The most balanced account is John Murphy, *Evatt, A Life* (New South, 2016).

140   Johnson, *American Cryptology: Book One*, pp. 18–19; Godfrey to Kinna, 24.12.48, FO 1093/516.

141   Andrew, *Defence of the Realm*, pp.367–72.

142   David Horner, *The Spy Catchers, The Official History of ASIO, 1949–1963* (Allen & Unwin, Sydney, 2014).

143   Memorandum by Sargant, 6.7.48, 'Australian Leakages', FO 1093/ 516.

144   Horner, *Spy Catchers*.

145   Murphy, *Evatt*.

146   *British Sigint*, Four, pp. 247–69.

147   Ibid., One, pp. 358–59; Ibid., Four, pp. 262–69; Johnson, *American Cryptology: Book Three*, pp. 159–61. Two useful accounts of these issues are Jenny Hocking, *Gough Whitlam: His Time* (Updated Edition) (Melbourne University Press, 2014) and John Blaxland, *The Protest Years: The Official History of ASIO, 1963–1975* (Allen & Unwin, 2015).

148   *British Sigint*, Four, pp. 283–94.

149   Ibid., One, pp. 334, 338–39.

150   Scott Lucas, *Britain and Suez, The Lion's Last Roar* (Manchester University Press, 1996).

151   GCHQ to GCOME 8.10.56, K/517/24; 'Supplement to LSIC (56) 13th Meeting', K/517/24.

152   D/0918, 29.11.56, 'Post-Mortem on Handling of Suez Crisis and Lessons for the Future', J/188/1

153   Palmer to Hooper, 7.1.57, D/353/4.

154   SUKLO to GCHQ, 9.1.57, I/09557, V. S, Palmer to Hooper, 17.1.57, D/353/4.

155   D/0918, 29.11.56, 'Post-Mortem' 'NSA Comments on GCHQ "Post-Mortem on Handling of Suez Crisis and Lessons for the Future", n.d., c.4.57, D/353/4.

156   *British Sigint*, Four, pp. 1160–63.

157   Memorandum by F. C. W. Figgs, 'Top Secret & Dinar', 24.5.64, ZW 83.

158   Bonsall to Figgs, 28.5.64, ZW 83.

159   Aldrich, 'GCHQ', pp. 277–99; *British Sigint*, Four, pp. 240–44.

160   Falklands Sigint History, pp. 16–21.

161   Entry 11 June 1985, William Odom Papers, Library of Congress, Box 25.

162   Cf. below.

163   *British Sigint*, Four, pp. 232–34.

164 Millward, 'Service of Middle East Reports to Australia', 19.12.56, Z/239/321/2, 'Extract from SUKO DSB's Letter dated 10th December 1956', K/517/24.

165 *British Sigint*, Two, pp. 683, 535–41,

166 Johnson, *American Cryptology: Book Three*, pp. 26–27

167 *British Sigint*, Two, pp. 581–83.

168 Ibid., pp. 539–41.

169 Ibid., pp. 18–609.

170 Ibid., pp. 599–600; Ibid., Three, pp. 997–1029;

171 Ibid., Two, p. 602.

172 Ibid., Four, pp. 395–98.

173 Ibid., Two, pp. 590–94, 600–4.

174 Ibid., Four, pp. 385–404.

175 Ibid., Three, pp. 997, 1012–13.

176 Cees Wiebes, 'Dutch Sigint during the Cold War, 1945–1994', pp. 243–84, in Cee Wiebes and Matthew Aid (eds), *Secrets of Sigint during the Cold War and Beyond* (Frank Cass and Co., London, 2001).

CHAPTER 9

1 *British Sigint*, One, pp.72–74.

2 Field Marshal Sir Gerald Templer, 'Review of Service Intelligence', 16.12.1960, T 296/277.

3 *Gloucestershire Echo*, 1 June 1953.

4 Hooper to Stephenson, 16.5.61, including undated memorandum by GCHQ, 'Summary of Evidence Available Outside UK Official Circles That the Government of the UK Indulges in Sigint Activities and That GCHQ is the UK Sigint Centre', T 296/278.

5 Personal Memoirs in GCHQ Archives.

6 Personal Memoirs in GCHQ Archives.

7 Personal Memoirs in GCHQ Archives.

8 Personal Memoirs in GCHQ Archives.

9 Memorandum by Denniston, 14.11.44, HW 62/21

10 Cooper to Rendle, 6.3.67 D/1102/1.

11 *British Sigint*, Two, pp. 126–47.

12 Personal Memoirs in GCHQ Archives.

13 CAB 301/11, Report of Bland Committee, 12.10.44, CAB 301/48.

14 Information from Tony Comer.

15 *British Sigint*, One, pp. 245–46.

16 Ibid., One, pp. 245–50.

17 CSC 2.9.49,'Recruitment under Normal Regulations to the Government Communication Headquarters (A Department of the Foreign Office)', Open Competition, 1950, CSC 6/55.

18 CSC, 9/65, 'Recruitment to the "A" Class and to the Departmental Specialist Class in Government Communication Headquarters (A Department of the Foreign Office)', CSC 6/70.

19 Rendle to Gedd, 5.6.63, CSC 5/1843.

20 Memorandum, 29.1.80, 'Selection of GCT 2s, Part 2, Review of Advertising and Selection Procedures', E/1100/28.

21 *British Sigint*, Three, p. 278 passim.

22 *Ibid.*, pp. 278–90.

23 *Ibid.*, p. 281.

24 Memorandum, 25.10.79, 'GCT Scheme: A Paper for Discussion with Staff Side', E/1100/28.

25 Ibid.

26 Minute by H, 4.1.80, E/1100/28.

27 Memorandum, 25.10.79, 'GCT'.

28 Minute by K1, 'Recruitment of Cadets', n.d., *c.* June 1982, E/1100/28.

29 Ibid.

30 Memorandum by S, 6.2.80, Minute by K1,, 'Recruitment of Cadets'.

31 Memorandum, 18.7.80, 'GCT Profile', E/1100/28.

32 GCHQ and the JTLS Cheltenham, 'Careers for Graduates', 1983, recruitment brochure in GCHQ Archives.

33 *British Sigint*, One, pp. 245, 248, 252.

34 Minute by K1, 'Recruitment of Cadets'.

35 Minutes of the Meeting of the Apprentices' Committee, 13.10.65, E/1000/12.

36 CSC 1964, GCHQ, 'Government Communication Headquarters, AIV and Assistant Departmental Specialist Posts Limited Competition, 1965', CSC 6/70; 12.68, 'Government Communication Headquarters Departmental Specialist Class: Technical Signals Officers', CSC 6/73.

37 'Professor Robert Churchhouse: 1927–2018 (1949, Mathematics)'. https://www.trinhall.cam.ac.uk/alumni/keep-in-touch/obituaries/robert-churchhouse/

38 Interview with David Pepper, 25.6.2018.

39 'Ralph Benjamin: An Interview'.

40 Tom Espiner, 26.10.2010, 'GCHQ pioneers on birth of public-key cryptography', ZDNet, https://www.zdnet.com/article/gchq-pioneers-on-birth-of-public-key-crypto/

41 Interview with John Adye, 20.6.2018.

42 Personal Memoirs in GCHQ Archives.

43 Simon Singh. 'Unsung Heroes of Cryptography', https://simonsingh.net/media/articles/maths-and-science/unsung-heroes-of-cryptography/ cf. Steven Levy, 'The Open Secret', *Wired*, 1/1999, 04.1.1999.

44 Ibid. The citation comes from a 1997 release by GCHQ which is no longer accessible on the internet, but is reproduced in James Ellis, 'The Story of Non-Secret Encryption', 1987, https://cryptome.org/jya/ellisdoc.htm

45 W. T. Gowers, 'The Two Cultures of Mathematics', in V. Arnold et al. (eds), *Mathematics, Frontiers and Perspectives* (American Mathematical Society, Providence, 2000).

46 *British Sigint*, Three, pp. 60, 64.

47 Smith, 'Bletchley Park and the Development of the Rockex.

48 Templer, 'Review of Service Intelligence'.

49 2.72, GCHQ, 'Graduate Electrical Engineers, CSC 6/77.

50 GCHQ and the JTLS Cheltenham, 'Careers for Graduates'.

51 Report of 'Inter-Departmental Languages Requirement Committee', 4.67, D/1102/1.

52 S.L.P. /P (59)11, 16.11.59, DEFE 10/343; Minute by K 31, 'Russian Language Training: Conference of Chief Instructors', 10.12.70, E/1105/6.

53 *British Sigint*, Young to Hooper, 7.2.67, FCO 79/2-; ML (67) Ist meeting, Appendix, 'Inter-Universities Chinese Language School', 28.2.67, ED 181/110.

54 Minute, 6.3.72, D/1104/5.

55 Memorandum by Templer, 16.12.1960, DEFE 23/23.

56 Minute in DK, 5.10.65, 'Interpretership Examinations', E/1105/6.

57 CSC, 5.68, 'Government Communications Headquarters (A Department of the Foreign Office). Language Specialist Class', CSC 6/73.

58 GCHQ and the JTLS Cheltenham, 'Careers for Graduates'.

59 Memorandum by Nicholl, 9.4.68,, D/1102/1.

60 S.L.P. /P. (59) 9, 5.8.39, DEFE 10/343.

61 Memorandum 'Linguist Specialist Open Competition, 1967', 29.6.67, D/1102/1.

62 *British Sigint*, Four, p. 448.

63 'Language Incentives, Record of a Meeting held in A/0610 on 28 February 1972', 22.3.72, E/1105/6.

64 'Language Allowances in the Administration Group and the LS Class', 9.6.82, E/1105/6.

65 'Note of a Meeting held on 25th January 1956, at the Civil Service Commission', Minute by E. J. D. Warne, CSC, to Mayes, 6/2/56, CSC 5/1105.

66 Memorandum 9.12.69, 'Supply of LS Class for J30', D/1102/1.

67 Memorandum J21T, 'Language Incentives', 17.4.72, E/1105/6.

68 Personal Memoirs in GCHQ Archives

69 GCHQ, 'General Interim Report No. 2, Electronic Computers, An account of early computers based on based on six lectures delivered at GCHQ between July and November 1949', HW 76/1.

70 *British Sigint*, Two, pp. 137–38.

71 Ibid., Three, pp. 202–5, 630–32.

72 Johnson, *American Cryptology: Book One*, pp. 195– 205; 'NSA Early Computer History', especially 'History of NSA General-Purpose Electronic Digital Computers' (1964) and 'NSA's Key Role in Major Developments in Computer Science, Parts One and Two' (2006), https://www.nsa.gov/news-features/declassified-documents/ nsa-early-computer-history/

73 'Notes of Discussion at Cheltenham on 11 March, 1957, with Dr. J. Morgan and Staff', by Milner Barry, T 222/1304.

74 *British Sigint*, Three, pp. 646–69.

75 Ibid., p. 649.

76 Ibid., Three, p. 654.

77 Ibid., p. 651.

78 Ibid., pp. 865–66.

79 Poulden to Carey, 12.11.71, CAB 184/15.

80 'Notes of Discussion at Cheltenham on 11 March, 1957, with Dr. J. Morgan and Staff', by Milner Barry, T 222/1304.

81 Poulden to Carey, 19.9.71, CAB 184/14; Richard Aldrich, 'GCHQ and UK Computer Policy, Teddy Poulden, ICL and IBM', pp. 240–61, in Malcolm Murfett (ed.), *Shaping British Foreign and Defence Policy in the Twentieth Century, a Tough Ask in Turbulent Times* (Palgrave Macmillan, 2014); Martin Campbell-Kelly, *ICL: A business and Technical History* (OUP, 1989); John Hendry, *Innovating for Failure: government policy and the early British computer industry* (MIT Press, 1990.

82 Foreign Office, 'Working Party on Computers', Third Meeting, 14.12.67, CAB 163/119.

83 'Something More about Computers', *Contact*, No. 24, 3rd Issue 1977, pp. 10–14; 'T Division GCHQ', *Contact*, No. 39, 3rd Issue, 1982, p. 15.

84 'CSOS Bude Part 1', *Contact*, No. 27, 3rd Issue, 1978, pp. 10–11.

85 'The Hewlett Packard 9845T Microcomputers for Local Aids on Stations', *Contact*, No. 36, 3rd Issue, 1981.

86 Personal Memoirs in GCHQ Archives.

87 'GCHQ Organisation -4, K Division', *Contact*, No. 33, 3rd Issue, 1980, p. 20.

88 'The Falklands Crisis: Review of Sigint Performance and Lessons'. P/8210/7/ 1 Part 1.

89 Memorandum by Poulden, 'Central Policy Review of the British Computing Industry, 29.6.71, CAB 184/12.

90 'The Hewlett Packard 9845T', *Contact*.

CHAPTER 10

1 FCO Historians, *Women and the Foreign Office, A History*, History Notes: Issue 20 (FC); Helen McCarthy, *Women of the World, The Rise of the Female Diplomat* (London, Bloomsbury, 2014).

2 Knox to Denniston, 10.8.40, HW 14/8.

3 Marion Hill, *Bletchley Park People* (The History Press, Stroud, 2008); Hill, p. 79.

4 Michie to Good, 13.7.97, 1.9.98, Donald Michie papers, ADD MS 89072/1/1, British Library.

5 I. J. Good, 'Early Work on Computers at Bletchley', *Annals of the History of Computing* 1/1, July 1979, p. 41.

6 Memorandum by Clarke, 'Naval Cryptography in War Time', c. 2.37, HW 3/1; Squadron-Leader Jones's Section, no date or author, HW 3/164.

7 LDO to A.D. (A), 25.2.44, HW 3/166; Squadron-Leader Jones's Section, no date or author, HW 3/164.

8 'History of C.M.Y. Section and The Development of Civil (International) W/T Interception during the War, 1939–1945', HW 3/162.

9 'History of Hut 3, Volume 1, HW 3/119, pp. 45–46, 122.

10 Nigel de Grey, 'Summary of Sigint Operations 1939–1945', HW 14/145.

11 Margaret Porter, 'Memories of a WW 2 WAAF W/Op', 10.8.03, Intelligence Corps Museum (ICM), Chicksands.

12 BPTA, *Other peoples' stories book three* (2001), transcript of interview with Joan Allen.

13 Yvonne Jones, n.d., 'R.A.F. Chicksands Priory', ICM, Chicksands.

14 Marjorie Arbury, 'Memories of a Y Operator', 9.7.2002, ICM, Chicksands.

15 Aileen Clayton, *The Enemy is Listening, The Story of the Y Service* (1982).

16 E. M. Kemp-Jones et al., *Civil Service Department, Management Studies 3, The Employment of Women in the Civil Service*, 14.6.71.

17 GCHQ, 'Careers for Graduates', 1970, GCHQ Archives.

18 Memorandum by K, 'Falklands Crisis Review', 20.7.82, P/8210/7/1 Pt. 1.

19 *Contact*, No. 2, Second Quarter 1971, 'Hawklaw', p. 13; *Contact*, No. 25, 1st Issue, 1978, 'Station Closures, CSOS Gilnahirk', p. 18–19; *Contact*, No. 12, 4th Quarter 1973, CSOS Cheadle', pp. 12–13.

20 *British Sigint*, Two, p. 81.

21 David French, *Military Identities: The Regimental System, the British Army and the British People, c. 1870–2000* (OUP, 2008).

22 Marie Hicks, *Programmed Inequality: How Britain Discarded Women Technologists and Lost its Edge in Computing* (Boston, MIT Press, 2018).

23 Joe Devanney and Catherine Haddon, *Women and Whitehall, Gender and the Civil Service since 1979*, Institute for Government, King's College, London, September 2015, pp. 12–13.

24 'Speech to 'Ladies of CIA''', 31.10.91, by Anne Z. Caracristi, Caracristi Papers, National Cryptologic Museum Library.

25 Ibid., p. 57–8.

26 History of Postal Censorship, pp. 409–10.

27 Lycett to Rozer, 2.5.48, HW 3/88. TNA WO 374/32200.

28 Elsdale to Harris, 25.5.28, HW 62/19; *London Gazette,* issues 33121, 5.1.26, 39080, 1.12.50.

29 Foreign Office to Civil Service Commission, 16.12.24, FO 366/815.

30 'Summary of Documents relating to Staff of G.C.& C.S.', Chief Clerk, 7.7.22, HW 3/35.

31 Martin Sugarman, 'Breaking the Codes: Jewish personnel at Bletchley Park', and 'A supplement to 'Breaking the Codes: Jewish personnel at Bletchley Park', *Jewish Historical Studies,* Vols 40 (2005) and 43 (2011), pp. 197–246, 213–222.

32 Cf. p. 559.

33 'Wybrow Case', no date or author, but 1950 by internal evidence, KV 2/3293; minute by Hayter, 8/3/49, FO 1093/390; Andrew, *Defence of the Realm,* pp. 365–6. For the Lavon affair, cf. Uri Bar Joseph, *Intelligence Intervention in the Politics of Democratic States, The United States, Israel and Britain,* Pennsylvania State University Press, 1995, pp. 149–254.

34 Minute by Burrows, 2.3.49, FO 1093/390.

35 Somerville to Hayes, 27.2.56, CSC 5/1139.

36 'Nationality Rules for Staff Employed on Special Signals Duties – Note by the Air Ministry', 1962, CAB 21/4744.

37 'Civil Servants as security risks on other than Communist or Fascist Grounds', 26.4.57, CAB 21/4530.

38 For introductions to the lengthy literature on positive vetting, cf. Lomas, *Attlee Governments,* Chapter Six, and Andrew, *Defence of the Realm,* pp. 389–99.

39 Security Conference of Privy Councilors, SCPC (55) 3rd meeting, 12.12.55, CAB 134/1325.

40 Security Conference of Privy Councilors, SCPC (55) 5th meeting, 22.12.55, CAB 134/1325.

41 James Southern, 'Homosexuality in the Foreign Office, 1967–1991', *FCO History Notes: Issue 19* (London, FCO).

42 Ibid.

43 https://www.gchq.gov.uk/speech/director-gchq-s-speech-at-stonewall-workplace-conference-as-delivered

44 Report of the Security Commission, D 16.12.81, PREM 19/1634; Daniel W. B. Lomas, 'Research Note: Security, Scandal, and the Security Commission report, 1981', INS, 2020.

45 Southern, 'Homosexuality'.

46 'Langeleben in the Beginning-1951', Draft History Project, Langeleben and the Intercept Business, Chapter One, www.langeleben.co.uk/draftproject/draft_004. htm

47 *Contact,* No. 4, 4th Quarter 1971, 'CSOS Flowerdown', pp. 11–12.

48 Ibid., No. 12, 4th Quarter 1973, CSOS Cheadle', pp. 4–22.

49 Ibid., No. 8, 4th Quarter 1972, 'CSOS Scarborough', pp. 14–31; ibid. No. 37, 4th Issue, 1981, 'CSOS Scarborough (UKC 117)–Part 2'.

50 Ibid., No. 23, 2nd Edition, 1977, 'UKC 100 Part Two', pp. 18–22; Contact, No. 24, 3rd Issue, 1977, 'UKC 100–Part 3', pp. 14–22.

51 David Thorp, *The Silent Listener* (History Press, 2012), pp. 10–23.

52 Draft History Project, Langeleben and the Intercept Business, Chapter Four, 'Langeleben 1958–59, As Recalled by Chris Rundle', op.cit.

53 Tony Cash, *The Coder Special Archive* (Hodgson, Kingston upon Thames, September 2012), Chapter Nine, pp. 9–16.

54 Ibid., Chapter Five.

55 *Contact*, No. 24, 3rd Issue, 1977, 'UKC 100 – Part 3', p. 16.

56 Ibid., No. 25, Ist Issue, 1978, 'Station Closures, CSOS Gilnahirk', p. 16.

57 Ibid., No. 6, Second Quarter 1972, 'Malta', p. 2.

58 Ibid., No. 3, 3rd Quarter, 1971, 'Singapore', p. 17.

59 Ibid., No. 1, First Quarter 1971, 'Ascension Island', pp. 10–20.

60 *British Sigint*, Two, p. 463.

61 Ibid., p. 461.

62 *Contact*, No. 10, 2nd Quarter 1973, Letter to the Editor, pp. 2–3.

63 *Contact*, No. 24, 3rd Issue 1977, 'Grouper II Training and Trials 1977/78', pp. 24–26.

64 *Contact*, No. 8th Quarter 1972, 'CSOS Scarborough', p. 23.

65 *Conflict*, p 40.

66 *British Sigint*, Three, pp. 269–77.

67 Ibid., p. 277.

68 Minute by Winnifrith, 11.11.59, T 215/391.

69 *British Sigint*, Three, p. 458.

70 Ibid., p. 459.

71 Ibid., p. 459.

72 Ibid., p. 456.

73 Michael Herman, *Intelligence Services in the Information Age, Theory and Practice* (Taylor & Francis, London, 2001), pp. 180–91.

74 *British Sigint*, Three, pp. 454–64; Ibid., Four, pp. 453–75.

75 *Contact*, No.1, First Quarter 1971, 'From the Director', p. 3.

76 *Conflict*, pp. 39, 42.

77 *Contact*, No. 6, Second Quarter 1972, 'CSOS Wincombe', p. 11.

78 'Language Allowances in the Administration Group and the LS Class', 9.6.82, E/1105/6.

79 Minutes of Evidence Taken Before the Eployment Committee of the House of Commons, 8.2.1984, pp. 50–70.

80 *British Sigint*, Five.

81 'Memories of the Cryptologic Business'.

82 *Conflict*, pp.35–6.

83 'Note for the Record', by Badham, 31.10.79, memorandum by Herbecq, 22.10.79, to PS/Minister of State, 'No Strike Agreements in the Civil Service', BA 19/721; Armstrong Affadavit.

84 *Conflict*, p 33.

85 *British Sigint*, Five.

86 'Secret War', *Sunday Times*, 5.2.84.

87 Ian Beesley, *The Official History of the Cabinet Secretaries*.

88 Ibid., pp. 442–9.

89 The best account of the union ban is Aldrich, 'GCHQ', though key evidence was published later, augmented by Charles Moore, *Margaret Thatcher: The Authorised Biography, Volume Two: Everything She Wants* (Penguin, 2016) and Beesley, *Cabinet Secretaries*. Susan Corby, 'The GCHQ Union Ban: 1984–1997: the unions' strategy and the outcome', *Labour History Review*, 65/3, Winter 2000, pp. 317–32, is a sound study. H. Lanning and Richard Norton-Taylor, *A Conflict of Loyalties: GCHQ, 1984–1991* (Cheltenham: New Clarion Press, 1991) contains useful material, but its comments on GCHQ leadership and the government, and union actions, are partial.

90 *Conflict*, pp.109–12.

91 Moore, *Thatcher*, pp. 138–42, 142–150.

CHAPTER 11

1 Memo 25.10.79, 'GCT Scheme: A Paper for Discussion with Staff Side', E/1100/28.

2 *Contact*, No. 12, 4th Quarter 1973, 'CSOS Cheadle', pp. 4–22; ibid., No. 20, 2nd Edition, 1976, 'No. 399 Signals Unit Royal Air Force Digby', pp. 7–12; ibid., No. 23, 2nd Edition, 1977, 'UKC 100 Part 2', pp. 18–22; ibid., No. 24. 3rd Issue, 1977, 'UKC 100 – Part 3', pp. 14–22; ibid., No. 36, 3rd Issue, 1981, 'CSOS Scarborough (UKC 117) – Part 1', p. 13. ibid., No. 37, 4th Issue, 1981, 'CSOS Scarborough (UKC 117) – Part 2'.

3 Ibid., No 27/3, 1978, 'CSOS Bude', pp. 2–14.

4 Alfred Price, *The History of US Electronic Warfare*, Volumes One (Association of Old Crows, Westford MA, 1984), Two (*The Renaissance Years, 1946 to 1968*) (1989) and Three, *Rolling Thunder Through the Allied Forces, 1964 to 2000* (2000).

5 *British Sigint*, Two, pp. 32–44.

6 Ibid., Four, p. 23.

7 Ibid., Three, p. 64

8 Personal Memoirs in GCHQ Archives.

9 Ibid.

10 Ibid.

11 'FOLKLORE: An Innovative Approach Toward a User Interface', *Cryptolog, The Journal of Technical Health*, 22/4, 1996, pp. 11–16, https://www.nsa.gov/Portals/70/documents/news-features/declassified-documents/cryptologs/cryptolog_134.pdf

12 'FALKLANDS: Notes of Meeting Held on 18 May 1982', 18.5.82, D/2304/14/4.

13 'The Falklands Crisis: Review of SIGINT Performance and Lessons', n.d., *c.* August 1982, P/8210/7/1.

14 Ibid.

15 Personal Memoirs in GCHQ Archives.

16 Ibid.

17 Interview with unnamed official.

18 Kit Braunholtz, email 14.8.2016, on Robert Churchhouse, 'A GCHQ memoir', 15.1.2010, https://18thcenturydiary.org.uk/a-gchq-memoir/

19 Interview with unnamed official.

20 Cavendish-Bentinct and Capel-Dunn, 'The Intelligence Machine'.

21 Minute 'Language Money for GCHQ's Executive and Clerical Classes', E/1105/6.

22 *British Sigint*, Two, p. 162.

23 LSIB/14/ 1979, 5.4.79, 'The State of Sigint, 1978', LSIB 1979.

24 Leonard Hooper, A 2, 'Suez Telegrams', 4.9.56, K/517/24.

25 Selwyn Lloyd to Jones, 20.9.56, K/517/24.

26 Le Bailly to Hooper, 16.4.78, ZIC /4/21.

27 Draft memorandum by Hooper, 'What Intelligence can and cannot do', n.d. but *c.* July 1974, ZIC /4/21.

28 Ibid.

CHAPTER 12

1 Johnson, *American Cryptology, Book One,* p. 118. For the best exposition of the conventional version of Berlin and espionage, cf. David. E. Murphy, Sergei A. Kondrashev, George Bailey, *Battleground Berlin, CIA vs. KGB in the Cold War* (Yale University Press, 1997).

2 Robert Louis Benson and Michael Warner, *Venona: Soviet Espionage and the American Response, 1939–1957* (NSA/CIA, Washington, 1996); Johnson, *American Cryptology, Book One.* pp. 277–78.

3 Carol B. Davis, *Candle in the Dark: COMINT and Soviet Industrial Secrets, 1946–1956* (CCH, 2017), quoting Robert Benson and John Schindler, 'LINK: The Greatest Intelligence Disaster in U.S. History', paper presented to 2003 Cryptologic History Symposium.

4 Peterson, *Bourbon*, pp. 29–297.

5 S/ARU/T3368, 14.10.49, *passim*, HW 75/482.

6 *Sigint History*, Two, pp. 802–10.

7 HW 75/24, HW 75/47–8, HW 75/73, HW 75/78.

8 Davis, *Candle*, pp. 12–15, 19, 47; *British Sigint*, Two, pp. 20–22.

9 See pp. 522–4.

10 Davis, *Candle*, p. 5.

11 Halford to C, 26.1.49, FO 1093/490.

12 Ibid.

13 COS Confidential Annex to COS (48) 155th Meeting, 3.11.48, 'Intelligence Requirements for "Cold War" Planning', FO 1093/370.

14 Ibid.

15 JIC (48) 19 (0) (2nd Revised Draft, 11.5.48, 'Sigint Intelligence Requirements – 1948', L/WS/1/1196.

16 Minutes, JIC Meeting, 24.3.55, JIC (55) 25th Meeting, CAB 159/18; 'Confidential Annex' to JIC (55) 34th Meeting, 28.4.55, CAB 159/19.

17 JIC (51) 126, 'Present State of our Intelligence on the Soviet Union, The European Satellites and China and Measures to Improve It', 7.1.52, CAB 158/13.

18 *British Sigint*, Three, pp. 44–60, 1143–8, 1176–83; Goodman, JIC, Volume One, XXX.

19 USAREUR Intelligence Estimate 1961 (U), Headquarters, United States Army, Europe, Office of the Deputy Chief of Staff, Intelligence, 1.1.61; William Burr and Robert A. Wampler (eds), *Lifting the Veil on Cosmic: Declassified US and British Documents on NATO Military Planning and Threat Assessments on the Warsaw Pact*, Parallel History Project on Cooperative Security, 2002.

20 LSIB(80) 3rd Meeting, Minutes, 5.11.80, LSIB 7/80, 17.10.80, 'The Concept of Sigint Support to Military Operations in Tension and War', LSIB 1980.

21 *Contact*, No. 37, 1/1982, 'WINTEX 81', pp. 9–11; *Contact*, 3/38, 'WINTEX 81 Part 2', pp. 20–23.

22 COS (57) 174, 29.7.57, 'Period of Planning for Global War', DEFE 5/77.

23 COS (61), 3rd Meeting, 10.1.61, DEFE 4/133.

24 Strong to Dickson, 24.1.58, JIC (58) 4 (Final), CAB 158/31. William Burr and Svetlana Savranskaya, 'Previously Classified Interviews with Former Soviet Authorities Reveal U.S. Strategic Intelligence Failure over Decades' National Security Archive, 11.9.09, https://nsarchive2.gwu.edu/nukevault/ebb285/), reprints a 1995 study by the Office of Net Assessment at the Pentagon, which offers useful material on Soviet attitudes on these issues during the middle and late Cold War.

25 JP (58) 34 Final, 26.3.58, DEFE 6/49; JIC (55) 7 (Final), 'The Soviet Strategic Air Plan in the Early Stages of a General War in the period up to 1959', 16.2.55, CAB 158/19.

26 USAREUR Intelligence Estimate–1961; Burr and Wampler (eds), *Lifting the Veil*.

27 JIC (59) 33, 'Warning of an Attack on the West in Global War up to the end of 1960, 1.4.59, CAB 158/36; JIC (6), 33 (Final) 'Warning and Timing of a Soviet Attack on the West in Global War', 21.10.60, CAB 158/40.

28 Ehlers, *Targeting the Third Reich*.

29 Kaplan, To Kill Nations; Len Scott and Stephen Twigge, *Planning Armageddon, Britain, The United States, and the Command of Western Nuclear Forces, 1945–1964* (Routledge, London, 2013).

30 Michael Warner, 'The Collapse of Intelligence Support for Air Power, 1944–52', *Studies in Intelligence*, 49/3, https://www.cia.gov/library/center-for-the-study-of-intelligence/csi-publications/csi-studies/studies/vol49no3/html_files/Intel_Air_Power_4.htm

31 Kevin O'Daly, 'Living in the shadow: Britain and the USSR's nuclear weapon delivery systems 1949–62', PhD diss., University of Westminster, 2016, pp. 115–47.

32 Donald E. Welzenbach and Gregory W. Pedlow, *The CIA and Overhead Reconnaissance: The U2 and Oxcart Programs, 1954–74* (Simon & Schuster, 2016; original, CIA, Washington, 1992); CIA history of the office of special activities to 1969, https://archive.org/details/HistoryOfTheOfficeOfSpecialActivitiesFromInceptionTo1969/page/n8

33 Stanley G. Zabetakis and John F. Peterson, 'The Diyarbikir Radar', 2.7.96. CIA Library, https://www.cia.gov/library/center-for-the-study-of-intelligence/kent-csi/vol8no4/html/v08i4a05p_0001.htm.

34 O'Daly, 'Living in the shadow', pp. 72–74, Aldrich, 'GCHQ', pp. 320–5.

35 'Soviet Research and Development 1957', 14.4.58, JIC (58) 42, CAB 158/32.

36 Joint Technical Committee Meeting, 7.9.54, DEFE 10/497; JIC to ACAS (I) 9.9.60, AIR 8/1953; Memorandum by JIB 18.8.60, 'Definition of Responsibilities for the Assessment of Intelligence in the Sphere of National Defence: Comment of JIB on an Undated Air Ministry Note', AIR 8/1953.

37 Templer, 'Review of Service'.

38 *Aviation News*, 21.20.57, 'How U.S. Taps Soviet Missile Secrets'.

39 Sigint Production Review, 1977, 4.4.78,

40 *British Sigint*, Three, pp. 44–60, 1143–48, 1176–83

41 Ibid., pp. 53; Johnson, *American Cryptology, Book One*, pp. 253–56.

42 Minute by Tovey, 9.8.68, 'DGI/DIS Colonel Discussion with Mr. Healey on Czech Crisis Intelligence', J/2300/18 Part 1.

43 Peter Davies, *The Authorised History of British Defence Economic Intelligence, A Cold War in Whitehall, 1925–1990* (Routledge, London, 2018); Huw Dylan, Defence Intelligence and the Cold War, Britain's Joint Intelligence Bureau, 1945–1964 (OUP, Oxford, 2014).

44 S/ARU-E/C125, 12.2.48, HW 75/127.

45 CREAM/ZIP/RUE/C91, 28.1.47, HW 75/105; S/ARU-E/C490, 19.1.1950, HW 75/160.

46 Minute, 'Czech Crisis and J Division', 22.11.68, J/3200/18/Annexe.

47 Production Review Meeting, 10.4.81, Memorandum by Johnson, 'Production Review 1984', 13.5.84; LSIB/1/81, 30/12/80, 'The State of Sigint 1981', LSIB 1981.

48 *Contact*, No. 12, 4th Quarter 1973, 'CSOS Cheadle', pp. 4–22.

49 Ibid., No. 8, 4th Quarter 1972, 'CSOS Scarborough', pp. 14–31; ibid., No. 36, 3rd Issue, 1981, 'CSOS Scarborough – Part 1', p. 13, ibid., No. 37, 4th Issue, 1981, 'CSOS Scarborough – Part 2'.

50 Ibid., No. 23, 2nd Edition, 1977, 'Part Two', pp. 18– 22, ibid., No. 24. 3rd Issue, 1977, ' Part 3', pp. 14–22.

51 Peter Hennessy, *Silent Deep, The Royal Navy Submarine Service since 1945* (Penguin, 2016).

52 Johnson, *American Cryptology*, Book One, p. 118

53 'Berlin Crisis, Record of a Meeting Held on 26th May, 1959', 26,5.59, D/2303/3.

54 Roy Marsden, 'Operation 'Schooner/Nylon/: RAF Flying in the Berlin Control Zone', INS, 13/4 ((1998), pp. 178–93; Kevin Paul Wright, 'Cold War Reconnaissance Flights along the Berlin Corridors and in the Berlin Control Zone 1960–90: Risk, Coordination and Sharing', INS, 30/5, 2014, pp. 615–36.

55 Tony Geraghty, *BRIXMIS: the untold exploits of Britain's most daring Cold War spy mission* (London: HarperCollins, 1997); Major General Peter Williams, 'BRIXMIS in the 1980s: The Cold War's "Great Game"', in British Commanders'-in-Chief Mission to the Soviet Force in Germany (BRIXMIS): Photographs and Documents, Parallel History Project on Cooperative Security, http://www.php.isn.ethz.ch/kms2.isn. ethz.ch/serviceengine/Files/PHP/29544/ipublicationdocument_ singledocument/ cfc33b48-d4eb-4ad4-a253-fb9dec50d345/en/BRIXMIS_ 1980s.pdf .

56 Tony Cunnane, *A Yorkshire Aviator's Autobiography*, 'No. 26 Signals Unit'.

57 'Post-Mortem of Handling of Suez Crisis and Lessons for the Future', 29.11.56, K/517/24/Middle East Crisis.

58 Lucas, *Britain and Suez*.

59 'Post-Mortem of Handling of Suez Crisis and Lessons for the Future', 29.11.56, K/517/24/Middle East Crisis.

60 Action at 1700 Meeting on 1st November, 1956, XII/I/48, Policy Suez Crisis 1956.

61 SUKLO to GCHQ, 22.11.56, 961/11, XII/1/48.

62 NSA Comments on GCHQ 'Post-Mortem on Handling of Suez Crisis and Lessons for the Future', no author or date, *c.* May 1957, J/188/I, Crisis Planning.

63 Memorandum by K1H, 14.12.56, '1 WRLS. REGT. – A point arising from the crisis', J/188/1.

64 SUKLO to GCHQ, 15.11.56, XII/I/48, Policy Suez Crisis 1956.

65 GCHQ London to GCHQ, 9.22.56, XII/I/48, Policy Suez Crisis 1956.

66 AD2 to Director, 8.11.56, XII/I/48, Policy Suez Crisis 1956.

67 3/ARU/9088, 9.6.57, 'Summary of Activities of Soviet Army Divisions in Hungary 24th October, 1956–31st April 1957', *passim*, ARU/C Reporting 1956.

68 'Report on 1615 Meeting on 7th November, 1956', XII/I/48, Policy Suez Crisis 1956.

69 *British Sigint*, Three, pp. 1159– 62.

70 'Report on 1615 Meeting on 7 th November, 1956', XII/I/48, Policy Suez Crisis 1956.

71 *British Sigint*, Three, pp. 1159–62.

72 James H. Hansen, 'Soviet Deception in the Cuban Missile Crisis', Center for the Study of Intelligence, CIA, 46/1, is the best account of Soviet *maskirovka*, as Dino Brugioni, *Eyeball to Eyeball, The Inside Story of the Cuban Missile Crisis* (New York, Random House, 1991) is of American intelligence during the crisis. Neither author had access to the Sigint record, and Brugioni's account rests largely on personal experience and interviews, and largely is unsourced. 'NSA and the Cuban Missile Crisis' (Ft. Meade, Maryland, Center for Cryptologic History, 1998), and Johnson, *American Cryptology: Book II, Centralization Wins*, pp. 317–30 are the best accounts of US Sigint.

73 Minute, 26.11.56, J/188/1 – Crisis Planning.

74 UKN 125 to SCA 2078 et al., 20.7.62, 2X-AR3U-S-C2338/62720//SE, Cuba/1962.

75 UKN 125 to SCA 2078. et al., 31.7.62, 2X-AR3U-S-C2366/620731//SE, 13.9.62, 2X-AR3U-C/2524/620923//SE, 4.10.62, 2X-AR3U-C/2597/621004//SE, Cuba/1962.

76 UKN 125 to SCA 2078. et al., 27.10.62, 2X-AR3U-S-C2682/621026//SE, Cuba/1962.

77 Kaplan, *Kill Nations*.

78 Petit to Tovey, 16.1.69, DIS, First Draft, 'Warning of Warsaw Pact Attack Against NATO in the Central Area of ACE', J/2300/18 Part 1.

79 Memorandum 25.5.68, 'J Division Post Mortem of the Czechoslovak Crisis (5th to 21st May)', J/2300/18 Part 1.

80 David Glantz, *Soviet Military Deception in the Second World War* (Frank Cass, 1988).

81 Anatoly Golitzyn, *New Lies for Old* (New York, Dodd, Mean and Co., 1984)

82 James H. Hansen, 'Soviet Deception in the Cuban Missile Crisis', CIA.

83 Memorandum by Tovey, 21.7.69, 'Service to BAOR and RAF Germany: Proposed Presentation of the Czech Crisis', J/2300/18, Pt. 2.

84 Memorandum by Tovey, 15.12.69, 'Czech Crisis Presentation: Secretary JIC's request for a 'Record'', J/2300/18 Pt. 2.

85 J 276/1, 1.12.69, J/2300/18, Pt. 2.

86 Memoranda by Tovey, 21.7.69, 'Service to BAOR and RAF Germany: Proposed Presentation of the Czech Crisis', 15.12.69, 'Czech Crisis Presentation: Secretary JIC's request for a "Record", and 26.1.70, 'The CPX of August 1968', J/2300/18, Pt. 2.

87 MOD Secretary to GCHQ, 20.8.68, P 0211002, Tovey to Murray, 21.1.69, J/4578/2300/18, J/2300/18 Part 1.

88 Memorandum by Tovey, 20.10.68, 'Post-Mortem on the Czech Crisis', J/2300/18 Part 1, Annexe.

89 Memorandum by Tovey, 11.9.68, 'Czech Crisis: Sigint Contribution', J/2300/18 Part 1.

90 Memorandum by Tovey, 20.10.68, 'Post-Mortem on the Czech Crisis'; J/2300/18 Part 1, Annexe.

91 Memorandum by Hooper, 5.8.68, J/2300/18 Part 1.

92 This paragraph is based on Memorandum 25.5.68, 'J Division Post Mortem of the Czechoslovak Crisis, and Memorandum by Tovey, 20.10.68, 'Post-Mortem on the Czech Crisis', J/2300/18 Part 1, Annexe.

93 Memorandum by Tovey, 20.10.68, 'Post-Mortem on the Czech Crisis'; J/2300/18 Part 1, Annexe; 3/A/CMJ/C33-69, 21.10.69, 'The Czechoslovakia Crisis, Part II. Activity by Warsaw Pact Forces Associated with Exercise Sumava', C33-69, Czech Summaries; 'The C 3/A/CMJ/C43-70, 8.6.70, The Czechoslovakia Crisis Part V. The Invasion of Czechoslovakia', CS43-70, Czech Summaries.

94 Documents No. 53–54, Vojtech Masty, Malcolm Byrne, Anna Locher and Christian Neunlist, 'An Inside History of the Warsaw Pact, 1955–1991: Documentary Companion to A Cardboard Castle?', Parallel History Project on Cooperative Security, https://www.fi les.ethz.ch/isn/108638/10_ACardboardCastle.pdf

95 Memorandum by Tovey, 20.10.68, 'Post-Mortem on the Czech Crisis'; J/2300/18 Part 1, Annexe.

96 Memorandum by Tovey, 9.8.68, 'DGI/DSI Colonel Discussions with Mr. Healey in Czech Crisis Intelligence', J/2300/18 Part 1.

97 Tovey to Rendle, 13.9.68, J/2300/18 Part 1.

98 Petit to Tovey, 12.8.68, DIS 9.8.68, 1500/DIS/26/5, 9.8.68, 'Military Intelligence Gathered on Czechoslovak/Soviet Military Confrontation and the Relevance to any Future Soviet Bloc Troop and Aircraft Movements Threatening NATO', J/2300/18 Part 1.

99 Petit to Tovey, 16.1.69, DIS, First Draft, 'Warning of Warsaw Pact Attack Against NATO in the Central Area of ACE', J/2300/18 Part 1.

100 Tovey to Rendle, 13.9.68, J/2300/18 Part 1. The Cierna-Bratislava discussions were between the Czechoslovak government and those of other Warsaw Pact nations.

101 Tovey to Petit, 17.12.68, J/4371/2300/18, J/2300/18 Part 1.

102 Minute by Tovey, 18.11.68, J/2300/18 Part 1.

103 Memorandum by Tovey, 20.10.68, 'Post-Mortem on the Czech Crisis'; J/2300/18 Part 1, Annexe.

104 Memorandum, 25.5.68, 'J Division Post Mortem'.

105 Memo, 6.11.68, 'Sigint and the Czech Crisis, 'A Strategy for J Division', J/2300/18 Part 1, Annexe.

106 Technical Supplement to 2/AA/24068-79 (RUA), Minsk ADD: 'Status of Fighter Direction Posts in the Riga ADZ as at 1 March 1979', 31.7.79.

107 2/AA/APP/J26K2-81 (RUJ), 'GSFG: 47 GTD, 3SA, Field Training Exercise, 4–9 August 1980', 13.5.81,.

108 2/AA/27092-81, 5.6.81, 'Soviet Baltic Fleet and Baltic Fleet Air Force Development Report, 1– 81', HS– 31.

109 2/AA/24043-79 (RUA), 10.5.79, 'Soviet Long Range Air Force Order of Battle', 3/AA/26168-79 (RUM), 13.12.79, 'GSFG: Ground Forces Order of Battle from Sigint 31 August 1979'; 2/AA/29102-81, 15.11.81, 'EGAF: Locations, Equipments and Pilot Strengths as at 31 Oct 1981', 2/AA/29074-81, 'GDR: Ground Forces Sigint Order of Battle as at 30 June 1981', 7.10.81.

110 2/AA/23512 79 (CMJ), 2.5.79, 2/AA/24070-79 (RUA), 'Operations by PX090 TU-126 Airborne Warning and Control (AWAC) Aircraft over the Western USSR sic, 1978', 13.6.79.

111 Douglas MacEachin, 'Predicting the Soviet Invasion of Afghanistan: The Intelligence Community's Record' (CIA, 2000); Interagency Intelligence Memorandum, October 1980, 'The Soviet Invasion of Afghanistan: Implications for Warning', https://www.cia.gov/library/readingroom/docs/DOC_0000278538.pdf

112 2/AA/22038-79 (RUJ), 6.8.79, 'Increased Soviet General Staff Communications with Kabul since 3 Aug 1979', 2/AA/23003-79 (RUH), 17.9.79, 'Soviet Reaction to Unrest in Afghanistan, 13–17 September 1979', 2/AA/22046-79, 28.9.79, 'Codeword Messages and increased Messages Affecting sic VTA and VDV', 2/AA/22058-79 28.11.79, 'Slightly Increased General Staff Communications to the Turkistan Central Asian and Transbajkal MDs, 25–28 Nov'.

113 3/AA/23137-79 (CMH), 13.12.79, 'Soviet Bloc Political and Military Activity Abroad, Number No. 48–79: 6–12 Dec 1979, 3/AA/23138-79 (CMH), 15.12.79, 'Soviet Activity in Afghanistan and the Southern USSR, 15/12/79', 3/AA/23140-79 (CMH), Soviet Military Activity in Afghanistan and the Southern USSR, 17/12/79, 17.12.79, 3/AA/23148-79 (RUH) Soviet Military Activity in the Southern USSR and Afghanistan 23/12/79'.

114 LSIB (80) 1st Meeting, 11.2.80, LSIB 1980, LSIB/6/84, 'The State of Sigint 1984', 20.7.84, LSIB 1984.

115 3/AA/23078-80 (RUH), 14.8.80, 'Exercise Activity in Transcaucasia and Turkestan MDs, August 1980', H3-17.

116 Ibid.

117 3/AA/22037-80 (RUJ) 12.9.80, 'Unusual Communications Involving Poland and Adjacent Areas', H3-17.

118 3/AA/29148, 4.11.80, 'Review of Eurcom Activity 26 October–1 November 1980', H3-17.

119 3/AA/29028-81 (CMY), 'Review of Eurcom Activity 8–14 February 81 sic', 17.2.81, 3/AA/29054-81, 'Review of Eurcom Activity 29 March–4 April 1981', 7.4.81; 2/AA/29071-81 (PLJ). 28.7.81, 'Polish Contingency Communications Close Down'.

120 Andrew, *Defence of the Realm*, pp. 836–45.

121 R. L. Garthoff, 'The KGB Reports to Gorbachev', INS, 11/2, April 1996, pp. 224–44; David Kahn, 'Soviet Comint in the Cold War', *Cryptologia*, 22/1, January 1998, pp. 1–24.

CHAPTER 13

1   C.C. 65 (33), 19.9.63, CAB 195/23/7; Minute by Healey to Commonwealth Secretary, 3.2.65, FO 371/181454.

2   The best account of Anglo-Zionist politics are Bernard Wasserstein, *The British in Palestine: The Mandatory Government and the Arab–Jewish Conflict, 1917–1929* (Royal Historical Society Studies in History Series, Number 10, RHS, London, 1978) and Michael J. Cohen, *Palestine and the Great Powers* (Princeton University Press, 1982).

3   'Visit to the Middle East by Mr. A. J. Kellar', 19.2.45, KV 4/384.

4   C. M. (47), 6th Conclusions, Minute 3, Confidential Annexe, 15.1.47, *passim*, CAB 128/11.

5   'Report on Visit to Middle East by Mr. A. J. Kellar', 7.46, KV 3/384.

6   High Commissioner to Secretary of State, telegram No. 1111, 3.10.46, Alan Cunningham Papers, MECA.

7   High Commissioner to Secretary of State, telegram No. 1119, 12.10.46, Alan Cunningham Papers, MECA.

8   'Visit to the Middle East by Mr. A. J. Kellar'.

9   Charles Tegart papers. 4/6. Diary Entry 30.12.1937, MECA.

10 SLU Clover to LSIC, BRAN/YD 300, 13.3.47, SLU Clover to SLU Fayid, BRAN/YD 945, 19.11.47, SLU Clover to SLU Cairo, BRAN/YD 966, 27.11.47, PALESTINE BRAN/YD 1947.

11 Minute by Stiebel, B.5.a., 18.7.47, KV 2/1435.

12 'Appendix to Part II, Messages Referred to in the Text', n.d. but *c.* July 1946 by internal evidence, CO 537/1715.

13 C to Loxley, 7.3.44, FO 1094/328.

14 West, *Liddell Diaries*, p. 235.

15 GC&CS to SLU Clover, G 1025, 17.10.45, PALESTINE PROC 1945.

16 D.D. 3 to D.D. C, 27.9.44, HW 14/112.

17 CO to GCCS, W 84, 20.10.45, BRAN CO 1945.

18 Barber to DD 1, 5.8.45, HW 14/133.

19 Report of the Bland Committee, 12.10.44, CAB 301/48.

20 GC&CS to Clover, 10.10.45, No. 1456, 16.11.45, PALESTINE PROC 1945;
    Trafford Smith to Chadwick, 7.9.46, minute by Trafford Smith, 4.7.46, *passim*,
    CO 537/1735.

21 SLU Clover to SLU Cairo, BRAN/YD 5.7.46, PALESTINE BRAN/YD 1946.

22 SLU Clover to LSIC, 5.7.46, CO 537/1735.

23 BRAN/CO 31, 28.11.45, BRAN CO 1945.

24 'Report on Visit to Middle East by Mr. A. J. Kellar'.

25 SLU Clover to LSIC BRAN/YD 375, 12.4.47, PALESTINE BRAN/YD 1947.

26 SLU Clover to SLU Cairo, BRAN/YD 804, 19.9.47, PALESTINE BRAN/YD
    1947.

27 'Report on Visit to the Middle East by Mr. J. C. Robertson, 14th April–14th June
    1947', KV 4/438. In the TNA version of this paragraph, all references to 'FOG'
    and 'CREAM' are redacted; I have replaced them.

28 GL Diary, pp. 156, 172, 174, 177.

29 SLU Clover to LSIC BRAN/YD 375, 12.4.47, PALESTINE BRAN/YD 1947.

30 SLU Clover to LSIC, BRAN/YD 162, 15.1.48, BRAN/YD 226, 29.1.48, SLU
    Clover to SLU Fayid, BRAN/YD 230, 29.1.48, BRAN Y D 01/48.

31 'Report on Visit to the Middle East by Mr. J. C. Robertson'.

32 SLU Clover to LSIC, BRAN/YD 561, 14.6.47, PALESTINE BRAN Y/D 1947.

33 SLU Clover to LSIC, BRAN/YD 903, 3.11.47 (two telegrams) PALESTINE
    BRAN/YD 1947.

34 SLU Cairo to GC&CS, W Number 120, 22.12.45, BRAN CO 1945.

35 GL Diary, p. 247.

36 High Commissioner to Secretary of State, 1.8.46, telegram No. 1258, Alan
    Cunningham Papers, MECA.

37 'Visit to the Middle East by Mr. A. J. Kellar'.

38 SLU Clover to LSIC, BRAN/YD 440, 25.4.47, PALESTINE BRAN/YD 1947;
    'Report on Visit to the Middle East by Mr. J. C. Robertson'.

39 SLU Clover to LSIC, 3.7.46, BRAN/YD 560, PALESTINE BRAN/YD 1946.

40 'Illegal Zionist Armed Forces in Palestine and the Complicity of the Jewish
    Agency', n.d., *c*. July 1946, CO 537/1735.

41 SLU Cairo to LSIC, BRAN/CO 114, 19.6.46, BRAN/CO 117, 19.6.46, BRAN/
    CO 118, 20.6.46, *passim*, BRAN/CO 1946.

42 'Notes on the White Paper of Evidence (CMD. 6863)', n.d. or author, but by MI5
    and *c*.31.7.46, by internal evidence, CO 537/1735.

43 'Illegal Zionist Armed Forces in Palestine and the Complicity of the Jewish
    Agency', n.d., *c*. July 1946, CO 537/1735.

44 Unsigned and undated, 'Implication of Ben-Gurion and Shertok in Hagana Activities', CO 537/1735.

45 Aaron Edwards, *Defending the Realm? The Politics of Small Wars in Britain since 1945* (OUP, 2013), pp. 25–40.

46 SLU Clover to LSIC, 28.6.46, BRAN/YD 543, PALESTINE BRAN/YD 1946.

47 SLU Clover to LSIC, BRAN/YD 556, 1.7.46, PALESTINE BRAN/YD 1946.

48 Hall to Attlee, 12.7.46, CO 537/1735.

49 Menachem Begin, *The Revolt, Story of the Irgun* (WF Allen, 1951).

50 'Illegal Zionist Armed Forces in Palestine and the Complicity of the Jewish Agency', n.d., *c.* July 1946, CO 537/1735.'Hayyim' was Weizmann and Sir John Shaw was the British Political Secretary in Jerusalem. The 'Executive' of the Jewish Agency meant power there. Rcksch perhaps was Yisrael Rokach, the mayor of Tel Aviv. 'Yemin' might be 'Yellin', for whom many candidates are possible.

51 SLU Clover to LSIC, BRAN/YD 585, 9.7.46, PALESTINE BRAN/YD 1946.

52 SLU Clover to LSIC, BRAN/YD 603, 15.7.46, PALESTINE BRAN/YD 1946.

53 SLU Cairo to LSIC, BRAN/CO 133, 15.7.46, BRAN/CO 1946.

54 SLU Clover to LSIC, BRAN/YD 564, 3.7.46, PALESTINE BRAN/YD 1946.

55 SLU Clover to LSIC, BRAN/YD 561, 3.7.46, PALESTINE BRAN/YD 1946.

56 SLU Clover to SLU Cairo, BRAN/YD 580, 8.7.46, PALESTINE BRAN/YD 1946.

57 Cabinet meeting, 11.7.46, CAB 67 (46), CAB 128/6/5.

58 SLU Clover to LSIC, BRAN/YD 627 23.7.46, PALESTINE BRAN/YD 1946.

59 Calder Walton, 'British Intelligence and Threats to British National Security after the Second World War', p. 158–60, in Matthew Grant (ed.), *The British Way in Cold Warfare: Intelligence, Diplomacy and the Bomb, 1945–1975* (Continuum, 2009)

60 'Summary of Letter from D.S.O. Palestine ref. DSO/S/P1 dated 26 July 1946', Robertson to Trafford Smith, 29.7.46, KV 2/1389.

61 SLU Clover to SLU Cairo, BRAN/YD 715, 14.8.46, PALESTINE BRAN/YD 1946.

62 SLU Clover to LSIC, BRAN/YD 800, 2.9.46, PALESTINE BRAN/YD 1946.

63 'Extract from CIRCUS report on Jewish Affairs dated 12.9.46 forwarded by D.S.O. Palestine', KV 2/1389.

64 SLU Clover to SLE Cairo, BRAN/YD 987, 30.10.46, PALESTINE BRAN/YD 1946.

65 Stephen Wagner, *Statecraft by Stealth: Secret Intelligence and British Rule in Palestine* (Ithaca, Cornell University Press, 2019).

66 'Notes on the White Paper of Evidence (CMD. 6863)', n.d. or author, but by MI5 and *c.* 31.7.46, by internal evidence, CO 537/1735.

67 Chief Secretary, Palestine, to Secretary of State, No. 1061, 12.7.46, CO 537/1735.
68 SLU Clover to LSIC, BRAN/YD 562, 3/7/46, PALESTINE BRAN/YD 1946.
69 Secretary of State to High Commissioner, telegram No. 1158, 8.7.46, CO 537/1735.
70 Hall to Attlee, 8.7.46, CO 537/1735.
71 High Commissioner to Secretary of State, No. 1156, 14.7.46, Jowitt to Hall, 15.7.46, CO 537/1735.
72 SLU Clover to PSIC, BRAN/YD 596, 11.7.46, PALESTINE BRAN/YD 1946.
73 Kellar to Trafford Smith, 30.7.46, High Commissioner to Secretary of State, telegram No. 1061, 12.7.46, CO 537/1735.
74 'Operations in Palestine, Illegal Zionist Armed Forces in Palestine and the Complicity of the Jewish Agency', minutes of ministerial meeting, 11.7.46, CO 537/1735.
75 'Illegal Zionist Armed Forces in Palestine and the Complicity of the Jewish Agency', n.d., c. July 1946, CO 537/1735.
76 Gutch to Trafford Smith, 19.8.46, CO 537/1735.
77 SLU Clover to LSIC, BRAN/YD 440, 25.4.47, PALESTINE BRAN/YD 1947.
78 Minute by Stiebel, B.5.a., 18.7.47, KV 2/1435.
79 SLU Clover to SLU Cairo, BRAN/YD 873, 23.9.46, PALESTINE BRAN/YD 1946.
80 For examples, cf. KV 2/1389–90.
81 SLU Clover to LSIC, BRAN/YD 181, 13.2.47, PALESTINE BRAN/YD 1947.
82 SLU Clover to SLU Cairo, BRAN/YD 165, 10.2.47, SLU Clover to LSIC, BRAN/YD 367, 380, 441, 31.4.47 (probably misdated for 31.3.47), 3.4.47, 25.4.47, PALESTINE BRAN/YD, 1947.
83 SLU Clover to LSIC, BRAN/YD 566, 598, 14.6.47, 28.6.47, PALESTINE BRAN /YD 1947.
84 SLU Clover to SLU Cairo, BRAN/YD 518, 24.5.47, PALESTINE BRAN/YD 1947.
85 SLU Clover to LSIC, BRAN/YD 362, 31.3.47, PALESTINE BRAN/YD 1947.
86 SLU Clover to LSIC, BRAN/YD 870, 17.10.47, PALESTINE BRAN/YD 1947.
87 Minutes by FitzGerald, 27.1.47, *passim*, CO 537/2405.
88 SLU Cairo to SLU Clover, BRAN/CO 180, 27.8.46, BRAN/CO 1946.
89 SLU Clover to SLU Cairo, BRAN/YD 408, 15.4.47, PALESTINE BRAN/YD 1947.
90 SLU Clover to SLU Cyprus, BRAN/YD 499, 20.5.47, PALESTINE BRAN/YD 1947.
91 For an analysis by the DSO and NLO of the role of intelligence in these operations, cf. SLU Clover to LSIC, BRAN 152, 12.1.48, BRAN Y D 01/48.
92 SLU Clover to SLU Fayid, BRAN/YD 221, 27.1.48, BRAN Y D 01/48.
93 SLU CAIRO to SLU Clover, BRAN/CO 99, 16.5.46, BRAN CO 1946.
94 CO to CRACKER W No. 33, 9.10.45, BRAN CO 1945.

95 High Commissioner to Secretary of State, No. 1255, 1.8.46, Cunningham Papers. MECA.

96 'Military Implications of Establishing Malaysia Without Singapore and Possibly without Brunei, Note by the Secretary', 27.6.63, DEFE 5/140; Saki Dockrill, *Britain's Retreat from East of Suez: The Choice Between Europe and the World* (Palgrave Macmillan, London, 2002).

97 David Easter, *Britain and the Confrontation with Indonesia, 1960–1966.*

98 Australian report.

99 Cf. pp. 595–601.

100 C.P. 64 (5), Minute by Butler, 6.1.64, 'Policy Towards Indonesia', CAB 129/11/6/5.

101 COS/58th Meeting/64, 29.9.64, DEFE 4/175; 'Measures to Control Indonesian Confrontation, Report by the Defence Planning Staff ', DP 70 (65) Final, 15.10.65, DEFE 25/170.

102 Easter, *Confrontation*; Alexander Nicholas Shaw, 'British counterinsurgency in Brunei and Sarawak, 1962–63: developing best practices in the shadow of Malaya', *Small wars & Insurgencies*, 27/4, 2016, pp. 702–25.

103 H. A. Majid, *Rebellion in Brunei: The 1962 Revolt, imperialism, confrontation and oil* (IB Tauris, London, 2007).

104 GSO (S) to D.D. GCHQ, 3.1.63, D/2201/30/1.

105 GSO (S) to D.D. GCHQ, 18.12.62, *passim*, D/2201/30/1.

106 GCO (S) to GCHQ, 14.12.14, 4780/14, *passim*, D 2201/30/1.

107 10.9.63, D 2201/30/2.

108 DSB to UKF 200, 26.12.62, D/2201/30/1.

109 GCHQ (London) to GCHQ, 10.12.62, DZ/B/32, /D/2201/30/1.

110 DSB to GCO (S), 26.12.62, D 2201/30/1.

111 DSB to GCHQ, 8.2.63, D/2201/30/1.

112 DSB to GCO (S), 19.2.63, D/2201/30/1.

113 29.11.63, D/2201/30/2.

114 GCO (S) to SLO (M), 2.9.66, D/2201/30/7.

115 DSD to GCHQ, 1.5.67, D/2304/5 pt II.

116 Ibid.

117 22.8.63, D/2201/30/1.

118 5.12.63, D/2201/30/2.

119 DSB to GCO (S), PR 300514Z/1/63, 30.1.63, D/2201/30/1.

120 GCHQ to MI8, and DSD (9), 22.11.63, D/2201/30/2.

121 Memorandum by Hooper, 'Borneo', 13.2.63, D/2201/30/1.

122 GCO (S) 2.4.65, 'Visit to Borneo by GCO, O.C. 7 Sigs Regt (Aust) and OC 121 Sig Sq, 29 March–1 April, Matters Arising', GCO (S) to SIN/901 PLUS, 29.4.65, D 2201/30/5.

123 Nicholl to Director, 11.2.63, D/2201/30/1.

124 *Contact*, No. 3, 3rd Quarter 1971, 'Singapore', pp. 14–15.

125 Australian report, June 1964.

126 Ibid.

127 DSD to GCHQ, 10.1.64, D/2201/30/2.

128 DSD to GCHQ, 3.7.64, D 2201/30/4.

129 DSD to GCHQ, 1.5.67, D/2304/5 pt II.

130 Australian report, June 1964.

131 DSD to UKC 200 and other recipients, 30.6.64, passim, D/2201/30/4.

132 C-in-C FE to MOD Sec, 9.7.64, D/2201/30/4.

133 8.1.65, 'Sigint Implications of the Current Indonesian Reinforcement of Kalimantan', D/2201/30/5.

134 'Record of a Meeting Held on 9th June to Discuss the Borneo Operation', D/2201/30/4.

135 LSIB (64) 2nd meeting, LSIB 1964.

136 GCO (S) to GCHQ, 1.2.65, D/2201/30/5.

137 15.11.63, 'Note for the File' by Hooper, 26.11.63, D/2201/3/2.

138 DSO (S) to GCHQ, 13.8.63, ZCZCRZA051, D/2201/30/4.

139 GCO (S) to GCHQ 9.3.65, GCO (S) 2.4.65, 'Visit to Borneo by GCO, O.C. 7 Sigs Regt (Aust)'.

140 GCO (S) to GCHQ, 24.5.65, D/2201/30/5.

141 GCO (S) to DSD,12.8.65, ZCZCHSA011, D/2201/30/5.

142 GCO (S) 2.4.65, 'Visit to Borneo by GCO, O.C. 7 Sigs Regt (Aust) and OC 121 Sig Sq, 29 March–1 April, Matters Arising', D/2201/30/5.

143 DSD to GCHQ, 1.5.67, D/2304/5pt II PRO 368.

144 David Easter, 'British Intelligence and Propaganda during the "Confrontation", 1963– 66', INS, 16.2.2001, pp. 83–102.

145 Australian report, March 1964.

146 Ibid., August 1964.

147 Ibid.

148 Ibid., September 1964.

149 Ibid.

150 Ibid., October 1964.

151 Ibid., September and December 1964.

152 DSD to GCHQ, 1.5.67, D/2304/5 pt II.

153 Australian report, October 1964.

154 Ibid., January 1965.

155 Ibid., March 1964.

156 Ibid., June 1964.

157 Ibid., September 1964.

158 Ibid.

159 Ibid.; DSD to GCHQ, 1.5.67, D/2304/5pt II PRO 368.

160 Van der Bijl, *Confrontation*, pp. 133–35.

161 COS/58th Meeting/64, 29.9.64, COS 61st Meeting/64, 15.10.64, DEFE 4/175.

162 JIC meeting, JIC (64) 49th Meeting, 1.10.64, CAB 159/42.

163 Australian report, June 1964.

164 Ibid., October and November 1964.

165 DSD to GCHQ, 8.1.65, D/2201/30/5.

166 8.1.65, 'Sigint Implications of the Current Indonesian Reinforcement of Kalimantan', D/2201/30/5.

167 Van der Bijl, *Confrontation*, p. 159.

168 GCO (S) to GCHQ 24.3.65, D/2201/30/5.

169 Ibid.

170 8.1.65, 'Sigint Implications of the Current Indonesian Reinforcement of Kalimantan', D/2201/30/5.

171 GCHQ to DSD, 9.3.65, GCO (S) to DSD, 10.3.65, D/2201/30/5.

172 Foreign Office to Djakarta Embassy, No. 1920, 16.10.65, DEFE 25/214.

173 DSO (S) to GCHQ/DSD, 2.6.66, D/2201/30/6.

174 Memorandum n.d., *c.* July 1966, 'The Bau Incursions – June 1966', D/2201/30/6.

175 GCO (S) to DSD, 13.9.66, JIC 66/72, 'Preliminary Draft', 'Intelligence Requirements Concerning East Malaysia and Brunei', 30.9.66, and 'Revised Draft', 8.10.66, D/2201/30/7.

176 DSO (S) to DSD, 19.2.66, D/2201/30/6.

177 Memorandum n.d., *c.* July 1966, 'The Bau Incursions'.

178 DSD to GCHQ, 1.5.67, D/2304/5 pt II PRO 368.

179 GCO (S) to DSD, 13.9.66, ZCZCRVA026, D/2201/30/7.

180 Van der Bijl, *Confrontation*, p. x.

181 Minutes by Grandy, 17.1.69, and Healey, 'Confrontation Operations', 20.1.69, AIR 8/2441.

182 Van der Bijl, *Confrontation*, p. x.

183 Robert J. Hanyok, *Spartans in Darkness, American SIGINT and the Vietnam War, 1945–1975* (CCH, 2002).

184 John Roosa, *Pretext for Mass Murder, The September 30th Movement and Suharto's Coup D'Etat in Indonesia* (University of Wisconsin Press, 2006), pp. 198–201, 208.

185 UKMIS New York to FCO, Telegram No. 909, 23.9.81, *passim*, PREM 19/643.

186 The best account of the war, using Argentine and British sources well, is Freedman, *Falklands*. Antony H. Cordesman, *The Lessons of Modern Wars, III, The Afghan and Falklands Confl icts* (Westview Press, 1991) and Norman Friedman, *Fighters over the Fleet, Naval Air Defence from Biplanes to the Cold War* (Seaforth, 2016), Chapter Twelve, are useful operational analyses of key issues. A useful English-language account of the Argentine navy is Mariano Sciaroni,

A Carrier at Risk: Argentinian Aircraft Carrier and Anti-Submarine Operations against Royal Navy's Attack Submarines during the Falklands/Malvinas War 1982 (Helion and Co., 2019).

187 COS (Misc) 105/742/1, 10.4.82, Navy Department, 'Operational and Support Planning – Operation Corporate', FCO 7/4472; Operation Corporate – Long Term Measures, 2.5.82, DEFE 25/466.

188 Friedman, *Fighters over the Fleet*.

189 GCHQ London to GCHQ, 29.4.82, D/2304/14/3.

190 'The Argentine Air Force', *Secret Air Intelligence Quarterly Review*, Summer 1970, pp. 24–25.

191 'An Examination of Argentine Air Effort during the Falklands Campaign'. Operational Research Branch, Strike Command, 9.83, DEFE 58/212.

192 COS 9/82, Operation Sutton, Directive to the Commander-in-Chief Fleet, 15.4.82, DEFE 24/2504.

193 Memorandum by Controller of the Navy, 27.4.82, 'Operation Corporate –HMS *Illustrious*', Evans to PSO/CDS, 'Operation Corporate– HMS Illustrious', 4.5.82, DEFE 24/2504.

194 Presentation to OD (SA) – 22 April 1982, DEFE 25/479.

195 'Naval Staff Assessment of the Balance of Fighting Capability between TGs 317.8/324.3 and the ARA', DEFE 25/564

196 Minute by Whitmore, 'Landing on the Falkland Islands', 14.5.82, PREM 19/647.

197 Presentation to OD (SA) – 22 April 1982, DEFE 25/479.

198 'Falklands: Record of Meeting Held on 29 April 1982', 29.4.82, D/2304/14/3.

199 'Falklands: Minutes of Meeting 26 April 1982', D/2304/14/3; GCHQ London to GCHQ 0202 1641728, 24.5.82, D/2304/14/5.

200 'Falklands: Record of Meeting Held on 20 April 1982', 21.4.82, D/2304/14/2; Flower, PUSD to Johnson, 20.5.82, D/2304/14– 4.

201 GCHQ London to GCHQ 4.5.82, D/2304/14/3; 'Falklands: Notes of Meeting held on 14 May 1982', 17.5.82, D/2304/14/4; 'Falklands: Notes of Meeting held on 21 May 1982', 24.5.82, D/2304/14/5.

202 *Contact*, No. 39, 3rd Issue, 1982, 'The Falklands Crisis 1982', p. 20.

203 'Record of a Meeting Held at 10 Downing Street on Tuesday 13 April 1982 At 0915 Hours PREM 19/617.

204 'Record of Meeting Held in 12 Downing Street on 12 April 1982, at 930', PREM 19/617.

205 Duff to Carrick, 16.4.82, D/2403-14-3.

206 'Telephone call between the Prime Minister and Sir Antony Parsons on Saturday 8 May 1982', PREM 19/626.

207 Armstrong to Thatcher, 11.5.82, AO8378, 'The Falkland Islands', PREM 19/647; COSC, Confidential Annexe to COS/24th Meeting/82 held on Monday 19 April 1982 at 9.30 a.m.', Confidential Annexe to COS/25th Meeting/82 held

on Tuesday 20 April 1982 at 10.00 a.m.', Confidential Annexe to COS/34th Meeting/82 held on Wednesday 28 April 1982 at 2.00 p.m.', FCO 7/4472.

208 Antony Duff to Johnson/Palliser, 16.4.82, D/2304/14/2. Eighty words of detail about GCHQ material are redacted in this letter.

209 22.6.82, D/2304/14/6; 'The Falklands: Operation Royce', *Contact*, No. 39, 3rd Issue, 1982, pp. 26– 27.

210 Memorandum by DCDS (1), 'Operation Corporate – The Intelligence Lessons', 21.12.82, P/8210/7/1 Pt. 1.

211 Memorandum, 'Falkland Islands: The Nicholl Report', 13.5.82, D/2304/14/4.

212 Nick Barker, *Beyond Endurance: An Epic of Whitehall and the South Atlantic Confl ict* (Leo Cooper, 2002), pp.30–31

213 GCHQ LDN to GCHQ, 0961700, 6.4.84, D/2304/14– 1.

214 GCHQ to Northwood, 9.6.82, D/2304/14/5; *History*; *Contact*, No. 39, 3rd Issue 1982, 'The Falklands Crisis 1982', pp. 21–22.

215 'Falkland Island Review Committee, Note of an oral evidence session', 25.10.82, CAB 292/47.

216 Michael S. Goodman, 'The Dog that Didn't Bark: The Joint Intelligence Committee and Warning of Aggression', *Cold War History*, 7/4, pp. 529– 51.

217 During the war, MOD said that DIS had assigned one officer to Latin America before the crisis, but after the war listed this number as two. MOD to GCHQ, 9.5.82, D/2403/14/3.

218 Y-3/AA/73087-82, 1902 25.1.82.

219 'Falkland Island Review Committee, Note of an oral evidence session', 15.10.82, CAB 292/47.

220 Carrington to Thatcher, 24.3.82, PREM 19/656; sentence redacted under Section 3 (4).

221 'Defence Implications of Argentine Action Against the Falkland Islands by MOD)', n.d., *c.* 26.3.82, PREM 19/656.

222 Minute by Foreign Secretary and Minister of State (Armed Forces), undated but 30 March by internal evidence, PREM 19/656.

223 GCHQ incoming telegram No. 36, 30.3.82, GCHQ outgoing telegram 31.3.82, D/2304/1A.

224 3/AA/73089-82, 30.3.82, D/2304/14/1.

225 Interview with Omand, 21 June 2018; *Sigint History*, pp.2–8; 'Illegal Landings on South Georgia: Chronology of Events', minute by Weyland, 21.4.2012, PREM 19/614.

226 'Falkland Island Review Committee, Note of an oral evidence session', 25.10.82, CAB 292/47.

227 Ibid.

228 D/Ops/Staff, 7.10,42, Operation Corporate – First Impressions', D. W. Brown, ACDS (ops), DEFE 25/477; Interview with Sir Michael Beacham – 1 Nov 83', AIR 20/13044.

229 *Sigint History*, p. 2–3.

230 *Sigint History*, p. 33.

231 'Falkland Crisis, Meeting held on 14 April 1982', 16.4.82, D/2304/14/2.

232 Memorandum, 'Sigint Alert Margay: Requirements of 22 SAS, Hereford', 5.5.82, D/2403/14/3; ibid., 17.5.82, D/2403/14-4; MOD to GCHQ, 6.6.82, 157130, D/2304/14/5.

233 GCHQ London to GCHQ, 4.4.82, #0002 0942032, D/2304/1/A.

234 Minute by Z, 3/4/82, 'Priority of Requirement for Intelligence on Argentine and the Falklands', D/2304/1/A.

235 GCHQ LDN to GCHQ, #0306, 0961700, 6.4.84, D/2304/1A.

236 GCHQ London to GCHQ, 29.4.82, D/2403/14/3; *Contact*, No. 39, 3rd Issue 1982, 'The Falklands Crisis 1982', pp. 20–21.

237 Ibid.

238 Fieldhouse to Tovey, 27.4.82, D/2403/14/3; Office of the Commander Task Force 317, 22. 10. 82, 'Report by CTF 317 on Intelligence Aspects of Operation Corporate', P/8210/7/1 Pt. 1.

239 Memorandum 1.6.82, 'Alert Margay –Financial Consequentials', D/2304-14-5.

240 Memorandum, 5.4.82, 'Falkland Islands – Cover and Reporting', D/2304/14 1.

241 Sigint *History*, p. 63.

242 'The Falklands Crisis: Review of Sigint Performance and Lessons'. P/8210/7/1 Pt. 1.

243 Memorandum by K, 'Falklands Crisis Review', 20.7.82, P/8210/7/1 Pt. 1.

244 Ibid.

245 Memorandum 'Alert Margay: Comms Status 19 April', 19.4.82, D/2403/14/2; memorandum, 26.4.82, 'Alert Margay: Communications Minimize', D/2403/14/3; cf. *Contact*, No. 37, 1st Issue 1982, 'The Duty Signal Officer GCHQ', pp.5–8.

246 *Sigint History*, p. 11.

247 *Sigint History*, p. 18.

248 Minute 'The Elint Effort on Alert Margay', 20.5.82, D/2403/14/4.

249 Interview with Herman, 22 June 2018.

250 Ibid.

251 *Sigint History*, p. 22.

252 'Falklands: Minutes of Meeting 26 April 1982', D/2304/14/3.

253 CTG 317.9 to MODUK/Navy, 26.4.82, D/2403/14/3; History, p. 24.

254 Memorandum by Fear, 'Alert Margay: Fort Grange Sigint Fit', 12.5.82, D/2304/14/4.

255 *Contact*, No. 39, 3rd Issue 1982, 'Operation Corporate/Sigint Alert Margay', p. 23.

256 Memorandum by, 'Falklands Contingency Plans', 8.6.82, D/2304/14/5.

257 C-in-C Fleet to GCHQ, #0037, 0981715, XXX, D/2304/14/1.

258 Memorandum by K, 'Crisis Handling at Northwood and GCHQ', 15.4.82, D/2304/14/2; Memorandum 14.5.82, 'New Moon: Alert Margay', D/2304/14/4.

259 *Sigint History*, p. 19, 43–44.

260 *Sigint History*, p. 8.

261 Memorandum by 7.4.82, 'Sigint Support to the Task Force', D/2403/14/1; *History* pp. 12, 27.

262 Hansard, House of Commons, 3.4.82, Volume 21, column 648.

263 'Falkland Island Review Committee, Note of an oral evidence session', 18. 10. 82, CAB 292/36.

264 Memorandum by Cooper, 'The Falklands: Sunday Times Insight Articles, 23 May 1982', D/2304/14/5.

265 BDS Washington to FCO, 5.5.82, D/2403/14/3.

266 Memorandum by Armstrong, 22.4.82, PREM 19/621.

267 A1 to PSO/CDS, 24.4.82, DEFE 25/492.

268 Interview with Sir David Omand, 21 June 2018.

269 S. Webb, 6.5.82, 'Note for the Record, Third Meeting with Editors on Falklands Emergency', SW/82/666, 9/31/F, PREM 19/626.

270 GCHQ to SUKLO, 1845 1381483, 10.4.82, D/2304/14/1; SUKLO to GCHQ, 0012 1071800, 1.4.82, D/2304/14/2.

271 Ibid.

272 Memorandum by K, 'Falklands Crisis Review', 23.8.82, P/8210/7/1 Pt. 1.

273 'Falklands: Notes of Meeting Held on 17 May 1982', 18.5.82, D/2304/14/4.

274 DCDS (I) to Tovey, 5.8.82, P/8210/7/1 Pt. 1.

275 Office of the Commander Task Force 317, 22. 10. 82, 'Report by CTF 317 on Intelligence Aspects of Operation Corporate', P/8210/7/1 Pt. 1.

276 Minute 'The Elint Effort on Alert Margay', 20.5.82, D-2403_ 14_ 4.

277 COSC, Confidential Annexe to COS/9thMeeting/82 held on Thursday 8 April 1982 at 930 a.m.', FCO 7/4472.

278 Presentation to OD (SA) – 22 April 1982, DEFE 25/479.

279 3/AA/97174-82, 15.4.82, 3/AA/97423-82, 23.4.83, 3/AA/97514-82, 26.4.82, H5-37.

280 'Falklands: Notes of Meeting on 22 April 1982', 23.4.82, D/2304/14/2.

281 (3/AA/97246-82, 18.4.82, 3/AA/97543-82, 26.4.82, 97000.

282 3/AA/97487-82, 24.4.82, 97000.

283 3/AA/090057-82, 30.4.82, H5-37; *Sigint History*, pp. 99–108, reproduces all of the relevant messages.

284 Presentation to OD (SA) – 22 April 1982, DEFE 25/479.

285 'Operation Corporate – Threat from Argentine Carrier', COS (Misc).
163/742/1, 26.4.82, DEFE 25/465; COSC, Confidential Annexe to COS/32nd
Meeting/82 held on Tuesday 27 April 1982 at 10.30 a.m.', COSC, Confidential
Annexe to COS/33rd Meeting/82 held on Wednesday 28 April 1982 at 10.45
a.m.' FCO 7/4472.

286 Pym to Thatcher, 1.5.82, DEFE 25/466.

287 Interview with Omand, 21 June 2018.

288 Telegram No. 1574, British Embassy Washington to FCO, 3.5.82, PREM 19/624.

289 GCHQ London to GCHQ, 13.5.82, D/2304/14/4.

290 CDS Brief as of 0600 11 May 1982, DEFE 25/467.

291 Office of the Commander Task Force 317, 22.10.82, 'Report by CTF 317 on
Intelligence Aspects of Operation Corporate', P/8210/7/1 Pt. 1.

292 *Sigint History*, p. 62.

293 GCU Northwood to GCHQ, No. 0005 1340245, 14.5.82, No. 0013 1471432,
27.5.82, D/2304/14 Tarpon Annex 1.

294 'Falklands: Notes of Meeting Held on 25 May 1982', 26.5.82, D/2304/14/5.

295 CDS to S of S, 21.4.82, DEFE 69/1098.

296 Presentation to OD (SA) – 22 April 1982, DEFE 25/479.

297 (3/AA/098229-82, 9.5.82, H5-37.

298 3/AA/899471-82, 13.6.82,

299 3/AA/298388-82, H5-37.

300 Memorandum by Sneyd, 'SPG 007-Deception Proposals-Liaison with
CinCFleet HQ Northwood', 4.82, DEFE 24/2504.

301 GCU Northwood to GCHQ No. 0017 1360655, 16.5.82, D/2304/14 Tarpon
Annex 2.

302 British Embassy Santiago to FCO, telegram No. 94, 12.4.82, PREM 19/616.

303 GCU Northwood to GCHQ, No. 0031 1402319, D/2304/14 Tarpon Annex 1.

304 GCHQ to DIRNSA, No. 3244, 4.5.82, D/2304/14/3.

305 DCDS (I) to Tovey, 5.8.82, P/8210/7/1 Pt. 1.

306 *Sigint History*, pp. 108–10.

307 GCHQ to TF 317, 3255 2871728,14.10.82, P/8210/7/1 Pt. 1.

308 *Sigint History*, pp. 14, 48.

309 CTG 317.0 to CTF 317, 25.5.82, DEFE 68/630.

310 CTF 317 TO CTG 310.0, 27.5.82, DEfE 68/630.

311 GCU Northwood to GCHQ, 1430440, 23.5.82, D/2304/14 Tarpon Annex 1.

312 'Falklands: Notes of Meeting on 1 June 1982', 2.6.82, D/2403/14/5.

313 3/AA/099127-82, 3.6.82,.

314 3/AA/098965-82, 30.5.82, 2/AA/090090-82, 4.6.82,

315 GCHQ London to GCHQ 0202 1641728, 24.5.82, Flower to Duff, 27.5.82,
D/2304/14/5.

316 GCHQ to SUKLO, 3271 1051742, 15.4.82, D/2403/14/2.

317 For a description of the system cf. MOD to GCHQ 1116 1291516, 9.5.82, D/2403/14/3.

318 SCDS (A) 1 to PS/CDS, 11.4.82, 'Operation Corporate – CDS and the New MOD Organisation', DEFE 25/461.

319 JIC meeting 27.4.82, JIC (82) 20, CAB 185/33.

320 Interview with senior official.

321 DCDS (I) to Tovey, 5.8.82, P/8210/7/1 Pt. 1.

322 Memorandum by Cumming, 18.5.82, 'Falklands Crisis: Letter of Appreciation from COS UKLF', D/2304/14-4.

323 Group Captain Edwards to Gp Capt Ops, 18.8.82, DEFE 58/274.

324 'The Falklands Crisis: Review of Sigint Performance and Lessons', P/8210/7/1 Pt. 1.

325 'The Falklands Conflict: Sigint Post-Mortem (First R Division Contribution)', 12.7.82, P/8210/7/1 Pt. 1.

326 UKH 292L to GCHQ,, 28.5.82, D/2304/14/5.

327 CTF 317 to CTG 317.8, 24.5.82, DEFE 68/630.

328 CTF 317 to CTG 317.1, 24.5.82, DEFE 68/630.

329 CTF 317 to CTU 317.1.1, 12.5.82, DEFE 68/630.

330 CTG 317.1 to CTU 317, 25.5.82, DEFE 68/630.

331 CTG 317 to CTU 317.1.1., 25.5.82, DEFE 68.630.

332 CTF 317 to CTG 317.1, 26.5.82, DEFE 68/630.

333 CTG 317.1 to CTF 317. 30.5.82, DEFE 68/630.

334 CTG 317.1 to CTF 317, 31.5.82, DEFE 68/630.

335 *Sigint History*, pp. 78–79; D. J. Thorp, *The Silent Listener: British Electronic Surveillance Falklands 1982* (Spellmount, Stroud, 2011), pp. 115–18.

336 Aldrich, 'GCHQ', pp. 407–16.

337 2/AA/090106-82, 13.6. 82, 2/AA/190108-82, 14.06.82, H5-34.

338 GCHQ LDN to GCHQ, 6.4.82, D/2304/1A.

339 3/AA/099242-82, 7.6.82,.

340 Group Captain Clerk to Air Cdre Ops, 13.7.82, DEFE 58/274.

341 *Sigint History*, pp. 47–48.

342 'Falklands: Record of Meeting Held on 19 April 1982', 19.4.82, D/2304/14/2.

343 GCHQ to SUKLO, 17.4.82, D/2304/1/2.

344 GCHQ to MOD, No. 2304/14, 17.4.82, D/2304/14/2.

345 3/AA/97367-82, 22.4.82, H5-37.

346 'Falklands: Notes of Meeting 26 April 1982', 27.4.82, D/2304/14/3, *Sigint History*, pp. 76–8.

347 Ibid.

348 GCHQ to C-in-C Fleet, 29.4.82, D/2304/14/3.

CHAPTER 14

1 Cf. pp. 275–8.

2 Ferris, *Intelligence and Strategy*, pp. 165–80.

3 AVIA 65/977 contains material on the development of Typex Mercury and 5 U.C.O.; cf. Ferris, 'British Enigma', for that of Typex and Rockex II.

4 Colonel H. C. B. Rogers, *The History of the Communications-Electronics Security Department and its Predecessors, c.* 1970, pp. 93–120.

5 Ibid., pp. 259, 267–8.

6 'Report of the Working Party on The Future of the Communications-Electronic Security Department', 13.5.69, CAB 163/125.

7 Allinson to Burroughs, 9.5.69, including 'Report of the CESD Working Party, Summary and Conclusions', CAB 163/125.

8 Rogers, *History of the Communications-Electronics Security Department*, p. 344.

9 Ibid., pp. 121–37, 321–34,

10 J. V. Boone and R. R. Peterson, *The Start of the Digital Revolution: SIGSALY Secure Digital Voice Communications in World War Two* (CCH, Fort Meade, MD, 2000).

11 Rogers, *History of the Communications-Electronics Security Department*, pp.471–73.

12 Bill Cunningham, 'From Telegrams … to eGrams, A Potted History of FCO Communications', FCO, 16.8.2004, pp. 20–21.

13 Ibid., pp. 16–20.

14 Rogers, *History of the Communications-Electronics Security Department*, pp. 335–75.

15 Ibid., p. 534.

16 Ibid. pp. 165–84, 451–69.

17 M. Savage, 'Houseman Part I: BRENT, Autumn 1988 to Autumn 1995', CESG Case Studies No. 3, November 1997; Peter Osborn, 'Pippa, Project Case History No. 4, n.d.

18 John Tiltman, 'Winterbotham's "The Ultra Secret", A Personal Comment', *Cryptologia*, December 1975, pp. 1–5, https://www.nsa.gov/Portals/70/documents/news-features/declassified-documents/cryptologs/cryptolog_15.pdf; Malcolm Kennedy Diary, 10.1.46.

19 Hansard, Commons, Fifth Series, Vol. CLXXIV, col. 674, 15.12.24.

20 Report on Postal Censorship, 1914–1919, DEFE 1/131, p. 77.

21 Basil Thomson, Director of Intelligence, No. E.A.S., 5.7.19, to Secretary for War, Churchill, WO 32/4899

22 Section Four, Official Secrets Act, 1920.

23 Blackwell (Home Office) to Grant (Eastern Telegraph Company), 11.5.26, 493263, Telegraph Museum, Porthcurno,

24 *British Sigint*, Four, pp. 88.

25 Nicholas Wilkinson, *Secrecy and the Media: the Official History of the United Kingdom's D-Notice System* (Routledge, 2009); Pauline Sadler, *National Security and the D-Notice System* (Routledge, 2018). Sadler correctly detected GCHQ's involvement in handling this issue.

26 *British Sigint*, Four, pp. 89–90.

27 Cmnd. 283, October 1957, 'Report of the Committee of Privy Counsellors appointed to inquire into the interception of communications', paras. 64–70, 141–2/

28 Cmnd, 3309, 19.5.67.

29 *British Sigint*, Four, pp. 87–99.

30 Section 11, Post Office Bill, July 1969.

31 Ferris, 'Whitehall's Black Chamber'.

32 DNI to Managing Director, Marconi Company, 17.6.20, *passim*, HIS 185, Marconi Archive, Bodleian Library.

33 Round to James, 8.5.18, Round to Buxton, 30.10.19, ADM 137/4692.

34 LSIB 57/57, 6.5.57, 'GCHQ Cover Story', LSIB 1957.

35 *British Sigint*, Four, p. 495.

36 Goodall, GCHQ, to Morrison, Cabinet Office, 6.6.74, 'Co-Ordinator's Working Party on World War II Intelligence Matters', CAB 190/74.

37 Duncan Campbell, 'My Life Unmasking British Eavesdroppers', 3.8.15, *The Intercept*, https://theintercept.com/2015/08/03/life-unmasking-british-eavesdroppers/

38 Aldrich, 'GCHQ', pp. 367–86; Report of the Security Commission, May 1983, CMND, 8876.

CHAPTER 15

1 Memorandum by Clark, 22.6.89, 'Royal Air Force and United States Radio Proving Flights', AHB 16-4-3.

2 LSIB/3/89, 19.4.89, 'The State of Sigint 1989', LSIB 1989.

3 LSIB/2/89, 18.4.89, 'Sigint Support to Military Operations 1989', LSIB 1989; LSIB/4/1991, 27.3.91, 'Future of the Services Component of the National Sigint Organisation', LSIB 1991.

4 Roger Hurn, 24.3.95, '"Accelerating Change", Special Study of GCHQ, Part 1: Main Report'.

5 'Review of Defence Requirements and Resources, Conducted by Sir Michael Quinlan 1994, GCHQ Precis'.

6 Roger Hurn, 24.3.95, '"Accelerating Change", Special Study of GCHQ, Part 1: Main Report'.

7 HC 65, 15.6.04, House of Commons Committee of Public Accounts, 'Government Communications Headquarters (GCHQ): New Accommodation Programme', Twenty-third Report of Session 2003–04, pp. 453, 469–70, *passim*.

8 Ibid.

9 Interview with Sir John Adye, 20.6.2018.

10 LSIB/6/91, 11.6.91, 'Minutes of Meeting Held on 11 April 1991', LSIB 1991.

11 Ibid.

12 John Perry Barlow, 'The Declaration of Independence of the Internet'.

13 Intelligence and Security Committee of Parliament, 'Uncorrected Transcript of Evidence', 7.11.13, http://isc.independent.gov.uk/publicevidence/7november2013

14 David Anderson, Q.C., 'Report of the Bulk Powers Review', CM 9326, 8.2016, pp. 152–56, 159–62, https://terrorismlegislationreviewer. independent.gov.uk/wp-content/uploads/2016/08/Bulk-Powers-Reviewfinal-report.pdf

15 Ibid.

16 Draft memoirs of Admiral Hall, Chapter on 1914–15, Hall 3/2, Reginald Hall Papers, Churchill College, Cambridge.

17 Andrew, *Defence of the Realm*, p. 147.

18 Viceroy to Secretary of State, telegram No. 17-U, 30.9.36, L/PO/10/31 i.

19 Minute by unknown Treasury official, 23.6.25, T 161/252, S. 27259.

20 Blackwell (Home Office) to Grant (Eastern Telegraph Company), 11.5.26, 493263, Telegraph Museum, Porthcurno.

21 'UK Debate Grows over "Orwellian" NSA and GCHQ Surveillance', *Guardian*, 9.10.2013.

22 Ibid.

23 David Anderson Q.C., 'A Question of Trust, Report of the Investigatory Powers Review', June 2015, pp. 4, 8, 268, https://www.daqc.co.uk/2015/06/11/a-question-of-trust-report-of-the-investigatory-powers-review/; David Anderson, 'A Democratic Licence to Operate, Report of the Independent Surveillance Review', to RUSI, July 2015, https://rusi.org/sites/default/files/20150714_whr_2-15_a_democratic_licence_to_operate.pdf

24 Ewan MacAskill, '"Extreme Surveillance" Becomes UK Law with Barely a Whimper', *Guardian*, 19.11.2016; 'Liberty's Briefing on the Investigatory Powers Act for Report Stage in the House of Commons', August 2016, https://www.libertyhumanrights.org.uk/sites/default/files/campaigns/resources/Liberty

25 'A Democratic License to Operate: Report of the Independent Surveillance Review', RUSI, July 2015, https://rusi.org/sites/default/files/20150714_whr_2-15_a_democratic_licence_to_operate.pdf

26 Intelligence and Security Committee of Parliament, 'Uncorrected Transcript of Evidence', 7.11.13, http://isc.independent.gov.uk/publicevidence/7november2013.

27 Cabinet Office, 'Cyber Security Strategy of the United Kingdom, safety, security and resilience in cyber space', CM 7642, 25.6.2009.

28 Robert Hannigan, 'Organising a Government for Cyber, The Creation of the UK's National Cyber Security Centre', RUSI Occasional Paper, February 2019, pp. 7–10.

29 'Securing Britain in an Age of Uncertainty, The Strategic Defence and Security Review, CM 7948, 10.2010, pp.47–49.

30 Cabinet Office, 'The UK Cyber Security Strategy, Protecting and promoting the UK in a digital world', November 2011.

31 Hannigan, 'Organising a Government', p. 14.

32 Ibid.

33 Hannigan, 'Organising a Government', pp. 10, 39.

34 Ibid., p. 14.

35 'Dr. Ian Levy', Enigma 2017, https://www.usenix. o r g /c o n f e r e n c e /e n i g m a 2 0 1 7 /s p e a k e r -o r -o r g a n i z e r /dr-ian-levy-national-cyber-security-centre-uk

36 'A new Approach for cyber security in the UK', 13.9.2016, https://www.ncsc.gov. uk/news/new-approach-cyber-security-uk

37 Hannigan, 'Organising a Government', pp. 40–42.

38 Ibid.

39 Iain Thompson, 3.2.17, 'GCHQ cyber-chief slams security outfits peddling 'medieval witchcraft', The Register, https://www.theregister.co.uk/2017/02/03/ security_ threat_ solutions/

40 Ian Levy, blog post, 1.11.16, 'Active Cyber Defence – tackling cyber attacks on the UK, https://www.ncsc.gov.uk/blog-post/active-cyber-defence-tackling-cyber-attacks-uk

41 NCSC Annual Report 2018, p. 10.

42 Ibid.

43 NCSC Annual Report 2018, pp.42–46; NCSC, 'Education and Skills, 11 to 19 year olds (CyberFirst)', https://www.ncsc.gov.uk/section/educationskills/11-19-year-olds; 'GCHQ CyberFirst', https://www.gchq-careers. co.uk/early-careers/ cyberfi rst.html.

CONCLUSION

1 'Director GCHQ's Speech at CYBERUK 2019', 2.5.2019, https://www.gchq.gov. uk/speech/director-s-speech-at-cyberuk-2019

2 HM Treasury, 'Policy Paper 2018', Table 1.6, 'Departmental Resource Budgets', 29.10.18.

Acknowledgements

I have incurred many debts in writing this book. I owe much to friends now passed – Mike Dockrill, Peter Freeman, Michael Handel, Keith Neilson, Brad Smith and Zara Steiner – and also to those still among us: Richard Aldrich, Chris Andrew, David Alvarez, Jim Beach, Liz Bruton, Ralph Erskine, Markus Faulkner, David French, Michael Herman, Peter Jackson, David Kahn, Andrew Lambert, Richard Poppelwell and Dave Sherman. I owe particular thanks to several friends and scholars who helped me to understand issues and to find evidence, particularly Seb Cox, Ed Kaplan, Dan Lomas and Steve Wagner. I have gained much from members of the Cryptologic History Center at the National Security Agency, especially David Hatch, Betsy Smoot and Bill Williams. I owe much to my friends in the Department of History, and the Centre for Military, Security and Strategic Studies at the University of Calgary. I received help from many people whom I do not know at GCHQ, which is characteristic of how that institution works. At GCHQ, however, Peter Freeman, Tony Comer and James Bruce provided advice, debate and help, as did many others, including Stu R., Annette E. and Tim N.. James Bruce, Annette E. and Stu R. were invaluable in finding and selecting the images which are fundamental to this work. Other members of GCHQ staff contributed to the production of this book: Daniel, Abby, James, Doug, Greg, Neil, Emma, Jenny, Phillip, Steve, and staff in the UKKPA and the NCSC, as did members of Five Eyes Sigint Agencies and UK government departments. I am grateful to my literary agent, Bill Hamilton, and to members of Bloomsbury's editorial team, especially Michael Fishwick, Kate Johnson and Sarah Ruddick, for seeing this work through to completion, which sometimes did not seem easy to envisage. Nuffield College, Oxford, kindly gave me a place to work for several months while in Britain. Without the love and support of Elizabeth, Morgan, Owen and Edmond, this work could not have been written. I dedicate it to them.

Index

A Note on the Author

John Ferris is a Fellow of the Royal Society of Canada. He is Professor of History at the University of Calgary, an Honorary Professor at the Department of International Politics of the University of Aberystwyth, and the Department of Law and Politics, Brunel University, and is an Associate Member of Nuffield College, Oxford. He has written or edited eight books and over 100 articles or chapters on diplomatic, intelligence, imperial, international, military and strategic history and strategic studies. He lives in Calgary.

A Note on the Type

The text of this book is set in Adobe Garamond. It is one of several versions of Garamond based on the designs of Claude Garamond. It is thought that Garamond based his font on Bembo, cut in 1495 by Francesco Griffo in collaboration with the Italian printer Aldus Manutius. Garamond types were first used in books printed in Paris around 1532. Many of the present-day versions of this type are based on the Typi Academiae of Jean Jannon cut in Sedan in 1615.

Claude Garamond was born in Paris in 1480. He learned how to cut type from his father and by the age of fifteen he was able to fashion steel punches the size of a pica with great precision. At the age of sixty he was commissioned by King Francis I to design a Greek alphabet, and for this he was given the honourable title of royal type founder. He died in 1561.

I did a lot of writing, then. I did a piece I called "Soul Tattoos" for a place called Theater X in Milwaukee, a small place that did experimental performance art. It got some reviews, too. One called it somewhat self-indulgent, but mostly they got what I wanted to say. I used it to attack the issue of how the media treats a female defendant. I got a lot off my chest, too; I was so sick of the myths that surrounded me and my case, the whole "killer bunny" thing.

And there were strange things happening! Christine Schultz's family sued me for three million dollars, did you know that? And Don Eisenberg's firm sued me for thirty-eight thousand dollars in a fee dispute. Imagine! So I declared bankruptcy. I was earning seventeen cents an hour in prison. Everyone wanted something from me.

My friends and family kept me going. Some of them visited me for years. Some still do. But others, inevitably, moved on. You can't fight psychic distancing with long-distance calls, and sometimes I struggled with myself not to blame them. They have lives to live, years pass, they get older, they take on other responsibilities.

Over the years, people die. Because I was in prison, I would find out from a letter or a phone call, but I couldn't be there to share in the grieving process, so to me these people were still alive. I was afraid to scratch them from my address book; it felt like killing so much memory, like a willful destruction of a life lived so long before.

I made new friends along the way. I made a lot of good friends in prison. But it's hard to know whether we were close only because we shared so much so fast; on the outside, I don't think prison friendships would last.

Misery loves company, I suppose.

If there's one thing I'm now sure of, it's that the way the system is set up, you're insane if you don't plea bargain. If I'd done so, I'd be out by now. So what if you didn't do it, if you're not guilty? Pleading innocent only keeps you in jail. Those who are guilty get out more quickly; because they know they're guilty, they have no hesitation in plea bargaining. They therefore draw ten years or less and they're out. There you have it—the most guilty people are the ones doing less time.

Pleading not guilty is an affirmation of belief in the system, believing that justice will prevail. No one who has been where I have been believes any such thing. Raw injustice happened to me. It has happened to so many of my friends.

I ask myself now, would this question of guilt or innocence matter any more after twenty, thirty, forty years in jail? Would anyone care?

My answer is, No.

I counsel anyone going into the system—plea bargain for your own sanity.

So what if you didn't do it? No one will believe what you say anyway. Freedom is the bottom line. After a third of your life in prison, you'd do anything to be free. And if you have to compromise all your principles, well, tough.

But me? I had a naive, ridiculous faith in the system.

21

THE BEMBENEK CIRCUS

Ambulance-chasers, sensation-seekers, crazies, the klieg-light vampires of the television wasteland, the riffraff and the lowlife, the ink-stained wretches of what passes these days for the fourth estate, the obsessives and the dogged chasers after elusive Truth—my case seems to attract them all. Why is it that I'm a magnet for all this swirling passion, all these gaudy characters? Why do people either seem to love me or hate me? I don't know. I'm isolated in here, dependent on what people tell me. I just want to be able to go home, but I'm at the center of the Bembenek Circus ...

■   ■   ■

Under Wisconsin law, you have two shots at winning a new trial: either present new evidence or show conflict of interest. For a prisoner, neither is easy. You are dependent on what your lawyers tell you. You have no access to documents. (It wasn't until I was in Canada and my lawyers there gave me a copy of the extradition warrant issued by Wisconsin that I finally saw some of the original police reports in my case.) Lawyers are not crazy about taking advice from a client anyway. Even less so when the jail is hours away by car and the client has to rely entirely on memory. They don't try to make things any easier, do they?

In my case, there was some new evidence. Or, put another way, the original case was starting to unravel.

For example, the medical examiner, Dr. Elaine Samuels, came forward in 1983 to dispute the hair and fiber evidence. She denied absolutely that she'd

279

ever recovered any blond hairs from the body. Because witnesses were sequestered, she hadn't known during the trial that those blond hairs in the police evidence had been attributed to her. She'd read about it only after the conviction. Samuels gave us an affidavit that she had found only hair consistent with the victim, and no "color-processed" (dyed) blond hair at all.

Then, in 1984, Judy Zess recanted her testimony; inconsistencies were pointed out in Fred's alibi; Fred was investigated for three or four instances of perjury; and there were some other things ...

Eisenberg thought the best strategy would be to go directly to the DA, E. Michael McCann, show him the new evidence and ask him to reopen the case. Eisenberg thought there was more than enough to persuade any fair-minded person at least to take another look. The timing wasn't great. McCann was running for a congressional seat at the time and didn't want to do anything controversial. Ironically, nine months went by, McCann lost the election anyway and then announced he wouldn't reopen the case.

After that, Eisenberg decided to file a motion for a new trial. The motion material seemed to be just thrown together. You should have seen this motion! It was a mess. A law student could have done better. He just threw it together and filed this half-baked, stupid thing. And then, a hearing on this motion before Judge Gram was scheduled. Three days prior to the hearing, Don's law license was suspended indefinitely for conflict of interest.

Wonderful timing. A blessing in disguise, I suppose.

I had to scramble to get someone else to represent me and to attempt to withdraw the motion. I was in a complete panic. There were still no phones in the prison at the time; I couldn't persuade the prison staff I needed special dispensation. It was awful. The only thing that saved me was that I was at the time looking into a divorce from Fred who was in Florida, and my divorce lawyer paid me a visit. I told him I urgently needed him to go to court to withdraw my motion for a new trial. He did that for me.

For a new lawyer I hired Thomas Halloran, a Milwaukee attorney.

It takes a new lawyer time to get acquainted with a case, particularly a case as complex as mine. Halloran, however, seemed to me to be a very slow reader. Six months went by. No action. He kept saying he was going to file a new motion, kept saying it, kept saying it ... and more months went by. His marriage broke up, he lost his partners, everything went wrong, every excuse was put forward. Two years later he finally filed the motion, but only because my parents pushed and pushed—this after they'd paid him seventeen thousand dollars.

Two years went by. Two *years*. Nine years and four different lawyers. People wonder how nine years can go by in prison without action! This is how.

Meanwhile, Eisenberg sued me for more money. They tried to garnishee my wages. Good luck, at seventeen cents an hour. He finally ended up in Florida. It must be getting crowded down there.

Then the Joseph Hecht scenario started.

I learned about Hecht from a friend of mine in Madison, a girl I'd gone to grade school with. She sent me some news reports of Hecht's case. She wrote: "This case sounds identical to yours, Laurie. Hecht was a hit man, he fits the description that Sean and Shannon gave, the victim was a cop's ex-wife, the motive was a matter of alimony.... He got into the house, there was no sign of forced entry, he shot the victim in front of her children. He even used the same caliber gun. It was the same MO all around. Maybe you should check into this?"

It did seem almost spooky.

I knew it was a long shot, but it was worth a try. I mean, I was in prison all these years knowing that, since I hadn't killed Christine Schultz, someone else had. I was waiting, hoping, that someone would come forward either to say, Yes I did it, or to say they knew who did it. I was always hoping something would break.

Enter Joe Hecht.

But how to investigate? I could hardly pop up to the men's prison to chat with Hecht. Halloran wasn't at that time up to speed on my case, and Eisenberg was gone. So my friend Bill Roddick, who had helped me so much over the years (he'd written two books on my case, *The Thirteenth Juror* and *After the Verdict*), said he'd see what he could do.

However, Hecht refused to see him, as I'd suspected he would. I'd been in prison long enough to know you don't just talk to anyone who comes by.

At that time, Halloran came up with the bright idea that I should take a polygraph test. Great, I thought. Why now? What will it help? People don't understand that those things cost thousands of dollars and are inadmissible as evidence in court to boot. Why would I want to take one? I had already passed a voice stress analysis that Don had required.

But a prisoner is always suspect. If you refuse, it looks as if you had something to hide. You just can't say no, so I did the damn thing, and passed, of course.

The one thing Halloran did do for me was to dispatch Joseph Broderick, his investigator, to talk to Hecht. And Hecht talked. I guess he was more willing to talk to a lawyer.

Hecht confessed. He said he'd killed Christine Schultz. He told Broderick. Then he told Halloran. Then he told another attorney they brought in for corroboration. All three times his story was the same.

Was I excited? Of course I was. But I'd been disappointed often enough to preserve some cynicism. After all, I wasn't there. I had to believe what Halloran told me. And Hecht did have one reason for confessing to the case falsely—according to Halloran, he said he was wanted in Texas for another murder, and that state had the death penalty. It could certainly be seen to be in his interest to want to stay in Wisconsin, which didn't.

Still, Broderick set off to attempt to verify Hecht's story.

Everything seemed to pan out. Hecht had been working at a gas station at the time. He said he was allowed only four sick days per year, and took three of the days on May 27, 28 and 29, 1981. Christine was murdered on May 28. Coincidence? His employment records verified his absence, according to Halloran. Hecht said he'd picked up a bag with the gun, a wig and some other stuff in a parking lot behind a carpet store. He described how he'd been told to look inside a stack of giant cardboard tubes used for rolling carpet, and had found the gun in the third tube from the left. Broderick went to check the store. It wasn't a carpet store at all. But when he looked into it, he found that it had indeed been a carpet place in 1981. So that checked out, too.

Hecht said he was paid half in cocaine and half in money. After the murder, he said, he spent a couple of days just partying. He rented a limo and ran it like a taxi, ran it to Chicago and back, partying and doing the cocaine. Broderick said he verified the limo rental. So it all seemed plausible. I don't, of course, know how much of it was true, but it did seem plausible.

One of the puzzles of the case had always been why Christine's legs hadn't been tied. Why bind someone at all if you're planning just to shoot them? Hecht's version of that seemed to make sense. He said he'd been planning to rape her but had been interrupted by noises from the kids' bedroom.

As to who had hired him, he wouldn't say. He had his own bizarre set of scruples. He said his code of ethics wouldn't allow him to snitch. This was consistent with his recent conviction—he would not tell police who hired him in the Madison murder, either.

Still, we thought that with my polygraph, his confession, the deposition from Samuels, Judy Zess' recantation and the other stuff, we had enough for a new trial.

So in we went. Back to the Milwaukee County Courthouse.

And Robert Donahoo, the assistant DA, produced a lunatic convict witness who said Hecht had told him he'd never killed anybody.

As if things weren't bad enough already, Jacob Wissler started to interfere.

■   ■   ■

Jacob Wissler! Where did he come from? Straight from hell. He's an evil, sick man, and he poisons everything he touches.

■   ■   ■

He first came into my life when the *Milwaukee Journal* printed a front page story about me in September 1983. He wrote me a letter. It was a normal enough letter, and we started to correspond. All his early letters were innocuous enough, and interesting in their way. We argued about politics, and I enjoyed that. He was a rightwing Republican conservative, and I blasted every Reagan policy in existence.

He saw me only twice, I believe. I was so distracted. My appeals had yielded up one disappointment after another. Not only was the legal process going badly, but my father almost died of stomach cancer at about that time. Wissler offered to come up and visit me, and I was so down, I was so desperate to see someone, anyone, that I accepted. It was better than no visits at all. My dad was in hospital and my mom couldn't manage the long drive to the prison. Wissler's early letters had been completely rational, and that's how I had communicated with him. Perhaps if I'd been able to talk to him on the phone I could have seen earlier that he wasn't cooking on all four burners. But, because I was filled with grief, I grabbed the chance to have a visit.

So he came to visit. He was just a visitor, not even a friend. I did give him a hug before he left, and said thanks for everything, but it wasn't like a sexual hug, just like you would hug a friend.

Soon, however, it became clear he was utterly obsessed. He claimed to be in love with me. His visit with me, this small contact, built in his mind into something towering, some grand obsession, something sick and twisted and poisonous. He wrote me love letters. Then he told the newspapers he'd sent me gifts and was in love with me. Then he wrote to me and threatened me and my family. He would send me as many as ten letters a day, and hundreds of Western Union telegrams and messages via Federal Express. He also sent copies of all this to my mom and dad, to my lawyers, to Bill Roddick and others, anyone who had anything to do with me.

When I refused to accept his mail, he started sending it anonymously. He even misrepresented himself as an attorney by using envelopes "obtained" from Eisenberg's office.

As I've said, this was happening at a desperately difficult time for me. Wissler was aware of my situation and used it to his advantage. It was obvious he knew a great deal about me and my case, though he always implied that he knew even more. "I hold the keys to your freedom," he would say. He claimed he had tapes that proved my innocence. Don Eisenberg advised me to keep up contact with him—just in case he really had information that would be useful.

What were these "tapes" he was supposed to have? Another product of his imaginings. Finally, my dad had enough, and told him to put up or shut up. Wissler responded by demanding that I first write a letter to him saying how much I cared for him and how much I appreciated his help. Only after getting such a letter would he hand over the tapes to my attorney.

Oh, how powerless I felt! How vulnerable! In order to gain a key to my freedom—*if* such a key existed in the first place—I would have to write to him and gush and thank him and tell him I loved him? In other words, lie? I felt dirty, used. But what could I do? What if he really did have this stuff? The evil man understood my dilemma. He manipulated everyone. I reluctantly wrote the letter he wanted. He responded by returning the letter by the next mail with the words *Fuck You!* scrawled on it. The very next day he began writing romantic letters again, as though nothing had happened. The tapes, of course, never existed.

In the months following, he paid fellow inmates to spy on me. He wanted to know even the most mundane things, like my hairstyle. Any information he had about me gave him the crazy sense that he owned a piece of me. He found out who visited me and harassed them all with calls in the middle of the night. He wanted to cut me off from friends and family, to leave me alone and isolated, so I'd turn to him out of desperation.

He was like having my own personal John F. Hinckley. He was a master of deception and confusion—a scam artist. With him, nothing was the way it seemed, nothing was real.

Through his inmate spies he once "heard" that I was having an affair with the female warden. This ridiculous allegation made him insanely jealous. He even phoned a bomb threat into the institution and was charged and finally arrested.

Where did he get all his money? He had no visible means of support—no nine to five job, no freelance occupation. Did someone hire him to muddy the waters?

Someone, after all, had killed Christine Schultz. Someone was responsible for my conviction. If there was a conspiracy, they could have wanted someone to damage me, and damage my case badly, drive me and my family crazy ... Could he have been hired by the other side? Is that too outlandish? Sometimes an individual can commit acts a government can't.

He once told Bill Roddick that "I hope she never gets out of prison, so the fantasy can continue."

Talk about going through hell! My family didn't need this! I tried everything. At first when he got creepy I responded, and that didn't work. Then I ignored him, and that didn't work. It was only his conviction on the bomb threat charge that finally put a damper on him.

■　　■　　■

Wissler interfered in the Hecht affair, too.

It started when he read that Hecht had confessed to the killing I'd been convicted for. Of course, Wissler couldn't stand it. He immediately threatened me.

"If you refuse to love me I'll pay Hecht hush money to shut up," he said.

I don't know whether he did or not. But he did go to the press and the DA and tell them he'd bribed Hecht to confess in the first place. And that this had been at my urging—that it had been my idea!

When we got to court, Hecht decided to plead the Fifth. Halloran told me that wasn't so bad for our case. Why plead the Fifth unless you have something to hide? But Wissler just wouldn't stop. He wrote letters to Hecht in prison, knowing of course that they'd be read, like all inmate mail. At Donahoo's request, these letters were confiscated by prison guards and tainted my evidence.

Hecht tried to escape before he testified. He almost got away, too, by pulling a gun on two guards who had transported him to a Madison hospital for a doctor's appointment. Or, put another way, he was almost killed, which would have been very convenient for the cops. Too bad for them: he tried to escape across a golf course in Madison, and TV cameras followed the attempt all the way. Wissler, of course, bragged about being involved in Hecht's escape attempt, claiming to have smuggled him the gun.

It was a mess. Halloran was trying to present his motion; Wissler was threatening the judge, threatening Hecht, threatening me; Hecht was trying to escape, then took the Fifth ... What a zoo.

Wissler then changed his tune and bragged that he'd paid Hecht not to testify. But by then he'd so muddied the waters that no one, including the trial judge, knew what to believe.

With Hecht's confession suspect, my chances for a new trial were virtually destroyed.

Wissler is now living and working in the Chicago area and says he doesn't want any publicity!

It wasn't until years later that the rest of the exculpatory evidence began to accumulate.

■　　■　　■

That this evidence did accumulate, and is accumulating still, is due to a lot of people and a tremendous amount of diligent work.

But more than anything, it is due to Ira Robins, my private investigator.

My own personal pitbull.

The persistent, unstoppable, irrepressible, irresistible Ira Robins.

■　　■　　■

Ira Robins has been with me—or I've been with Ira—for so long now I've almost forgotten what life was like "B.I." (Before Ira.)

I first met him through Kathy Braun. He'd done some work in the past for her family, and came to see her in prison concerning her family's company.

I was more or less between lawyers—that is, officially I still had Halloran, but he didn't seem to be actually doing anything.

Ira urged me to hire Attorney Gerry Boyle. He seemed to be a good criminal lawyer. We arranged a meeting, but it didn't go well. He wanted me to agree to questioning under sodium pentathol before he'd agree to represent me pro bono. I was dismayed. For years I had been put in the position of being forced to prove my innocence. Over and over again with every new lawyer, a new lie detector test. If I balked they took it as a sign of guilt. I was weary of it. I'd already taken two lie detector tests—and to what end? They cost me thousands of dollars, were always inadmissable in court and they never got me out of prison. So I thanked Mr. Boyle and said "good-bye." He walked out, taking his huge belly and perpetual tan with him.

Then Ira hooked up somehow with Marty Kohler and that's how I got Marty as a lawyer.

■　　■　　■

What's motivating Ira? At first, he was interested, and when Ira gets interested he gets tenacious. Oh, is he stubborn! But I saw a turning point in Ira when the assistant DA, Donahoo, tried to make a fool of him, tried to attack his credibility, paint him as some kind of a nutbar. That was a big mistake. Ira began to take my case as a personal challenge after that, to the point of obsession. He lives, eats and breathes this case now. I needed an Ira, and there he was. He'll always have my gratitude for that.

Someone asked him on TV when he'd give up.

"The only way they're going to stop me is to ice me," he said.

That's a very Ira sort of thing to say.

■ ■ ■

Some people say he's fanatical. But oh, how I needed a fanatic, needed some-one obsessed! The years went by, the weary years, and time rolled on and people changed; unless you're a victim or a villain or a saint, it's so hard to keep the white heat of anger burning for so many long, tired years ...

■ ■ ■

My good friends were now starting to fade. Even Bill Roddick, bless him, who was such a good friend, who did so much, who did so much to help keep costs down for me and my family, even Bill got to the point where he just gave up. I could see it in Bill about 1985 or so. Finally, the enthusiasm just wasn't there. I could tell even from his conversations. At first he would talk about "when you get out of prison," but then a point came where "when" wasn't said anymore; he seemed resigned to the fact that I'd spend the rest of my years without ever getting out. I found this transformation in him depressing and discouraging, but I never blamed him, even then. He'd just reached burn-out.

Luckily for me, that was just when Ira was getting fired up.

Ira and I have been together so many years now, I know him like I'd know an old shoe. We've had our differences. He's not the easiest guy to get along with, believe me. He's prickly and quick to temper and has very strong opin-ions, and he pushes, pushes, pushes. But he's been through so much, he's suf-fered personally and financially, he's been evicted several times, his bills pile up, the phone gets cut off, he gets bounced from one place to another. The Mil-waukee authorities humiliate him when they can. And sure, he complains. Ira is not one to suffer in silence. My parents paid him, I don't know, only about four hundred dollars initially, and every time he gets really hard up he hits them for a couple of hundred more. But he deserved it and deserves it, because he's earned it many times over.

There are friends of his who grow weary of his constant borrowing. They say, Ira, nobody told you to do the Bembenek case full time, you *could* go get a job. But he just can't stop.

I've thought about him a lot. When I escaped and was unable to contact him, I hoped he didn't hate me. I thought, my case was his life, and now that I'm gone he doesn't know whether he'll ever see me again, and maybe he's really crushed ... I didn't *know*. I wanted to call him and I couldn't.

Many people assume he's in love with me. What an easy out! Every time someone's on my side, they diminish it by bringing in sex. It's the easiest way for McCann to discredit a person on my side. "Oh, he's in love with her, what can you expect?" This infuriates me more than anything; it is a last poisonous residue of the "killer bunny" image—men who are on my side must be there because I've ensnared them sexually and not because the evidence of my innocence is overwhelming. I hypnotized them, manipulated and charmed them. From prison yet!

In Ira's case, it's just not true. I've known Ira for years. He visited me socially for a while, but only because it was easier for him to get in that way than through arranging "professional visits." He and I talked about things other than the case, and we came to understand about each other that we're polar opposites.

■   ■   ■

Ira has threatened to quit a million times. He can be a bit of an emotional terrorist, believe me. Every so often he'll say, that's it, I'm gone, I've had enough ... But he never does.

Some people have asked me what he'll do when I do get out of prison. What'll he do when it's all over? And of course I don't know.

If something has become your life, if someone's cause is your life, is your primary motivation just to ... continue it? Could it be that Ira ... wouldn't *want* me out? I hated myself for thinking this way, but hey—I have my paranoid moments after all I've been through.

So I've looked for signs like that. And found nothing.

Nothing. No such signs are there.

I was ashamed of doubting him.

Ira has never, publicly, berated me, unlike my fair-weather friends—Fred and Eisenberg. When they love me, I'm innocent. As soon as an argument ensues, they run to the media to announce my guilt. Ira and I have had our personal arguments, our private disagreements, but he's never repeated anything to the media, he's been utterly loyal, he always defends me.

As I have defended him.

■　　■　　■

Marty Kohler helped me get my case going again through the courts.

By the time I acquired him, I was dead in the water. The storm of publicity had died down; I was in my sixth year in prison, and nothing was happening or seemed about to happen. I felt like I was trapped inside Beckett's play "Waiting for Godot." Kohler took a look at the case and, in his phrase, "it didn't pass the smell test," by which he meant he felt intuitively that my conviction has been wrong. He began to explore what remedies I had left.

I had already tried to get a retrial under the "new evidence" provisions, and that road was now closed. You get only one kick at that can, even if you get even more new evidence. Just in case some court thought differently, Donahoo tried to insist that any such new evidence must have been presented within a year of the trial. Why? Is an old injustice more acceptable than a recent one? He never said. The court ignored him, in any case. And then they denied the motion on other grounds.

I was left with proving a Conflict of Interest. Under federal law, there was a two-part test for conflict. First, you had to prove a conflict existed, and then that the conflict damaged the defense in some way. The state law was much tougher, and better for the defendant: all you had to do was prove the existence of a conflict. The state supreme court had ruled that a lawyer cannot accept money from one suspect to represent another suspect. In other words, you can't represent two suspects in one case.

Fred was paying Don Eisenberg. And clearly Fred had been a suspect.

Kohler asked me how many attorney-client meetings I had had with Eisenberg with Fred in the room. It would be easier, I said, to say how many I had when he wasn't there. He was there for most of them—all but two, I think. Kohler was appalled. He was even more so when I pointed out that most of our meetings had been not in chambers or private spaces but in restaurants and bars.

Kohler also argued that Fred should have kept away for no other reason than that he was an active member of the Milwaukee Police Department. But of course I hadn't known that. Eisenberg hadn't told me. And Fred surely didn't. I thought he was there to help. And he was helpful—there were so many questions Eisenberg asked that I didn't know how to answer, specific things like which child would be the more credible witness? Was there an alarm in the house? It was Fred's house, Fred's kids, Fred's ex-wife—his world. I had no answers.

Marty Kohler seemed pretty good. And it helped that he had an associate lawyer named Ann Reilly, who was a wonderful help. I think women tend to think differently, and can communicate on a different level. I appreciated having her around. She was a caring, compassionate attorney.

Because Eisenberg had been a Wisconsin lawyer, and under Wisconsin law we would only have to prove that a conflict existed, not that it damaged the defendant, we thought we'd developed a compelling case. It should have been enough. No one denied that Fred was a suspect.

Marty filed the motion. We got a good judge, and Marty was pleased until Donahoo objected and pointed out that state law required us to go before the trial court. To my dismay, Donahoo was able to require us to reappear before the original trial judge, Judge Skwierawski.

And it happened again.

We'd been promised two full court days for witnesses, but the motion was fragmented into seventeen different appearances, and the impact of the argument, the logic and the force of it, were utterly diminished.

It was so expensive! We had three expert witnesses who were to testify on my behalf. One was a member of the board of the lawyers' self-regulatory organization, the Board of Attorney's Professional Responsibility; another taught ethics at Marquette Law University. But we had to pay them, get them together, get them back again, over and over. Eisenberg and Fred flew up from Florida. That motion took months. It was so frustrating.

One of the things we were alleging was a connection between Fred and Horenberger. Fred denied it, but we had evidence that they knew one another, and it was certainly possible that Horenberger was the man who'd actually pulled the trigger that night. We pointed out that according to a MPD written report, one Daniel L. Gilbert had been found near the scene and that Gilbert and Horenberger had later robbed Zess. These are two seriously bad people. So, imagine how I felt one day when the van that brought me to court, handcuffed to a chain around my waist, stopped and the sheriff loaded Horenberger and Gilbert into the van. Wonderful.

My motion was denied, of course.

22

IN THE NICK OF TIME

I met Nick, Dominic Gugliatto, through his sister, Maribeth. She was in Taycheedah, serving a fairly short sentence. When I was doing my Bachelor's degree work I spent every afternoon from one to four in the prison library, and it was there that Maribeth approached me. She knew who I was. She was very friendly and bubbly and we chatted, and we seemed to get along. Later there were press reports that we'd been cellmates (another myth becomes "fact"), but we didn't even live in the same housing unit. She lived in the one I facetiously call "Tara"—it's got big white pillars—and soon afterwards she was transferred to another institution. Anyway, she was pleasant and we got along.

I saw Nick first on a Sunday.

I'm pretty much of a materialist and I don't believe in much hocus-pocus, but those who believe in fate will say something was "meant to be," that you'll meet someone if you are meant to. I do know it was unusual for me to have a Sunday visit. I usually avoided them because during the week, visits are three hours long. They're only two on weekends, and the weekends are more crowded, to boot. But for some reason, I was sitting there this Sunday with a visitor.

We were sitting outside, in a grassy area with picnic tables scattered about, and this guy passed by our table on his way somewhere.

He had on white tennis shorts and a white shirt, like a tennis outfit, and my testosterone radar went off right away.

Ooooooh, who's *that!!!*

I watched and saw him sit down at Maribeth's table. There were a number of people at the table, so I didn't know who he was.

Maribeth and I just happened to finish our visits at the same time, and we walked out together.

"Who was the guy in the white shorts?" I asked her.

"That's my brother Nick," she said.

And I said, "Well, is he gay or is he married?" Because, you know, at my age that's all I run into.

"Neither," she said. "And, by the way, he noticed you, too."

I told Maribeth to tell Nick that if he wrote to me, I'd write him back. But he had to write first, to make the first move. I didn't want to seem like the proverbial pathetic, lonely prisoner, because, alas, it was only too true. I had my dignity. I wasn't going to write anybody first.

Maribeth called home and told Nick what I'd said, and he started to write to me, and one thing led to another, as it does in these matters.

I was kind of pleased about it, to tell the truth. I was flattered. And excited, too—I was having fun. Nick asked me to call him, and I did, and then we agreed he should begin visiting, and I put him on my Visitors List, and he started to come up.

Oh, was I surprised! Surprised and delighted that I was, after so many years, still *capable* of feeling happy—that these long-dormant (or long-suppressed) feelings were still there. There was a joyous reawakening going on; I had lived so long in isolation. Ironically, only a few months before I had staunchly, emphatically (and a little defiantly) defended my solo life, my living without a male presence in my life. I'd told Kris Radish of *Wisconsin Woman Magazine* that I had come to the conclusion once and for all that there was no way to have a loving relationship in prison, and that was that.

Well, I'd just finished saying how impossible it was, and here I was. It was ridiculous, but delicious, too.

I had tried to get interested in one man or another over the years—there were a couple of times and a couple of different guys—but it just never worked out. Why? I was in, and they were out. I'd call them and a girl answers the phone, you know—stuff like that inevitably happened. I had adjusted to my small, little life and I was comfortable with it that way, like an old shoe.

In retrospect I can see how I was defending myself from more heartbreak. Maybe I was getting a little warped, I don't know, but I was dealing with it.

I'm certainly not sexually interested in women; after all these years I would know by now.

So I reveled in my new emotional state.

First I grew to like Nick, and then I felt myself falling in love with him. It's a wonderful feeling, a giddy feeling, but ... I was still a prisoner.

I remember one day I was walking back to the housing unit after a visit and through the fence I could see his truck driving away down the highway and I started to panic. I thought, "Oh no, here I go, I don't want to have to yearn for somebody, not here, I don't want to want someone I can't have, I don't want to do this, to put myself through this ..."

In prison, it's a survival trick to try to eliminate from your life all the things you desire, so it doesn't hurt that badly. You put your life on hold, you freeze-frame your feelings, you shut down your heart.

I thought I had done that.

But here I was—my heart hadn't dried up and blown away as dust after all. I was shocked! And delighted. And worried. All my pals noticed a change in me at once. I was a lot more open, a lot happier. I was no longer acting as if I had PMS thirty days a month. I was just a lot ... nicer.

People would say to me, "You must be in love or something," and I would just smile. At the same time I was fighting it because I knew what it would mean. I knew for a lifer, falling in love was ridiculous.

Finally, Nick told me he loved me. I'd been waiting for him to say it first. So then we talked about my future—if I would ever get paroled, and he didn't seem to care about any of that. He asked me to marry him. He'd been hinting that if I got out of prison he was afraid I wouldn't need him anymore; he seemed to need the marriage to make himself feel more secure. So I wasn't really surprised when he popped the question.

When I broached the subject with my mom and dad they were concerned. They didn't want me to marry in a place like that, and we quarreled.

"God, no, don't do this, don't do this to us," my mom said.

"You don't understand," I'd respond. "This is the one little thread of happiness I've had in ten years, and you want to deprive me of it. Why can't you just be glad? Even if this is temporary, it's bringing me happiness now, and that's all you should care about ..."

We were all being unfair, I think. It was difficult.

Prison weddings are strange, of course, a peculiar version of the real thing. I've been to a few. Most prison marriages don't last. The prison system requires that you take counseling if you're contemplating marriage; they want to make sure you know exactly what you're doing, what you're getting involved in.

I argued that I was getting to know Nick in a way that I might not have on the outside. Outside, when you're dating someone, you might go to a bar, or go dancing, or to a movie, but you don't necessarily ever really just sit and talk like you do on visits.

I pointed out that when I married for the first time it was to someone I didn't even know. But when a person visits you in prison three times a week for three hours and you do nothing but talk, with no phones ringing and no TV on, no distractions, you can get to know that person very well. We wrote letters. We phoned every day, and talked. There's more contact than people realize. It was a good argument, anyway.

Well, wrong again.

I now understand that you can't know someone really well until you live with them, until you see them in daily routines, see whether they stay drunk or sober, see them under stress, see how they behave with others. On prison visits, everything's wonderful, everyone puts their best foot forward.

A couple of friends of mine tried to tell me this, but I didn't want to listen. "I don't care," I said. "I might be in prison for the rest of my life, and this is making me happy now." I was also thinking of my parents getting older, and of the burdens they had taken on, and of their weariness. I needed so much help all the time. It was always, "Can you send me this, do this or that for me ..." I thought perhaps a husband could take over some of these small duties, and that would make their lives a little easier.

I had several long talks with my mom and dad. They were being really protective, as usual.

"I know what you're objecting to," I said, "but I have to go on, I have to hang on to something, because I haven't been living, really, I've just been existing, and now I feel I'm alive again."

They thought it over, and it wasn't easy for them. But they liked Nick when they met him. They weren't too happy with the fact that he was divorced with several kids, but then their generation worries more about divorce than mine does.

Nick even offered a prenuptial agreement, whatever I wanted, whatever would make things easier for them. He seemed sincere enough. I thought if he wanted to marry me in prison then he really loved me.

We went ahead, and I bought a wedding dress from a catalogue; we would have been married in the prison chapel, and in the pictures it would have looked just like any other wedding, like any normal wedding. We went ahead on the assumption that my appeal would be denied. If it was denied, we'd get married in prison; if not, we could do it "out there."

■   ■   ■

But while my emotional juices were flowing again, and I was squeezing out increments of happiness like wringing water from a damp cloth, in the veins of the legal system there ran only acid.

Acid that seemed to eat away at my future.

Again.

They were pinching off avenues of emotional escape, and that's why I was led to contemplate a real escape.

■　　■　　■

It was a difficult summer.

First, the Wisconsin Department of Corrections arbitrarily changed the classification of all lifers. This was like tying us down and beating us on the head with a shovel.

Without warning, they changed the system for lifers retroactively. It was obscene. It was like Nazi Germany. They went round to all the institutions, all the camps, seized all the lifers at four in the morning and took them, in shackles, back to maximum security to be reclassified.

By this time I had a network of other lifers, and it wasn't just me. We were all in the same boat.

Legislatively, they amended the Wisconsin Administrative Code to reclassify all lifers into various categories and created subjective criteria that the institution's review committee would apply to us to decide how dangerous we were. If the victim of the crime was bound or sexually assaulted, for example, that would put the lifer in Category One, which would add about fifty years to her sentence. The one U.S. Constitutional Right that has always been honored, is the right of a prisoner to never be arbitrarily incarcerated for longer than whatever sentence the judge imposed. A person sentenced to five years, for instance, could never have the term increased to fifteen years. Yet this was, in effect, what they were doing to us. Category One lifers were required to spend a minimum of fifteen years in a maximum security prison, then a number of years in a medium security facility and then a number of years in a minimum security prison.

We filed a Class Action against this horrid new law, but there was no hope for me. The light at the end of the tunnel had turned into an oncoming train.

The reclassification was eventually overturned by a higher court, but I couldn't know that would happen. At the time I was being told that I would never get out of prison.

Then we had a lockdown for two weeks.

A lockdown happens when, for reasons best known to themselves, the prison authorities decide to cancel all routines. They "lock down" everyone—lock them into their cells. Meals are brought to cells. No one moves. Nobody goes to work. All recreation is canceled. All study is canceled. The place screeches to a halt. You just wait.

There was no communication. They told us nothing. They brought in drug-sniffing dogs, the whole thing. It was really melodramatic, really stupid. They'd been watching late-night television too much. Everybody felt pushed to the brink.

After the lockdown, they began giving me a particularly hard time in the visitors' room.

You must understand the arbitrary nature of prison authority. They can, in practice, do what they want. You're allowed visits, but if they decide you shouldn't have them, they'll find a way to cancel them. They will fabricate Conduct Reports, make up infractions, change the rules so you can't help but break them, because you have no idea what they are this month, this week, this hour.

There is a rule against sexual conduct anywhere in the institution, of course. There are good reasons for this. The whole issue of consent becomes difficult in prison. If you find two people in bed, well, perhaps they want to be in bed together, but one might just be stronger than the other. If a woman has a strong arm around her neck, she'll be prepared to smile and tell the world she's enjoying it. In order to prevent rapes that result from grotesque power imbalances, prisons try instead to prevent all sexual conduct whatever. So prisoners cannot kiss or hold hands with another prisoner or you risk being charged and thrown into the hole.

Of course, people do it and get away with it, but officially it's prohibited.

This prohibition carries over into the visitors' room. And, depending on the personality of the guard, it can get insanely picayune and hyper-technical. You're allowed to hold hands with your visitor, and when the visitor walks in you're allowed one hug and one kiss. Again, when they leave, one hug and one kiss. This kiss is a fast little smooch, too—no standing there for fifteen minutes.

Naturally, people try to get around the rules. Understand, these are people who have been deprived of sex for three, eight, ten years; when you get a visitor and you're in love, it is only human to want to snuggle, to hug, to touch. Always under the watchful eye of the visitors' room guard.

One particular guard refused to use the common sense and judgment of some of the others, who used to look the other way unless the conduct was utterly outrageous. What's the difference if someone has an arm around a loved one? But the guard watching over us was like a hawk. You couldn't have your hand anywhere, on any part of your visitor's body.

Once Nick had his hand on my back, between my shoulder blades, and the guard said, "Bembenek, that's a warning!"

"What do you mean, that's a warning?" I said. I was genuinely puzzled. A hand on my back, in the middle of a crowd of other people?

"That's Sexual Conduct. Take his hand off your back."

I argued. "Wait a minute! The administrative code does not define 'back' as a sexual part. It defines sexual part very clearly. Breast, buttock, scrotum and vagina—you cannot have your hand on any of those—but I don't think back is defined as a sexual part."

"I'm giving you a warning," she said. "This is going on your card."

I was stupid to argue. You can't win. After two warnings you get a Conduct Report, and then the guards have the power simply to remove a person from your Visitors List.

I warned Nick. I told him how arbitrary they could be, how once they get an idea in their heads they'll never let it go. I had to keep warning him. It was depressing. Here was someone I loved, and I spent so much time saying, "Watch it, don't, don't do that ..." But it's hard for someone who hasn't been in prison to understand. He didn't take it seriously.

One day in the spring (it was still cold enough for me to be wearing long jeans and a denim jacket), the guard saw Nick with his hand on my hip. We must have been goofing around or something, because I don't even remember the incident, and there was certainly nothing sexual about it. But I got a Conduct Report on the incident anyway.

I sent it home to my mother, using it as stationery. It was stupid and petty and mean-spirited. But petty as it was, they gave it to me with both barrels. They denied me the use of the library; they forbade me to use the telephone; they prevented me from playing tennis on the beaten-up old tennis court; I wasn't allowed to jog; I was allowed no recreation at all.

I complained to the superintendent about this. It didn't help, of course. Complaining never helps, but I can't stop myself—the ability and willingness to complain was the only sense of "self" I had left, and I wasn't going to give it up without a struggle.

Complaining about sexual conduct was even more than usually useless. The guards tolerated lesbian behavior. I don't know why exactly—perhaps because lesbians don't get pregnant—but the institution consistently discriminated against heterosexuals.

You think I'm making this up? Not at all. I watched it closely for nine years, and I know.

I pushed and pushed. I wrote to the superintendent: "Why is it that you have lesbian couples visiting, and they're all over one another, kissing and doing this and that, but you don't enforce the rules? Why?"

She wrote back and said: "If you can't conduct yourself in the proper manner I can have your visitor removed from your list."

Great, I thought, now she's threatening to remove someone I'm supposed to get married to next month.

Nick found all this hard to believe.

"Behave," I said. "They're looking for an excuse to remove you from my list."

"They can't do that!" he said.

And I said, "Not in America, right? Maybe we're living in the Soviet Union after all, maybe that's where this prison is ..."

He was offended.

I began to wear a little metal button on my jacket, a likeness of Lenin. After *glasnost* there was this catalogue of all these cool things from Russia. I had a little Red Army button with a hammer and sickle on it. All the other inmates were shocked. *Oh, Bembenek, the Communist!* After that, inmates would come up to me and say, "Who's that?" And I'd say, "Lenin." Puzzled, they'd say, "John?" I'd say, "No! Vladimir!"

■   ■   ■

One of the Last Straws of Summer:

The other disappointment was this: I had worked six years to get my BA— I would be the first female prisoner in Wisconsin to earn a university Bachelor's Degree. After I finished my course work, my professor from Kavenik entered my name on the list of graduates, so the crazy newspapers printed an article about not only getting "first degree" but a "college degree" as well (sick humor). I looked forward to attending graduation with the AA graduates from PREP at the end of July. But as "Bembenek luck" would have it, my prof discovered I neglected one of my BOK (Breadth of Knowledge) requirements for graduation: two years of a foreign language. Still on the list to attend graduation, I hurriedly finished Russian 101 in two months and began Russian 102, working on it eight hours a day.

Kathy tried to cheer me up. "Don't worry about it, Laur," she said. "There are three other PREP students who are currently finishing their summer course, but the warden is letting them go to graduation."

"Yes, but they aren't me," I replied pessimistically.

"Switala will let you go," Kathy said. "And by the way, stand up straight. You're slouching again."

I had begun to walk with my shoulders rounded, hunched over—a physical manifestation of oppression. Show me a round-shouldered prisoner and I'll show you a prisoner doing life.

The warden refused to let me attend graduation. Now that's what I call positive reinforcement for productive behavior.

■ ■ ■

This was the sequence: First, the lifer reclassification. Then the lockdown. Then they blasted me with this punitive action in the visiting room. And, to top it all off, I couldn't attend the graduation ceremony.

"I can't stand this," I told myself. "I can't live like this anymore."

Then my appeal was denied.

That was it. The last hope. The tunnel had caved in completely.

■ ■ ■

I remember a conversation in the visitors' room with Nick.

"Let's say everything fails," he asked. "How much time are we talking about? How long will you still be in?"

"Nick," I said, "I've never tried to mislead you. I've tried to explain. I don't know whether you had stars in your eyes or if you really believed this appeal was going to happen, but I'm telling you, we're in for a long haul. A long, long haul. Lifers have no mandatory release date."

He just ... How to explain where an idea comes from? He thought about it, and I thought about it, and gradually we came to understand that the only way I would ever live again was to go over the wall. It was a mutual decision.

■ ■ ■

It's important that you understand. I didn't just wake up one day and decide to take off, decide that I really wanted to get it off with Nick and hit the road. I'd been desperate for so many years, but there had always been one last chance, one last, slim hope that the system of justice would come to its senses, would understand that a travesty had been perpetrated in the name of the law.

Instead, like a strangler in the night, they kept hauling the garrote tighter and tighter until ... until it was breathe, or die.

■   ■   ■

I know there are people saying that I was the one who talked Nick into helping me escape, that I manipulated him, somehow, into going against his judgment. They like to portray me as having this strange sexual allure, as if I can make men do anything I want, as if I am this Svengali-like figure. (You'd be so disappointed! But I guess the truth is really boring.)

I don't know why two lovers planning an escape to freedom wouldn't be just as good a story as a man being sexually hypnotized against his will, but there it is. We just wanted to be together, and we thought of it together. We were in love!

Nick, I think, was a romantic. He wasn't very happy with his life at the time. He'd been working at the same factory for about eleven or twelve years, and the job was going nowhere. His ex-wife was giving him problems. He saw this, I think, as a chance to start all over again. It was a romantic thing, to run away together ...

And it was, and it is, romantic, not just for Nick, but for me, too.

I was at the point where I couldn't *not* escape. I came to believe that I'd try it, even if I knew in advance I'd have only one night of freedom. That would be enough. I'd add five more years to my sentence for one free night. I needed it that badly. It was juvenile, of course, I know that. But it's how I felt. The letter from the superintendent was the last straw.

Only one thing gave me pause: what if I didn't make it? What if I got caught within the compound? What if I never made it over the fence? I'd be going to the hole for 360 days, and for nothing ...

Most prisoners, most women prisoners, don't try to escape because they have kids, and they wouldn't be able to see them again. That's a major controling factor.

I just hoped to God everybody would understand. I worried about my parents and about Ira. Maybe everybody would be really mad at me. I didn't know; I only knew I had to try in order to survive. As it turned out, they weren't mad at all. Most of them said afterwards, "That was the best thing you could ever have done."

Run, Bambi, run!

The last day was terrible. I knew it was the last time I would see these people, my friends ... and yet I couldn't act as if anything was wrong, or anything was different. I couldn't tip off the prison officials. I'm generally very private and stoic about my emotions, so when I do cry my friends know there is something seriously wrong. I'm generally embarrassed about public displays of emotion.

So when my parents left for the last time ... There was a baseball diamond in the yard in front of the housing unit, and I walked out into the middle of the field and I broke down and sobbed, I wept and wept, the tears staining my shirt. I had a good cry, then I put my sunglasses on and walked back to the housing unit.

My parents mean everything to me. But if I had to wait ... how long could they keep going? How long? It was hell for them, too. By leaving, I was going to free everybody else. I knew them well. I knew that if I was free, they would take comfort from that.

And I think, honestly, my mom was glad I wasn't going to be married in prison.

If I looked out of sorts that last day, at least I had an excuse. My friends blamed love. "Oh well," my good friend Debbie laughed, "she's in love, she's a little distracted ..."

Every Sunday afternoon I played tennis, so on this Sunday I had to play as usual. Everyone knew I lived for tennis, and I couldn't, on this day of all days, do anything out of the ordinary. In the middle of the first set, my doubles partner Laurie Fox said sharply to me, "Laurie!"

It was my turn to serve, and she'd caught me staring into the middle distance, my mind miles away.

The escape was going to be that night.

23

ON THE LAM

When you're in the same place for nine years you get to know everything, every inch of every room, everybody's routines. Human beings are creatures of habit, and one of a prisoner's habits is watching the watchers. You get to know which guards head for the kitchen for coffee as soon as they come on duty, which ones bury their noses in newspapers or gab on the phone for hours. When you're planning an escape, you have to know who is going to be on shift. It would be riskier with some people than others. I had to think all that through.

And even then, you have to be flexible. Someone may call in sick, they might switch jobs without notice. You have to be prepared to cancel your plans at the last moment.

In truth, I could have taken off at any time during the last eight years or so, but I needed the psychological push, the sense that I had, truly, lost all hope of ever being free again.

Every summer I worked on the outdoor maintenance crew. Although we eventually got tractor mowers, at first we used to mow the lawns by hand. What a sight—a crew of women, side by side, with hand-mowers. Monday we'd start at one end of the prison compound and by Friday we'd be at the other. These were big lawns, over two hundred acres of them. Because of the unvarying nature of the routine, every Thursday I found myself at the North Gate. I mowed away by myself. Near the gate was a dump for garbage and cut trees and whatnot. The highway was beside the dump. I used to stand and watch the beer trucks drive by. Mostly, I was there alone, not even within sight of the cameras (we all got to know the cameras, and how far they could see). There was a supervisor who checked on our whereabouts periodically, but I knew that if someone met me on a Thursday, I could just ... go. There is always a crack in any system. Always. If you wanna go, you can go.

I thought it all through. They say prison is a crime school, and this is so true! I learned a *lot* over the years. I'd seen people escape before, often enough, and nine times out of ten they'd go right back to where they came from, to their children or their families or their homes. And, of course, they were picked up right away. I knew that if I left, I'd leave Wisconsin for good. The best thing would be to go, just to go immediately, and not to stop.

■　　■　　■

I finished my tennis game in the late afternoon.

I knew there was a 5:30 PM "count." Everything revolved around these counts.

They did "counts" all the time, checking to see that we were all accounted for. We had counts at 7:30 AM, 12:30 PM, 5:30 PM and 9:30 PM. So I had to go either well before or just after a count, otherwise they would know I was missing immediately. The count at 9:30 PM was no good—after that, they counted every hour on the hour, all night long. The guard shift changed at 10:00, then they patrolled the corridors and went past every cell with a flashlight, walkie-talkies blaring and keys jangling while we tried to sleep. The rule was that the guard counting us had to see skin. I learned to sleep with one foot hanging out of the blanket.

After the 9:30 count cleared, we had several options. We had access to a basement card room in the Housing Unit, but I hated the noise and smoke. Or, until about 11:00 PM, we could take a shower or use the telephone in the hall-way. But every hour, on the hour, we were all counted.

There were some women who escaped through the windows in their cells. I had once lived in a cell where that would have been possible. On some floors the windows had no bars, but the window stays prevented anyone from open-ing the windows more than about four inches—just enough for some rather inadequate ventilation. In a cell I once shared with Kathy Braun, the window just flew right open. The stays were broken, or perhaps they were never put on by mistake. I certainly could have escaped from that room. Other women who sawed through the stays, tied their sheets together and out they went.

I remember two women who went to great lengths to get out. They stole a file from maintenance and cut through the bars. They worked at it for a long time. And when they'd escaped, what did they do? They hitchhiked to Madison, an hour and a half away, went immediately to the first party they could find and bragged about what they'd done. Someone from the party called the police and they were caught the same night.

So I knew what *not* to do. No parties. Take off and keep going!

If I'd waited until 9:30 it would have been dark, but there was that matter of the hourly count. I decided on that odd time between dark and light, dusk, when you can see, but not very well. Better than dark, in some ways.

Ironically, two things actually helped my escape. The Security Director insisted that when a prisoner was doing laundry she had to stay in the laundry room until she was done. Of course, this was done to inconvenience everybody; how boring to sit and watch a dryer going round for hours. Most people would otherwise have gone to the card room instead. It worked to my advantage in this case, because it allowed me to be absent from my floor, the third. They would simply assume I was doing my laundry for a couple of hours. And to help me further, the Captain was conducting a white glove building inspection that evening. All the guards were preoccupied with dustball reports.

Right after the 5:30 count, I signed out with my floor officer and told her I was going to the laundry room. This was consistent with my routine. I carried my sweaty tennis clothes with me.

There was a window in the laundry that was not secured. Who knows why? Maybe they'd painted it and forgotten to put the stays back on. But there it was, calling out to me like one of the sirens.

It was not as small as the newspapers reported the next day. I think the prison exaggerated the smallness of the window to minimize their fault, and implied I had somehow wriggled through a hole about six inches square. Actually, it was about two feet by two feet. It was high off the ground, but I was in wonderful shape because I'd been running five miles every day and doing aerobics four nights a week, not to mention my tennis matches.

There I was, pushing myself through the window, on my way Out.

I can honestly say I've never been so scared in my entire life. My heart was pounding so hard it was like drums beating in my ears.

Security vans patroled the grounds, but they, too, had their routines. Through simple observation I'd learned when they had deliveries to make and other things to do.

I was afraid of them, of course.

I was also afraid of the screwy inmates. Someone could easily have spotted me. Of course, anyone with half a brain wouldn't have said anything, but prisons are full of the other kind, too—people who will blurt out anything that comes into their heads. "Hey, everybody! I just saw somebody!" They would! There are people so bored they have nothing to do but look out the window. You have to anticipate that.

There was an apple orchard behind the housing unit, and I knew the cameras couldn't see past it. If I could only get into the woods past the orchard, I'd be safe. Well, maybe not safe, but cool ...

In the first few seconds after I got out I paused in the woods behind the Housing Unit to catch my breath and make sure no one had seen me. There is a large stone grotto with a statue of the Virgin Mary. So much for separation of Church and State.

I wore a leather jacket, to protect me from branches in the woods, so I got through the woods without a scratch. I'd never been in those woods before, and it was scary. Woods at night are always creepy, and when you're in a hurry, even more so. I didn't want to lose an eye to a low-hanging branch; nor did I want to fall into a hidden ravine and break a leg. I didn't know whether there were any ravines. The woods sloped generally uphill from the housing unit to the highway beyond. To freedom.

I was still within the perimeter of the fence.

It was hot, and very dark in the woods. I sweated profusely; I had the hood of my sweatshirt over my head. My heart was pounding. I was afraid I would hyperventilate because I was panting like a horse. The air seemed thick and rank. I just wanted to get through those woods!

I went up, and farther up, and eventually I could see light at the end of the woods, I was running toward the light, scrambling over fallen trees, crossing one small ravine on a deadfall bridge, like a balance beam, but I just went, driving myself, trying not to panic, trying to keep going.

I reached the fence. It was tall, maybe nine or ten feet, with barbed wire at the top. I wrapped my belt around the barbed wire and I pulled it taut, and no sooner had I done so than I heard a car coming.

I didn't know if it was Nick, but I couldn't risk being seen at the top of the fence, so I jumped down, ran for cover and waited. It could be a prison van doing a perimeter check.

When the truck had passed, I tried again.

This time I became hooked on the barbed wire. It snagged my pants, and I felt it tear into my leg. I yanked at it, and the barbs raked my leg, but I freed myself.

I left half my pant leg on the wire. Talk about fiber evidence!

Later, I saw three or four big gashes in my leg. It looked as though I'd been attacked by a mountain lion—four big claw marks in the flesh. I worried about infection, but it healed eventually.

I was out!

I had to run for cover.

The truck that had passed hadn't been Nick after all. We two amateurs had got the timing down pat. Nick showed up right on time.

A witness at his trial later swore he'd seen Nick parked near the fence where he picked me up. It still amazes me what lies people will tell, just to get into the papers or on television. Nick *never* parked anywhere—we had worked that out ahead of time. Drive up and down twenty times if you must, I'd warned him, but don't ever stop, it will only attract attention. He'd agreed, and did as I suggested.

He pulled up, I jumped in, and we sped off. To freedom!

I'd made it! It was an amazing feeling. My heart was still going. My adrenaline levels must have been off the charts! Ecstasy mingled with fear.

I scrunched down and started peeling layers of clothes off to cool myself. I took my leather jacket off, then my sweatshirt, down to a tank top. Hand in hand, with Guns 'n Roses blasting on the tape player, we just drove straight through to Canada. It took us all night.

■　　■　　■

We reached the Canadian border, and I looked across at Another Country beyond. The trees looked the same, and so did the roads. The highway signs had little crowns on them, but everything else looked the same. I knew, though, that it wasn't so. I knew that beyond that gate the Milwaukee Police Department had no jurisdiction, no weight, no authority. It was a place that was Donahoo-free. Skwierawski had no say there. They had never heard of McCann there. It was a refuge, a place empty of malice.

It was our first big test. Nick gripped the wheel, but looked otherwise relaxed—good old happy-go-lucky Nick! I was so nervous! We'd driven all night but I was wide awake, running on pure adrenaline. We couldn't get stopped here, surely? We just couldn't! Not after all our efforts!

We pulled up at the border crossing post.

The officer approached Nick's side of the car. "Hi!" he said. "Where are you going?"

■　　■　　■

Would the word have been out by then? I thought we'd still be pretty safe. They'd do a thorough search of the grounds before they even notified the sheriff. I had looked into it surreptitiously earlier, and discovered that they generally delay issuing an APB for something like forty-eight hours, to allow a thorough search of the immediate locality. But I wondered if all those years behind bars had made me ignorant of the new high-tech systems available. After all, I had never even seen a fax machine. What if news of the escape had been sent by fax to the border?

It was mid-morning by the time we got to Canada. There were some things in our favor. I was in good shape and I was suntanned, so I didn't look like the stereotypical jailbird. We were sitting there holding hands like an ordinary couple.

"What's your business in Canada?" the border officer asked.

Could I have told them an earful! Refuge, I wanted to say.

"We're on honeymoon," I said.

"Okay then, have a nice time," she said, smiling and waving us off.

Freedom! I rolled down the window and let the breeze speed through my hair. The sun beat furiously over the tops of the pine trees. The sky was a brilliant blue.

I looked over at Nick and said, "Well, maybe there is a God." Me, an unwavering atheist for so many years!

■　　■　　■

Even had they demanded our ID at the border, we would have been all right. Nick had come prepared.

It turned out to be surprisingly simple. In Milwaukee County they don't cross-reference birth and death certificates. Every baby gets a birth certificate, but if that baby dies in infancy the death certificate isn't cross-referenced to the birth certificate. The trick, therefore, is to go to a cemetery and look for a child who died young but who would have been about your age had she lived. You write the name and birth date down. Then you have to consult the death notice in the newspaper to find out the mother's maiden name. Death notices commonly say something like, "Beloved daughter of so and so, née so and so." You have to have the maiden name to apply for a copy of the birth certificate. It has to be a baby, unfortunately. Most adults have other identification that is cross-referenced to birth dates; if you apply for a birth certificate for someone who also has a social security number, they can trace you easily enough.

Once you have a birth certificate, you can apply for a real social security number under that baby's name—which means you can get a job.

We got "our" birth certificates. I was Jennifer Lee Voelkel, a name from a tombstone, and Nick was Tony Gazzana.

Later, some people expressed outrage about what we'd done. It bordered to them on the sacrilegious, the morbid. After we were recaptured, the newspapers published a picture of the dead baby's tombstone, which did seem morbid, and went to the parents for comment. We didn't mean to be hurtful. It was the only means we had to acquire ID.

Afterwards, the parents of the real Tony Gazzana became our friends. Nick met with the Gazzanas after he was deported and apologized. They even signed a petition we sent to Canada's Immigration Minister, Barbara McDougall, to dispute her ministry's contention that I was a danger to the Canadian public. "We don't find Laurie a danger here, please don't in Canada," they said. They came over to our side.

The Voelkels were upset with me, and I'm sorry, but I meant no harm. I hardly ever used the name, anyway. Nick and I were posing as husband and wife, so I traveled and worked under the alias Jennifer Gazzana.

■　　■　　■

It's true, it was illegal to acquire false ID. It was the only illegal thing I did all the time I was on the run. The Canadian immigration and justice lawyers for the ministry, trying to establish that I was a menace to public safety, made much of the fact that I had got jobs under false pretenses. What did they want me to do? Say, "Hi, I'm Laurie Bembenek, I'm a fugitive, can you give me a job?" But Nick and I never stole anything. We never robbed banks, held up gas stations, pilfered from newspaper boxes, short-changed anyone, drove without a license or even jaywalked. I worked at two jobs, six days a week to survive, and we lived frugally in Thunder Bay. Never for a moment did we consider committing a crime.

I never want to commit a crime.

I want desperately to be ordinary.

I want to work, and pay my own way.

■　　■　　■

Meanwhile, in Milwaukee, the cops, in typical Milwaukee fashion, wiretapped my mom's phone, opened my parent's mail and waited outside my parents' house for me to come "home."

For months afterwards they waited there. They were so obvious! They would sit in front of the house, and my mom and dad felt like prisoners in their own home. One time a large furniture truck pulled up across the street, and before you could turn around it was surrounded by squad cars. It was as if they'd dropped out of the sky.

What goes through their minds? Did they really think I'd come home in a furniture van posing as a sofa bed? My mom and dad thought that was a real hoot.

■   ■   ■

You know what my dad said, when they asked him on television how he felt about my escape?

"I hope she's safe," he said.

Then he added, "If I saw her I would tell her to keep on running, because it may not be freedom but at least it's a taste of freedom ..."

■   ■   ■

I can't tell you how hard it is living on the run. It's like being on guard at all times. You have to be aware of everything you say, everything you do. For twenty-four hours a day you have to be another person. If somebody calls you Jennifer you have to respond right away. You have to remember to call yourself Jennifer. I might be telling you a story and say something like, "I said to myself, now Laurie, smarten up ..." But I had to learn to say Jennifer instead of Laurie. Usually when you sign your name you do it without thinking. On the run, you have constantly to think the idiotic question: "Who am I?"

To everyone but me, the escape itself seemed astonishingly easy. So much so that most people assumed I'd had lots of help. They accused Kathy Braun of giving me tips on how to escape—but it wasn't like that at all. Nobody advised me. I couldn't do that to my friends, implicate anybody, so none of them had even an inkling of my plans. They could all take a polygraph test and pass easily. As far as they were concerned, I just had to disappear one night. I hated having to do that.

And in Thunder Bay I missed Kathy and my other friends from Tay-cheedah. Nick didn't have a clue what I was going through. How could he? Only another prisoner would have understood what things were like, how the little things affected me. Like the price of cigarettes. I'd been in prison for a decade, and then had the double-whammy of going to Canada, where things are incredibly more expensive. Cigarettes were about a buck and a half in the U.S., and about six bucks in Canada. Nick smoked over a pack a day, which meant over two hundred dollars a month going up in smoke! We argued about that constantly.

I lost so many simple skills. I'd lost any ability to figure out directions, east and west, north and south. It took me weeks just to figure out how to take the bus to work in the mornings. I know that sounds absurd, but when you're in the same little compound for years and years, and when you do go somewhere you're taken by the police, you don't have to take responsibility for anything. You wouldn't believe how many bus stops I waited at for buses that never came.

I also lost the ability to make choices. You're not presented with any choices in prison. You're told when to eat, what to eat, what to do ... you don't get a variety pack. I drove Nick crazy. We'd go to a restaurant and I'd keep looking at the menu, and I'd say "I want this. No, wait, I'll have this. No, no, can you come back in a minute?" I couldn't decide. We'd go to a grocery store and I couldn't decide what to buy. There were too many choices.

■　　■　　■

Jennifer and Tony Gazzana spent the day looking for a place to stay. Wide-eyed, I looked around. So this was the outside world! Hot dog vendors, people shopping, kids on bikes. So this was life! I slipped off my sandal to feel the warm cement of the sidewalk under my foot. I kept thinking I was dreaming. We finally bought a newspaper and went to a coffee shop to mark off some likely prospects for apartments. We did that right away because you need a permanent address to apply for a job. And we needed to work—we didn't have much money.

That night we stayed in a hotel. Fortunately, they never asked for ID. We paid cash. Hotels made me nervous. Nick said I was paranoid. Prison does that to a person. So we bought some beer and a pizza and looked for news of my escape on TV. Nothing was reported.

One of the things the cruder reporters always seem to want to ask me is: "Did you make love all night?" And you know what they're thinking: "Did you have good sex? Did you screw like minks? You'd been without for nine years—what was it *like*?"

They always want to ask me about sex.

Once, years before, I'd made a facetious remark to a reporter. She'd asked me about the first thing I'd do after I was released, and I said, "Have sex." I was joking, for God's sake! But the quote took on a life of its own, and eventually made its squalid way into *People* magazine and, of course, taken out of context and blown out of proportion, it winds up making me sound like a nympho.

So we were in love, and we went to bed, and in the morning we went and found ourselves an apartment.

A woman named Jenny Beck rented us a place. It was a basement apartment, small and somewhat dark. Jenny had done all the work herself—from the paneling to the plumbing. She is a very small woman, and the place was built for midgets. I once went to a rummage sale and saw a beautiful sofa for fifty dollars. I wanted it, because the apartment only had two chairs so Nick and I couldn't sit and cuddle. We measured the sofa and it wouldn't fit through the damn door. I wanted to cut it in half!

I picked up the first job I could get. I was scared. I was scared all the time, in fact. I was scared of starving, of going through all our money. I didn't want to end up as a public charge at some shelter someplace. Especially after seeing the prices. So four days after we arrived, I got a job in the Fort William side of Thunder Bay, as a cook in a Greek restaurant.

What a joke! That's one of the things I would have loved to have shared with Kathy and my friends. A cook! I have a domestic deficiency. I don't know how to cook! I've been locked up for ten years. I can barely fry an egg. Even before I got sent up, Fred did the cooking.

But the Columbia Grill and Tavern trained me. They showed me how to make souvlaki and gyros and Greek salads.

After a while, because I was still obsessed with this irrational fear that we'd starve and because everything seemed so expensive to me, and because Nick wasn't working, I got a second job, in a gym. I'd go home, change into my aerobics clothes and walk to my second job. I couldn't drive; I didn't have a license yet.

I wished constantly that I had Kathy there to share things with, the small things that mean so much to a prisoner. Every animal I ran into on the street I would bend down and pet. I'd attract stray cats. We got a cat of our own. I'd walk barefoot in the grass, go for long walks in the night, smell the air, watch the stars, stand in the rain, walk down the hill to the convenience store at night and get something, anything, a popsicle.

Very simple things were so wonderful. Jenny had raspberry bushes in the back yard, so Tony/Nick and I had fresh berries on our breakfast cereal. She gave me a homemade apple pie one day and as I baked it, the most delicious smell filled our apartment. I hadn't smelled anything so good in years! I even made grape jelly one evening and really thought I was the cat's pajamas. I know these things sound silly to the average individual, but another lifer would understand.

I worried about so much. About running out of money. About seeming conspicuous. About saying the wrong thing, asking the wrong question. I was worried about getting drunk and blurting something out. I became very conservative about drinking. Apparently, over the years I have turned into a control freak. I had to be constantly aware of what was going on and who was saying what.

For weeks I'd keep my ears open, listening for news of our escape. I looked at the supermarket tabloids. Nothing. Thunder Bay seemed like a million miles from Milwaukee. Nobody had even heard of me. People at work would talk about this and that, and occasionally the topic of prisons would come up, but the only U.S. prisoner they seemed to know was Charles Manson. Most mornings cops would come in for coffee, and I would serve them thinking, "*Act normal, Bembenek!*"

I didn't try to change my appearance too much. It would have been too expensive for one thing, and it would have meant frequent trips to the beauty shop. I didn't want to go back to being blond, anyway. Over the years I've been everything—short brown hair, long brown hair, blond hair—I didn't know what to do. So I left it alone.

Why, I was asked later, Thunder Bay? There was no particular reason. We just landed there. I barely knew how we got there. I just let Nick drive. But I loved Thunder Bay. It was so beautiful. I was seduced by it.

Of course, that was easy. I was suffering from sensory deprivation. In prison you're so starved for beauty, for anything natural. I could see Mount Mackay on the way to work every morning, and in the other direction, in Lake Superior, there is a huge mound called the Sleeping Giant. Up the hill from our apartment there was a beautiful little hilltop park, with a gorgeous view.

Everything was gorgeous to me.

Thunder Bay was a good choice, I think. It was small enough for me to handle. If we'd gone directly to Toronto, I would have been lost, unable to cope. The pace would have been too frenzied. We heard about Toronto in Thunder Bay, and all the stories were negative: its cost of living was outrageous, its people harsh and unpleasant. People in Thunder Bay certainly implied that no one in their right minds would want to live there.

■　　■　　■

"Tony" had a real driver's license. I'm an artist, so I bought some art supplies and made up more ID for him, (it looked quite authentic when laminated, I must say), and with that and his birth certificate, he got himself a real Ontario driver's license under the name Tony Gazzana, with picture ID and all.

The next thing we had to do was get rid of our car. Not so easy, that. We couldn't sell the damn thing without returning to the border and filling out some forms. Obviously we didn't want to chance that. So we bought a Canadian Datsun. After that, if we'd been pulled over by a cop, we had legitimate papers. I wanted every last detail to be worked out.

You have to think of everything. It's complicated finding out the simplest thing, getting the simplest questions answered. In the U.S., everyone has a Social Security number. I knew they likely existed in Canada, but I didn't know what they were called. How can you ask? You can't stop someone on the street and ask them. And how many digits should it be? We had a three, a two and a four in the U.S. How many in Canada? Fortunately, I found a place that let me take an application form home to fill in, and I saw there were nine little boxes for the Social Insurance number. You have to think of all this just to get a job. And it's hard to get a job without a phone, but you can't get a phone without a job. It's a circular process. If you're legal, of course, none of this is a problem.

■   ■   ■

And Nick? Nick and me?

I don't want to say anything bad about Nick. We were in love, and he was there when I needed him. He helped me get out, and I'm grateful for it.

But I learned that you can't get to know someone in prison.

We were both naive, I think.

I had been in prison for too long. That was years of learning to live without material possessions. I learned actively to reject any attachment to possessions; in prison, attachment leads surely to disappointment. Someone would steal your goods, or break them accidentally or maliciously, and if you had allowed yourself to care, the loss would hurt you. Successful prisoners learn to live entirely internal lives. So I wanted to talk, and to hug, and to take walks, and to go to the park and sit quietly, listening to the silence, taking pleasure in freedom. I needed no music but the wind. I had no desire to watch television, no need for a phone, no urgent need at all to fill the blessed silence.

To me, silence was not an emptiness but a peaceful relief. Silence was a rich part of my freedom.

Nick, on the other hand, was like most people—immersed, saturated, in the material world. He was unhappy without a phone, without a VCR, without a stereo, a television, expensive fishing, golfing and hunting gear. He had to have the best brand of coffee, he's gotta have his White Russians. He was the kind of person who wouldn't mind hiking, but he was uncomfortable without the best hiking boots money could buy. Being penniless, as we were, depressed him.

I tried to warn him before we escaped. I didn't want him to participate blindly. I was afraid he'd blame me. I told him how hard it would be. I told him, "You're going to be homesick. You might lose the custody of your kids. If we get caught you're going to jail, you could do five years." He just kept saying, "I don't care, I love you ..." He treated it as a romantic escapade and never really realized how much he'd have to do without.

Until he was immersed in it. Then, oh, Mr. Unhappiness!

But, as I said, we were both naive. And we hadn't known how unalike we were.

When he got back to Milwaukee, he told some friends, "Laurie has been in jail too long. She's forgotten how to have a good time. She never wanted to go dancing or have fun. She just wanted to go sit in a park and talk."

He never understood that for me that *was* having a wonderful time.

We were penniless, and I got two jobs so we could get by; I was determined to be a good citizen. At first, he went to a lot of job interviews, but he never managed to land one. I never knew why. Something always went wrong. It was never his fault. After a while, he stopped trying so hard. He went fishing several times a week, then he wanted to go moose hunting. He wanted to play, to have a good time. I couldn't figure out why he didn't want to come home to me. I slept alone in prison, and now I was sleeping alone again.

Eventually he got a job selling vacuum cleaners, but it didn't last. It seemed to cost him more in gas than it brought in, anyway.

We had lots of fights, I'm sorry to say. One night, a Sunday night, I was standing at the bus stop in the rain, weary and footsore. Nick was off fishing, I didn't know where, and it slowly dawned on me "What is wrong with this picture? Is this why I escaped from prison? Oh, I'm having so much fun!"

Nick didn't get back until one in the morning. I was terrified he'd been in an accident, had been arrested. I wondered whether I should pack and get to the bus station. But he came back, saying he had been delayed because he had stopped to help a truck out of a ditch. He later admitted that it was a lie.

I guess it was just that he hadn't been inside, hadn't been a prisoner, that he was careless. He used to hang out with friends at a local hardware store, and he once told his friends there that it was my birthday. But it was August—Laurie Bembenek's birthday. Jennifer's birthday is in January! It caused trouble later when we were at a party and people started talking about jewelry with Zodiac signs on it. Someone asked me what my sign was. I had to say Capricorn, and some woman at the party said, "But Tony just said it was your birthday last week?" (I'm a Leo.) Luckily she was half in the bag, and it just went away. How easy it is to get trapped by something so seemingly insignificant. Tony/Nick just thought I was being paranoid when I worried about it.

My main priority was to make Nick happy. I never wanted him to regret what he'd done. I was so grateful to him for helping me. Because of him I was free.

Many times I wished I'd escaped with another inmate. A convict would have understood.

24

RECAPTURED

I never saw the program that did me in.

We did have a TV—Nick insisted on it, so he bought one at a rummage sale. But the last thing I wanted to do after nine years in prison was to watch more TV; I wanted to see the outdoors, to be outside as much as I could. Our set wasn't the best in the world—it only got a couple of channels and we didn't have cable—so if there was indeed something on "America's Most Wanted," I didn't see it. I went to work the next morning as usual.

We'd been planning to move. I knew we were pushing our luck staying in one place as long as we did. One day in the early fall I saw an ad in the newspaper for Banff National Park. They were hiring for the winter ski season and listed a whole range of jobs. I was sure if we went there we could *both* get work. And if Nick and I were on the same schedule and both working, life would be easier and we'd get on better together. I typed up letters of application and mailed them off.

Everything's in the timing, isn't it? We'd been planning to go right away but decided to wait another week, to see what Banff's response would be. If there was no response in a week ... off we'd go.

By September, it was getting colder, already a touch of winter in the air. I took the bus to work as usual. I remember standing around after the breakfast rush with the other waitresses, waiting for the lunch crowd to come in. We were gossiping and laughing when a man in a suit and tie walked in.

He walked toward us and asked to see the owner. Louie wasn't there—he usually came in a little later—and so Ann, a waitress who had worked there since I was in rubber pants, said she'd give him a message. She assumed this person was a salesman. Instead, he asked to talk to her privately. Thelma, another of the waitresses, said to me, "These salesmen are so damn pushy, eh?"

We could see this fellow talking to Anne at the rear of the restaurant. He showed her something and I could see her shaking her head, no. I didn't think anything of it.

Then he came back to where we were all standing. Oh God! He showed me his badge and said, "Can I talk to you for a minute?" He was a Thunder Bay cop.

Well, let me tell you! Talk about a heart attack! I almost had a massive coronary on the spot. Of course I knew at once why he was there.

I thought, Calm down and it'll be okay, just calm down ... My life was flashing before my eyes and I was thinking, Okay, this is it, it's over.

We went to a booth and sat down. He spoke first.

"I asked if anyone from the States was working here, and you're from the States?"

"Yes," I said, stating the obvious.

"What are you doing here?"

Nick and I had several stories prepared. It had gotten somewhat complicated because to some people Nick had said that I was a Canadian, and to others that we were both Americans and he'd been transferred to Thunder Bay. Different people heard different stories, and it was sometimes difficult remembering which story was which, and keeping track of the different versions. Oh God.

I said, "My husband got a job transfer."

"Oh? How long have you been here?"

"Oh, since about June, or something like that."

He asked me for identification, and I dug it out of my purse. Oh God. Oh God.

"What's your date of birth?" he asked. Cops always ask you for your date of birth, even when you've just handed them a birth certificate.

"January 7, 1961," I said, remembering to be Jennifer.

"Where are you from?"

"Chicago. I was born in Milwaukee but I moved to Chicago when I was a baby." Everyone at the restaurant thought I was from Chicago.

He didn't ask for my work permit, which was just as well because I didn't have one. Nor did he ask for my visa, which was also just as well, for the same reason. He asked my husband's name and my address. At first I was going to lie about my address, but I made a split-second decision—what happens if he asks someone on the way out where I live, and they tell him? So I told him.

Then he pulled out The Picture.

It was a fax, a poor reproduction, but it was definitely me and Nick. I was just dying.

"Have you ever seen this before?"

I tried to look thoughtful, and squinted at the picture.

"No," I said, "Nooooo ... I don't think so."

"Is that your husband?"

"Not at all," I said. I had a curly perm by now, so I looked different.

"Okay, I guess I'll tell them we got the wrong girl," he said, and got up, and walked to the front of the restaurant.

But by then Louie was at the cash register and the cop pulled the picture out again. I saw Louie shaking his head, no, no ... He must have asked him the same question. After another minute, out the door he went.

Well!

I was thinking, Oh my God oh my God oh my God what am I going to do? I couldn't just run out of there. Everybody in the restaurant would then know.

Think, Laurie, think!

The first thing was to reach Tony, Nick, I no longer knew what to call him. Was he home? Noooo! I called all over Thunder Bay looking for him, and he was nowhere to be found. I finally called the hardware store where he usually hung out and left a message.

"It's extremely important, it's an emergency, if he shows up tell him to call me immediately, okay?"

How long should I wait? Maybe they've got him already? In the States, the cops would "sit on" the restaurant; they'd park nearby, and if the suspect went flying out of there, that's your man. Surely that's what they were doing right now? Meanwhile, the lunch crowd came in, a real stampede, everyone wanting food right away. Suddenly I had twelve tables to wait on and no time at all to think.

My mind was spinning. I didn't know my left hand from my right. I gave people menus, took orders—God knows what I served them. The refrain was going through my mind: oh my God oh my God oh my God oh my God! I was trying to act normally, whatever that was. I didn't want to panic, because when you panic you get stupid, do something stupid, like flying out of there.

The phone rang. Anne answered and called me over.

"Jennifer, it's Tony."

I talked quickly. "Look," I said, "we've got to get out of here right now, come and pick me up immediately, it's the cops, we've got to get out of here ..."

"Okay," Nick said, and hung up.

I guess I had a troubled look on my face, and one of the waitresses asked me what was wrong.

"Look, I'm sorry, I had a death in the family," I said. "I have to go." What an old excuse! I hated lying to them because they were my friends, but what could I do? Louie gave me an odd look.

I put my coat on, and since it was raining outside I put my hood up, and left out the back door. I looked up and down the alley and saw no cops. With my hood up I don't know whether they would have noticed me anyway. I walked to the corner and looked around. Nick wasn't there yet.

I waited. After a minute he arrived. And what did he do? He pulled up in front and leaned on the horn! *Beep beep beep*! Why not just let everyone in Thunder Bay know you're here, Nick? Why not rent a giant neon sign?

Up the block I waved and he saw me and pulled up. I got into the car, by this time completely panicked.

I said, "We've got to get out of here right now, right away, don't even pull over, let's go!"

And he said, calmly, "Now wait, wait a minute, explain to me what happened, don't panic. Let's decide what to do."

I told him about the cop and the picture.

After a while he said, "So let's go to Banff."

"Okay."

But there was a problem. I'd been making our fake ID at the apartment, and there was incriminating material lying around. If they got a warrant to search the flat they'd be able to trace us easily. Not only would they have our aliases, but they'd know for sure who we really were and how we'd done what we did.

What bad timing! We'd been planning to get rid of the stuff, but we hadn't quite finished with it. Worse—the Wednesday after we got busted we got Canadian ID, the real stuff. A week later and we'd have been free and clear. One week later! I could have screamed. The only way they could have traced us after that would have been through fingerprints. We could have worked normally, lived normal lives. Oh, the might-have-beens!

And that's all I ever wanted to do, to be legal.

I didn't want to commit any crimes or rob banks. I just wanted to be legal, be normal, like everybody else. Get a work permit, work, earn money, have a real life. One more week ...

But this scrambling ... collecting all this stuff takes time! You can only do things so fast. People don't understand. They would say, "You were there for three months! Why didn't you go to Europe?" I'd say, "Because we were waiting for passports. You can't get passports overnight. You need paper to get paper."

■　　■　　■

So many times I'd sit on the bus and look at all the people around me and think, God, I'd trade places with any of them, just to be normal and legal and legitimate, and not have to look over my shoulder, worrying about my actions, my words. Any face, any of those faces on the bus would do. I'd trade my life with any of them.

Any day, at any time, they could come and take me away.

■　　■　　■

We sat in the car, arguing. I didn't want to go back to the apartment, and he did.

"You're panicking," he said. "If they really thought that was you in that picture, they'd have picked you up right away." That sounded reasonable. But what if they were sitting on the house?

"Okay," I said. "We'll drive up High Street and look down our street. We'll be able to see the whole block, and if there are any strange cars outside the house, we're taking right off, we're not going in."

Even then Nick argued. "I can't leave my fishing rods! Those are nine hundred dollar fishing rods! And the boat motor! I have to return Charlie's boat motor!"

Meanwhile, he was driving toward the apartment. *He wants his goddamn fishing rods, he tells me I'm panicking, we should fetch the incriminating stuff ...* So I said, "Okay, maybe you're right."

Of course, we should never have gone home.

Looking back, it seems obvious.

There were no strange cars anywhere near our apartment. After more discussion, I persuaded Nick to park in the garage—at least that way our car wouldn't be quite so obvious. I went in to begin throwing things together in suitcases, and to change into my jeans.

It took the cops a while. The Thunder Bay cop went and had lunch or something, and only called the RCMP after that. Then the RCMP called Immigration to see if there were work permits in the names of Jennifer and Tony Gazzana, and of course there weren't. So the Mounties, while they didn't know who we were, figured they at least had a pair of illegals on their hands.

Nick took some of our things from the apartment out to the car. But he left the back door open.

In a basement flat, you can't look out to see if anyone's there. I heard a little *tap tap tap* on the back door. I assumed it was Nick, though I was puzzled—is he carrying something back into the house and he can't get the door? It was just a little *tap tap*, not like a true knock on the door. I peeked around, and saw nothing. I came out of the apartment and peered up at the outside door. If the door had been closed I'd never have answered. They could have waited all day. (Though Nick, of course, was still at large, in the garage.) I'd be holed up in the basement and we'd tunnel out—or something! Nick had left the door open, and an RCMP cop was standing there.

I thought, Well, game over. At the same time, I didn't recognize the cop. It wasn't the same person who'd been at the restaurant.

He was very polite. "Are you Jennifer Gazzana?"

And I said, "Yeeah," cautiously.

I was thinking, Oh, holy shit!

I knew if he went in it would be the end. We had been frantically packing, and there was stuff all over the apartment. The place looked trashed. It wouldn't have taken a genius to see that someone was trying to leave in one awful hurry. The Thunder Bay cop arrived, smiling.

I thought, If he comes in, that's it, that's all.

I didn't know if he needed a warrant or not. I didn't know Canada's laws.

"Can I come in?" he asked.

I said nothing. We stood there for a moment.

"We do have the right," he said. "We *can* come in."

I wasn't in a position to argue. I just didn't know. Nor could I afford to seem uncooperative. He started saying something about work permits and I was thinking, Oh man ...

And then Nick came in.

That was the end of that. I had told Nick to shave his mustache off, but he has a distinctive face; he's got this big nose and there's no hiding it, not much you can do to change his appearance. The cop looked at the pictures and said, "That's our boy! Now, who are you?"

All of a sudden everybody was there—the RCMP, the local cops, the Immigration officers, three jurisdictions.

Ohhhh man, I thought, it's over.

You know, I was so exhausted that there was almost a sense of relief. Finally, we can relax.

I can't tell you how exhausting it was to live like that. I felt like the horse in Orwell's *Animal Farm*. It was way too much for me.

We walked into the apartment, and the Thunder Bay cop who'd been at the restaurant earlier looked around and said, "Hmmm, looks like we're in a hurry to leave," or something like that, and I sat down at the table and I thought, Oh well ...

It was so low-key! In the States, the cops would have been busting down the door with sawn-off shotguns, screaming, *"Hit the floor! Freeze!"* (the Kent State approach). But not these guys. They were quite casual.

The Thunder Bay cop asked me, "Could I please see the ID you showed me earlier today?"

I dug into my purse. Now, I could have had a gun in there. I didn't, of course—we didn't own any weapons and I wouldn't do something like that anyway—but he didn't know that. I also dug into a couple of drawers to pull out some clothing. I mean, I could have had an arsenal in there! If I'd been the desperate criminal everyone thought I was, they'd all have been dead, for real. I was shocked, to tell the truth, at how casual they were.

One of the cops looked at me and said, "You used to be a cop, didn't you?"
And I said, "Yeah."
"Run, Bambi, Run!" he said, and started to laugh. Hysteria.
I just sat at the table and said to myself, Great, this is just great! Oh God!

They radioed for more people. I looked at Nick and he looked at me and we just shrugged. They wanted to know all kinds of things—when we came over the border, our previous address, how long we'd been there.

We had a bank account, and they went through it carefully. How did we get this money? Did we commit robberies?

"Not at all," I said. "There was a payroll check from both my employers deposited on a weekly basis, the same amount, you can easily see we didn't do anything like that."

"Do you have any weapons?" they asked. "Drugs? Stolen property?"

We said no, and they said, okay. Again, in the States they would have been tearing that place apart, looking for who knows what, creating more problems than they solved, wrecking the poor place. Not here. They just politely asked us questions. I was quite surprised.

Finally, they formally placed us under arrest—the RCMP, the cop from the restaurant and the Immigration officer.

I watched all this in wonder. These guys were really nice! In the States, we would have been in shackles, in separate cars, on our way to jail in minutes. But not here. One of the Thunder Bay cops asked me what we wanted to do with our cat—he was really concerned about it. The cat was walking around being friendly, not knowing what was going on. I didn't want to just leave him. The cops let me write a little note to my landlady asking her to take care of our cat and saying how sorry I was. What would Jenny think? Oh God!

Then we went outside, to the squad cars. We came out into the air, and there were cops in the front and back yards. The weather was dramatic, strange—it was snowing, but there were also flashes of lightning and rumbles of thunder.

Nick and I were together in the same squad car on the way to the local jail. That was another thing they'd never do in the States. There, they would have separated us at once, so we couldn't talk. But they let us travel together in the same squad, and we chatted quietly as we drove. I promised I would never make any incriminating statements to the police against him and warned him not to talk to any cops until he got a lawyer.

That night the news went over the wire, and the next morning I woke up and the tiny Thunder Bay jail was surrounded. Every tripod and satellite dish in the world was there. *People* magazine was there, all three networks, TimeLife, "20/20," "60 Minutes," "Hard Copy," "A Current Affair" and "Inside Edition." It was a mess. The poor jail didn't know what was going on. They'd never seen anything like this before; they were just shocked.

Of course, the media people were demanding to be let in.

No, they said, this is Canada. I don't know where you people are from, but you don't get in.

It was just a little rinkydink bucket anyway, a very tiny jail, but they wouldn't let anybody in. Good for them.

■　　■　　■

But—and this makes me sick at heart, this is how institutionalized I have become—I didn't feel normal until I was back in jail.

When I was back inside, I thought, I'm home again ... I know how to do this, I can do jail ...

All the time I was out there, while I was free, I wanted to keep pinching myself, I felt like I was dreaming, I felt unreal, I was disoriented. So often I would stop myself and think, No, I'm going to wake up any minute now, this isn't real.

Jail feels real to me. Freedom doesn't.

When I finally got back in, I lay down on my bunk, took a nap and thought, So I'm back in. That's normal.

I hate this. I've become like a caged bird who can't handle freedom. It sickens me.

Perhaps, I comfort myself, three months of freedom wasn't enough. Perhaps being on the run isn't really being free. Perhaps with more time my sense of self would return from where I have hidden it. Perhaps there is still a chance I can become me again. I don't know. I hope so, but it terrifies me that perhaps the "me" of myself has shriveled and died ...

■　　■　　■

As I lay on my bunk, small things filled my head. The little things that others would not have noticed. For instance, every day after an eight-hour shift at the restaurant I would have a bagful of loonies, dollar coins, from tips, and we'd go grocery shopping. We'd be at the cash register and I'd hand over a fistful of loonies. It used to drive Nick crazy. "Laurie," he said (forgetting to call me Jennifer), "will you stop this? It looks like we've been panhandling all day. Stop paying in change!" He thought it was socially inappropriate behavior. It was just money to me.

That would happen all the time. I never got the hang of acting normally. I kept asking Nick, "Am I acting weird?" Mostly he would comfort me, tell me I was doing okay.

■　　■　　■

I don't usually believe in fate. I'm not a spiritual person. But, what happened next ... Matters got rather strange ...

I hadn't thought through my legal situation very well. I just assumed I'd be returned at once, that I'd be on the next plane out and back in Taycheedah the next day. That's certainly what the Immigration people implied. I knew I had to go to a hearing, but I didn't know what for.

"Is this a hearing where I need a lawyer?" I asked.

"Oh no," they said. They'd rather I didn't, of course.

Okay, I thought, I won't bother.

Thunder Bay doesn't have a major-league jail. It's a twenty-foot by seven-foot cellblock for women, with a picnic table bolted to the bars, a little black-and-white TV in the corner, three cells with three bunks each, a shower and a little table in the corner where they stack *True Romance* magazines. That's it, that's all—you eat, sleep and shower in that little cage and you don't go anywhere. The only pleasant aspect is the view; there's a pretty view of Lake Superior from the window.

There are no phones, no exercise treadmill or bicycle. Nothing.

The cops came the next morning and said, "You're going to a hearing. Are you dressed? You're going to court."

I brushed my teeth and waited and waited. Two hours went by, and nothing happened.

So I thought, Wait a minute! The misinformation is starting already. I'd better get myself a lawyer.

A tiny guard called Debbie came into the cellblock. She was really nice, a very pretty woman, a pleasant person.

I asked her, "How does a person go about getting a lawyer if we can't make a phone call? I'm not from here so I don't know any lawyers."

She said, "Oh, we'll call a lawyer for you. We have a list of legal-aid lawyers. I'll call Mary Kelly for you, she's really good, everyone seems to like her."

I was impressed. A woman lawyer, good!

About four hours later I was less impressed. Nothing had happened. No one came. I was thinking, Yeah, right, you'll call a lawyer for me. Already the lies are starting.

But I was wrong. Debbie had been calling all over, looking for Kelly. Kelly was at her cottage and didn't return the call. Finally Debbie returned.

"I can't find Kelly so I'll call the next lawyer on the list," she said.

And that was Dave Dubinsky.

Now Dave was six months out of law school, twenty-six years old. He is such a doll, like a brother to me, I just love this guy. He looked fresh-faced and sweet as he walked into the lawyer visiting room. It was pretty overwhelming for him. By now the papers were printing their garbage and the media circus was in full cry. He fought his way through the scrum to get to me. Dubinsky was so young and dressed so casually that he didn't look like a lawyer, and they didn't bother him.

We talked for a while, and he said, "Let me talk to my partner, Ron Lester, and we'll come back tonight."

So they did. And it all fell into place for me. Without me even trying.

Understand this, what it felt like. For nine years I'd been clawing and scraping and doing everything in my power, begging and borrowing, to try to get out of jail, calling and writing and hounding people, trying everything, exhausting myself. And now, for the first time, I sat back and did absolutely nothing and people helped me anyway. It blew my mind.

What an incredible sense of relief! I couldn't get Legal Aid because I'm not a Canadian, but these lawyers didn't care about money. They recognized that a terrible injustice had occurred and wanted to help.

Ron Lester and Dave Dubinsky gave me back a bit of myself. And I love them for it.

Lester came in with a copy of the Immigration Act, and he said, "You know, this might be a long shot, but I think you have a legitimate refugee claim."

■　　■　　■

My parents and Nick's parents flew up to join us. The Immigration Act requires a hearing within forty-eight hours after arrest, and the ministry assigned some-one from its Sault Ste. Marie office and from Mississauga, near Toronto, to act for them. Ron told us from the start that Nick didn't have the same case; he was being deported right away.

My lawyers warned me that the refugee-hearing process might take a very long time, and that the time I spent in jail in Canada would not count against my sentence in Wisconsin.

"Well," I said, "what have I got to lose? I already have a life sentence. And the longer I'm away from that horrible place the better." I wasn't in any hurry to go back.

Nick was deported November 16, 1990. He got bailed out December 1, 1990, and he had his preliminary hearing December 6, being bound over for trial. The charge? Aiding and Abetting Escape from Lawful Custody. They set his bail at one hundred thousand dollars! Wisconsin is really insane. His sister borrowed money for him.

I tried to tell him to plea bargain at once. I pleaded with him.

"Believe me, Nick, I've been through this system for nine years, listen to me. You're guilty, so don't even think you're going to be acquitted. Plea bargain at once, and get it over with."

Instead, he entered a not guilty plea.

Nick fired his first lawyer, who had wanted to blame me for the whole thing. It was the old Svengali defense—this manipulative woman had some-how hypnotized him, somehow forced him to do this from prison, had held a (metaphoric) gun to his head and forced him. Nick didn't buy that. He knew it had been a mutual decision.

I argued with him again. I said, "Just get a public defender, plead guilty, and you'll get a nice little deal. And by the time I'm done in Canada you'll be out." But noooo! He wouldn't listen.

They found him guilty anyway, just like I said they would. He was con-victed on September 4, 1991 and went to jail. In November 1991 Nick stopped writing to me.

■   ■   ■

I spent five months in the cellblock of the Thunder Bay jail. Jenny Beck, Louie Kabezes, and other local friends faithfully visited me, including my co-workers from the restaurant and my other boss, Debbie Pedre from the fitness center. All were very supportive and encouraging and kind. A regular customer, Doug Smith, even got a group of carollers together at Christmas and they sang outside beneath the jail windows.

It was a long, tough five months, not knowing what my future held, alone and heartbroken. With no access to cream rinse or conditioner for my new perm, my hair looked like a psychotic gerbil's nest. With no access to Vaseline or Chapstick, the jail's dry heat turned my lips into a chapped, cracked and bleeding mess. The other problem was that smoking was not allowed anywhere in the jail for the staff with the exception of the cellblocks—so they'd all come into our cellblock to smoke day and night, which bothered me. The canteen list was very limited and offered only Old Spice deodorant—which reminds me thoroughly of my dad—but no women's products at all. We received a change of clean clothes once a week, consisting of one pair of panties, socks, a bra, some sweatpants and a sweatshirt.

Soon I was disappointed to learn that only the male inmates were allowed to work—not women. The men also had a separate cellblock for mentally ill prisoners, but the women did not—so we occasionally shared the cellblock with women from the Lakehead Psychiatric Hospital across the street. I caught a nasty virus from one of them because she failed to cover her mouth when she coughed. With no access to cough drops or cough syrup, I waited five days to see the doctor and coughed all night every night. The other women, for the most part, were Native Canadians (aboriginals). I never did see one single black person in Thunder Bay, but there seemed to be a large Native population.

The days *crawled* by. Like a Sumo wrestler (held in a cage and force fed), I managed to put on ten pounds in five months because the food was dynamite. While in Canada I acquired a taste for gravy on my french fries—like they don't have enough calories already—and the jail gave us a snack at 9:00 PM like tea and big chocolate macaroon muffins, still warm from the oven!

■   ■   ■

In Thunder Bay, we went back and forth to court a couple of times. The U.S. media was raising hell about not having access to the hearings. Normally, immigration hearings are closed to the public. The media can petition for access provided they don't disrupt the proceedings. Initially, they were not allowed in, and it was driving them wild. So the first couple of hearings dealt mostly with that.

Dave Dubinsky stood up in court. "We have a tradition here in Canada," he said. "We try people in the courtroom, not in the newspapers."

No wonder I love this guy!

Ron Lester had been approached by the Justice Ministry about becoming a judge. He'd been looking at it for a while, and told me he was thinking of accepting. He was feeling burned-out by practicing criminal law, and he wanted out. At the same time, he said, he didn't want to leave me in the middle of my fight without a good lawyer.

I believe it sincerely bothered him, and this was really a switch. I was so unaccustomed to concern, especially from lawyers. It had become clear to me that in the U.S. a good lawyer won't even talk to you if you don't have three hundred thousand dollars in your pocket. They just don't seem to care. If you have the retainer, fine, if not, goodbye.

But now—an ethical lawyer! A lawyer with a conscience! A lawyer who cares about his clients! I couldn't believe it!

It was Ron that picked out a refugee claim as a possible defense.

When he told the case presenting officer that this is what he was going to do, alarm bells went off in the Justice Department. Or I suppose they did, because shortly after that the Minister of Immigration and Citizenship, Barbara McDougall, issued a certificate calling me a danger to the public. Ron Lester then knew that he urgently needed someone who was a criminal lawyer with a knowledge of constitutional and immigration law.

Ron called his friend David McCombs, a criminal lawyer, in Toronto.

"No, I can't do this," David told Ron. "She needs *the* expert on immigration. Let me call Frank Marrocco. He wrote the book on immigration—literally. It's called *The Annotated Immigration Act*."

■   ■   ■

Frank Marrocco showed up at my next hearing in Thunder Bay, and the Immigration Department adjudicator just about fell off his chair. They wanted to ship me back right away, and having Frank Marrocco walk in was an unpleasant surprise for them.

I had hearings in December, and that same month I took a polygraph test, a thorough examination of my veracity conducted by a well know Toronto firm called International Corporate Investigators Inc. The specialist they used was John J. J. McClinton, a certified forensic polygraphist. His conclusion was pretty clear: "It is the final opinion of the polygraphist," his report said, "based upon the polygraphic interview of the examinee, that Lawrencia Bembenek was telling the truth when she denied shooting Christine Schultz in her home with a thirty-eight caliber handgun on May 28, 1981. This truthful polygraphic opinion is substantiated by the statistically significant total examination scores of +8 recorded for Lawrencia Bembenek ..."

Bear in mind that a total score of -6 or lower, means the subject is not truthful; a score between +5 and -5 is inconclusive; and +6 or greater means a judgment of truthful.

There were more hearings in January and March. On March 26, 1991, I got a change of venue and was sent to Toronto.

I have been in Toronto ever since. It's where I write these words.

■　　■　　■

From my jail cell in Thunder Bay, I wrote to my mom:

Dear mom
Did you ever think for one second
after I was born
that the baby you carried home in your arms
would someday be a cop, a convict, a refugee?
You just don't know how many times
I looked out a window
at an ordinary woman walking down the street
with a bag of groceries or a small dog
and wished I was that woman—
wished I was anybody but me;
just someone plain, anonymous, legitimate
normal and free.
Did you ever think for one second
when you saved me from drowning
in Canada twenty-three years ago
that someday
Canada would in turn
try to save my life?

I love you and dad so much!
Laurie

25

FREEDOM FOR A DAY

I was transferred to this grim place, Toronto's Metro West Detention Centre, in March 1991. Population: over six hundred. One morning, in September, I went out, as usual, for "Yard" (a kind of outdoor "airing" given prisoners in this otherwise recreation-free environment).

I wasn't expecting any trouble. After all these years, I know how to live with women, how to get along, and I seldom had any problems.

I was sitting by myself in the sun when four women came over and sat down beside me. I mean, *right next to me*, a deliberate provocation. Oh oh, I thought, I don't know these people, something is about to go down. I knew that whatever it was, it would be something ugly.

The woman closest to me was covered with homemade tattoos and pus-filled needle track-marks. I found out who she was later—a hard-bitten old con who had spent time in the Pen. Most people knew her as an old lesbian junkie prostitute from the Parkdale area of Toronto. She was a truly repulsive person. I heard her bragging about stealing from her dealer and then stabbing him fifteen times. "Yeah, well, I stole twelve grams of heroin from the fucking goof ..." A true gem, a charmer.

But these are the people you have to live with.

She'd read about me, and for some reason something clicked in the mush the heroin had made of her brains.

She started in—"You fucking copper ..."—and she began to spit at me. Her three friends joined in.

This, I didn't need. I normally remain passive in these situations. I'll defend myself when attacked, but I won't throw the first punch. It's seldom worth getting into any kind of fight, and here even more so. I have too much to lose. Although it took everything I had not to react, I remained still. I'm particularly vulnerable here, I thought. The last thing I need just before one of my hearings is to get into a physical altercation in Yard. What if I accidentally hurt this woman? There would go my refugee claim. There was a concrete floor out there. If she fell and cracked her head ... I could already see the headline: "Bembenek kills Canadian inmate."

People don't understand what jail is like, what the provocations are. Any incident would be torn out of context, and I'd be portrayed, again, as a violent, crazy person.

I didn't feel physically threatened, because I can take care of myself, but I didn't want to have to, I wanted to avoid it. So I struggled not to react.

They pushed me. People like this always feel powerful in groups.

So all I said was, "Give me a break, eleven years ago I was a cop ..."

She just sneered. "Once a cop, always a cop."

"Look," I said, trying to be reasonable, "I've done more time than all you clowns put together."

It was unpleasant, but there was no violence. Still, I stopped going to Yard after that. It was the only time I had all day to get fresh air, and now even that was taken away from me.

A few days later the guards intercepted kites (unauthorized letters) these people were writing to each other. They were full of death threats. You should have seen them: "We'll kill her, we'll stab her in the shower, I'd be proud to go to Seg for killing a cop ..."

The institution moved fairly swiftly; they didn't want an incident any more than I did. They moved her to another range, where we wouldn't bump into each other. I was blamed, of course. I was the rat because they moved her. The inmates' golden rule is, "Don't go to the cops for anything."

I agonized over this. Should I continue going to Yard? If I don't go, they'll have won, they'll have dictated to me. If I do go, there's going to be a fight, I know it. I wrestled with myself, not knowing what to do.

It was at that time that they let me out.

Cruelly, cruelly, for a day.

And then they put me back.

■　　■　　■

It came out of the blue, one Thursday afternoon while I was at "hobbycraft."

I lived for hobbycraft. I was not allowed to work because they were convinced I was Houdini, so the only thing they allowed me to do in this prison was go to the hobbycraft room twice a week—Tuesday afternoons and Thursday afternoons. There I could get out my brushes and my paints and, using whatever surface I could find—some old cardboard, scraps of plywood or particle board—I'd try to lose myself in my painting. (The *Toronto Sun* later published a page of my paintings under the heading "The Artful Dodger." *Please!*)

Wouldn't you know, of course, that the Immigration people would choose to hold their weekly review of my detention every Thursday, too? Under the terms of the Immigration Act, detentions must be reviewed every seven days, but it didn't really matter which day it was held. It seemed perverse of them to insist on holding it on my hobbycraft day.

The hearing cannot be waived. Everyone knows it's a waste of time and money, but they hold it anyway. It usually takes only a few minutes. An adjudicator and a case-presenting officer go to the prison; the CPO tells you what a jerk and a menace to the public you are, and then they leave. It doesn't do much for morale, let me tell you.

That Thursday, the art teacher came to pick me up as usual. The hobbycraft room is on the men's side of Metro West, a good five-minute walk away. Of course, you can't go anywhere unescorted. As with any art class, it takes a while to set up, get the paints ready and jars open and canvas in place and so on, and so you don't have very much time for actual painting. No sooner did I start that day, September 12, 1991, when the guard arrived. "I need Bembenek for Immigration."

The teacher said, "Well, when you're finished, could you bring her back?"

I begged the guard to wait for me. "It only takes thirty seconds or so," I said. If he left, I wouldn't be able to go back to my painting.

"Okay," he said.

But when we got there, only one person was in the room—Terry Mackay, the adjudicator that day. There was a national civil servants' strike going on, and they hadn't been able to find a CPO willing to cross the picket line. A CPO must be present for a detention review.

Mackay explained the problem. "Thanks," I said, and left.

"You weren't kidding about the thirty seconds," the guard said.

He took me back to hobbycraft.

About twenty minutes later, another guard showed up.

"We need Bembenek again," he said.

It was maddening. I went stomping back. I stalked into the room, and there was a new person there, a CPO I'd never seen before. I stood, waiting for the wham-bam-thank-you-ma'am, but he just sat there. Then the adjudicator said, "I want to ask you some questions."

I thought, That's odd. What's this? It's a game you learn to play in prison: Do I get my hopes up? No! He doesn't mean anything by it. You have to struggle to maintain mental strength, and not getting your hopes up is a basic strategy—you have to come to terms with the fact that you're not going anywhere.

I was thinking, Nah! It can't mean anything!

Mackay spoke quietly. "There is quite a lot happening in the U.S. right now regarding your case. Would you be more willing to return there if they ordered a new trial?"

I suppose rumors of the John Doe investigation they had launched in Milwaukee had been circulating. But this left me in something of a pickle. I'd applied to stay in Canada as a refugee. That meant I was maintaining that I mistrusted the U.S. judicial system, that I believed it would not give me a fair trial. I couldn't now say I thought it would treat me fairly. On the other hand, his question was innocent; he was thinking of granting me bail, and he wanted me to say that I wouldn't flee. I was between a rock and a hard place. I gave him some outrageous two-step answer, babbling for twenty seconds without really saying anything. A hypothetical answer for a hypothetical question.

Then he said, "Well, let me ask you this: if bail was granted, would you return for your hearings?"

"Of course," I said, meaning it fervently. "If someone put up money for me for bail, there's no way I couldn't return. That would be a real slap in the face for that person. I wouldn't do that to anybody, anybody."

And I added, "In any case, where am I going to go? When I first came to Canada, no one looked twice at me. Now, my face is all over. There's no place I *can* go. The point is, I want to stay.

"People from the Justice Department say to me, 'We can't let you out because you have a history of escape.' Well, no kidding! How do you think I got here? But it's a circular argument—when I escaped the first time I had absolutely nothing to lose, and nor did anyone else. I didn't compromise anyone. And no one lost money because of me.

"You can't compare that to the situation now.

"Since then, a great deal of exculpatory evidence has been documented. If I ran now, I would lose everything—the faith that my lawyers have in me, and all my supporters, the growing presumption of my innocence. There's simply no way I could contemplate taking off. I'd have to be crazy—I have a very good chance now."

Mackay said, "I have the tendency to agree with you, Miss Bembenek, and I'm going to order your release."

Well, I just about fell off my chair.

He looked at the CPO and asked, "Do you have any submissions on this?"

The CPO said, "No submissions."

I was numb. Once a week, very formally, they sat me down and told me what a horrible person I am, what a danger to the public, how I'm an escape risk, a fugitive, a runaway who would never come back, a real menace that no one could trust. On and on they'd go.

This time this person just said, "No submissions."

What was this?

He said nothing more, just looked down at his papers.

My heart was thumping. I couldn't believe that somebody, after all this time, was ordering my release. A tear rolled down my face.

Metro West was a very punitive environment, really tough. The year I had so far spent there was harder than nine years at Taycheedah. Metro West was just a holding tank, a detention center, never meant for long stays. It's not equipped to hold inmates for years like prisons are. It has no humanity. You can't go anywhere, you can't do anything, you can't have anything—any of the little creature comforts that you might have had in other prisons are forbidden here. Three or four times a week they get everyone up and line us up, and you think you're at Dachau or something. You get strip-searched, then they search your cell and take away the one pen more than you're supposed to have, tip through all your stuff, take whatever they feel like. We're allowed virtually no possessions.

People weren't supposed to stay there as long as I had.

I was thinking about all this, about this awful place, and tears were running down my face. I was just stunned. The CPO left to take a phone call, and I said to Mackay, "Honest to God, you will not regret this decision. I'll not do anything to make you regret this. I've been begging to be allowed to live in a less punitive environment. Can I shake your hand, can I please shake your hand?"

I wanted to hug the guy! I wanted to have his baby! Let me hug you! Please!

I shook his hand.

"I've been thinking about this for a long time," he said. "You're right, where could you go? You've got a good chance right now."

"I know," I said. "That's the other point, I want to stay in Canada."

I thanked him a thousand times, I think, in about a minute.

He set the conditions on my bail: stay at the Elizabeth Fry Society Halfway House, do volunteer work at the Salvation Army (I wasn't allowed to work without a work permit), ten thousand dollars cash bail and ten thousand dollars surety. He also added the stipulation that I report to the Immigration office every day.

"I'll report ten times a day if that's what it takes, if that's what you want," I said. "It's okay, I'll do anything."

So he signed the papers and started to walk out.

I called after him, "Don't I get a copy?"

"No," he said, and left.

■   ■   ■

They returned me to my cell, my mind utterly boggled. I didn't say anything to anyone. I couldn't. I had nothing to prove this had really happened, nothing tangible, no copy of the release order.

Just then one of my lawyers, David Liblong, came by with a reporter from CBC TV. I went down to the visiting room, my mind spinning. David walked in and picked up the phone on the other side of the glass wall.

"David!" I said, trying not to look agitated. "You won't believe what just happened! They just ordered my release at a detention review!"

Liblong's eyeballs popped. "Holy shit!" he said. "Please, don't tell anyone!"

The reporter was asking me questions, and I didn't know what I was saying ... I must have sounded like someone who ought to switch right away to decaf. It was unreal!

I couldn't think. I couldn't sleep. I paced like a tiger. I lay awake all night. It was so unreal. I was sure there was someone in the background with authority over Terry Mackay who would put a stop to this as soon as he heard about it. On the other hand, they were on strike, so maybe it was going to happen.

I called my mom and told her, and I was crying, and she said, "Should we come up, Sweetie?"

"No," I said, "don't come, just wait, it's too soon, too much can happen."

Of course, they didn't listen, they were on the next plane. I was afraid it would fall apart, and I didn't want them to take on any more pain. On my own, I could handle it.

I didn't pack anything in the morning. I didn't tell anyone. What was I to do? I tried to call my lawyers at home, but no one was there. They weren't in the office, either.

Then the superintendent came to my cell and she put her hand through the bars, and she said, "Well, good luck, Laurie ..." And then I thought, If she's heard about it, it must be true!

I bundled my little possessions together, my few precious little things, my Russian studies book, my Immigration Act, my law course, a few toiletries, some lotion, a little shampoo. I put them into a pillow case, because I didn't have a bag.

Nine o'clock came. I went out for Yard and played ping-pong for a while because I couldn't sit still, and then a guard came and hollered, "Bembenek!"

This is it! They don't come to Yard unless it's important.

I went running in and they took me to A&D—Arrivals and Departures—where everyone gets processed. That's where all your money and possessions are, and the paperwork gets done. I had some paintings I'd done and two boxes full of junk. Some of it I'd never seen—sometimes people would send me stuff and the prison would simply confiscate it. I had to carry all this stuff—the paintings, these boxes, my little bag of possessions. The only clothes I had to wear in Canada were the dress and high heels I'd been wearing to hearings. I didn't want to be teetering around on these golf-tees carrying boxes and paintings, so I asked if I could wear jeans and my prison-issue top. "No," they said, "if you have clothes you must change into them here."

The International Center, where the Immigration Ministry is headquartered, had sent Pinkerton guards in a van for me. They had to wait until I'd changed into my dress.

Bad, bad timing. In the five minutes it took me to change into my dress, the guy at the desk got a phone call.

He came up to the Pinkerton sergeant and said, "Can I talk to you?" in that "Oh no!" tone of voice that you learn to recognize, that all prisoners know and love. They whispered together for a few minutes. The Pinkerton man came back with a stunned look on his face. "You're not going," he said.

I was standing at the door, waiting for the electronic gate to open so I could get into the van. I was in my dress, carrying my boxes.

"I don't understand," he said. "I've got your release order right here, this is as good as a court order. But ... we were told to return to the International Center without you."

And I thought, I knew it! I knew it I knew it I knew it!

And so they left.

The superintendent didn't know what to do with me. She put me for a while in the little bullpen near the entrance. I sat there in my dress, in this filthy and horrible place, cold concrete ... She said, "I don't know what's going on,

Laurie. If we knew, we'd tell you. I don't know what game they're playing. But we have to take you back upstairs."

They took me back up to the range, one step farther away from the door, away from freedom. I was still in my dress. I couldn't call anyone, because they turn the phones off over lunch.

I was just hanging by a thread.

What were they trying to do? After ten years, this was the first time I'd be out legally, and they were telling me, Yes, No, Yes, No ...

I tried to eat, but my stomach was in knots. About an hour went by, I think—I don't really know because we are not allowed clocks. Then they came for me again.

They said, "Let's try this again, Bembenek."

"Are you sure this time?"

We went back to the main floor, I signed out my money, and this time I made it out the door. I was in the van, driving away. They had sent three Pinkerton guards to come and get me. One of these swashbucklers looked down at me—I was in nylons—and said, "Oh, these shackles are really going to hurt your ankles ..."

I was being released, and she wanted to shackle me? Please! I imagined teetering along on high heels, in shackles, carrying boxes and paintings. It was ridiculous, and eventually she saw it, too. She left the shackles off.

We arrived at the International Center, and they wouldn't let us in. Civil servants' strike. Pickets. It was the media circus from hell—satellite dishes everywhere. Crowds of picketers rushed the van and wouldn't let us go.

The van engine was turned off and we sat. It was very hot without the air-conditioning on, 100 degrees or so, and we sat sweltering. The cameras zoomed up to the van, attaching themselves to the window like flies. Picketers circled outside, chanting, "Even Bambi eats better than we do! What kind of justice is that?"

Finally they agreed that management could escort prisoners across the picket line. But management was out to lunch, and didn't come back for another hour.

Inside the International Center, more hours went by. I sat in some kind of waiting room, doing nothing. The Pinkerton guard dozed off. Other people, guards, workers, came by. It seemed every person on staff made some excuse to come look at me. They'd stand there and just stare! I didn't know what to do. I was reduced to some kind of zoo animal. They were deliberately stalling. They wanted as long a delay as possible while they figured out ways of stopping my release.

Isn't it interesting that when a court order is in their favor they insist on implementing it at once?

My lawyers were almost reduced to violence, they were so frustrated. They were about ready to punch someone.

At 4:00 PM, it was over. David Liblong and John Callaghan rushed in. "That's it, you're released, let's go!"

We bulldozed our way out through the media crowd. They were chasing us down the hallways. I'm surprised they didn't go ass over teakettle, walking backwards with those giant cameras. I bet they could land planes with those lights.

There was considerable confusion when we went out the wrong door and we had to hunt through the parking lot looking for our car, a scrum of reporters following us. Frank Marrocco was in the back seat, and we zigzagged our way through the crowd of reporters as Callaghan drove out of the lot.

Frank smiled at me. "Well," he said, "you made it."

"I told you you should've let *me* argue," I laughed.

We pulled out into the street. I rolled down the window and I breathed in the air ... the free air.

■   ■   ■

The lawyers had rented a conference room at a nearby Holiday Inn to get away from the reporters and regroup. I followed Frank into the Holiday Inn, thinking, Oh God the next headline is that I head right for a hotel room with Frank Marrocco as soon as I'm out on bail! Michelle Nash and John Callaghan and other members of the legal team came, and my dear friend Louie, my employer from Thunder Bay, who was putting up the surety. We heard my parents had flown in, but we didn't know where they were.

I looked around at everything, as delighted as a child. The Holiday Inn looked like a palace! I was delighted with the mineral water, with the coffee in neat little cups, with all the ordinary things that were extraordinary to me. John Callaghan asked me how I felt. "Freaked out!" I said. I didn't even know. I gave Louie a big hug.

But of course it wasn't over. The lawyers were huddling over in a corner, and I heard the words "extradition order." "What extradition order?" I asked, and they all looked at me, with that look on their faces. My heart started to constrict.

"No," someone said, "no, it's impossible, you can't extradite a refugee claimant. How can you? The claim hasn't been determined yet."

Frank, who knew better, reached for a phone and called a colleague, Doug Hunt. He handed the phone to me.

"Hi," said this voice. "I'm Doug Hunt. Do you want me to represent you?"

I was confused. I didn't know what was going on. Represent me in what? Didn't I already have lawyers? "What are we talking about?" I asked. "What's happening?" I didn't know. It hadn't registered that the State of Wisconsin was already seeking extradition.

■　　■　　■

The blood started to thud in my brain. They would not leave me alone! They had heard I was being released on bail—were the fax machines humming while I sat there during the delay at the International Center—and they wanted me back inside. A year had gone by since my capture, but now they decided it was "urgent" they extradite me. I could hear them laughing. I could hear the shrill vindictive laughter echoing down the years. I thought of all the mean, pinched people who wanted to control my life. The idea of my freedom seemed to give them all nightmares. I felt the dead weight of the State on the back of my neck. This wasn't supposed to be how America was!

■　　■　　■

John Paul Barry and David Liblong took me to Elizabeth Fry. I went through orientation, reading the house rules, getting a lock for a locker, figuring out what the curfews were. They assigned me a room.

It was so quiet! The silence was deafening. That was my first impression. Jail is so noisy! Sometimes, when I talk to people on the phone, they hear what sounds like someone getting macheted in the background, but it's normal prison noise. The TV is blasting and people are yelling over it. The silence was wonderful. Everything was carpeted, soft and pretty. Oh God, I thought, my own little bed, with its own little nightlight so I could read before I went to sleep. I could turn it off when I wanted to! There was even a little kitchen, and you could go in and make your own stuff. My roommate, who was also American, was baking lemon meringue pies for everyone.

I kicked off my shoes, because I can't walk in real shoes anymore—nor can I walk on carpeting, because I keep tripping. I was walking around in my pantyhose. I was exhausted. I hadn't eaten anything all day. I was sweaty and wanted to shower.

The lawyers had left. I was trying to make my bed and get situated, poking about at all the wonders—a cabinet, a little closet, drawers, a mirror, places to put things.

Then the residence staff told me my parents had arrived.

We sat in the lounge, my dad with his arm around me. It was so wonderful, but I was exhausted, and they saw that.

They stayed for about an hour, I think. My mom took pity on me and said, "Well, we've got time now, we can talk a lot. We'll let you get some sleep and come back tomorrow. Shower and change and sleep and we'll be here for a week if necessary."

So they left. There was a bowl of fresh fruit in the kitchen—fresh fruit is like gold in prison—and I grabbed a green apple. And then the lawyers came back with a suitcase of clothes. Lawyer Arthur Jacques' wife had gone out to get me clothes ...

I had a lump in my throat. I probably didn't thank them enough. Everyone was being so ... nice ... I didn't know how to act. I'd become so accustomed to harsh treatment—the normal inmate-guard relationship—that being with pleasant people who seemed to like me was quite disconcerting and upsetting. I changed clothes. Some of the stuff in the suitcase I couldn't figure out—fashions had changed in ten years. I put on a top and pants made out of T-shirt material.

After I'd changed, we used the phone in the Elizabeth Fry office for a conference call to Doug Hunt. He needed information: he had to go into court the next morning on the extradition matter, and he had to be prepared.

That's when it started to sink in.

Shit, they're serious. Court in the morning.

Even so, I was more cynical than the lawyers. They were still saying, "This has never been done before, this is unprecedented ..." and I was thinking, Yeah, story of my life ...

One of the things I liked about Hunt was that he gave me straight information. Right until the end, Don Eisenberg kept painting a rosy picture. Don's favorite comment was, "We'll talk about that after the acquittal." You're not mentally prepared if your lawyer keeps insisting nothing bad will happen.

Doug Hunt pointed out that the criteria they had to satisfy to get an extradition warrant was extraordinarily simple. They had to prove a conviction, which was easy, and make a positive identification, which wasn't so hard. Doug warned that the judge might feel compelled, using those criteria, to issue the warrant.

J. P. Barry called David Liblong at home, got him out of bed and down to the office. "We've got to go over the case," J. P. told him. "Work all night to be prepared."

This is how these guys worked for me. They're incredible! I kept saying, "Thank you, thank you!" I was so grateful. I still find it hard to believe ...

I went back up to my little room and sorted out my stuff. There were all kinds of things I hadn't seen. I hung a few things up and figured out what to wear to court. It was like Christmas—three or four pairs of shoes!

In my boxes from Metro West was all sorts of odd junk. The most exciting part was, I got to open my own mail for the first time in ten years.

I fell asleep an hour or so after midnight.

I wanted so much to stay there, it was so quiet ...

■　　■　　■

The next morning they picked me up at six, and we went over to Doug Hunt's office, on the thirty-eighth floor of one of the bank towers. The morning had a dreamlike quality. I had never met Doug Hunt, but he was now to be representing me in court, trying to stop them from sending me back. We sat for a few hours and went over the information again.

At nine, my herd of lawyers and I got into the elevator—that's what it felt like, this whole legal entourage. There was Doug, with five assistants. John Callaghan and David Liblong and John Paul Berry were there. Frank showed up, too, and we walked over to the courthouse, a whole regiment of legal talent.

We walked up York Street toward the courthouse. I was thinking, Oh no, please, I don't want to get arrested again, I don't want to go back in that place.

The judge was Patricia German, a tiny little woman. Doug Hunt told me she was sympathetic but felt compelled to issue the warrant because of the ease of meeting the criteria.

She insisted on doing the bail hearings right away, and that took all morning.

She was pleasant. She called me "young lady" and offered to let me use the bathroom in her chambers (it was a Saturday and the others were closed). On the way out, she told the RCMP, "Now make sure she gets a nice lunch." She seemed to be going that extra mile to show me she was sympathetic.

The RCMP were ticked off. "We've got better things to do with our time than this bullshit," one of them said. They refused to cuff me. Clearly they thought the whole thing was ludicrous. I was fingerprinted again and we went to lunch in the staff lounge. They picked up ribs and fries and we sat around and had lunch. We chatted about the case. They had read about the gun, the so-called murder weapon, and what procedures had been followed.

"A bullshit case" was their verdict.

■ ■ ■

Once again the Justice Department lawyers made a big production of the fact that I'd worked for a living in Thunder Bay, using false ID! They implied that if I'd used false ID there was nothing I wouldn't do. I still don't understand what they thought I should have done. Of course I wasn't using my real name. Would they rather I'd robbed banks for a living?

Around 6:00 PM we adjourned until the next morning. Doug Hunt asked if I could go back to Elizabeth Fry for another night. The judge made an approving sort of face, as if she was going to go along with this idea, but the Justice Department lawyers went wild.

"Your Lordship! This is a convicted killer! The most horrible crime imaginable, in Canada as well as the U.S."

A whole tirade. I looked at them, wondering what was going on in their heads. I wondered if they heard the wounds their words caused, and whether they cared. Perhaps they armored themselves in some way against feelings. I wondered if their husbands and wives and children and sisters saw this side of them, or whether they had simply somehow persuaded themselves I was some subhuman monster. I hoped they could live with themselves in the mornings.

The judge said she would have to remand me back to Metro West.

My heart went cold.

I went over to my dad and hugged him and I started to cry. I cried and cried, I felt so desolate, sobbing and holding onto his shoulders, those shoulders that were now so much more frail than when we had started this awful journey, ten years before. I felt the bones of his shoulders and it all poured out, the frustration and the sadness, and he just stood there and hugged me back. The courtroom was so quiet you could have heard a pin drop. Even the reporters were quiet, for once. I think they felt the desolation, too. How could they help but feel it? It was choking the air.

I went back, and it was really bad. When the door opened and the guards saw me, they just shook their heads. They couldn't believe I was back. "What the hell is going on here, you just got bail yesterday?"

I felt worse than I had when we were caught in Thunder Bay. It was such a cruel joke. To put up with this horrible place for all these months, and then get that one, short, tantalizing night—it would have been better not to have left at all. I had made the prisoner's fatal mistake. I had allowed myself to hope.

■   ■   ■

There were three of us in my cell, now. One was a crazy girl, burned out from cocaine, crazy and hyper and restless, sitting on my clothes, pressing on my space, filling the air with craziness ...

Please, please, oh, let me out of here!

But no one came.

26

THE RETURN

Well, it's over.

I'm back in this ... this place.

For months, for so many months, I simply endured what they did to me. They would take me to court, then take me away again. I went to a hearing, and then they put me back in jail. I came and I went. Lawyers argued, judges listened (typing away on their little computers), prosecutors ranted. It was a routine. It wasn't a life, but it was a routine.

For months I went to court in the little death box on wheels they call a Metro Police transportation van. One week ... they had seventeen women stuffed into the back of one of the police wagons, five on either side, hand-cuffed together. I was in my suit, and nylons, but there was no room, and the policewoman said, "Too bad. You're gonna have to sit on the floor." There were already four other women on the floor—and then they wonder why we look like criminals. You do everything in your power to look presentable in court, but you're filthy and wrinkled and there's nothing you can do about it. They get us up at 5:30 AM, I'm in court at 9:00, it's over by 10:30, and I sit in the bullpen until 6:00 PM. In the evening, on the way back, they picked up a woman who was obviously mentally ill. She was in her underwear—no shoes or socks or pants, and this in December. Couldn't they have found her some pants? What is she going to a jail for anyway? She should be going to a mental health facility.

But why should they care?

And so "home," to that grim place, and to bed.

Again, and again.

For all that time, my lawyers were fighting for me. They spent hours, days, weeks, months fighting for me. I became a little legal cottage industry all on my own—these guys used to have other clients! They fought because they thought what had happened to me was outlandish, and because they liked the idea of justice and because—well, let's face it, they liked the challenge, too. Frank is a chess player, and he understands intricate moves.

I watched them in the hallways sometimes. They argued and gesticulated, getting angry at the obstinacy of the other side—*Why can't they see it the way we can?*

But it's over now. The shining towers of freedom I thought I saw in their arguments were just a mirage after all. I thought Canada could be my home, a refuge; I wanted so badly to become a citizen of some place where I could be free! But it was not to be. Mirages are just dreams, after all, and dreams are dangerous for inmates, because they let the daylight in, and you can see the bars and the bare concrete, stretching down the years... If I am to win my freedom, it will have to be here, where they first took it from me. So I came back, of my own accord, to continue the fight.

■   ■   ■

I have many memories of Canada, good and bad. Among the bad are my memories of Metro West Detention Centre and their strip searches, the most pointless and dehumanizing of all prison procedures. Some jail rules are at least understandable—making us eat spaghetti with a spoon at least helps cut down stabbing incidents among inmates—but strip searches make no sense at all except to humiliate people. In Thunder Bay and Toronto they routinely stripped and searched inmates during cell searches, a completely purposeless activity. In Toronto, you could be stripped three times a day. Wherever you went in prison, you were strip searched afterwards. Cell search in the morning: strip search. After work in the laundry or kitchen: strip search. After hobbycraft: strip search. After Elizabeth Fry volunteer visit: strip search. After a lawyer's visit: strip search. Come back from court: strip search. And the guards looked on the activity as normal, not even caring that male officers were present; they only looked puzzled when I complained that I was not an exhibitionist and hated taking off my clothes in front of strangers. Most of the guards just shrugged, and said they didn't like strip searching people either, but they were just following orders. Orders! There's an excuse familiar from history!

But of course I have good memories too, and among them were the friends I made and the people who worked so hard on my behalf.

A friend told me how Frank Marrocco really got involved in my case (I was too timid to ask Frank directly).

At first, I was told, Frank wasn't too impressed when McCombs called him. Frank's been around a long time, and believes that plenty of guilty people insist they're innocent. So he believed that if he was going to get involved at all, it would be to give me a quick opinion, for a good fee, and then take himself out.

But the thing that struck him immediately was the testimony of the boys—12-year-old Sean insisting he'd seen the murderer and it wasn't me. That made him think.

Also, Frank is of that rare breed, a criminal lawyer who knows constitutional law. And the Immigration minister's certificate offended him constitutionally. It was such a circular argument the minister was making—she declared me a danger to the public on the basis of the very conviction I was claiming gave me a good basis for a refugee claim! I was claiming that my conviction was erroneous. She said I was dangerous because I was convicted. Frank agreed to argue this at the hearings.

So he flew to Thunder Bay to meet me. And I guess he saw I wasn't a complete wingnut. Then he spent two thousand dollars on Xerox bills and took all the documents away with him. He read everything—transcripts, police reports, everything. And again, what struck him was that at first everybody had been looking for a man. All the police reports mentioned a male suspect.

He began to get interested.

Immigration Minister Barbara McDougall, confronted with a challenge, withdrew her certificate and asked for submissions for both sides. Frank prepared a brief to her outlining all the exculpatory evidence that had been uncovered in my case to date.

She re-issued the certificate, once again declaring me a danger to the public. But at least Frank's brief was now on the record. Finally, somewhere, I had on the record some of the evidence that supported me.

We were challenging the validity of the second certificate when Ron Lester was called to the bench as a judge. Suddenly I was without a lawyer. So, almost by accident, Frank found himself arguing the merits of my case and not just its constitutional aspects.

This is what he told my friend:

"So I started to get into it. I could have turned it back, and told her it was none of my business, that it was an American case, and nothing to do with me.

But I thought, I have to live with myself. If one day I was to wake up, and she was fifty-five instead of thirty-three, and she's lost her adult life instead of just her twenties, and she is then proven innocent, or someone eventually confesses, well, that would have haunted me for the rest of my life.

"I believed in her and I just couldn't do that ...

"I'm no saint, God knows, but if I could have done something to save her and refrained ... no, I couldn't do that."

Many law firms would have insisted he drop the case, or at least get paid for it. But by this time he was in, and bringing his friends and colleagues in, and the firm not only allowed but encouraged it.

I still find it all hard to believe.

So I then had Frank and John Callaghan for the immigration (refugee) case, which was being held before a two-man tribunal of the immigration department, not a judge. Frank looks like a lawyer. He used to be a Crown prosecutor, on a per diem basis, and he can't always get the prosecutor out of his bones. Sometimes when he was questioning me I'd say, "Frank! What's this cross examination!" He kept asking me about stuff that's ten years old, and I didn't mean to give fuzzy answers but I couldn't always be positive. Then he got a prosecutorial sort of expression that said, "What do you mean you don't remember! You were there!" He wanted me to remember so badly.

Frank's a chess player and was always thinking a couple of moves ahead. For instance, at the immigration hearings (unlike courtrooms in Canada) television cameras were allowed. So Frank was playing to two audiences, the immigration tribunal, arguing my case there, and the television audience back in Milwaukee—they played my evidence in full on air there, and this was finally helping to turn public opinion in my favor.

And John Callaghan? He didn't look old enough to be a lawyer. I had to laugh every time I saw him in court, in his robes (in Canada lawyers wear robes), looking like a kid, with a face like Tom Hanks. But *smart*!

Doug Hunt, of Fasken Campbell Godfrey, was my counsel for the extradition matter, before the Ontario courts. He's a desert storm all by himself. The immigration proceedings gave rise to a habeas corpus application—that was David McCombs, of Carter McCombs and Minden. (There was another habeas corpus application attached to the extradition case.) Then there was Arthur Jacques, a colleague of Frank's, who is a barracuda. David Liblong and J. P. Barry were student lawyers, and then there was Michelle Nash, who knew everything about the case there was to be known and ... oh, there were others: the Milwaukee chapter of the National Organization of Women applied for intervener status in the hearings, and retained a lawyer named Michelle Fuerst.

In the U.S. I had Sheldon Zenner out of Chicago, who was (and is) acting for me in the John Doe action. And Mary Woehrer, in Milwaukee, who was helping me by representing Ira Robins. She is formally counsel for the applicants for the John Doe—Dr. Irwin, who was the chief medical examiner at the time of the murder, and Ira. She also assists Zenner.

A regular industry, no? All these actions—the extradition case, the refugee hearings, habeas corpus actions arising from both, the John Doe.

A John Doe hearing is sort of like a one-person Grand Jury. This one has a specific frame of reference, which is police misconduct—they are looking for proof of evidence tampering. The prosecutor is investigating the investigation; that is, he's looking at police procedures rather than my guilt or innocence. All these proceedings had one basis: my apparent inability to get justice in the courts that tried me. The prosecutor will probably report about mid-year 1992.

Frank believed I had a strong case in the immigration hearings. Although one side effect of stringing out the Canadian hearings was to give the John Doe hearings more time, that wasn't why they strung them out. They did so because they thought they could win.

At least, in our many submissions and petitions and motions in the various Canadian tribunals and courts, we slowly got on an official record some of the exculpatory evidence no one had ever recognized before. At least people now know what kind of "evidence" convicted me. They can now begin to see how oddly intransigent the Milwaukee authorities were about re-opening my case.

My Chicago attorney, Sheldon Zenner, wrote to the DA before the Canadian immigration hearings started, and suggested letting the FBI look into the case. The DA refused. Why? During the course of my trial, they didn't hesitate to call in the FBI about evidence like the mysterious clothesline.

The Justice Department in Canada complained that my lawyers used the immigration hearings just to retry the murder case in Canada. But I had to try to establish that I might have been framed as a consequence of my attempts to expose corruption and police misconduct in the Milwaukee police force. We had to get someone to pay attention to the facts.

And, as Frank put it, "You can't be blind to that fact that the Special Prosecutor may find someone, someone who will just walk through his door ... I believe someone, whoever, down there in Milwaukee will wake up to the fact that the best thing he can do is make a deal ... After all, *someone* did the murder."

Frank also told a friend of mine this:

"The ultimate objective of all these actions, of everything we do, or every argument, is to get the door open and let her walk out.

"How we do that, and where it happens, is not material.

"We can't let our own egos get in the way. It would be grand to win here in Canada. But if the best way to get her free is to let her do so in the U.S., so be it. You can never afford to ignore the moral dimension, to forget that it is her freedom that is the real issue. I can't afford to let the process get in the way of her fate. Winning a good case, setting a good precedent, is not the point of this. Prying open the gates for her is the point."

In February 1992, he advised me to come back. And here I am.

■   ■   ■

My friends held rallies for me in Milwaukee. There was a jog-a-thon to raise money for my defense, there were bake sales and craft sales and fund raising drives, there were write-in campaigns and telephone drives and mail drops and ... people worked so *hard* for me. It's not just my parents and my sisters, Colette and Melanie, and Ira and my old friends, Donna and Wally, from the Boston Store days; there are hundreds of others and I hope they know that they have been sustaining me, that their efforts have been keeping me alive, that I love them all for it with a fierce affection, and that if I get out—when I get out—it will be partly because of them, who have kept the long vigil and not given up.

My parents have mortgaged their house twice for me.

And yet—what do they say?

"It's not the money, because money is just money, but it's her youth, how do you put a price on that? On ten years? You can't replace it. So we've been fighting for her ..."

Their loyalty makes me weep, for all that has been done to *them*.

The last time they came to visit me in Toronto, the airline clerk insisted on changing their tickets to first class because "you need a little tender loving care." He asked them to tell me that "she should hang in there, we're all pulling for her, remember to tell her that ..."

Maybe things *are* changing.

■   ■   ■

Of course, there are people who will believe whatever they want—that Elvis is still alive, despite a mountain of evidence. There was a bumper sticker in Milwaukee after my escape, which said, "Bambi's with Elvis."

Too true!

Once, sometime in 1991, reporters called Fred Schultz to get his comment about something, some trivial matter. The man who cleans his pool answered the phone. Fred didn't want to be bothered. "Say I'm in Kuwait," he said. So the man did.

What did the press do? They printed it, of course. Every news outlet in Milwaukee ran with it. Even my Canadian lawyers asked me what Fred was doing in Kuwait.

I knew right away that he wasn't of course. It was just common sense. So I said to them: "Get outta here! He is not!"

And they said, "He is, it was on the news ..."

"The news! You believe the news! Please!"

They were pretty embarrassed.

It's not always as benign as that, however. You must understand how vulnerable I am in prison. People feel they can say anything they want, and they do!

Recently, Fred Horenberger, who was (and is) a prime suspect for Christine Schultz's murder, committed suicide in the course of an armed robbery. He got caught, took hostages, and killed himself after a standoff.

What happens? Horenberger's brother goes on television and says that Judy Zess and Horenberger and I had frequent sex orgies together. Not to worry that I never once met Horenberger, never mind that in Horenberger's own handwriting there is a document admitting Zess was fabricating allegations against me, and several documents that proved I had never met Horenberger. None of those things prevent this cowardly creep, Horenberger's brother, from libeling me all over again. Why doesn't the press feel it necessary to check? Why do they allow lies like that to be broadcast? Is it enough to have Ira Robins on afterwards denying it, but identifying Ira as one of my partisans, when the facts were checkable?

Why can anyone come off the street and say anything they like about me, and they'll print it? Why does the press feel cavalierly free to manufacture stories when the facts don't say what they think they should? No one should be that vulnerable.

What am I supposed to do? I get so angry at this stuff. The lawyers always advise me to do nothing, because reacting to a libel only draws attention to it— those who hadn't seen it the first time will surely see it then. But why should they get away with it? I'm not for censorship, just for some responsibility, for some professional standards.

Well, maybe things are changing, now. I even have some of the media on my side.

But I still don't know how long my fight will take, or whether I'll ever be free again.

I'm back where it all began. The struggle continues. The love of my family and my friends, and my inner knowledge of my innocence, sustain me.

Those things, at least, are not mirages.

■　■　■

Well, now you know me a little better.

As I said at the beginning, I'm no Joan of Arc, no cringing virgin, no saint. I was something of a wild child, and I made lots of mistakes. I'm also mouthy and independent and, I think, I have become quite strong.

But I'm also just an ordinary person, like your sister, or your daughter.

I'm just a person who would like her life back.

Is that so much to ask?

I have learned so many things I wish I'd never had to learn. I learned about the system of justice; I learned that it protects its own, cannot bring itself to admit its mistakes, that many of its practitioners seem more concerned with process than justice.

So much heartbreak, so much despair, so unnecessary, so many lives broken on the wheel of crude ambition and coverup, on the rack of process ...

I will be out, soon, I hope. But I will never recapture any sense that the system is benign. It has taken ten years of my life, and every day I listen to its partisans demanding to take more, more, more.

Going on is possible.

Survival is possible.

Even happiness is possible, I hope.

But I'm not at all sure about forgiveness.